Lecture Notes in Artificial Intelligence 9494

Subseries of Lecture Notes in Computer Science

More information about this series at http://www.springer.com/series/1244

Béatrice Duval · Jaap van den Herik
Stephane Loiseau · Joaquim Filipe (Eds.)

Agents and Artificial Intelligence

7th International Conference, ICAART 2015
Lisbon, Portugal, January 10–12, 2015
Revised Selected Papers

Springer

Editors
Béatrice Duval
LERIA - UFR Sciences
Angers Cedex 01
France

Jaap van den Herik
Leiden University
Leiden
The Netherlands

Stephane Loiseau
LERIA - UFR Sciences
Angers Cedex 01
France

Joaquim Filipe
Polytechnic Institute of Setúbal
Setúbal
Portugal

ISSN 0302-9743   ISSN 1611-3349   (electronic)
Lecture Notes in Artificial Intelligence
ISBN 978-3-319-27946-6   ISBN 978-3-319-27947-3   (eBook)
DOI 10.1007/978-3-319-27947-3

Library of Congress Control Number: 2015950896

LNCS Sublibrary: SL7 – Artificial Intelligence

This Springer imprint is published by SpringerNature
The registered company is Springer International Publishing AG Switzerland

Preface

The present book includes extended and revised versions of a set of selected papers from the 7th International Conference on Agents and Artificial Intelligence (ICAART 2015), held in Lisbon, Portugal, during January 10–12, 2015, which was sponsored by the Institute for Systems and Technologies of Information, Control and Communication (INSTICC) in cooperation with the ACM Special Interest Group on Artificial Intelligence (ACM SIGAI), the Association for the Advancement of Artificial Intelligence (AAAI), the Spanish Association for Artificial Intelligence (AEPIA), the European Society for Fuzzy Logic and Technology (EUSFLAT), the European Coordinating Committee for Artificial Intelligence (ECCAI), the Italian Association for Artificial Intelligence, and the Portuguese Association for Artificial Intelligence (APPIA). ICAART 2015 was also technically co-sponsored by the IEEE Computer Society.

The purpose of the International Conference on Agents and Artificial Intelligence is to bring together researchers, engineers, and practitioners interested in the theory and applications in the areas of agents and artificial intelligence. Two related tracks were held simultaneously, covering both applications and current research work. One track focused on agents, multi-agent systems and software platforms, distributed problem solving and distributed AI in general. The other track focused mainly on artificial intelligence, knowledge representation, planning, learning, scheduling, perception, reactive AI systems, and evolutionary computing.

ICAART 2015 received 187 paper submissions from 45 countries in all continents, of which 19 % were presented at the conference as full papers, and their authors were invited to submit extended versions of their papers for this book. In order to evaluate each submission, a double-blind review was performed by the Program Committee. Finally, only the 19 best papers were included in this book.

We would like to highlight that ICAART 2015 also included four plenary keynote lectures, given by internationally distinguished researchers, namely: Chris Reed (University of Dundee, UK), Joseph Halpern (Cornell University, USA), Nick Jennings (University of Southampton, UK), and Robert Kowalski (Imperial College London, UK). We must acknowledge the invaluable contribution of all keynote speakers who, as renowned researchers in their areas, presented cutting-edge work and thus enriched the scientific content of the conference.

We especially thank the authors, whose research and development efforts are recorded here. The knowledge and diligence of the reviewers were essential to ensure the quality of the papers presented at the conference and published in this book. Finally, a special thanks to all members of the INSTICC team, whose involvement was fundamental for organizing a smooth and successful conference.

September 2015

Béatrice Duval
Jaap van den Herik
Joaquim Filipe
Stephane Loiseau

Organization

Conference Co-chairs

Stephane Loiseau   LERIA, University of Angers, France
Joaquim Filipe   Polytechnic Institute of Setúbal/INSTICC, Portugal

Program Co-chairs

Béatrice Duval   LERIA, University of Angers, France
Jaap van den Herik   Leiden University, The Netherlands

Program Committee

Giovanni Acampora	Nottingham Trent University, UK
Jose Aguilar	Universidad de Los Andes, Venezuela
Varol Akman	Bilkent University, Turkey
Isabel Machado Alexandre	Instituto Universitário de Lisboa (ISCTE-IUL) and Instituto de Telecomunicações, Portugal
Vicki Allan	Utah State University, USA
Klaus-Dieter Althoff	German Research Center for Artificial Intelligence/University of Hildesheim, Germany
Frédéric Amblard	IRIT – Université Toulouse 1 Capitole, France
Cesar Analide	University of Minho, Portugal
Diana Arellano	Filmakademie Baden-Württemberg, Germany
Tsz-Chiu Au	Ulsan National Institute of Science and Technology, Republic of Korea
Jean-Michel Auberlet	IFSTTAR (French Institute of Science and Technology for Transport, Development and Networks), France
Snorre Aunet	Norwegian University of Science and Technology, Norway
Javier Bajo	Technical University of Madrid, Spain
Florence Bannay	IRIT – Toulouse University, France
Suzanne Barber	The University of Texas, USA
Kamel Barkaoui	Cedric-CNAM, France
Senén Barro	University of Santiago de Compostela, Spain
Punam Bedi	University of Delhi, India
Nabil Belacel	National Research Council Canada, Canada
Christoph Benzmüller	Freie Universität Berlin, Germany
Carole Bernon	University of Paul Sabatier – Toulouse III, France

Daniel Berrar	Tokyo Institute of Technology, Japan
Bruno Bouchard	LIARA Laboratory, Université du Québec à Chicoutimi, Canada
Noury Bouraqadi	Ecole Des Mines De Douai, France
Sheryl Brahnam	Missouri State University, USA
Ramón F. Brena	Tecnológico De Monterrey, Campus Monterrey, Mexico
Paolo Bresciani	Fondazione Bruno Kessler, Italy
Stefano Bromuri	University of Applied Sciences Western Switzerland, Switzerland
Alberto Bugarín	University of Santiago de Compostela, Spain
Aleksander Byrski	AGH University of Science and Technology, Poland
Giacomo Cabri	Università di Modena e Reggio Emilia, Italy
Silvia Calegari	Università Degli Studi Di Milano Bicocca, Italy
David Camacho	Universidad Autónoma de Madrid, Spain
Rui Camacho	Universidade do Porto, Portugal
Valérie Camps	IRIT – Université Paul Sabatier, France
Amilcar Cardoso	University of Coimbra, Portugal
John Cartlidge	University of Bristol, UK
José Jesús Castro-Schez	Escuela Superior de Informática, Universidad de Castilla-La Mancha, Spain
Patrick De Causmaecker	Katholieke Universiteit Leuven, Belgium
François Charpillet	Loria – Inria Lorraine, France
Amitava Chatterjee	Jadavpur University, India
Mu-Song Chen	Da-Yeh University, Taiwan
Adam Cheyer	SRI International, USA
Marco Chiarandini	University of Southern Denmark, Denmark
Anders Lyhne Christensen	Instituto Superior das Ciências do Trabalho e da Empresa, Portugal
Davide Ciucci	Università degli Studi di Milano Bicocca, Italy
Carlo Combi	Università degli Studi di Verona, Italy
Diane Cook	Washington State University, USA
Daniel Corkill	University of Massachusetts Amherst, USA
Chris Cornelis	University of Granada, Spain
Gabriella Cortellessa	ISTC-CNR, Italy
Paulo Cortez	University of Minho, Portugal
Massimo Cossentino	National Research Council, Italy
Evandro Costa	UFAL, Brazil
Darryl N. Davis	University of Hull, UK
Alok Kanti Deb	Indian Institute of Technology, India
Andreas Dengel	German Research Center for Artificial Intelligence (DFKI GmbH), Germany
Louise Dennis	University of Liverpool, UK
Enrico Denti	Alma Mater Studiorum – Università di Bologna, Italy
Ioan Despi	UNE, Australia
Michel Dojat	INSERM and Université Grenoble Alpes, France
Agostino Dovier	Università degli Studi di Udine, Italy

Julie Dugdale   Laboratoire d'Informatique de Grenoble, France
Paul Dunne   University of Liverpool, UK
Béatrice Duval   LERIA, University of Angers, France
Michael Dyer   University of California Los Angeles, USA
Stefan Edelkamp   Universität Bremen, Germany
Thomas Eiter   Technische Universität Wien, Austria
Fabrício Enembreck   Pontifical Catholic University of Paraná, Brazil
Esra Erdem   Sabanci University, Turkey
Christophe Feltus   Luxembourg Institute of Science and Technology,
                           Luxembourg
Stefano Ferilli   University of Bari, Italy
Alberto Fernández   University Rey Juan Carlos, Spain
Antonio   Universidad de Castilla-la Mancha, Spain
  Fernández-Caballero
Edilson Ferneda   Catholic University of Brasília, Brazil
Klaus Fischer   German Research Center for Artificial Intelligence DFKI
                           GmbH, Germany
Stan Franklin   University of Memphis, USA
Claude Frasson   University of Montreal, Canada
Naoki Fukuta   Shizuoka University, Japan
Maurizio Gabbrielli   University of Bologna, Italy
Sarah Alice Gaggl   Technische Universität Dresden, Germany
Salvatore Gaglio   Università degli Studi di Palermo, Italy
Maria Ganzha   SRI PAS and University of Gdansk, Poland
Catherine Garbay   CNRS, France
Alfredo Garro   Università della Calabria, Italy
Max Gath   Universität Bremen/Center for Computing
                           and Communication Technologies, Germany
Andrey Gavrilov   Novosibirsk State Technical University,
                           Russian Federation
João CarlosGluz   Universidade do Vale do Rio dos Sinos, Brazil
Daniela Godoy   Universidad Nacional del Centro de la Pcia. de Buenos
                           Aires, Argentina
Guido Governatori   NICTA, Australia
Dominic Greenwood   Whitestein Technologies AG, Switzerland
Perry Groot   Radboud University Nijmegen, The Netherlands
Sven Groppe   University of Lübeck, Germany
Renata Guizzardi   Federal University of Espirito Santo (UFES), Brazil
Rune Gustavsson   Blekinge Institute of Technology, Sweden
Hisashi Hayashi   Toshiba Corporation, Japan
Pedro Rangel Henriques   University of Minho, Portugal
Frans Henskens   University of Newcastle, Australia
Jaap van den Herik   Leiden University, The Netherlands
Andreas Herzig   University of Toulouse, CNRS, France
Rattikorn Hewett   Texas Tech University, USA
Vincent Hilaire   UTBM, France

Xudong Luo	Sun Yat-Sen University, China
José Machado	University of Minho, Portugal
Jerusa Marchi	Universidade Federal de Santa Catarina, Brazil
Elisa Marengo	Free University of Bozen-Bolzano, Italy
Mourad Mars	Institute of Computer Science and Mathematics of Monastir, Tunisia
Nicola Di Mauro	Università di Bari, Italy
Fiona McNeill	Heriot-Watt University, UK
Paola Mello	Università di Bologna, Italy
Daniel Merkle	University of Southern Denmark, Denmark
Marjan Mernik	University of Maribor, Slovenia
Bernd Meyer	Monash University, Australia
John-Jules Meyer	Utrecht University, The Netherlands
Ambra Molesini	Alma Mater Studiorum – Università di Bologna, Italy
José Moreira	Universidade de Aveiro, Portugal
Pedro Moreira	Escola Superior de Tecnologia e Gestão – Instituto Politécnico de Viana do Castelo, Portugal
Maxime Morge	University of Lille, France
Bernard Moulin	Université Laval, Canada
Haralambos Mouratidis	University of East London, UK
Christian Müller-Schloer	Leibniz Universität Hannover, Germany
Radhakrishnan Nagarajan	University of Kentucky, USA
Konstantinos Nikolopoulos	Bangor University, UK
Jens Nimis	Hochschule Karlsruhe - Technik und Wirtschaft, Germany
Luis Nunes	Instituto Universitário de Lisboa (ISCTE-IUL) and Instituto de Telecomunicações (IT), Portugal
Andreas Oberweis	Karlsruhe Institute of Technology (KIT), Germany
Michel Occello	Université Pierre-Mendès-France, France
Dimitri Ognibene	King's College London, UK
Sancho Oliveira	Instituto Universitário de Lisboa (ISCTE-IUL), Portugal
Andrea Omicini	Alma Mater Studiorum – Università di Bologna, Italy
Stanislaw Osowski	Warsaw University of Technology, Poland
Nandan Parameswaran	University of New South Wales, Australia
Andrew Parkes	University of Nottingham, UK
Krzysztof Patan	University of Zielona Gora, Poland
Manuel G. Penedo	University of A Coruña, Spain
Célia da Costa Pereira	Université de Nice Sophia Antipolis, France
Wim Peters	University of Sheffield, UK
Aske Plaat	Tilburg University, The Netherlands
Agostino Poggi	University of Parma, Italy
Ramalingam Ponnusamy	Anna University - Chennai – Rajiv Gandhi College of Engineering, India
David Powers	Flinders University, Australia
Marco Prandini	University of Bologna, Italy

Mariachiara Puviani	Università di Modena e Reggio Emilia, Italy
Martin Rehák	Czech Technical University in Prague, Czech Republic
Luis Paulo Reis	University of Minho, Portugal
Lluís Ribas-Xirgo	Universitat Autònoma de Barcelona, Spain
Miguel Rocha	University of Minho, Portugal
Fátima Rodrigues	Instituto Superior de Engenharia do Porto (ISEP/IPP), Portugal
Daniel Rodriguez	University of Alcalá, Spain
Andrea Roli	Università di Bologna, Italy
Juha Röning	University of Oulu, Finland
Rosaldo Rossetti	Laboratório de Inteligência Artificial e Ciência de Computadores, LIACC/FEUP, Portugal
Ruben Ruiz	Universidad Politécnica de Valencia, Spain
Fariba Sadri	Imperial College London, UK
Lorenza Saitta	Università degli Studi del Piemonte Orientale "Amedeo Avogadro", Italy
Manuel Filipe Santos	University of Minho, Portugal
Jorge Gomez Sanz	Universidad Complutense de Madrid, Spain
Fabio Sartori	Università degli Studi di Milano Bicocca, Italy
Jurek Sasiadek	Carleton University, Canada
Christoph Schommer	University Luxembourg, Campus Kirchberg, Luxembourg
Stefan Schulz	Medical University of Graz, Austria
Michael Schumacher	University of Applied Sciences Western Switzerland, Switzerland
Frank Schweitzer	ETH Zurich, Switzerland
Valeria Seidita	University of Palermo, Italy
Hasan Selim	Dokuz Eylul University, Turkey
Ivan Serina	University of Brescia, Italy
Emilio Serrano	Universidad Politécnica de Madrid, Spain
Giovanni Sileno	University of Amsterdam, The Netherlands
Flavio S. CorreaDa Silva	University of Sao Paulo, Brazil
Viviane Silva	Universidade Federal Fluminense, Brazil
Ricardo Silveira	Universidade Federal de Santa Catarina, Brazil
David Sislak	Czech Technical University in Prague – Agent Technology Center, Czech Republic
Alexander Smirnov	SPIIRAS, Russian Academy of Sciences, Russian Federation
Marina V. Sokolova	Instituto de Investigación en Informática de Albacete, Spain
Kim Solin	The University of Queensland, Australia
Armando J. Sousa	Universidade do Porto, Portugal
Fernando Da Fonseca De Souza	Centro de Informática – Universidade Federal de Pernambuco, Brazil
Antoine Spicher	LACL – Université Paris-Est Créteil, France
Bruno Di Stefano	Nuptek Systems Ltd., Canada
Bernd Steinbach	Freiberg University of Mining and Technology, Germany

Kathleen Steinhofel	King's College London, UK
Daniel Stormont	The PineApple Project, USA
Thomas Stützle	Université Libre de Bruxelles, Belgium
Zhaohao Sun	PNG University of Technology; Federation University Australia, Australia Boontawee Suntisrivaraporn, Sirindhorn International Institute of Technology, Thailand
Pavel Surynek	Charles University in Prague, Czech Republic
Yasuhiro Suzuki	Nagoya University, Japan
Ryszard Tadeusiewicz	AGH University of Science and Technology, Poland
Antonio J. Tallón-Ballesteros	University of Seville, Spain
Nick Taylor	Heriot-Watt University, UK
Patrícia Tedesco	Universidade Federal de Pernambuco/FADE, Brazil
Mark Terwilliger	Lake Superior State University, USA
José Torres	Universidade Fernando Pessoa, Portugal
Bogdan Trawinski	Wroclaw University of Technology, Poland
Paola Turci	University of Parma, Italy
Anni-Yasmin Turhan	Technische Universität Dresden, Germany
Franco Turini	KDD Lab, University of Pisa, Italy
Paulo Urbano	Universidade de Lisboa, Portugal
Visara Urovi	University of Applied Sciences Western Switzerland, Sierre (HES-SO), Switzerland
Marco Valtorta	University of South Carolina, USA
Athanasios Vasilakos	University of Western Macedonia, Greece
Srdjan Vesic	CNRS, France
Serena Villata	Inria Sophia Antipolis, France
Marin Vlada	University of Bucharest, Romania
George Vouros	University of Piraeus, Greece
Christel Vrain	University of Orléans, France
Yves Wautelet	KU Leuven, Belgium
Rosina Weber	iSchool at Drexel, USA
Stephan Weiss	NASA/Jet Propulsion Laboratory, USA
Cees Witteveen	Delft University of Technology, The Netherlands
T.N. Wong	The University of Hong Kong, Hong Kong, SAR China
John Woodward	University of Stirling, UK
Franz Wotawa	Graz University of Technology, Austria
Bozena Wozna-Szczesniak	Jan Dlugosz University, Poland
Ning Xiong	Mälardalen University, Sweden
Feiyu Xu	Deutsches Forschungszentrum für Künstliche Intelligenz (DFKI), Germany
Yiyu Yao	University of Regina, Canada
Li-Yan Yuan	University of Alberta, Canada
Bruno Zanuttini	GREYC, Normandie Université, UNICAEN, CNRS UMR 6072, ENSICAEN, France

Laura Zavala   Megar Evers College of the City University of New York,
                             USA
Alejandro Zunino   Universidad Nacional del Centro de la Provincia de
                             Buenos Aires, Argentina

Additional Reviewers

Sviatlana Danilava   University of Luxembourg, Luxembourg
Luke Day   King's College London, UK
Alevtina Dubovitskaya   HES-SO Valais; EPFl, Switzerland
Agnieszka Jastrzebska   Warsaw University of Technology, Poland
Sebastian Niemann   Leibniz Universität Hannover, Germany
Andrea Pazienza   Università degli Studi di Bari Aldo Moro, Italy
Mariusz Popieluch   University of Queensland, Australia
Hércules Antônio do   Universidade Católica de Brasília, Brazil
  Prado
Tahiry Rabehaja   Macquarie University, Australia
Fabrizio Riguzzi   University of Ferrara, Italy
Ouala Abdelhadi Ep   King's College London, UK
  Souki
Henning Spiegelberg   University of Hanover, Germany
Michaël Thomazo   TU Dresden, Germany
Suguru Ueda   National Institute of Informatics, Japan
Filippo Vella   National Research Council of Italy, Italy

Invited Speakers

Chris Reed   University of Dundee, UK
Joseph Halpern   Cornell University, USA
Nick Jennings   University of Southampton, UK
Robert Kowalski   Imperial College London, UK

Contents

Agents

A Hybrid POMDP-BDI Agent Architecture with Online Stochastic
Planning and Desires with Changing Intensity Levels 3
   Gavin Rens and Thomas Meyer

Dynamic *JChoc*: A Distributed Constraints Reasoning Platform
for Dynamically Changing Environments 20
   Imade Benelallam, Zakarya Erraji, Ghizlane EL Khattabi,
   and El Houssine Bouyakhf

Stream X-Machines for Agent Simulation Test Case Generation 37
   Ilias Sakellariou, Dimitris Dranidis, Marina Ntika, and Petros Kefalas

Building Self-adaptive Systems by Adaptation Patterns Integrated into
Agent Methodologies. 58
   Mariachiara Puviani, Giacomo Cabri, Nicola Capodieci,
   and Letizia Leonardi

Artificial Intelligence

A Logic for Reasoning About Decision-Theoretic Projections. 79
   Gavin Rens, Thomas Meyer, and Gerhard Lakemeyer

Identifying Critical Positions Based on Conspiracy Numbers 100
   Mohd Nor Akmal Khalid, E. Mei Ang, Umi Kalsom Yusof,
   Hiroyuki Iida, and Taichi Ishitobi

Infinite Horizon Multi-armed Bandits with Reward Vectors:
Exploration/Exploitation Trade-off. 128
   Madalina M. Drugan

Solving PCSPs Using Genetic Algorithms Guided by Structural Knowledge . . . 145
   Lamia Sadeg, Zineb Habbas, and Wassila Aggoune-Mtalaa

Activity Recognition for Dogs Based on Time-series Data Analysis 163
   Tatsuya Kiyohara, Ryohei Orihara, Yuichi Sei, Yasuyuki Tahara,
   and Akihiko Ohsuga

Machine Breakdown Recovery in Production Scheduling with Simple
Temporal Constraints. 185
   Roman Barták and Marek Vlk

From Information Assistance to Cognitive Automation: A Smart Assembly
Use Case   207
    Mario Aehnelt and Sebastian Bader

A Heuristic for Constrained Set Partitioning in the Light of Heterogeneous
Objectives   223
    Gerrit Anders, Florian Siefert, and Wolfgang Reif

Using Process Calculi for Plan Verification in Multiagent Planning   245
    Jan Jakubův, Jan Tožička, and Antonín Komenda

Speeding up Planning in Multiagent Settings Using CPU-GPU
Architectures   262
    Fadel Adoe, Yingke Chen, and Prashant Doshi

LS²C - A Platform for Norm Controlled Social Computers   284
    Flavio S. Correa da Silva, David S. Robertson,
    and Wamberto W. Vasconcelos

Construction of a Planar PLCA Expression: A Qualitative Treatment
of Spatial Data   298
    Kazuko Takahashi, Mizuki Goto, and Hiroyoshi Miwa

Offline Norm Evolution   316
    Magnus Hjelmblom

Parsing with Partially Known Grammar   334
    Ife Adebara, Veronica Dahl, and Sergio Tessaris

Author Index   347

Agents

A Hybrid POMDP-BDI Agent Architecture with Online Stochastic Planning and Desires with Changing Intensity Levels

Gavin Rens[1,2]($\boxtimes$) and Thomas Meyer[2,3]

[1] School of Mathematics, Statistics and Computer Science,
University of KwaZulu-Natal, Durban, South Africa
`grens@csir.co.za`
[2] Centre for Artificial Intelligence Research, CSIR Meraka, Pretoria, South Africa
[3] Department of Computer Science, University of Cape Town,
Cape Town, South Africa
`tmeyer@cs.uct.ac.za`

Abstract. We propose an agent architecture which combines Partially observable Markov decision processes (POMDPs) and the belief-desire-intention (BDI) framework to capitalize on their complimentary strengths. Our architecture introduces the notion of intensity of the desire for a goal's achievement. We also define an update rule for goals' desire levels. When to select a new goal to focus on is also defined. To verify that the proposed architecture works, experiments were run with an agent based on the architecture, in a domain where multiple goals must continually be achieved. The results show that (i) while the agent is pursuing goals, it can concurrently perform rewarding actions not directly related to its goals, (ii) the trade-off between goals and preferences can be set effectively and (iii) goals and preferences can be satisfied even while dealing with stochastic actions and perceptions. We believe that the proposed architecture furthers the theory of high-level autonomous agent reasoning.

Keywords: POMDP · BDI · Online planning · Desire intensity · Preference

1 Introduction

Imagine a scenario where a planetary rover has four main tasks and one task it can do when it does not interfere with performing the main tasks. The main tasks could be, for instance, collecting gas (for industrial use) from a natural vent at the base of a hill, taking a temperature measurement at the top of the hill, performing self-diagnostics and repairs, and reloading its batteries at the solar charging station. The less important task is to collect soil samples wherever the rover is. The rover is programmed to know the relative importance of collecting soil samples. The rover also has a model of the probabilities with which its

© Springer International Publishing Switzerland 2015
B. Duval et al. (Eds.): ICAART 2015, LNAI 9494, pp. 3–19, 2015.
DOI: 10.1007/978-3-319-27947-3_1

various actuators fail and the probabilistic noise-profile of its various sensors. The rover must be able to reason (plan) in real-time to pursue the right task at the right time while considering its resources and dealing with unforeseen events, all while considering the uncertainties about its actions (actuators) and perceptions (sensors).

We propose an architecture for the proper control of an agent in a complex environment such as the scenario described above. The architecture combines belief-desire-intention (BDI) theory [1,2] and partially observable Markov decision processes (POMDPs) [3,4]. Traditional BDI architectures (BDIAs) cannot deal with probabilistic uncertainties and they do not generate plans in real-time. A traditional POMDP cannot manage goals (major and minor tasks) as well as BDIAs can. Next, we analyse the POMDPs and BDIAs in a little more detail.

One of the benefits of agents based on BDI theory, is that they need not generate plans from scratch; their plans are already (partially) compiled, and they can act quickly once a goal is focused on. Furthermore, the BDI framework can deal with multiple goals. However, their plans are usually not optimal, and it may be difficult to find a plan which is applicable to the current situation. That is, the agent may not have a plan in its library which exactly 'matches' what it ideally wants to achieve. On the other hand, POMDPs can generate optimal policies on the spot to be highly applicable to the current situation. Moreover, policies account for stochastic actions and partially observable environments. Unfortunately, generating optimal POMDP policies is usually intractable. One solution to the intractability of POMDP policy generation is to employ a *continuous planning* strategy, or *agent-centred search* [5]. Aligned with agent-centred search is the *forward-search* approach or *online* planning approach in POMDPs [6].

The traditional BDIA maintains goals as *desires*; there is no reward for performing some action in some state. The reward function provided by POMDP theory is useful for modeling certain kinds of behavior or preferences. For instance, an agent based on a POMDP may want to avoid moist areas to prevent its parts becoming rusty. Moreover, a POMDP agent can generate plans which can optimally avoid moist areas. But one would not say that avoiding moist areas is the agent's goal. And POMDP theory maintains a single reward function; there is no possibility of weighing alternative reward functions and pursuing one at a time for a fixed period—all objectives must be considered simultaneously, in one reward function. Reasoning about objectives in POMDP theory is not as sophisticated as in BDI theory. A BDI agent cannot, however, simultaneously avoid moist areas *and* collect gold; it has to switch between the two or combine the desire to avoid moist areas with every other goal.

We argue that maintenance goals like avoiding moist areas (or collecting soil samples) should rather be viewed as a *preference* and modeled as a POMDP reward function. And specific tasks to complete (like collecting gas or keeping its battery charged) should be modeled as BDI desires.

Given the advantages of POMDP theoretic reasoning and the potentially sophisticated means-ends reasoning of BDI theory, we propose to combine the best features of these two theories in a coherent agent architecture. We call it the Hybrid POMDP-BDI agent architecture (or HPB architecture, for short).

In BDI theory, one of the big challenges is to know *when* the agent should switch its current goal and *what* its new goal should be [7]. To address this challenge with an intuitive explanation, we propose that an agent should maintain intensity levels of desire for every goal. (This intensity of desire could be interpreted as a kind of emotion.) The goal most intensely desired should be the current goal sought (the intention). We also define the notion of how much an intention is satisfied in the agent's current belief-state.

Typically, BDI agents do not deal with stochastic uncertainty. Integrating POMDP notions into a BDIA addresses this. For instance, an HPB agent will maintain a (subjective) belief-state representing its probabilistic (uncertain) belief about its current state. Planning with models of stochastic actions and perceptions is thus possible in the proposed architecture. The tight integration of POMDPs and BDIAs is novel, especially in combination with desires with changing intensity levels.

Section 2 briefly reviews the necessary theory. The proposed agent architecture is presented in Sect. 3 and formally defined. Section 4 shows an implementation of the architecture on an example domain and evaluates the performance on various dimensions, confirming that the approach may be useful in some domains. In Sect. 5, we propose one approach to making the specification of goals and preferences more general or flexible. The last section discusses some related work and points out some future directions for research in this area.

2   Preliminaries

The basic components of a BDI architecture [8,9] are

- a set or knowledge-base B of beliefs;
- an option generation function 'wish', generating the objectives the agent would ideally like to pursue (its desires);
- a set of desires D (goals to be achieved);
- a 'focus' function which selects intentions from the set of desires;
- a structure of intentions I of the most desirable options/desires returned by the focus function;
- a library of plans and subplans;
- a 'reconsideration' function which decides whether to call the focus function;
- an execution procedure, which affects the world according to the plan associated with the intention;
- a sensing or perception procedure, which gathers information about the state of the environment; and
- a belief update function, which updates the agent's beliefs according to its latest observations and actions.

Exactly how these components are implemented result in a particular BDI architecture.

Algorithm 1 (adapted from [10, Fig. 2.3]) is a basic BDI agent control loop. π is the current plan to be executed. *getPercept*($\cdot$) senses the environment and

---

Algorithm 1. Basic BDI agent control loop.

Input: B_0: initial beliefs
Input: I_0: initial intentions
1 $B \leftarrow B_0$;
2 $I \leftarrow I_0$;
3 $\pi \leftarrow null$;
4 **while** *alive* **do**
5 $\quad p \leftarrow getPercept()$;
6 $\quad B \leftarrow update(B, p)$;
7 $\quad D \leftarrow wish(B, I)$;
8 $\quad I \leftarrow focus(B, D, I)$;
9 $\quad \pi \leftarrow plan(B, I)$;
10 $\quad execute(\pi)$;

Algorithm 2. Control loop for an agent with reconsideration.

Input: B_0: initial beliefs
Input: I_0: initial intentions
1 $B \leftarrow B_0$;
2 $I \leftarrow I_0$;
3 $\pi \leftarrow null$;
4 **while** *alive* **do**
5 $\quad p \leftarrow getPercept()$;
6 $\quad B \leftarrow update(B, p)$;
7 $\quad$ **if** *reconsider*(B, I) **then**
8 $\quad\quad D \leftarrow wish(B, I)$;
9 $\quad\quad I \leftarrow focus(B, D, I)$;
10 $\quad\quad$ **if** *not sound*(π, I, B) **then** $\pi \leftarrow plan(B, I)$
11 $\quad$ **if** *not empty*(π) **then**
12 $\quad\quad \alpha \leftarrow head(\pi)$;
13 $\quad\quad execute(\alpha)$;
14 $\quad\quad \pi \leftarrow tail(\pi)$;
15 $\quad I \leftarrow succeeded(I, B)$;
16 $\quad I \leftarrow impossible(I, B)$;

---

returns a percept (processed sensor data) which is an input to $update(\cdot)$. $plan(\cdot)$ returns a plan from the plan library to achieve the agent's current intentions. $wish : B \times I \rightarrow D$ generates a set of desires, given the agent's beliefs, current intentions and possibly its innate motives. It is usually impractical for an agent to pursue the achievement of all its desires. It must thus filter out the most valuable and achievable desires. This is the function of $focus : B \times D \times I \rightarrow I$, taking beliefs, desires and current intentions as parameters. Together, the processes performed by *wish* and *focus* may be called deliberation, formally encapsulated by the *deliberate* procedure.

Algorithm 2 (adapted from [11]) has some more sophisticated controls. It controls when the agent would consider *whether* to re-deliberate, with the *reconsider* function (line 7) placed just before deliberation would take place. *reconsider*(·) is a Boolean function which tells the agent *whether* to reconsider its intentions (every time line 7 is reached).

The agent tests at every iteration through the main loop whether the currently pursued intention is still possibly achievable, using *impossible*(·). In the algorithm, serendipity is also taken advantage of by periodically testing—using *succeeded*(·)—whether the intention has been achieved, without the plan being fully executed. This agent is considered 'reactive' because it executes one action per loop iteration; this allows for deliberation between executions. The soundness (or applicability) of the plan to achieve the current intention is checked at every iteration of the loop.

There are various mechanisms which an agent might use to decide when to reconsider its intentions. See, for instance, [1,7,12–16].

In a partially observable Markov decision process (POMDP), the actions the agent performs have non-deterministic effects in the sense that the agent can only predict with a likelihood in which state it will end up after performing an action. Furthermore, its perception is noisy. That is, when the agent uses its sensors to determine in which state it is, it will have a probability distribution over a set of possible states to reflect its conviction for being in each state.

Formally [17], a POMDP is a tuple $\langle S, A, T, R, Z, P, b^0 \rangle$ with

- S, a finite set of states of the world (that the agent can be in),
- A a finite set of actions (that the agent can choose to execute),
- a transition function $T(s, a, s')$, the probability of being in s' after performing action a in state s,
- $R(a, s)$, the immediate reward gained for executing action a while in state s,
- Z, a finite set of observations the agent can perceive in its world,
- a perception function $P(s', a, z)$, the probability of observing z in state s' resulting from performing action a in some other state, and
- b^0 the initial probability distribution over all states in S.

A belief-state b is a set of pairs $\langle s, p \rangle$ where each state s in b is associated with a probability p. All probabilities must sum up to one, hence, b forms a probability distribution over the set S of all states. To update the agent's beliefs about the world, a special function $SE(z, a, b) = b_n$ is defined as

$$b_n(s') = \frac{P(s', a, z) \sum_{s \in S} T(s, a, s') b(s)}{Pr(z|a, b)}, \tag{1}$$

where a is an action performed in 'current' belief-state b, z is the resultant observation and $b_n(s')$ denotes the probability of the agent being in state s' in 'new' belief-state b_n. Note that $Pr(z \,|\, a, b)$ is a normalizing constant.

Let the *planning horizon h* (also called the *look-ahead depth*) be the number of future steps the agent plans ahead each time it plans. $V^*(b, h)$ is the *optimal* value of future courses of actions the agent can take with respect to a finite horizon h starting in belief-state b. This function assumes that at each step the action that will maximize the state's value will be selected.

Because the reward function $R(a,s)$ provides feedback about the utility of a particular state s (due to a executed in it), an agent who does not know in which state it is in cannot use this reward function directly. The agent must consider, for each state s, the probability $b(s)$ of being in s, according to its current belief-state b. Hence, a *belief* reward function $\rho(a,b)$ is defined, which takes a belief-state as argument. Let $\rho(a,b) \overset{def}{=} \sum_{s \in S} R(a,s)b(s)$.

The optimal *state-value* function is define by

$$V^*(b,h) \overset{def}{=} \max_{a \in \mathcal{A}} \left[\rho(a,b) + \gamma \sum_{z \in Z} Pr(z \mid a,b)V^*(SE(z,a,b), h-1) \right],$$

where $0 \leq \gamma < 1$ is a factor to discount the value of future rewards and $Pr(z \mid a,b)$ denotes the probability of reaching belief-state $b_n = SE(z,a,b)$. While V^* denotes the optimal value of a belief-state, function Q^* denotes the optimal *action-value*:

$$Q^*(a,b,h) \overset{def}{=} \rho(a,b) + \gamma \sum_{z \in Z} Pr(z \mid a,b)V^*(SE(z,a,b), h-1)$$

is the value of executing a in the current belief-state, plus the total expected value of belief-states reached thereafter.

3   The HPB Architecture

A hybrid POMDP-BDI (HPB) agent maintains (i) a belief-state which is periodically updated, (ii) a mapping from goals to numbers representing the level of desire to achieve the goals, and (iii) the current intention, the goal with the highest desire level. As the agent acts, its desire levels are updated and it may consider choosing a new intention based on new desire levels.

The *state* of an HPB agent is defined by the tuple $\langle B, D, I \rangle$, where B is the agent's current belief-state (i.e., a probability distribution over the states S, defined below), D is the agent's current desire function and I is the agent's current intention. We'll have more to say about D and I a little later.

An HPB agent could be defined by the tuple $\langle Atrb, G, A, Z, T, P, Util \rangle$, where

- *Atrb* is a set of attribute-sort pairs (for short, the *attribute set*). For every $(atrb : sort) \in Atrb$, $atrb$ is the name or identifier of an attribute of interest in the domain of interest, like *BattryLevel* or *Direction*, and *sort* is the set from which $atrb$ can take a value, for instance, real numbers in the range $[0, 55]$ or a list of values like $\{North, East, West, South\}$. So $\{(BattryLevel : [0, 55]), (Direction : \{North, East, West, South\})\}$ could be an attribute set.

  Let $\mathcal{N} = \{atrb \mid (atrb : sort) \in Atrb\}$ be the set of all attribute names. We define a state s induced from *Atrb* as one possible way of assigning values to attributes: $s = \{(atrb : v) \mid atrb \in \mathcal{N}, (atrb : sort) \in Atrb, v \in sort\}$ such that if $(atrb : v), (atrb' : v') \in s$ and $atrb = atrb'$, then $v = v'$. The set of all possible states is denoted S.

- G is a set of goals. A goal $g \in G$ is a subset of some state $s \in S$. For instance, $\{(BattryLevel : 13), (Direction : South)\}$ is a goal, and so are $\{(BattryLevel : 33)\}$ and $\{(Direction : West)\}$. It is even possible to have one goal overlap or be a subset of another goal. For instance, one is allowed to have $\{(BattryLevel : 13), (Direction : South)\} \in G$ and simultaneously $\{(BattryLevel : 13)\}$, $\{(BattryLevel : 14), (Direction : South)\} \in G$. In this architecture, it is assumed that the set of goals is given.
- A is a finite set of actions.
- Z is a finite set of observations.
- T is the transition function of POMDPs.
- P is the perception function of POMDPs.
- $Util$ consists of two functions $Pref$ and $Satf$ which allow an agent to determine the utilities of alternative sequences of actions. $Util = \langle Pref, Satf \rangle$.

$Pref$ is the preference function with a range in $\mathbb{R} \cap [0, 1]$. It takes an action a and a state s, and returns a value reflecting the preference for performing a in s. That is, $Pref(a, s) \in [0, 1]$. Numbers closer to 1 imply greater preference and numbers closer to 0 imply less preference. Except for the range restriction of $[0, 1]$, it has the same definition as a POMDP reward function, but its name indicates that it models the agent's preferences and not what is typically thought of as rewards. An HPB agent gets 'rewarded' by achieving its goals. The preference function is especially important to model action costs; the agent should prefer 'inexpensive' actions. $Pref$ has a local flavor. Designing the preference function to have a value lying in $[0,1]$ may sometimes be challenging, but we believe it is always possible.

$Satf$ is the satisfaction function with a range in $\mathbb{R} \cap [0, 1]$. It takes a state s and an intention I, and returns a value representing the degree to which the state satisfies the intention. That is, $Satf(I, s) \in [0, 1]$. It is completely up to the agent designer to decide how the satisfaction function is defined, as long as numbers closer to 1 mean more satisfaction and numbers closer to 0 mean less satisfaction. $Satf$ has a global flavor.

The desire function D is a total function from goals in G into the positive real numbers $\mathbb{R}^+$. The real number represents the intensity or level of desire of the goal. For instance, $(\{(BattryLevel : 13), (Direction : South)\}, 2.2)$ could be in D, meaning that the goal of having the battery level at 13 and moving in a southerly direction is desired with a level of 2.2. $(\{(BattryLevel : 33)\}, 56)$ and $(\{(Direction : West)\}, 444)$ are also examples of desires in D.

I is the agent's current intention; an element of G; the goal with the highest desire level. This goal will be actively pursued by the agent, shifting the importance of the other goals to the background. The fact that only one intention is maintained makes the HPB agent architecture quite different to standard BDIAs.

Figure 1 shows a flow diagram representing the operational semantics of the HPB architecture.

The satisfaction an agent gets for an intention in its current belief-state is defined as

$$Satf_\beta(I, B) \overset{def}{=} \sum_{s \in S} Satf(I, s)B(s),$$

where $Satf(I, s)$ is defined above and $B(s)$ is the probability of being in state s. The definition of $Pref_\beta$ has the same form as the reward function ρ over belief-states in POMDP theory:

$$Pref_\beta(a, B) \overset{def}{=} \sum_{s \in S} Pref(a, s)B(s),$$

where $Pref(a, s)$ was discussed above.

We propose the following desire update rule.

$$D(g) \leftarrow D(g) + 1 - Satf_\beta(g, B) \tag{2}$$

Rule 2 is defined so that as $Satf_\beta(g, B)$ tends to one (total satisfaction), the intensity with which the incumbent goal is desired does not increase. On the other hand, as $Satf_\beta(g, B)$ becomes smaller (more dissatisfaction), the goal's intensity is incremented. The rule transforms D with respect to B and g. A goal's intensity should drop the more it is being satisfied. The update rule thus defines how a goal's intensity changes over time with respect to satisfaction.

Note that desire levels never decrease. This does not reflect reality. It is however convenient to represent the intensity of desires like this: only *relative* differences in desire levels matter in our approach and we want to avoid unnecessarily complicating the architecture.

An HPB agent controls its behaviour according to the policies it generates. *Plan* is a procedure which generates a POMDP policy π of depth h. Essentially, we want to consider all action sequences of length h and the belief-states in which the agent would find itself if it followed the sequences. Then we want to choose the sequence (or at least its first action) which yields the highest preference and which ends in the belief-state most satisfying with respect to the intention.

During planning, preferences and intention satisfaction must be maximized. The main function used in the *Plan* procedure is the HPB action-value function Q^*_{HPB}, giving the value of some action a, conditioned on the current belief-state B, intention I and look-ahead depth h:

$$Q^*_{HPB}(a, B, I, h) \overset{def}{=} \alpha Satf_\beta(I, B) + (1 - \alpha)Pref_\beta(a, B)$$
$$+ \gamma \sum_{z \in Z} Pr(z \mid a, B) \max_{a' \in A} Q^*_{HPB}(a', B', I, h - 1),$$

$$Q^*_{HPB}(a, B, I, 1) \overset{def}{=} \alpha Satf_\beta(I, B) + (1 - \alpha)Pref_\beta(a, B),$$

where $B' = SE(a, z, B)$, $0 \leq \alpha \leq 1$ is the goal/preference 'trade-off' factor, γ is the normal POMDP discount factor and SE is the normal POMDP state estimation function. To keep things simple for this introductory paper, we define

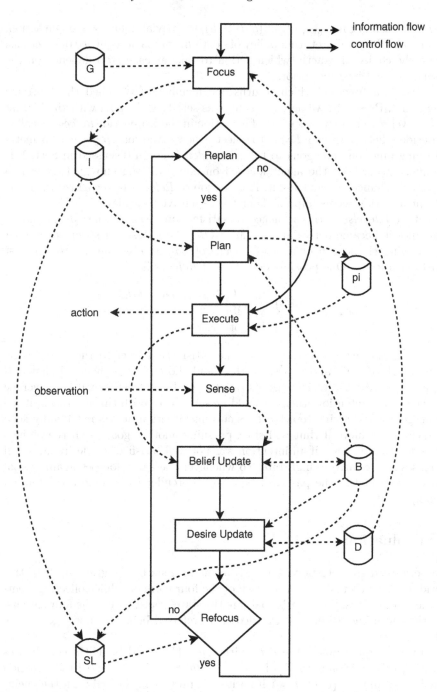

Fig. 1. Operational semantics of the HPB architecture. SL stands for *Satf_levels*. Note that *Satf_levels* depends on the current belief-state and intention, but not on desire levels. Planning is also independent of desire levels. The focus function depends on desire levels, but not on satisfaction. Whether to refocus depends on satisfaction levels, but not on desire levels.

Plan to return arg $\max_{a \in A} Q^*_{HPB}(a, B, I, h)$, the trivial policy of a single action. In general, *Plan* could return a policy of depth h, that is, a sequence of h actions, where the choice of exactly which action to take at each step depends on the observation received just prior.

Focus is a function which returns one member of G called the (current) intention I. Presently, we define it simply as selecting the goal with the highest desire level. After every execution of an action in the real-world, *Refocus* is called to decide whether to call *Focus* to select a new intention. *Refocus* is a meta-reasoning function analogous to the *reconsider* function discussed in Sect. 2. It is important to keep the agent focused on one goal long enough to give it a reasonable chance of achieving it. It is the job of *Refocus* to recognize when the current intention seems impossible or too expensive to achieve.

Let *Satf_levels* be the sequence of satisfaction levels of the current intention since it became active and let *MEMORY* be a designer-specified number representing the length of a sub-sequence of *Satf_levels*—the *MEMORY* last satisfaction levels. One possible definition of *Refocus* is

$$Refocus(c, \theta) \stackrel{def}{=} \begin{cases} \text{`no' if } |Satf\_levels| < MEMORY \\ \text{`yes' if } c < \theta \\ \text{`no' otherwise,} \end{cases}$$

where c is the average change from one satisfaction level to the next in the agent's '*MEMORY*', and θ is some threshold chosen by the agent designer. If the agent is expected to increase its satisfaction by at least, say, 0.1 on average for the current intention, then θ should be set to 0.1. With this approach, if the agent 'gets stuck' trying to achieve its current intention, it will not blindly keep on trying to achieve it, but will start pursuing another goal (with the highest desire level). Note that if an intention was not well satisfied, its desire level still increases at a relatively high rate. So whenever the agent focuses again, a goal not well satisfied in the past will be a top contender to become the intention (again).

4 Evaluation

We performed some tests on an HPB agent in a six-by-six grid-world. In this world, the agent's task is to visit each of the four corners, while collecting items on the way. That is, the agent's goals are the states representing the four corners, but the collecting of items is regarded as a preferred behavior, not a goal to be pursued.

States are quadruples $\langle x, y, d, t \rangle$, with $x, y \in \{1, \cdots, 6\}$ being the coordinates of the agent's position in the world, $d \in \{North, East, West, South\}$ the direction it is facing, and $t \in \{0, 1\}$, $t = 1$ if an item is present in the cell with the agent, else $t = 0$. The agent can perform five actions $\{left, right, forward, see, collect\}$, meaning, turn left, turn right, move one cell forward, see whether an item is present and collect an item. The only observation possible when executing one

of the physical actions is *obsNil*, the null observation, and *see* has possible observations from the set $\{0, 1\}$ for whether the agent sees the presence of an item
(1) or not (0).

Next, we define the possible outcomes for each action: When the agent turns
left or right, it can get stuck in the same direction, turn 90° or overshoots by
90°. When the agent moves forward, it moves one cell in the direction it is facing
or it gets stuck and does not move. The agent can see an item or see nothing (no
item in the cell), and collecting is deterministic (if there is an item present, it
will be collected with certainty, if the agent executes *collect*). All actions except
collect are designed so that the correct outcome is achieved 95 % of the time and
incorrect outcomes are achieved 5 % of the time.

So that the agent does not get lost too quickly, we have included an automatic
localization action, that is, a sensing action returns information about the agent's
approximate location. The action is automatic because the agent cannot choose
whether to perform it; the agent localizes itself after every regular/chosen action
is executed. However, just as with regular actions, the localization sensor is noisy,
and it correctly reports the agent's location with probability 0.95, else the sensor
reports a location adjacent to the agent with probability uniformly distributed
over 0.05.

Errors in the agent's actions and perceptions are thus modeled, not ignored.

In the experiments which follow, the threshold θ is set to 0.05, *MEMORY*
is set to 5 and $h = 4$. Desire levels are initially set to zero for all goals. Four
experiments were performed. First, collecting items but not intentionally visiting corners, second and third, visiting corners while collecting items (with
different values for the goal/preference 'trade-off' factor), and fourth, visiting
corners but not collecting items. For each experiment, 10 trials were run with
the agent starting in random locations and performing 100 actions per trial.
We let $Satf(I, s) = 1 - dist/10$ where 10 is the maximum Manhattan distance
between two cells in the world and $dist$ is the Manhattan distance between the
cells represented by I and s, and we let

$$Pref(a, s) = (1 - dist/10 + collUtil + sensUtil)/100,$$

where $dist$ is the Manhattan distance between the cell representing s and the
closest cell containing an item, $collUtil$ is 98 if a is *collect* and there is actually
an item in the cell represented by s, else 0, and $sensUtil$ is 1 if the agent tries
to *see*, else 0.[1] The division by 100 is to bring the value of $Pref(\cdot)$ within the
limits of 0 and 1.

First, we see how an HPB agent behaves when it has no goal state ($\alpha = 0$),
but continually only 'prefers' to collect items. That is, we let

$$Q^*_{HPB}(a, B, I, h) \stackrel{def}{=} Pref_\beta(a, B) + \gamma \sum_{z \in Z} Pr(z \mid a, B) \max_{a' \in A} Q^*_{HPB}(a', B', I, h - 1).$$

---

[1] $Pref(\cdot)$ is designed such that the agent collects a maximum number of items (ignoring
goals). The agent collects more when it is encouraged to sense where items are, hence
$sensUtil$ is 1 if the agent tries to *see*.

On average, it collects 7.4 of 12 possible items. The left-most results column of Table 1 shows how often corners are (unintentionally) visited.

Next, if the HPB agent prefers to collect items *while* equally trying to reach corners ($\alpha = 0.5$), it collects 4.3 of 12 possible items and the corners it visits is summarized in the second-from-left results column of Table 1.

Table 1. The average number of times each corner was visited (on separate occasions), percentage of times all corners were visited, and percentage of items (out of 12) collected.

Corner	Times visited			
	$\alpha = 0$	$\alpha = 0.5$	$\alpha = 0.75$	$\alpha = 1$
(1,1)	2.2	2.8	2.7	2.9
(1,6)	2.1	2.6	2.7	3.2
(6,1)	2.0	2.7	2.6	3.0
(6,6)	1.7	2.6	2.9	3.0
All	8.0 %	10.7 %	10.9 %	12.1 %
Items coll'ed	62 %	36 %	29 %	0 %

Then, we observe the agent's behavior if we set $\alpha = 0.75$. In this case, the agent collects 3.5 items on average, and its corner-visiting behavior—as given in the second-from-right column of Table 1—is proportional to the value of α, as expected.

Finally, we ignore the collection of items by setting $\alpha = 1$. That is, we let

$$Q^*_{HPB}(a, B, I, h) \stackrel{def}{=} Satf_\beta(I, B) + \gamma \sum_{z \in Z} Pr(z \mid a, B) \max_{a' \in A} Q^*_{HPB}(a', B', I, h - 1).$$

The right-most results column of Table 1 shows the average number of times each corner was visited when collecting items is not a preference. No items were collected.

These experiments highlight five important features of an HPB agent: (1) While the agent is pursuing goals, it can concurrently perform rewarding actions not directly related to its goals. (2) Each of several goals can be pursued individually until satisfactorily achieved. (3) Goals must periodically be re-achieved. (4) The trade-off between goals and preferences can be set effectively. (5) Goals and preferences can be satisfied even while dealing with stochastic actions and perceptions.

5   Towards Generalizing Goals

Considering exactly one preference, and pursuing exactly one goal at a time does not leave the agent designer with much flexibility. Moreover, are we justified in making such an absolute distinction between *preferences* and *goals*?

In an attempt to generalize the specification of goals and preferences, one might define $I \subseteq G$ to be the agent's current *set* of intentions. So here, there is not necessarily a single goal assigned the status of *intention*, but a set of goals are intentions; every goal (intention) in I is simultaneously pursued.

Instead of the agent having a particular preference, the design process could be made more flexible if the agent may be designed to exhibit preferential behavior—as loosely defined earlier via $Pref(\cdot)$—with respect to one or more goals.

And we let $Util = \langle \kappa, Satf \rangle$, where κ is a cost function in $\mathbb{R} \cap [0,1]$ and $Satf$ is a *set* of satisfaction functions $\{Satf^g \mid g \in G\}$. κ has the same definition as a POMDP reward function, but models the agent's action costs and not what is typically thought of as rewards. Rewards are gained to the degree the agent's goals are satisfied: Every $Satf^g$ is a satisfaction function with domain in S and range in $\mathbb{R} \cap [0,1]$, that is, $Satf^g(s) \in [0,1]$. $Satf^g$ measures the degree to which g is satisfied.

Every goal $g_i \in G$ will be weighted by α_{g_i} according to the importance of g_i to the agent. Let $\{\alpha_{g_1}, \alpha_{g_2}, \ldots, \alpha_{g_n}\}$ be the weights of the goals in $G = \{g_1, g_2, \ldots, g_n\}$ such that α_{g_i} is the weight of g_i, $\alpha_{g_i} > 0$ for all i, and $\sum_{i=1}^{n} \alpha_{g_i} = 1$. Then the generalized action-value function can be defined as

$$Q^*_{HPB}(a, B, I, h) \stackrel{def}{=} i(I,1)\alpha_{g_1} Satf^{g_1}_\beta(B) + \cdots + i(I,n)\alpha_{g_n} Satf^{g_n}_\beta(B) - \kappa_\beta(a, B)$$
$$+ \gamma \sum_{z \in Z} Pr(z \mid a, B) \max_{a' \in A} Q^*_{HPB}(a', B', I, h-1),$$

$$Q^*_{HPB}(a, B, I, 1) \stackrel{def}{=} i(I,1)\alpha_{g_1} Satf^{g_1}_\beta(B) + \cdots + i(I,1)\alpha_{g_n} Satf^{g_n}_\beta(B) - \kappa_\beta(a, B),$$

where

- $Satf^g_\beta(\cdot)$ and $\kappa_\beta(\cdot)$ are the expected (w.r.t. a belief-state) values of $Satf^g(\cdot)$, respectively, $\kappa(\cdot)$,
- $i(I,j) = 1$ if $j \in I$, else $i(I,j) = 0$ if $j \notin I$,
- $B' = SE(a, z, B)$,
- γ is the normal POMDP discount factor and
- SE is the normal POMDP state estimation function.

Focus could now be defined as follows. If $g \notin I$ and for all $g' \in I$, $D(g) > D(g')$, then add g to I. And for every $g \in I$, if $Remove(g, I)$ returns 'yes', then remove g from I. It is the job of $Remove(g, I)$ to recognize when g seems impossible or too expensive to achieve, and thus needs to be removed from I.

Let $Satf\_levels(g)$ be the sequence of satisfaction levels of some goal $g \in I$ since g became active (i.e., was added to I). For every goal, its satisfaction levels are maintained if and only if the goal is currently an intention.

From preliminary simulations, it seems that the definition of *Focus*, just given, is inadequate for the proposed generalization. It does, however, provide a stepping-stone in the ongoing research.

6   Related Work and Conclusion

Our work focuses on providing high-level decision-making capabilities for robots and agents who live in dynamic stochastic environments, where multiple goals and goal types must be pursued. We introduced a hybrid POMDP-BDI agent architecture, which may display emergent behavior, driven by the intensities of their desires. In the past decade, several BDIAs have been augmented with capabilities to deal with uncertainty. The HPB architecture is novel in that, while the agent is pursuing goals, it can concurrently perform rewarding actions not directly related to its goals, and goals must periodically be re-achieved, depending on the goals' desire levels, which change over time and in proportion to how close the goals are to being satisfied.

The ideas presented in Sect. 5 and the associated preliminary simulations indicate that generalizing our agent architecture will be an interesting and challenging endeavour.

[18,19] have incorporated online plan generation into BDI systems, however the planners deal only with deterministic actions and observations.

[20] use POMDP theory to coordinate teams of agents. However, their framework is very different to our architecture. They use POMDP theory to determine good role assignments of team members, not for generating policies online.

[21] provide a rather sophisticated architecture for controlling the behavior of an emotional agent. Their agents reason with several classes of emotion and their agents are supposed to portray emotional behavior, not simply to solve problems, but to look believable to humans. Their architecture has a "continuous planner [...] that is capable of partial order planning and includes emotion-focused coping [...]" Their work has a different application to ours, however, we could take inspiration from them to improve the HPB architecture.

[22] take a different approach to use POMDPs to improve BDI agents. By leveraging the relationship between POMDP and BDI models, as discussed by [23], they devised an algorithm to extract BDI plans from optimal POMDP policies. The main difference to our work is that their policies are pre-generated and BDI-style rules are extracted for all contingencies. The advantage is that no (time-consuming) online plan/policy generation is necessary. The disadvantage of their approach is that all the BDI plans must be stores and every time the domain model changes, a new POMDP must be solved and the policy-to-BDI-plan algorithm must be run. It is not exactly clear from their paper [22] how or when intentions are chosen. Although it is interesting to know the relationship between POMDPs and BDI models [23,24], we did not use any of these insights in developing our architecture. However, the fact that the HPB architecture does integrate the two frameworks, is probably due to the existence of the relationship.

[25] also introduced a hybrid POMDP-BDI architecture, but without a notion of desire levels or satisfaction levels. Although their basic approaches to combine the POMDP and BDI frameworks is the same as ours, there are at least two major differences: Firstly, they define their architecture in terms of the GOLOG agent language [26]. Secondly, their approach uses a computationally intensive method for deciding whether to refocus; performing short policy look-aheads to

ascertain the most valuable goal to pursue.[2] Our approach seems much more efficient.

[27] incorporate probabilistic graphical models into the BDI framework for plan selection in stochastic environments. An agent maintains epistemic states (with random variables) to model the uncertainty about the stochastic environment, and corresponding belief sets of the epistemic state are defined. The possible states of the environment, according to sensory observations, and their relationships are modeled using probabilistic graphical models: The uncertainty propagation is carried out by Bayesian Networks, and belief sets derived from the epistemic states trigger the selection of relevant plans from a plan library. For cases when more than one plan is applicable due to uncertainty in an agent's beliefs, they propose a utility-driven approach for plan selection, where utilities of actions are modeled in influence diagrams. Our architecture is different in that it does not have a library of pre-supplied plans; in our architecture, policies (plans) are generated online.

None of the approaches mentioned maintain desire levels for selecting intentions. The benefit of maintaining desire levels is that intentions are not selected only according what they offer with respect to their *current* expected reward, but also according to when last they were achieved.

Although [20,27] call their approaches hybrid, our architecture can arguably more confidently be called hybrid because of its more intimate integration of POMDP and BDI concepts.

We could take some advice from [28]. They provide a systematic methodology to incorporate emotion into a decision-theoretic framework, and also provide "a principled, domain-independent methodology for generating heuristics in novel situations".

Policies returned by *Plan* as defined in this paper are optimal. A major benefit of a POMDP-based architecture is that the literature on POMDP planning optimization [6,29–35] (for instance) can be drawn upon to improve the speed with which policies can be generated.

Our architecture cannot yet control how often one goal is sought relative to other goals. It would be advantageous to be able to do this.

Evaluating the proposed architecture in richer domains would highlight problems in the architecture and indicate new directions for research and development in the area of hybrid POMDP-BDI architectures.

References

1. Bratman, M.: Intention, Plans, and Practical Reason. Harvard University Press, Massachusetts (1987)
2. Rao, A., Georgeff, M.: BDI agents: From theory to practice. In: Proceedings of the ICMAS 1995, pp. 312–319. AAAI Press (1995)

---

[2] Essentially, the goals in G are stacked in descending order of the value of $V^*_{HPB}(B, g, h^-)$, where $h^- < h$ and B is the current belief-state. The goal on top of the stack becomes the intention.

3. Monahan, G.: A survey of partially observable Markov decision processes: theory, models, and algorithms. Manage. Sci. **28**, 1–16 (1982)
4. Lovejoy, W.: A survey of algorithmic methods for partially observed Markov decision processes. Ann. Oper. Res. **28**, 47–66 (1991)
5. Koenig, S.: Agent-centered search. Artif. Intell. Mag. **22**, 109–131 (2001)
6. Ross, S., Pineau, J., Paquet, S., Chaib-draa, B.: Online planning algorithms for POMDPs. J. Artif. Intell. Res. (JAIR) **32**, 663–704 (2008)
7. Schut, M., Wooldridge, M., Parsons, S.: The theory and practice of intention reconsideration. Exp. Theor. Artif. Intell. **16**, 261–293 (2004)
8. Wooldridge, M.: Intelligent agents. In: Weiss, G. (ed.) Multiagent Systems: A Modern Approach to Distributed Artificial Intelligence. MIT Press, Massachusetts (1999)
9. Wooldridge, M.: An Introduction to Multiagent Systems. Wiley, Chichester (2002)
10. Wooldridge, M.: Reasoning About Rational Agents. MIT Press, Massachusetts (2000)
11. Schut, M., Wooldridge, M.: Principles of intention reconsideration. In: Agents 2001: Proceedings of the 5th International Conference on Autonomous Agents, pp. 340–347. ACM Press, New York (2001)
12. Pollack, M., Ringuette, M.: Introducing the tileworld: experimentally evaluating agent architectures. In: Proceedings of the AAAI 1990, pp. 183–189. AAAI Press (1990)
13. Kinny, D., Georgeff, M.: Commitment and effectiveness of situated agents. In: Proceedings of the 12th International Joint Conference on Artificial Intelligence (IJCAI-91), pp. 82–88 (1991)
14. Kinny, D., Georgeff, M.: Experiments in optimal sensing for situated agents. In: Proceedings of the 2nd Pacific Rim Internatioanl Conference on Artificial Intelligence (PRICAI 1992) (1992)
15. Schut, M., Wooldridge, M.: Intention reconsideration in complex environments. In: Proceedings of the 4th International Conference on Autonomous Agents (AGENTS 2000). ACM, New York (2000)
16. Schut, M., Wooldridge, M.: The control of reasoning in resource-bounded agents. Knowl. Eng. Rev. **16**, 215–240 (2001)
17. Kaelbling, L., Littman, M., Cassandra, A.: Planning and acting in partially observable stochastic domains. Artif. Intell. **101**, 99–134 (1998)
18. Walczak, A., Braubach, L., Pokahr, A., Lamersdorf, W.: Augmenting BDI agents with deliberative planning techniques. In: Bordini, R.H., Dastani, M., Dix, J., El Fallah Seghrouchni, A. (eds.) PROMAS 2006. LNCS (LNAI), vol. 4411, pp. 113–127. Springer, Heidelberg (2007)
19. Meneguzzi, F., Zorzo, A., Móra, M., Luck, M.: Incorporating planning into BDI systems. Scalable Comput. Pract. Experience **8**, 15–28 (2007)
20. Nair, R., Tambe, M.: Hybrid bdi-pomdp framework for multiagent teaming. J. Artif. Intell. Res. (JAIR) **23**, 367–420 (2005)
21. Lim, M.Y., Dias, J., Aylett, R.S., Paiva, A.C.R.: Improving adaptiveness in autonomous characters. In: Prendinger, H., Lester, J.C., Ishizuka, M. (eds.) IVA 2008. LNCS (LNAI), vol. 5208, pp. 348–355. Springer, Heidelberg (2008)
22. Pereira, D., Gonçalves, L., Dimuro, G., Costa, A.: Constructing bdi plans from optimal pomdp policies, with an application to agentspeak programming. In: Henning, G., Galli, M., Goneet, S. (eds.) XXXIV Conferência Latinoamericano de Informática, Santa Fe. Anales CLEI 2008, pp. 240–249 (2008)

23. Simari, G., Parsons, S.: On the relationship between mdps and the bdi architecture. In: Proceedings of the Fifth International Joint Conference on Autonomous Agents and Multiagent Systems, AAMAS 2006, pp. 1041–1048. ACM, New York (2006)
24. Simari, G., Parsons, S.: Markov Decision Processes and the Belief-Desire-Intention Model. Springer Briefs in Computer Science. Springer, Heidelberg (2011)
25. Rens, G., Ferrein, A., Van der Poel, E.: A BDI agent architecture for a POMDP planner. In: Lakemeyer, G., Morgenstern, L., Williams, M.A. (eds.) Proceedings of the 9th International Symposium on Logical Formalizations of Commonsense Reasoning (Commonsense 2009), University of Technology, pp. 109–114. UTSe Press, Sydney (2009)
26. Boutilier, C., Reiter, R., Soutchanski, M., Thrun, S.: Decision-theoretic, high-level agent programming in the situation calculus. In: Proceedings of the Seventeenth National Conference on Artificial Intelligence (AAAI 2000) and of the Twelfth Conference on Innovative Applications of Artificial Intelligence (IAAI 2000), pp. 355–362. AAAI Press, Menlo Park (2000)
27. Chen, Y., Hong, J., Liu, W., Godo, L., Sierra, C., Loughlin, M.: Incorporating PGMs into a BDI architecture. In: Boella, G., Elkind, E., Savarimuthu, B.T.R., Dignum, F., Purvis, M.K. (eds.) PRIMA 2013. LNCS, vol. 8291, pp. 54–69. Springer, Heidelberg (2013)
28. Antos, D., Pfeffer, A.: Using emotions to enhance decision-making. In: Walsh, T. (ed.) Proceedings of the 22nd International Joint Conference on Artificial Intelligence (IJCAI 2011), pp. 24–30. AAAI Press, Menlo Park (2011)
29. Murphy, R.: Introduction to AI Robotics. MIT Press, Massachusetts (2000)
30. Roy, N., Gordon, G., Thrun, S.: Finding approximate POMDP solutions through belief compressions. J. Artif. Intell. Res. (JAIR) **23**, 1–40 (2005)
31. Paquet, S., Tobin, L., Chaib-draa, B.: Real-time decision making for large POMDPs. In: Kégl, B., Lee, H.-H. (eds.) Canadian AI 2005. LNCS (LNAI), vol. 3501, pp. 450–455. Springer, Heidelberg (2005)
32. Li, X., Cheung, W., Liu, J.: Towards solving large-scale POMDP problems via spatio-temporal belief state clustering. In: Proceedings of IJCAI-05 Workshop on Reasoning with Uncertainty in Robotics (RUR 2005) (2005)
33. Shani, G., Brafman, R., Shimony, S.: Forward search value iteration for POMDPs. In: de Mantaras, R.L. (ed.) Proceedings of the 20th International Joint Conference on Artificial Intelligence (IJCAI 2007), pp. 2619–2624. AAAI Press, Menlo Park (2007)
34. Cai, C., Liao, X., Carin, L.: Learning to explore and exploit in pomdps. In: NIPS, pp. 198–206 (2009)
35. Shani, G., Pineau, J., Kaplow, R.: A survey of point-based pomdp solvers. Auton. Agent. Multi-Agent Syst. **27**, 1–51 (2013)

Dynamic *JChoc*: A Distributed Constraints Reasoning Platform for Dynamically Changing Environments

Imade Benelallam[1,2], Zakarya Erraji[1(✉)], Ghizlane EL Khattabi[1], and El Houssine Bouyakhf[1]

[1] LIMIARF FSR, University Mohammed V, Rabat, Morocco
imade.benelallam@ieee.org,
{zakarya.erraji,elkhattabi.ghizlane}@gmail.com, bouyakhf@mtds.com
[2] INSEA, Rabat, Morocco

Abstract. In Artificial Intelligence, a large number of problems (i.e. distributed resource management, distributed air traffic management, Distributed Sensor Network [1]) can be modeled and solved as Distributed Constraint Satisfaction Problems (DisCSPs). As many real world problems change continuously and incessantly over time, some methods have been developed (e.g. DynABT), for solving problems which exhibit this dynamic behavior. Meanwhile, there was no available framework that helped users to develope intelligent multi-agent systems based on Dynamic and Distributed Constraints Reasoning (DCR) techniques.

In this paper, we propose a new platform, called JChoc, supporting the dynamic aspect for DisCSPs. JChoc is an easy to use platform, based on an elegant Multi-agent communication sub-platform (e.i JADE). It deals with agents with local complex problems and allows a realistic use of agents on a real distributed and dynamic framework.

A real distributed problem is addressed to illustrate how the platform can be used to solve dynamically changing problems. However, the experimental results show the defectiveness of our platform.

Keywords: Dynamically changing environments · Constraint programming (CP) · Multi-agent systems · Distributed problem solving · Agent models and architectures · Distributed constraints reasoning · Realistic use · Constraint satisfaction problem (CSP) · Distributed CSP (DisCSP)

1 Introduction

Since the onset of real time electronic devices, mobiles, ubiquitous, and intelligent computing, new combinatorial problems have emerged in the AI community such as: distributed resource management, distributed air traffic management, Distributed Sensor Network [1], disaster rescue [2] and distributed Meeting Scheduling Problems (SMP), for which it is not suitable to collect all data of problem in one site, to solve it by a centralized algorithm. The reasons are communication time and cost of translation of each sub-problem in a

© Springer International Publishing Switzerland 2015
B. Duval et al. (Eds.): ICAART 2015, LNAI 9494, pp. 20–36, 2015.
DOI: 10.1007/978-3-319-27947-3_2

common format. In addition, to give a single agent all data of the problem can also be excluded for reasons of security and confidentiality. Therefore, some of the AI communities are motivated to take an interest in Distributed Constraint Reasoning (DCR), giving birth to other distributed formalism [5], whose work focused on developing techniques for modeling and solving distributed combinatorial problems with or without optimization criterion. Distributed Constraint Satisfaction Problems (DisCSP), Distributed Constraint Optimization Problems (DCOP) and Dynamic Distributed Constraints Satisfaction Problems provide a useful framework of multiagent systems for distributed and dynamic resolution of combinatorial problems [3–5, 16, 17].

In this context, an agent must have a communication platform that allows the exchange of information or dialogue to coordinate their decision-making. This reliable communication tool allows agents to send and receive messages according to a given distributed protocol. However, various sophisticated solvers have been developed: DisChoco [18], Disolver [6], MELY [7], Frodo [8]. Those solvers rely on several algorithms for solving DisCSP problems such as Asynchronous Backtracking (ABT [4], ABT Family [9]), Asynchronous Forward Checking (AFC) [10] and Nogood-based Asynchronous Forward-Checking (AFC-ng) [11]. Asynchronous Distributed Constraints Optimization (ADOPT) [12], Asynchronous Forward Bounding (AFB) [13], Asynchronous Branch-and-Bound (BnB-ADOPT) [14] and Dynamic Backtracking for distributed constraint optimization (DyBop) [15] were developed to solve DCOP problems. As well as the authors recognise that most of these tools are specially developed for simulation context. This fact can be clearly observed from its experimental setups. Given the difficulty that researchers are facing, they often make many simplifying assumptions (i.e. simple agent (one variable per agent), agents as multi-thread, single physical platform, communication via simulated perfect FIFO channels, etc.) about the underlying distributed problem, which might affect the predictions obtained from the simulation in non-trivial ways. Switching from the simulation to the actual development practice often leads to loss of accuracy. Hence, bridging the gap between simulation and actual development and deployment within distributed constraints solvers and include dynamic aspect are the motivations for presenting the different ideas discussed in the present paper.

In this paper we focus on the development of a Multi-agent platform for Distributed Constraint Reasoning and Dynamic Distributed Constraints Problems, namely JChoc DisSolver. This proposed platform allows non-expert user to address and solve easily, not only distributed constraint satisfaction problems, but also real Dynamic Distributed Constraint Satisfaction Problems.

This document is organized as follows. Section 2 presents a brief definition of Distributed Constraint Satisfaction Problem (DisCSP) and Dynamic and Distributed Constraint Satisfaction Problem (DDisCSP) with an example. In Sect. 3, we present related work. Section 4 presents the global architecture of JChoc platform. In Sect. 5, we show how use this platform in a distributed environment even if it changes dynamically. And finally, in Sect. 6 we conclude the paper by experiment this platform within a real Distributed and Dynamic Constraints Satisfaction Problems.

2   Preliminaries

2.1   Distributed Constraint Satisfaction Problems

Constraint Programming distinguishes between the description of the constraints involved in a problem on the one hand, and the algorithms and heuristics used to solve the problem on the other hand. Modeling and solving problems is through a very elegant mathematical formalism, called the Constraint Satisfaction Problems CSPs.

The Distributed Constraint Satisfaction Problem (DisCSP) is represented by a constraint network where variables and constraints are distributed among multiple automated agents.

Definition: A finite DisCSP is defined by a 5-tuple(A, X, D, C, ψ), where:

- $A = \{A_1, ..., A_p\}$ is a set of p agents.
- $X = \{x_1, ..., x_n\}$ is a set of n variables such that each variable x_i is controlled by one agent in A.
- $D = \{D(x_1), ..., D(x_2)\}$ is a set of current domains, where $D(x_i)$ is a finite set of possible values for variable x_i.
- $C = \{c_1, ..., c_m\}$ is a set of m constraints that specify the combinations of values allowed for the variables they involve. We note that the constraints are distributed among the automated agents. Hence, constraints divide into two broad classes: inter-agent and intra-agent.
- $\psi : X \longmapsto A$ is a function that maps each variable to its agent.

A solution to a DisCSP is an assignment of a value from its domain to every variable of the distributed constraint network, in such a way that every constraint is satisfied. Solutions to DisCSPs can be found by searching through the possible assignments of values to variables such as ABT algorithm [4].

Many hard practical problems can be seen as DisCSPs. Most Distributed Reasoning platform however assume that problem are static. This has a limitation for dynamic problems that change over time, for example timetabling shifts in a large hospital where availability staff change over time. Also in a dynamic environment a DisCSP may change over time, these changes could be due to addition/deletion of variables, constraints, or agents. The Distributed and Dynamic Constraint Satisfaction Problems (DDisCSPs) can be described as a five tuple (A, X, D, C, δ) where:

- A, X, D and C remain as described in DisCSP.
- δ is the change function which introduces changes.

Many DDisCSPs approaches (e.i : DynABT [25], DynBDA [26]) are proposed to solve such problems, and can be easily implemented in This platform.

2.2   Meeting Scheduling Problem as a DisCSP

The Distributed Meeting Scheduling Problem (MSP) is a real distributed problem where agents may not desire to deliver their personal information to a centralized agent to solve the whole problem [20,21].

The MSP involves a set of n agents having a personal private calendar and a set of m meetings each taking place in a specified location. Each agent, $A_i \in A$, knows the set of the k_i among m meetings he/she must attend. It is assumed that each agent knows the traveling time between the locations where his/her meetings will be held. The traveling time between locations where two meetings m_i and m_j will be hold is denoted by $TravellingTime(m_i, m_j)$. Solving the problem consists in satisfying the following constraints: (i) all agents attending a meeting must agree on when it will occur, (ii) an agent cannot attend two meetings at same time, (iii) an agent must have enough time to travel from the location where he/she is to the location where the next meeting will be held.

We illustrate in Fig. 1 the encoding of the instance of the meeting scheduling problem in the distributed constraint network formalism. This figure shows 4 agents where each agent has a personal private calendar and a set of meetings each taking place in a specified location. Thus, we get the following DisCSP:

- $A = \{A_1, A_2, A_3, A_4\}$ each agent A_i corresponds to a real agent,
- For each agent $A_i \in A$ there is a variable m_{ik}, for every meeting m_k that A_i attends,
- $X = \{m_{11}, m_{13}, m_{14}, m_{21}, m_{22}, m_{32}, m_{33}, m_{34}, m_{44}\}$.
- $D = \{D(m_{ik}) | m_{ik} \in X\}$ where,
  * $D(m_{11}) = D(m_{13}) = D(m_{14}) = \{s \mid s \text{ is a slot in } calendar(A_1)\}$.
  * $D(m_{21}) = D(m_{22}) = \{s \mid s \text{ is a slot in } calendar(A_2)\}$.
  * $D(m_{32}) = D(m_{33}) = D(m_{34}) = \{s \mid s \text{ is a slot in } calendar(A_3)\}$.
  * $D(m_{44}) = \{s \mid s \text{ is a slot in } calendar(A_4)\}$.
- For each agent A_i, there is a private arrival-time constraint (c_{kl}^i intra-agent constraint) between every pair of its local variables (m_{ik}, m_{il}) (e.g. Omar must attend tree meetings m_1, m_2 and m_3). For each two agents A_i, A_j that attend the same meeting m_k there is an equality inter-agent constraint (c_k^{ij}) between the variables m_{ik} and m_{jk}, corresponding to the meeting m_k on agent A_i and A_j (e.g. Omar and Jean participate in the same meeting m_1). Then, $C = \{c_{kl}^i, c_k^{ij}\}$.

Given this example, a Distributed Constraint Reasoning (DCR) platform must allow agents to have a reliable communication tool that allows sending and receiving messages, in order to find the feasible solutions.

3   Related Work

Recently, B. Lutati and et al. [23] have proposed a MAS platform, called AgentZero. This tool can be considered as a new addition to the available MAS tools in general and to the DCR research field in particular. The authors claim that AgentZero is generic and applicable to many domains, specifically introducing benefits for the DCR simulation domain. However, the platform has been designed only for simulation use and used only by researchers in Distributed Constraint Reasoning. So developing and setting computer software for real problems based on DCR is not simple and remains a difficult task for users in general.

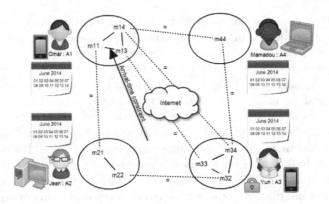

Fig. 1. Meeting scheduling problem modeled as DisCSP.

In [8] A. Petcu. Proposes a Framework for Open Distributed Optimization (FRODO). The framework is implemented in Java, and simulates a multiagent environment in a single Java virtual machine. Each agent in the environment is executed asynchronously in a separate execution thread, and communicates with its peers through message exchange. FRODO comes with several built in algorithms and a suite of problem generators for benchmarking.

The authors of [24] proposed a open-source tool for solving DCR, called DCOPolis. DCOPolis is an open-source framework designed to abstract algorithm implementation from the underlying platform (i.e. hardware, network, operating system). This allows a single implementation of an algorithm to be run in simulation (i.e. on top of the NS2 network simulator with AgentJ). DCOPolis differs from existing DCR frameworks and simulators, however, it supports a novel type of simulation in which the runtime of any distributed algorithm can be accurately estimated on a single physical computer.

Researchers in DCR are concerned with developing new algorithms, and comparing their performance with existing algorithms. Therefore, in [18] the authors present an open source Java library, called DisChoco which aims at implementing DCR algorithms from an abstract model of agent. DisChoco allows to represent both DisCSPs and DCOPs, as opposed to other platforms. A single implementation of a DCR algorithm can run as simulation on a single machine. DisChoco is a elegant platform, but all the different issues of realistic uses and actual deployment have not been addressed.

Developing intelligent software applications based on DCR algorithms is a difficult task, because the programmer must explicitly juggle between many very different concerns, including centralized programming, distributed programming, asynchronous and concurrent management of distributed structures, communication concerns and others. In addition, there are very few open-source tools for solving DCR problems in a physically distributed environment. In this paper we have been looking for a singular platform that would possess not only simulation qualities, but especially designed for realistic and actual deployment. JChoc platform is a new added value which allows bridging the gap between simulation and realistic use. To our knowledge, this is the first DCR platform respecting FIPA standards and specifications.

4   JChoc Platform

4.1   JChoc Description

The best way to prove the effectiveness of a proposed distributed constraint reasoning algorithm, is to use it in a realistic multi-platform agent. This is how we can reduce the gap between theory and practice. JChoc is a distributed constraints multiagent platform proposed for solving combinatorial problems within a specific distributed environment. It can also be used to analyze and test the algorithms proposed by constraints programming community. This platform is presented in the form of programming environment (API) and applications to help different types of users. Hence, JChoc can be easily appropriated by two main actors:

- Developers to design and develop applications (e.i. client application, web application, mobile application, etc.) within distributed constraints programming based on JChoc API;
- Non-expert user to interact directly with applications based on distributed constraints programming.

This proposed platform has several advantages:

- A distributed constraints problem can be easily addressed and solved in a realistic environment by unsophisticated users;
- The performances of the proposed protocols (i.e. ABT, AFC, Adopt, etc.) can be actually tested and proved in a realistic communication channel (i.e. WLAN WPAN WMAN WWAN);
- It offers a modular software architecture which accepts extensions easily (i.e. security, confidentiality, cryptography, etc.);
- Thanks to the extensibility of JADE communication model [19], JChoc allows the development of multiagent systems and applications consistent with Foundation for Intelligent Physical Agents (FIPA)[1] standards and specifications;
- Thanks to the robustness of Choco platform [22], complex agent (i.e. multiple variables per agent) can easily address and solve its local sub-problem and use solutions as a compiled domain.

This platform consists of several modules presented as services. The main constraint programming services offered are based Distributed Constraint Reasoning Protocols (DCRP) and Choco Solver (CS). Choco is a platform for research in centralized constraint programming and combinatorial optimization. This choice of Choco enabled us to benefit from the modules already implemented in it. In the next section, we will study the different elements of JChoc platform.

---

[1] http://www.fipa.org/.

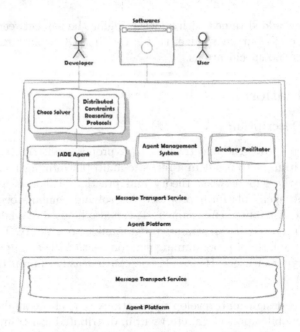

Fig. 2. The JChoc architecture.

4.2 JChoc Architecture

JChoc architecture is motivated by FIPA specifications, it allows the development of multiagent systems and applications conforming to MAS standards. It is implemented in JAVA and provides classes that implement and inherit from JADE and Choco platforms to define the behavior of specific agents. Figure 2 represents the main JChoc architectural elements. This platform has five main modules.

- DCRP ≪Distributed Constraint Reasoning Protocols≫ provides distributed constraints protocols as service. This element defines new types of messages and implements the behavior of the agent when receiving and sending a specific type of information (e.i. ABT, AFC, Adopt, etc.);
- CS ≪Choco Solver≫ provides the ability to address and resolve local CSP sub-problem;
- DF ≪Director Facilitator≫ provides a service of "yellow pages" to the platform;
- ACC ≪Agent Communication Channel≫ manages the communication between agents;
- AMS ≪Agent Management System≫ oversees the registration of agents, their authentication, their access and the use of the system.

These five modules are activated at each time the platform is started.

The JADE agent is also a key player in our platform. Thanks to JADE an Agent Identifier (AID) identifies an agent uniquely.

JChoc uses extensively a sniffing tool for debugging, or simply documenting conversations between agents. The sniffer subscribes to AMS agent to be notified of all platform events and of all message exchanges between a set of specified agents. When the user decides to monitor an agent or a group of agents, every message directed to, or coming from, that agent/group is tracked and displayed in the sniffer GUI. The user can select and view the details of every individual message, save the message or serialize an entire conversation as a binary file.

5   Using Dynamic JChoc

5.1   Using JChoc in Distributed Environment

In this section we present how to use the JChoc platform in real distributed environment. The MSP problem depicted in Fig. 1 is used to illustrate this proposed platform. Initially we generate a sub-problem for each agent involved in the global DisCSP problem, modeled by an expert as an XML file, which allows standardizing the syntactic structure of the sub-problems. A sub-problem containing only the information necessary for a single agent, so he can participate in solving the global problem in a real distributed environment.

Figure 3 shows an example of representation of the MSP sub-problem defined above in the XDisCSP format. Each variable has a unique ID, which is the concatenation of the ID of its owner agent and index of the variable in the agent. This is necessary when defining constraints (scope of constraints). For constraints, we used two types of constraints: TKC for Totally Known Constraint and PKC for Partially Known Constraint. Constraints can be defined in extension or as a Boolean function. Different types of constraints are predefined: equal to $eq(M_i, M_j)$, different from $ne(M_i, M_j)$, greater than or equal $ge(M_i, M_j)$, greater than $gt(M_i; M_j)$,etc. In this sub-problem there is 1 complex agent A_3 which controls exactly 3 variables. The domain of A_3 contain 14 values $D_3 = \{1...14\}$. There are three constraints of Arrival time $ge(abs(sub(M_i, M_j)))$: the first constraint is between $M_{3.2}$ and $M_{3.3}$ the second one is between $M_{3.3}$ and $M_{3.4}$ and the third is between $M_{3.2}$ and $M_{3.4}$, three constraints of equality $eq(M_i, M_j)$: between $M_{1.4}$ and $M_{3.4}$, between $M_{1.3}$ and $M_{3.3}$, between $M_{2.2}$ and $M_{3.2}$ after defining our sub-problem we can configure our solver.

Once the sub-problem is generated, we can test the functioning of the platform in a physically distributed environment. So we chose machines that simulate the different agents of the problem, and filed each sub-problem in a machine, before launching it.

Figure 4 shows how the master launches its communication interface listening on the network. We start with instantiate the dissolver object (line 7), This class models the distributed problem when JChoc is used to solve a problem in a real distributed environment. All information on distributed problem is encapsulated in this object (identities of agents, inter-agent constraints, protocol, etc.). Then, we define the type of master (line 8) (ABT in this case). Finally, we trigger the container and we launch the master (lines 10–11).

```
1   <?xml version="1.0" encoding="UTF-8"?>
2   <instance>
3       <presentation name="MSP" type="DisCSP"
4           model="Complex" constraintModel="TKC" format="XDisCSP 1.0" />
5       <domains nbDomains="2">
6           <domain name="D1" nbValues="7">1..7</domain>
7       </domains>
8       <variables nbVariables="3">
9           <variable name="M3.2" id="1" domain="D1" description="M.2" />
10          <variable name="M3.3" id="2" domain="D1" description="M.3" />
11          <variable name="M3.4" id="1" domain="D1" description="M.4" />
12      </variables>
13      <constraints nbConstraints="3">
14          <constraint model="TKC" name="C0" reference="ArrivalTime" scope="M3.2 M3.3 2" arity="2">
15              <parameters>M3.2 M3.3 2</parameters>
16          </constraint>
17          <constraint model="TKC" name="C1" reference="ArrivalTime"
18              scope="M3.3 M3.4 2" arity="2">
19              <parameters>M3.3 M3.4 2</parameters>
20          </constraint>
21          <constraint model="TKC" name="C2" reference="ArrivalTime"
22              scope="M3.2 M3.4 2" arity="2">
23              <parameters>M3.2 M3.4 2</parameters>
24          </constraint>
25      </constraints>
26      <predicates nbPredicates="2">
27          <predicate name="ArrivalTime">
28              <parameters>int Mi, int Mj, int cte</parameters>
29              <expression>
30                  <functional>ge(abs(sub(Mi,Mj)), cte)</functional>
31              </expression>
32          </predicate>
33          <predicate name="eq">
34              <parameters>int Mi, int Mj</parameters>
35              <expression>
36                  <functional>eq(Mi,Mj)</functional>
37              </expression>
38          </predicate>
39      </predicates>
40      <agents_neighbours>
41          <agents_parent>
42              <agent name="A1">
43                  <constraints nbConstraints="2">
44                      <constraint model="TKC" name="C0" reference="eq" scope="M1.4 M3.4" arity="2">
45                          <parameters>M1.4 M3.4</parameters>
46                      </constraint>
47                      <constraint model="TKC" name="C1" reference="eq" scope="M1.3 M3.3" arity="2">
48                          <parameters>M1.3 M3.3</parameters>
49                      </constraint>
50                  </constraints>
51
52              </agent>
53              <agent name="A2">
54                  <constraints nbConstraints="1">
55                      <constraint model="TKC" name="C0" reference="eq" scope="M2.2 M3.2" arity="2">
56                          <parameters>M2.2 M3.2</parameters>
57                      </constraint>
58                  </constraints>
59              </agent>
60          </agents_parent>
61          <agents_children>
62              <agent name="A4" id="5" variable="M3.4" />
63          </agents_children>
64      </agents_neighbours>
65  </instance>
```

Fig. 3. Definition of DMS sub-problem in XDisCSP format.

Figures 5, 6, 7 and 8 show how to launch JChoc agents. We start with instantiate the DisSolver object (line 7), followed by the agent and distributed sub-problem declaration which specifies the resolution algorithm to be used (line 8–9). Next, the declaration of the container containing the master with its IP address (line 10). Eventually, we launch the agent (line 11).

The master waits for the confirmation of creation of all agents before ordering the start of the search. Thus, the problem can be solved using a specified implemented protocol (ABT for example).

```
1  import JChoc.DisSolver;
2
3  public class Master
4  {
5      public static void main(String[] args)
6      {
7          DisSolver js = new DisSolver();
8          js.setType("MasterABT");
9          js.setGui(true);
10         js.setNumberOfAgents(4);
11         js.run();
12     }
13
14 }
```

Fig. 4. How the master launches its communication interface.

```
1  import JChoc.DisSolver;
2
3  public class Omar
4  {
5      public static void main(String[] args)
6      {
7          DisSolver js1 = new DisSolver();
8          js1.setType("AgentABT");
9          js1.addAgent("A1", "Problem1.xml",true,true);
10         js1.setContainer("192.168.1.8");
11         js1.run();
12     }
13 }
```

Fig. 5. How to implement and launch JChoc DisSolver in Omar agent (A1).

```
1  import JChoc.DisSolver;
2
3  public class Jean
4  {
5      public static void main(String[] args) {
6          DisSolver js1 = new DisSolver();
7          js1.setType("AgentABT");
8          js1.addAgent("A2", "Problem2.xml",true,true);
9          js1.setContainer("192.168.1.8");
10         js1.run();
11     }
12 }
```

Fig. 6. How to implement and launch JChoc DisSolver in Jean agent (A2).

```
1  import JChoc.DisSolver;
2
3  public class Yun
4  {
5      public static void main(String[] args) {
6          DisSolver js1 = new DisSolver();
7          js1.setType("AgentABT");
8          js1.addAgent("A3", "Problem3.xml",true,true);
9          js1.setContainer("192.168.1.8");
10         js1.run();
11     }
12 }
```

Fig. 7. How to implement and launch JChoc DisSolver in Yun agent (A3).

```
1   import JChoc.DisSolver;
2
3   public class Mamadou
4   {
5       public static void main(String[] args) {
6           DisSolver js1 = new DisSolver();
7           js1.setType("AgentABT");
8           js1.addAgent("A4", "Problem4.xml",true,true);
9           js1.setContainer("192.168.1.8");
10          js1.run();
11      }
12  }
```

Fig. 8. How to implement and launch JChoc DisSolver in Mamadou agent (A4).

```
1   <?xml version="1.0" encoding="UTF-8"?>
2   <instance>
3       <presentation name="MSP" type="DisCSP"
4       model="Complex" constraintModel="TKC"
5       format="XDisCSP 1.0" />
6       <domains nbDomains="1">
7           <domain name="D1" nbValues="20">1..20</domain>
8       </domains>
9       <variables nbVariables="1">
10          <variable name="X4.1" id="1" domain="D1" description="X.4" />
11      </variables>
12      <predicates nbPredicates="0">
13      </predicates>
14      <constraints>
15      </constraints>
16      <agents_neighbours>
17          <agents_parent>
18              <agent name = "A1">
19                  <constraints nbConstraints="1">
20                      <constraint model="TKC" name="C1" reference="R1"
21                      scope="X1.1 X4.1" arity="2" change = "add.4">
22                          <parameters>X1.1 X4.1</parameters>
23                      </constraint>
24                  </constraints>
25              </agent>
26              <agent name = "A2">
27                  <constraints nbConstraints="1">
28                      <constraint model="TKC" name="C1" reference="R2"
29                      scope="X2.1 X4.1" arity="2" change = "no">
30                          <parameters>X2.1 X4.1</parameters>
31                      </constraint>
32                  </constraints>
33              </agent>
34              <agent name = "A3">
35                  <constraints nbConstraints="1">
36                      <constraint model="TKC" name="C1" reference="R3"
37                      scope="X3.1 X4.1" arity="2" change = "remove.3">
38                          <parameters>X3.1 X4.1</parameters>
39                      </constraint>
40                  </constraints>
41              </agent>
42          </agents_parent>
43          <agents_children>
44              <agent name="A5" id="1" variable="X4.1" />
45          </agents_children>
46      </agents_neighbours>
47      <relations>
48          <relation name="R1" semantics="conflicts">2 8|8 20|5 7|9 20|17 14|
49                      5 16|16 7|9 10|19 2|4 13|18 1|1 19|20 6|16 2|
50                      5 18|11 14|10 2|19 19|19 18</relation>
51          <relation name="R2" semantics="conflicts">6 16|14 2|19 15|20 2|8 2|
52                      4 2|17 20|18 6|7 7|7 10|3 18|18 10|13 15|9 18|
53                      14 16|19 6|13 18|3 14|14 20</relation>
54          <relation name="R3" semantics="conflicts">16 12|20 6|8 17|17 5|4 18|
55                      12 18|19 5|20 17|15 13|6 5|17 18|3 1|17 12|1 16|
56                      2 1|8 5|13 3|17 10|6 20|7 9</relation>
57          <relation name="R4" semantics="conflicts">|1 6|5 2|7 19|15 1|17 15|
58                      13 7|2 5|8 5|1 14|2 16|4 14|12 14|9 19|3 4|
59                      19 18|10 8|9 4|1 2</relation>
60      </relations>
61  </instance>
```

Fig. 9. Definition of dynamic sub-problem in XDisCSP format.

5.2 Using JChoc in Dynamic Distributed Environment

The use of JChoc platform in a dynamic environment is not very different to that in the case of distributed static problems. The difference is seen in the xml file that defines the sub-problem of each agent.

To see the platform's exploitation in the Dynamic case of Distributed Satisfaction Problems, we take a random example composed of five agents, each agent has one variable. Figure 9, shows a model of representation of a dynamic sub-problem of an agent that has two constraints with two other agents, 3 s after launching, one of the constraints is going to be removed, then after 4 s, another link with a third agent will be added.

In addition of the definition of variables, domains and constraints, we define the constraints that will be either added or removed.

After the generation of the dynamic sub-problem, we can launch the resolution following the same approach as before, but instead to insert the name of an XML file of a static sub-problem as argument, we insert the name of dynamic sub-problem XML.

6 Experimental Results

6.1 Configuration Example

To experiment the JChoc platform in a physically distributed environment, we chose five machines with features **2.93 GHz, CORE(TM) 2 duo** with **2 GB RAM** that simulate agents. These machines are connected via the **WLAN** of our laboratory. We also chose *ABT* algorithm to solve Meeting Scheduling problems (MSP). In Fig. 1 above, we depict an example of problem solved by this platform in a live distributed environment network. This figure illustrates an instance of MSP viewed as DisCSP where each agent has a personal private calendar and a set of meetings each taking place in a specified location. In that example, there are four agents, A_1, A_2, A_3 and A_4, and four meetings, m_1, m_2, m_3 and m_4. Each agent has its own calendar divided into **14** slots. The time required for traveling among places where meetings can be scheduled is **2 slots**.

We have intentionally limited the number of agents to 4 for this problem needs, but the number of the agents can be easily extended to **N≫4** for the neediest problems.

Figures 10 and 11 show the GUI of the sniffer agent at the start and the end of ABT resolution. The canvas provides a graphical representation of the messages exchanged between sniffed **ABTagents**, where each arrow represents a message and each color identifies a type of conversation. For example agent A_1 sends an **OK?** message to informs A_2 that he has done a new assignment $m_{1.1}$**:1** (line 5).

If no new consistent value is found (line 10), A_3 generates a new **nogood** $m_{1.3}$**:3** $\wedge$ $m_{1.4}$**:5** $\Rightarrow$ $m_{2.2} \neq 5$ by the resolution of existing nogoods. Eventually, the system can stabilize in a state where each agent has a value and no constraint is violated. This state is a global solution and the network has reached quiescence, meaning that no message is traveling through it (lines 37, 40, 43, 46). Once the solution is found, the master should be advised to spread the stop order to all agents (lines 49–52) (Fig. 11).

A solution to this example is:

$$A_1 \longrightarrow (m_{1.1} : 3; m_{1.3} : 7; m_{1.4} : 1), A_2 \longrightarrow (m_{2.1} : 3; m_{2.2} : 5), A_3 \longrightarrow (m_{3.2} : 5; m_{3.3} : 7; m_{3.4} : 1), A_4 \longrightarrow (m_{4.4} : 1).$$

6.2   Platform Scalability

The scalability of JChoc is the ability of the system, network, and process to handle a growing amount of work in a capable manner and its ability to be enlarged to accommodate that growth. In order to experiment our platform, we consider a large number of MSP instances. These Meeting Scheduling Problem are characterized by $< m, p, n, d, h, t, a >$, where m is the number of meetings, p is the number of participants, n is the number of inter-agent constraints d determines the number of days. Different time slots are available for each meeting, and h is the number of hours per day, t is a duration of the meeting and a is the percentage of availability for each participant. We present our results for the class $< m, p, n, 5, 10, 1, 90\% >$ and we vary three parameters: m, p, n (each agent has 2 meetings):

As shown in experimental results, in Fig. 7, the performance of our platform is measured in terms of network load (number of messages) and run-time execution. From these preliminary results we see that JChoc platform performs rapidly in small instances ($\#p \in [4, 14]$). The number of messages increases for $\#p \in [15, 18]$ and reduces for $\#p > 18$. This scalability behavior is due to complexity of MSP problems. When the instance is hard the problem can be solved rapidly (Fig. 12).

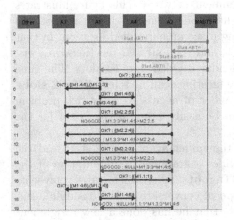

Fig. 10. The start on sniffer agent GUI.

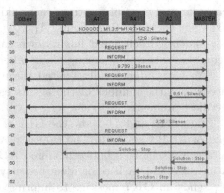

Fig. 11. The finish on sniffer agent GUI.

#p	#m	#n	#messages	Time (ms)
4	8	3	11	17070
5	10	5	11	17204
6	12	6	14	16144
7	14	7	14	17073
8	16	8	19	19180
9	18	9	24	20210
10	20	10	22	18294
11	22	11	32	20197
12	24	12	27	18516
13	26	15	30	20370
14	28	33	51	26073
15	30	35	105	31103
16	32	29	69	28914
17	34	33	175	38324
18	36	35	139	43172
19	38	38	141	37121
20	40	43	94	33457

Fig. 12. Performance of JChoc platform using ABT protocol on the Meeting Scheduling Problem (MSP).

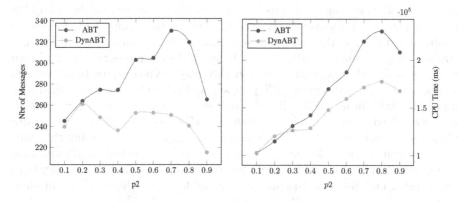

Fig. 13. ABT vs DynABT.

6.3   Platform Scalability in a Dynamic Changed Environement

To compare the performance of the DDisCSPs with a platform that supports dynamic aspect and an other that doesn't. We made our experiments using ABT that cant solve such problem dynamically and resolve the problem when changes are available, and DynABT that can adapt changes and continuous problem's solving. We have introduced a rate change δ as a percentage of the total constraints in the problem ($\delta = 20\,\%$). In these experiments we generated problems randomly, with parameters $(a, i, n, d, p1, p2)$ using the platform generator, where: a is the number of agents = 20, i: the number of instances = 10, n: the number of variables $= 20$, $p1$: the density of constraints $= 20\%$, and $p2$: the tightness of constraints with value 10%–90% step 10%, the range of tightness 10%–40% contains solvable problems, 50% contains both solvable and unsolvable problems, and 60%–90% problems are unsolvable.

The Fig. 13 shows the number of messages sent and CPU Time, measured for both ABT and DynABT implemented on JChoc platform and using our laboratory's wireless network, that allows the communication between Agents in the same environment and conditions. All results obtained show that Dyn-ABT significantly outperforms ABT in a dynamic changed environment. This comparison shows the benefits of solving dynamic distributed problems in a real distributed changed environment with an algorithm that support dynamic aspect implemented in a suitable Platform. The platform is user friendly and lets users implement their Multi-agents applications for dynamic environment.

7   Conclusion

In this paper, we have proposed a modular, reliable, deployable and distributed software architecture, called JChoc DisSolver, which can be used easily for several real dynamic combinatorial problems. The main purpose of our platform is to break down the barriers to building new and innovative applications. The possibility of combining the expressiveness of Choco, the extensibility of JADE and our powerful Dynamic Distributed Constraint Reasoning Add-On bring a strong added value in the development of innovative applications based on Constraints Programming paradigm. The JChoc platform presented in this paper has been designed to support extensions: security, cryptography. In our experiments, We have implemented ABT protocol and solved the Meeting Scheduling problem (MSP) in a real distributed environment. In a dynamic environment, we have solved dynamic problems with DynABT, to show the benefits of our platform that supports the dynamic aspect. We found that, by using this platform, we can adopt easily any proposed protocol for solving distributed constraint problem even if environment changes dynamically. Future investigations are focusing on enhancing the platform, by adding other layers that will allow users to implement their multi-robots applications easily. The platform will allow the communication between robots in a dynamically changing environment.

References

1. Béjar, R., Domshlak, C., Fernández, C., Gomes, C., Krishnamachari, B., Selman, B., Valls, M.: Sensor networks and distributed csp: communication, computation and complexity. Artif. Intell. **161**(1–2), 117–148 (2005)
2. Kitano, H., Tadokoro, S., Noda, I., Matsubara, H., Takahashi, T., Shinjou, A., Shimada, S.: Robocup rescue: search and rescue in large-scale disaster as a domain for autonomous agents research. In: IEEE International Conference on System, Man, and Cybernetics (1999)

3. Yokoo, M., Hirayama, K.: Distributed breakout algorithm for solving distributed constraint satisfaction problems. In: Proceedings of the First International Conference on MultiAgent Systems. MIT Press (1995)
4. Yokoo, M., Durfee, E., Ishida, T., Kuwabara, K.: Distributed constraint satisfaction for formalizing distributed problem solving. In: International Conference on Distributed Computing Systems, pp. 614–621 (1992)
5. Yokoo, M.: Distributed constraint satisfaction. In: Foundation of Cooperation in multiagent Systems (2001)
6. Hamadi, Y.: Disolver : a distributed constraint solver. In Technical Report MSR-TR-2003-91, Microsoft Research (2003)
7. Galley, M.: Distributed constraint programming platform using sjavap (2000). http://cs.fit.edu/Projects/asl/#MELY
8. Petcu, A.: Frodo: a framework for open/distributed optimization. In Technical Report EPFL:2006/001, LIA, EPFL, CH-1015 Lausanne (2006). http://liawww.epfl.ch/frodo/
9. Bessiere, C., Brito, I., Maestre, A., Meseguer, P.: Asynchronous backtracking without adding links: a new member in the abt family. Artif. Intell. **161**, 7–24 (2005)
10. Meisels, A., Zivan, R.: Asynchronous forward-checking for discsps. Constraints **12**, 131–150 (2007)
11. Ezzahir, R., Bessiere, C., Wahbi, M., Benelallam, I., Bouyakhf, E.: Asynchronous interlevel forward-checking for discsps. In: Principles and Practice of Constraint Programming (CP 2009) (2009)
12. Modi, P., Shen, W., Tambe, M., Yokoo, M.: Adopt: asynchronous distributed constraints optimization with quality guarantees. Artif. Intell. **161**(1–2), 149–180 (2005)
13. Gershman, A., Meisels, A., Zivan, R.: Asynchronous forward bounding for distributed cops. J. Artif. Intell. Res. **34**, 61–88 (2009)
14. Yeoh, W., Felner, A., Koenig, S.: Bnb-adopt: an asynchronous branch and bound dcop algorithm. In: AAMAS08: Proceedings of the 7th International Joint Conference on Autonomous Agents and Multiagent Systems, pp. 591–598 (2008)
15. Ezzahir, R., Bessiere, C., Benelallam, I., Bouyakhf, E., Belaissaoui, M.: Dynamic backtracking for distributed constraint optimization. Proceeding of the 2008 conference on ECAI 2008, pp. 901–902. The Netherlands, IOS Press, Amsterdam (2008)
16. Yokoo, M.: Algorithms for distributed constraint satisfaction problems: a review. Auton. Agents Multiagent Syst. **3**, 185–207 (2000)
17. Yokoo, M., Durfee, E., Ishida, T., Kuwabara, K.: The distributed constraint satisfaction problem: formalization and algorithms. IEEE Trans. Knowl. Data Eng. **10**(5), 673–685 (1998)
18. Wahbi, M., Ezzahir, R., Bessiere, C., Bouyakhf, E.: Dischoco 2: a platform for distributed constraint reasoning. In: DCR 2011, pp. 112–121 (2011). http://www.lirmm.fr/coconut/dischoco/
19. JADE Java agent developpement framework (2013). http://jade.tilab.com/
20. Meisels, A., Lavee, O.: Using additional information in discsp search. In: DCR 2004 5th Workshop on Distributed Constraints Reasoning (2004)
21. Wallace, J.R., Freuder, C.E.: Constraintbased multi-agent meeting scheduling: effects of agent heterogeneity on performance and privacy loss. In: DCR 2002 3rd Workshop on Distributed Constraint Reasoning, pp. 176–182 (2002)
22. Jussien, N., Rochart, G., Lorcal, X.: Choco: an open source java constraint programming library. In: CPAIOR 2008 Workshop on Open-Source Software for Integer and Constraint Programming (OSSICP 2008), France, Paris (2008)

23. Lutati, B., Levit, V., Meisels, A.: Agentzero: a framework for simulating and evaluating multiagent algorithms. In: Shehory, O., Sturm, A. (eds.) In Agent-oriented Software Engineering, pp. 309–327. Springer, Heidelberg (2014)
24. Sultanik, E., Lass, R., Regli, W.: Dcopolis: a framework for simulating and deploying distributed constraint optimization algorithms. In: CP-DCR (2007)
25. Omomowo, Bayo, Arana, Inés, Ahriz, Hatem: DynABT: dynamic asynchronous backtracking for dynamic DisCSPs. In: Dochev, Danail, Pistore, Marco, Traverso, Paolo (eds.) AIMSA 2008. LNCS (LNAI), vol. 5253, pp. 285–296. Springer, Heidelberg (2008)
26. Mailler, R.: Comparing two approaches to dynamic, distributed constraint satisfaction. In: Proceedings of the Fourth International Joint Conference on Autonomous Agents and Multiagent Systems, pp. 1049–1056. ACM (2005)

Stream X-Machines for Agent Simulation Test Case Generation

Ilias Sakellariou[1]([✉]), Dimitris Dranidis[2], Marina Ntika[3], and Petros Kefalas[2]

[1] Department of Applied Informatics, University of Macedonia,
156 Egnatia Street, 54636 Thessaloniki, Greece
iliass@uom.edu.gr
[2] Department of Computer Science, The University of Sheffield International Faculty,
City College, L. Sofou 3, 54624 Thessaloniki, Greece
{dranidis,kefalas}@city.academic.gr
[3] South East European Research Centre,
Research Centre of the University of Sheffield International Faculty, City College,
24 Proxenou Koromila Street, 54622 Thessaloniki, Greece
mantika@seerc.org

Abstract. Applying the Stream X-Machine formal method in the development of multi-agent simulations has a number of significant advantages, since it combines the power of executable specifications and test case generation. The present work supports this argument by reporting on the combined use of two tools that involve Stream X-Machines (SXM): the first is a domain specific language for effortlessly encoding agent behaviour using SXMs in a well known agent simulation platform. The second tool, supports among other things, automated test case generation using SXMs. The main benefits of using the specific formal approach in such a practical setting is that it offers a clear intuitive way of specifying agent behaviour and the automated generation of "agent simulation test scenarios" that can be used for validation.

Keywords: Formal methods · NetLogo · Agent based simulation · Test case generation

1 Introduction

Agent based simulation has been applied to a wide range of scientific fields, such as biology, pedestrian simulations, and economics [9]. This explosive interest has resulted to the proposal in the literature of a large number of agent simulation platforms [1,18] and development methodologies.

However, the work concerning approaches that combine various aspects of the standard software engineering process in building simulations is rather limited. One important issue when developing any system is systematic testing, i.e. the generation of an (ideally) exhaustive set of test cases that will allow checking the conformance of a system to its specification. Another important aspect is validation, i.e. checking whether the system exhibits the intended behaviour.

B. Duval et al. (Eds.): ICAART 2015, LNAI 9494, pp. 37–57, 2015.
DOI: 10.1007/978-3-319-27947-3_3

Validation could be performed by executing the system with some representative scenarios, thus allowing the developer to investigate the simulation system behaviour.

Towards this direction, this paper advocates the use of *Stream X-Machines* (SXM) to develop agent simulations. SXMs extend finite state machines by augmenting them with memory and by labelling the transitions with partial functions instead of simple input symbols. One of the main benefits in using the specific formalism is that SXMs offer a testing method that under certain design-for-test conditions ensures the conformance of a system to its specification [14]. Furthermore, there exist tools that allow encoding of executable SXM specifications of agents in simulation environments, and most importantly, in the current context, tools that allow automated test case generation.

This work reports on the combined use of two SXM related software artefacts on the same agent model: one that supports direct simulation execution of agents defined as SXMs (TXStates) and a tool for automated test case generation (JSXM).

TXStates is a domain specific language (DSL) that acts as a layer for specifying and executing agents represented as SXMs in NetLogo [25]. The TXStates DSL has evolved for a number of years and earlier versions of it have been used to develop medium to large scale simulations, including some that concern behaviour under the influence of emotions [22]. The current work presents in full the latest complete version of TXStates.

The model developed in TXStates can then be transformed to a JSXM model. JSXM [11] is a tool, supporting modelling and execution of SXMs and most importantly automated test case generation, based on the SXM testing theory.

The approach (and not yet a methodology) this work proposes, is to use TXStates to develop a simulation based on an SXM model through the usual iterative development process, and then use JSXM to produce test cases for the same model. The generated test case scenarios can (a) be used to show that the JSXM and the TXStates model are equivalent and (b) act as input scenarios to the simulation environment, providing visual output that the user can use in order to visually validate the modelled agents. The latter presents a complete set of "simulation scenarios" that can assist the user in finding inconsistencies between the system the modeller *intended to represent* and the implemented model, thus performing validation.

This paper is an extension of the paper [21] presenting in more detail the approach and reporting on advances regarding the integration of the JSXM and TXStates tools. The rest of the paper is organised as follows. Section 2 outlines our approach. Section 3 provides an overview of the SXM formal modelling technique, how SXM concepts are mapped to agent concepts and an introduction to SXM testing. The TXStates DSL is presented in Sect. 4. Section 5 describes the model used as a working example in the current paper. The process of moving from specification to testing using the JSXM tool is described in Sect. 6. Related work is presented in Sect. 7. Finally, Sect. 8 concludes the work and presents future work.

2   The SXM Approach

Developing a complex agent simulation is a challenging task, mainly due to the fact that the modeller has to consider all possible interactions between the modelled agent and the environment, and ensure that these are dealt with in the model. In many cases, and especially in simulation environments where execution is usually cheap, discovering the set of interactions and ensuring that the agent behaves correctly relies on developing the simulation in an iterative manner, i.e. an implement—visualise—revise cycle. However, when agents become complex, such a cycle demands tools that would facilitate code changes and at the same time provide a clear, intuitive representation of the behaviour. The TXStates DSL aims at exactly that. Offering the ability of encoding agent behaviour as stream X-Machines maintains clarity and allows users to easily modify the encoded behaviour. The execution layer provided by the DSL allows to "run" the simulation and detect any inconsistencies at an initial level.

To ensure that the simulated agent behaves correctly, testing the model has to be performed in a systematic manner. For this purpose, the modeller expresses the *corresponding model* in JSXM in order to produce test cases. We refer to this as a *corresponding model* since the modeller has to include in the former various environment conditions in order to compensate for the functionality provided by the simulation environment. The model expressed in JSXM is used to generate test cases that serve two purposes. The first concerns that of ensuring that the two models are equivalent [14]. Secondly, the generated test cases are used as "simulation scenarios" that allow the systematic validation of the agent by visualizing the agent behaviour with TXStates. Thus model developers can confirm that the simulated agent behaves as the modeller expected, i.e. validate the model.

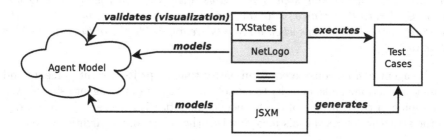

Fig. 1. The SXM approach to simulation development.

Figure 1, depicts the approach taken by this work. The *intended model* that the user aims at, is modelled in TXStates. This model acts as a guide for developing the JSXM model that is used for generating test cases. The test cases then are executed by the TXStates DSL in order to prove *equivalence* of the two models. When this is achieved, the same test cases act as simulation scenarios, which, when visualized by TXStates, allow the user to observe the behaviour of the developed simulation in a range of situations and thus validate the model.

3   Modelling and Testing Agents as SXMs

State machines have been used extensively to derive agent simulation implementations since they provide a rather intuitive way to model agent behaviour. SXMs extend finite state machines with a memory structure and transitions labelled with functions and thus allow more powerful modelling of a system. For completeness, the definition of SXMs is presented below.

Definition 1. *A stream X-machine* [13] *is an 8-tuple* $Z = (\Sigma, \Gamma, Q, M, \Phi, F, q_0, m_0)$, *where:*

- *Σ and Γ are the input and output alphabets, respectively.*
- *Q is the finite set of states.*
- *M is the (possibly) infinite set called memory.*
- *Φ is a set of partial functions φ, called processing functions; each such function maps an input and a memory value to an output and a possibly different memory value, $\varphi : M \times \Sigma \to \Gamma \times M$.*
- *F is the next state partial function, $F : Q \times \Phi \to Q$, which given a state and a processing function determines the next state. F is often described as a state transition diagram.*
- *q_0 and m_0 are the initial state and initial memory respectively.*

Intuitively, an SXM Z can be thought as a finite automaton with the arcs labelled by functions from the set Φ. The automaton $A_Z = (\Phi, Q, F, q_0)$ over the alphabet Φ is called *the associated automaton* of Z and is usually described by a state-transition diagram.

Definition 2. *A computation state is defined as the tuple (q, m), with $q \in Q$ and $m \in M$. The computation step is defined as $(q, m) \overset{\varphi}{\vdash} (q', m')$ with $q, q' \in Q$ and $m, m' \in M$ such that $\varphi(m, \sigma) = (\gamma, m')$ and $F(q, \varphi) = q'$. The computation is the series of computation steps when all inputs are applied to the initial computation state (q_0, m_0).*

An agent can be considered as an entity that maps its current percepts and state to an action. Thus, in order to model the behaviour of an agent using SXMs, a mapping of the concepts of the former to the latter is necessary. However, due to the structure of SXMs this mapping is rather clear and straightforward:

- The input alphabet Σ forms the agent percepts.
- The agent's internal world representation and all parameters that affect its behaviour are mapped to the SXM memory M and current state. In other words, M holds the agent beliefs, while with appropriate encoding of states, it can also hold the agent's current goal.
- Agent behaviour is modelled as a set of functions Φ and the transition diagram F.
- Finally, agent actions are mapped to the output Γ.

3.1   Background on Testing with SXM

SXMs have the significant advantage of offering a testing method that, under certain design-for-test conditions, ensures the conformance of a system under test (SUT) to a specification. This section provides details regarding test case generation to ensure completeness of the paper.

The goal of the testing method is to devise a finite test set $X \subset \Sigma^*$ of input sequences that produce identical results when applied to the specification and the SUT *only if* they both compute identical functions. The main assumption that needs to be made for the SUT is that it consists of correct elementary components, i.e. the processing functions are correctly implemented. Furthermore, it is estimated that the number of states in the SUT is $n' \geq n$, where n is the number of states of the specification. Let $k = n' - n$.

Input sequences attempt to drive the SUT to all the states, then exercise from those states paths of transitions of length $k + 1$ and finally uniquely identify the reached states. If the output sequences produced by the SUT are different than the ones produced by the specification faults are revealed.

The SXM testing method [13,14] relies on the following design-for-test condition:

- **Output-distinguishability:** Processing functions should be distinguishable by their different outputs on some memory-input pair, i.e. for every $\phi_1, \phi_2 \in \Phi$, $m \in M$ and $\sigma \in \Sigma$ such that $(m, \sigma) \in \text{dom}\,\phi_1$ and $(m, \sigma) \in \text{dom}\,\phi_2$, if $\phi_1(m, \sigma) = (\gamma, m_1)$ and $\phi_2(m, \sigma) = (\gamma, m_2)$ then $\phi_1 = \phi_2$.

The testing method for SXMs is an extension of the W-method for finite state machines. The test generation is a two stage process: (1) the W method [5] is applied on the associated automaton A_Z to produce a set $T \subset \Phi^*$ of sequences of processing functions, which are then (2) translated into sequences of inputs for Z using a so-called test function $t : \Phi^* \to \Sigma^*$.

T is obtained by constructing a state cover set S and a characterization set W of A_Z. $S \subset \Phi^*$ contains sequences to reach all states of A_Z, while $W \subset \Phi^*$ contains sequences to distinguish between any two distinct states of A_Z. Each sequence $t \in T$ consists of three sub-sequences, i.e., $t = syw$, where $s \in S$ drives the automaton to a specific state, $y \in \Phi^*$ attempts to exercise transition-paths up to length of $k+1$ and w distinguishes the resulting state from any other state. Thus $T = S\Phi[k + 1]W = S(\bigcup_{0 \leq i \leq k+1} \Phi^i)W$.

Based on [14], the maximum number of test sequences, i.e., $card(T)$, is less than $n^2 \cdot r^{k+2}/(r - 1)$, where $n = card(Q)$, $r = card(\Phi)$. The total length l of the test set is less than $card(T) \cdot n'$, where $n' = k + n$.

Since SXMs have memory, there may exist sequences of processing functions that are accepted by the associated automaton A_Z but they cannot be driven by any input sequence. These sequences are called non-realizable.

Definition 3. *A sequence $p \in \Phi^*$ is called* realizable *in q and m if $p \in L_{A_Z}(q)$ and $\exists s \in \Sigma^*$ such that $(m, s) \in \text{dom}\,\|p\|$. The set of realizable sequences of Z in q and m is notated as $LR_Z(q, m)$. Let LR_Z be defined as $LR_Z(q_0, m_0)$.*

The definitions of the state cover and the characterization sets are extended to handle realizable sequences of processing functions.

A state is r-reachable if it can be reached by a realizable sequence $p \in LR_Z$.

Definition 4. *A set $S_r \subseteq LR_Z$ is called a r-state cover of Z if for every r-reachable state q of Z there exists a unique $p \in S_r$ that reaches the state q.*

The set of memory values that can be attained at a state q is notated as $MAtt(q)$ and it consists of all memory values that are the result of realizable sequences that end at state q, i.e. $MAtt(q) = \{m \in M \mid \exists p \in LR_Z \land \exists s \in \Sigma^*, \|p\|(m_0, s) = (q, m)\}$.

Any two states have to be *separable*, i.e. distinguished by two realizable sequences with *overlapping* domains.

Definition 5. *A pair of states (q_1, q_2) is separable if there exists a finite set of sequences Y such that $\forall m_1 \in MAtt(q_1)$, there exists $p_1 \in LR(q_1, m_1) \cap Y$ and $p_2 \in LR(q_2, m_2) \cap Y$ such that $dom\,p_1 \cap dom\,p_2 \neq \emptyset$.*

Essentially, at each state the same sequence of inputs will trigger one of the two sequences of processing functions. By the observed outputs we can tell which sequence of processing functions has been triggered and thus identify the state.

Definition 6. *A set $W_s \subseteq \Phi^*$ is called a separating set of Z if it separates (distinguishes) between every pair of separable states of Z.*

If S_r reaches all states of Z and W_s separates all pairs of states in Z. the testing method reduces to a variant of the W-method:

$$T = UW_s = ((S_r\Phi[k+1]) \cap L_{A_Z})W_s$$

Furthermore, the testing method requires that all sequences of $U = (S_r\Phi[k+1]) \cap L_{A_Z}$ are realizable, i.e. it is required that $U \subseteq LR_Z$. Note that the sequences of processing functions of maximum length $k+1$ that follow the r-state cover are limited to those that are accepted by the associated automaton.

The final test suite for checking functional equivalence is:

$$X = t(T) = t(UW_s)$$

The sequences of inputs in $X \subset \Sigma^*$ are fed to the SXM in order to produce the corresponding expected sequences of outputs $Y \subset \Gamma^*$.

4   MAS Simulation with TXStates

TXStates is an internal DSL for the NetLogo Agent Simulation environment, that allows encoding SXM agent specifications in a natural manner. NetLogo [25] is "a cross-platform multi-agent programmable modelling environment" aiming at MAS simulation. In NetLogo, the environment consists of a static grid of *patches*, useful for describing the environment, since they are capable of interacting with other entities. This "world" is inhabited by *turtles* that are entities that "live" and interact within it. They are organised in groups called *breeds*, i.e. user defined teams sharing some characteristics. Agent behaviour is specified by the domain specific NetLogo programming language, supports two main programming constructs: functions (called *reporters*) and *procedures*. The language includes a large set of primitives for turtles motion, environment inspection, standard program control, etc. NetLogo v5 introduced *tasks*, the version of anonymous functions or closures of NetLogo.

Although a powerful modelling tool, as indicated by the constantly increasing number of publications that use NetLogo as the platform of choice, NetLogo has been criticised for not providing modelling constructs that allow encoding of more complex agents. The TXStates DSL provides an answer to this and contributes to the list of tools to support complex agent behaviour encoding, such as BOD [2] and IODA [17], adding the dimension of automatic test case generation for agents.

4.1   TXStates Models SXMs

The TXStates supports encoding all modelling constructs of SXM definition presented in Sect. 3. Since the emergent phenomena that manifest in multi-agent simulations demand a trial and error approach and constant changes in the model, an iterative modelling approach is recommended and ease of encoding becomes a very important requirement.

In essence, TXStates extends the NetLogo programming language with the necessary constructs to build executable SXM models. The DSL is *internal* since it relies on the syntax of NetLogo and all the code is implemented using the NetLogo language, possibly at the cost of execution speed, but offering tight coupling with the underlying language and without interrupting the normal development cycle a modeller follows in the specific platform. We decided not to implement an external DSL, since in order to arrive to an executable simulation, apart from the SXM model, the developer has to provide other parts of the simulation, such as environment setup, visualization and agent perception mechanisms. Having an external DSL would mean that the developer would have to work on two different platforms simultaneously, thus complicating the development process.

The implementation relies on storing agent specific information on turtle-own variables, since each agent must carry its own agent (execution) state. Thus, memory M is mapped to a data structure stored in a turtle-own variable called *memory* that consists of attribute - value pairs. The DSL provides special care for its management to facilitate model development (Table 1). Table 1 the procedure x-mem-set <V> <Val> is a destructive update with value <Val> for attribute (or memory element) <V>.

In a similar manner, percepts that correspond to SXM input Σ are stored in a variable *percept* and although *percepts* is a relatively simple data structure, the library provides a set of programming constructs (Table 1) to access/add percepts depending on environment changes.

Table 1. TXStates primitives for X-Machine memory handling and percept updates.

Memory primitives	Percept primitives
x-init-memory	x-add-percept <P>
x-mem-initial-var <V> <Val>	x-percept-add-value <P> <Val>
x-mem-set <V> <Val>	x-has-percept? <P>
x-mem-value <V>	x-percept-value <P>
	x-oneof-percept-value <P>
	x-all-percept-values <P>

Probably the most interesting features of the DSL are encoding the set of processing functions Φ, output Γ, states Q and the transition diagram F. These are described in the sections that follow.

4.2   Encoding Agent Actions

Processing functions of the set Φ are encoded as NetLogo reporters (NetLogo jargon for functions), that return results in a specific format, the latter being handled by the TXStates meta-interpreter. There are no arguments to these reporters since by SXM definition, functions operate on input and memory and produce output and memory updates and thus all these functions are assumed to work on the memory structures described in the previous section.

Since, processing functions are *partial functions*, they must return (report in NetLogo terms) either output and memory updates, prefixed by a special *success token* or a special *failure token*. These special tokens are used by the TXStates meta-interpreter to determine possible transitions. Thus, each such NetLogo reporter should return:

- **x-false**, a keyword handled by the meta-interpreter, indicating that the function is not applicable (*failure token*),
- **x-true** <xmOutput> <xmMemUpdates>, indicating that the function is applicable *success token* and will produce <xmOutput> output and change memory according to the <xmMemUpdates>.

The <xmOutput> corresponds to the SXM output Γ and in the simulation context defines the list of actions that the agent has to perform. This list consists of NetLogo tasks, prefixed by the keyword x-action, included in delimiters #< and >#. Thus, <xmOutput> has the form:

```
#< x-action task [...] x-action task [...]   ... >#
```

The second "argument" <xmMemUpdates> is a list of memory updates, i.e. invocations of x-mem-set commands described in Table 1, again delimited by #< and >#. Thus, <xmMemUpdates> has the following form:

```
 #< x-mem-set <Memory Var> <Value> x-mem-set ... >#
```

Empty <xmOutput> and <xmMemUpdates> are denoted as #< >#. It should be mentioned that the above are *lists*, and not sets, i.e. the changes described either as environment effects or memory updates will be performed in the order they appear.

There are no limitations regarding the code that a processing function can include, as long (a) it returns results in the form indicated above (b) does not include side-effects, i.e. changes in the simulation environment and agent state, outside those explicitly encoded as return values of an x-true function result. Since the meta-interpreter evaluates all functions, producing candidate memory and output results and then decides on which function to apply, the presence of side-effects outside x-true lists would produce unexpected behaviour. Allowing arbitrary NetLogo code in a processing function contributes towards the tight integration to the TXStates DSL to the underlying platform.

A processing function encoded in TXStates is presented in Fig. 2. The function checks whether the agent has certain percepts, executes the NetLogo procedure bee-move and updates the memory variable "position" to reflect the change in the "beliefs" of the agent that it has moved. The condition that appears in the ifelse is known as a "guard" and defines the domain of the partial function.

```
to-report moveTowardsAttackFormation
 ifelse
 x-percept-value "hornet" and x-mem-value "alert" = "hiveInDanger" and
 p-distance x-percept-value "hornetPos" x-mem-value "position"
   > p-distance x-percept-value "hornetPos" x-percept-value "closerToHornet"
   [report x-true
    #< x-action task [bee-move x-percept-value "closerToHornet"] >#
    #< x-mem-set "position" x-percept-value "closerToHornet" >#  ]
   [report x-false]
end
```

Fig. 2. Example of a processing function demonstrating the use of TXStates primitives.

4.3   State and Transition Diagram Specification

SXM states Q and the transition diagram F are encoded quite naturally in the TXStates DSL. A single transition labelled by a processing function, is represented as # x-func <XMFunc> goto <StateName>, where <XMFunc> is a NetLogo reporter as described in Sect. 4.2 and <StateName> is the name of a state, i.e. a simple string. An SXM that consists of multiple states each state being a set of transitions and can be defined as follows:

```
x-diagram
 state <StateNameA>
  # x-func <XMFunc A1> goto <StateName A1>
  ...
  # x-func <XMFunc An> goto <StateName An>
 end-state
 ...
```

```
state <StateNameK>
 # x-func <XMFunc K1> goto <StateName K1>
 ...
 end-state
end-x-diagram
```

In such a specification, the first state that appears in the definition of the x-diagram is considered to be the *initial state* q_0.

4.4 Executing the Agent Specification

Executing the agent specifications presented in the previous sections is the responsibility of the TXStates *meta-interpreter*. The latter is invoked by calling the execute-state-machines command, usually in each simulation cycle. Before invocation, the user must ensure that the agent percepts been updated, through appropriate calls of the corresponding primitives in Table 1.

The *meta-interpreter* is responsible for handling state transitions and action execution and implements the computation described in Definition 2, with each invocation of the execute-state-machines command corresponding to a single *computation step* of Definition 2. Thus at each cycle, the meta-interpreter:

1. Forms the list of functions $\Phi_{state} \subseteq \Phi$ that label transitions in the current SXM state q, i.e. $\Phi_{state} = \phi \in \Phi : (q, \phi, q'') \in F$, in the order they appear in the agent specification.
2. Form the list $\Phi_{trig} \subseteq \Phi$ that contains all functions from Φ_{state} whose guards are satisfied. In the case that the trigger list is empty, execution ends with an error message.
3. Select the *first* function ϕ_i from the list Φ_{trig} .
4. Execute actions specified by ϕ_i.
5. Apply memory updates specified by ϕ_i.
6. Perform a transition to state q' that corresponds to function $(q, \phi_i, q') \in F$.

In order to simplify the encoding of guards, an ordering is imposed to the function application; currently the selection function chooses the *first function* in the state definition that triggers in step 3. This imposes a *priority ordering* on the transitions in a state, with the transitions that appear higher in the state definition having a larger priority. Imposing a priority ordering ensures that the model is always deterministic, i.e. it is always clear which state transition will occur, an issue that is very important when dealing with simulation environments, since it maintains reproducibility. In the *corresponding* JSXM model, the same behaviour is achieved by having a richer set of guards in the functions.

The TXStates DSL[1] is provided as a NetLogo library that users can include in their models and specify behaviour. The major advantage of using TXStates is that developers can develop models in an iterative fashion, modifying the X-Machine model quite easily and viewing directly the results of their changes. Thus, complex model development can be greatly facilitated.

---

[1] http://users.uom.gr/~iliass/projects/TXStates/.

5   Case Study: Modelling the Japanese Bee

The working example we selected in the present work concerns the behaviour of Japanese bees under the presence of a giant Asian Hornet scout in the hive [19]. The phenomenon is an excellent example of collective behaviour under attack in insects, since bees form the so called "bee ball" around the scout hornet, and by doing so increase the temperature inside the ball to a level non tolerable by the hornet, but tolerable by the bee itself.

We have implemented a simulation using SXMs that mimic the behaviour of both the hornet and the bees during this phenomenon. Rather informally, bees that do not perceive any danger, are in a non-alert state, i.e. they keep working as usual. Upon perception of a hornet in the hive, bees start moving towards the hornet in order to form the attack assemblage. However, since the perception radius of bees is limited and in order to engage as large a population as possible, bees become aware ("inAlert") when perceiving another bee approaching the hornet, or another bee alerted. Bees in alert that do not directly perceive the hornet try to follow an approaching bee or move randomly. While approaching, the bee has to detect when it reached the attack formation: this case occurs either when it is close to the bee, or when there is a bee in its adjacent patches (neighbourhood) is an attacking bee. Upon reaching the attack formation, the bee starts the attack, i.e. produces heat if the environment temperature is below 49 °C, and does nothing otherwise. Obviously, since the hornet moves and possibly kills other bees, bees attacking have to understand whether the hornet has been relocated, in order to adjust their position.

Modelling such a phenomenon in an agent based simulation is rather straightforward, having bees and the scout hornet modelled as a single agent. The model has been studied before in [15] and we closely follow the approach authors have taken in that paper, although providing a different implementation and a modified state diagram.

The behaviour of the bee is modelled as a set of states, as for example *workInHive, inAlert, attacking*, etc. reflecting the state of the bee under the presence of a hornet in the hive, or other bees in alert. The state transition diagram is shown in Fig. 3. This diagram was encoded in the TXStates DSL quite naturally as shown in Fig. 4.

As shown in the diagram of Fig. 3, state transitions are labelled by functions. For instance, the function in Fig. 2 implemented in TXStates labels the self transition of the state "approachingHornet". Input reflects information the agent perceives from the environment. For example, when the agent perceives a hornet, the tuple (*hornet, true*) is member of the input of the agent and this becomes true when the hornet is positioned inside the radius of perception of the bee.

The NetLogo implementation of the Bee model using TXStates is approximately 290 lines of code including the state diagram and the SXM functions, while the code for the hornet and the set up of the environment is approximately 170 lines.

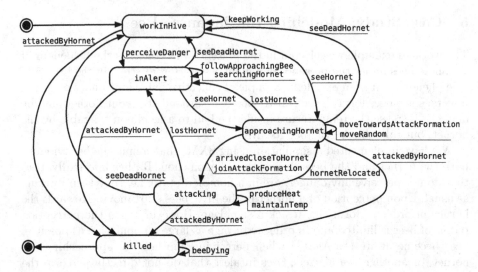

Fig. 3. The state diagram representing the Japanese bee. Labels in transitions represent processing functions that based on percepts and memory are triggered to alter the environment and the agent's internal memory.

```
to-report state-def-of-bees
  report x-diagram
    state "workInHive"
     # x-func "attackedByHornet" goto "killed"
     # x-func "seeHornet" goto "approachingHornet"
     # x-func "perceiveDanger" goto "inAlert"
     # x-func "keepWorking" goto "workInHive"
    end-state
    ... (more states)
    state "killed"
     # x-func "beeDying" goto "killed"
    end-state
  end-diagram
end
```

Fig. 4. Encoding the state transition diagram of the Japanese Bee in TXStates. Due to space limitations, part of this encoding is shown below.

6   Generating the Test Cases

JSXM [11] is a tool, developed in Java, that allows the specification of SXM models, their animation and most importantly automated test case generation. The test cases that are generated by JSXM are in XML format and they are independent of the technology or programming language of the implementation. In the following sections we briefly describe the JSXM modelling language and the associated tool suite.[2]

---

[2] The tool can be downloaded from http://www.jsxm.org.

6.1   The Model in JSXM

The JSXM modelling language is an XML-based language with Java in-line code. An extract of the JSXM code for representing the model of Fig. 3 is shown in Fig. 5. Information regarding *states*, *transitions* and *input/output* is included in the corresponding XML elements. *Memory* elements are specified with in-line Java code, that allows the definition of any complex Java data structure as the

```
<states>
 <state name="workInHive" />
 <state name="approachingHornet" />
 ...(more)
 <state name="killed" />
</states>
<initialState state="workInHive" />

<transitions>
 <transition from="workInHive" function="attackedByHornet"
        to="killed" />
 <transition from="workInHive" function="seeHornet"
        to="approachingHornet"/>
 ... (more)
</transitions>

<input name="percept">
  <arg name="deadHornet" type="xs:boolean"/>
  <arg name="hornet" type="xs:boolean"/>
  <arg name="hornetPosX" type="xs:byte"/>
  <arg name="hornetPosY" type="xs:byte"/>
  ... (more percepts)
  <arg name="lethalBite" type="xs:boolean"/>
</input>

<memory>
 <declaration>
  byte positionX, positionY; byte hornet_posX, hornet_posY;
 </declaration>
 <initial>
  positionX=0; positionY=0; hornet_posX=-1; hornet_posY=-1;
 </initial>
</memory>

<function name="arrivedCloseToHornet" input="percept" output="action"
                  xsi:type="OutputFunction" >
 <precondition>
 !(percept.get_lethalBite()) && percept.get_hornet()
 && !(percept.get_deadHornet())
 && abs(positionX-percept.get_hornetPosX()) +
          abs(positionY-percept.get_hornetPosY()) <= 2
 </precondition>
 <effect>
 hornet_posX=percept.get_hornetPosX();
 hornet_posY=percept.get_hornetPosY(); action.msg="arrivedClosedToHornet";
 </effect>
</function> ... (more functions)
```

Fig. 5. JSXM model of the Japanese Bee.

memory of the system. The same applies for the definition of *processing functions*, that are specified by defining their inputs, outputs, preconditions (specifying the domain of the function) and effects on the memory. Due to space limitations only one processing function (*arrivedCloseToHornet*) is shown in Fig. 5.

As mentioned in Sect. 2, the JSXM model implemented is the *corresponding model* of the one implemented in TXStates. There are two issues that have to be considered:

- The SXM testing method requires that the model is deterministic i.e. in each state, the choice of a processing function is performed deterministically. It should be noted, that deterministic choice in function application to a state is imposed in the TXStates model by introducing to the meta-interpreter a *priority ordering* (Sect. 4.4).
- The simulation environment imposes constraints on inputs. For instance, although `hornetPosX` is of type byte (Fig. 4), the simulation environment size could constrain this to a smaller range of values.

Thus, functions in the JSXM model require a richer set of guards to deal with the above two cases. As an example, Fig. 6 depicts the *seeHornet* function in TXStates and in the corresponding JSXM Model. The TXStates and JSXM guards regarding the perception of a hornet that is still alive (`!percept.get_deadHornet()`) are equivalent, the JSXM function contains two sets of additional guards:

```
-- TXStates Function --
to-report seeHornet
  ifelse x-percept-value "hornet" and (not x-percept-value "deadHornet")
    [report x-true #< x-action task [bee-show "saw_Hornet"] >#
                   #< x-mem-set "hornet-pos" (x-percept-value "hornetPos")># ]
    [report x-false]
end


-- JSXM Function --
<function name="seeHornet" input="percept" output="action"
        xsi:type="OutputFunction">
 <precondition>
  percept.get_hornet() && !percept.get_deadHornet()
  && !percept.get_lethalBite()
  && abs(positionX - percept.get_hornetPosX())
     + abs(positionY - percept.get_hornetPosY()) < 10
 </precondition>
 <effect>
  hornet_posX = percept.get_hornetPosX();
  hornet_posY = percept.get_hornetPosY(); action.msg="saw_Hornet";
 </effect>
</function>
```

Fig. 6. The see-hornet function in TXStates and JSXM.

- The guard `!percept.get_lethalBite()` that is required for ensuring that the JSXM model is deterministic, in order to distinguish the *seeHornet* function from the *attackedByHornet* function in the same state. In TXStates this is done by placing the latter function before the former in the state description.

- The guard `abs(positionX-percept.get_hornetPosX()) + abs(positionY - percept.get_hornetPosY())<10` that states that the hornet must be in the perception radius (10 units) of the bee in order for the latter to perceive it. This is constraint imposed by the simulation environment, since the perception mechanisms of the agent implemented ensure this and thus there is no need to encoded it the corresponding TXStates function.

The environment constraint stated above is applicable only in the case of the specific function. Naturally there exist a number of constraints that are *global* i.e. applicable to all function. A classic example is the size of the simulation world that constraints inputs regarding the positions of agents, free positions that the bee can move to in a single move, that have to be in the close neighbourhood of the bee, etc. To avoid repeating these global constraints on every function specification in JSXM, these are encoded once and applied to all processing functions.

6.2   Test Generation

The JSXM tool implements the SXM testing method (Sect. 3.1) for the generation of the test set. For the test generation process the modeller needs to provide:

- a JSXM specification of the SXM model Z.
- an r-state cover S_r and a separating set W_s
- the estimated difference k of states between the SUT and the specification.

The r-state cover for the specific case study consists of the following sequences of processing functions: $\langle\rangle$, $\langle attackedByHornet\rangle$, $\langle perceiveDanger\rangle$, $\langle seeHornet\rangle$, $\langle seeHornet, arrivedCloseToHornet\rangle$. All states of the state diagram are reached by these sequences. It should be noted that the r-state cover is computed automatically by the JSXM tool.

The separating set W_s consists of the following sequences: $\langle attackedBy Hornet\rangle$, $\langle beeDying\rangle$, $\langle keepWorking\rangle$, $\langle seeDeadHornet\rangle$, $\langle lostHornet\rangle$, $\langle search ingHornet\rangle$, $\langle followApproachingBee\rangle$, $\langle moveTowardsAttackFormation\rangle$, $\langle hor netRelocated\rangle$, $\langle produceHeat\rangle$, $\langle maintainTemp\rangle$. At each reached state the execution of these processing functions produces outputs that uniquely separate the reached state by all the other states. Automatically computing the separating set W_s is still an open research issue.

For the input-output test cases to be produced, all the input sequences are fed to the JSXM animator, which acts as an oracle, and the resulting output sequences are recorded. The resulting test cases (pairs of input and output sequences) are stored in an XML file in a programming language independent format. For the specific case study the JSXM tool has generated 62 test cases for $k = 0$.

6.3   From Test Cases to Simulation Scenarios

The test cases produced by the JSXM tool are then processed in order to prove that (a) the TXStates and JSXM models are *equivalent*, and (b) produce simulation scenarios for validation. Since the sequences of test cases are in XML, XSLT transformations are applied in order to obtain the NetLogo code necessary for performing both these tasks. In the case of proving *equivalence*, the XSLT transformations produce a sequence of `x-add-percepts` calls, as NetLogo tasks, that "inject" the input values as percepts in the usual cycle of the agent with no other changes in the environment. Then the output of the NetLogo model is checked against the expected output recorded in the sequence.

In the specific case, all tests but one succeeded completely proving the two models equivalent. The test that partially failed regarded the sequence of functions ⟨*attackedByHornet, beeDying, beeDying*⟩, where the last two function calls are self-transitions on the final state. However, since in the simulation environment, when a bee "Dies" it is removed from the simulation, the second call to *BeeDying* failed, simply because there was no bee to execute the function.

A similar process is used to produce the simulation scenarios used for *validation*. Since the input to each JSXM function actually describes the state of the

```
<call>
<function name="seeHornet" />
 <input name="percept">
  <temperature type="xs:byte">30 </temperature>
  <freePosX type="xs:byte"> 0 </freePosX>
  <freePosY type="xs:byte"> 1 </freePosY>
  <deadHornet type="xs:boolean"> false </deadHornet>
  <hornetPosX type="xs:byte"> 0 </hornetPosX>
  <hornetPosY type="xs:byte"> -9 </hornetPosY>
   ...
  <lethalBite type="xs:boolean"> false </lethalBite>
  <beeInAlert type="xs:boolean"> false </beeInAlert>
 </input>
<output name="action"> <msg type="xs:string">saw_Hornet</msg> </output>
</call>
```

Fig. 7. Part of a test sequence generated by the JSXM tool. In the specific setting, the bee is expected to follow the transition guarded by the "seeHornet" function and output that it has perceived a hornet.

Fig. 8. Two snapshots of the scenario case obtained by the function call of Fig. 7. Bees are labelled with their current SXM state.

environment, appropriate XSLT transformations produce the necessary NetLogo code to set up the exact state of the environment described. For instance, in the case of the test generated by JSXM shown in Fig. 7, execution of the code places the bee at position $(0, 0)$, sets the temperature to 30, and places a live hornet at position $(0, -9)$. Then the agent TXStates implementation is executed and the resulting actions are matched against the output of the test case, while visually providing feedback to the modeller involving the state change of the bee. Thus the modeller can validate that this is the expected behaviour of the bee in the specific scenario. Figure 8, presents an example of the visual output that the modeller sees, that corresponds to the function call *seeHornet*. The image on the left presents how the environment is set up for the function to be applicable and the one on the right the state of the world after a single run.

7   Related Work

From the various Multi-Agent Systems (MAS) design methodologies that exist, relatively few deal explicitly with simulation design, and among these even fewer are applicable for producing NetLogo code. The Behavior Oriented Design (BOD) [2] and the Interaction-Oriented Design of Agent simulations (IODA) [17] are examples of such methodologies that are also currently supported by corresponding NetLogo tools. Going into the specifics of both these methodologies exceeds the scope of this section work, however, they both lack support for any automated test generation process.

A number of DSL and DMSL approaches to programming MAS have been reported in the literature. For instance, [4,12] present approaches to domain specific modelling languages (DSML), for developing multi agent systems. These approaches differ from TXStates since they focus on describing MAS models using high level concepts such as agent roles and interactions, and provide and model transformations to code. The present work addresses mainly and problem of modelling and validating a single agent in a MAS simulation setting, and provide what could be considered as unit testing/validation of that agent model. To the best of our knowledge, these modelling frameworks do not address this problem.

A number of diverse approaches for testing agent based systems are found in the literature. As mentioned, our focus lies mainly on two aspects. On one hand, whilst testing the communication and coordination in a society of agents is of interest when developing MAS, testing a single agent against its specification is of paramount importance. Under this scope, a number of unit testing frameworks have been proposed. However, there is a variety of views as to what constitutes a unit to be tested. On the other hand, tools that offer automated test generation and execution capabilities are limited.

Caire et al. [3] present a testing framework that offers a skeleton code for the developer to build test cases, considering as a testable unit either a single agent or any of its internal behaviours as a black box. The framework was developed as part of the PASSI [8] development methodology. An agent system's behaviour was initially captured in a Multi-Agent Zoomable Behaviour Description diagram - introduced by the authors - which is in essence an Activity Diagram extended with Agent UML notations. The tool also provides a test agent for automatic test case execution.

SUnit [24] is a framework that is built on top of the Seagent [10] MAS development platform. The tool allows for testing of agent interactions and plans, which are considered as the units to be tested. SUnit extends the JUnit[3] testing framework, and was developed with the purpose of facilitating test driven development of MAS. SUnit provides a mock agent infrastructure, which the developer uses to automatically run the manually written tests.

Coelho et al. [7] suggest that the modular unit in a MAS is a single agent, and thus, propose the notion of a Mock Agent that is built specifically for testing the agent under test. Therefore, each Mock Agent is a manual fake implementation of an actual agent that interacts with the agent (role) under test. Coehlo et al. in [6] later proposed JAT (Jade Agent Testing Framework), a test automation framework built on top of the JADE[4] MAS development platform, and is aimed to facilitate the developer in creating the Mock Agent code and automatically executing the test scenarios.

The above work focuses on automating the execution rather than the generation of test cases. The latter capability is provided in the work of Zhang et al. [27] who proposed a model-based testing framework that allows for automatic test generation and execution. The framework uses the design artefacts produced with the Prometheus [20] agent development methodology. The framework was integrated [28] in the Prometheus Design Tool[5] (PDT). In this case, an agent consists of events, plans and belief-sets, and each of these were considered as a unit to be tested by the authors, in contrast to our work that tests the dynamic internal behaviour of a single agent as a whole rather than its individual components.

A different approach on model based test generation is provided by Seo et al. [23] and Zheng and Alagar [29]. The former used Statecharts extended with roles descriptions, event types and memory to model a MAS. Based on the diagram, all possible transitions to all concrete events were manually calculated, and then fed to a tool developed by Seo et al. that generated the test sequences. The latter used Extended State Machines (ESM) to formally model an agent and then used this model to generate a set of unit test cases. Each test set consisted of a set of state cover sequences and a set of transition cover sequences. However, in both these cases, no further discussion exists on automating the test execution process. More importantly, in our case, the SXM testing theory provides for more coverage than state and transition coverage, additionally allowing for proof of functional equivalence of the models.

Automated test case generation and execution are useful in supporting model verification to some significant extend. Visualization on the other hand is considered as one of the most predominant validation techniques for simulations.

---

[3] http://junit.org/.

[4] http://jade.tilab.com/.

[5] http://www.cs.rmit.edu.au/agents/pdt/.

A validation framework proposed by [16] identifies animation assessment as one of the basic methodological elements. To further support a preliminary model validation, Xiang et al. [26] applied a model-to-model comparison technique. They initially built a conceptual model of the Natural Organic Matter (NOM) evolution, and then implemented a corresponding simulation. By using various verification methods and by visualizing 450 simulation runs of their model with different random seeds, they validated their model against the conceptual one. They subsequently compared their results with another existing implementation of the same conceptual model. The authors argue that the good agreement between the results of these two different implementation supports the validity of their implementation. In our case, the generated test cases facilitate the validation via visualization process, by providing the developer with an easy way of selecting specific test scenarios of interest.

8 Conclusions

This work presents a systematic approach to the problem of developing, testing and validating agent simulations. Towards this direction, the current work:

- describes a DSL that can be used to specify and execute an SXM model, that encodes the behaviour of an agent in the simulation, and
- shows how an existing tool for automated test case generation that employs the same formal modelling approach can be used for generating a set of "simulation scenarios."
- reports on the necessary changes in the TXStates model needed to obtain the JSXM model in order to produce the test cases.

Thus, this paper demonstrates how the SXM formal modelling technique is employed in a practical setting to develop simulations.

The XSLT transformations provide a way to automatically test equivalence of the two models developed models. These are general and can be applied to any model with minor changes, thus removing the need of manually crafted code as reported in [21]. Although the necessary changes of the transformations are minimal we are planning to extend the tool in order to fully automated the process.

One of our immediate aims is to provide a way to semi-automatically translate large parts of the TXStates model to the JSXM modelling language, including both the generation of the richer set of guards for processing functions, and the set of global constraints related to the simulation world that are applied in all functions. The task has also a theoretical interest, since it demands a systematic way of imposing mutual exclusiveness of guards on a set of processing functions, by modifying the former.

Finally, it is our intention to extend this approach to other agents simulation and agent programming platforms. One future direction is to investigate whether BDI agents can be modelled as SXMs and apply the specific testing approach to such systems.

Acknowledgements. This research has been co-financed by the European Union (European Social Fund-ESF) and Greek national funds through the Operational Program Education and Lifelong Learning of the National Strategic Reference Framework (NSRF)-Research Funding Program: Thalis-Athens University of Economics and Business-SOFTWARE ENGINEERING RESEARCH PLATFORM.

References

1. Allan, R.J.: Survey of agent based modelling and simulation tools. Technical report DL-TR-2010-007, DL Technical reports (2010)
2. Bryson, J.J.: The behavior-oriented design of modular agent intelligence. In: Kowalczyk, R., Müller, J.P., Tianfield, H., Unland, R. (eds.) NODe-WS 2002. LNCS (LNAI), vol. 2592, pp. 61–76. Springer, Heidelberg (2003)
3. Caire, G., Cossentino, M., Negri, A., Poggi, A., Turci, P.: Multi-agent systems implementation and testing. In: Fourth International Symposium: From Agent Theory to Agent Implementation. Citeseer (2004)
4. Challenger, M., Demirkol, S., Getir, S., Mernik, M., Kardas, G., Kosar, T.: On the use of a domain-specific modeling language in the development of multiagent systems. Eng. Appl. Artif. Intel. **28**, 111–141 (2014). http://linkinghub.elsevier.com/retrieve/pii/S0952197613002297
5. Chow, T.S.: Testing software design modelled by finite state machines. IEEE Trans. Softw. Eng. **4**, 178–187 (1978)
6. Coelho, R., Cirilo, E., Kulesza, U., von Staa, A., Rashid, A., Lucena, C.: Jat: a test automation framework for multi-agent systems. In: ICSM 2007, IEEE International Conference on Software Maintenance, pp. 425–434. IEEE (2007)
7. Coelho, R., Kulesza, U., von Staa, A., Lucena, C.: Unit testing in multi-agent systems using mock agents and aspects. In: Proceedings of the 2006 International Workshop on Software Engineering for Large-scale Multi-agent Systems, pp. 83–90. ACM (2006)
8. Cossentino, M., Potts, C.: A case tool supported methodology for the design of multi-agent systems. In: International Conference on Software Engineering Research and Practice (SERP 2002) (2002)
9. Davidsson, P., Holmgren, J., Kyhlbäck, H., Mengistu, D., Persson, M.: Applications of agent based simulation. In: Antunes, L., Takadama, K. (eds.) MABS 2006. LNCS (LNAI), vol. 4442, pp. 15–27. Springer, Heidelberg (2007)
10. Dikenelli, O., Erdur, R.C., Gumus, O.: Seagent: a platform for developing semantic web based multi agent systems. In: Proceedings of the 4th International Joint Conference on Autonomous Agents and Multiagent Systems, pp. 1271–1272. ACM (2005)
11. Dranidis, D., Bratanis, K., Ipate, F.: JSXM: a tool for automated test generation. In: Eleftherakis, G., Hinchey, M., Holcombe, M. (eds.) SEFM 2012. LNCS, vol. 7504, pp. 352–366. Springer, Heidelberg (2012)
12. Hahn, C.: A domain specific modeling language for multiagent systems. In: Proceedings of the 7th International Joint Conference on Autonomous Agents And Multiagent Systems, vol. 1, pp. 233–240. International Foundation for Autonomous Agents and Multiagent Systems (2008). http://dl.acm.org/citation.cfm?id=1402420
13. Holcombe, M., Ipate, F.: Correct Systems: Building a Business Process Solution. Springer, London (1998)

14. Ipate, F., Holcombe, M.: An integration testing method that is proven to find all faults. Int. J. Comput. Math. **63**, 159–178 (1997)
15. Kefalas, P., Stamatopoulou, I., Sakellariou, I., Eleftherakis, G.: Transforming communicating X-machines into P systems. Natural Comput. **8**(4), 817–832 (2009)
16. Klügl, F.: A validation methodology for agent-based simulations. In: Proceedings of the 2008 ACM Symposium on Applied Computing, pp. 39–43. ACM (2008)
17. Kubera, Y., Mathieu, P., Picault, S.: IODA: an interaction-oriented approach for multi-agent based simulations. Auton. Agents Multi-agent Syst. **23**(3), 303–343 (2011)
18. Nikolai, C., Madey, G.: Tools of the trade: a survey of various agent based modeling platforms. J. Artif. Soc. Soc. Simul. **12**(2), 2 (2009). http://jasss.soc.surrey.ac.uk/12/2/2.html
19. Ono, M., Igarashi, T., Ohno, E., Sasaki, M.: Unusual thermal defence by a honeybee against mass attack by hornets. Nature **377**(6547), 334–336 (1995)
20. Padgham, L., Winikoff, M.: Developing Intelligent Agent Systems: A Practical Guide, vol. 13. Wiley, New York (2005)
21. Sakellariou, I., Dranidis, D., Ntika, M., Kefalas, P.: From formal modelling to agent simulation execution and testing. In: ICAART 2015 - Proceedings of the 7th International Conference on Agents and Artificial Intelligence, Lisbon, Portugal, pp. 87–98, SciTePress, January 2015
22. Sakellariou, I., Kefalas, P., Stamatopoulou, I.: Evacuation simulation through formal emotional agent based modelling. In: ICAART 2014 - Proceedings of the 6th International Conference on Agents and Artificial Intelligence, vol. 2, pp. 193–200, SciTePress, March 2014. http://dx.doi.org/10.5220/0004824601930200
23. Seo, H.-S., Araragi, T., Kwon, Y.-R.: Modeling and testing agent systems based on statecharts. In: Núñez, M., Maamar, Z., Pelayo, F.L., Pousttchi, K., Rubio, F. (eds.) FORTE 2004. LNCS, vol. 3236, pp. 308–321. Springer, Heidelberg (2004)
24. Tiryaki, A.M., Öztuna, S., Dikenelli, O., Erdur, R.C.: SUNIT: a unit testing framework for test driven development of multi-agent systems. In: Padgham, L., Zambonelli, F. (eds.) AOSE VII/AOSE 2006. LNCS, vol. 4405, pp. 156–173. Springer, Heidelberg (2007)
25. Wilensky, U.: NetLogo. In: Center for Connected Learning and Computer-Based Modeling, Northwestern University, Evanston, IL (1999). http://ccl.northwestern.edu/netlogo/
26. Xiang, X., Kennedy, R., Madey, G., Cabaniss, S.: Verification and validation of agent-based scientific simulation models. In: Agent-Directed Simulation Conference, pp. 47–55 (2005)
27. Zhang, Z., Thangarajah, J., Padgham, L.: Automated unit testing for agent systems. ENASE **7**, 10–18 (2007)
28. Zhang, Z., Thangarajah, J., Padgham, L.: Automated unit testing intelligent agents in PDT. In: Proceedings of the 7th International Joint Conference on Autonomous Agents And Multiagent Systems: Demo Papers, pp. 1673–1674. International Foundation for Autonomous Agents and Multiagent Systems (2008)
29. Zheng, M., Alagar, V.: Conformance testing of BDI properties in agent-based software. In: APSEC 2005: 12th Asia-Pacific Software Engineering Conference, pp. 457–464, December 2005

Building Self-adaptive Systems by Adaptation Patterns Integrated into Agent Methodologies

Mariachiara Puviani[✉], Giacomo Cabri, Nicola Capodieci, and Letizia Leonardi

Università di Modena e Reggio Emilia, Modena, Italy
{mariachiara.puviani,giacomo.cabri,nicola.capodieci,
letizia.leonardi}@unimore.it
http://www.unimore.it

Abstract. Adopting patterns, i.e. reusable solutions to generic problems, turns out to be useful to rely on tested solutions and to avoid reinventing the wheel. To this aim, we proposed to use adaptation patterns to build systems that exhibit self-adaptive features. However, these patterns would be more usable if integrated in a methodology exploited to develop a system. In this paper we show how our Catalogue of adaptation patterns can be integrated into methodologies for adaptive systems; more in detail, we consider methodologies which support the development of multi-agent systems that can be considered good examples of adaptive systems. The paper, in particular, shows the integration of our Catalogue of adaptive patterns into the PASSI methodology, together with the graphical tool that we developed to support it.

Keywords: Multi-agent system · Adaptation pattern · Methodology

1 Introduction

Intelligent software systems are playing an important role in many fields, but they are becoming more and more complex, requiring appropriate approaches for their development and maintenance. In particular, their complexity and the fact that they often cannot be stopped, introduce the need for some form of adaptation to the changes in the surrounding environment or in general in the execution conditions. So, self-adaptation is more and more a required feature of the complex intelligent systems, and must be carefully taken into consideration during the development, from a software engineering point of view, becoming one of the challenges for the discipline [14].

We define *Self-adaptation* as the ability of a software system or an application to automatically modify its structure and behaviour at runtime in order to ensure, maintain or recover some functional or non-functional properties, even in the case of unexpected changes to operating conditions or user requirements.

M. Puviani—The work is supported by the "Linea strategica SMART ICT FOR SMART SOCIAL WORLDS" of the Università di Modena e Reggio Emilia.

© Springer International Publishing Switzerland 2015
B. Duval et al. (Eds.): ICAART 2015, LNAI 9494, pp. 58–75, 2015.
DOI: 10.1007/978-3-319-27947-3_4

In the literature, we can find two approaches to develop self-adaptive systems: *parameter* adaptation and *compositional* adaptation [21]. Parameter adaptation means adapting the system's behaviour through changing parameters, while compositional adaptation is meant as a change of components (in terms of behaviour or whole structure). In our work, we focus on *compositional* adaptation, but in a more specific way: we do not aim to simply change the components in a system, but we aim to modify their behaviour (defined as the *pattern* that describes it) inside the system. This leads to conceive the adaptation of a system as the capability of changing its internal structure in order to make it behave differently, not only as the possibility of changing the system's components.

Anyway, there is a *lack* of support for designing and implementing self-adaptive systems, in terms of reusable and well-defined *components* and how composing them, so designers often start from scratch the development of a self-adaptive system. From this point of view, the availability of adaptation patterns is considered as useful means to introduce adaptation into a system. Further, the integration of adaptation patterns into a more general framework not only will help suggesting developers how to include adaptivity in their systems, but also this would take advantage of the methodologies and the tools exploited in the framework, leading to a fast and less error-prone development.

The general aim of our work is to propose a comprehensive approach that will guide developers during the development phases, from the system's specification to the system's implementation, in a complete framework for developing self-adaptive systems. To this purpose, we have defined four general steps for our work:

1. analysis of existing methodologies, choice of few of them and integration of our Catalogue of adaptation patterns into the chosen ones;
2. modification of the tools that support the chosen methodologies, for the creation of adaptive systems;
3. creation of a middleware that will merge the concepts coming from methodologies' tools, by means of Java classes;
4. evaluation of the framework, experimenting the creation of self-adaptive systems.

In a previous work [27], we have presented a preliminary result of the first step. In this paper, we extend the presentation of the results of the first step and add some results of the second and of the third steps, in particular related to a specific methodology.

With regard to the first step, we will show how our Catalogue of adaptation patterns can be integrated, in particular, into one existing methodology, PASSI; we will exploit the SPEM notation [34] to specify when and how our Catalogue can be considered in the development process proposed by a specific methodology.

With regard to the second step, we will present the graphical tool we have developed in order to support the previously mentioned integration.

With regard to the third step, we will show how the graphical tool produces a set of Java classes.

The reminder of this paper is as follows: in Sect. 2, we present the Catalogue of adaptation patterns, explaining its importance in connection with adaptive systems and methodologies. Further on, in Sect. 3 we introduce agent-oriented methodologies, along with the criteria we used to select a few of them, and we show how and where our Catalogue of adaptation patterns can be included into one of the chosen methodology, PASSI (Sect. 4); moreover, we present the developed graphical tool to exploit adaptation patterns in the PASSI methodology and to produce the needed Java classes. In Sect. 5, we present some work related to our approach and at the end, in Sect. 6 we conclude the paper and present some future works.

2   The Catalogue of Adaptation Patterns

Closed to self-adaptation are *Service-based systems* and *Agent-based systems*.

In literature, design patterns (or simply *patterns*) are defined as reusable solutions to recurring design problems and are a mainstream of software reuse practice [15,22]. They crystallize a general solution to a common problem, so software developers can benefit from their reuse to develop systems. An *adaptation pattern* is a conceptual scheme that describes a specific adaptation mechanism. It specifies how the component/system architecture can express adaptivity.

An important task to develop a well performing self-adaptive system, is to understand which pattern to choose. In order to define how a pattern works in a self-adaptive system and which kind of systems is covered by a specific pattern, we wrote a Catalogue of adaptation patterns [28]. In this Catalogue, the different patterns are presented, and each of them describes the features of a specific adaptive system.

The adaptive behaviour inside a component or an ensemble is described in terms of feedback loops. In the Catalogue, the patterns are proposed with a specific description by means of a template, and with examples of use of the patterns in real systems, in order to simplify the selection of the right pattern to use. The use of a pattern permits the developer to be guided to make the system exhibit the required behaviour, even when unexpected situations occur.

The use of adaptation patterns to create self-adaptive systems has been tested in different fields and in many applications [20,29], and guarantees correct results in systems that are frequently changing, not only in their internal conditions, but also in the environment where they are operating.

The use of a methodology could be very useful to develop self-adaptive systems. However, the current methodologies consider adaptation only at level of single components, instead of at the system's level. That is the reason why we consider necessary to introduce our Catalogue of adaptation patterns into methodologies: in fact, this will enact adaptivity at the level both of single component and of the entire system. By this integration, our Catalogue of adaptation patterns will support the methodologies in the creation of an adaptive system where the structural adaptation of the whole system is considered very relevant.

3   Agent-Oriented Methodologies for Adaptive Systems

In order to support application developers during the creation of an adaptive system, it is necessary to provide a methodology that support adaptation mechanisms starting from the system requirements. The initial idea is not to propose a methodology from scratch, but to have as a base a stable and well known methodology.

Moreover, we consider that "agents" are one of the most useful paradigms to build intelligence distributed systems, so we would like to use that paradigm to create adaptive systems. To do that, we started from the study of agent-oriented methodologies as a starting point to introduce adaptation features while building a system.

Considering MASs (Multi Agent Systems), it is generally accepted that analysis and design of agent-based systems require an Agent-Oriented Software Engineering (AOSE) methodology. There are now many mature AOSE methodologies [4,19], including MaSE [13], Tropos [6], Gaia [36], Prometheus [24], INGENIAS [25], ADEM[1], ADELFE [5], SODA [1] and PASSI [11].

After different studies [32], we found out that to create a unified methodology that may have the most powerful features of every of the starting ones, is very difficult. For example, we are not able to prove if a new unified methodology covers all the possible scenarios, as happened for MAR&A [7], that is a composed methodology, but is not applicable to adaptive systems. Moreover, not all the composing methodologies use the same language or the same concepts, and translating them into unified terms will not be always easy. Furthermore, creating a new methodology for adaptive systems from scratch will not be easy as well. It may be yet another methodology, and there is no guarantee that it will be able to build all the adaptive systems.

All these reasons suggested us to not create a methodology dedicated to self-adaptive system, or to compose a methodology, but to start from well known and well defined methodologies, and to insert our Catalogue of adaptation patterns into them in order to have self-adaptive features.

Starting from our previous work [30], we found out that some AOSE methodologies, even if they are well known, are not up to date, or no more utilised to develop intelligent complex agents systems. So we selected only few methodologies that we consider suitable to build a self-adaptive system. The methodologies that we selected have some common features:

- they are updated (e.g. a new version of the methodology has been released in the last years);
- they have been tested in different distributed systems;
- they use well known paradigms like UML and the SPEM approach [31,34] that will be very useful in order to introduce adaptation patterns;
- they use the concept of "role" to define adaptation patterns in a system;
- they have a supporting tool, or specific indication for the development of a system.

---

[1] http://www.whitestein.com/adem.

The methodologies we selected for our work are: ADELFE, PASSI2 and SODA. For space reasons, in this paper we describe only PASSI2, along with explaining where introducing our Catalogue of adaptation patterns.

As said before, an common point of these methodologies is that all of them have been described using the SPEM (Software Process Engineering Meta-model) approach [23]. This will be useful in order to insert our Catalogue of adaptation patterns in terms of SPEM fragments. In this way, it will be possible to better define the concepts presented in patterns and to insert them into the different methodologies.

To improve reading of the paper, in Fig. 1 we report the definitions of some common notations used by SPEM.

WorkProduct		Anything produced, consumed, or modified by a process.
WorkDefinition		Operation that describes the work performed in the process.
Activity		The main subclass of WorkDefinition, it describes a piece of work performed by one ProcessRole.
ProcessRole		Defines a performer for a set of WorkDefinitions in a process. It represents abstractly the "whoole process" or one of its components.
ProcessPackage		
Phase		A specialization of WorkDefinition. Its precondition defines the phase entry criteria and its goal defines the phase exit criteria.
Document		A WorkProduct
UMLModel		A WorkProduct

Fig. 1. SPEM notations.

4   Integrating Catalogue of Adaptation Patterns into Methodologies

In this section we present how to integrate our Catalogue of the adaptation patterns, in particular, in the PASSI methodology. Moreover, the last subsection sketches the interfaces of the graphical tool we developed to support the exploitation of the patterns in that methodology.

4.1   Integration in PASSI2

PASSI2 (Process for Agent Society Specification and Implementation) [12] is the evolution of PASSI [11], a methodology that aims at covering all the phases of a system development from the requirements' analysis to the deployment configuration, coding, and testing.

It is based on a meta-model describing the elements that constitute the system to be designed (agents, tasks, communications, roles) and what are the relationships among them. The importance of this description is in the lack of a universally accepted meta-model of MASs (differently from object-oriented systems) that makes unclear any agent design process that does not precisely define the structure of the system it aims to produce. PASSI2 has been designed keeping in mind the possibility of designing systems with the following peculiarities: (i) highly distributed, (ii) subject to a (relatively) low rate of requirements changes, (iii) openness (at runtime external systems and agents that are unknown at design time will interact with the system to be built). Robotics, workflow management, and information systems are the specific application areas where it has been wildly applied.

PASSI2 is composed of three models that address different design concerns and several phases, as we can see in Fig. 2. An important aspect of PASSI2 is that it uses standards as UML and adapts it to the need of representing agent systems through its extension mechanisms (constraints, tagged values and stereotypes).

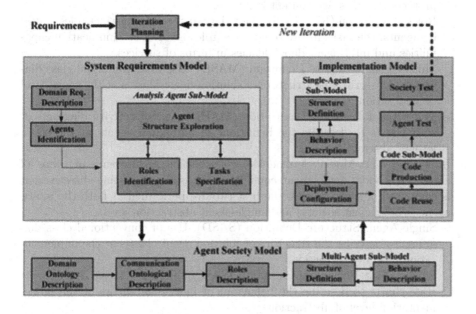

Fig. 2. PASSI2 models and phases.

Synthetically, the models and phases of PASSI2 are:

1. System Requirements Model. A model of the system requirements in terms of agency and purpose. Developing this model involves:

- Domain req. Description (DD). A functional description of the system using conventional use-case diagrams.
- Agents Identification (AId). Separation of responsibility concerns into agents, represented as UML packages.
- Roles Identification (RId). Use of sequence diagrams to represent each agent's responsibilities through role-specific scenarios.
- Agent Structure Exploration (ASE). An analysis-level description of the agent structure in terms of tasks required for accomplishing the agent's functionalities.
- Tasks Specification (TSp). Specification through state/activity diagrams of the capabilities of each agent.

2. Agent Society Model. A model of the social interactions and dependencies among the agents involved in the solution. Developing this model involves five phases:

- Domain Ontology Description (DOD). Use of class diagrams to describe domain categories (concepts), actions that could affect their state and propositions about values of categories.
- Communication Ontology Description (COD). Use of class diagrams to describe agents' communications in terms of referred ontology, interaction protocol and message content language.
- Roles Description (RD). Use of class diagrams to show distinct roles played by agents, the tasks involved what the roles involve, communication capabilities and inter-agent dependencies in terms of services.
- Multi-Agent Structure Definition (MASD). Use of conventional class diagrams to describe the structure of solution agent classes at the social level of abstraction.
- Multi-Agent Behavior Description (MABD). Use of activity diagrams or state-charts to describe the behaviour of individual agents at the social level of abstraction.

3. Implementation Model. A model of the solution architecture in terms of classes, methods, deployment configuration, code and testing directives; it is composed of seven phases, the first two are performed at both the multi-agent (whole agent society) and single-agent abstraction level:

- Single-Agent Structure Definition (SASD). Use of conventional class diagrams to describe the structure of solution agent classes at the implementation level of abstraction.
- Single-Agent Behavior Description (SABD). Use of activity diagrams or state-charts to describe the behaviour of individual agents at the implementation level of abstraction.
- Deployment Configuration (DC). Use of deployment diagrams to describe the allocation of agents to the available processing units and any constraints on migration, mobility and configuration of hosts and agent-running platforms.
- Code Reuse (CR). A library of patterns with associated reusable code to allow the automatic generation of significant portions of code.

- Code Production (CP). Source code of the target system that is manually completed.
- Agent Test. Verification of the single behaviour with regards to the original requirements of the system solved by the specific agent.
- Society Test. Validation of the correct interaction of the agents, performed in order to verify that they actually concur in solving problems that need cooperation. This test is done in the most real situation that can be simulated in the development environment.

The Iteration Planning phase is positioned at a higher level of abstraction, above the logical sequence of models and phases. It is at the base of every iterative incremental process and in our case consists of the analysis of the Problem Statement and all the other available documents (for instance outputs of previous iterations) in order to identify the requirements (and related risks) that should be faced in the next iteration (that is considered as the nineteen phase).

An important concept in PASSI2 is that of "role". A *role* is defined by the set of responsibilities defining the subjective behaviour of an agent in an interaction (conversation) with another one or in providing some service in one or more scenarios; an agent may play one or more roles at the same time. Roles are very important because they are considered a useful paradigm that can used to define the different patterns in a system [26].

Two are the main phases that involved roles: the *Role Identification phase*, into the System Requirements Model (Fig. 3), and the *Role Description phase* into the Agent Society Model (Fig. 4).

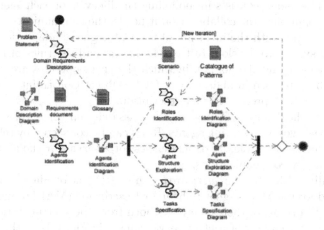

Fig. 3. PASSI2: System Requirements Model activities and resulting work products.

The *Roles Identification* phase produces a set of sequence diagrams that specify scenarios from the agents' identification use case diagram. In this phase, our Catalogue of adaptation patterns is added as input, in order to create specific

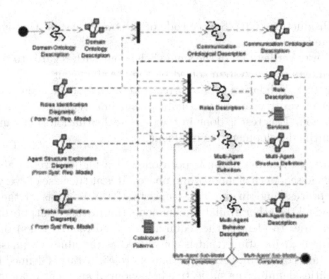

Fig. 4. PASSI2: Agent Society Model activities and resulting work products.

roles able to describe an adaptive system. In that phase, roles are identified in the sense that agents' external manifestations are captured in sequence diagrams where agents participate playing one or more roles concurring to the evolution of the system dynamic.

Our Catalogue of adaptation patterns is also introduced in the *Roles Description* phase. This phase consists in modelling the lifecycle of each agent, looking at the roles it can play, the collaboration it needs, the communications in which it participates and, with the inclusion of the Catalogue of adaptation patterns, the adaptive system to develop. In the RD diagram all the rules of the society, laws of the society and the domain in which the agent operates are introduced. They could be expressed in plain text or OCL (Object Constraint Language) in order to have a more precise, formal description.

In PASSI2, the defined RD diagram is a class diagram where roles are classes grouped in packages representing agents. Roles can be connected by relationships representing changes of role, by dependencies for a service or the availability of a resource and by communications.

Specifically, in the *Agent Society Model*, the Catalogue of adaptation patterns is introduced for the Multi-Agent Behaviour Description (MABD), where agents are described in terms of their behaviour both from the social-exterior point of view and the internal flow of control, as we can see in Fig. 4. Here the Catalogue is necessary to identify which role to choose to obtain the system adaptation in the considered environment.

PASSI2 does not have a real Code Production Phase, but each programmer has to complete the code of the application starting from the design of the skeletons produced by the methodology.

The PASSI2 design methodology is supported by a specific design tool, granting a large number of automatisms during the design, and a pattern repository for the reuse practice; these are determinant in cutting down the time and cost for developing systems [10]. The toolkit is PTK (PASSI ToolKit). The PTK add-in can generate the code for all the skeletons of the agents, tasks and other classes included in the project. The pattern repository consists of a series of reusable portions of agents and tasks. The repository also includes a list of tasks that can be applied to existing agents.

4.2   The Graphical Tool

We developed a graphical tool to be used as a complementary extension for PTK, with the purpose of allowing the designer of adaptive system to rapidly prototype different patterns to be applied to the same sets of tasks within the considered adaptive system. Our contribution aims to extend the concept of *Agent-Structure Exploration* as defined by the PASSI methodology (see Fig. 2), hence to focus the necessary design aspects needed to foster the dynamic creation of hierarchical structures of *autonomic components*. The word *component* is from now on used a substitute of agent, so that we are now able to operate a first distinction on the concept of Agent-Structure by dividing the agents of the considered population into two mutually exclusive categories: *Autonomic Managers* and *Service Components* (resp. AMs and SCs).

From the role description, the following phase of the PASSI methodology deals with "Behaviour Description", hence implying an unspecified relation between roles and behaviours. In our implementation, we detailed the relation between these two concepts, by proposing a logic that is consistent with the taxonomy of adaptation patterns as proposed in [28]. We defined a role as a collection of sequential and/or parallel behaviours and the concept of behaviour is an (implementation-wise) extension of the concept of Behaviour as intended in the JADE agent platform [3]. We therefore extended the definition of PTK so to support the definition of roles, behaviours, components and adaptive patterns so to have a tool able to generate the necessary artifacts for describing more complete adaptive systems.

As presented in Sect. 2, an *adaptation pattern* is a conceptual scheme that describes a specific adaptation mechanism. It specifies how the component/system architecture can express adaptivity.

In [28], a taxonomy of adaptation patterns is defined in such a level of detail that we are able to translate most of the relevant aspects in an Object Oriented Programming point of view, with Java as our language of choice. In particular, we are now able to design abstract classes, interfaces and basic implementations of them (called default implementations) so to have re-usable structures of classes that the designer of adaptive systems can rely on.

According to [28] a clear definition of the components interfaces helps us in understanding the mechanism of components' composition. The interfaces of a component can be described as a tuple of six elements:

- Input, used to receive information (e.g. service's request);
- Output, used to send information (e.g. service's reply);
- Sensor, that makes the component able to achieve information from the external (e.g. others components and/or the environment);
- Effector, that makes the component be able to manage the external (e.g. to act on the environment and manage other components);
- Emitter, used to emit status information to an external manager. This interface permits also to share information taken from the environment (using sensors) or other components;
- Controller, that makes it possible to an external adaptation manager to change and adapt the component's internal state.

According to our implementation, these elements refer to the generic concept of Component, hence the class Component is subsequently sub-classed into the classes *Service Component* and *Autonomic Manager*, with the latter one having the implicit role of adaptation manager. Service Components have a list of different sensors and actuators and those are mainly used for reading or applying modifications to the environment in which the ensemble is inserted. The list of sensors and actuators belonging to an Autonomic Manager is used to create connections with SCs or other AMs. Other important lists, associated with the

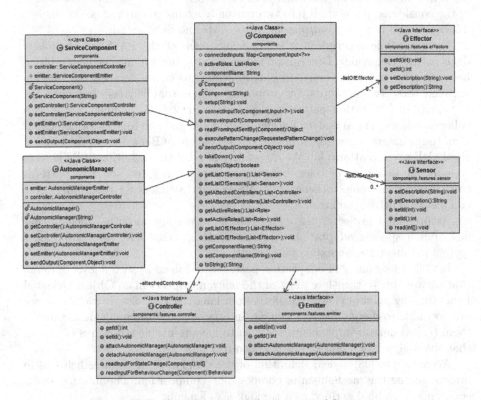

Fig. 5. UML Class diagram of the concept of Component.

component, are related to active roles, components attached to the emitter and components attached to the controller. Trivially, all the methods that allow us to modify these lists are accessible through the class hierarchy. The concept of component is an extension of the class *Agent* from the Jade agent platform, hence the component inherits methods such as *setup* and *takeDown* that refer to standard agent operations to be executed just after their creation or just before their removal from the considered context (i.e. registering to or de-registering from a directory facilitator or other user-implemented yellow pages services).

A summarizing class diagram is in Fig. 5.

As shown in Fig. 5, components have the possibility to actively participate into a change of pattern. A pattern is a description of which component is connected to which other components inside the same adaptive system. More specifically, we can define a pattern by specifying for each component (AMs and SCs), which components are attached to the their emitters and controllers. By doing so we are able to re-create any combination of adaptation pattern that are referred as *taxonomies* in [28]. A pattern may or may not have an associated role, but is always bounded to a context. A context is an attribute of the environment and it is characterized by a list of *rules* and a list of *laws*. The difference between these latter ones is mostly case specific; however, as rule of thumb, we can specify that rules are used to regulate the single behaviour within a role, while laws deal with regulating the inter-component interactions (e.g.: negotiations, elections etc.). As previously specified, roles are collections of behaviours: this implies being able to use existing classes from the JADE package for defining behaviours as dynamically activated local computation within the agents/components: these computations can be sequential, parallel, cyclic or (using a JADE terminology) *one-shot*.

These considerations have been summarized in Fig. 6.

Now that we have a more detailed view on the concept of pattern and component, we were able to proceed in creating the extension for the PTK. We called this extension *Component Hierarchy Builder (CHB)*. Both these toolkits use tree structures as a mean of representing the considered system: a screen shot of both of them is in Fig. 7.

The PASSI toolkit (PTK) allows the designer to describe agent structures in terms of agents, tasks (as behaviours) and their relations. Agents can be characterized in low level implementation details: therefore for each agent we can specify which interfaces implements as well as defining attributes and methods' prototypes. Our extension of this PTK feature does not capture this level of details, instead it complements it in order to have generic and reusable agents in the form of components. During the creation of a component in CHB, the user can decide to insert a new Autonomic Manager or a new Service Component and, for each, can specify which sensor and effectors are going to be used.

In PTK, tasks are behaviour and viceversa. In our implementation, tasks are not directly defined: instead roles are collection of behaviours and components can add scheduled roles by picking from all the roles that the user inserted in the CHB tree (Fig. 8).

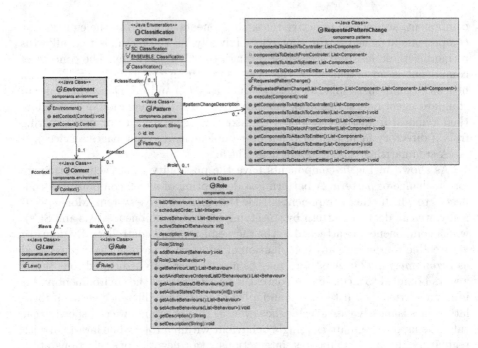

Fig. 6. UML Class diagram of the concept of Context, Pattern and Role.

In the example scenario depicted in Fig. 8, we can see a generic Service Component that is representing a mobile robot: it has proximity sensors and an effector constituted by a differential wheeled motor. As far as its scheduled roles are concerned, it has the task to explore an area and to operate the role of *Listener*. In order to know more about the listener role we have to open the corresponding CHB panel regarding roles and behaviours (see Fig. 9). The listener role is composed of two parallel behaviours that basically describe how the Service Component listens to its connected autonomic managers and (if necessary) enacts the requested state changes.

In Fig. 9, we can see how for each behaviour composing the role, we can specify the sub-class of JADE's Behaviour class that better suits the component's needs.

Using CHB, the user can specify adaptation pattern by indicating the connection topology among components, as specified as list of attached components in both controllers and emitters. This can be seen in Fig. 10, in which an example master-slave pattern is implemented and from the screen shot we can see how a generic Autonomic Manager is connected to both the Service Components that were previously inserted in the designed component structure.

Instead of generating code, CHB is able to serialize all the inserted information (components, patterns, context, roles etc.) inside a macro object that is called *adaptive system*. Such macro object can be serialized and deserialized so to allow the operations of modifications, export and import of previously saved component structures.

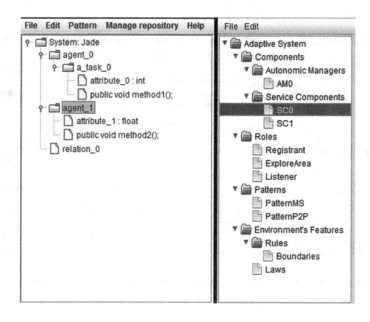

Fig. 7. Tree views of both PTK (left) and our proposed CHB (right).

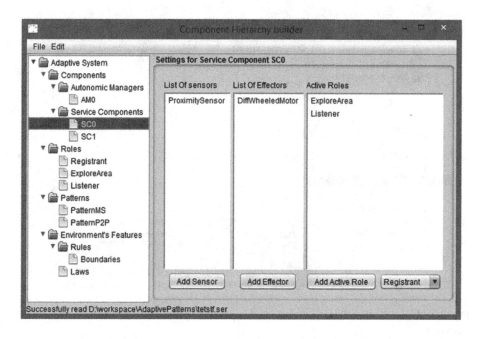

Fig. 8. A screen shot for the creation of a Service Component.

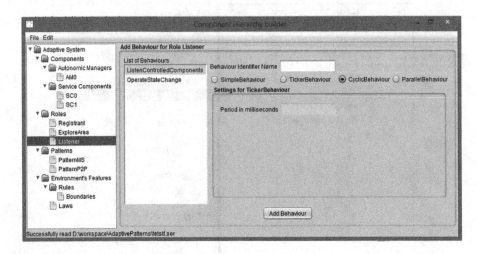

Fig. 9. A screen shot for the creation of a roles as collection of behaviours.

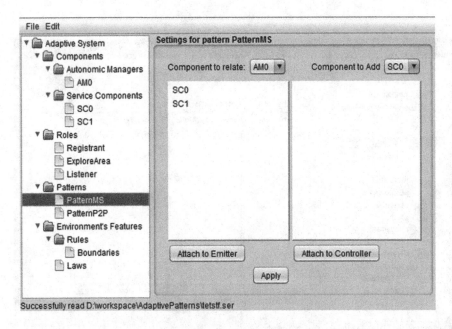

Fig. 10. A screen shot for the creation of a pattern: point of view of the Autonomic Manager.

5   Related Work

In literature, many approaches on patterns for self-adaptation exist, like the one of [8,33,35]. However, in this paper we do not focus on the use of adaptation patterns to create self-adaptive systems, but on the definition of a useful methodology to create this kind of systems, with the aid of the patterns' approach.

In the last years, engineering research has tackled a well-defined problem and has carefully selected and combined existing solutions into a comprehensive development framework for self-adaptive systems.

A lot of projects like MADAM project[2] and the MUSIC project[3] tried to address adaptation in different scenarios, from both the theoretical and the practical perspective. For example, the MUSIC project [18] would like to introduce a model-driven development methodology [17] for self-adaptive context-aware applications. Different from us, this approach was to write a new methodology instead of exploiting the power of existing ones.

Other approaches as CARISMA [9] and RAINBOW [16] propose self-adaptation middleware or architectural styles to develop self-adaptive software, but they do not propose any methodology that will guide developers from the collection of requirements to implementation. Moreover, MOCAS (Model of Components for Adaptive Systems) propose a generic state-based component model which enables the self-adaptation of software components along with their coordination [2]; but like the other approaches, there are not concrete guidelines, considered as a methodology.

6   Conclusions

In this paper, we have proposed an approach to enrich methodologies for addressing adaptation in building self-adaptive systems. We considered, in specific, agent-oriented methodologies and we introduced in some of them our Catalogue of adaptation patterns that help in defining self-adaptive systems. In this paper we have shown how the patterns can be integrated in PASSI2, but our approach can be exploited in any methodologies for building adaptive systems. The possibility of easily inserting our Catalogue of adaptation patterns inside a methodology is based on the SPEM approach and permits harnessing the power of the chosen methodologies. Moreover, we have completed the methodologies process introducing our Catalogue of adaptation patterns also in the supporting tools, in order to have all the steps completed. Then we have created a framework that permits matching the methodologies' concepts into agents' infrastructures.

As an ongoing work we are testing these modified methodologies in different scenarios, to have quantitative and qualitative results of the effectiveness of the methodologies.

---

[2] Mobility and Adaptation-enabling Middleware, supported by the European Union under research grant 004159 lasting from September 2004 to March 2007.

[3] Self-Adapting Applications for Mobile Users in Ubiquitous Computing Environments, supported by the European Union under research grant IST-035166 lasting from October 2006 to March 2010.

References

1. aliCE Research Group et al. SODA home page (2009)
2. Ballagny, C., Hameurlain, N., Barbier, F.: Mocas: a state-based component model for self-adaptation. In: Third IEEE International Conference on Self-Adaptive and Self-Organizing Systems, SASO 2009, pp. 206–215. IEEE (2009)
3. Bellifemine, F., Poggi, A., Rimassa, G.: JADE-a FIPA-compliant agent framework. In: Proceedings of PAAM, London, vol. 99, p. 33 (1999)
4. Bergenti, F., Gleizes, M.-P., Zambonelli, F.: Methodologies and Software Engineering for Agent Systems: The Agent-Oriented Software Engineering Handbook, vol. 11. Springer, US (2004)
5. Bernon, C., Gleizes, M.-P., Peyruqueou, S., Picard, G.: ADELFE: a methodology for adaptive multi-agent systems engineering. In: Petta, P., Tolksdorf, R., Zambonelli, F. (eds.) ESAW 2002. LNCS (LNAI), vol. 2577, pp. 156–169. Springer, Heidelberg (2003)
6. Bresciani, P., Perini, A., Giorgini, P., Giunchiglia, F., Mylopoulos, J.: Tropos: an agent-oriented software development methodology. Auton. Agent. multi-agent Syst. 8(3), 203–236 (2004)
7. Cabri, G., Puviani, M., Leonardi, L.: The MAR&A methodology to develop agent systems. In: ICAART, pp. 501–506 (2009)
8. Cabri, G., Puviani, M., Zambonelli, F.: Towards a taxonomy of adaptive agent-based collaboration patterns for autonomic service ensembles. In: CTS, pp. 508–515. IEEE (2011)
9. Capra, L., Emmerich, W., Mascolo, C.: Carisma: context-aware reflective middleware system for mobile applications. IEEE Trans. Softw. Eng. 29(10), 929–945 (2003)
10. Chella, A., Cossentino, M., Sabatucci, L.: Tools and patterns in designing multi-agent systems with PASSI. WSEAS Trans. Commun. 3(1), 352–358 (2004)
11. Cossentino, M.: From requirements to code with the PASSI methodology. Agent-Oriented Methodologies 3690, 79–106 (2005)
12. Cossentino, M., Seidita, V.: Passi2-going towards maturity of the passi process (2009)
13. DeLoach, S.A., Wood, M.F., Sparkman, C.H.: Multiagent systems engineering. Int. J. Softw. Eng. Knowl. Eng. 11(03), 231–258 (2001)
14. Fernandez-Marquez, J.L., Marzo Serugendo, G.D., Snyder, P.L., Valetto, G.: A pattern-based architectural style for self-organizing software systems. Drexel University, Department of Computer Science. Technical report, 6 (2012)
15. Gamma, E., Helm, R., Johnson, R., Vlissides, J.: Design Patterns. Addison Wesley, Reading (1995)
16. Garlan, D., Cheng, S.-W., Huang, A.-C., Schmerl, B., Steenkiste, P.: Rainbow: architecture-based self-adaptation with reusable infrastructure. Computer 37(10), 46–54 (2004)
17. Geihs, K., Reichle, R., Wagner, M., Khan, M.U.: Modeling of context-aware self-adaptive applications in ubiquitous and service-oriented environments. In: Cheng, B.H.C., Lemos, R., Giese, H., Inverardi, P., Magee, J. (eds.) Self-Adaptive Systems. LNCS, vol. 5525, pp. 146–163. Springer, Heidelberg (2009)
18. Hallsteinsen, S., Geihs, K., Paspallis, N., Eliassen, F., Horn, G., Lorenzo, J., Mamelli, A., Papadopoulos, G.A.: A development framework and methodology for self-adapting applications in ubiquitous computing environments. J. Syst. Softw. 85(12), 2840–2859 (2012)

19. Henderson-Sellers, B., Giorgini, P.: Agent-oriented methodologies. IGI Global (2005)
20. Mayer, P., Klarl, A., Hennicker, R., Puviani, M., Tiezzi, F., Pugliese, R., Keznikl, J., Bure, T.: The autonomic cloud: a vision of voluntary, peer-2-peer cloud computing. In: 2013 IEEE 7th International Conference on Self-Adaptation and Self-Organizing Systems Workshops (SASOW), pp. 89–94. IEEE (2013)
21. McKinley, P.K., Sadjadi, S.M., Kasten, E.P., Cheng, B.H.C.: Composing adaptive software. Computer **37**(7), 56–64 (2004)
22. Morandini, M., et al.: On the use of the goal-oriented paradigm for system design and law compliance reasoning. In: iStar, vol. 586, pp. 71–75. CEUR-WS.org (2010)
23. Object Management Group. SPEM (1997). http://www.omg.org/technology/documents/formal/spem.htm
24. Padgham, L., Winikoff, M.: Developing Intelligent Agent Systems: A Practical Guide, vol. 13. Wiley, New York (2005)
25. Pavón, J., Gómez-Sanz, J.J., Fuentes, R.: The INGENIAS methodology and tools. Agent-Oriented Methodologies **9**, 236–276 (2005)
26. Puviani, M., Cabri, G., Leonardi, L.: Enabling self-expression: the use of roles to dynamically change adaptation patterns. In: FOCAS 2014. IEEE Computer Society (2014)
27. Puviani, M., Cabri, G., Leonardi, L.: Integrating adaptation patterns into agent methodologies to build self-adaptive systems. In: 7th International Conference on Agents and Artificial Intelligence (ICAART 2015), pp. 99–106. SciTePress-Science and Technology Publications (2015)
28. Puviani, M., Cabri, G., Zambonelli, F.: A taxonomy of architectural patterns for self-adaptive systems. In: Proceedings of the International C* Conference on Computer Science and Software Engineering, pp. 77–85. ACM (2013)
29. Puviani, M., Cabri, G., Zambonelli, F.: Agent-based simulations of patterns for self-adaptive systems. In: ICAART 2014 - Proceedings of the 6th International Conference on Agents and Artificial Intelligence, ESEO, Angers, Loire Valley, France, 6–8 March 2014, vol. 1, pp. 190–200. IEEE Computer Society (2014)
30. Puviani, M., Cossentino, M., Cabri, G., Molesini, A.: Building an agent methodology from fragments: the MEnSA experience. In: Proceedings of the 2010 ACM Symposium on Applied Computing, pp. 920–927. ACM (2010)
31. Puviani, M., Marzo Serugendo, G.D., Frei, R., Cabri, G.: Methodologies for self-organising systems: a SPEM approach. In: Proceedings of the 2009 IEEE/WIC/ACM International Joint Conference on Web Intelligence and Intelligent Agent Technology, vol. 02, pp. 66–69. IEEE Computer Society (2009)
32. Puviani, M., Di Marzo, G., Serugendo, R.F., Cabri, G.: A method fragments approach to methodologies for engineering self-organizing systems. ACM Trans. Auton. Adapt. Syst. (TAAS) **7**(3), 33 (2012)
33. Ramirez, A.J., Cheng, B.H.C.: Design patterns for developing dynamically adaptive systems. In: Proceedings of the 2010 ICSE Workshop on Software Engineering for Adaptive and Self-Managing Systems, pp. 49–58. ACM, May 2010
34. Seidita, V., Cossentino, M., Gaglio, S.: Using and extending the SPEM specifications to represent agent oriented methodologies. In: Luck, M., Gomez-Sanz, J.J. (eds.) AOSE 2008. LNCS, vol. 5386, pp. 46–59. Springer, Heidelberg (2009)
35. Weyns, D., Malek, S., Andersson, J., Schmerl, B.: Introduction to the special issue on state of the art in engineering self-adaptive systems. J. Syst. Softw. **85**(12), 2675–2677 (2012)
36. Zambonelli, F., Jennings, N.R., Wooldridge, M.: Developing multiagent systems: the gaia methodology. ACM Trans. Softw. Eng. Methodol. (TOSEM) **12**(3), 317–370 (2003)

Artificial Intelligence

A Logic for Reasoning About
Decision-Theoretic Projections

Gavin Rens[1,2]([⊠]), Thomas Meyer[2,3], and Gerhard Lakemeyer[4]

[1] School of Mathematics, Statistics and Computer Science,
University of KwaZulu-Natal, Durban, South Africa
grens@csir.co.za
[2] Centre for Artificial Intelligence Research, CSIR Meraka, Pretoria, South Africa
tmeyer@cs.uct.ac.za
[3] Department of Computer Science, University of Cape Town,
Cape Town, South Africa
[4] Knowledge-based Systems Group, RWTH Aachen University, Aachen, Germany
gerhard@cs.rwth-aachen.de

Abstract. A decidable logic is presented, in which queries can be posed
about (i) the degree of belief in a propositional sentence after an arbitrary
finite number of actions and observations and (ii) the utility of a finite
sequence of actions after a number of actions and observations. The
main contribution of this work is that a POMDP model specification
is allowed to be partial or incomplete with no restriction on the lack
of information specified for the model. The model may even contain
information about non-initial beliefs. Essentially, entailment of arbitrary
queries (expressible in the language) can be answered. A sound, complete
and terminating decision procedure is provided.

Keywords: Logic · POMDP · Projection · Decision-theory

1 Introduction

Symbolic logic is good for representing information compactly and it is good for
reasoning with that information. However, only in the last two or three decades
has research gone into developing ways to employ logic for representing stochastic information. One formalism for modelling agents in stochastic domains and
for determining 'good' sequences of actions is the *partially observable Markov
decision process* (POMDP) [1,2]. The popularity of the POMDP approach is,
arguably, due to its relative simplicity and intuitiveness, and its general applicability to a wide range of stochastic domains. In this paper, we propose the
Stochastic Decision Logic (SDL), a modal logic with a POMDP semantics. It
combines the benefits of POMDP theory and logic for posing entailment queries
about stochastic domains.

In POMDPs, actions have nondeterministic results and observations are
uncertain. In other words, the effect of some chosen action is somewhat unpredictable, yet may be predicted with a probability of occurrence, and the world

© Springer International Publishing Switzerland 2015
B. Duval et al. (Eds.): ICAART 2015, LNAI 9494, pp. 79–99, 2015.
DOI: 10.1007/978-3-319-27947-3_5

is not directly observable: some data are observable and the agent infers how likely it is that the world is in some particular state. The agent may thus believe to some degree—for each possible state—that it is in that state, but it is never certain exactly which state it is in. In fact, the agent typically maintains a probability distribution over the states, reflecting its conviction of being in each state.

Traditionally, to make any deductions in POMDP theory, a domain model must be completely specified. Another contribution of this work is that it allows the user to determine whether or not a set of sentences is entailed by an arbitrarily precise specification of a POMDP model. By "arbitrarily precise specification" we mean that the transition function, the perception function, the reward function or the initial belief-state might not be completely defined by the logical specification provided. Another view is that the logic allows for the (precise) specification of and reasoning over classes of POMDP models.

This work is not meant to be a logic-based version of all POMDP theory; it is meant to be a logic with POMDP semantics for online reasoning in stochastic domains.

Full-scale planning will not be considered here. However, as a preliminary step, projections concerning epistemic situations and expected rewards will be possible. That is, at this stage, we have not developed a procedure to produce a reward-maximizing policy conditioned on observations. There is, however, a procedure to determine whether some hypothesised situation follows from a knowledge base of the system and some beliefs about the system state. More precisely, with the SDL, an agent can (i) determine the degree of belief in a propositional sentence after an arbitrary finite number of actions and observations and (ii) the utility of a finite sequence of actions after a number of actions and observations.[1]

Imagine a robot that is in need of an oil refill. There is an open can of oil on the floor within reach of its gripper. If there is nothing else in the robot's gripper, it can grab the can (or miss it, or knock it over) and it can drink the oil by lifting the can to its 'mouth' and pouring the contents in (or miss its mouth and spill). The robot may also want to confirm whether there is anything left in the oil-can by weighing its contents with its 'weight' sensor. And once holding the can, the robot may wish to replace it on the floor. There are also rewards and costs involved, which are explained in the Examples section of the paper. The domain is (partially) formalized as follows. The robot has the set of (intended) actions $\mathcal{A} = \{\text{grab}, \text{drink}, \text{weigh}, \text{replace}\}$ with expected intuitive meanings. The robot can perceive observations only from the set $\Omega = \{\text{Nil}, \text{Light}, \text{Medium}, \text{Heavy}\}$. Intuitively, when the robot performs a weigh action (i.e., it activates its 'weight' sensor) it will perceive either Light, Medium or Heavy; for other actions, it will perceive Nil. The robot experiences its world (domain) through two Boolean features: $\mathcal{F} = \{\text{full}, \text{holding}\}$ meaning that the robot believes the oil-can is full and respectively that it is currently holding something in its gripper.

In the following informal examples, several syntactic elements are mentioned which are formally defined in Sect. 2.1. $\mathbf{B}\varphi \geq p$ is read 'The degree of belief in φ

---

[1] By "utility", we mean 'expected rewards'.

is greater than or equal to p'. $\mathbf{U}\Lambda > r$ is read 'The utility of performing action sequence Λ is greater than r'. Given a complete formalization $\mathcal{K}$ of the scenario sketched here, a robot may have the following queries:

- Is the degree of belief that I'll have the oil-can in my gripper greater than or equal to 0.9, after I attempt grabbing it twice in a row? That is, does [grab + obsNil] [grab + obsNil] $\mathbf{B}$ holding ≥ 0.9 follow from $\mathcal{K}$?
- After grabbing the can, then perceiving that it has medium weight, is the utility of drinking the contents of the oil-can, then placing it on the floor, more than 6 units? That is, does [grab + obsNil] [weigh + obsMedium] $\mathbf{U}$[drink][replace] > 6 follow from $\mathcal{K}$?

Related Work: Recently, some researchers have investigated formal languages for compactly representing POMDPs [3–9]. They also mention that with a logical language for specifying models, decision-making algorithms can exploit the structure found in these logical specifications. They are not presented as *logics*, though, and logical theorem proving is thus not possible for them.

[10] present a modal logic to deal with imprecision in robot actions and sensors. Their models do not contain an accessibility relation, which makes it hard to understand what it means for an action to be executed. They cannot deal with utilities of actions, and no system for determining truth of statements is provided.

[11] supply a theory for reasoning with noisy sensors and effectors, with graded belief. They use the situation calculus [12] to specify their approach but some elements fall outside the logical language. They do not address utilities of actions.

$\mathcal{ESP}$ [13] is closely related to Bacchus et al.'s approach with some improvements. It is founded on $\mathcal{ES}$ [14], which is a fragment of the situation calculus. The semantics of SDL is arguably simpler than that of $\mathcal{ESP}$, because SDL fixes its semantics on POMDPs. In the long-run, this may be a disadvantage of SDL, though. With any logic based on the situation calculus or first-order logic, decidability of entailment comes into question. The SDL's entailment procedure is decidable.

[15] states "The representation in this paper can be seen as a representation for POMDPs" about his Independent Choice Logic using the situation calculus (ICL$_{SC}$). Belief-states can be expressed and belief update can be performed (but maintenance of belief-states is not a necessary component of the system). Even programs that are sequences of actions conditioned on observations can be expressed for agents to adopt. The ICL$_{SC}$ is a relatively rich framework, with acyclic logic programs which may contain variables, quantification and function symbols. For certain applications, the SDL may be preferred due to its comparative simplicity, and it may be easier to understand by people familiar with POMDPs. Finally, decidability of inferences made in the ICL$_{SC}$ are, in general, not guaranteed.

[16] present a logic called $\mathcal{E}+$ for reasoning about agents with sensing, qualitative nondeterminism and probabilistic uncertainty in action outcomes. Planning

with sensing and uncertain actions is also dealt with. The application area is plan generation for agents with nondeterministic and probabilistic uncertainty. Noisy sensing is not dealt with, that is, sensing actions are deterministic. They mention that although they would like to be able to represent action rewards and costs as in POMDPs, $\mathcal{E}+$ does not yet provide the facilities.

PRISM is a framework for model-checking representations of systems with a probabilistic character [17]. [17] show how MDPs can be represented with an extension of Probabilistic Computation Tree Logic [18]. PRISM can then determine whether the occurrence of some event satisfies a given probability bound. To our knowledge, PRISM has not been extended to represent POMDPs. Moreover, by definition, model-checking requires full specification of a system. However, we could learn something from the implementation of PRISM (www. prismmodelchecker.org) for the future development of the SDL, or PRISM could be extended with ideas from the SDL.

There is another sense in which an incomplete model can be dealt with; it can be learnt. [19] outline the Bayes-Adaptive POMDP framework to reinforcement learning, which allows them to "explicitly target the exploration-exploitation problem in a coherent mathematical framework." Our work is different in that we do not tackle the learning problem; our work suggests a way for an agent to make decisions with incomplete models without considering whether its actions will also help it explore wisely. There are problems for which an agent should explore its environment and learn while working on its task. But there may also be problems for which the agent should not explore (anymore?) and simply work on the task at hand with the given information (domain model).

When it comes to the projection task (in the first-order setting), work by [20] concerning "filtering" in the incremental update of the belief-state, may be important to look at.

Next, our logic is defined. Then in Sect. 3, we describe a decision procedure for checking entailment queries. In Sect. 4, a framework for domain specification is described and some practical examples of the logic are provided.

2   The Stochastic Decision Logic

The SDL's foundations are in the Specification Logic of Actions with Probability [21] and the Specification Logic of Actions and Observations with Probability [22].

2.1   Syntax

The syntax is carefully designed to provide the required expressiveness, and no more.

The vocabulary of our language contains six sorts of objects:

1. a finite set of *fluents* $\mathcal{F} = \{f_1, \ldots, f_n\}$,
2. a finite set of names of atomic *actions* $\mathcal{A} = \{\alpha_1, \ldots, \alpha_n\}$,
3. a countable set of *action variables* $V_\mathcal{A} = \{v_1^a, v_2^a, \ldots\}$,

4. a finite set of names of atomic *observations* $\Omega = \{\varsigma_1, \ldots, \varsigma_n\}$,
5. a countable set of *observation variables* $V_\Omega = \{v_1^o, v_2^o, \ldots\}$.
6. all *real numbers* $\mathbb{R}$,

We refer to elements of $\mathcal{A} \cup \Omega$ as *constants*. We work in a multi-modal setting, in which we have modal operators $[\alpha]$, one for each $\alpha \in \mathcal{A}$. And $[\![\alpha + \varsigma]\!]$ is a *belief update operator* (or *update operator* for short). Intuitively, $[\![\alpha + \varsigma]\!]\Theta$ means 'Θ holds in the belief-state resulting from performing action α and then perceiving observation ς'. For instance, $[\![\alpha_1 + \varsigma_1]\!]$ $[\![\alpha_2 + \varsigma_2]\!]$ expresses that the agent executes α_1 then perceives ς_1 then executes α_2 then perceives ς_2. $\mathbf{B}$ is a modal operator for belief and $\mathbf{U}$ is a modal operator for utility.

We first define a language $\mathcal{L}$, then a useful sublanguage $\mathcal{L}_{SDL} \subset \mathcal{L}$. The reason why we define $\mathcal{L}$ is because it is easier to define the truth conditions for $\mathcal{L}$; the truth conditions for $\mathcal{L}_{SDL}$ then follow directly.

Definition 1. *First the propositional fragment:* $\varphi ::= f \mid \top \mid \neg\varphi \mid \varphi \wedge \varphi$, *where* $f \in \mathcal{F}$.

Then the fragment Φ used in formulae of the form $\varphi \Rightarrow \Phi$ (see the definition of Θ below). Let $\alpha \in (V_\mathcal{A} \cup \mathcal{A})$, $v^a \in V_\mathcal{A}$, $\varsigma \in (V_\Omega \cup \Omega)$, $v^o \in V_\Omega$, $p \in [0,1]$, $r \in \mathbb{R}$ and $\bowtie \in \{<, \leq, =, \geq, >\}$.[2]

$$\Phi ::= \varphi \mid \alpha = \alpha \mid \varsigma = \varsigma \mid Reward(r) \mid Cost(\alpha, r) \mid$$
$$[\alpha]\varphi \bowtie p \mid (\varsigma|\alpha) \bowtie p \mid (\forall v^a)\Phi \mid (\forall v^o)\Phi \mid \neg\Phi \mid \Phi \wedge \Phi.$$

where φ is defined above.

$[\alpha]\varphi \bowtie p$ *is read 'The probability x of reaching a φ-world after executing α is such that $x \bowtie p$'. Whereas $[\alpha]$ is a modal operator, $(\varsigma|\alpha)$ is a predicate; $(\varsigma|\alpha) \bowtie p$ is read 'The probability x of perceiving ς, given α was performed is such that $x \bowtie p$'.*

The language of $\mathcal{L}$ is defined as Θ:

$$\Lambda ::= [\![\alpha]\!] \mid \Lambda[\![\alpha]\!]$$
$$\Theta ::= \top \mid \alpha = \alpha \mid \varsigma = \varsigma \mid Cont(\alpha, \varsigma) \mid \mathbf{B}\varphi \bowtie p \mid \mathbf{U}\Lambda \bowtie r \mid \varphi \Rightarrow \Phi \mid$$
$$[\![\alpha + \varsigma]\!]\Theta \mid (\forall v^a)\Theta \mid (\forall v^o)\Theta \mid \neg\Theta \mid \Theta \wedge \Theta \mid \Theta \vee \Theta,$$

where φ and Φ are defined above.

The scope of quantifier $(\forall v')$ is determined in the same way as is done in first-order logic. A variable v appearing in a formula Θ is said to be bound by quantifier $(\forall v')$ if and only if v is the same variable as v' and is in the scope of $(\forall v')$. If a variable is not bound by any quantifier, it is free. In $\mathcal{L}$, variables are not allowed to be free; they are always bound.

$Cont(\alpha, \varsigma)$ is read 'Consciousness continues after executing α and then perceiving ς'. $\mathbf{B}\varphi \bowtie p$ is read 'The degree of belief x in φ is such that $x \bowtie p$'. Performing $\Lambda = [\![\alpha_1]\!][\![\alpha_2]\!] \cdots [\![\alpha_z]\!]$ means that α_1 is performed, then α_2 then ...

---

[2] $[0,1]$ denotes $\mathbb{R} \cap [0,1]$.

then α_z. $U\Lambda \bowtie r$ is thus read 'The utility x of performing Λ is such that $x \bowtie r$'. Evaluating some sentence Ψ after a sequence of z update operations, means that Ψ will be evaluated after the agent's belief-state has been updated according to the sequence

$$\underbrace{[\![\alpha + \varsigma]\!] \cdots [\![\alpha' + \varsigma']\!]}_{z \text{ times}}$$

of actions and observations. $\varphi \Rightarrow \Phi$ is read 'It is a general law of the domain that Φ holds in all situations (worlds) which satisfy φ'.

Definition 2. *The language of SDL, denoted $\mathcal{L}_{SDL}$, is the subset of formulae of $\mathcal{L}$ excluding formulae containing subformulae of the form $\neg(\varphi \Rightarrow \Phi)$.*

For instance, sentences of the form $\neg(\varphi \Rightarrow \Phi) \wedge (\varphi' \Rightarrow \Phi') \wedge \Theta \notin \mathcal{L}_{SDL}$, but $(\varphi \Rightarrow \Phi) \wedge (\varphi' \Rightarrow \Phi') \wedge \Theta \in \mathcal{L}_{SDL}$. And, for instance, $\neg(\forall v')(\varphi \Rightarrow \Phi) \vee (\varphi' \Rightarrow \Phi') \vee \Theta \notin \mathcal{L}_{SDL}$, but $(\forall v')(\varphi \Rightarrow \Phi) \vee (\varphi' \Rightarrow \Phi') \vee \Theta \in \mathcal{L}_{SDL}$. The reason why $\mathcal{L}_{SDL}$ is defined to exclude $\neg(\varphi \Rightarrow \Phi)$ is because such sentences cause unnecessary technical difficulties in the decision procedure. Rens's doctoral thesis [23, Chap. 8] contains a detailed explanation.

$\perp$ abbreviates $\neg\top$, $\theta \rightarrow \theta'$ abbreviates $\neg\theta \vee \theta'$ and $\leftrightarrow$ abbreviates $(\theta \rightarrow \theta') \wedge (\theta' \rightarrow \theta)$. In grammars φ and Φ, $\phi \vee \phi'$ abbreviates $\neg(\neg\phi \wedge \neg\phi')$, but in grammar Θ, $\vee$ is defined directly, because otherwise its definition in terms of $\neg$ and $\wedge$ would involve formulae of the form $\neg(\varphi \Rightarrow \Phi)$, which are precluded in $\mathcal{L}_{SDL}$. $\rightarrow$ and $\leftrightarrow$ have the weakest bindings, with $\Rightarrow$ just stronger; and $\neg$ the strongest. Parentheses enforce or clarify the scope of operators conventionally.

$c = c'$ is an equality literal, $Reward(r)$ is a reward literal, $Cost(\alpha, r)$ is a cost literal, $[\alpha]\varphi \bowtie p$ is a dynamic literal, $(\varsigma|\alpha) \bowtie p$ is a perception literal, and $\varphi \Rightarrow \Phi$ is a law literal. $Cont(\alpha, \varsigma)$ is a continuity literal, $\mathbf{B}\varphi \bowtie p$ is a belief literal and $U\Lambda \bowtie r$ is a utility literal. The negation of all these literals are also literals with the associated names.

2.2 Semantics

Formally, a partially observable Markov decision process (POMDP) is a tuple $\langle \mathcal{S}, \mathcal{A}, \mathcal{T}, \mathcal{R}, \mathcal{Z}, \mathcal{P}, b^0 \rangle$: a finite set of states $\mathcal{S} = \{s_1, s_2, \ldots, s_n\}$; a finite set of actions $\mathcal{A} = \{a_1, a_2, \ldots, a_k\}$; the *state-transition function*, where $\mathcal{T}(s, a, s')$ is the probability of being in s' after performing action a in state s; the *reward function*, where $\mathcal{R}(a, s)$ is the reward gained for executing a while in state s; a finite set of observations $\mathcal{Z} = \{z_1, z_2, \ldots, z_m\}$; the *observation function*, where $\mathcal{P}(s', a, z)$ is the probability of observing z in state s' resulting from performing action a in some other state; and b^0 is the initial probability distribution over all states in $\mathcal{S}$.

Let b be a total function from $\mathcal{S}$ into $\mathbb{R}$. Each state s is associated with a probability $b(s) = p \in \mathbb{R}$, such that b is a probability distribution over the set $\mathcal{S}$ of all states. b can be called a *belief-state*.

An important function in POMDP theory is the function that updates the agent's belief-state, or the *state estimation* function SE. $SE(a, z, b) = b_n$, where $b_n(s')$ is the probability of the agent being in state s' in the 'new' belief-state b_n, relative to a, z and the 'old' belief-state b. Notice that $SE(\cdot)$ requires an action, an observation and a belief-state as inputs to determine the new belief-state.

When the states an agent can be in are *belief*-states (as opposed to objective, single states in $\mathcal{S}$), the reward function $\mathcal{R}$ must be lifted to operate over belief-states. The *expected* reward $\rho(a, b)$ for performing an action a in a belief-state b is defined as $\sum_{s \in \mathcal{S}} \mathcal{R}(a, s) b(s)$.

Let $w : \mathcal{F} \to \{0, 1\}$ be a total function assigning a truth value to each fluent. We call w a *world*. Let C be the set of $2^{|\mathcal{F}|}$ *conceivable worlds*, that is, all possible functions w.

Definition 3. *An SDL structure is a tuple $\mathcal{D} = \langle T, P, U \rangle$ such that*

- $T : \mathcal{A} \to \{T_\alpha \mid \alpha \in \mathcal{A}\}$, *where* $T_\alpha : (C \times C) \to [0, 1]$ *is a total function from pairs of worlds into the reals. That is, T provides a transition (accessibility) relation T_α for each action in $\mathcal{A}$. For every $w^- \in C$, it is required that either* $\sum_{w^+ \in C} T_\alpha(w^-, w^+) = 1$ *or* $\sum_{w^+ \in C} T_\alpha(w^-, w^+) = 0$.[3]
- $P : \mathcal{A} \to \{P_\alpha \mid \alpha \in \mathcal{A}\}$, *where* $P_\alpha : (C \times \Omega) \to [0, 1]$ *is a total function from pairs in $C \times \Omega$ into the reals. That is, P provides a perceivability relation P_α for each action in $\mathcal{A}$. For all $w^+ \in C$, if there exists a $w^- \in C$ such that $T_\alpha(w^-, w^+) > 0$, then $\sum_{\varsigma \in \Omega} P_\alpha(w^+, \varsigma) = 1$, else $\sum_{\varsigma \in \Omega} P_\alpha(w^+, \varsigma) = 0$;*
- U *is a pair $\langle Re, Co \rangle$, where $Re : C \to \mathbb{R}$ is a reward function and Co is a mapping that provides a cost function $Co_\alpha : C \to \mathbb{R}$ for each $\alpha \in \mathcal{A}$.*

As in POMDPs, in the SDL, an agent typically does not know in which world $w \in C$ it actually is, but for each w it has a degree of belief that it is in that world. From now on, let $b : C \to [0, 1]$ be a probability distribution over C, still referred to as a *belief-state*. The degree of belief in w is denoted by the probability measure $b(w)$.

Definition 4. *The probability of reaching the next belief-state b' from the current belief-state b, given α and ς, is $Pr_{NB}(\alpha, \varsigma, b) = \sum_{w' \in C} P_\alpha(\varsigma, w') \sum_{w \in C} T_\alpha(w, w') b(w)$.*

The above definition is from standard POMDP theory.

Definition 5. *We define a belief update function $BU(\alpha, \varsigma, b) = b'$:*

$$b'(w') = \frac{P_\alpha(w', \varsigma) \sum_{w \in C} T_\alpha(w, w') b(w)}{Pr_{NB}(\alpha, \varsigma, b)},$$

for $Pr_{NB}(\alpha, \varsigma, b) \neq 0$.

---

[3] Either the action is executable and there is a probability distribution (the summation is 1) or the action is inexecutable (the summation is 0). Letting the sum equal a number not 1 or 0 would lead to badly defined semantics.

$BU(\cdot)$ has the same intuitive meaning as the state estimation function $SE(\cdot)$ of POMDP theory.

Given the opportunity to be slightly more clear about the specification of rewards in the SDL, we interpret $\mathcal{R}(a,s)$ of POMDPs as $R(s) - C(a,s)$, where $R(s)$ provides the positive reward portion of $R(a,s)$ and $C(a,s)$ provides the punishment or cost portion. By this interpretation, we assume that simply being in a state has an intrinsic reward (independent of an action), however, that punishment is conditional on actions and the states in which they are executed. There are many other ways to interpret $\mathcal{R}(a,s)$, and $\mathcal{R}(a,s)$ is not even the most general reward function possible; a more general function is $\mathcal{R}(s,a,s')$ meaning that rewards depend on a state s, an action executed in s and a state s' reached due to performing a in s. The SDL adopts one of several reasonable approaches. In the semantics of the SDL, we equate a state s with a world w and an action a as $\alpha \in \mathcal{A}$, and interpret $\mathcal{R}(a,s)$ as $Re(w) - Co_\alpha(w)$. We derive a reward function over belief-states for the SDL in a similar fashion as we did with $\rho(a,b)$ of POMDP theory, however, including the notion of cost: $RC(\alpha,b) = \sum_{w \in C}(Re(w) - Co_\alpha(w))b(w)$.

Let $\alpha, \alpha' \in \mathcal{A}$, $\varsigma, \varsigma' \in \Omega$, $p \in [0,1]$ and $r \in \mathbb{R}$. Let $f \in \mathcal{F}$ and let Θ be any sentence in $\mathcal{L}$. Let $\bowtie \in \{<, \leq, =, \geq, >\}$. If $\Theta \in \mathcal{L}$ is *satisfied* at world w and belief-state b in SDL structure $\mathcal{D}$, we write $\mathcal{D}bw \models \Theta$. Some of the conditions for satisfaction are reproduced below.

$\mathcal{D}bw \models \alpha = \alpha' \iff \alpha$ and α' are the same element;

$\mathcal{D}bw \models \varsigma = \varsigma' \iff \varsigma$ and ς' are the same element;

$\mathcal{D}bw \models Reward(r) \iff Re(w) = r$;

$\mathcal{D}bw \models Cost(\alpha, c) \iff Co_\alpha(w) = c$;

$\mathcal{D}bw \models [\alpha]\varphi \bowtie p \iff \sum_{\substack{w' \in C \\ \mathcal{D}bw' \models \varphi}} T_\alpha(w, w') \bowtie p$;

$\mathcal{D}bw \models (\varsigma | \alpha) \bowtie p \iff P_\alpha(w, \varsigma) \bowtie p$;

$\mathcal{D}bw \models Cont(\alpha, \varsigma) \iff Pr_{NB}(\alpha, \varsigma, b) \neq 0$;

$\mathcal{D}bw \models \mathbf{B}\varphi \bowtie p \iff \sum_{\substack{w' \in C \\ \mathcal{D}bw' \models \varphi}} b(w') \bowtie p$;

$\mathcal{D}bw \models \mathbf{U}[\![\alpha]\!] \bowtie r \iff RC(\alpha, b) \bowtie r$;

$\mathcal{D}bw \models \mathbf{U}[\![\alpha]\!]\Lambda \bowtie r \iff \left(RC(\alpha, b) + \sum_{\varsigma \in \Omega} Pr_{NB}(\alpha, \varsigma, b) \cdot r' \right) \bowtie r$, where

$\qquad\qquad\qquad \mathcal{D}b'w \models \mathbf{U}\Lambda = r'$ for $b' = BU(\alpha, \varsigma, b)$;

$\mathcal{D}bw \models \varphi \Rightarrow \Theta \iff$ for all $w' \in C$, if $\mathcal{D}bw' \models \varphi$ then $\mathcal{D}bw' \models \Theta$;

$\mathcal{D}bw \models [\alpha + \varsigma]\Theta \iff Pr_{NB}(\alpha, \varsigma, b) \neq 0$ and $\mathcal{D}b'w \models \Theta$, where $b' = BU(\alpha, \varsigma, b)$;

$\mathcal{D}bw \models (\forall v^a)\Upsilon \iff \mathcal{D}bw \models \Upsilon|_{\alpha_1}^{v^a} \wedge \ldots \wedge \Upsilon|_{\alpha_n}^{v^a}$;

$\mathcal{D}bw \models (\forall v^o)\Upsilon \iff \mathcal{D}bw \models \Upsilon|_{\varsigma_1}^{v^o} \wedge \ldots \wedge \Upsilon|_{\varsigma_n}^{v^o}$,

where Υ is a formula from the grammar Φ or Θ, and we write $\Upsilon|_c^v$ to mean the formula Υ with all occurrences of variables $v \in (V_\mathcal{A} \cup V_\Omega)$ appearing in it replaced by constant $c \in \mathcal{A} \cup \Omega$ of the right sort.

A sentence $\Theta \in \mathcal{L}$ is *satisfiable* if there exists a structure $\mathcal{D}$, a belief-state b and a world w such that $\mathcal{D}bw \models \Theta$, else Θ is *unsatisfiable*. Let $\mathcal{K} \subset \mathcal{L}$. We say that $\mathcal{K}$ *entails* Θ (denoted $\mathcal{K} \models \Theta$) if for all structures $\mathcal{D}$, all belief-states b, all $w \in C$: if $\mathcal{D}bw \models \kappa$ for every $\kappa \in \mathcal{K}$, then $\mathcal{D}bw \models \Theta$. When $\mathcal{K}$ is a finite subset of $\mathcal{L}_{SDL}$ and $\Psi \in \mathcal{L}_{SDL}$, it is easy to show that $\mathcal{K} \models \Psi \iff \bigwedge_{\kappa \in \mathcal{K}} \kappa \wedge \neg \Psi$ is unsatisfiable. The SDL decision procedure for entailment is based on this latter correspondence.

3   The Decision Procedure for SDL Entailment

Informally, a query is satisfiable if there exists a way of filling in missing domain information about rewards, transitions, perceptions, etcetera, so that the query is true. And a query should be valid if all ways of extending the supplied model information makes the query true.

We provide a sketch of the (formal) decision procedure for checking whether entailments of the form $\mathcal{K} \models \Psi$ hold. Our strategy is to set up a tableau tree for $\bigwedge_{\kappa \in \mathcal{K}} \kappa \wedge \neg \Psi$, and then check whether or not every leaf node of the tree after full expansion implies a contradiction. If every leaf node implies a contradiction, then $\bigwedge_{\kappa \in \mathcal{K}} \kappa \wedge \neg \Psi$ is unsatisfiable and $\mathcal{K} \models \Psi$ holds.

There are two phases in the decision procedure. The first phase uses a tableau approach to (i) catch 'traditional' contradictions, (ii) separate formulae into literals and (iii) prepare the literals for processing in the second phases. We shall call this the *tableau* phase. The second phase creates systems of inequalities, checking their feasibility. We shall call this the *systems of inequalities* (SI) phase.

An *activity sequence* is either 0 or a sequence of the form $0 \xrightarrow{\alpha_1, \varsigma_1} e_1 \xrightarrow{\alpha_2, \varsigma_2} e_2 \cdots \xrightarrow{\alpha_z, \varsigma_z} e_z$. Intuitively, an activity sequence represents a hypothetical sequence of actions and associated perceptions. The e_i represent belief-states; e_z is an integer which uniquely identifies the belief-state reached after the occurrence of the sequence $\alpha_1, \varsigma_1, \alpha_2, \varsigma_2, \cdots \alpha_z, \varsigma_z$ of actions and observations. The e_i are called *activity points*—because they represent an agent's state of mind at some point after a sequence of activities.

In the following discussion, and also later, we employ some abbreviations: The set of fluents $\mathcal{F} = \{\texttt{full}, \texttt{holding}\}$ is abbreviated to $\{f, h\}$. The set of actions $\mathcal{A} = \{\texttt{grab}, \texttt{drink}, \texttt{weigh}\}$ is abbreviated to $\{g, d, w\}$. The set of observations $\Omega = \{\texttt{Nil}, \texttt{Light}, \texttt{Medium}, \texttt{Heavy}\}$ is abbreviated to $\{N, L, M, H\}$.

Given some initial belief-state, every clause of a sentence specifies a final belief-state/activity point. For instance, $\mathbf{B}(f \wedge h) = 0.35 \wedge \mathbf{B}(f \wedge \neg h) = 0.35 \wedge \mathbf{B}(\neg f \wedge h) = 0.2 \wedge \mathbf{B}(\neg f \wedge \neg h) = 0.1$ specifies the belief-state $\{(w_1, 0.35), (w_2, 0.35), (w_3, 0.2), (w_4, 0.1)\}$, where $w_1 \models f \wedge h, \ldots, w_4 \models \neg f \wedge \neg h$. And $[\![g + N]\!][\![w + M]\!]\mathbf{B}h > 0.85$ specifies belief-state $BU(w, M, BU(g, N, b^0))$, where b^0 is some initial belief-state. Now it is obvious that

$$\mathbf{B}(f \wedge h) = 0.35 \ \wedge \ \mathbf{B}(f \wedge \neg h) = 0.35 \ \wedge \mathbf{B}(\neg f \wedge h) = 0.2 \ \wedge \ \mathbf{B}(\neg f \wedge \neg h) = 0.1$$
$$\rightarrow [\![g + N]\!][\![w + M]\!]\mathbf{B}h > 0.85 \ \wedge \ [\![g + N]\!][\![w + M]\!]\mathbf{B}h \leq 0.85$$

is a contradiction, because in the belief-state reached after the sequence g, N, w, M, an agent cannot have a degree of belief in h both greater-than and less-than-or-equal-to 0.85. This is a very simple example, but the need for the maintenance of activity sequences and activity points becomes much more apparent when one understands that an activity point plays a part in identifying the variables representing the probabilities of being in the different possible worlds at that point.

3.1   The Tableau Phase

A *labeled formula* is a pair (Σ, Ψ), where $\Psi \in \mathcal{L}_{SDL}$ is any formula, and Σ is an activity sequence. If Σ is $0 \xrightarrow{\alpha_1, \varsigma_1} e_1 \cdots \xrightarrow{\alpha_z, \varsigma_z} e_z$, then the concatenation of Σ

and $\xrightarrow{\alpha',\varsigma'} e'$, denoted as $\Sigma \xrightarrow{\alpha',\varsigma'} e'$ is the sequence $0 \xrightarrow{\alpha_1,\varsigma_1} e_1 \cdots \xrightarrow{\alpha_z,\varsigma_z} e_z \xrightarrow{\alpha',\varsigma'} e'$. A *node* Γ is a set of labeled formulae. The initial node to which the tableau rules must be applied, is called the *trunk*. A *tree* T is a set of nodes. A tree must include the trunk and only nodes resulting from the application of *tableau rules* to the trunk and subsequent nodes. If one has a tree with trunk $\{(0,\Psi)\}$, we shall say one has *a tree for* Ψ.

A node Γ is a *leaf* node of tree T if no tableau rule has been applied to Γ in T. A node Γ is *closed* if $(\Sigma, \bot) \in \Gamma$ for any Σ. It is *open* if it is not closed. A tree is closed if all of its leaf nodes are closed, else it is open. A rule may not be applied to (i) a closed leaf node or (ii) a formula to which it has been applied higher in the tree.

Some of the tableau rules follow. Let Γ be a leaf node.

- rule $\wedge$: If Γ contains $(\Sigma, \Psi \wedge \Psi')$ or $(\Sigma, \neg(\Psi \vee \Psi'))$, then create child node $\Gamma' = \Gamma \cup \{(\Sigma,\Psi), (\Sigma,\Psi')\}$, respectively, $\Gamma' = \Gamma \cup \{(\Sigma, \neg\Psi), (\Sigma, \neg\Psi')\}$.
- rule $\vee$: If Γ contains $(\Sigma, \Psi \vee \Psi')$ or $(\Sigma, \neg(\Psi \wedge \Psi'))$, then create child nodes $\Gamma' = \Gamma \cup \{(\Sigma,\Psi)\}$ and $\Gamma'' = \Gamma \cup \{(\Sigma, \Psi')\}$, respectively, child nodes $\Gamma' = \Gamma \cup \{(\Sigma, \neg\Psi)\}$ and $\Gamma'' = \Gamma \cup \{(\Sigma, \neg\Psi')\}$.
- rule $\Rightarrow \wedge$: If Γ contains $(\Sigma, \varphi \Rightarrow \Phi \wedge \Phi')$, then create child node $\Gamma' = \Gamma \cup \{(\Sigma, \varphi \Rightarrow \Phi), (\Sigma, \varphi \Rightarrow \Phi')\}$.
- rule Ξ: If Γ contains $(\Sigma, [\alpha+\varsigma]\Psi)$, then: if Γ contains (Σ', Ψ') such that $\Sigma' = \Sigma \xrightarrow{\alpha,\varsigma} e$, then create node $\Gamma' = \Gamma \cup \{(\Sigma',\Psi)\}$, else create child node $\Gamma' = \Gamma \cup \{(\Sigma \xrightarrow{\alpha,\varsigma} e', \Psi)\}$, where e' is a fresh integer.
- rule $\neg\Xi$: If Γ contains $(\Sigma, \neg[\alpha+\varsigma]\Psi)$, then create child node $\Gamma' = \Gamma \cup \{(\Sigma, \neg Cont(\alpha,\varsigma) \vee [\alpha+\varsigma]\neg\Psi)\}$.

Definition 6. *A branch is* saturated *if and only if every rule that can be applied to its leaf node has been applied. A tree is* saturated *if and only all its branches are saturated.*

3.2 The SI Phase

Let Γ be an open leaf node of a saturated tree T. $SI(\Gamma)$ is the system of inequalities generated from the formulae in Γ (as explained below). After the tableau phase is completed, the SI phase begins.

> For each open leaf node Γ_k^j of T, do the following. If $SI(\Gamma_k^j)$ is infeasible, then create new leaf node $\Gamma_{k+1}^j = \Gamma_k^j \cup \{(0, \bot)\}$.

Definition 7. *A tree is called* finished *after the SI phase is completed.*

Definition 8. *If a tree for* $\neg\Psi$ *is closed, we write* $\vdash \Psi$. *If there is a finished open tree for* $\neg\Psi$, *we write* $\nvdash \Psi$.

The generation of $SI(\Gamma)$ from the formulae in Γ is explained in the rest of this section. All variables are assumed implicitly non-negative.

Let $C^{\#} = \{w_1, w_2, \ldots, w_n\}$ be an ordering of the worlds in C. Let ω_k^e be a variable representing the probability of being in world w_k at activity point e (after a number of activity updates). The equation

$$\omega_1^0 + \omega_2^0 + \cdots + \omega_n^0 = 1$$

is in $SI(\Gamma)$ and represents the initial probability distribution over the worlds in C. We may denote an activity sequence as $\Sigma \xrightarrow{\alpha,\varsigma} e$ to refer to the last action α, observation ς and activity point e in the sequence. We may also denote an activity sequence as Σe to refer only to the last activity point in the sequence; if Σ is the empty sequence, then e is the initial activity point 0.

In the next four subsections, we deal with (i) law literals involving dynamic and perception literals, (ii) activity sequences, (iii) belief literals and (iv) laws involving reward and cost literals, and utility literals.

Action and Perception Laws. For every formula of the form $(\Sigma, \phi \Rightarrow [\alpha]\varphi \bowtie q) \in \Gamma$ and $(\Sigma, \phi \Rightarrow \neg[\alpha]\varphi \bowtie q) \in \Gamma$, for every j such that $w_j \models \phi$ (where j represents the world in which α is executed),

$$c_1 pr_{j,1}^{\alpha} + c_2 pr_{j,2}^{\alpha} + \cdots + c_n pr_{j,n}^{\alpha} \bowtie q, \text{ respectively, } c_1 pr_{j,1}^{\alpha} + c_2 pr_{j,2}^{\alpha} + \cdots + c_n pr_{j,n}^{\alpha} \not\bowtie q$$

is in $SI(\Gamma)$, such that $c_k = 1$ if $w_k \models \varphi$, else $c_k = 0$, and the $pr_{j,k}^{\alpha}$ are variables. Adding an equation

$$pr_{j,1}^{\alpha} + pr_{j,2}^{\alpha} + \cdots + pr_{j,n}^{\alpha} = \lceil pr_{j,1}^{\alpha} + pr_{j,2}^{\alpha} + \cdots + pr_{j,n}^{\alpha} \rceil$$

for every j such that $w_j \models \phi$, will ensure that either $\sum_{w' \in W} R_{\alpha}(w_j, w') = 1$ or $\sum_{w' \in W} R_{\alpha}(w_j, w') = 0$, for every $w_j \in C$, as stated in Definition 3.

Let $m = |\Omega|$. Let $\Omega^{\#} = (\varsigma_1, \varsigma_2, \ldots, \varsigma_m)$ be an ordering of the observations in Ω. With each observation in $\varsigma \in \Omega^{\#}$, we associate a variable pr_j^{ς}, where j represents the world in which ς is perceived. For every formulae of the form $(\Sigma, \phi \Rightarrow (\varsigma|\alpha) \bowtie q) \in \Gamma$ and $(\Sigma, \phi \Rightarrow \neg(\varsigma|\alpha) \bowtie q) \in \Gamma$, for every j such that $w_j \models \phi$,

$$pr_j^{\varsigma|\alpha} \bowtie q, \text{ respectively, } pr_j^{\varsigma|\alpha} \not\bowtie q$$

is in $SI(\Gamma)$. Adding an equation

$$pr_j^{\varsigma_1|\alpha} + pr_j^{\varsigma_2|\alpha} + \cdots + pr_j^{\varsigma_m|\alpha} = \lceil (pr_{1,j}^{\alpha} + pr_{2,j}^{\alpha} + \cdots + pr_{n,j}^{\alpha})/n \rceil$$

for every j such that $w_j \models \phi$, ensures that for all $w_j \in C$, if there exists a $w_i \in C$ such that $R_{\alpha}(w_i, w_j) > 0$, then $\sum_{\varsigma \in \Omega} Q_{\alpha}(w_j, \varsigma) = 1$, else $\sum_{\varsigma \in \Omega} Q_{\alpha}(w_j, \varsigma) = 0$, as stated in Definition 3.

Belief Update. Let $\Pi(e_h, \alpha, \varsigma)$ be the abbreviation for the term

$$\sum_{j=1}^{n} pr_j^{\varsigma|\alpha} \sum_{i=1}^{n} pr_{i,j}^{\alpha} \omega_i^{e_h},$$

which is the probability of reaching the belief-state after performing belief update $[\![\alpha + \varsigma]\!]$ at activity point e_h. And let $BT(e_h, k, \alpha, \varsigma)$ be the abbreviation for the term

$$\frac{pr_k^{\varsigma|\alpha} \sum_{i=1}^n pr_{i,k}^\alpha \omega_i^{e_h}}{\Pi(e_h, \alpha, \varsigma)},$$

which is the probability of being in world w_k after performing belief update $[\![\alpha + \varsigma]\!]$ at activity point e_h, where $n = |C|$.

Suppose Σ is $0 \xrightarrow{\alpha_0, \varsigma_0} e_1 \xrightarrow{\alpha_1, \varsigma_1} e_2 \cdots \xrightarrow{\alpha_{z-1}, \varsigma_{z-1}} e_z$ and $\Sigma \neq 0$. For every formulae of the form $(\Sigma, \Psi) \in \Gamma$, the following equations are in $SI(\Gamma)$.

$$\omega_k^{e_{h+1}} = BT(e_h, k, \alpha_h, \varsigma_h) \text{ for } k = 1, 2, \ldots, n \text{ and } h = 0, 1, \ldots, z-1,$$
$$\Pi(e_h, \alpha_h, \varsigma_h) \neq 0 \text{ for } h = 0, 1, \ldots, z-1 \text{ and}$$
$$\omega_1^{e_h} + \omega_2^{e_h} + \cdots + \omega_n^{e_h} = 1 \text{ for } h = 0, 1, \ldots, z, \text{ where } e_0 \text{ is } 0.$$

Observe that the e_h are integers and we enforce the constraint that $e_i < e_j$ iff $i < j$.

Continuity and Belief Literals. For every formula of the form $(\Sigma e, Cont(\alpha, \varsigma))$ $\in \Gamma$ or $(\Sigma e, \neg Cont(\alpha, \varsigma)) \in \Gamma$,

$$\Pi(e, \alpha, \varsigma) \neq 0, \text{ respectively, } \Pi(e, \alpha, \varsigma) = 0$$

is in $SI(\Gamma)$.

For every formula of the form $(\Sigma e, \mathbf{B}\varphi \bowtie p) \in \Gamma$,

$$c_1 \omega_1^e + c_2 \omega_2^e + \cdots + c_n \omega_n^e \bowtie p,$$

is in $SI(\Gamma)$, where $c_k = 1$ if $w_k \models \varphi$, else $c_k = 0$.

Rewards, Costs and Utilities. For every formula of the form $(\Sigma, \phi \Rightarrow Reward(r)) \in \Gamma$ and $(\Sigma, \phi \Rightarrow \neg Reward(r)) \in \Gamma$, for every j such that $w_j \models \phi$,

$$R_j = r, \text{ respectively, } R_j \neq r$$

is in $SI(\Gamma)$.

For every formula of the form $(\Sigma, \phi \Rightarrow Cost(\alpha, r)) \in \Gamma$ and $(\Sigma, \phi \Rightarrow \neg Cost(\alpha, r)) \in \Gamma$, for every j such that $w_j \models \phi$,

$$C_j^\alpha = r, \text{ respectively, } C_j^\alpha \neq r$$

is in $SI(\Gamma)$.

Let $RC(\alpha, e) \stackrel{def}{=} \omega_1^e(R_1 - C_1^\alpha) + \omega_2^e(R_2 - C_2^\alpha) + \cdots + \omega_n^e(R_n - C_n^\alpha)$. For every formula of the form $(\Sigma e, \mathbf{U}[\![\alpha]\!] \bowtie q) \in \Gamma$,

$$RC(\alpha, e) \bowtie q$$

is in $SI(\Gamma)$.

To keep track of dependencies between variables in inequalities derived from utility literals of the form $(\Sigma, \mathbf{U}[\![\alpha]\!]\Lambda \bowtie q)$, we define a *utility tree*. A set of utility trees is induced from a set Δ which is defined as follows (examples follow the formal description). For every formula of the form $(\Sigma e, \mathbf{U}[\![\alpha]\!]\Lambda \bowtie q) \in \Gamma$, let $(e \xrightarrow{\alpha,\varsigma} e^\varsigma, \Lambda) \in \Delta$, for every $\varsigma \in \Omega$, where e^ς is a fresh integer. Then, for every $(\xi, [\![\alpha]\!]\Lambda) \in \Delta$ (where Λ is not empty), for every $\varsigma \in \Omega$, if $(\xi', \Psi) \in \Delta$ such that $\xi' = \xi \xrightarrow{\alpha,\varsigma} e^{\varsigma'}$, then $(\xi', \Lambda) \in \Delta$, else $(\xi \xrightarrow{\alpha,\varsigma} e^\varsigma, \Lambda) \in \Delta$, where e^ς is a fresh integer. This finishes the definition of Δ. The following example should clarify the meaning Δ and utility trees.

Suppose $\Omega = \{\varsigma_1, \varsigma_2\}$ and

$$(\Sigma \xrightarrow{\alpha',\varsigma'} 13, \mathbf{U}[\![\alpha_5]\!] = 88),$$

$$(\Sigma \xrightarrow{\alpha',\varsigma'} 13, \mathbf{U}[\![\alpha_1]\!][\![\alpha_2]\!] > 61),$$

$$(\Sigma \xrightarrow{\alpha',\varsigma'} 13, \mathbf{U}[\![\alpha_1]\!][\![\alpha_3]\!][\![\alpha_2]\!] < 62),$$

$$(\Sigma \xrightarrow{\alpha',\varsigma'} 13, \mathbf{U}[\![\alpha_1]\!][\![\alpha_4]\!] = 63),$$

$$(\Sigma \xrightarrow{\alpha',\varsigma'} 23, \mathbf{U}[\![\alpha_1]\!][\![\alpha_2]\!] \geq 64) \text{ and}$$

$$(\Sigma \xrightarrow{\alpha',\varsigma'} 23, \mathbf{U}[\![\alpha_2]\!][\![\alpha_1]\!] = 65)$$

are in some leaf node Γ'. Then $(\Sigma \xrightarrow{\alpha',\varsigma'} 13, \mathbf{U}[\![\alpha_5]\!] = 88)$ is not involved in the definition of Δ', nevertheless, $RC(\alpha_5, 13) = 88$ is in $SI(\Gamma')$.

With respect to the other utility literals,

$$(13 \xrightarrow{\alpha_1,\varsigma_1} 24, [\![\alpha_2]\!]), (13 \xrightarrow{\alpha_1,\varsigma_2} 25, [\![\alpha_2]\!]),$$

$$(13 \xrightarrow{\alpha_1,\varsigma_1} 24, [\![\alpha_3]\!][\![\alpha_2]\!]), (13 \xrightarrow{\alpha_1,\varsigma_2} 25, [\![\alpha_3]\!][\![\alpha_2]\!]),$$

$$(13 \xrightarrow{\alpha_1,\varsigma_1} 24, [\![\alpha_4]\!]), (13 \xrightarrow{\alpha_1,\varsigma_2} 25, [\![\alpha_4]\!]),$$

$$(23 \xrightarrow{\alpha_1,\varsigma_1} 26, [\![\alpha_2]\!]), (23 \xrightarrow{\alpha_1,\varsigma_2} 27, [\![\alpha_2]\!]),$$

$$(23 \xrightarrow{\alpha_2,\varsigma_1} 28, [\![\alpha_1]\!]) \text{ and } (23 \xrightarrow{\alpha_2,\varsigma_2} 29, [\![\alpha_1]\!])$$

are in Δ'. And due to $(13 \xrightarrow{\alpha_1,\varsigma_1} 24, [\![\alpha_3]\!][\![\alpha_2]\!]), (13 \xrightarrow{\alpha_1,\varsigma_2} 25, [\![\alpha_3]\!][\![\alpha_2]\!]) \in \Delta'$, the following are also in Δ'.

$$(13 \xrightarrow{\alpha_1,\varsigma_1} 24 \xrightarrow{\alpha_3,\varsigma_1} 30, [\![\alpha_2]\!]),$$

$$(13 \xrightarrow{\alpha_1,\varsigma_1} 24 \xrightarrow{\alpha_3,\varsigma_2} 31, [\![\alpha_2]\!]),$$

$$(13 \xrightarrow{\alpha_1,\varsigma_2} 25 \xrightarrow{\alpha_3,\varsigma_1} 32, [\![\alpha_2]\!]) \text{ and}$$

$$(13 \xrightarrow{\alpha_1,\varsigma_2} 25 \xrightarrow{\alpha_3,\varsigma_2} 33, [\![\alpha_2]\!]).$$

Note how an activity point is represented by the same integer (for instance, 24) if and only if it is reached via the same sequence of actions and observations (for instance, $13 \xrightarrow{\alpha_1,\varsigma_1}$).

The set of utility trees is generated from Δ as follows. Δ is partitioned such that $(e \xrightarrow{\alpha,\varsigma} e', \Lambda)$, $(e'' \xrightarrow{\alpha',\varsigma'} e''', \Lambda') \in \Delta$ are in the same partitioning if and only if $e = e''$. Each partitioning represents a unique utility tree with the first activity point as the root of the tree. For example, one can generate two utility trees from Δ'; one with root 13 and one with root 23. Each activity sequence of the members of Δ represents a (sub)path starting at the root of its corresponding tree. Figure 1 depicts the two utility trees generated from Δ'.

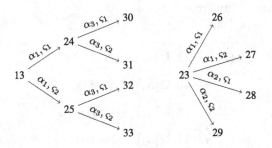

Fig. 1. The two utility trees generated from Δ'.

Before considering the general case, we illustrate the method of generating, from the utility trees in Fig. 1, the required inequalities which must be in $SI(\Gamma')$.

The formula $(\Sigma \xrightarrow{\alpha',\varsigma'} 13, \mathbf{U}[\![\alpha_1]\!][\![\alpha_2]\!] > 61) \in \Gamma'$ is represented by

$$RC(\alpha_1, 13) + \Pi(13, \alpha_1, \varsigma_1)RC(\alpha_2, 24) + \Pi(13, \alpha_1, \varsigma_2)RC(\alpha_2, 25) > 61$$

in $SI(\Gamma')$. To generate this inequality, the utility tree rooted at 13 is used: See that α_1 is executed at activity point 13, α_2 is executed at activity point 24 if ς_1 is perceived and α_2 is executed at activity point 25 if ς_2 is perceived. Moreover, the latter two rewards must be weighted by the probabilities of reaching the respective new belief-states/activity points.

The formula $(\Sigma \xrightarrow{\alpha',\varsigma'} 13, \mathbf{U}[\![\alpha_1]\!][\![\alpha_4]\!] = 63) \in \Gamma'$ is represented by

$$RC(\alpha_1, 13) + \Pi(13, \alpha_1, \varsigma_1)RC(\alpha_4, 24) + \Pi(13, \alpha_1, \varsigma_2)RC(\alpha_4, 25) = 63.$$

in $SI(\Gamma')$. This time, α_4 is executed at the activity points 24 and 25.

Next, the utility tree rooted at 23 is used to find the representation of $(\Sigma \xrightarrow{\alpha',\varsigma'} 23, \mathbf{U}[\![\alpha_1]\!][\![\alpha_2]\!] \geq 64) \in \Gamma'$. Looking at the utility tree, one can work out that

$$RC(\alpha_1, 23) + \Pi(23, \alpha_1, \varsigma_1)RC(\alpha_2, 26) + \Pi(23, \alpha_1, \varsigma_2)RC(\alpha_2, 27) \geq 64$$

must be in $SI(\Gamma')$.

For $(\Sigma \xrightarrow{\alpha',\varsigma'} 23, \mathbf{U}[\![\alpha_2]\!][\![\alpha_1]\!] = 65) \in \Gamma'$,

$$RC(\alpha_2, 23) + \Pi(23, \alpha_2, \varsigma_1)RC(\alpha_1, 28) + \Pi(23, \alpha_1, \varsigma_2)RC(\alpha_1, 29) \geq 64$$

is in $SI(\Gamma')$.

Formula

$$(\Sigma \xrightarrow{\alpha', \varsigma'} 13, \mathbf{U}[\![\alpha_1]\!][\![\alpha_3]\!][\![\alpha_2]\!] < 62) \in \Gamma', \tag{1}$$

is represented by the inequality shown in Fig. 2. The size of the utility tree rooted at 13 is due to (1). Hence, the whole tree is employed to generate the inequality.

$$RC(\alpha_1, 13) \begin{array}{l} + \Pi(13, \alpha_1, \varsigma_1)\left(RC(\alpha_3, 24) \begin{array}{l} + \Pi(24, \alpha_3, \varsigma_1)\ RC(\alpha_2, 30) \\ + \Pi(24, \alpha_3, \varsigma_2)\ RC(\alpha_2, 31) \end{array} \right) \\ \\ + \Pi(13, \alpha_1, \varsigma_2)\left(RC(\alpha_3, 25) \begin{array}{l} + \Pi(25, \alpha_3, \varsigma_1)\ RC(\alpha_2, 32) \\ + \Pi(25, \alpha_3, \varsigma_2)\ RC(\alpha_2, 33) \end{array} \right) \end{array} < 62$$

Fig. 2. The inequality representing $(\Sigma \xrightarrow{\alpha', \varsigma'} 13, \mathbf{U}[\![\alpha_1]\!][\![\alpha_3]\!][\![\alpha_2]\!] < 62) \in \Gamma'$.

In general, for every utility literal of the form

$$(\Sigma e_z, \mathbf{U}[\![\alpha_1]\!][\![\alpha_2]\!] \cdots [\![\alpha_y]\!] \bowtie q)$$

in leaf node Γ, an inequality can be generated from an associated utility tree and the inequality must be in $SI(\Gamma)$. We do not have space to go into the details, but please see the thesis [23, Chap. 8] for details.

Theorem 1. *The decision procedure is sound, complete and terminating. The SDL is thus decidable with respect to entailment as defined above.*

Proof. Please refer to the thesis [23, Chap. 8] for the proof.

Although the SDL vocabulary is finite, the need to deal with probabilistic information makes the above decidability result non-trivial.

4   Domain Specification

First we present a framework for domain specification with the logic, then we look at some examples of SDL entailment in use.

4.1   The Framework

The framework presented here should be viewed as providing guidance; the knowledge engineer should adapt the framework as necessary for the particular domain being modeled. On the practical side, in the context of the SDL, the domain of interest can be divided into five parts:

Static laws (denoted as the set *SL*) have the form $\phi \Rightarrow \varphi$, where ϕ and φ are propositional sentences, and ϕ is the condition under which φ is always satisfied. They are the basic laws and facts of the domain. For instance, "A full battery allows me at most four hours of operation", "I sink in liquids" and "The charging station is in sector 14". Such static laws cannot be explicitly stated in traditional POMDPs.

Action rules (denoted as the set *AR*) must be specified. In this paper, we ignore the frame problem [24]; a solution in the current setting requires careful machinery and space prohibits giving it the attention it deserves. We have made preliminary progress in this direction [25]. For this paper, we identify two kinds of action rules.

The basic kind is the *effect axiom*. For every action α, effect axioms take the form

$$\phi_1 \Rightarrow [\alpha]\varphi_{11} = p_{11} \wedge \cdots \wedge [\alpha]\varphi_{1n} = p_{1n}$$
$$\phi_2 \Rightarrow [\alpha]\varphi_{21} = p_{21} \wedge \cdots \wedge [\alpha]\varphi_{2n} = p_{2n}$$
$$\vdots$$
$$\phi_j \Rightarrow [\alpha]\varphi_{j1} = p_{j1} \wedge \cdots \wedge [\alpha]\varphi_{jn} = p_{jn},$$

where (i) for every rule i, the sum of transition probabilities $p_{i1}, \ldots, p_{in}$ must lie in the range $[0, 1]$ (preferably 1), (ii) for every rule i, for any pair of effects φ_{ik} and $\varphi_{ik'}$, $\varphi_{ik} \wedge \varphi_{ik'} \equiv \bot$ and (iii) for any pair of conditions ϕ_i and $\phi_{i'}$, $\phi_i \wedge \phi_{i'} \equiv \bot$.

The knowledge engineer must keep in mind that if the transition probabilities do not sum to 1, the specification is incomplete. Suppose, for instance, that for rule i, $p_{i1} + \cdots + p_{in} < 1$. Then one or more transitions from a ϕ_i-world has not been mentioned and some logical inferences will not be possible.

The second kind of action rule is the *inexecutability axiom*. We shall assume that the set of effect axioms for an action is complete, that is, that the knowledge engineer intends that the conditions of these axioms are the only conditions under which the actions can be executed. Note that $[\alpha]\top > 0$ implies that α is executable. Therefore, if there is an effect axiom for α with condition ϕ, then one can assume the presence of an executability axiom $\phi \Rightarrow [\alpha]\top > 0$. However, we must still specify that an action is inexecutable when none of the effect axiom conditions is met. Hence, the following *inexecutability* axiom is assumed present.[4]

$$\neg(\phi_1 \vee \cdots \vee \phi_j) \Rightarrow [\alpha]\top = 0$$

where $\phi_1, \ldots, \phi_j$ are the conditions of the effect axioms for α.

Perception rules (denoted as the set *PR*) must be specified. Let $E(\alpha) = \{\varphi_{11}, \varphi_{12}, \ldots, \varphi_{21}, \varphi_{22}, \ldots, \varphi_{jn}\}$ be the set of all effects of action α executed under all executable conditions. For every action α, perception rules typically take the form

---

[4] Inexecutability axioms are also called *condition closure* axioms.

$$\phi_1 \Rightarrow (\varsigma_{11} \mid \alpha) = p_{11} \wedge \cdots \wedge (\varsigma_{1m} \mid \alpha) = p_{1m}$$
$$\phi_2 \Rightarrow (\varsigma_{21} \mid \alpha) = p_{21} \wedge \cdots \wedge (\varsigma_{2m} \mid \alpha) = p_{2m}$$
$$\vdots$$
$$\phi_k \Rightarrow (\varsigma_{k1} \mid \alpha) = p_{k1} \wedge \cdots \wedge (\varsigma_{km} \mid \alpha) = p_{km},$$

where (i) the sum of perception probabilities $p_{i1}, \ldots, p_{im}$ of any rule i must lie in the range $[0, 1]$ (preferably 1), (ii) for any pair of conditions ϕ_i and $\phi_{i'}$, $\phi_i \wedge \phi_{i'} \equiv \bot$ and (iii) $\phi_1 \vee \phi_2 \vee \cdots \vee \phi_k \equiv \bigvee_{\varphi \in E(\alpha)} \varphi$. If the sum of perception probabilities $p_{i1}, \ldots, p_{im}$ of any rule i is 1, then any observations not mentioned in rule i are automatically *unperceivable* in a ϕ_i-world. However, in the case that the sum is not 1, this deduction about unperceivability cannot be made. Then the knowledge engineer should keep in mind that a perception rule of the form

$$\phi_i \rightarrow \cdots \wedge (\varsigma \mid \alpha) = 0 \wedge \cdots$$

implies that ς is unperceivable in a ϕ_i-world given that the world is reachable via α. Hence, if $p_{i1} + \cdots + p_{im} \neq 1$ and unperceivability information is available, it should be included with a subformula of the form $(\varsigma \mid \alpha) = 0$.

Utility rules (denoted as the set UR) must be specified. Utility rules typically take the form

$$\phi_1 \Rightarrow Reward(r_1), \quad \ldots, \quad \phi_j \Rightarrow Reward(r_j),$$

meaning that in all worlds where ϕ_i is satisfied, the agent gets r_i units of reward. And for every action α,

$$\phi_1 \Rightarrow Cost(\alpha, r_1), \quad \ldots, \quad \phi_j \Rightarrow Cost(\alpha, r_j),$$

meaning that the cost for performing α in a world where ϕ_i is satisfied is r_i units. The conditions are disjoint as for action and perception rules.

The fifth part of the domain specification is the agent's initial belief-state IB. That is, a specification of the worlds the agent should believe it is in when it becomes active, and probabilities associated with those worlds should be provided. In general, an initial belief-state specification should have the form

$$\mathbf{B}\varphi_1 \bowtie p_1 \quad \wedge \quad \mathbf{B}\varphi_2 \bowtie p_2 \quad \wedge \quad \cdots \quad \wedge \quad \mathbf{B}\varphi_n \bowtie p_n,$$

where (i) $\bowtie \in \{<, \leq, =, \geq, >\}$ and (ii) the φ_i are mutually exclusive propositional sentences (i.e., for all $1 \leq i, j \leq n$ s.t. $i \neq j$, $\varphi_i \wedge \varphi_j \equiv \bot$). For a *full/complete* specification of a *particular* initial belief-state, all the $\bowtie$ must be $=$ and $p_1 + p_2 + \ldots + p_n$ must equal 1.

The union of SL, AR, PR and UR is referred to as an agent's *background knowledge* and is denoted BK. In practical terms, the question to be answered in the SDL is whether $BK \models IB \rightarrow \Theta^-$ holds, where $BK \subset \mathcal{L}_{SDL}$, IB is as described above, and $\Theta^- \in \mathcal{L}_{SDL}^{\not\rightarrow}$ is some sentence of interest, where $\mathcal{L}_{SDL}^{\not\rightarrow}$ is the subset of formulae of $\mathcal{L}_{SDL}$ excluding law literals.

4.2 Examples

This section states three entailment queries based on the oil-drinking scenario. Except for the initial belief-state, the following is a full specification of the POMDP model.[5]

Action Rules.

$\neg h \Rightarrow [g](f \wedge h) = 0.8 \wedge [g](\neg f \wedge h) = 0.1 \wedge [g](\neg f \wedge \neg h) = 0.1; \quad h \Rightarrow [g]\top = 0.$
$h \Rightarrow [d](\neg f \wedge h) = 0.95 \wedge [d](\neg f \wedge \neg h) = 0.05; \quad \neg h \Rightarrow [d]\top = 0.$
$f \wedge h \Rightarrow [w](f \wedge h) = 1; \quad f \wedge \neg h \Rightarrow [w](f \wedge \neg h) = 1;$
$\neg f \wedge h \Rightarrow [w](\neg f \wedge h) = 1; \quad \neg f \wedge \neg h \Rightarrow [w](\neg f \wedge \neg h) = 1.$

Perception Rules.

$\top \Rightarrow (N \mid g) = 1 \wedge (N \mid d) = 1.$
$f \wedge h \Rightarrow (L \mid w) = 0.1 \wedge (M \mid w) = 0.2 \wedge (H \mid w) = 0.7.$
$\neg f \wedge h \Rightarrow (L \mid w) = 0.5 \wedge (M \mid w) = 0.3 \wedge (H \mid w) = 0.2.$
$\neg h \Rightarrow (\forall v^{\varsigma})\neg(v^{\varsigma} = N) \rightarrow (v^{\varsigma} \mid w) = \frac{1}{3}.$

Utility Rules.

$f \Rightarrow Reward(0); \quad \neg f \wedge h \Rightarrow Reward(10); \quad \neg f \wedge \neg h \Rightarrow Reward(-5).$
$\top \Rightarrow (\forall v^{\alpha})(v^{\alpha} = g \vee v^{\alpha} = d) \rightarrow Cost(v^{\alpha}, 1); \quad f \Rightarrow Cost(w, 2); \quad \neg f \Rightarrow Cost(w, 0.8).$

The robot gets 10 units of reward for holding the can while it is not full (implying the robot drank the oil), and it gets -5 units of reward for not holding the can while it is not full. Otherwise, the robot gets no rewards. It costs two units to weigh the can when the can is full, else it costs 0.8 units. Grabbing and drinking always costs one unit.

Suppose that the initial belief-state is specified as

$$\mathbf{B}f = 0.7 \wedge \mathbf{B}(\neg f \wedge h) = 0.2 \wedge \mathbf{B}(\neg f \wedge \neg h) = 0.1.$$

Note that it is not fully specified. We determined that BK entails

$$\mathbf{B}f = 0.7 \wedge \mathbf{B}(\neg f \wedge h) = 0.2 \wedge \mathbf{B}(\neg f \wedge \neg h) = 0.1 \rightarrow [\![g + N]\!][\![w + M]\!]\mathbf{B}h > 0.85.$$

That is, the agent's degree of belief that it is holding the can is greater than 0.85 after grabbing the can and then weighing and perceiving that it has medium weight follows from BK, given an initial belief-state $\mathbf{B}f = 0.7 \wedge \cdots = 0.1$. We draw the reader's attention to the fact that sensible entailments can be queried, even with a partially specified initial belief-state.

In the next example, we provide a complete specification of the initial belief-state, but we under-specify the perception probabilities. Suppose that instead of perception rule $f \wedge h \Rightarrow (L \mid w) = 0.1 \wedge (M \mid w) = 0.2 \wedge (H \mid w) = 0.7 \in BK$, we have only $f \wedge h \Rightarrow (H \mid w) = 0.7 \in BK'$. Also assume the perception rule $f \wedge h \Rightarrow (M \mid w) \geq 0.2 \in BK'$. (That is, we modify BK to become BK'.) Then

---

[5] Probabilities used for specifying the initial belief-state are assumed given by a knowledge engineer or computed in an earlier process.

$$\mathbf{B}(f \wedge h) = 0.35 \ \wedge \ \mathbf{B}(f \wedge \neg h) = 0.35 \ \wedge \mathbf{B}(\neg f \wedge h) = 0.2 \ \wedge \ \mathbf{B}(\neg f \wedge \neg h)$$
$$= 0.1 \ \rightarrow \ [\![g + N]\!][\![w + M]\!]\mathbf{B}h > 0.85$$

is entailed by BK'.

Finally, we have shown that BK entails

$$\mathbf{B}f = 0.7 \wedge \mathbf{B}(\neg f \wedge h) = 0.2 \wedge \mathbf{B}(\neg f \wedge \neg h) = 0.1 \ \rightarrow \ [\![g + N]\!]\mathbf{U}[\![d]\!][\![d]\!] \leq 7,$$

where, the initial belief-state is under-specified. This example shows that non-trivial entailments about the utility of sequences of actions can be confirmed, even without full knowledge about the initial belief-state.

5   Concluding Remarks

We presented a modal logic with a POMDP semantics for representing stochastic domains and reasoning about noisy actions and observations. Entailment queries can be answered as a solution to certain kinds of projection problems, even with incomplete domain specifications. The procedure for deciding entailment is proved sound, complete and terminating. As a corollary, the entailment question for the SDL is decidable.

Our work can likely be enhanced in several dimensions by further studying the ongoing research in the field of probabilistic logics, stochastic/probabilistic satisfiability, relational (PO)MDPs and symbolic dynamic programming [7–9, 20, 26]. As espoused by [27], for instance, there are advantages to being able to model a domain with relational predicates and not only propositions. We could thus consider lifting the SDL to a first-order fragment.

Automatic plan generation is highly desirable in cognitive robotics and for autonomous systems modeled as POMDPs. In future work, we would like to take the SDL as the basis for developing a language or framework with which plans can be generated, in the fashion of DTGolog [28].

POMDP methods do not deal with the problem of belief maintenance over incomplete models, and this is why the problem is interesting, provided that the solution can lead to methods that are at least, minimally effective. [29]'s article seems like a good starting point for the investigation to determining the computational complexity of the procedure, our next task.

References

1. Smallwood, R., Sondik, E.: The optimal control of partially observable Markov processes over a finite horizon. Oper. Res. **21**, 1071–1088 (1973)
2. Monahan, G.: A survey of partially observable Markov decision processes: theory, models, and algorithms. Manage. Sci. **28**, 1–16 (1982)
3. Boutilier, C., Poole, D.: Computing optimal policies for partially observable decision processes using compact representations. In: Proceedings of the Thirteenth National Conference on Artificial Intelligence (AAAI 1996), pp. 1168–1175. AAAI Press, Menlo Park (1996)

4. Geffner, H., Bonet, B.: High-level planning and control with incomplete information using POMDPs. In: Proceedings of the Fall AAAI Symposium on Cognitive Robotics, pp. 113–120. AAAI Press, Seattle (1998)
5. Hansen, E., Feng, Z.: Dynamic programming for POMDPs using a factored state representation. In: Proceedings of the Fifth International Conference on Artificial Intelligence, Planning and Scheduling (AIPS 2000), pp. 130–139 (2000)
6. Wang, C., Schmolze, J.: Planning with POMDPs using a compact, logic-based representation. In: Proceedings of the Seventeenth IEEE International Conference on Tools with Artificial Intelligence (ICTAI 2005), pp. 523–530. IEEE Computer Society, Los Alamitos (2005)
7. Sanner, S., Kersting, K.: Symbolic dynamic programming for first-order POMDPs. In: Proceedings of the Twenty-Fourth National Conference on Artificial Intelligence (AAAI 2010), pp. 1140–1146. AAAI Press (2010)
8. Lison, P.: Towards relational POMDPs for adaptive dialogue management. In: Proceedings of the ACL 2010 Student Research Workshop, ACLstudent 2010, pp. 7–12. Association for Computational Linguistics, Stroudsburg (2010)
9. Wang, C., Khardon, R.: Relational partially observable MDPs. In: Fox, M., Poole, D. (eds.) Proceedings of the Twenty-Fourth AAAI Conference on Artificial Intelligence (AAAI 2010). AAAI Press, Atlanta (2010)
10. De Weerdt, M., De Boer, F., Van der Hoek, W., Meyer, J.J.: Imprecise observations of mobile robots specified by a modal logic. In: Proceedings of the Fifth Annual Conference of the Advanced School for Computing and Imaging (ASCI 1999), pp. 184–190 (1999)
11. Bacchus, F., Halpern, J., Levesque, H.: Reasoning about noisy sensors and effectors in the situation calculus. Artif. Intell. **111**, 171–208 (1999)
12. McCarthy, J.: Situations, actions and causal laws. Technical report, Stanford University (1963)
13. Gabaldon, A., Lakemeyer, G.: $\mathcal{ESP}$: A logic of only-knowing, noisy sensing and acting. In: Proceedings of the Twenty-Second National Conference on Artificial Intelligence (AAAI 2007), pp. 974–979. AAAI Press (2007)
14. Levesque, H., Lakemeyer, G.: Situations, si! Situation terms no! In: Proceedings of the Conference on Principles of Knowledge Representation and Reasoning (KR 2004), pp. 516–526. AAAI Press (2004)
15. Poole, D.: Decision theory, the situation calculus and conditional plans. Linköping Electron. Art. Comput. Inf. Sci. **8**, 34 (1998)
16. Iocchi, L., Lukasiewicz, T., Nardi, D., Rosati, R.: Reasoning about actions with sensing under qualitative and probabilistic uncertainty. ACM Trans. Comput. Logic **10**, 5:1–5:41 (2009)
17. Kwiatkowska, M., Norman, G., Parker, D.: Advances and challenges of probabilistic model checking. In: Proceedings of the Forty-Eighth Annual Allerton Conference on Communication, Control and Computing, pp. 1691–1698. IEEE Press (2010)
18. Hansson, H., Jonsson, B.: A logic for reasoning about time and reliability. Formal Aspects Comput. **6**, 512–535 (1994)
19. Ross, S., Pineau, J., Chaib-draa, B., Kreitmann, P.: A bayesian approach for learning and planning in partially observable markov decision processes. J. Mach. Learn. Res. **12**, 1729–1770 (2011)
20. Shirazi, A., Amir, E.: First-order logical filtering. Artif. Intell. **175**, 193–219 (2011)
21. Rens, G., Meyer, T., Lakemeyer, G.: SLAP: Specification logic of actions with probability. J. Appl. Logic **12**, 128–150 (2014)

22. Rens, G., Meyer, T., Lakemeyer, G.: A logic for specifying stochastic actions and observations. In: Beierle, C., Meghini, C. (eds.) FoIKS 2014. LNCS, vol. 8367, pp. 305–323. Springer, Heidelberg (2014)

23. Rens, G.: Formalisms for Agents Reasoning with Stochastic Actions and Perceptions. Ph.D. thesis, School of Mathematics, Statistics and Computer Science, University of KwaZulu-Natal (2014)

24. McCarthy, J., Hayes, P.: Some philosophical problems from the standpoint of artificial intelligence. Mach. Intell. 4, 463–502 (1969)

25. Rens, G., Meyer, T., Lakemeyer, G.: On the logical specification of probabilistic transition models. In: Proceedings of the Eleventh International Symposium on Logical Formalizations of Commonsense Reasoning (COMMONSENSE 2013), University of Technology, Sydney. UTSe Press (2013)

26. Saad, E.: Probabilistic reasoning by SAT solvers. In: Sossai, C., Chemello, G. (eds.) ECSQARU 2009. LNCS, vol. 5590, pp. 663–675. Springer, Heidelberg (2009)

27. Wang, C., Joshi, S., Khardon, R.: First order decision diagrams for relational MDPs. J. Artif. Intell. Res. (JAIR) 31, 431–472 (2008)

28. Boutilier, C., Reiter, R., Soutchanski, M., Thrun, S.: Decision-theoretic, high-level agent programming in the situation calculus. In: Proceedings of the Seventeenth National Conference on Artificial Intelligence (AAAI 2000) and of the Twelfth Conference on Innovative Applications of Artificial Intelligence (IAAI 2000), pp. 355–362. AAAI Press, Menlo Park (2000)

29. Littman, M., Majercik, S., Pitassi, T.: Stochastic boolean satisfiability. J. Autom. Reasoning 27, 251–296 (2001)

Identifying Critical Positions Based on Conspiracy Numbers

Mohd Nor Akmal Khalid[1], E. Mei Ang[1]([✉]), Umi Kalsom Yusof[1],
Hiroyuki Iida[2], and Taichi Ishitobi[2]

[1] School of Computer Sciences, Universiti Sains Malaysia,
11800 George Town, Pulau Pinang, Malaysia
akmal1040401@gmail.com, emei1225@yahoo.com, umiyusof@cs.usm.my
[2] School of Information Science, Japan Advance Institute of Science and Technology,
1-1 Asahidai, Nomi, Ishikawa 923-1292, Japan
{iida,itaichi}@jaist.ac.jp

Abstract. Research in two-player perfect information games has been one of the focuses of computer-game related studies in the domain of artificial intelligence. However, focus on an effective search program is insufficient to give the "taste" of actual entertainment in the gaming industry. Instead of focusing on effective search algorithm, we dedicate our study in realizing the possibility of applying strategy changing technique. However, quantifying and determining this possibility is the main challenge imposed in this study. For this purpose, the Conspiracy Number Search algorithm is considered where the maximum and minimum conspiracy numbers are recorded in the test bed of simple Tic-Tac-Toe and Othello game application. We analysed these numbers as the measures of critical position identifier which determines the right moment for possibility of applying strategy changing technique. For Tic-Tac-Toe game, the conspiracy numbers are analysed through operators formally defined in this article as ↑ *tactic* and ↓ *tactic* while variance of the conspiracy numbers are analysed in Othello game. Interesting results are obtained with convincing evidences but future works are still needed in order to further strengthen our hypothesis.

Keywords: Tic-Tac-Toe · Othello · Conspiracy numbers

1 Introduction

In the domain of speculative play, understanding the game or mastering the game intricacy is the most important aspect for achieving successful outcome in the respective competitive combat [1]. However, the main challenge in the domain of speculative play is to identify a (critical) position for applying a speculative play. The opponent-model search [2–4] is such a speculative play, but without the knowledge of when is the most optimum position to apply it during a game. In other words, determining when one should change his strategy from minimax to any speculative way is the puzzling issue.

© Springer International Publishing Switzerland 2015
B. Duval et al. (Eds.): ICAART 2015, LNAI 9494, pp. 100–127, 2015.
DOI: 10.1007/978-3-319-27947-3_6

The mechanics of computer-games in two-player perfect information games or two-player games in short, such as board games (e.g. tic-tac-toe, othello, checkers, chess, etc.), involve using a tree searching algorithm to evaluate and decide the possible moves to take. However, even in the best known search algorithms, the search space possesses exponential time complexity with the growing depth of the tree [5]. Innovative search algorithms, search enhancements, and learning ideas have been applied by ample research efforts towards creating a computer program that dominates the games against their opponents with better strength and performance [6], as well as overcoming the time complexity limitation of the tree search [7]. In order to better understand the nature of any computer-game, studying the progress of the games is important for improving the game's value as a form of entertainment.

When progressing on the board game, different positions made by a player throughout the game's time horizon can effect the outcome of the endgame. Usually, playing well throughout the game when competing against top human players is not enough but playing optimally during the endgame (or certain parts of the games) is very important [8,9]. Focusing on a certain stage of the game is essential in order to apply different speculative play to boost its *excitement*. However, the outcome of the computer-games (lose, win, or draw) is unclear until the game ends. Predicting this outcome during the progress of computer-games is mainly dependent on the likeliness of a position to result in either winning, losing, or draw. This situation is formally defined as *critical* position, where at a certain point of the game progress, the game outcome is measurable and eventually becomes certain and inevitable.

Identifying *critical position* of a progressing computer game involve comprehending the computer players tendency of changing its strategy during a particular moment of the game play. In other words, knowing the right moment of based on this *critical position* at a certain state of the game enables the possibility of applying speculative play which essentially produces *interesting* outcome of the game [10]. Thus, identifying this *critical position* is highly dependent on the quantifying capabilities of the indicator. Therefore, a suitable search algorithm that acts as an indicator during the games progress is necessary in order to identify its *critical position*.

A well-known search indicators studied by several researchers in the late-80s is the Conspiracy-Number Search (CNS). Introduced by McAllester [11,12], CNS is a best-first search algorithm for minimax tree framework, which determines the cardinality of the smallest set of leaf nodes which have to "conspire" to change their values in order to change the minimax value of the root. This present a suitable opportunity for determining the moments for applying speculative play (e.g. opponent model), thus acts as the motivating factor of selecting CNS for this study. One of the ideas underlying CNS is that the distribution of the values over the leaf nodes of the tree, and the shape of the tree, should influence the selection of the next node to be investigated [7]. However, focus on CNS as a search algorithm in computer-games research was faced with discouraging results [5,13–16]. Later, Allis *et al.* [17] derived and specialized CNS concepts to the AND/OR tree framework where the study matured into Proof-Number Search (PNS). Although CNS is different compared to PNS, CNS's conceptual frameworks bear certain correlation to PNS.

This study concerns a matter of critical position identification, not a matter of program strength improvement in games (See some approaches, e.g., done by Jonathan Schaeffer). Hence, we have chosen a game as simple as possible in order to clearly explain the proposed idea. Further investigation would be, as suggested, to implement the proposed idea in more complicated games such as chess. To our best knowledge, no other research has been done with CNs to identify *critical positions* instead of using as game-tree search heuristics (stability of the root node's minimax value). In this paper, any part of speculative play is not described. However, the relation between CN and strategic change at *critical position* (in case where the position is going to be disadvantageous position) should be very important in the context of speculative play.

2   Conspiracy-Number Search

In the minimax tree framework, the first player tries to maximize his or her advantage, while the second player tries to minimize it [18,19]. CNS searches the tree in a manner that at least $c > 1$ of the leaf values have to change in order to change the decision at the root [5]. Intuitively, when expanding a minimax tree further, the accuracy and stability of the root value depend on how much it changes. Major changes on the root value make it unreliable [12]. Therefore, the concept of *conspiracy* is used to measure the root value's stability and its likelihood to change by narrowing the range of the plausible values of the root [13]. The likelihood of the root taking a particular value is reflected in that value's associated conspiracy number. This conspiracy number measures the size of the "conspirators" needed to bring about a certain change in root value; the more conspirators needed for a given change, the less likely the change [12]. This is done by keeping track so the number of leaf nodes whose value must be changed (when searched deeper) to change the root's node value by a certain amount or taking on that new value. A change in the value of a certain set of leaf nodes is called conspiracy between those leaf nodes.

The algorithm is a probabilistic search in nature where there is no guarantee that the correct solution will be found when it terminates, but the most likely one instead. The conceptual framework behind the CNS is to grow search trees for which one has confidence by measuring the number of value through the conspiracy numbers. The search is guided in a best first manner, where the tree searched so far is kept in memory. An example is probably the best way to illustrate the function of a conspiracy number. The following is taken from [5,13]: Assume that the branching factor is 2, the range of values are from 1 to 6, the root node is the MAX node, inside the nodes are their names and their minimax values, and the simple tabular for storing conspiracy numbers of the root. From Fig. 1, it can be observed that the leaves or terminal node have to at least change their value to cause the value of the root to become 1, 2, 4, 5, or 6.

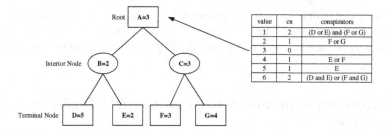

Fig. 1. Illustration of a minimax tree adopting CNS algorithm.

For example, only leaf E has to change its value to 5 in order for the root value to become 5.

As described by Schaeffer [13], there is a simple method of computing the conspiracy numbers. At the terminal node t, the conspiracy number associated with node t value is 0 and for all other values is 1. For the interior node, if the value x of a MAX node is to be increased to $x' > x$, only one of the successor nodes need to change its value to x'. It is clear that the conspiracy number for x' is the minimum amongst all other successors. This is denoted as $\uparrow needed_i$. If the value x is to be decreased to $x' < x$, all successors with values greater than x' must change their value to one lower than x'. That is the reason why the number of conspirators for these nodes are summed. This is denoted as $\downarrow needed_i$. The rules of calculating conspiracy numbers are given as the following (v is the associated conspiracy number of the node and m is the minimax value of the node):

$$CN(v) = 0, \quad \text{if } v = m,$$

At MAX node:

$$CN(v) = \sum_{\text{all sons } i} \downarrow needed_i(v), \quad \text{for all } v < m,$$

$$CN(v) = \min_{\text{all sons } i} \uparrow needed_i(v), \quad \text{for all } v > m.$$

At MIN node:

$$CN(v) = \min_{\text{all sons } i} \downarrow needed_i(v), \quad \text{for all } v < m,$$

$$CN(v) = \sum_{\text{all sons } i} \uparrow needed_i(v), \quad \text{for all } v > m.$$

Since its introduction, variants of CNS have been proposed by several researchers. $\alpha - \beta$ Conspiracy Search proposed by McAllester and Yuret [20] establishes lower and upper bound of the search. The MAX strategy establishes a lower bound and the MIN strategy establishes an upper bound. Thus, the conspiracy numbers can be used to measure the "safety" of these two strategies. Lorenz *et al.* [5] proposed a Controlled-Conspiracy Number Search where instead of variable depth, an $\alpha - \beta$ quiescence search is used and search bound is provided. The conspiracy number vectors are compressed into 3-tuples, allowing the CCNS to be independent of the granularity of the evaluation function (e.g. positional play in chess).

3   Conspiracy-Number Search as Critical Position Identifier

Determining *critical position* is vitals due to the following reasons: First, the specific outcome of the game can be estimated in advance (e.g. *resignation*) and this estimation can be utilized for game outcome prediction. Second, the *critical positions* are expected to expose the possibilities of tactic changes, denoted as ↑ *tactics* or ↓ *tactics*, respectively. The ↑ *tactics* implies that the computer player tries to force a draw when it's losing, while ↓ *tactics* implies that the computer player tries to force a draw when achieving a win is impossible. Third, *critical positions* can be used to estimate the moment for computer player to apply speculative play and change the outcome of the game.

However, why do we use CNS instead of the positional scoring (evaluation function) alone during the game's progression? The positional scoring act as a guiding function for an individual player to determine his/her state in the game's progress [21]. Although it might be suitable for identifying *critical positions*, it still lack of the probabilistic element in abstracting the player's decision to determine the next game state. Basically, positional scoring shows how the game progresses (i.e. which player is leading the game) but the CN-values potentially show its probable changes. Thus, the goal of *critical position* is to determine the possibility of improving or deteriorating the positional score value of a move (evaluate for probable impact of next moves), while positional scoring makes use of the *evaluation features* of a move (evaluate for probable gain of next moves) [21].

3.1   Tic-Tac-Toe: Experimental Results and Discussion

CNS requires two types of conspiracy numbers needed to maintain, ↑ *needed* and ↓ *needed*. We consider this as a scalar measures in the computer-game's search progress to analyze and justify the rationale of the hypothesis mentioned earlier. A simple Tic-Tac-Toe game is used as the test bed of our study.

This experiment is tested with fixed-depth minimax algorithm applying CNS as a scalar measures for recording the conspiracy numbers of the root values for each game moves. For every player X with search depth i there is an opposing player O with search depth j, where $2 \leq i \leq 6$ and $2 \leq j \leq 6$. Therefore, there are 25 total game sets (both player X and player O have five depths). Player X is assumed to be the first player to start the game in every case, since if player O starts the results will be just the reverse. The rules of the games are as follows:

- For player O, the score is negative. For player X, the score is positive.
- Player X tries to maximize the score, while player O tries to minimize the score.
- For each row, if there are both X and O, then the score for the row is 0.
- If the whole row is empty, then the score is 1.
- If there is only one X, then the score is 10. If there is only one O, then the score is −10.
- If there are two X, then the score is 100. If there are two O, then the score is −100.
- If there are 3 X, then the score is 1000. If there are three O, then the score is −1000.

Tables 1 and 2 shows the recorded maximum conspiracy numbers (*MaxCN*) and minimum conspiracy numbers (*MinCN*) for every game sets, respectively. The odd and even numbers (highlighted in light gray) of the game's progress are relevant to player X and player O, respectively. In all cases of game sets, the game outcomes is a draw. To counter this, we consider the final score of any player as win, lose, or draw as final score of 100, −100, and 0, respectively. Table 3 shows the final scores of every game of player X versus player O.

Observing Tables 1 and 2, the MaxCN of player X decreases steadily (in most cases) while the MaxCN for player O decreases abruptly. To simplify the results interpretation, the following rules are adopted: The MaxCN of current player p is considered abruptly decreased if $|MaxCN_{p_{i+1}} - MaxCN_{p_i}| > |MaxCN_{p_{i+1}}|$, where i equals to the game progress (e.g. moves). The value of MaxCN implies instability and changes in the root value is more likely. In other words, possibility of losing or winning is high since the likeliness of the root value to change is high. However, the fact that the outcome is inevitable (either win or lose) but not known, this stage simulates the *critical position* which is highly recommended for applying speculative play.

For MinCN, however, a different interpretation is needed. The abruptly decreased MinCN utilizes the same rule as MaxCN: The MinCN of current player p is considered abruptly decreased if $|MinCN_{p_{i+1}} - MinCN_{p_i}| > |MinCN_{p_{i+1}}|$, where i equals to the game's progress (e.g. moves). This situation is the *critical position* for tactic changes (↑ *tactic* or ↓ *tactic*). In the case of abrupt inclining of MaxCN, the root value stabilizes and tactic change of the current player from better to worst (from winning to a draw or a draw to losing) is more likely. This particular situation is when the ↓ *tactic* occurs. In the case of abrupt inclining of MinCN, the root value is limited to the available MinCN value only. Thus, this situation implies the likelihood of identifying the tactic change of the current player from worst to better (from losing to a draw or from a draw to winning). This particular situation is when the ↑ *tactic* occurred.

For instance, consider player X with search depth 2 against player O with search depth 3. Generally, player O can be regarded to outperform player X due to lookahead superiority. Figures 2 and 4(a) simulates the mentioned game's progress situation. During the first move, player X chooses the middle position of the board leaving player O with limited options. The MaxCN and MinCN of

Table 1. Maximum Conspiracy numbers of player X against player O with depth variations.

Maximum Conspiracy Numbers									
Depth	**Game Progress**								
(p1,p2)	**1**	**2**	**3**	**4**	**5**	**6**	**7**	**8**	**9**
2,2	8	7	6	5	4	3	2	1	1
2,3	8	22	6	8	4	4	2	1	1
2,4	8	62	6	16	4	4	2	1	1
2,5	8	128	6	17	4	4	2	1	1
2,6	8	288	6	17	4	4	2	1	1
3,2	56	7	26	5	10	3	2	1	1
3,3	56	22	26	8	10	5	2	1	1
3,4	56	62	26	16	10	5	2	1	1
3,5	56	128	26	17	10	5	2	1	1
3,6	56	288	26	17	10	5	2	1	1
4,2	136	7	89	5	17	3	2	1	1
4,3	136	22	89	8	17	3	2	1	1
4,4	136	62	89	16	17	3	2	1	1
4,5	136	128	89	17	17	3	2	1	1
4,6	136	288	89	17	17	3	2	1	1
5,2	360	7	206	5	17	3	2	1	1
5,3	360	22	206	8	17	3	2	1	1
5,4	360	62	206	16	17	3	2	1	1
5,5	360	128	206	17	17	3	2	1	1
5,6	360	288	206	17	17	3	2	1	1
6,2	648	7	295	5	17	3	2	1	1
6,3	648	22	295	8	17	3	2	1	1
6,4	648	62	295	16	17	3	2	1	1
6,5	648	128	295	17	17	3	2	1	1
6,6	648	288	295	17	17	3	2	1	1

p1 = player X, p2 = player O

Table 2. Minimum Conspiracy numbers of player X against player O with depth variations.

Minimum Conspiracy Numbers									
Depth	**Game Progress**								
(p1,p2)	**1**	**2**	**3**	**4**	**5**	**6**	**7**	**8**	**9**
2,2	1	6	1	4	1	3	0	0	0
2,3	1	4	1	4	1	1	0	0	0
2,4	1	13	1	8	1	0	0	0	0
2,5	1	13	1	5	1	0	0	0	0
2,6	1	23	1	1	1	0	0	0	0
3,2	6	6	4	4	0	0	0	0	0
3,3	6	4	4	4	0	0	0	0	0
3,4	6	13	4	8	0	0	0	0	0
3,5	6	13	4	5	0	0	0	0	0
3,6	6	23	4	1	0	0	0	0	0
4,2	4	6	3	4	1	3	0	0	0
4,3	4	4	3	4	1	1	0	0	0
4,4	4	13	3	8	1	0	0	0	0
4,5	4	13	3	5	1	0	0	0	0
4,6	4	23	3	1	1	0	0	0	0
5,2	13	6	5	4	0	3	0	0	0
5,3	13	4	5	4	0	1	0	0	0
5,4	13	13	5	8	0	0	0	0	0
5,5	13	13	5	5	0	0	0	0	0
5,6	13	23	5	1	0	0	0	0	0
6,2	13	6	5	4	0	3	0	0	0
6,3	13	4	5	4	0	1	0	0	0
6,4	13	13	5	8	0	0	0	0	0
6,5	13	13	5	5	0	0	0	0	0
6,6	13	23	5	1	0	0	0	0	0

p1 = player X, p2 = player O

player X is currently 8 and 1 respectively. After considering the vertical, diagonal, and horizontal spaces, player O chooses the upper left corner of the board and currently possess MaxCN and MinCN of 22 and 4 respectively. Consequently, player X chose the upper middle side of the board, which effects MaxCN to decrease steadily, while MinCN remain the same. Next, player O chooses the lower middle of the board which abruptly reduces player O's MaxCN to 8 while MinCN remains the same. This situation imposes that player O is in a *critical position*, even if its intent is to prevent player X from winning. Therefore, player O is in the state of ↓ *tactic* and is advised to apply different tactic. In the next

Table 3. Final scores based on depths of player X against player O

Final Score		Player O				
		2	3	4	5	6
Player X	2	0	0	0	0	0
	3	0	0	0	0	0
	4	−100	−100	−100	−100	−100
	5	−100	−100	−100	−100	−100
	6	−100	−100	−100	−100	−100

move, player X chooses the lower left corner of the board which has forced player O into another bad position. During the consequent move, player O's MaxCN reduces steadily while MinCN is abruptly reduced to 1, which implies that player O has applied ↑ *tactic* where, instead of losing, it tries to force player X into a draw. Thus, the final outcome of the game is a draw.

Another example is the case of player X with search depth 5 against player O with search depth 4 which is given in Figs. 3 and 4(b). During the first move, player X chooses the middle position of the board leaving player O with limited options. The MaxCN and MinCN of player X is currently 360 and 4 respectively. The high value of MaxCN is because of the deeper search depths. In the next move, player O chooses the upper left corner of the board and obtains a MaxCN and MinCN of 62 and 13 respectively. Consequently, player X chooses the upper middle side of the board, making MaxCN and MinCN decreases steadily. During the rest of the moves, the evolution of MaxCN of both player X and player O abruptly reduces, forcing both players into "dilemmas" where both ↓ *tactic* and ↑ *tactic* occur. This situation can be hypothetically defined as the state where both players are able to apply different tactics. On the other hand, observing the MinCN of both player X and player O during fifth and sixth moves implies that both player adopted the ↓ *tactic*. However, player O's leading score plays its part and forces player X to lose the game (assumed final score is winning).

The challenge in the study of speculative play is to identify *critical positions* at which one should consider to apply a kind of speculative strategy such as opponent-model search in order to change the situation: from behind to even or better. Another challenge in GM-level man-machine matches is to identify (no more promising) positions to resign. Therefore, the experiments suggested in this study provide the main foundation for identifying the *critical positions*, although further investigation is expected.

3.2 Othello: Experimental Results and Discussion

Othello takes place between two players, White player and Black player. The default board used in this experiment is 8 × 8 board of 64 squares which is set up by two black discs and two white discs initially as shown as Fig. 8. Black player is always assumed to be the first player to start first and both players must

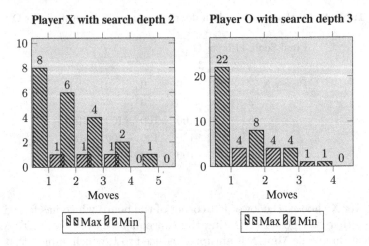

Fig. 2. MaxCN and MinCN for player X with search depth 2 against player O with search depth 3.

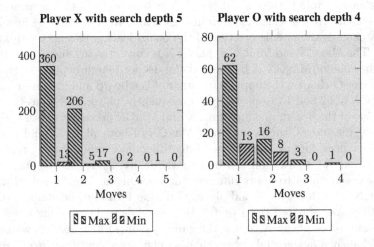

Fig. 3. MaxCN and MinCN for player X with search depth 5 against player O with search depth 4.

not pass or skip turn unless there are no legal moves available [22]. The game continues until neither players are able to move nor all the 64 squares have been played. The Othello program developed in this study is a novice player program with weighted squares strategy [22] that computed the numeric difference of the discs ownership with a given fitness value on certain significant squares on board. These significant squares (usually corners) are given with special names and assigned with evaluation fitness. Each of these squares are assigned with an evaluation fitness value. This fitness value behaves as a penalty to the position scoring function. The penalty calculation is clearly explained in the Appendix A.

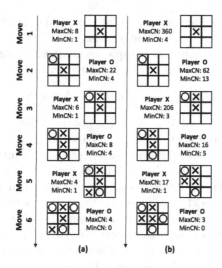

Fig. 4. Simulation of Tic-Tac-Toe games.

The main purpose of adopting an evaluation function in Othello is to apply a scheme that prefers good positions and avoids bad positions to the players. The player's position scoring, S can be obtained with Eq. 1.

$$S = B - W \qquad (1)$$

where B: sum of the black discs on board W: sum of the white discs on board Penalty, P is applied differently to the maximizing (Black) and minimizing (White) players.

$$P_{final} = \begin{cases} S + P & \text{Black player} \\ S - P & \text{White player} \end{cases} \qquad (2)$$

where P_{final}: final position score. The position scoring function of the Othello game are as follows:

- A positive P_{final} value refers to Black player who is leading in the game whereas negative P_{final} value referring to White player who is winning in the game. Draw position of Black and White player can be denoted as zero P_{final} value.
- Black player favours larger positive position scores (maximizing current node's score) while White player favours larger negative position scores (minimizing current node's score).
- Zero position score means that Black and White player are in draw position.

Othello game ends in 60 moves with 64 squares on board deducted with 4 initial discs positions [22]. The game progress of Othello is divided into three phases with approximating dividing lines [23] in this study. The first 20 game progresses are the opening phase following by next 20 game progress of middle phase. The last 20 game progresses are in endgame phase.

In order to analyse the flow of conspiracy numbers changed with the game, the variance of MaxCN and MinCN is calculated as Eq. 3.

$$CN_{variance} = MaxCN - MinCN \tag{3}$$

The variance of MaxCN and MinCN represents the difference of these two conspiracy numbers over the game progress. The idea of analysing the conspiracy numbers variance is to ease the observation of the conspiracy number values changed. By identifying MaxCN and MinCN itself, it is hard to observe the change especially when the Othello program developed in this study is much weaker than the Tic-Tac-Toe program in the previous section. The Tic-Tac-Toe program has the perfect evaluation function which has made the change of MaxCn and MinCN values easier to observe. Moreover, the *critical positions* can be identified through as describe as following. There are four possible outcomes which can be obtained from the variance which is as follows:

- $CN_{variance}$ is a positive value. The value of MaxCN is larger than the value of MinCN, this represents that the current player has to check many nodes in order to obtain higher position score than current nodes. Therefore, the difficulties of current player to obtain higher position score than current position score is high whereas it is easy to obtain a lower position score. If the current player is a minimizing player (White player), it has higher advantage to make a good move and vice versa.
- $CN_{variance}$ is a negative value. The value of MaxCN is lower than the value of MinCN. In this case the current player just has to check few nodes to obtain higher position score than current nodes. Thus, the difficulties of current player to obtain higher position score than current position score is low while obtaining lower position score became hard. If the current player is a maximizing player (Black player), it has higher advantage to choose a better move and vice versa.
- $CN_{variance}$ is a zero value. The zero value ratio represents that the MaxCn is equal with MinCN which both MaxCn and MinCN can be in either equally large or small values. The players have equal number of nodes to be searched for higher or lower position score than current position score. These uncertainties have led to the high possibilities of winning or losing. Therefore, the outcome is inevitable (either win or lose) but not known. In contrast to previous Tic-Tac-Toe experiment, this stage simulates the *critical position* which is highly recommended for applying strategy changing technique.
- $CN_{variance}$ is infinity value. Infinity value indicates that the game has reached to a terminal node where there are no available next move to be played. Positive refers to MaxCN returned infinity value whereas negative $CN_{variance}$ refers to MinCN returned infinity value. When an infinity $CN_{variance}$ value is obtained, it means that the players have to search infinity nodes to get higher or lower position score and the players have no available or valid moves to play next.

In contrast with the Tic-Tac-Toe study, four game set is selected to be evaluated in this section. The opening position in this study is the default opening position as shown as Fig. 8 at the Appendix A. This Othello study is conducted on 3 and 4 search depth for Black player with 3 and 4 search depth for White player under three conditions. They are separately evaluated at the next subsections. The Othello is analysed in the first subsection study by the $CN_{variance}$ value and position scoring. The strategy changing technique is applied to either Black or White player in the next subsection which is followed by applying the technique to both Black and White players. The possible timing for resignation can be identified from first or second subsections and they are discussed in the third subsection. The strategy changing technique in this study is defined by deepening the current search depth by two for both players. This technique is applied to the computer program that has lower search depth than its opponent player.

Game Analysis using $CN_{variance}$ and Position Scoring. Four game set have conducted with different search depth for each player without any strategy changing technique as listed in Table 4.

Table 4. Game set.

Game set	Search depth	
	Black player	White player
1	3	3
2	3	4
3	4	3
4	4	4

The conspiracy numbers and position scoring results of both players from Game set 1 are shown in Figs. 5 and 6. The situations of ↑ *tactic* and ↓ *tactic* are analysed before the endgame phase (40th game progress and following) of the game.

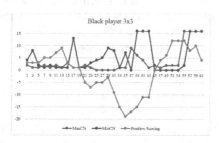

Fig. 5. Game set 1: Black player with search depth 3.

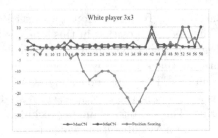

Fig. 6. Game set 1: White player with search depth 3.

Black player's MaxCN abruptly decreases from 3 to 1 at 17th game progress. At this stage, the position scores of Black player have decrease from 3 to 1 where ↓ *tactic* occurs. Next, Black players MinCN reduces abruptly at 5th game progress from 8 to 2 and its position scores remain the same as 3. ↑ *tactic* occurs at this situation by keeping the position scores stable. In contract to the Tic-Tac-Toe study, abruptly decreased MinCN in this study does not always represent ↑ *tactic*. Black players MinCN at 33rd game progress abruptly decreases from 8 to 1 but Black player has lost from 9 discs to 15 discs to White player. White players MaxCN abruptly decreases from 3 to 1 at 16th and 38th game progress. Its position scores change from 0 to −4 (draw to winning) and from −28 to −24 (wining more discs to winning lesser discs). This might be due to the Othello program developed in this study which is a weak program without perfect evaluation function comparing to the Tic-Tac-Toe program that has the perfect evaluation function.

Figures 10, 11, 12 and 13 at Appendix B show the $CN_{variance}$ for the game and the position scoring of Black and White players. A trend line is presented in each figure with the second order polynomial equation of $y = ax^2 + bx + c$. Observing the $CN_{variance}$ of Black player from Figs. 10(a), 11(a) and 13(a), Black player has increasing trend at the game progress from 1st to 20th in the opening phase. This increasing trend represents that MaxCN value is slowly increasing which means that many nodes have to be searched by Black player for higher position score than current position score. Hence, it is difficult to obtain higher position score than current position score. As a maximizing player, Black player has lost its advantage to choose better moves and headed towards a losing position. This assumption can be predicted at the middle phase of the game as shown as Figs. 10(b), 11(b) and 13(b). Next, the $CN_{variance}$ of Black player from Fig. 12(a) shows a decreasing trend at the opening phase that have led the Black player slowly winning against White player at the middle phase as shown as Fig. 12(b). In contract to Black player, increasing $CN_{variance}$ trend at opening phase predicts that White player is getting advantages at the middle phase.

Next, future outcome at the next few game progress can be predicted by examining current $CN_{variance}$. High positive $CN_{variance}$ denotes high difficulty in acquiring higher position score than current score whereas high negative $CN_{variance}$ denotes high difficulty in acquiring lower position score than current score. A conclusion can be drawn that players with a high $CN_{variance}$ value have higher disadvantages in obtaining a better position score.

To summarize, short-term (next few game progress) outcome prediction can be made by observing current $CN_{variance}$ as listed at Eq. 4.

$$Outcome = \begin{cases} Disadvantages & \text{If } CN_{variance} \text{ is high} \\ Advantages & \text{If } CN_{variance} \text{ is zero} \end{cases} \quad (4)$$

While the trend at the opening phase is used to predict long-term (future trend) outcome as shown at Eqs. 5 and 6.

Increasing $CN_{variance}$ trend,

$$Outcome = \begin{cases} Advantages & \text{If White player} \\ Disadvantages & \text{If Black player} \end{cases} \quad (5)$$

Decreasing $CN_{variance}$ trend,

$$Outcome = \begin{cases} Advantages & \text{If Black player} \\ Disadvantages & \text{If White player} \end{cases} \quad (6)$$

Critical positions are identified from both players before the endgame phase. These *critical positions* indicate a situation where the player has high uncertainties in predicting the future short-term or long-term outcome of the move played. Table 5 shows the number of *critical positions* identified in each game set.

Table 5. Position Scoring and Number of Critical Positions in each game set.

Game set	Num. of Critical Pos. (Position Scores — Search depth)	
	Black player	White player
1	7 (20—3)	**5 (44—3)**
2	5 (8—3)	**2 (56—4)**
3	**1 (43—4)**	11 (21—3)
4	4 (17—4)	**0 (46—4)**

Second player (White player) always has advantages in winning when both players have equal search depth. Based on the results shown at Table 5, the winning player has lower number of *critical positions* which means that player has lower uncertainties in predicting the future trend of the moves played and vice versa. Therefore, large numbers of *critical positions* encountered will led that player into a situation where the future trend of the move played is unpredictable. Based on above experiment, the player with higher number of conspiracy numbers lost the game. For example, Fig. 10(c) shows that the move is played on *critical position* at 13th game progress which has led Black player into a worst situation and slowly losing until the endgame phase.

Incorporating Strategy Changing for Black or White Player only. Generally, human expert players require longer time to think carefully at a harder position and vice versa. As for computer players, a strategy needs to be changed at a hard position. In this study, the strategy changing is closely related to the player's search depth. Player with deeper search depth is a stronger player. At a *critical position*, not only the search depth will be deepened; the trend of $CN_{variance}$ also needs to be concerned as well. According to Eq. 5, increasing $CN_{variance}$ benefits White player while decreasing $CN_{variance}$ benefits Black player. When a *critical position* is identified, the trend of $CN_{variance}$ before the *critical position* has to be examined. If it is an increasing trend, Black player's search depth will increase (strategy changing technique) else the search depth will remain or change to the initial search depth. On the other hand, White player's search depth will increase on a decreasing trend and remain or change to the initial search depth on an increasing trend.

To examine the results of the assumption whether deeper search depth is required at a *critical position*, the strategy changing technique is applied to Black player in game set 1, 2 and 4 (where Black player loses at previous experiments) and to White player in game set 3 when a *critical position* is identified. The experimental results are shown in Tables 6 and 7. The grey shaded area indicates that the strategy changing technique is applied on that player. The grey shaded numbers of *critical positions* of Table 7 only record the total number of *critical positions* that applied strategy changing whereas Table 6 and white shaded players recorded the total numbers of *critical positions*. The player that does not involve in the strategy change at that game set is shaded as white.

Table 6. Position Scoring and Number of Critical Positions (before endgame phase) in each game set.

Game set	Num. of Critical Pos. (Position Scores — Search depth,d)	
	Black player	**White player**
1	3(35—$d+2$*)	8 (29—3)
2	3 (0—$d+2$*)	2 (46—4)
3	0 (43—4)	8 (21—$d+2$*)
4	3 (17—$d+2$*)	0 (46—4)

*$d+2$: the initial search depth deepens by 2 on a
critical position by referring to Equation 5 and 6.

Figures 14, 15, 16 and 17 at Appendix C show the $CN_{variance}$ for the game and the position scoring of Black and White players with a trend line. By observing the result and $CN_{variance}$ trend of Game set 1, changing the strategy at the *critical positions* is a beneficial method. Black player increases its search depth by 2 (initial search depth 3) at each identified *critical position* that has increasing $CN_{variance}$ trend before the *critical position*, and it slowly moved to better

Table 7. Position Scoring and Number of Critical Positions (before endgame phase) that apply strategy changing technique in each game set.

Game set	Num. of Critical Pos. (Position Scores — Search depth,d)	
	Black player	**White player**
1	1(35—d+2*)	8 (29—3)
2	1 (0—d+2*)	2 (46—4)
3	0 (43—4)	2 (21—d+2*)
4	1 (17—d+2*)	0 (46—4)

*d+2: the initial search depth deepens by 2 on a *critical position* by referring to Equation 5 and 6.

position at the middle phase. At the end, the game has turned into a more balancing game (final position scoring from 20–44 to 35–29). In this game set, Black player is able to find and play a better move with deeper search depth. Therefore, bad moves that will lead to hard situations can be avoided.

Game set 2 is a unique condition where the game ended at the middle phase. White player wins the game although the strategy changing technique is applied to Black player. In this game set, Black player has encounter a positive infinity $CN_{variance}$ at 29th game progress before endgame phase which means that Black player has to search infinity node in order to find larger position scores. This situation represents that Black player has searched to a terminal node. Therefore, Black player has lost its advantage since a terminal node indicates no available moves.

Game set 3 and 4 does not have any changes in terms of the position scoring. However, the numbers of *critical positions* identified are reduced. For example, the number of *critical positions* of White player had reduced from 11 to 8 (Game set 3), Black player's from 4 to 3 (Game set 4). In this case, strategy changing technique does not help the player in winning the game as Game set 1. However, by increasing the search depth, Black player in game set 4 that has increased search depth are able to search to a terminal node with positive infinity $CN_{variance}$ value (stage 13th), 2 stages earlier than Game set 4 that has no strategy changing technique (stage 15th). Due to Black player had identified a positive infinity $CN_{variance}$ value before endgame phase, Black player has lost its advantages and White player wins the game at the end. Out of the 3 *critical positions* identified by Black player, the search depth is increased at the second *critical position* but it changed back the initial search depth at the third *critical position* before endgame phase. Therefore, the position score does not improve. On the other hand, the significant difference between Game set 3's Figs. 12(b) (without strategy changing) and 15(b) (with strategy changing) is the observation of negative infinity $CN_{variance}$ value before endgame phase. The negative infinity $CN_{variance}$ value is identified at 44th stage in Fig. 12(b) whereas it is identified in Fig. 16(b) at 34th stage. By applying strategy changing technique,

White player is able to observe a negative infinity $CN_{variance}$ value before the endgame phase.

The main idea of changing the strategy at *critical positions* is to keep game balance. This can be done by increasing the search depth on the weaker player in observing the $CN_{variance}$ value. However, the results of changing the strategy on weaker player do not always help in winning the game. It may lead to a losing position as shown as Game set 2, 3 and 4 in this section where positive or negative infinity $CN_{variance}$ can be observed at the earlier stage.

Resignation. Infinity the $CN_{variance}$ values indicates that the player that observed the values have no available moves and have high disadvantages. Therefore, this stage might be the stage where that particular player can resign. Figure 15(a) and (b) of Game set 1 with strategy changing has spotted continuously positive infinity $CN_{variance}$ values which are 29th to 35th stage in Fig. 15(a) and 28th to 36th stage in Fig. 15(b). After that, Fig. 15(c) and (d) show that the position scoring is decreasing starting at 28th stage towards the endgame and White player wins the game. According to Game set 3 with strategy changing technique, negative infinity $CN_{variance}$ values are identified at 33rd to 43rd stage in Fig. 16(a) and 34th to 40th stage in Fig. 16(b). The continuous negative infinity $CN_{variance}$ values represent that White player has losing its advantages continuously. This situation was proved by Fig. 16(c) and (d) where the position scoring is slowly increasing at 33rd stage towards the endgame. Game set 4 also shows the similar situation where positive infinity $CN_{variance}$ values are identified and the position scoring is decreasing towards the endgame with White player wins the game. Therefore, a conclusion can be drawn that when continuously positive (negative) infinity $CN_{variance}$ values are observed, Black (White) player has lost its advantages due to there are no available moves. Hence, this might be the time for Black (White) player to resign.

As summary, the resignation timing is highly dependent to the strength of the players where stronger player has deeper search depth and vice versa. Stronger player is able to foresee the future of the move played by analysing $CN_{variance}$ values which the outcome of the moves played can be either winning or losing. With deeper search depth, the players are able to identify the timing to resign where continuous positive or negative infinity $CN_{variance}$ values are observed.

Weak program (Othello program in this study) that has poor evaluation function will lead to low position scoring accuracy. Therefore, the Othello studies might be affected when its evaluation function is strong. Changing strategy when $CN_{variance}$ is equal to zero might be too aggressive. According to Tables 1 and 2, Player O with search depth 2 (and Player X's search depths are 2, 4, 5 and 6) encountered four *critical positions* where $CN_{variance}$ is equal to zero throughout 25 game set. Therefore, changing search depth at *critical positions* defined as $CN_{variance}$ is equal to zero might be hard to be applied on strong program like the Tic-Tac-Toe program in this study due to there might be no or very less number of *critical positions* can be identified in a game. In this case, changing strategy when $CN_{variance}$ is equal to zero might need to be revised in order to fit both strong and weak game programs.

4 CNS Correlations to PNS

Application of PNS in the previous work such as [24] raised questions whether any correlations exists in the application of CNS as a *critical position* identifier. Theoretically, experimental results obtained from the previous section empowered the possibility of correlation between CNS and PNS as indicators in their respective tree search framework. This section attempts to identify that correlation and give a better picture on the importance of these two indicators. The following section will give a short description on the basis of PNS.

4.1 The Basis of PNS

PNS, like its ancestor CNS, is a best-first search algorithm in which the tree searched so far is stored in memory. The main difference is that PNS aims at proving the true value of root, where the interim minimax values are not considered [17]. The PNS heuristic determines the most promising leaf by selecting a *most-proving node* or *most-promising node* (MPN), which can contribute to either a proof or a disproof of the root if a leaf node is solved. The MPN can be formally defined as the node which, with the least possible effort, potentially contributes most to the establishment of the minimax value of the root. The MPN can be found by manipulating two criteria of the search tree: (1) its shape (determined by the branching factor of every internal node), and (2) the values of the leaves. The basic and un-enhanced PNS is an uninformed search method that does not require any game-specific knowledge beyond its rules [7].

The PNS produces two special values for each node n in order to find MPN. First, the proof number (denoted as $pn(n)$ where pn is the proof number of node n) which is the smallest number of leaf nodes in the subtree starting with n that have to be proven in order to prove that n is a win. Second, the disproof number (denoted as $dn(n)$ where dn is the disproof number of node n) which is the minimum number of leaf nodes that have to be disproved in order to prove that n is a loss.

Calculating the values of pn and dn for each node in the tree is performed in a bottom-up manner. Usually, In a terminal node t, the game-theoretic value is known or the corresponding position has no legal moves. If t is a win, then $pn(t) = 0$ and $dn(t) = 1$. If t is a loss, then $pn(t) = 1$ and $dn(t) = 0$. If t is unknown, then $pn(t) = dn(t) = 1$. In this case, the terminal node t is called a temporary terminal node. For the internal MAX node, it is sufficient to have one child that proves the value of v. The pn of a MAX node is equal to the minimum of the pn of its children. For dn, the only way to disprove v is to disprove v for all its children. So, the dn for MAX node is equal to the sum of the dn of all its children. It is the reverse for the internal MIN node.

However, PNS is famously known for searching the AND/OR tree framework instead of the minimax tree framework. The AND/OR tree is a type of tree where the nodes have only three possible values: true, false, and unknown [24]. Using PNS, the *pn* for an AND/OR tree represents the minimum number of unsolved leaf nodes that need to be solved in order to win in the root. Similarly, the *dn* for an AND/OR tree represents the minimum number of unsolved leaf nodes that need to be solved in order to lose in the root. The PNS always considers the MPN in which the internal nodes can be decided recursively if the terminal node value was decided. Thus, PNS can be used to decide the value of the root node by deciding values of other nodes as soon as possible [24].

4.2   General Correlation of the Elements of CNS and PNS

As described by Ishitobi *et al.* [24], *pn* is related to the difficulty, which relates to the minimum number of unsolved nodes that need to be solved. So, maximum *pn* shows the complexity to solve these unsolved nodes. On the other hand, *dn* is related to the minimum number of unsolved nodes that need to be disproved. Therefore, maximum *dn* shows the complexity to disprove. In other word, both the maximum *pn* and maximum *dn* are an effective measures of difficulty to solve nodes as soon as possible for the AND/OR tree framework.

The MaxCN and MinCN show a correlation to maximum *pn* and maximum *dn* in the minimax tree framework. In the CNS context, MaxCN and MinCN identify the *critical position* in the game's progress for an expected outcome. MaxCN indicates the unlikeliness of root value in achieving a value. Therefore, high value of MaxCN implies the high likeliness of winning or losing. MinCN indicates that the likeliness of root value to achieve a value is limited to the value of MinCN. So, high value of MinCN implies the possibility of target change of the possible estimated outcome. Considering the relation to maximum *pn* and maximum *dn*, we find that high values of MaxCN and MinCN are an effective measures of difficulty of a particular value to be likely. Figure 7 depicts the correlation of CNS and PNS.

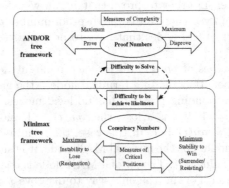

Fig. 7. Correlation between CNS and PNS.

5   Concluding Remarks

In this article, we presented four main contributions:

- The application of conspiracy numbers as the critical position identifier in the context of tic-tac-toe game (two-players perfect information games) and Othello game (two-players weak information games).
- The theoretical correlation of maximum and minimum conspiracy numbers to maximum proof numbers and maximum disproof numbers.
- The application of conspiracy numbers variance in *critical positions* with strategy changing technique that defined by increasing search depth by two.
- The timing of players resignation at a worst situation that the players are not able to change the situation.

In the results presented, we successfully identified the *critical positions* through maximum and minimum conspiracy numbers in most cases of game sets. However, not all game sets support the findings anticipated from the value of the conspiracy numbers variance especially in the Tic-Tac-Toe game. Therefore, further revisions on conspiracy numbers variance are needed in order to identify the perfect timing to change the players strategy. However, Othello game results returned valuable information where the timing of players resignation is able to identify by conspiracy numbers variance. By determining this *critical position* and resignation timing, possible application of strategy changing technique can be explored and exploited to improve the overall game *excitement*. Further explorations on larger and more perfect game searches (Othello with perfect evaluation function, chess, and endgames of difficult positional chess) is the outlook which we will focuses in future studies in order to give a more accurate and extensive understanding on the role of CNS as critical position identifier. Similarly, future work on CNS as critical position identifier will potentially reinforce claims made on its correlation to PNS.

Acknowledgement. This research is funded by a grant from the Japan Society for the Promotion of Science, in the framework of the Grant-in-Aid for Challenging Exploratory Research (grant number26540189).

A   Appendix

Experiment Design

This Othello study is conducted by the default opening position on 8×8 board with 64 squares as shown in Fig. 7. Figure 8 denotes the significant squares that are given special names.

C-squares are adjacent to the corner D while X-squares are diagonally adjacent to the corner D. A-squares and B-squares are the edges of the board [23]. E-squares are adjacent to A-squares and B-squares. The evaluation function is defined as follows (Fig. 9):

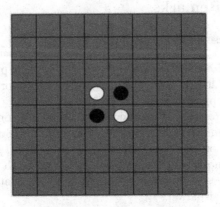

Fig. 8. Othello opening position.

D	C	A	B	B	A	C	D
C	X	E	E	E	E	X	C
A	E					E	A
B	E					E	B
B	E					E	B
A	E					E	A
C	X	E	E	E	E	X	C
D	C	A	B	B	A	C	D

Fig. 9. Significant squares on board.

Table 8. Fitness value of each significant square.

Squares on board	Fitness value
Corner D	40
C-squares	−40
X-squares	−40
A-squares	−30
B-squares	−30
E-squares	−20

*d+2: the initial search depth deepens by 2 on a *critical position* by referring to Eqs. 5 and 6.

- D-squares are good and high priority positions.
- C-squares and X-squares are bad positions which may give chances to the opponent player accessing corner D.
- A-squares are good positions if there exist no opponent's discs at the adjacent squares.
- B-squares are bad positions where the opponent player might has chances to access to A-squares.

Table 8 shows the fitness values that have been assigned to each significant square on board.

B   Appendix

Game Analysis using CN Variance and Position Scoring
Applicable to all the figures
The trend line drawn in position scoring Figs. 10(c), 11(c), 12(c) and 13(c) is closely related to the CN$_{variance}$ trend line at Figs. 10(a), 11(a), 12(a) and 13(a) whereas the trend line drawn in position scoring Figs. 10(d), 11(d), 12(d) and 13(d) is closely related to the CN$_{variance}$ trend line at Figs. 10(b), 11(b), 12(b) and 13(b). CN$_{variance}$ trend line in Figs. 10(a), (b), 11(a), (b), 12(a), (b) and

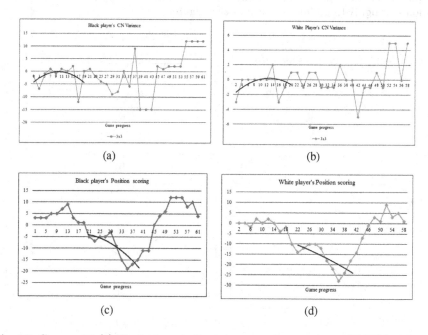

Fig. 10. Game set 1 (a) Black player's Conspiracy numbers variance (b) White player's Conspiracy numbers variance (c) Black player's position scoring (d) White player's position scoring. A trend line is drawn in each figure.

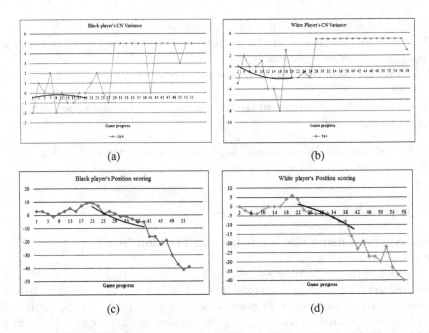

Fig. 11. Game set 2 (a) Black player's Conspiracy numbers variance (b) White player's Conspiracy numbers variance (c) Black player's position scoring (d) White player's position scoring. A trend line is drawn in each figure.

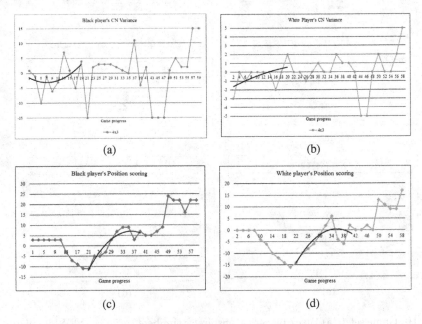

Fig. 12. Game set 3 (a) Black player's Conspiracy numbers variance (b) White player's Conspiracy numbers variance (c) Black player's position scoring (d) White player's position scoring. A trend line is drawn in each figure.

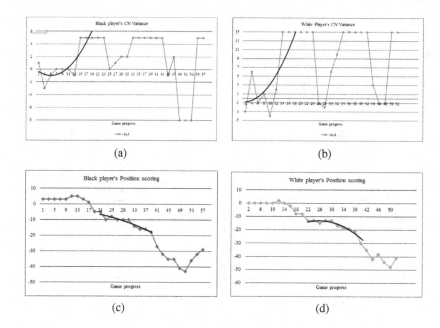

(a)   (b)

(c)   (d)

Fig. 13. Game set 4 (a) Black player's Conspiracy numbers variance (b) White player's Conspiracy numbers variance (c) Black player's position scoring (d) White player's position scoring. A trend line is drawn in each figure.

13(a), (b) can be used to predict the trend of position scoring in Figs. 10(c), (d), 11(c), (d), 12(c), (d) and 13(c), (d).

Increasing $CN_{variance}$ trend line in Figs. 10(a), (b), 11(a), (b), 12(a), (b) and 13(a), (b) will lead to decreasing trend in position scoring which can be observed by Figs. 10(c), (d), 11(c), (d), 12(c), (d) and 13(c), (d). However, trend line observation is not applicable when there are infinity $CN_{variance}$ values.

C   Appendix

Incorporating Strategy Changing for Black or White Player Only
Applicable to all the figures
The trend line drawn in position scoring Figs. 14(c), 15(c), 16(c) and 17(c) is closely related to the $CN_{variance}$ trend line at Figs. 14(a), 15(a), 16(a) and 17(a) whereas the trend line drawn in position scoring Figs. 14(d), 15(d), 16(d) and 17(d) is closely related to the $CN_{variance}$ trend line at Figs. 14(b), 15(b), 16(b) and 17(b). $CN_{variance}$ trend line in Figs. 14(a), (b), 15(a), (b), 16(a), (b) and 17(a), (b) can be used to predict the trend of position scoring in Figs. 14(c), (d), 15(c), (d), 16(c), (d) and 17(c), (d).

Increasing $CN_{variance}$ trend line in Figs. 14(a), (b), 15(a), (b), 16(a), (b) and 17(a), (b) will lead to decreasing trend in position scoring which can be observed

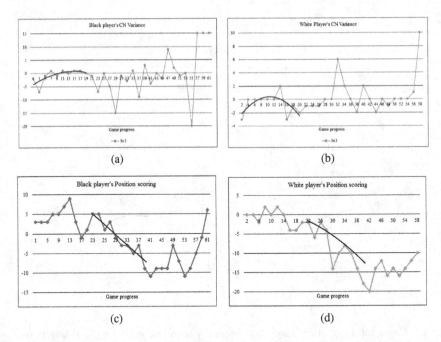

Fig. 14. Game set 1 (a) Black player's Conspiracy numbers variance (b) White player's Conspiracy numbers variance (c) Black player's position scoring (d) White player's position scoring. A trend line is drawn in each figure.

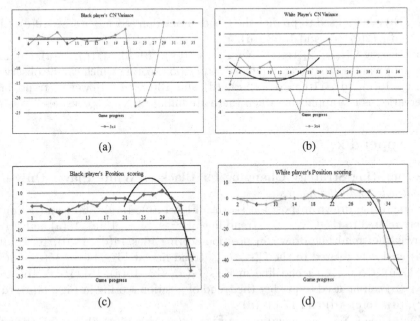

Fig. 15. Game set 2 (a) Black player's Conspiracy numbers variance (b) White player's Conspiracy numbers variance (c) Black player's position scoring (d) White player's position scoring. A trend line is drawn in each figure.

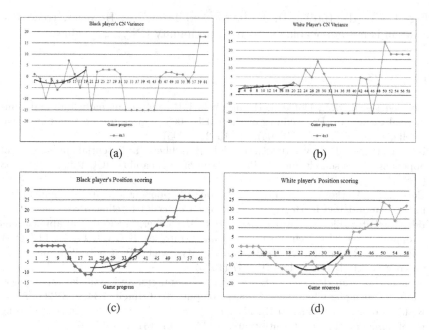

Fig. 16. Game set 3 (a) Black player's Conspiracy numbers variance (b) White player's Conspiracy numbers variance (c) Black player's position scoring (d) White player's position scoring. A trend line is drawn in each figure.

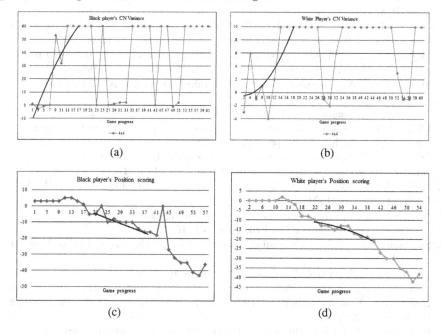

Fig. 17. Game set 4 (a) Black player's Conspiracy numbers variance (b) White player's Conspiracy numbers variance (c) Black player's position scoring (d) White player's position scoring. A trend line is drawn in each figure.

by Figs. 14(c), (d), 15(c), (d), 16(c), (d) and 17(c), (d). However, trend line observation is not applicable when there are infinity $CN_{variance}$ values.

References

1. van den Herik, H.J., Donkers, H., Spronck, P.H.: Opponent modelling and commercial games. In: Proceedings of the IEEE 2005 Symposium on Computational Intelligence and Games (CIG05), pp. 15–25 (2005)
2. Iida, H., Uiterwijk, J., van den Herik, H.J., Herschberg, I.: Potential applications of opponent-model search: Part 1. The domain of applicability. ICCA J. **16**, 201–208 (1993)
3. Carmel, D., Markovitch, S.: Learning models of opponent's strategy in game playing. Technion-Israel Institute of Technology, Center for Intelligent Systems (1993)
4. Iida, H., Uiterwijk, J., van den Herik, H.J., Herschberg, I.: Potential applications of opponent-model search. Part 2: risks and strategies. ICCA J. **17**, 10–14 (1994)
5. Lorenz, U., Rottmann, V., Feldmann, R., Mysliwietz, P.: Controlled conspiracy number search. ICCA J. **18**, 135–147 (1995)
6. Schaeffer, J., van den Herik, H.J.: Games, computers, and artificial intelligence. Chips Challenging Champions Games Comput. Artif. Intell. **134**, 1–8 (2002)
7. Kishimoto, A., Winands, M.H., Müller, M., Saito, J.T.: Game-tree search using proof numbers: the first twenty years. ICGA J. **35**, 131–156 (2012)
8. Jansen, P.: Using knowledge about the opponent in game-tree search. Ph.D. thesis, Carnegie Mellon University (1992)
9. Donkers, J.: Nosce Hostem: Searching with Opponent Models. Ph.D. thesis, Universiteit Maastricht (2003)
10. Ramon, J., Jacobs, N., Blockeel, H.: Opponent modeling by analysing play. In: Proceedings of Workshop on Agents in Computer Games. Citeseer (2002)
11. McAllester, D.A.: A new procedure for growing min-max trees. Technical report, Artificial Intelligence Laboratory, MIT, Cambridge, MA, USA (1985)
12. McAllester, D.A.: Conspiracy numbers for min-max search. Artif. Intell. **35**, 287–310 (1988)
13. Schaeffer, J.: Conspiracy numbers. Adv. Comput. Chess **5**, 199–218 (1989)
14. Elkan, C.: Conspiracy numbers and caching for searching and/or trees and theorem-proving. In: IJCAI, pp. 341–348 (1989)
15. Schaeffer, J.: Conspiracy numbers. Artif. Intell. **43**, 67–84 (1990)
16. van der Meulen, M.: Conspiracy-number search. ICCA J. **13**, 3–14 (1990)
17. Allis, L.V., van der Meulen, M., van den Herik, H.J.: Proof-number search. Artif. Intell. **66**, 91–124 (1994)
18. Neumann, L.J., Morgenstern, O.: Theory of Games and Economic Behavior, vol. 60. Princeton University Press Princeton, NJ (1947)
19. Shannon, C.E.: Xxii. programming a computer for playing chess. Philos. Mag. **41**, 256–275 (1950)
20. McAllester, D.A., Yuret, D.: Alpha-beta-conspiracy search (1993)
21. Buro, M.: From simple features to sophisticated evaluation functions. In: van den Herik, H.J., Iida, H. (eds.) CG 1998. LNCS, vol. 1558, pp. 126–145. Springer, Heidelberg (1999)
22. Rosenbloom, P.S.: A world-championship-level othello program. Artif. Intell. **19**, 279–320 (1982)

23. Landau, T.: Othello: Brief & basic. US Othello Association 920, pp. 22980–23425 (1985)
24. Ishitobi, T., Cincotti, A., Iida, H.: Shape-keeping technique and its application to checkmate problem composition. In: Ninth Artificial Intelligence and Interactive Digital Entertainment Conference (2013)

Infinite Horizon Multi-armed Bandits with Reward Vectors: Exploration/Exploitation Trade-off

Madalina M. Drugan$^{(\boxtimes)}$

Artificial Intelligence Lab, Vrije Universiteit Brussel, Pleinlaan 2,
1050 Brussels, Belgium
mdrugan@vub.ac.be

Abstract. We focus on the effect of the exploration/exploitation trade-off strategies on the algorithmic design off multi-armed bandits (MAB) with reward vectors. Pareto dominance relation assesses the quality of reward vectors in infinite horizon MABs, like the UCB1 and UCB2 algorithms. In single objective MABs, there is a trade-off between the exploration of the suboptimal arms, and exploitation of a single optimal arm. Pareto dominance based MABs fairly exploit all Pareto optimal arms, and explore suboptimal arms. We study the exploration vs exploitation trade-off for two UCB like algorithms for reward vectors. We analyse the properties of the proposed MAB algorithms in terms of upper regret bounds and we experimentally compare their exploration vs exploitation trade-off on a bi-objective Bernoulli environment coming from control theory.

Keywords: Multi-armed bandits · Multi-objective optimisation · Pareto dominance relation · Infinite horizon policies

1 Introduction

Multi-armed bandits (MAB) is a machine learning paradigm used to study and analyse resource allocation in stochastic and noisy environments. The *multi-objective multi-armed bandits* (MOMAB) problem is an extension of MAB to reward vectors and imports techniques from multi-objective optimisation for an efficient exploration/exploitation mechanism. Some of these techniques were also imported in other related learning paradigms: multi-objective Markov Decision Processes [1,2], and multi-objective reinforcement learning [3,4].

Multi-objective MAB with stochastic reward vectors with finite set of arms, let $\mathcal{A}$ the set of these K arms, where $K \leq 2$, receive for one arm pull a random vector of rewards, one component per objective. The random vectors have a stationary distribution with support in the D-dimensional hypercube $[0, 1]^D$, and the vector of true expected rewards $\boldsymbol{\mu}_i = (\mu_i^1, \ldots, \mu_i^D)$ is unknown, where D is the number of objectives. All rewards $\mathbf{X}_t^i$ obtained from any arm i are independently

© Springer International Publishing Switzerland 2015
B. Duval et al. (Eds.): ICAART 2015, LNAI 9494, pp. 128–144, 2015.
DOI: 10.1007/978-3-319-27947-3_7

and identically distributed according to an an unknown law. Reward vectors obtained from different arms are also assumed to be independent.

MOMAB algorithm chooses the next machine to play based on the sequence of past plays and obtained reward vectors. *Pareto dominance relation* [5] is a partial order relation for (reward) vectors that considers that a reward vector can be optimal one objective and sub-optimal in other objectives, leading to many vector rewards of the same quality. There could be several arms considered to be the best according to their reward vectors. *Pareto front* is the set of optimal arms of the same quality. An adequate performance indicator for MOMABs is the regret of pulling suboptimal arms and it measures the distance between a suboptimal reward vector and the Pareto front [6]. An alternative measure of performance for MOMABs is a regret function that indicates the variance in using each Pareto optimal arm. Similarly with multi-objective optimization, all Pareto optimal arms are considered equally important and the variance in using all these arms should be minimized. Section 2 gives background information on MOMABs.

Exploration/exploitation trade-off is an essential mechanism in MABs: exploration means pulling the suboptimal arms that might have been unlucky, whereas exploitation means pulling as much as possible the optimal arms. The two mechanisms are not trivial and their balance means an efficient MABs that explore enough the suboptimal arms to ensure that they are not erroneously classified as such, and exploit very often the optimal arm to minimize the regret in pulling suboptimal arms. In this paper, we study the exploration vs exploitation trade-off in two infinite horizon MOMABs with the goal of minimizing the regret. The exploration vs exploitation trade-off is different for single objective MABs and for MOMABs. In MOMABs, by design, we should pull equally often all the arms in the Pareto front. Thus, the exploitation now means the fair usage of Pareto optimal arms, and furthermore, the quality of each suboptimal arm is now assessed using all the Pareto optimal arms.

We propose several MOMAB algorithms that are an extension of the classical single objective MAB algorithms, i.e. UCB1 and UCB2 [7], to reward vectors. We consider the Pareto UCB1 [6] to be an exploratory variant of UCB1 because each round only *one* Pareto optimal arm is pulled. In Sect. 3, we propose an exploitative variant of the Pareto UCB1 algorithm where, each round, *all* the Pareto optimal arms are pulled. We show that the analytical properties, i.e. upper confidence bound of the Pareto projection regret, for the exploitative Pareto UCB1 are improved when compared with the exploratory variant of the same algorithm because this bound is independent of the cardinality of the Pareto front.

Section 4 proposes two multi-objective variants of UCB2 for reward vectors corresponding to the two exploitation vs exploration mechanisms. The exploitative Pareto UCB2 introduced in Sect. 4.1 is an extension of UCB2 where, each epoch, all the Pareto optimal arms are pulled equally often. The exploratory Pareto UCB2 algorithm, see Sect. 4.2, pulls each epoch a single Pareto optimal arm. We compute the upper bound of the Pareto projection regret for the exploitative Pareto UCB2 algorithm.

Section 5 experimentally compares the proposed MOMAB algorithms on a stochastic bi-objective environments showing the superior performance of UCB2 based MOMABs but no practical advantage in using explorative or exploitative variants of the same MOMAB. Section 6 concludes the paper.

2   Multi-objective Multi-armed Bandits Paradigm

We consider the general case where a reward vector can be better than another reward vector in one objective, and worse in another objective. Expected reward vectors are compared according to the **Pareto dominance relation** [5]. A vector μ is *dominating*, another vector ν, $\nu \prec \mu$, iff there exists at least one objective o for which $\nu^o < \mu^o$ and for all other objectives j, $j \neq i$, we have $\nu^j \leq \mu^j$. The vector μ is *non-dominated* by ν, $\nu \not\prec \mu$, iff there exists at least one objective o for which $\nu^o < \mu^o$. Let $\mathcal{A}^*$ be the Pareto front, i.e. non-dominated by any arm in $\mathcal{A}$.

The goal of a MOMAB algorithm is to simultaneously minimise the regret of not selecting the Pareto optimal arms by fairly playing all the arms in the Pareto front. In order to measure the performance of these algorithms, we define two Pareto regret metrics. The first regret metric measures the loss in pulling arms that are not Pareto optimal and is called the *Pareto projection regret*. The second metric, the *Pareto variance regret*, measures the variance in pulling each arm from the Pareto front $\mathcal{A}^*$.

The Pareto Projection Regret expresses the expected loss due to the play of suboptimal arms. For this purpose, it uses the Euclidean distance between the mean reward vector μ_i of an arm i and its projection ν_i into the Pareto front. A vector ϵ_i with equal components ϵ_i, i.e. $\epsilon_i = (\epsilon_i, \epsilon_i, \cdots, \epsilon_i)$, is added to μ_i such that ϵ_i is the smallest value for which $\nu_i = \mu_i + \epsilon_i$ becomes Pareto optimal. The Euclidean distance Δ_i between μ_i and its projection ν_i into the Pareto front equals:

$$\Delta_i = \|\nu_i - \mu_i\|_2 = \|\epsilon_i\|_2 = \sqrt{D}\epsilon_i \tag{1}$$

where the last equality holds because we have D objectives and all components of ϵ_i are the same.

Since by definition Δ_i is always non-negative, the resulting regret is also non-negative. Note that the for a Pareto optimal arm $\nu_i = \mu_i$ and $\Delta_i = 0$.

Let $T_i(n)$ be the number of times that arm i has been played after n plays in total. Then the Pareto projection regret $R_p(n)$ after n plays is defined as:

$$R_p(n) = \sum_{i \notin \mathcal{A}^*} \Delta_i \mathbb{E}[T_i(n)] \tag{2}$$

where Δ_i is defined in Eq. 1 and where $\mathbb{E}$ is the expectation operator. A similar regret metric was introduced in [6].

The Pareto Variance Regret Metric measures the variance of a Pareto-MAB algorithm in pulling all optimal arms. We use the superscript $*$ when we mean a Pareto optimal arm. Let $T_i^*(n)$ be the number of times an optimal arm i is pulled during n total arm pulls. Let $\mathbb{E}[T_i^*(n)]$ the expected number of times the Pareto optimal arm i is pulled. The Pareto variance regret is defined as

$$R_v(n) = \frac{1}{|\mathcal{A}^*|} \sum_{i \in \mathcal{A}^*} \left(\mathbb{E}[T_i^*(n)] - \frac{\mathbb{E}[T^*(n)]}{|\mathcal{A}^*|} \right)^2 \tag{3}$$

where $\mathbb{E}[T^*(n)]$ is the expected number of times that *any* Pareto optimal arm is selected, and $|\mathcal{A}^*|$ is the cardinality of the Pareto front $\mathcal{A}$.

If all Pareto optimal arms are played in a fair way, i.e. an equal number of times, then $R_v(n)$ is minimized. For a perfect fair, or equal, usage of the Pareto optimal arms, we have $R_v(n) \leftarrow 0$. If a Pareto MAB-algorithm identifies only a subset of $\mathcal{A}^*$, then $R_v(n)$ is large. A similar measure, called unfairness, was proposed in [6] to measure variance of a Pareto-MAB algorithm in pulling all Pareto optimal arms.

3   Exploration vs Exploitation Trade-off in Pareto UCB1

The Pareto UCB1 algorithm [6] is an UCB1 algorithm using the Pareto dominance relation to partially order the reward vectors. The index of Pareto UCB1 has two terms: the mean reward vector, and the second term related to the size of a one-sided confidence interval of the average reward according to the Chernoff-Hoeffding bounds. In this section, we propose a Pareto UCB1 algorithm with a theoretical improved exploration vs exploitation trade-off because its performance does not depend on the size of Pareto front. In each round, all the Pareto optimal arms are pulled instead of pulling only one arm. This means that the proposed Pareto UCB1 algorithm has an aggressive exploitation mechanism of Pareto optimal arms to improve it upper regret bound. We call this algorithm *exploitative Pareto UCB1*, as opposite with the Pareto UCB1 algorithm from [6], here called *exploratory Pareto UCB1*.

Algorithm 1. Exploitative Pareto UCB1.

1: Play each arm i once
2: $t \leftarrow 0$; $n \leftarrow K$; $n_i \leftarrow 1, \forall i$
3: **while** the stopping criteria is NOT met **do**
4:     $t \leftarrow t + 1$
5:     Select the Pareto front at the round t, $\mathcal{A}^{*(t)}$, such that $\forall i \in \mathcal{A}^{*(t)}$ the index
       $\hat{\mu}_i + \sqrt{\frac{2 \ln(n \sqrt[4]{D})}{n_i}}$ is non-dominated
6:     Pull each arm i once, where $i \in \mathcal{A}^{*(t)}$
7:     $\forall i \in \mathcal{A}^{*(t)}$, update $\hat{\mu}_i$, and $n_i \leftarrow n_i + 1$
8:     $n \leftarrow n + |\mathcal{A}^{*(t)}|$
9: **end while**

3.1   Exploitative Pareto UCB1

The pseudo-code for *exploitative Pareto UCB1* is given in Algorithm 1. At initialization, each arm is played once. Let $\hat{\boldsymbol{\mu}}_i$ be the estimation of the true but unknown expected reward vector $\boldsymbol{\mu}_i$ of an arm i. In each iteration, we compute for each arm i its index, i.e. the sum of the estimated reward vector $\hat{\boldsymbol{\mu}}_i$ and the associated confidence value of arm i

$$\hat{\boldsymbol{\mu}}_i + \sqrt{\frac{2\ln(n\sqrt[4]{D})}{n_i}} = \left(\hat{\mu}_i^1 + \sqrt{\frac{2\ln(n\sqrt[4]{D})}{n_i}}, \dots, \hat{\mu}_i^D + \sqrt{\frac{2\ln(n\sqrt[4]{D})}{n_i}}\right)$$

At each time step t, the Pareto front $\mathcal{A}^{*(t)}$ is determined using the indexes $\hat{\boldsymbol{\mu}}_i + \sqrt{\frac{2\ln(n\sqrt[4]{D})}{n_i}}$. Thus, for all arms not in the Pareto front $i \notin \mathcal{A}^{*(t)}$, there exists a Pareto optimal arm $h \in \mathcal{A}^{*(t)}$ that dominates arm i:

$$\hat{\boldsymbol{\mu}}_h + \sqrt{\frac{2\ln(n\sqrt[4]{D})}{n_h}} \succ \hat{\boldsymbol{\mu}}_i + \sqrt{\frac{2\ln(n\sqrt[4]{D})}{n_i}}$$

Each iteration, exploitative Pareto UCB1 selects *all* Pareto optimal arm from $\mathcal{A}^{*(t)}$ and pull them for an equal number of iterations. Thus, by design, this algorithm is fair in selecting Pareto optimal arms. Next, the estimated vector of the selected arm $\hat{\boldsymbol{\mu}}_h$ and the corresponding counters are updated. A possible stopping criteria is a given fix number of iterations.

The following theorem provides an upper bound for the Pareto regret of the efficient Pareto UCB1 strategy. The only difference is that a suboptimal arm is pulled $|\mathcal{A}^*|$ times less often than in the exploratory Pareto UCB1 algorithm. This fact is reflected by the multiplicative constant, $\sqrt[4]{D}$, in the index of the algorithm.

Theorem 1. *Let exploitative Pareto UCB1 from Algorithm 1 be run on a K-armed D-objective bandit problem, $K > 1$, having arbitrary reward distributions $\mathbf{P}_1, \dots \mathbf{P}_K$ with support in $[0,1]^D$. Consider the Pareto regret defined in Eq. 1. The expected Pareto projection regret of after any number of n plays is at most*

$$\sum_{i \notin \mathcal{A}^*} \frac{8 \cdot \ln(n\sqrt[4]{D})}{\Delta_i} + \left(1 + \frac{\pi^2}{3}\right) \cdot \sum_{i \notin \mathcal{A}^*} \Delta_i$$

Proof. This prove follows closely the prove from [6]. Let $\mathbf{X}_{i,1}, \dots, \mathbf{X}_{i,n}$ be random D-dimensional variables generated for arm i with common range $[0,1]^D$. The expected reward vector for the arm i after n pulls is $\bar{\mathbf{X}}_{i,n} = 1/n \cdot \sum_{t=1}^n \mathbf{X}_{i,t}$, where $\forall j$, $\bar{X}_{i,n}^j = 1/n \cdot \sum_{t=1}^n X_{i,t}^j$.

Chernoff-Hoeffding bound. We use a straightforward generalization of the standard Chernoff-Hoeffding bound to D objectives environments. Consider that $\forall j$, $1 \le j \le D$, $\mathbb{E}[X_{i,t}^j \mid X_{i,1}^j, \dots, X_{i,t-1}^j] = \mu_i^j$. There, $\bar{\mathbf{X}}_{i,n} \not\prec \boldsymbol{\mu}_i + a$ if there exists *at least* a dimension j for which $\bar{X}_{i,n}^j > \mu_i^j + a$. Translated in Chernoff-Hoeffding bound, using union bound, we have for all $a \geq 0$

$$\mathbb{P}\{(\bar{\mathbf{X}}_{i,n} \not< \boldsymbol{\mu}_i + a)\} = \mathbb{P}\{(\bar{X}_{i,n}^1 > \mu_i^1 + a) \vee \ldots \vee (\bar{X}_{i,n}^D > \mu_i^D + a)\} \leq De^{-2na^2} \tag{4}$$

Following the same line of reasoning

$$\mathbb{P}\{(\bar{X}_{i,n}^1 < \mu_i^1 - a) \vee \ldots \vee (\bar{X}_{i,n}^D < \mu_i^D - a)\} \leq De^{-2na^2} \tag{5}$$

Let $\ell > 0$ an arbitrary number. We take $c_{t,s} = \sqrt{2 \cdot \ln(t\sqrt[4]{D})/s}$, and we upper bound $T_i(n)$ on any sequence of plays by bounding for each $t \geq 1$ the indicator $(I_t = i)$. We have $(I_t = i) = 1$ if arm i is played at time t and $(I_t = i) = 0$ otherwise. Then,

$$T_i(n) = 1 + \sum_{t=K+1}^{n} \{I_t = i\} \leq \ell + \sum_{t=K+1}^{n} \{I_t = i, T_i(t-1) \geq \ell\}$$

$$\leq \ell + \sum_{t=K+1}^{n} \frac{1}{|\mathcal{A}^*|} \cdot \sum_{h=1}^{|\mathcal{A}^*|} \{\bar{\mathbf{X}}_{h,T_h^*(t-1)}^* + c_{t-1,T_h^*(t-1)} \not\succ \bar{\mathbf{X}}_{i,T_i(t-1)} + c_{t-1,T_i(t-1)}\}$$

$$\leq_{\substack{s_h^* \leftarrow T_h^*(t-1) \\ s_i \leftarrow T_i(t-1)}} \ell + \sum_{t=1}^{\infty}\sum_{s=1}^{t-1}\sum_{s_i=\ell}^{t-1} \frac{1}{|\mathcal{A}^*|} \sum_{h=1}^{|\mathcal{A}^*|} \{\bar{\mathbf{X}}_{h,s_h^*}^* + c_{t-1,s_h^*} \not\succ \bar{\mathbf{X}}_{i,s_i} + c_{t-1,s_i}\} \tag{6}$$

From the straightforward generalization of Chernoff-Hoeffding bound to D objectives, we have that

$$\mathbb{P}\{\bar{\mathbf{X}}_i^{(t)} \not\prec \boldsymbol{\mu}_i + c_s^{(t)}\} \leq \frac{D}{D} \cdot t^{-4} = t^{-4}$$

and

$$\mathbb{P}\{\bar{\mathbf{X}}_h^{*(t)} \not\succ \boldsymbol{\mu}_h^* - c_{s_h^*}^{(t)}\} \leq t^{-4}$$

For $s_i \geq \frac{8 \cdot \ln(n\sqrt[4]{D})}{\Delta_i^2}$, we have that

$$\nu_i^* - \mu_i - 2 \cdot c_{t,s_i} = \nu_i^* - \mu_i - 2 \cdot \sqrt{\frac{2 \cdot \ln(n\sqrt[4]{D})}{s_i}} \geq \nu_i^* - \mu_i - \Delta_i$$

Thus, we take $\ell = \lceil \frac{8 \cdot \ln(n\sqrt[4]{D})}{\Delta_i^2} \rceil$, and we have

$$\mathbb{E}[T_i(n)] \leq \lceil \frac{8 \cdot \ln(n\sqrt[4]{D})}{\Delta_i^2} \rceil +$$

$$\sum_{t=1}^{\infty}\sum_{s=1}^{t-1} \sum_{s_i=\lceil \frac{8 \cdot \ln(n\sqrt[4]{D})}{\Delta_i^2} \rceil}^{} \sum_{h=1}^{|\mathcal{A}^*|} (\mathbb{P}\{\bar{\mathbf{X}}_h^{*(t)} \not\succ \boldsymbol{\mu}_h^* - c_{s_h}^{(t)}\} + \mathbb{P}\{\bar{\mathbf{X}}_i^{(t)} \not\prec \boldsymbol{\mu}_i + c_{s_i}^{(t)}\})$$

$$\leq \frac{8 \cdot \ln (n \cdot \sqrt[4]{D})}{\Delta_i^2} + 1 + \sum_{t=1}^{\infty} \sum_{s=1}^{t} \sum_{s_i=1}^{t} \sum_{h=1}^{|\mathcal{A}^*|} t^{-4} \frac{t^{-4}}{|\mathbb{A}^*|} \leq$$

$$\frac{8 \cdot \ln (n\sqrt[4]{D})}{\Delta_i^2} + 1 + 2 \cdot \sum_{t=1}^{\infty} t^2 \cdot |\mathcal{A}^*| \frac{t^{-4}}{|\mathcal{A}^*|} = \frac{8 \cdot \ln (n\sqrt[4]{D})}{\Delta_i^2} + 1 + 2 \cdot \sum_{t=1}^{\infty} t^{-2}$$

Approximating the last term with the Riemann zeta function $\zeta(2) = \sum_{t=1}^{\infty} t^{-2} \approx \frac{\pi^2}{6}$ we obtain the bound from the theorem. $\qquad \square$

For a suboptimal arm i, we have $\mathbb{E}[T_i(n)] \leq \frac{8}{\Delta_i^2} \ln(n\sqrt[4]{D})$ plus a small constant. Like for the standard UCB1, the leading constant is $8/\Delta_i^2$ and the expected upper bound of the Pareto regret for the exploitative Pareto UCB1 is logarithmic in the number of plays n. Unlike exploratory Pareto UCB1 [6], the expected regret bound for exploitative Pareto UCB1 does not depend on the cardinality of the Pareto front $\mathcal{A}^*$ which is usually not known beforehand, and it increases with the number of objectives.

Note that for $D = 1$ the algorithm reduces to the standard UCB1. Thus, exploitative Pareto UCB1 performs similarly with the standard UCB1 for small number of objectives. However, for large Pareto front where all almost all the arms K are Pareto optimal arms, $|\mathcal{A}|^* \approx K$, the exploitative Pareto UCB1 algorithm pulls once (almost) all arms making the exploitative Pareto UCB1 algorithm impractical.

3.2   Exploratory Pareto UCB1

The exploratory version of Pareto UCB1 algorithm was introduced in [6] and it is a straightforward extension of the UCB1 algorithm to reward vectors. The main difference between the exploratory Pareto UCB1 and the exploitative Pareto UCB1, cf Algorithm 1, is in lines 6–8 of the algorithm. For the exploratory Pareto UCB1 algorithm, each iteration, a single Pareto optimal arm is selected uniformly at random and pulled. The counters are updated accordingly, meaning that $n \leftarrow n + 1$.

Another difference is the index associated to the mean vector that is larger than for the exploitative Pareto UCB1. Thus, the Pareto set is now the non-dominated vectors $\hat{\mu}_i + \sqrt{\frac{2\ln(n\sqrt[4]{D|\mathcal{A}^*|})}{n_i}}$.

The regret bound for the exploratory Pareto UCB1 algorithm using Pareto regrets is logarithmic in the number of plays for a suboptimal arm and in the size of the reward vectors, D. In addition, this confidence bound is also logarithmic in the cardinality of Pareto front, $|\mathcal{A}^*|$.

4   Exploration vs Exploitation Trade-Off in Pareto UCB2

In this section, we propose Pareto MAB algorithms that extend of the standard UCB2 algorithm to reward vectors. Pareto UCB2 algorithms play the optimal arms in epochs with a length that exponentially increase with the number of pulls to play good arms longer each epoch. In single objective MABs, the UCB2 algorithm is acknowledged to have a better upper regret bound than the UCB1 algorithm [7]. We show that Pareto UCB2 algorithms have a better upper Pareto projection regret bound than the Pareto UCB1 algorithms.

The first proposed Pareto UCB2 algorithm, see Sect. 4.1, plays in an epoch *all* Pareto optimal arms equally often. We call this algorithm exploitative Pareto UCB2. The second Pareto UCB2 algorithm introduced in Sect. 4.2 plays only *one* Pareto optimal arm per epoch. We call this algorithm exploratory Pareto UCB2.

Algorithm 2. Exploitative Pareto UCB2.

Require: $0 < \alpha < 1$; the length of a epoch r is an exponential function $\tau(r) = \lceil (1+\alpha)^r \rceil$
1: Play each arm once
2: $n \leftarrow K$; $r_i \leftarrow 1, \forall i$
3: **while** the stopping condition is NOT met **do**
4:     Select the Pareto front at the epoch r, $\mathcal{A}^{*(r)}$, such that $\forall i \in \mathcal{A}^{*(r)}$, the index $\hat{\boldsymbol{\mu}}_i + a_n^{\tau(r_i)}$ is non-dominated
5:     **for all** $i \in \mathcal{A}^{*(t)}$ **do**
6:         Pull the arm i exactly $\tau(r_i + 1) - \tau(r_i)$
7:         Update $\hat{\boldsymbol{\mu}}_i$, and $r_i \leftarrow r_i + 1$
8:         $r \leftarrow r + 1$ and $n \leftarrow n + \tau(r + 1) - \tau(r)$
9:     **end for**
10: **end while**

4.1 Exploitative Pareto UCB2

In this section, we present the *exploitative Pareto UCB2* algorithm and we analyse its upper confidence bound. The pseudo-code for this algorithm is given in Algorithm 2.

As an initial step, we play each arm once. The plays are divided in epochs, r, of exponential length until a stopping criteria is met a fix number of arm' pulls. The length of an epoch is an exponential function $\tau(r) = \lceil (1+\alpha)^r \rceil$. In each epoch, we compute for each arm i an index given by with the sum of expected rewards plus a second term for the confidence value

$$\hat{\boldsymbol{\mu}}_i + a_n^{\tau(r_i)} \leftarrow \left(\hat{\mu}_i^1 + a_n^{\tau(r_i)}, \ldots, \hat{\mu}_i^D + a_n^{\tau(r_i)} \right)$$

where $a_n^{\tau(r_i)} = \sqrt{\frac{(1+\alpha)\cdot \ln(e \cdot n/(D \cdot \tau(r_i)))}{2 \cdot \tau(r_i)}}$, and r_i is the number of epochs played by the arm i. A Pareto front $\mathcal{A}^{*(r)}$ is selected from all vectors $\hat{\boldsymbol{\mu}}_i + a_n^{\tau(r_i)}$. Thus, $\forall i \in \mathcal{A}$, exists $h \in \mathcal{A}^{*(t)}$, such that we have

$$\hat{\boldsymbol{\mu}}_h + a_n^{\tau(r_h)} \succ \hat{\boldsymbol{\mu}}_i + a_n^{\tau(r_i)}$$

Each arm $i \in \mathcal{A}^{*(t)}$ is selected and played $\tau(r_i + 1) - \tau(r_i)$ consecutive times. The mean value and the epoch counter for all Pareto optimal arms are updated accordingly, meaning that $r_i \leftarrow r_i + 1$. The total epoch counter, r, and the total number of arms' pulls n are also updated.

The following theorem bounds the expected regret for the Pareto UCB2 strategy from Algorithm 2.

Theorem 2. *Let exploitative Pareto UCB2 from Algorithm 2 be run on K-armed bandit, $K > 1$, having arbitrary reward distributions $\mathbf{P}_1, \ldots \mathbf{P}_K$ with support in $[0, 1]^D$. Consider the regret defined in Eq. 1.*

The expected regret of a strategy π after any number of $n \geq \max_{\hat{\mu}_i \notin \mathcal{A}^*} \frac{D}{2 \cdot \Delta_i^2}$ plays is at most

$$\sum_{i:\hat{\mu}_i \notin \mathcal{A}^*} \left(D \cdot \frac{(1+\alpha) \cdot (1 + 4 \cdot \alpha) \cdot \ln(2 \cdot e \cdot \Delta_i^2 \cdot n/D)}{2 \cdot \Delta_i} + \frac{c_\alpha}{\Delta_i} \right)$$

where

$$c_\alpha = 1 + \frac{D^2 \cdot (1+\alpha) \cdot e}{\alpha^2} + D^{\alpha+2} \cdot \left(\frac{\alpha+1}{\alpha} \right)^{(1+\alpha)} \cdot \left(1 + \frac{11 \cdot D \cdot (1+\alpha)}{5 \cdot \alpha^2 \cdot \ln(1+\alpha)} \right)$$

Proof. This prove is based on the homologue prove of [7]. We consider $n \geq \frac{D}{2 \cdot \Delta_i^2}$, for all i. From the definition of $\tau(r)$ we can deduce that $\tau(r) \leq \tau(r-1) \cdot (1-\alpha) + 1$.

Let $\tau(\tilde{r}_i)$ be the largest integer such that

$$\tau(\tilde{r}_i - 1) \leq \frac{D \cdot (1 + 4 \cdot \alpha) \cdot \ln(2 \cdot e \cdot n \cdot \Delta_i^2/D)}{2 \cdot \Delta_i^2}$$

We have that for an suboptimal arm i

$$T_i(n) \leq 1 + \frac{1}{|\mathcal{A}^*|} \cdot \sum_{r \geq 1} (\tau(r) - \tau(r-1)) \cdot \{\text{arm } i \text{ finished its } r\text{-th epoch}\}$$

$$\leq \tau(\tilde{r}_i) + \frac{1}{|\mathcal{A}^*|} \cdot \sum_{r > \tilde{r}_i} (\tau(r) - \tau(r-1)) \cdot \{\text{arm } i \text{ finished its } r\text{-th epoch}\}$$

The assumption $n \leq D/(2 \cdot \Delta_i^2)$ implies $\ln(2e \cdot n\Delta_i^2/D) \geq 1$. Therefore, for $r > \tilde{r}_i$, we have

$$\tau(r-1) > \frac{D \cdot (1 + 4\alpha) \cdot \ln(2e \cdot n\Delta_i^2/D)}{2 \cdot \Delta_i^2} \tag{7}$$

and

$$a_n^{\tau(r-1)} = \sqrt{\frac{(1+\alpha)\ln(e \cdot n/(D \cdot \tau(r-1)))}{2\tau(r-1)}} \leq_{Eq\ 7} \frac{\Delta_i}{\sqrt{D}} \sqrt{\frac{(1+\alpha)\ln(e \cdot n/(D \cdot \tau(r-1)))}{(1+4\alpha)\ln(2e \cdot n\Delta_i^2/D)}}$$

$$\leq \frac{\Delta_i}{\sqrt{D}} \cdot \sqrt{\frac{(1+\alpha)\ln(2e \cdot n\Delta_i^2/D))}{(1+4\alpha)\ln(2e \cdot n\Delta_i^2/D)}} \leq \frac{\Delta_i}{\sqrt{D}} \cdot \sqrt{\frac{1+\alpha}{1+4\alpha}}$$

Because $a_t^{\tau(r)}$ is increasing in t, by definition, if the suboptimal arm j finishes to play the r-th epoch then $\forall h, 1 \leq h \leq |\mathcal{A}^{*(r)}|, \exists s_h \geq 0, \exists t \geq \tau(r-1) + \tau(s_h)$ such that arm i is non-dominated by any of the Pareto optimal arms in $|\mathcal{A}^{*(r)}|$. This means that

$$\bar{\mathbf{X}}_h^{*\tau(s_h)} + a_t^{s_h} \not\succ \bar{\mathbf{X}}_i^{\tau(r-1)} + a_t^{\tau(r-1)}$$

implies that one of the following conditions holds

$$\bar{\mathbf{X}}_i^{\tau(r-1)} + a_n^{\tau(r-1)} \not\succ \nu_i^* - \frac{\alpha \cdot \Delta_i}{\sqrt{D} \cdot 2}$$

or

$$\bar{\mathbf{X}}_h^{*\tau(s_h)} + a_{\tau(r-1)+\tau(s_h)}^{\tau(s_h)} \not\succ \mu_h^* - \frac{\alpha \cdot \Delta_i}{\sqrt{D} \cdot 2}$$

Then,

$$\mathbb{E}[T_i(n)] \leq \tau(\tilde{r}_i) + \sum_{r \geq \tilde{r}_i} \frac{\tau(r) - \tau(r-1)}{|\mathcal{A}^*|} \cdot \sum_{h=1}^{|\mathcal{A}^*|} \mathbb{P}\{\bar{\mathbf{X}}_i^{\tau(r-1)} + a_n^{\tau(r-1)} \not\succ \nu_i^* - \frac{\alpha \cdot \Delta_i}{\sqrt{D} \cdot 2}\} + \quad (8)$$

$$\sum_{i \geq 0} \sum_{r \geq 1} \frac{\tau(r) - \tau(r-1)}{|\mathcal{A}^*|} \cdot \sum_{h=1}^{|\mathcal{A}^*|} \mathbb{P}\{\bar{\mathbf{X}}_{s_h}^{\tau(r-1)} + a_{\tau(r-1)-\tau(s_h)}^{\tau(s_h)} \not\succ \mu_h^* - \frac{\alpha \cdot \Delta_i}{\sqrt{D} \cdot 2}\}$$

Let's expand Eq. 8 using Chernoff and union bound. For the first term between the parenthesis, we have that

$$\mathbb{P}\{\bar{\mathbf{X}}_i^{\tau(r-1)} + a_n^{\tau(r-1)} \not\succ \nu_i^* - \frac{\alpha \cdot \Delta_i}{\sqrt{D} \cdot 2}\} = \sum_{j=1}^{D} \mathbb{P}\{\bar{X}_i^{j\tau(r-1)} + a_n^{\tau(r-1)} > \mu_i^j + \Delta_i - \frac{\alpha \cdot \Delta_i}{\sqrt{D} \cdot 2}\} \leq$$

$$D \cdot e^{-2 \cdot \tau(r-1) \cdot \Delta_i^2 \cdot (1 - \frac{\alpha}{2 \cdot \sqrt{D}} - \frac{1}{\sqrt{D}} \cdot \frac{1+\alpha}{1+4 \cdot \alpha})^2} \leq_{\alpha < 1/10} D \cdot e^{-\frac{\tau(r-1) \cdot \Delta_i^2 \cdot \alpha^2}{2 \cdot D}}$$

If $g(x) = \frac{x-1}{1+\alpha}$ and $c = \frac{\Delta_i^2 \cdot \alpha^2}{D}$, and $g(x) \leq \tau(r-1)$ then

$$\sum_{r \geq 1} \frac{\tau(r) - \tau(r-1)}{|\mathcal{A}^*|} \cdot \sum_{h=1}^{|\mathcal{A}^*|} \mathbb{P}\{\bar{\mathbf{X}}_i^{\tau(r-1)} + a_n^{\tau(r-1)} \not\succ \nu_i^* - \frac{\alpha \cdot \Delta_i}{\sqrt{D} \cdot 2}\} \leq$$

$$\sum_{r \geq 1} \sum_{i \geq 0} \frac{\tau(r) - \tau(r-1)}{|\mathcal{A}^*|} \cdot \sum_{h=1}^{|\mathcal{A}^*|} D \cdot e^{-\tau(r-1) \cdot \Delta_i^2 \cdot \alpha^2 / D} =$$

$$D \cdot |\mathcal{A}^*| \cdot \sum_{r \geq 1} \sum_{i \geq 0} \frac{\tau(r) - \tau(r-1)}{|\mathcal{A}^*|} \cdot e^{-\tau(r-1) \cdot \Delta_i^2 \cdot \alpha^2 / D} \leq$$

$$\frac{D}{|\mathcal{A}^*|} \cdot |\mathcal{A}^*| \cdot \int_0^\infty e^{-c \cdot g(x)} dx \leq \frac{D^2 \cdot (1 + \alpha) \cdot e}{\Delta_i^2 \cdot \alpha^2}$$

Let's now expand the second term of the parenthesis in Eq. 8

$$\mathbb{P}\{\bar{\mathbf{X}}_s^{\tau(r-1)} + a_{\tau(r-1)-\tau(s)}^{\tau(s)} \not\succ \mu_h^* - \frac{\alpha \cdot \Delta_i}{\sqrt{D} \cdot 2}\} =$$

$$\sum_{j=1}^{D} \mathbb{P}\{\bar{X}_s^{j\tau(r-1)} + a_{\tau(r-1)-\tau(s)}^{\tau(s)} < \mu_h^{j*} - \frac{\alpha \cdot \Delta_i}{\sqrt{D} \cdot 2}\} \le$$

$$D \cdot e^{-\tau(i) \cdot \frac{\alpha^2 \cdot \Delta_i^2}{D \cdot 2}} \cdot e^{-(1+\alpha) \cdot \ln \frac{e \cdot (\tau(r-1)+\tau(i))}{D \cdot \tau(i)}} \le$$

$$D^{\alpha+2} \cdot e^{-\tau(i) \cdot \frac{\alpha^2 \cdot \Delta_i^2}{D \cdot 2}} \cdot \left(\frac{\tau(r-1)+\tau(i)}{\tau(i)}\right)^{-(1+\alpha)}$$

Thus,

$$\sum_{i \ge 0} \sum_{r \ge 1} \frac{\tau(r)-\tau(r-1)}{|\mathcal{A}^*|} \cdot \sum_{h=1}^{|\mathcal{A}^*|} \mathbb{P}\{\bar{\mathbf{X}}_s^{\tau(r-1)} + a_{\tau(r-1)-\tau(s)}^{\tau(s)} \not< \mu_h^* - \frac{\alpha \cdot \Delta_i}{\sqrt{D} \cdot 2}\} \le$$

$$D^{\alpha+2} \cdot \sum_{i \ge 0} e^{-\tau(i) \cdot \frac{\alpha^2 \cdot \Delta_i^2}{D \cdot 2}} \cdot \int_0^\infty \left(1 + \frac{x-1}{(1+\alpha) \cdot \tau(i)}\right)^{-(1+\alpha)} dx \le$$

$$D^{\alpha+2} \cdot \frac{\alpha}{(1+\alpha)-1} \cdot \left(\frac{\alpha+1}{\alpha}\right)^{(1+\alpha)} \cdot \sum_{i \ge 0} \tau(i) \cdot e^{-\tau(i) \cdot \frac{\alpha^2 \cdot \Delta_i^2}{D \cdot 2}}$$

Following the rationale from the prove of Theorem 2 from [7], we can bound further the first term of Eq. 8 to

$$\sum_{i \ge 0} \tau(i) \cdot e^{-\tau(i) \cdot \frac{\alpha^2 \cdot \Delta_i^2}{D \cdot 2}} \le 1 + \frac{11 \cdot D \cdot (1+\alpha)}{5\alpha^2 \cdot \Delta_i^2 \cdot \ln(1+\alpha)}$$

Using the bounds above, we now bound the expected regret for an arm i in Algorithm 2

$$\mathbb{E}[T_i(n)] \le \tau(\tilde{r}_i) - 1 + \frac{c_\alpha}{\Delta_i^2}$$

where

$$c_\alpha = 1 + \frac{D^2 \cdot (1+\alpha) \cdot e}{\alpha^2} + D^{\alpha+2} \cdot \left(\frac{\alpha+1}{\alpha}\right)^{(1+\alpha)} \cdot \left[1 + \frac{11 \cdot D \cdot (1+\alpha)}{5 \cdot \alpha^2 \cdot \ln(1+\alpha)}\right]$$

and the upper bound on $\tau(\tilde{r}_i)$

$$\tau(\tilde{r}_i) \le \tau(\tilde{r}_i - 1)(1+\alpha) + 1 \le \frac{D \cdot (1+\alpha) \cdot (1+4\alpha) \cdot \ln(2en\Delta_i^2/D)}{2 \cdot \Delta_i^2} + 1$$

This concludes our prove. □

The bound of the expected regret for Pareto UCB2 is similar with the bound for the standard UCB2 within a constant that depends on the number of objectives D. The intuition is that now the algorithm has to run D times longer to achieve a similar regret bound for the Pareto UCB2. For α small, the Pareto projection regret of this Pareto algorithm is bounded by $\frac{1}{2 \cdot \Delta_i^2}$. This is a better bound than of the Pareto UCB1 algorithm, $\frac{8}{\Delta_i^2}$.

The difference between single objective UCB2 and Pareto UCB2 is in the constant c_α which is smaller than the same constant for the standard UCB2 for $\alpha > 0$. This means that the constant c_α converges faster to infinity when $\alpha \to 0$.

4.2 Exploratory Pareto UCB2

In this section, we introduce the *exploratory Pareto UCB2* algorithm. In fact, the only difference between the exploratory and exploitative variants of Pareto UCB2 is in lines 5 from Algorithm 2. Now a single arm from the Pareto front at epoch r, $\mathcal{A}^{*(r)}$, is selected and played the entire epoch, i.e. for $\tau(r_i + 1) - \tau(r_i)$ consecutive times.

Since the length of the epochs is exponential, a single Pareto optimal arm is played longer and longer. Thus, the exploitation mechanism of Pareto optimal arms of the exploratory Pareto UCB2 algorithm is poor, and the upper Pareto projection regret depends on the cardinality of the Pareto front.

5 Numerical Simulations

In this section, we compare the performance of five Pareto MAB algorithms: (1) a baseline algorithm, (2) two Pareto UCB1 algorithms and (3) two Pareto UCB2 algorithms. The five compared MOMABs are: (1) tPUCB1 is the exploitative Pareto UCB1 algorithm introduced in Sect. 3.1, (2) rPUCB1 is the exploratory Pareto UCB1 algorithm summarised in Sect. 3.2, (3) tPUCB2 is the exploitative Pareto UCB2 algorithm summarised in Sect. 4.1, (4) rPUCB2 is the exploratory Pareto UCB2 algorithm summarised in Sect. 4.2. Hoeffding race algorithm [8], hoef, is considered a baseline algorithm for multi-armed bandits where all the arms are pulled equally often and the arms with the non-dominated empirical mean reward vectors are chosen.

Each algorithm runs 100 times with a fixed budged, or arm' pulls, of $N = 10^6$. By default, we set the α parameter for the two Pareto UCB2 algorithms to 1.

The test environment is bi-objective and contains the mean vectors of 54 points outputted with a multi-objective genetic algorithm that optimised the functioning of the wet clutch [9]. In Fig. 1, we give 54 points generated with the wet clutch application, each point representing a trial of the machine and the jerk time obtained in the given time. The problem was a minimisation problem

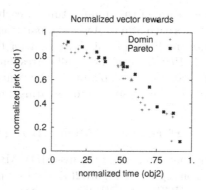

Fig. 1. All the points generated by the bi-objective wet-clutch application.

Table 1. Fifty-four bi-dimensional reward vectors labelled from 1 to 54 for the wet clutch application. The first sixteen reward vectors are labelled from μ_1^* till μ_{16}^* and are Pareto optimal, while the last thirty-four reward vectors are labelled from μ_{17} till μ_{54} and they are suboptimal.

$\mu_1^* = (0.116, 0.917)$	$\mu_2^* = (0.218, 0.876)$	$\mu_3^* = (0.322, 0.834)$	$\mu_4^* = (0.336, 0.788)$	$\mu_5^* = (0.379, 0.783)$
$\mu_6^* = (0.383, 0.753)$	$\mu_7^* = (0.509, 0.742)$	$\mu_8^* = (0.512, 0.737)$	$\mu_9^* = (0.514, 0.711)$	$\mu_{10}^* = (0.540, 0.710)$
$\mu_{11}^* = (0.597, 0.647)$	$\mu_{12}^* = (0.698, 0.540)$	$\mu_{13}^* = (0.753, 0.374)$	$\mu_{14}^* = (0.800, 0.332)$	$\mu_{15}^* = (0.869, 0.321)$
$\mu_{16}^* = (0.916, 0.083)$	$\mu_{17} = (0.249, 0.826)$	$\mu_{18} = (0.102, 0.892)$	$\mu_{19} = (0.497, 0.722)$	$\mu_{20} = (0.251, 0.824)$
$\mu_{21} = (0.249, 0.826)$	$\mu_{22} = (0.102, 0.892)$	$\mu_{23} = (0.497, 0.722)$	$\mu_{24} = (0.251, 0.824)$	$\mu_{25} = (0.575, 0.596)$
$\mu_{26} = (0.651, 0.448)$	$\mu_{27} = (0.571, 0.607)$	$\mu_{28} = (0.083, 0.903)$	$\mu_{29} = (0.696, 0.350)$	$\mu_{30} = (0.272, 0.784)$
$\mu_{31} = (0.601, 0.521)$	$\mu_{32} = (0.341, 0.753)$	$\mu_{33} = (0.507, 0.685)$	$\mu_{34} = (0.526, 0.611)$	$\mu_{35} = (0.189, 0.857)$
$\mu_{36} = (0.620, 0.454)$	$\mu_{37} = (0.859, 0.314)$	$\mu_{38} = (0.668, 0.388)$	$\mu_{39} = (0.334, 0.782)$	$\mu_{40} = (0.864, 0.290)$
$\mu_{41} = (0.473, 0.722)$	$\mu_{42} = (0.822, 0.316)$	$\mu_{43} = (0.092, 0.863)$	$\mu_{44} = (0.234, 0.796)$	$\mu_{45} = (0.476, 0.709)$
$\mu_{46} = (0.566, 0.596)$	$\mu_{47} = (0.166, 0.825)$	$\mu_{48} = (0.646, 0.349)$	$\mu_{49} = (0.137, 0.829)$	$\mu_{50} = (0.511, 0.611)$
$\mu_{51} = (0.637, 0.410)$	$\mu_{52} = (0.329, 0.778)$	$\mu_{53} = (0.649, 0.347)$	$\mu_{54} = (0.857, 0.088)$	

that we have transformed into a maximisation problem, by first normalising each objective with values between 0 and 1, and then transforming it into a maximisation problem. The best set of incomparable reward vectors is called the Pareto optimal reward set, i.e. there are 16 such reward vectors. In our example, $|\mathcal{A}^*|$ is about one-third from the total number of arms, i.e. 16/54, and is a mixture of convex and non-convex regions. In Table 1, we show the mean values of the 54 reward vectors. In order to generate a stochastic bi-objective environment, we have associated to each reward value a normal distribution.

The Performance of the Algorithms. We use four metrics to measure the performance of the five tested Pareto MAB algorithms. Two of these metrics are the Pareto projection regret, cf. Eq. 2, and the Pareto variance regret, cf. Eq. 3, presented in Sect. 2. We also use two additional metrics two explain the dynamics of the Pareto MAB algorithms.

The third metric measures the percentage of times each Pareto optimal arm is pulled. Thus, for all Pareto optimal arms, $i \in \mathcal{A}^*$, we measure $\mathbb{E}[T_i^*(n)]$ the expected number of times the arm i is pulled during n total arm pulls. Note that $\mathbb{E}[T_i^*(n)]$ is a part of Eq. 3 and it gives a detailed understanding of the Pareto variance regret.

The last metric is a measure of the running time of each algorithm, and it is given by the number of times each arm in $\mathcal{A}$ was compared against the other arms in $\mathcal{A}$ in order to compute the Pareto front. Note that for the exploratory algorithms, i.e. *rPUCB1* and *rPUCB2*, each arm pull corresponds to one estimation of the Pareto front, whereas, for the exploitative algorithms, i.e. *tPUCB1* and *tPUCB2*, one estimation of $\mathcal{A}^*$ corresponds to the arms' pulls of the entire set.

5.1   Comparing the Performance of MOMAB Algorithms

In Fig. 2, we compare the performance of the five MOMAB algorithms. According the Pareto projection regret, cf. Figure 2(a), the best performing algorithm is the exploitative Pareto UCB2, cf. tPUCB2, the second best algorithm is the

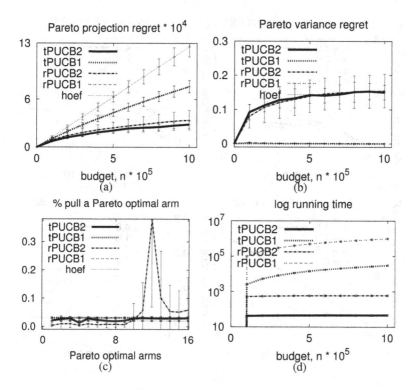

Fig. 2. The performance of the five MOMAB algorithms on the wet clutch problem: (a) the Pareto projection regret, (b) the Pareto variance regret, (c) the percentage of times each Pareto optimal arm is pulled, and (d) the running time in terms of comparisons between arms and Pareto front for each MOMAB algorithm.

exploratory Pareto UCB2, cf rPUCB2, and the worst algorithm is the Hoeffding race algorithm, cf. hoef. Note that the Pareto UCB1 family of algorithms has a (almost) linear regret whereas Pareto UCB2 algorithms have a logarithmic regret, like the single objective UCB2 algorithm. The worst performance of the exploitative Pareto UCB1 algorithm can be explained by the poor explorative behaviour of the algorithm. The performance of the explorative Pareto UCB1 is in-between linear and logarithmic and can be explained by the improved exploratory technique of pulling all the Pareto optimal arms each round. Both Pareto UCB2 algorithms perform better than Pareto UCB1 algorithms because the Pareto optimal arms are explored longer each round.

In opposition, according to the Pareto variance regret, cf. Fig. 2(b), the worst performing algorithms are the exploitative and exploratory Pareto UCB2 algorithms and the best algorithms are the exploratory and exploitative Pareto UCB1 algorithms but also the Hoeffding race algorithm. It is interesting to note that the difference in Pareto variance and projection regret between the exploratory and exploitative variance of the same algorithms is small. In general, Pareto

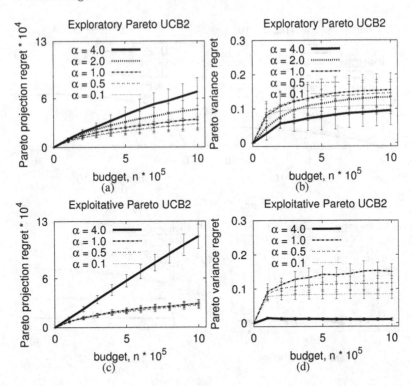

Fig. 3. The performance of the two version of Pareto UCB2 algorithms, i.e. exploratory and exploitative Pareto UCB2, given for the five values of the $\alpha = \{0.1, 0.5, 1.0, 2.0, 4.0\}$ parameter.

UCB1 algorithms have a larger Pareto projection regret then the Pareto UCB2 algorithms, but a smaller Pareto variance regret.

Figure 2(c) explains these contradictory results with the percentage of pulls for each of the Pareto optimal arms. As noticed in Sect. 4.2, the exploratory Pareto UCB2, cf rPUCB2, pulls the same Pareto optimal arm each epoch longer and longer, generating the peak in the figure on one random single Pareto optimal arm. In contrast, the exploitative Pareto UCB2, cf. tPUCB2, is fair in exploiting the entire Pareto front. In the sequel, the exploratory Pareto UCB1 algorithm, cf rPUCB1, has more variance in pulling Pareto optimal arms than the exploitative Pareto UCB2 algorithm, cf. tPUCB1, and this fact is reflected also in the Pareto variance regret measures from Fig. 2(b). The percentage of time *any* of the Pareto optimal arms is pulled is: (1) 83 % ±8.5 for exploitative Pareto UCB2, (2) 77 % ± 10.9 for explorative Pareto UCB2, (3) 49 % ± 4.9 for exploitative Pareto UCB1, and (4) 49 % ± 4.9 for the explorative UCB1. Note the large difference between the efficiency of Pareto UCB2 and Pareto UCB1 algorithms.

In Fig. 2(d), we show that the running time, i.e. number of comparisons between arms, for exploratory MOMABs, i.e. the exploratory Pareto UCB1 and the exploratory Pareto UCB2, are order of magnitude larger than the exploitative MOMAB algorithms, i.e. the exploitative Pareto UCB1 and the exploitative Pareto UCB2. The running time for Pareto UCB1 algorithms which compute the Pareto front often is larger than the running time for Pareto UCB2 algorithms that compute the Pareto front once in the beginning of an epoch. The most computationally efficient is the exploitative Pareto UCB2 and the worst algorithm is the exploratory Pareto UCB1.

5.2 Exploration vs Exploitation Mechanism in Pareto UCB2 Algorithms

In our second experiment, we measure the influence of the parameter α on the performance of Pareto UCB2 algorithms. Figure 3 considers five values for this parameter $\alpha = \{0.1, 0.5, 1.0, 2.0, 4.0\}$ that indicates the length of an epoch. The largest variance in performance we have for the exploratory Pareto UCB2. The smaller is the size of an epoch, the better the performance of the exploratory Pareto UCB2 algorithm is in terms of Pareto projection regret and Pareto variance regret. Note that for epochs' length of 1, the performance of Pareto UCB2 resembles the perofrmance of Pareto UCB1, meaning that an arm or a set of arms are pulled each epoch. The same parameter α has little influence on the performance of exploitative Pareto UCB2 where all the Pareto arms are pulled each epoch.

Our conclusion is that the exploration vs exploitation trade-off is better in the exploitative Pareto algorithms where all the Pareto optimal arms are pulled often. In opposition, exploratory Pareto UCB2 has a small Pareto projection regret but a large Pareto variance regret since the algorithm pulls a single Pareto optimal arm during exponentially large epochs.

6   Conclusions

In this paper, the classical UCB1 and UCB2 algorithms are extended to reward vectors using Pareto dominance relation. We propose exploitative Pareto UCB1 that pulls each round all the Pareto optimal arms. The exploratory version of the same algorithm uniform at random selects each round only one arm Pareto optimal arm. We show that this difference has an important impact on the upper Pareto projection regret bound of exploitative Pareto UCB1. Now, the upper regret bound is independent of the cardinality of the Pareto front, which is large for many objective environments, and, furthermore, unknown beforehand. Based on the same line of reasoning, we propose the exploratory and exploitative Pareto UCB2 algorithms. Exploratory Pareto UCB2 pulls each epoch a single Pareto optimal arm selected at random. Exploitative Pareto UCB2 pulls all the Pareto optimal arms in a single epoch. We upper bound the Pareto projection regret of exploitative Pareto UCB2. We experimentally compare these MOMAB algorithms on a bi-objective environment showing that the best performing algorithm is Pareto UCB2, both exploitative and exploratory versions.

Acknowledgements. Madalina M. Drugan was supported by the IWT-SBO project PERPETUAL (gr. nr. 110041).

References

1. Lizotte, D., Bowling, M., Murphy, S.: Efficient reinforcement learning with multiple reward functions for randomized clinical trial analysis. In: Proceedings of the Twenty-Seventh International Conference on Machine Learning (ICML) (2010)
2. Wiering, M., de Jong, E.: Computing optimal stationary policies for multi-objective markov decision processes. In: Proceedings of Approximate Dynamic Programming and Reinforcement Learning (ADPRL), pp. 158–165. IEEE (2007)
3. van Moffaert, K., Drugan, M.M., Nowé, A.: Hypervolume-based multi-objective reinforcement learning. In: Purshouse, R.C., Fleming, P.J., Fonseca, C.M., Greco, S., Shaw, J. (eds.) EMO 2013. LNCS, vol. 7811, pp. 352–366. Springer, Heidelberg (2013)
4. Wang, W., Sebag, M.: Multi-objective Monte Carlo tree search. In: Asian Conference on Machine Learning, pp. 1–16 (2012)
5. Zitzler, E., Thiele, L., Laumanns, M., Fonseca, C.M., da Fonseca, V.: Performance assessment of multiobjective optimizers: an analysis and review. IEEE Trans. Evol. Comput. **7**, 117–132 (2003)
6. Drugan, M., Nowe, A.: Designing multi-objective multi-armed bandits: a study. In: Proceedings of International Joint Conference of Neural Networks (IJCNN) (2013)
7. Auer, P., Cesa-Bianchi, N., Fischer, P.: Finite time analysis of the multiarmed bandit problem. Mach. Learn. **47**, 235–256 (2002)
8. Maron, O., Moore, A.: Hoeffding races: accelerating model selection search for classification and function approximation. In: Advances in Neural Information Processing Systems, vol. 6, pp. 59–66. Morgan Kaufmann (1994)
9. Vaerenbergh, K.V., Rodriguez, A., Gagliolo, M., Vrancx, P., Nowe, A., Stoev, J., Goossens, S., Pinte, G., Symens, W.: Improving wet clutch engagement with reinforcement learning. In: International Joint Conference on Neural Networks (IJCNN). IEEE (2012)

Solving PCSPs Using Genetic Algorithms Guided by Structural Knowledge

Lamia Sadeg[1,3], Zineb Habbas[2], and Wassila Aggoune-Mtalaa[4(✉)]

[1] Ecole Nationale Superieure d'Informatique, Algiers, Algeria
`l_sadeg@esi.dz`
[2] LCOMS, University of Lorraine, Ile du Saulcy, 57045 Metz Cedex, France
`zineb.habbas@univ-lorraine.fr`
[3] Laboratory of Applied Mathematics, Military Polytechnic School, Algiers, Algeria
[4] Luxembourg Institute of Science and Technology, Belval, Luxembourg
`wassila.mtalaa@list.lu`

Abstract. Solving a Partial Constraint Satisfaction Problem consists in assigning values to all the variables of the problem such that a maximal subset of the constraints is satisfied. An efficient algorithm for large instances of such problems which are NP-hard does not exist yet. Decomposition methods enable to detect and exploit some crucial structures of the problems like the clusters, or the cuts, and then apply that knowledge to solve the problem. This is the focus of the present work which uses the knowledge to improve an adaptive genetic algorithm proposed in previous studies. The approach is designed to be generic in order that any decomposition method can be used and different heuristics for the genetic operators are possible. To prove the effectiveness of the method, three heuristics for the crossover step are investigated.

Keywords: Optimization problems · Partial Constraint Satisfaction Problems · Graph decomposition · Adaptive Genetic Algorithm (AGA) · AGA guided by decomposition

1 Introduction

A Partial Constraint Satisfaction Problem (PCSP) is a partial version of a CSP for which only a subset of constraints called hard constraints have to be satisfied. The rest of the constraints of the problem called soft constraints can be violated in the condition that a penalty is involved. In other words, PCSPs are CSPs for which penalties are assigned to soft constraints that are not satisfied. When addressing a PCSP, the objective is to assign values to all variables such as to minimize the total penalty, also called the cost of the solution, induced by the violated constraints. A large class of Problems can be modeled as a PCSP including for example Maximum Satisfiability Problems, Boolean Quadratic Problems or Coloring Problems. In this paper, the Frequency Assignment Problem (FAP), one of the most well known combinatorial Problems, is taken as experimental target to validate our approach. Indeed, the focus of this work is on binary

© Springer International Publishing Switzerland 2015
B. Duval et al. (Eds.): ICAART 2015, LNAI 9494, pp. 145–162, 2015.
DOI: 10.1007/978-3-319-27947-3_8

PCSPs where any constraint involves two variables. When looking for a global solution of the PCSP, generic solvers are sometimes surprisingly competitive but other times, these solvers really fail to address large size problems because of some difficult subproblems that lurk beneath. PCSPs (and particularly FAPs) have been solved by a number of different exact approaches (enumerative search, Branch & Bound for instance) and numerous heuristics or metaheuristics [1–3]. However all these approaches have often a limited success when coping with real large instances. Nowadays solving approaches propose to explore the structure of the associated constraint graph [4,5]. In particular, methods exploiting tree decompositions [6] are known to be among the best techniques with regard to theoretical time complexity. Unfortunately these methods have not shown a real efficiency for large problems thus proving a practical interest. In [7], a generic approach based on decomposition was introduced. The aim was to solve large size problems in a short time but not necessarily at optimality. The computational results, using an Adapative Genetic Algorithm (AGA) were relatively promising. In this paper, the new idea is to exploit structural knowledges coming from the decomposition method in an innovative way. A recent study has shown the benefits of such an approach for improving a local search method [8,9]. In particular, the tree decomposition was explored. In this work, the approach is more generic since any decomposition can be used. Therefore, a new generic algorithm is proposed. It is called AGAGD_x_y for Adaptive Genetic Algorithm Guided by Decomposition. AGAGD_x_y uses a given decomposition method to detect crucial substructures of the problem and then applies that knowledge to boost the performance of the AGA itself. The name of the algorithm is indexed by x and y, where x is for the generic decomposition and y is for the generic genetic operator. In this paper three heuristics named Crossover_clus, Crossover_cut and Crossover_clus_cut are presented.

The paper is organized as follows. Section 2 gives a formal definition of a PCSP. Section 3 presents the decomposition method chosen to validate this approach. In Sect. 4 an efficient Adaptive Genetic Algorithm for solving PCSPs is proposed. The proposition of an Adaptive Genetic Algorithm Guided by Decomposition AGAGD_x_y is presented in Sect. 5. The first computational and promising results are presented in Sect. 6. The paper ends with a conclusion and perspectives for further research.

2   Partial Constraint Satisfaction Problem (PCSP)

Definition 1 (Constraint Satisfaction Problem). *A Constraint Satisfaction Problem (CSP) is defined as a triple* $P = <X, D, C>$ *where*

- $X = \{x_1, ..., x_n\}$ *is a finite set of n variables.*
- $D = \{D_1, ..., D_n\}$ *is a set of n finite domains. Each variable x_i takes its value in the domain D_i.*
- $C = \{c_1, ..., c_m\}$ *is a set of m constraints. Each constraint c_i is defined as a set of variables $\{x_i, ..., x_j\}$, $i, j = 1, ..., n$ called the scope of c_i. For each constraint c_i a relation R_i specifies the authorized values for the variables. This*

relation R_i can be defined as a formula or as a set of tuples, $R_i \subseteq \prod_{(x_k \in c_i)} D_k$ (subset of the cartesian product).

A **solution of a CSP** *is a complete assignment of values to each variable $x_i \in X$ denoted by a vector $< d_1, d_2, \ldots, d_n >$ (where $d_i \in D_i \ \forall i \in 1 \ldots n$) which satisfies all the constraints of C.*

Remark 1. The cardinality of c_i is called the *arity* of constraint c_i. CSPs with constraints involving at most two variables are named binary CSPs.

Let us recall that in this work, only binary CSPs are considered. In the rest of the paper, a constraint $c = \{x_i, x_j\}$ is denoted by (x_i, x_j).

Definition 2 (Binary Partial Constraint Satisfaction Problem). *A binary Partial Constraint Satisfaction Problem is defined as a quadruplet $P = < X, D, C, P >$ where*

- *$< X, D, C >$ is a binary CSP,*
- *$P = \{p_1, \ldots, p_m\}$ is a set of m penalties. Each penalty p_i is a value associated with a constraint c_i, $i = 1, \ldots, m$.*

The objective when solving a PCSP is to select an authorized value for each variable $x_i \in X$ such that the sum of the penalties of the violated constraints called also the cost of the solution s and defined as follows:

$$cost(s) = \sum_{i=1}^{m} p_i \ where \ c_i \ is \ violated$$

has to be minimized.

Definition 3 (Constraint Graph). *Let $\mathcal{P} = < X, D, C, P >$ be a PCSP. Let $G = (V, E)$ be the undirected weighted graph associated with $\mathcal{P}$ as follows: with each variable $x \in X$ we associate a node $v_x \in V$ and for each constraint $(x_1, x_2) \in C$ we define an edge $v_{x_1} v_{x_2} \in E$ and a weight w associated with its penalty defined in P.*

Remark 2. Among the set of constraints, those that must not be violated are called "hard" constraints while the others are "soft" constraints.

3 Decomposition Techniques

3.1 Generalities on Decomposition Techniques

The objective of a decomposition method is to split a large problem into a collection of interconnected but easier sub-problems. The decomposition process depends on the nature of the problem and how it is modelled [10]. In this study, the focus is on decomposition techniques which include graph decompositions such as graph partitioning or graph clustering particularly adapted to optimization problems which are modelled by graphs.

The originality of the approach proposed in this paper is the use of information resulting from the decomposition of the problem to guide its resolution. It is meant to be generic, thus not conditioned by any particular decomposition method. However as the aim of this first work is rather to validate the new AGAGD_x_y algorithm, the well known powerful clustering algorithm due to Newman [11] is considered as target decomposition method.

3.2 Newman Algorithm

Many clustering algorithms have been proposed in recent years. A common property that summarizes all these algorithms is the community structure: the nodes of the networks are grouped into clusters with a high internal density and clusters are sparsely connected. To detect structure communities in networks, an algorithm based on an iterative removal of edges is proposed in [12]. The main drawback of this algorithm is its computational time that limits the use of this algorithm to problems with a few thousand nodes at most. A more efficient algorithm for detecting community structure is presented in [11] which runs on current computers in a reasonable time for networks of up to a million vertices. The principle of this new algorithm (denoted Newman algorithm) is based on the idea of modularity. The first algorithm presented in [12], [11] splits the network into communities, regardless of whether the network has naturally such a division. To define the meaningfulness of a decomposition, a quality function denoted Q or modularity is associated. In [11] Q is simply optimized instead of considering different iterative removals of edges. However looking for all possible divisions for optimizing Q is infeasible for networks larger than 20 or 30 nodes. Different heuristic or metaheuristic algorithms can be used to approximate this problem. Newman algorithm starts by considering n clusters or communities, for which each community contains only one node. The communities are then repeatedly joined in pairs. The algorithm chooses at each step the join that results in the smallest decrease of Q. The algorithm progresses like a dendrogram at different nodes. The cuts through this dendrogram at different levels give the divisions of the graph into a certain number of communities of different sizes. The best cut is chosen by looking for the maximal value for Q. This new version of the algorithm is in $O(n^2)$ on sparse graphs.

3.3 Detected Structural Knowledge

This subsection defines the general concepts linked with decomposition techniques which will be used in the rest of the paper to present the AGAGD_x_y algorithm.

Definition 4 (Partition, Cluster). *Given a graph $G = < V, E >$, a **partition** $\{C_1, C_2, \ldots, C_k\}$ of G is a collection of subsets of V that satisfies the following:*

$$- \bigcup_{i=1}^{k} C_i = V$$
- $\forall i,j = 1,\ldots,k : C_i \cap C_j = \emptyset$

Each subset of variables C_i of the partition of G is called a **cluster**.

Definition 5 (Cut). *Let $\{C_1, C_2, \ldots, C_k\}$ be a partition of a graph $G = < V,E >$, and let C_i and C_j be two clusters. We denote by $Cut(C_i, C_j)$ the set of vertices $\{u \in V_i, \exists v \in V_j \text{ and } uv \in E\} \cup \{v \in V_j, \exists u \in V_i \text{ and } uv \in E\}$.*

Definition 6 (Separator). *Let $G = < V,E >$ be a graph and $P = \{C_1, C_2, \ldots, C_k\}$ a partition of this graph. Let C_i be a cluster in P. The separator of C_i denoted $Sep(C_i)$ is the set of vertices defined by: $Sep(C_i) = \{u \in V_i, \exists v \notin V_i \text{ and } uv \in E\}$. In other words, $Sep(C_i)$ is the set of the bordering nodes of C_i.*

Remark 3. Let $\mathcal{P} = < X, D, C, P >$ be a PCSP and $G = < V, E >$ its weighted graph representation where $V = X$, $E = C$ and $|V| = n$. In the rest of this paper $G[V_S]$ will denote the subgraph $< V_S, E_S >$ induced by the subset of nodes V_S in V.

Example 1. Figure 1 illustrates the important concepts related to structural knowledge: a constraint graph is decomposed into a partition $\{C_1, C_2, C_3, C_4, C_5, C_6\}$ of 6 clusters, where $Cut(C_1, C_5) = \{b, c, e, f\}$ and $Sep(C_1) = \{a, b, c, d\}$.

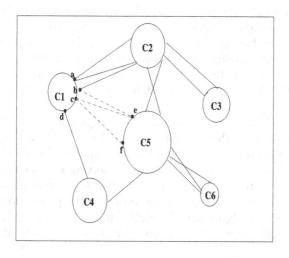

Fig. 1. Example of sep and cut notions

4   Adaptive Genetic Algorithm for PCSPs (AGA)

4.1   Motivation

This section presents an Adaptive Genetic Algorithm (AGA) specific to PCSPs. Standard genetic algorithms of the literature fail to find the optimum in a reasonable time. This is generally due to the fact that crossover and mutation probabilities are predetermined and fixed. The population becomes premature and falls in local convergence early. To avoid this drawback, in the proposed AGA, mutation and crossover probabilities change during the execution process, in order to improve the exploration of the search space.

4.2 Presentation of the Adaptive Genetic Algorithm (AGA) for PCSPs

Notations.

- p_{m_0}: initial mutation probability
- p_{c_0}: initial crossover probability
- $p_{m_{min}}$: mutation probability threshold
- $p_{c_{max}}$: crossover probability threshold
- Δp_m: mutation probability rate
- Δp_c: crossover probability rate.

AGA is formally given by Algorithm 1.

The performance of AGA is tightly dependent on its crossover and mutation operators. The mutation operator is used to replace the values of a certain number of genes, randomly chosen in the parent population, in order to improve the fitness of the resulting chromosome. The mutation occurs with a probability p_m, named mutation probability. The crossover operation is used to generate a new offspring by exchanging the values of some genes, to improve the fitness of a part of the chromosome. A crossover appears only with a probability p_c called the crossover probability. A good value for p_c avoids the local optima (diversification) while p_m enables the GA to improve the quality of the solutions (intensification).

In the proposed AGA, both parameters are dynamically modified to reach a good balance between the intensification and the diversification. More precisely, the crossover (respectively the mutation) operator is called each time p_c (respectively p_m) reaches a certain threshold, setting the Boolean value p_c-ok (respectively p_m-ok) to true. These probabilities are nevertheless bounded by $p_{m_{min}}$ and $p_{c_{max}}$, to avoid too much disruption in the population, which slows the convergence of the algorithm. Since all chromosomes of a given population are independent, crossover and mutation operations are processed concurrently.

Crossover in AGA. The crossover operator aims to modify the solution while reducing the degradation of its cost. It replaces, in the current solution, the elements and their neighborhood which have a bad fitness by ones which have a fitness of good quality in an individual selected by the tournament method.

Mutation in AGA. Contrarily to the mutation in a classical genetic algorithm which objective is to perturb the solution, the mutation operator in AGA aims at

Algorithm 1. AGA(*Pb*: a PCSP, *s*: a solution).

Input:$G < V, E, W >$: constraint graph for a PCSP, p_{m_0}, p_{c_0}, $p_{m_{min}}$, $p_{c_{max}}$, Δp_m, Δp_c, nb: mutation parameter

1: $p \leftarrow$ **Initial_Population**;
2: **if** local mimima **then**
3:    $p_m \leftarrow p_m - \Delta p_m$
4:    $p_c \leftarrow p_c + \Delta p_c$
5:    **if** $p_m < p_{m_{min}}$ **then**
6:       $p_m \leftarrow p_{m_{min}}$
7:    **end if**
8:    **if** $p_c > p_{c_{max}}$ **then**
9:       $p_c \leftarrow p_{c_{max}}$
10:    **end if**
11: **else**
12:    $p_m \leftarrow p_{m_0}$
13:    $p_c \leftarrow p_{c_0}$
14: **end if**
15: old_p $\leftarrow$ p
16: **repeat**
17:    **for all** i=1 to size(old_p) **do**
18:       in parallel
19:       parent_i $\leftarrow$ the ith chromosome in old_p
20:       parent_j $\leftarrow$ the selected chromosome in old_p using the tournament algorithm
21:       **if** p_c_ok **then**
22:          offspring_i $\leftarrow$ **Crossover**(parent_i, parent_j), where offspring_i will be the ith chromosome in a future population.
23:       **else**
24:          offspring_i $\leftarrow$ parent_i
25:       **end if**
26:       **if** p_m_ok **then**
27:          offspring_i $\leftarrow$ **Mutation**(offspring_i, nb)
28:       **end if**
29:    **end for**
30: **until** convergence

enhancing the solution cost. Indeed, this new mutation applies the local search method 1_opt to several elements of the solution (randomly chosen), until it is no more possible to enhance the cost during a certain number of successive iterations. The aim of this operation is twofold. First, it aims to enhance the quality of the population, for a large number of offsprings. Second, in the case where the solution 1_opt of a good quality solution is optimum, the solution has to converge to optimality.

5   Adapative Genetic Algorithm Guided by Decomposition: AGAGD_x_y

5.1   Presentation of AGAGD

Algorithm 2. AGAGD_x_y (*Pb*: a PCSP, *s*: a solution).

1: **Input:** $G = < V, E >$ is a weighted constraint graph associated with Pb
2: **Decompose_x**$(G, C = \{C_1, \ldots, C_k\})$
3: **AGA_y**(Pb, C, s)

This section aims to present the new AGAGD_x_y algorithm. The formal description of AGAGD_x_y is given by Algorithm 2. This algorithm consists of two major steps, as follows:

- The first step (Procedure **Decompose**) partitions the constraint network corresponding to the initial problem *Pb* in order to identify some relevant structural components such as clusters, cuts, or separators. The multicut decomposition method used in this paper has been presented in Sect. 3.
- The second step of the algorithm is related to the algorithm AGA_y. It is indexed by y, meaning that several variants can be considered. In AGA, the crossover involves at each time, a unique variable and its neighborhood. That explains why the number of the crossover steps needed can be very high before obtaining a convergence state. In AGA_y rather than operating a crossover on a single variable at each step, it applies it on more crucial parts of the problems, such that clusters, cuts, separators or any other relevant structural knowledge. Formally AGA_y corresponds to AGA for which the crossover procedure is replaced by **crossover_y**.

It is clear that several versions of crossover_y can be studied. In the present work, three different heuristics are introduced as described further.

5.2   Definition

Definition 7 (Fitness of a cluster). *Given a PCSP $\mathcal{P} = < X, D, C, P >$, its weighted constraint graph $G = < V, E >$ and a partition $P = \{C_1, C_2, \ldots, C_k\}$ of G. Let s be a current solution of $\mathcal{P}$ and C_i a cluster in P. Let us consider $G_i[C_i] = < V_i, E_i >$ the subgraph induced by C_i in G. The fitness of the cluster C_i is defined by:*

$$Fitness[C_i, s] = \sum_{(v_i, v_j) \in E_i} w(v_i, v_j)$$

where $(v_i, v_j) \in E_i$ and (v_i, v_j) is unsatisfied in s.

Remark 4. To obtain the definition of the fitness of a cut, one should replace the word cluster by the word cut in Definition 7.

5.3 Crossover_clus

In the heuristic Crossover_clus, the operation is performed on the clusters which are relevant structural knowledge that includes a small number of variables tightly connected. The separator is a set of bordering variables of a given cluster, which connects it to other clusters. This is an important structure that can give an indication about the role of a cluster and its neighborhood. The heuristic is described by Algorithm 3.

In the first loop (Lines 1–3), the cluster to be changed in the parent chromosome is the one which has the largest fitness as compared with those of the chromosome chosen by the tournament heuristic. To ensure that the crossover is performed on the cluster with the worst fitness, the heuristic must take into account both the fitness of the cluster (loop 1) and the fitness of its separator set (see the second loop in Lines 4–11). The main advantage of this second loop is that it avoids a deterioration of the overall fitness of the solution and then allows the algorithm to converge faster.

5.4 Crossover_cut

The cut plays a dual role with respect to the cluster. It is either lightweight (Min_weight heuristic) or has a low cardinality (Min_edge heuristic). This heuristic formalized by Algorithm 4 behaves globally as the previous one. The cut to be changed by the crossover operation is the one that presents both the worst fitness of the cut and the worst fitness of its variables in adjacent clusters.

Algorithm 3. Crossover_clus(p_1, p_2, $\{C_1, C_2, \ldots, C_k\}$).

1: **for all** i = 1 to k **do**
2:    Temp[i] ← Fitness[C_i, p_1] - Fitness[C_i, p_2]
3: **end for**
4: **for all** i = 1 to k **do**
5:    let $sep = Sep(C_i)$
6:    **for all** j = 1 to $|sep|$ **do**
7:       **if** $value(sep[j], p_1) \neq value(sep[j], p_2)$ **then**
8:          Temp[i] ← Temp[i] + Fitness[$(sep[j], p_1)$]
9:       **end if**
10:    **end for**
11: **end for**
12: Let C_j the cluster corresponding to the largest element in Temp.
13: **for all** i = 1 to n **do**
14:

$$offspring[i] \leftarrow \begin{cases} p_2[i] \text{ if } i \in C_j \\ p_1[i] \text{ otherwise} \end{cases}$$

15: **end for**

Algorithm 4. Crossover_cut(p_1, p_2, $\{C_1, C_2, \ldots, C_k\}$).

1: $l \leftarrow 1$
2: **for all** $i = 1$ to k **do**
3:   **for all** $j = i$ to k **do**
4:     Let $cut = Cut(C_i, C_j)$
5:     **if** $cut \neq \emptyset$ **then**
6:       Temp[l] $\leftarrow$ Fitness(cut,p_1) $-$ Fitness(cut,p_2)
7:       **for all** $h = 1$ to $|cut|$ **do**
8:         **if** $value(cut[h], p_1) \neq value(cut[h], p_2)$ **then**
9:           Temp[l]$\leftarrow$ Temp[l]$+$ Fitness $(cut[h]), p_1)$
10:         **end if**
11:       **end for**
12:     **end if**
13:     $l++$
14:   **end for**
15: **end for**
16: Let cut be the largest cut according to Temp.
17: **for all** i $= 1$ to n **do**
18:
$$
offspring[i] \leftarrow \begin{cases} p_2[i] \text{ if } i \in cut \\ p_1[i] \text{ otherwise} \end{cases}
$$

19: **end for**

5.5   Crossover_clus_cut

This heuristic is a compromise between the two former primitives as described by Algorithm 5. If the parent to be changed has a better fitness than those of the chromosome selected by the tournament, the Crossover_cut heuristic is applied, otherwise the heuristic Crossover_clus is used. Indeed, if the parent has a good fitness, it is better not to disturb it too much by making a change only on a small number of variables (cut). Conversely, if the parent to be changed has a worse fitness than the parent chosen by the tournament, then the first one probably contains good clusters while the second one contains bad clusters. In this case, it is wise to improve its quality by changing a bad cluster into a better one.

Algorithm 5. Crossover_clus_cut(p_1, p_2, $\{C_1, C_2, \ldots, C_k\}$).

1: **if** $Fitness[p_1] > Fitness[p_2]$ **then**
2:   Crossover_clus(p_1, p_2, $\{C_1, C_2, \ldots, C_k\}$)
3: **else**
4:   Crossover_cut(p_1, p_2, $\{C_1, C_2, \ldots, C_k\}$)
5: **end if**

---

6   Experimental Results

6.1   Application Domain: MI-FAP

The Frequency Assignment Problem (FAP) and more especially the Minimum Interference-FAP (MI-FAP) are well known hard optimization problems which are used here as application target.

Motivation. FAP is a combinatorial problem which appeared in the sixties [13] and, since then, several variants of the FAP differing mainly in the formulation of their objective have attracted researchers. The FAP was proved to be *NP-hard* [14]. More details on FAP can be found in [15,16].

Currently, MI-FAP is the most studied variant of FAP. It consists in assigning a reduced number of frequencies to an important number of transmitters/receivers, while minimizing the overall set of interferences in the network.

MI-FAP Modeling. MI-FAPs belong to the class of binary PCSPs (Partial Constraint Satisfaction Problems). More formally, a MI-FAP can be designed as the following PCSP $< X, D, C, P, Q >$, where:

- $X = \{t_1, t_2, \ldots, t_n\}$ is the set of all transmitters.
- $D = \{D_{t_1}, D_{t_2}, \ldots, D_{t_n}\}$ is the set of domains where each D_{t_i} gathers the possible frequencies at which a transmitter t_i can transmit.
- C is the set of constraints which can be *hard* or *soft*: $C = C_{hard} \cup C_{soft}$. *Soft* constraints can be violated at a certain cost, but *hard* constraints must be satisfied. Each constraint can involve either one transmitter t_i (and then we denote it c_{t_i}), or a pair of transmitters t_i, t_j, (in that case the constraint is denoted $c_{t_i t_j}$).
- $P = \{p_{t_i t_j} | i, j = 1, ..., n\}$, where $p_{t_i t_j}$ is a penalty associated to each unsatisfied soft constraint $c_{t_i t_j}$.
- $Q = \{q_{t_i} | i = 1, ..., n\}$, where q_{t_i} is a penalty associated to each unsatisfied soft constraint c_{t_i}.

Let $f_i \in D_{t_i}$ and $f_j \in D_{t_j}$ frequencies assigned to $t_i, t_j \in X$. The constraints of a MI-FAP are as follows:

- Hard constraints: these constraints must be satisfied
    1. $f_i = v$, $v \in D_{t_i}$ (*hard* pre-assignment).
    2. $|f_i - f_j| = l$, $l \in \mathbb{N}$ (f_i and f_j must be separated by a distance).
- Soft constraints: a failure to meet these constraints involves penalties.
    1. $f_i = v$, $v \in D_{t_i}$ (*soft* pre-assignment).
    2. $|f_i - f_j| > l$, $l \in \mathbb{N}$ (minimum suitable distance between f_i and f_j).

Solving a MI-FAP consists in finding a complete assignment that satisfies all the hard constraints and minimises the quantity:

$\sum\limits_{c_{t_i t_j} \in UC} p_{t_i t_j} + \sum\limits_{c_{t_i} \in UC} q_{t_i}$ where $UC \in C$ is the set of Unsatisfied Soft Constraints,

$\forall t_i, t_j \in X$.

6.2 Experimental Protocol

All the implementations have been achieved using C++. The experiments were run on the cluster Romeo of University of Champagne-Ardenne[1]. Decompositions are done with the edge.betweenness.community function of igraph package in R language [17], available at[2]. This function is an implementation of the Newman algorithm [11], presented in Sect. 3. This decomposition can be used under several criteria. In this paper two particular criteria have been considered: the first one aims to minimize the total number of edges of the cut while the second one aims to minimize the global weight of the cut. In the rest of this paper, the methods associated with these two criteria are denoted min_edge and min_weight, respectively.

The tests were performed on real-life instances coming from the well known CALMA (Combinatorial ALgorithms for Military Applications) project [18]. The characteristics of MI-FAP CALMA instances appear in Table 1. For each instance, the characteristics of the graph and the reduced graph as well as the best costs obtained so far are given. The set of instances consists of two parts: the Celar instances are real-life problems from military applications while the Graph (Generating Radio Link Frequency Assignment Problems Heuristically) instances are similar to the Celar ones but are randomly generated. Here, only the so-called MI-FAP instances were used.

Table 1. Benchmarks characteristics.

Instance	Graph		Reduced graph		Best_cost
	$|V|$	$|E|$	$|V|$	$|E|$	
Celar06	200	1322	100	350	3389
Celar07	400	2865	200	816	343592
Celar08	916	5744	458	1655	262
Graph05	200	1134	100	416	221
Graph06	400	2170	200	843	4123
Graph11	680	3757	340	1425	3080
Graph13	916	5273	458	1877	10110

6.3 Experimental Results Obtained with AGA

This section presents the results obtained by solving the whole problem with the AGA (Algorithm 1). The parameters, experimentally determined, are the following: $p_m = 1$, $p_c = 0.2$, $\Delta p_m = \Delta p_c = 0.1$, $p_{m_{min}} = 0.7$, $p_{c_{max}} = 0.5$, $population\_size = 100$. Three variables are calculated. The first one is the best

---

[1] https://romeo.univ-reims.fr/.

[2] http://cran.r-project.org/web/packages/igraph/igraph.pdf.

deviation, denoted best_dev, which is the standard deviation (Eq. (1)) of the best result obtained among all executions from the optimal. The second cost is the average deviation, denoted avg_dev, which is the standard deviation of the average cost obtained among all executions from the optimal cost. The third column named cpu(s) is the average time needed to find the best cost. The number of executions is fixed to 50.

$$standard\_dev(cost) = \frac{(cost - optimal\_cost)}{(optimal\_cost \times 100)} \tag{1}$$

Table 2 shows very clearly the efficiency of the AGA algorithm. Indeed, optimal solutions are reached for the majority of the instances, while near-optimal solutions are found for the rest of the instances. Moreover, AGA algorithm is stable. Indeed, most of the average deviations are either null or do not exceed 7 % on the most difficult instances.

Table 2. Performances of AGA.

Instance	best_dev	avg_dev	cpu(s)
Celar06	**0.00**	**0.38**	28
Celar07	0.02	0.05	212
Celar08	**0.00**	0.76	396
Graph05	**0.00**	**0.00**	27
Graph06	0.02	0.12	196
Graph11	1.26	3.60	1453
Graph13	3.77	6.94	2619

6.4   Experimental Results Obtained with AGAGD_x_y

This section presents experimental results obtained with AGAGD_x_y described in Sect. 5. In order to test this generic algorithm, three variants were implemented, AGAGD_Newman_clus, AGAGD_Newman_cut and AGAGD_Newman_clus_cut. Newman means here that the decomposition due to Newman has been considered. More precisely, two variants have been considered namely the min_weight and min_edge.

Experiments on AGAGD_Newman_clus. Two versions of Crossover_clus called Crossover_clus1 and Crossover_clus2 have been implemented. The second version corresponds exactly to the implementation of Algorithm 3, while the first one is a relaxed version where the crossover operator considers only the fitness of the cluster to be changed. Tables 3 and 4 present the results of the AGAGD_Newman_clus1 and AGAGD_Newman_clus2 heuristics both for min_weight and min_edge variants. The reported results show clearly that AGAGD_Newman_clus2 outperforms particularly AGAGD_Newman_clus1 in terms of average deviation (avg_dev). This can be due to the fact that the cluster chosen by AGAGD_Newman_clus1 presents certainly a bad fitness, but its separators can have a good fitness in adjacent cuts. Then a modification of these separators can lead to a degradation of the global fitness. For this reason, only the second version of the heuristic is considered in the next part of this paper.

Table 3. Performances of AGAGD_Newman_clus1.

Instance	min_weight			min_edge		
	best_dev	avg_dev	cpu(s)	best_dev	avg_dev	cpu(s)
Celar06	0.29	11.21	15	0.35	13.83	14
Celar07	3.11	30.33	80	3.03	21.46	80
Celar08	2.67	17.93	269	7.63	32.44	188
Graph05	0.00	14.02	24	0.00	26.69	22
Graph06	0.07	18.67	139	0.07	17.89	146
Graph11	7.11	69.93	676	5.68	80.77	1007
Graph13	17.59	70.82	2247	1.04	60.68	1905

Table 4 shows that AGAGD_Newman_clus2 presents in some cases an important gain in terms of CPU time as compared with the results obtained with AGA (Table 2). However, even though the results are quite significant with respect to the best_dev, the average performance (avg_dev) is unfortunately poorer, which qualifies this algorithm as "non stable". This instability problem is due to a premature convergence of AGAGD_Newman_clus caused by the crossover operator that modifies a large number of variables at once (clusters), which significantly reduces the diversity of the population after a few generations (Fig. 2).

Table 4. Performances of AGAGD_Newman_clus2.

Instance	min_weight			min_edge		
	best_dev	avg_dev	cpu(s)	best_dev	avg_dev	cpu(s)
Celar06	0.38	11.18	17	0.35	11.86	17
Celar07	0.11	41.49	85	0.06	15.61	111
Celar08	1.52	11.83	290	6.87	29.38	197
Graph05	0.00	2,71	24	0.00	4.52	22
Graph06	0.07	15.74	200	0.00	11.83	172
Graph11	1.62	44.96	820	0.81	30.94	957
Graph13	13.67	50.92	2004	6.73	39.61	2171

Experiments on AGAGD_Newman_cut. Table 5 presents the results obtained with the AGAGD_Newman_cut algorithm for both min_weight and min_edge variants. These results clearly show a worse performance than the previous algorithm both in terms of CPU time and best_dev and avg_dev. Indeed in this version, unlike the AGAGD_Newman_clus, the algorithm converges very slowly (Fig. 2). By performing the crossover on the cuts, which are by definition less dense regions of the problem, the cost of the solution tends to deteriorate. When this degradation is significant, the mutation operator struggles to repair it. Therefore, the quality of the chromosomes tends to worsen over the generations and the convergence of the algorithm becomes very slow.

Table 5. Results of AGAGD_Newman_cut.

Instance	min_weight			min_edge		
	best_dev	avg_dev	cpu(s)	best_dev	avg_dev	cpu(s)
Celar06	5.10	21.54	237	3.98	22.57	301
Celar07	50.15	426.71	812	41.66	469.29	1102
Celar08	30.53	50.01	1029	39.31	72.90	1079
Graph05	0.00	3.61	43	0.00	9.95	52
Graph06	0.02	10.57	443	0.04	27.04	337
Graph11	3.70	226.64	1807	46.20	335.55	1104
Graph13	16.22	118.82	5439	145.79	281.76	1724

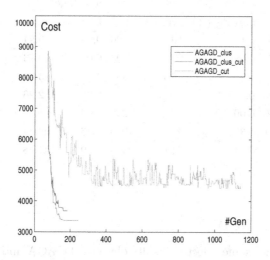

Fig. 2. Graph11 instance: comparing AGAGD_Newman_y.

AGAGD_Newman_clus_cut. Two dual methods were presented in the previous sections which both show their advantages and drawbacks. To benefit from the two methods, an hybrid heuristic called AGAGD_Newman_clus_cut is tested, in which the crossover can either be performed on the cluster or on the cut. Table 6 presents the results of this heuristic both for min_weight and min_edge variants. The results obtained show that this variant presents an important gain in terms of CPU time as compared with those obtained by using AGA (Table 2), especially for the min_edge variant. One can observe a significant improvement of the results as compared with those obtained with the two previous approaches. Notice that some performances in terms of best_dev were reached, while they were never obtained with AGA (Table 2) (see Celar07 and Graph13). However, although the average performances avg_dev are improved as compared with those obtained with AGAGD_Newman_clus2 (Table 4) and AGAGD_Newman_cut (Table 5), they still remain worse than those obtained with AGA (Table 2). This is explained by the large number of variables involved in the crossover. This means that AGAGD_Newman_clus_cut offers a good compromise between AGAGD_Newman_clus and AGAGD_Newman_cut because the integration of the two crossover operators Crossover_clus and Crossover_cut allows the algorithm to converge relatively quickly, while maintaining some diversification level. This avoids a premature convergence, thanks to the Crossover_clus crossover (Fig. 2) while a minimum diversification is maintained. This has enabled to achieve almost near optimal results and even optimal ones quickly Table 6.

Table 6. Performances of AGAGD_Newman_clus_cut.

Instance	min_weight			min_edge		
	best_dev(%)	avg_dev	cpu	best_dev	avg_dev	cpu
Celar06	0.14	10.50	26	0.29	9.94	23
Celar07	0.08	25.18	193	0.00	10.73	149
Celar08	1.9	8.77	357	4.19	13.74	281
Graph05	0.00	1.80	31	0.00	2.26	26
Graph06	0.00	8.82	272	0.00	1.57	219
Graph11	1.36	49.64	1036	2.56	24.48	900
Graph13	4.61	41.63	2428	1.29	41.48	1556

6.5   AGA vs AGAGD

Table 7 summarizes some selected results obtained by AGA and AGAGD algorithms. While we notice the degradation of the parameter avg_dev in AGAGD, let us note nonetheless improving some best_cost and reduced time resolution especially on the most difficult instances.

Table 7. Comparing AGA and AGAGD.

Instance	AGA			AGAGD		
	best_dev(%)	avg_dev	cpu	best_dev	avg_dev	cpu
Celar06	0.00	0.38	28	0.14	10.50	26
Celar07	0.02	0.05	212	0.00	10.73	149
Celar08	0.00	0.76	396	1.9	8.77	357
Graph05	0.00	0.00	27	0.00	1.80	31
Graph06	0.02	0.12	196	0.00	1.57	219
Graph11	1.26	3.60	1435	0.81	30.94	957
Graph13	3.77	6.94	2619	1.29	41.48	1556

7 Conclusion & Perspectives

The aim of this work was to solve Partial Constraint Satisfaction Problems close to the optimum in the shortest time possible. To this aim, an Adaptive Genetic Algorithm Guided by Decomposition called AGAGD_x_y was proposed. The name of the algorithm is indexed by x and y, where x is for the decomposition and y is for the genetic operator. In fact, the AGAGD_x_y algorithm is doubly generic because it fits several decomposition methods and can accept several heuristics as crossover operator as well. For the decomposition step, two variants of the well known decomposition algorithm due to Newman were used, namely the min_edge and min_weight variants. As crossover operators, three heuristics called Crossover_clus, Crossover_cut and Crossover_clus_cut were proposed.

The first results obtained on MI-FAP problems are promising. Indeed, the execution time was everywhere significantly reduced as compared with that obtained with the previous AGA algorithm, while a decrease of average quality of the solutions must be accepted in some cases.

These early positive investigations encourage to follow this direction of research and enhance the current results. In the short term, it is planned to investigate other heuristics in order to improve the crossover operator. Moreover, a local repairing method can be associated with AGAGD_x_y after each crossover step. Last, it would be also interesting to deploy this approach on other multi-cut decomposition or tree decomposition methods as well as on other PCSP applications.

References

1. Maniezzo, V., Carbonaro, A.: An ants heuristic for the frequency assignment problem. Comput. Inf. Sci. **16**, 259–288 (2000)
2. Kolen, A.: A genetic algorithm for the partial binary constraint satisfaction problem: an application to a frequency assignment problem. Stat. Neerl. **61**(1), 4–15 (2007)

3. Voudouris, C., Tsang, E.: Partial constraint satisfaction problems and guided local search. Technical report, Department of Computer Science, University of Essex (1995) Technical Report CSM-25
4. Allouche, D., de Givry, S., Schiex, T.: Towards parallel non serial dynamic programming for solving hard weighted CSP. In: Cohen, D. (ed.) CP 2010. LNCS, vol. 6308, pp. 53–60. Springer, Heidelberg (2010)
5. Colombo, G., Allen, S.M.: Problem decomposition for minimum interference frequency assignment. In: Proceedings of the IEEE Congress on Evolutionary Computation, Singapore (2007)
6. Koster, A., Van Hoessel, S., Kolen, A.: Solving partial constraint satisfaction problems with tree decomposition. Netw. J. **40**(3), 170–180 (2002)
7. Sadeg-Belkacem, L., Habbas, Z., Benbouzid-Sitayeb, F., Singer, D.: Decomposition techniques for solving frequency assignment problems (FAP) a top-down approach. In: International Conference on Agents and Artificial Intelligence (ICAART 2014), pp. 477–484 (2014)
8. Fontaine, M., Loudni, S., Boizumault, P.: Exploiting tree decomposition for guiding neighborhoods exploration for VNS. RAIRO Oper. Res. **47**(2), 91–123 (2013)
9. Ouali, A., Loudni, S., Loukil, L., Boizumault, P., Lebbah, Y.: Cooperative parallel decomposition guided VNS for solving weighted CSP. In: Blesa, M.J., Blum, C., Voß, S. (eds.) HM 2014. LNCS, vol. 8457, pp. 100–114. Springer, Heidelberg (2014)
10. Schaeffer, S.E.: Graph clustering. Computer Science Review **1**, 27–64 (2007)
11. Newman, M.: Fast algorithm for detecting community structure in networks. Phys. Rev. **69**(6), 066133 (2004)
12. Girvan, M., Newman, M.: Community structure in social and biological networks. In: Proceedings of the National Academy of Sciences of the USA, pp. 7821–7826 (2002)
13. Metzger, B.H.: Spectrum management technique. 38th National ORSA Meeting, Detroit (1970)
14. Hale, W.K.: Frequency assignment: theory and applications. Proc. IEEE **68**(12), 1497–1514 (1980)
15. Aardal, K., Van Hoessel, S., Koster, A., Mannino, C., Sassano, A.: Models and solution techniques for frequency assignment problems. Ann. Oper. Res. **153**, 79–129 (2007)
16. Audhya, G.K., Sinha, K., Ghosh, S.C., Sinha, B.P.: A survey on the channel assignment problem in wireless networks. Wirel. Commun. Mob. Comput. **11**, 583–609 (2011)
17. Csardi, G., Nepusz, T.: The Igraph software package for complex network research. InterJournal Complex Syst. **1695**, 1–9 (2005)
18. CALMA-website: Euclid Calma project (1995). ftp://ftp.win.tue.nl/pub/techreports/CALMA/

Activity Recognition for Dogs Based on Time-series Data Analysis

Tatsuya Kiyohara[✉], Ryohei Orihara, Yuichi Sei, Yasuyuki Tahara,
and Akihiko Ohsuga

Graduate School of Information Systems, University of Electro-Communications,
Chofu-city, Tokyo, Japan
t-kiyohara@ohsuga.is.uec.ac.jp, ryohei.orihara@toshiba.co.jp,
{sei,tahara,ohsuga}@is.uec.ac.jp

Abstract. Dogs are one of the most popular pets in the world, and
more than 10 million dogs are bred annually in Japan now [4]. Recently,
primitive commercial services have been started that record dogs' activities and report them to their owners. Although it is expected that an
owner would like to know the dog's activity in greater detail, a method
proposed in a previous study has failed to recognize some of the key
actions. The demand for their identification is highlighted in responses
to our questionnaire. In this paper, we show a method to recognize the
actions of the dog by attaching only one off-the-shelf acceleration sensor
to the neck of the dog. We apply DTW-D which is the state-of-the-art
time series data search technique for activity recognition. Application of
DTW-D to activity recognition of an animal is unprecedented according
to our knowledge, and thus is the main contribution of this study. As a
result, we were able to recognize eleven different activities with 75.1 %
classification F-measure. We also evaluate the method taking account of
real-world use cases.

Keywords: Activity recognition · Accelerometer · Time series data
mining · Sensor data mining · Acceleration sensor · Dynamic Time
Warping (DTW) · DTW-D

1 Introduction

There are services for dog owners that record dog's activity in the form of life
logs and report it to them. Examples of the services include the one provided by
Whistle Lab's "Whistle" [12] and NTT docomo's "pet fit" [7]. These commercial services recognize raw actions such as "walking", "running", "resting" and
"sleeping". These services themselves are evidences of the demand to learn pets'
behavior when the owners are away. However, the variety of actions recognizable
by the current commercial services is limited and far from being satisfactory.
In our analysis, which will be verified in Sect. 2 by analyzing the results of a
questionnaire, there are three aspects of the demand for pet activity monitoring.
The first aspect arises from the interest in short-term healthcare. The second

© Springer International Publishing Switzerland 2015
B. Duval et al. (Eds.): ICAART 2015, LNAI 9494, pp. 163–184, 2015.
DOI: 10.1007/978-3-319-27947-3_9

aspect originates from the interest in long-term healthcare. The third and final aspect is related to problematic behavior of pets.

For example, vomit reporting is desired for a pet monitoring system because the action is directly related to internal health condition. The action should be detected from the aspect of short-term healthcare.

Eye-scratching is an action that can lead to a serious disease if repeated multiple times. If a pet monitoring system reports the number of times the action is occurred, early treatment by a veterinarian is possible and a serious condition can be avoided. Therefore the detection of the action is desirable from the aspects of long-term healthcare.

In Japan, approximately 70 % of the dogs share the life space with human beings. In such circumstances, the pet may exhibit problematic behavior such as biting the furniture and entering the places where it should not, especially in the absence of owner. The owners need to know the problematic actions in order to take appropriate corrective measures, hence the third aspect of the demand for pet monitoring. An action related to this aspect is jumping. It is problematic because it could reflect pets' intention to touch things at higher place, which are kept there by the owners so that the pets could not play with them. Although there is a study on monitoring the actions of a dog, the accuracy of detection for those actions is not high.

In this article, we propose a method to monitor dog's behavior, which is especially effective in the recognition of those actions whose demand of detection is high, according to our analysis of the demands of the owners. The remainder of this paper is organized as follows. In Sect. 2, we will investigate and analyze a questionnaire to see whether there is a background to the kind of needs. In Sect. 3, we will write about the work related to the activity recognition of the dog and the search technique of time series data. In Sect. 4, we will present the algorithm for the calculation of Euclid distance, DTW distance and DTW-D distance. Section 5 is dedicated to the description of the experiments. We will describe the experimental environment, experimental procedure. In Sect. 6, we will show experimental results of our approach and exsisting approach as a base-line. In Sect. 7, we will discuss the conclusions and recommendations for future work.

2 Questionnaire Survey for Needs

2.1 Questionnaire Result

We performed a questionnaire survey with pet owners in order to investigate which actions of the pets should be recognized by a remote pet monitoring system. The questionnaire listed 22 typical actions of the pets and the owners were asked to tell if they were interested in knowing their occurrence when they were away. Furthermore, a free-format comment field was provided to collect the reasons why the owners were interested in knowing those actions. Figure 1 shows the questionnaire results and Table 1 shows the comments filled in the free-format field. The action that gathered the most interest from the owners

Table 1. Comments in free-format field.

How much is my dog relaxed?
What kind of facial expression does the dog have?
When the owner is away, what kind of action does the dog often take?
I keep some cats. I am not worried about the state of my house when I am away, because the cats usually sleep. When I had a dog before, I was worried how the dog was doing. I think it depends on animal species
It would be nice to talk to a dog at home via a mobile device, when the owner is away
(Dog)
Showing the stomach
Going around
Running around as energetically as possible
Shaking the tail buzzingly
Excited with the sound that promises food items even if they are invisible
(Cat)
Making rumbling sound at the throat
Putting the face into a paper or plastic bag
Climbing the curtain when excited
Waiting at the door for a family member to come home
Grooming
The reaction to the sound of phone calls and intercom during the absence of the owner
I am concerned if the dog gets into trouble while I am away
My dog silently vomits without having a cough. That makes it difficult for me to notice the vomiting instantly. I want to notice abnormality as early as possible
Because my dog is elderly, I am very interested in knowing the behavior of the dog during the absence of my family. In addition, I am concerned if the dog does some action that leads to an illness
I currently keep my cat in the room. When I go home, the room is so messy that I can imagine what the cat has been doing
Because the dog spends the daytime alone everyday, I leash the dog. So the range that the dog can move within is narrow. Sometimes my dog can neither jump nor walk. But, I think if the dog spends time without doing any mischievous act, there would be no need of the leash... [in order to realize the situation] it would be nice if the whole of the dog's behavior could be recognized
I want to see how the dog behaved during the earthquake
I want to know the action of the dog when it thunders during the absence of me and my family. Because the dog comes to see me to the door when I go home, I want to know when the dog begins to move. Is it when I open the front door, I stop the bicycle, or I open the gate?

is vomiting. In addition, the questionnaire result and the free-format description suggest that many owners are concerned with the health condition of their pets.

2.2 Questionnaire Analysis

Let us focus on behaviors in which more than 70 % of the owners are interested. "vomiting" and "shivering" directly reflect the health conditions of dogs, thus their monitoring is desirable from the aspect of short-term healthcare. "coughing" can suggest respiratory diseases if its frequency is unusually high and so its monitoring is desirable from the aspect of long-term healthcare. "scratching" can lead to a serious disease if done repeatedly and therefore its monitoring is also desirable from the aspect of long-term healthcare. "barking", "chewing", "drinking", "eating", "urinating", "defecating" and "jumping" are potentially problematic actions. "barking" could make the neighbors complain. "chewing" may indicate damage to the furniture. The problem with "drinking" and "eating" is that a pet might eat or drink something that the owner does not want it to. "urinating" and "defecating" could mean a blunder. With "jumping", a dog may try to take things at high places. As a result, the eleven behaviors in which more than 70 % of owners are interested are related to the three aspects introduced in Sect. 1.

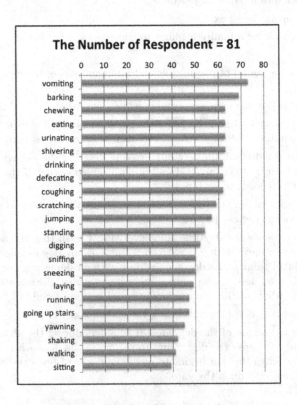

Fig. 1. Results of questionnaire.

3   Related Work

3.1   Activity Recognition for Dogs

There is a study on activity recognition [5]. They use PCA-based feature extraction and empirical cumulative density function (ECDF) [3]. They sample acceleration data at 30 Hz. The acceleration data are divided into one-second frames and each frame is analyzed separately. A frame has 50 % overlap with its predecessor and is created with sliding window procedure based on [9]. Each frame is labeled using the movie which is recorded by one annotator. The feature vector of each frame is trained and tested using 10-fold cross validation and is classified in each of the 16 actions and one rejection class using k-NN (k=1). They show the result as a confusion matrix. In their study, jumping in which 70 % of the owners are interested is not recognizable. Furthermore, seven actions are with less than 50 % recognition accuracies in their study, and recognition accuracy is less than 80 % for 12 actions. Therefore, we must say that there is room for improvement in the recognition accuracy.

3.2   Time Series Data Mining

Searching and Mining Trillions of Time Series Subsequences Under Dynamic Time Warping. There is a problem of finding a subsequence that is similar to a query sequence in a large scale time series data. The problem is solved by calculating the distance between the sequences and the query using Dynamic Time Warping (DTW). However, the computational cost of DTW is high. As time series data, that is to be searched, becomes longer, the number of calculations of DTW increases linearly. As a result, the computational time for the search becomes enormous. The study proposed a method to solve the problem by eliminating unpromising candidates at early stages.

DTW-D: Time Series Semi-supervised Learning from Single Example. Time series data with little up-and-downs tend to become close to any data in DTW distance. Because of this, a sequence with significant temporal change could be classified as data without one. In order to avoid a situation like this, Chen et al. proposed a distance measure called DTW-D.

4   Algorithm for Similarity Caluculation

Suppose there are two sequences $X = \langle x_i | i = 1, ..., N \rangle, Y = \langle y_j | j = 1, ..., M \rangle$. We would like to measure the distance between X and Y in order to measure the similarity of the sequences of X and Y in waveforms. The smaller the distance, the more similar X and Y. Some distances are commonly used.

4.1 Euclidean Distance

Euclidean Distance (ED) is the classic scale for measuring the similarity among the time series data. It is measuring the distance between the time series data of the same length. It is determined by summing up the distances between the data at the same time index.

$$ED = \sqrt{\sum_{i=1}^{N}(x_i - y_i)^2}, \quad (N = M) \tag{1}$$

Figure 2 is a figure of alignment of the Euclid distance.

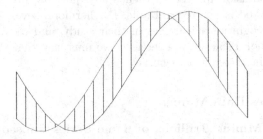

Fig. 2. Alignment of the Euclid distance.

4.2 Classical DTW

A weak point of the ED is that it tends to be large when the time series data are out of phase. Dynamic Time Warping is a technique used to find distance more flexibly between time series data than ED. Figure 3 shows alignment of the data points that is used to calculate the DTW distance.

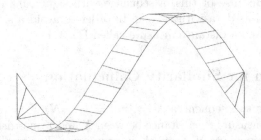

Fig. 3. Alignment of the DTW distance.

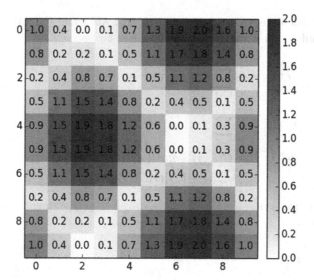

Fig. 4. Cost matrix.

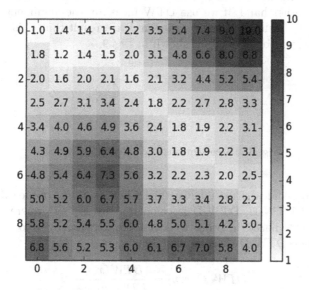

Fig. 5. Accumulated cost matrix.

At first, we calculate cost matrix $C \in \mathbb{R}^{N \times M}$ which is defined by the distance between each element using Eq. (2). An example of the cost matrix is shown in Fig. 4.

$$C(i, j) := c(x_i, y_j) = abs(x_i - y_j),$$
$$(i = 1, ..., N, \ j = 1, ..., M) \tag{2}$$

Then, we calculate accumulated cost matrix AC using Eq. (3). An example of the accumulated cost matrix is shown in Fig. 5.

$$AC(i,\ 1) = \sum_{k=1}^{i} c(x_k,\ y_1)$$

$$AC(1,\ j) = \sum_{l=1}^{j} c(x_1,\ y_l)$$

$$AC(i,\ j) = C(i,\ j) + min\{AC(i-1,\ j-1),$$
$$AC(i-1,j), AC(i,j-1)\},\ (i,\ j \geq 2) \tag{3}$$

DTW distance is $AC(N,\ M)$. We have shown the above-mentioned algorithm in Algorithm 1.

4.3   DTW-D

Let us consider to calculate the distance between each sequence R, G, B in Fig. 6. If we use ED measure, the alignment of data points will be similar to that in Fig. 7. On the other hand, if we use DTW measure, the alignment will be like that in Fig. 8. In both cases, the counter-intuitive result that G is more similar to R than B is, will be derived, as shown in Fig. 9.

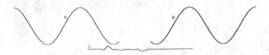

Fig. 6. Three sequences to calculate distance.

In order to avoid a situation like this, Chen et al. [2] proposed a distance measure called DTW-D. DTW-D is calculated by Eq. (4) where ϵ is a small positive constant placed in order to avoid the division by zero. As shown in Fig. 10, based on DTW-D, B is more similar to R than G is.

$$DTW\text{-}D(x,y) = \frac{DTW(x,y)}{ED(x,y) + \epsilon} \tag{4}$$

Fig. 7. Alignment of the ED between R and B, R and G (Color figure online).

Algorithm 1. Calculate DTW Distance.

Input: sequence $X = \langle x_i | i = 1, \ldots, N \rangle$,
$\qquad\qquad Y = \langle y_j | j = 1, \ldots, M \rangle$
Output: DTW Distance $AC(N, M)$
1: /*Calculate Cost Matrix*/
2: **for** $i = 1$ to N **do**
3:    **for** $j = 1$ to M **do**
4:       $C(i, j) \Leftarrow abs(x_i - y_j)$
5:    **end for**
6: **end for**
7: /*Calculate Accumulated Cost Matrix*/
8: $AC(1, 1) \Leftarrow C(1, 1)$
9: **for** $i = 2$ to N **do**
10:    $AC(i, 1) \Leftarrow AC(i-1, 1) + C(i, 1)$
11: **end for**
12: **for** $j = 2$ to M **do**
13:    $AC(1, j) \Leftarrow AC(1, j-1) + C(1, j)$
14: **end for**
15: **for** $i = 2$ to N **do**
16:    **for** $j = 2$ to M **do**
17:       $AC(i, j) \Leftarrow C(i, j) + min\{AC(i-1, j-1), AC(i-1, j), AC(i, j-1)\}$
18:    **end for**
19: **end for**
20: **return** $AC(N, M)$

Fig. 8. Alignment of the DTW distance between R and B, R and G (Color figure online).

	ED					DTW		
	R	G	B			R	G	B
R	0	3.4	6.7		R	0	3.3	3.4
G		0	3.5		G		0	3.2
B			0		B			0

Fig. 9. ED and DTW Distance in the three Sequence [R, G, B] (Color figure online).

	DTW/ED					DTW-D=DTW/ED		
	R	G	B			R	G	B
R	0	3.3/3.4	3.4/6.7		R	0	0.97	0.51
G		0	3.2/3.5		G		0	0.91
B			0		B			0

Fig. 10. DTW-D distance is the distance that DTW distance divided by ED.

Table 2. Information of the experimental subjects and environments.

Name	Yuzu	Gummi	Cool	Oreo	Orfeu	Shoko
Breed	Pembroke welsh corgi			Toy poodle		
Sexuality	Female	Male	Male	Male	Male	Female
Age	4-year	2-year	10-month	8-month	1-year	2-year
Weight	10.7 kg	10.2 kg	7.8 kg	2.7 kg	2.6 kg	2.4 kg
Length	60 cm	60 cm	58 cm	43 cm	43 cm	40 cm
Height	30 cm	30 cm	28 cm	30 cm	30 cm	28 cm
Character	Wise	Friendly	Selfish	Obedient	Active	Gentle

5   Experimental Protocol

5.1   Experimental Environments

The experimental subjects and environments shown in Table 2. The conditions of the experiment are as follows. The acceleration data was collected at sampling frequency 25 Hz. The video was recorded in order to put the ground truth label. We prepared the acceleration sensor shown in Fig. 12 on the left side. The sensor was attached to the neck of the dog as shown in the Fig. 12 on the right side. The acceleration sensor which we used for the experiment is AX3 Watch of Axivity [1]. The sensor is equipped with 3 axes MEMS which works as an accelerometer. Sampling frequency can be selected from several predetermined values provided by the tool between 12.5 Hz and 800 Hz. It has a mounted NAND flash memory of 512 MB to store the data. The maximum recording time is 14 days at 100 Hz, and 30 days at 12.5 Hz. Measurement range of the acceleration is ±16 g. This sensor has IP68-rated dust- and water-proof capability that is standardized by International Electrotechnical Commission 60529. Acceleration data is transferred to the PC from the sensor by using USB. We have shown the definition of the activity of the dog in Table 3.

Figure 13 shows appearance and dimension of the subjects.

5.2   Experimental Procedure

Our Approach. Using ELAN [6], which is a tool for video annotation, every sample of the acceleration data is labeled. The label consists of one of 8 activities shown in Table 3. "unspecified" label is given to the behavior that cannot be judged as one of the 8 activities. Let us call a subsequence of 25 samples a frame. A new frame is created by sliding the 25-sample window forward by one sample. As a result, adjoining two adjoining frames shares 24 samples of each other, that is 96 % of the frames. When the same ground truth label appears in more than 20 samples in a frame, that is 80 % of the frame, the whole frame is given the ground truth label. This is because, average F-measure became maximum at 80 % in 52 % through 100 %. Otherwise, the frame is labeled "mixed" and used for a test, but that frame is not listed in a result. We choose one frame from all frames and set it aside as a test frame. Remaining frames is assumed to be training frames. The test and training frames are chosen so that there are no shared samples. The distance between the training and test frames is calculated using each of the Euclidean, DTW, and DTW-D methods to compare each measure's appropriateness for the task. We include Euclidean Distance which is known to be prone to noises here because we are interested in how DTW-D can improve the performance against one of its base measures. We infer a label of a test frame from the label of the training frame nearest to the test frame. In other words, we used the nearest neighbor method. This is because, in a preliminary study comparing performance of k-nearest neighbor methods for the data, average F-measure became maximum at $k = 1$ in $k = 1, 3, 5$. Recognition accuracy is calculated through cross validation. Overview of the experimental setting is shown in Fig. 11.

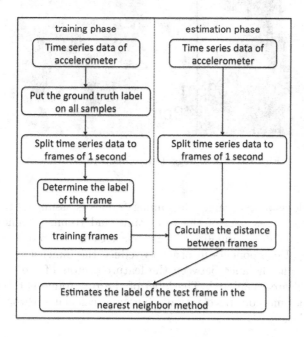

Fig. 11. Overview of the experimental setting.

Existing Approach. The existing PCA-based approach was also applied to our data set. Each parameters were chosen to be as close as possible to the existing study. A new frame is created by sliding the 25-sample window forward by 13 samples. As a result, adjoining two adjoining frames shares 12 samples of each other, that is 48 % of the frames. When the same ground truth label appears in more than 19 samples in a frame, that is 76 % of the frame, the whole frame is given the ground truth label. We choose one frame from all frames

Fig. 12. The appearance of the sensor and how the dog wears it.

Fig. 13. Size of dogs. (left) Oreo, (right) Yuzu.

and set it aside as a test frame. Remaining frames is assumued to be training frames. In some cases part of the test frame and training frames have 48% overlap. Each frame is normalized by inverse ECDF. We projected them into first 25 principal components in order to reduce the dimension of the feature of the frames. The distance between the feature vectors of the test frame and training frames are calculated. The label of the test frame is estimated using nearest neighbor method. Recognition accuracy is calculated through leave-one-out cross validation.

5.3   Experimental Results and Discussion

Analyses of the Result of Our Approach. Table 4 show accuracies of our approach obtained through the experiments using data of the six dogs. Tables 5, 6, 7, 8, 9 and 10 show accuracies obtained through the experiments using data of each dog alone. In Tables 4, 5, 6, 7, 8, 9 and 10, a cell is marked red if the corresponding distance measure gives the best result among the three measures. In Tables 5, 6, 7, 8, 9 and 10, an activity is omitted if the dog did not exhibit the activity.

Table 3. Definition of behavior (the number of DTW-D frames & PCA-based frames shown in parentheses, comparing existing approach).

walking: (2781 & 216 frames)
Walking. Movement of the left and right limb is alternating and not aligned.
eating: (5223 & 401 frames)
Put food in the mouth, and swallow.
sitting: (4140 & 319 frames)
Sitting quietly with buttocks on the floor or ground.
laying: (5746 & 442 frames)
Lying down and put his head against a fixed object such as a floor or ground.
sniffing: (370 & 29 frames)
Sniffing the smell of the floor or ground.
running: (961 & 74 frames)
Running. Movement of the left and right limb is almost aligned in flat.
jumping: (660 & 50 frames)
Foot of all is away from such as a floor or ground.
drinking: (1068 & 82 frames)
Drinking such as water from the dish on the floor or ground.
shaking: (670 & 50 frames)
Shaking itself to shake off the water.
scratching: (47 & 5 frames)
Scratching eyes by foreleg. Scratching the front side from the chest by hindleg.
up-stairs:
Go upstairs that movement of the left and right limb is almost aligned on the stairs.

Table 4. Precision, recall and F-measure at ED, DTW distance and DTW-D distance of 6 dogs.

All	Precision			Recall			F-measure		
	ED	DTW	DTW-D	ED	DTW	DTW-D	ED	DTW	DTW-D
unspecified	0.7912	0.8124	0.8129	0.7378	0.7611	0.7667	0.7635	0.7859	0.7891
walking	0.7381	0.7184	0.6911	0.7007	0.7432	0.8043	0.7189	0.7306	0.7434
eating	0.7933	0.7862	0.8039	0.7764	0.8122	0.8401	0.7847	0.7990	0.8216
sitting	0.4934	0.5437	0.6438	0.7733	0.7724	0.6763	0.6024	0.6382	0.6597
laying	0.8105	0.8629	0.9307	0.9568	0.9579	0.9541	0.8776	0.9079	0.9422
sniffing	0.2960	0.3512	0.5224	0.3591	0.3583	0.3822	0.3245	0.3547	0.4414
scratching	0.1622	0.3678	0.3158	0.1071	0.2857	0.3750	0.1290	0.3216	0.3429
running	0.8689	0.8512	0.6575	0.4372	0.4940	0.6896	0.5817	0.6252	0.6732
jumping	0.8212	0.8298	0.5855	0.4243	0.5111	0.6444	0.5595	0.6326	0.6136
drinking	0.8161	0.7924	0.7607	0.8631	0.9020	0.9421	0.8390	0.8436	0.8418
shaking	0.3761	0.3759	0.3802	0.3369	0.3333	0.3832	0.3554	0.3533	0.3817
up-stairs	0.8481	0.8790	0.6200	0.4786	0.5190	0.6333	0.6119	0.6527	0.6266

According to Table 4, the DTW-D has yielded high F-measures as compared to the DTW and ED. Using DTW-D, subtle differences in the actions of the dog are recognized more precisely than using the DTW and ED. With DTW-D, it is expected that the accuracy of activity recognition will be stable even when the number of actions to be recognized increases. If an action appears only in a part of a frame, such as jumping, it is difficult for a statistical method to detect the difference in the feature value from other actions.

It can be explained that a few samples with significant feature can be obscured by many ordinary samples in a statistical method. On the other hand, the methods that calculate the similarity of waveforms, such as DTW, are able to detect the difference resulting in superior accuracy.

"Scratching" has resulted an extremely low F-measure. There are only 47 frames of "scratching" in the data. The recall cannot be good simply because of the shortage of the data. The resulted few true positives are further overwhelmed by vast amount of false positives, yielding the poor precision. This can explain the remarkably poor F-measure.

From Tables 5, 6, 7, 8, 9 and 10, we can see the following trends.

- Acurracy for Shoko is poorer than for other dogs. Because she was gentle, we were unable to gather enough data from her.
- Behaviors such as drinking, eating, laying and running yield better F-measures than other activities for most dogs, with a few exceptions for Shoko.
- Behaviors such as shaking, sniffing, sitting, walking and up-stairs have large inter-dog variances for their F-measures.
- As we have already seen, F-measures for scratching are poor for all the dogs.
- Although F-measures for jumping are not particularly high, their inter-dog variance is small with an exception of one from Shoko.

Table 5. Precision, recall and F-measure at ED, DTW distance and DTW-D distance of Yuzu.

Yuzu	Precision			Recall			F-measure		
	ED	DTW	DTW-D	ED	DTW	DTW-D	ED	DTW	DTW-D
unspecified	0.8000	0.8124	0.8030	0.7487	0.7708	0.7802	0.7735	0.7911	0.7915
walking	0.5439	0.5470	0.5186	0.3489	0.4134	0.5650	0.4251	0.4709	0.5408
eating	0.8293	0.8336	0.8657	0.8418	0.8422	0.8560	0.8355	0.8379	0.8608
sitting	0.5056	0.5400	0.6281	0.7674	0.7489	0.6421	0.6096	0.6275	0.6350
laying	0.8405	0.8759	0.9348	0.9523	0.9568	0.9475	0.8929	0.9146	0.9411
sniffing	0.4974	0.5412	0.5635	0.4642	0.5185	0.5037	0.4802	0.5296	0.5319
scratching	0.2188	0.2222	0.2126	0.1818	0.2078	0.3506	0.1986	0.2148	0.2647
jumping	0.8944	0.9145	0.6688	0.4864	0.6299	0.7749	0.6301	0.7460	0.7180
shaking	0.3000	0.3568	0.3028	0.1846	0.2031	0.2954	0.2286	0.2588	0.2991

Table 6. Precision, recall and F-measure at ED, DTW distance and DTW-D distance of Gummi.

Gummi	Precision			Recall			F-measure		
	ED	DTW	DTW-D	ED	DTW	DTW-D	ED	DTW	DTW-D
unspecified	0.7397	0.7937	0.8268	0.7535	0.7591	0.7029	0.7466	0.7760	0.7598
walking	0.8623	0.8220	0.8285	0.9086	0.9254	0.9602	0.8849	0.8706	0.8895
eating	0.7292	0.7385	0.8922	0.9355	0.9392	0.9243	0.8196	0.8269	0.9080
running	0.8442	0.8848	0.7980	0.5985	0.6225	0.8656	0.7004	0.7308	0.8304
jumping	0.7500	0.7500	0.6340	0.4259	0.4630	0.5988	0.5433	0.5725	0.6159
sniffing	0.3437	0.3631	0.5187	0.4217	0.4076	0.5562	0.3787	0.3841	0.5368
shaking	0.0000	0.0000	0.0000	0.0000	0.0000	0.0000	0.0000	0.0000	0.0000
up-stairs	0.8382	0.8832	0.8489	0.8702	0.9237	0.9008	0.8539	0.9030	0.8741

Table 7. Precision, recall and F-measure at ED, DTW distance and DTW-D distance of cool.

Cool	Precision			Recall			F-measure		
	ED	DTW	DTW-D	ED	DTW	DTW-D	ED	DTW	DTW-D
unspecified	0.8816	0.8977	0.8747	0.7867	0.8095	0.8284	0.8315	0.8513	0.8509
walking	0.9064	0.8805	0.7990	0.9036	0.9262	0.9579	0.9050	0.9028	0.8713
eating	0.6851	0.6886	0.8180	0.8923	0.9097	0.8259	0.7751	0.7839	0.8219
sitting	0.6717	0.7240	0.8449	0.8960	0.8924	0.8224	0.7678	0.7994	0.8335
laying	0.9065	0.9257	0.9678	1.0000	0.9996	0.9929	0.9509	0.9612	0.9802
sniffing	0.6361	0.6554	0.7064	0.5094	0.5661	0.5993	0.5658	0.6075	0.6484
running	0.9903	0.9947	0.9146	0.9067	0.8311	1.0000	0.9466	0.9056	0.9554
jumping	0.9245	0.9505	0.5753	0.3769	0.3692	0.6462	0.5355	0.5319	0.6087
drinking	0.9013	0.8631	0.6591	0.9874	1.0000	1.0000	0.9424	0.9265	0.7946
shaking	0.7558	0.7532	0.6525	0.6019	0.5370	0.7130	0.6701	0.6270	0.6814
up-stairs	0.8542	0.8276	0.5068	0.5256	0.6154	0.9487	0.6508	0.7059	0.6607

Table 8. Precision, recall and F-measure at ED, DTW distance and DTW-D distance of Oreo.

Oreo	Precision			Recall			F-measure		
	ED	DTW	DTW-D	ED	DTW	DTW-D	ED	DTW	DTW-D
unspecified	0.6622	0.6950	0.7520	0.7295	0.7278	0.6695	0.6942	0.7110	0.7083
walking	0.1852	0.3244	0.3531	0.0877	0.2561	0.4386	0.1190	0.2863	0.3912
eating	0.8297	0.8296	0.8671	0.8912	0.8904	0.8773	0.8594	0.8589	0.8722
sitting	0.2473	0.2278	0.3036	0.4071	0.3186	0.1504	0.3077	0.2657	0.2012
sniffing	0.6923	0.8256	0.8750	0.5000	0.5635	0.6667	0.5806	0.6698	0.7568
running	0.8523	0.8480	0.6328	0.2809	0.3621	0.7272	0.4226	0.5075	0.6767
jumping	0.7778	0.8182	0.6047	0.2090	0.2687	0.7761	0.3294	0.4045	0.6797
drinking	0.9755	0.9740	0.8387	0.9899	0.9982	0.9991	0.9827	0.9859	0.9119
shaking	0.8015	0.8536	0.9096	0.8907	0.9089	0.9777	0.8437	0.8804	0.9424

Table 9. Precision, recall and F-measure at ED, DTW distance and DTW-D distance of Orfeu.

Orfeu	Precision			Recall			F-measure		
	ED	DTW	DTW-D	ED	DTW	DTW-D	ED	DTW	DTW-D
unspecified	0.8621	0.8757	0.8732	0.8306	0.8354	0.8073	0.8461	0.8550	0.8389
walking	0.7623	0.7495	0.6702	0.9202	0.9255	0.9103	0.8338	0.8282	0.7720
eating	0.8384	0.8437	0.8515	0.7349	0.7886	0.9076	0.7832	0.8152	0.8786
sitting	0.4464	0.4872	0.5503	0.6649	0.6569	0.4654	0.5342	0.5595	0.5043
sniffing	0.1593	0.2283	0.4599	0.3243	0.4144	0.3874	0.2136	0.2944	0.4205
running	0.9129	0.9507	0.8217	0.7249	0.7628	0.8353	0.8081	0.8464	0.8284
jumping	0.9853	1.0000	0.8500	0.6262	0.6776	0.7944	0.7657	0.8078	0.8213
drinking	0.6811	0.7061	0.8682	0.9848	0.9827	0.9697	0.8053	0.8217	0.9162
shaking	0.9583	0.9565	0.8519	0.9583	0.9167	0.9583	0.9583	0.9362	0.9020
up-stairs	0.9710	0.9200	0.6606	0.6569	0.6765	0.7059	0.7836	0.7797	0.6825

Table 10. Precision, Recall and F-measure at ED, DTW Distance and DTW-D Distance of Shoko.

Shoko	Precision			Recall			F-measure		
	ED	DTW	DTW-D	ED	DTW	DTW-D	ED	DTW	DTW-D
unspecified	0.8482	0.8689	0.8752	0.8887	0.8855	0.8351	0.8680	0.8771	0.8547
walking	0.3763	0.4058	0.4976	0.1762	0.2819	0.5268	0.2400	0.3327	0.5118
eating	0.6282	0.6187	0.5637	0.5840	0.6197	0.6483	0.6053	0.6192	0.6030
sitting	0.6096	0.6444	0.7638	0.8103	0.8140	0.6414	0.6957	0.7193	0.6973
sniffing	0.3423	0.3233	0.4797	0.1250	0.1414	0.2336	0.1831	0.1968	0.3142
scratching	0.0000	0.8000	0.4186	0.0000	0.4571	0.5143	0.0000	0.5818	0.4615
running	0.8431	0.7538	0.4375	0.5599	0.6458	0.8385	0.6729	0.6957	0.5750
jumping	0.8667	0.6500	0.1917	0.1733	0.1733	0.3067	0.2889	0.2737	0.2359
drinking	0.7839	0.7957	0.8729	0.9249	0.9224	0.9183	0.8486	0.8544	0.8951
shaking	0.9431	0.9470	0.8543	0.8286	0.8929	0.9214	0.8821	0.9191	0.8866
up-stairs	1.0000	1.0000	0.8889	0.0092	0.0092	0.2202	0.0182	0.0182	0.3529

Table 11. Precision, recall and F-measure at the existing study.

PCA-based	Precision	Recall	F-measure
Unspecified	0.2952	0.3346	0.3137
Walking	0.1232	0.1574	0.1382
Eating	0.3384	0.2793	0.3060
Sitting	0.1740	0.2351	0.2000
Laying	0.3100	0.1614	0.2123
Sniffing	0.0244	0.0345	0.0286
Running	0.0208	0.0270	0.0235
Jumping	0.0423	0.0600	0.0496
Drinking	0.1429	0.0244	0.0417
Shaking	0.0000	0.0000	0.0000
Scratching	0.0000	0.0000	0.0000

Comparison with the Existing Approach. Table 11 show accuracies of the existing approach obtained through the experiments using data of Yuzu and Oreo. Comparing this with Tables 4, 5 and 8, it can be said that our approach has resulted higher F-measures than the existing approach. This could be explained by a theory that the amount of data might be too small to perform the statistical feature extraction. We also think that valuable information of the data could have been lost by the interpolation used in the existing approach.

6 Evaluations Based on Real-World Use Cases

6.1 Possible Scenarios of Our Approach

We have carried out three experiments. They are corresponding to possible usage scenarios of the virtual dog monitoring service powered by our approach.

1. The service is available for deployment immediately after the purchase by the owner. In this case, the system uses only manufacturer-supplied data as the training data.
2. The service is available for deployment after measurement of activities of the target dog. In this case, the system uses the private data along with the manufacturer-supplied data as the training data.
3. The service is available for deployment after the owner select the breed of the target dog. In this case, the system uses some of the manufacturer-supplied training data, which came from the same breed of the target dog.

6.2 Evaluation for Scenario 1

We perform the experiment corresponding to the scenario 1.

In this case let us see how the recognition accuracy is affected by the amount of data. In order to do so we calculate the average F-measure for each of these conditions, where data of 1, 2, 3, 4 or 5 dogs are used. Figure 14 shows the results obtained from each method. DTW performs best, then Euclidean Distance, and DTW-D performs worst. Figure 15 is F-measures for each activity. The performance is poor for "sniffing", "scratching", "drinking" and "up-stairs" with all methods. Furthermore, DTW-D exhibits the extremely poor result for "laying".

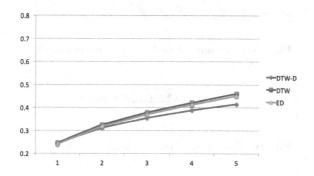

Fig. 14. Data amount vs. average F-measure: scenario 1.

Although we believe this is not important in real use cases, DTW-D's poor performance for "laying" can be explained as the following. In Fig. 16, we are comparing two data against each other, where the data contain little movement, as in the case of "laying". The vertical axis represents the value of the acceleration. For such cases the DTW almost equals the Euclidean Distance, meaning that DTW-D almost equals 1 for true cases. DTW-Ds maximum is 1. Thus, this has resulted the wrong classification.

6.3 Scenario 2

We perform the experiment corresponding to the scenario 2.

We use data from the target dog along with ones from other dogs. In the following experiment, the data from the target dog are cross-validated, meaning that the training data do not include test data. In this case let us see how the recognition accuracy is affected by the amount of data from other dogs. In order to do so we calculate the average F-measure for each of these conditions, where data of 0, 1, 2, 3, 4 or 5 other dogs are used. Figure 17 shows the results obtained from each method. DTW-D performs best, then DTW, and Euclidean Distance performs worst. Interestingly, as opposed to the scenario 1, more data implies lower F-measures. Figure 18 is F-measures for each activity. DTW-D performs uniformly well.

We explain why the F-measure of "laying" has been improved from scenario 1. The vertical axis of Fig. 19 represents the value of the acceleration. Using the

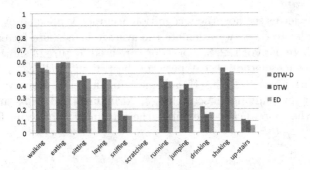

Fig. 15. F-measure of each activity in scenario 1.

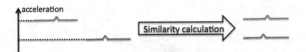

Fig. 16. F-measure of each activity in scenario 1.

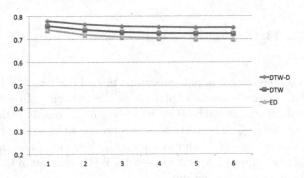

Fig. 17. Data amount vs. average F-measure: scenario 2.

private data, the DTW for true laying is sufficiently smaller than the Euclidean Distance, typically being 0. Therefore, the DTW-D for true laying is also smaller, yielding the better result.

6.4   Evaluation for Scenario 3

In this scenario the owner is allowed to choose a breed to select data to be used for activity recognition. Data from the target dog are not used. In this case let us see how the recognition accuracy is affected by choosing the right or wrong breed. In order to do so we calculate the average F-measure for each of these conditions, where data of two dogs of the same breed are used, and where data of three dogs of the different breed are used. Figure 20 is the result for the DTW-D. Although choosing the right breed has resulted the slightly better

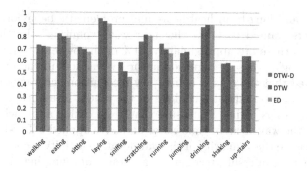

Fig. 18. F-measure of each activity in scenario 2.

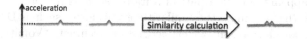

Fig. 19. F-measure of each activity in scenario 2.

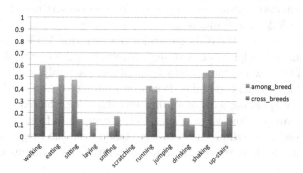

Fig. 20. Evaluation of scenario 3 in DTW-D.

F-measure, there are no statistically significant differences between the two. This is an interesting finding. Euclidean distance and the DTW give the similar trend.

7   Conclusion and Future Works

7.1   Conclusion

As seen in the emergence of commercial services that recognize *simple* behaviors of the dogs and to record them as life log, the desire to record the behavior of the dog has been increasing. However, the activity recognition ability of the services is limited and the need to record more detailed actions will arise in the future. We have investigated the needs and analyzed what kind of actions of the dog should be recognized by a pet monitoring system. As a result, we have found that there are three aspects of the demand for pet activity monitoring, namely, short- and long-term healthcare and problematic behavior. The action that the owners wanted to know the most was "vomiting". Furthermore, we have found that there are approximately 70 % of the owners who would like to monitor "jumping", whose recognition accuracy was low in the existing study [5]. We observed that the reason behind low recognition accuracy of "jumping" was that they used statistical technique in the study. In addition, in our data set, our approach has higher F-measure than the existing approach. Therefore, we focused on the waveform of time-series data. We applied DTW-D, which is a method to measure the similarity of the waveform, to activity recognition in dogs for the first time. As a result, recognition accuracy for "jumping" is particularly improved as compared to the previous study.

It can be said that it is difficult for a statistical method to differentiate an action which appears only in a part of a frame, such as jumping. On the other hand, methods that calculate the similarity of waveforms such as DTW perform well for the actions and result better recognition accuracy. "Vomiting" which is the most desired action to be monitored, is also a brief action. We are optimistic to detect it better with DTW-D.

We have evaluated our method in possible real-world settings. The evaluation has revealed the following findings potentially valuable for practical uses. First, as a similarity measure, DTW-D generally outperforms DTW and Euclidean Distance. Second, in order to achieve high F-measure, data from the target dog are required. Third, when using data from other dogs only, the more training data of other dogs means the higher F-measure. On the other hand, when using data from other dogs along with one from the target dog, the more training data of other dogs means the lower F-measure. When using data from other dogs only, aligning the breed from which the data were taken with the target dog, does not help, if it means the decrease of the data amount. Data amount matters more than breed.

7.2   Future Work

Measurement of Heart Rate and Respiratory Rate at Rest. By measuring the respiratory rate and heart rate at rest, it is possible to detect the heart or lungs diseases at early stages. It also makes it possible for dogs to receive the appropriate treatment by a veterinarian. For human beings, there is a study by Poh et al. [10]. However, because this study measures the transition of the reflection of light in the skin, application of this method to dogs with lots of hair is difficult. Therefore, we think that the measurement of heart rate by acceleration sensor is effective.

Pet Location Monitoring in a Room. Whether the behavior becomes problematic or not depends on the place where the pet is kept. If the detailed position of the dog in the room was available, it would further enhance the usefulness of the activity recognition. The research of Paasovaara et al. [8] could be a hint. Their study proposed the concept of human-dog interaction with social media.

They monitored the reaction of the user with a mock-up system to evaluate the concept. They planned to use a RFID device for indoor position detection.

Improvement of Recognition Accuracy. We cannot say that our approach has been sufficiently validated by experiments shown in this paper, both in terms of the number of individual dogs and the variety of breeds. Ultimately we would like to have higher F-measures for any unknown dogs. However, as the first step, we will carry out an experiment using many dogs of the same breed and do cross validation between individuals to verify the robustness of the approach among the same breed.

Further Inspection of the Validity of Our Approach. The validation of this paper, it is not sufficient to breeds, number of dogs of both. The ultimate goal is to be higher F-measure for any unknown dogs. However, as the most recent goal is carried out cross-validation among the same breed, whereby we want to verify the robustness among the same breed.

Acknowledgements. This work was supported by JSPS KAKENHI Grant Numbers 24300005, 26330081, 26870201.

In performing this study, We would like to thank everyone that has helped us questionnaire survey.

References

1. Axivity Ltd. (2011). http://www.axivity.com. Accessed 28 August 2014
2. Chen, Y., Hu, B., Keogh, E., Batista, G.E.A.P.A.: DTW-D: time series semi-supervised learning from a single example. In: Proceedings of the 19th ACM SIGKDD International Conference on Knowledge Discovery and Data Mining, Chicago, IL, USA, pp. 383–391 (2013)
3. Hammerla, N.Y., Kirkham, R., Andras, P., Plöotz, T.: On preserving statistical characteristics of accelerometry data using their empirical cumulative distribution. In: Proceedings of the 2013 International Symposium on Wearable Computers, Zurich, Switzerland, pp. 65–68 (2013)
4. Japan Pet Food Association(JPFA) (2013). http://www.petfood.or.jp. Accessed 28 August. (in Japanese)
5. Ladha, C., Hammerla, N., Hughs, E., Olivier, P., Plötz, T.: Dog's Life: wearable activity recognition for dogs. In: Proceedings of the 2013 ACM International Joint Conference on Pervasive and Ubiquitous Computing, Zurich, Switzerland, pp. 415–418 (2013)
6. MPI for Psycholinguistics: ELAN, ver. 4.6.2, Max Planck Institute for Psycholinguistics, Wundtlaan, Nijmegen, Nederland (2013)
7. NTT DOCOMO, INC. (2014). http://www.docomopet.com. 28 August 2014. (in Japanese)
8. Paasovaara, S., Paldanius, M., Saarinen, P., Hakkila, J., Vaananen-Vainio-Mattila, K.: The Secret life of my dog design and evaluation of paw tracker concept. In: Proceedings of the 11th International Conference on Human-Computer Interaction with Mobile Devices and Services, Bonn, Germany, pp. 231–240 (2011)

9. Plötz, T., Moynihan, P., Pham, C., Olivier, P.: Activity recognition and healthier food preparation. In: Chen, L., Nugent, C.D., Biswas, J., Hoey, J. (eds.) Activity Recognition in Pervasive Intelligent Environments, pp. 313–327. Atlantis Press, Paris (2010)
10. Poh, M.Z., McDuff, D., Picard, R.: A medical for non-contact health monitoring. In: Special Interest Group on Computer Graphics and Interactive Techniques Conference, Vancouver, BC, Canada (2011). Article No. 2
11. Rakthanmanon, T., Campana, B., Mueen, A., Batista, G., Westover, B., Zhu, Q., Zakaria, J., Keogh, E.: Searching and mining trillions of time series subsequences under dynamic time warping. In: Proceedings of the 18th ACM SIGKDD International Conference on Knowledge Discovery and Data Mining, Beijing, China, pp. 262–270 (2012)
12. Whistle Labs Inc (2013). http://www.whistle.com. Accessed 28 August 2014

Machine Breakdown Recovery in Production Scheduling with Simple Temporal Constraints

Roman Barták and Marek Vlk[✉]

Faculty of Mathematics and Physics, Charles University in Prague,
Malostranské nám. 25, 118 00 Prague 1, Czech Republic
{bartak,vlk}@ktiml.mff.cuni.cz

Abstract. One of the problems of real-life production scheduling is dynamics of manufacturing environments with new production demands coming and breaking machines during the schedule execution. Simple rescheduling from scratch in response to unexpected events may require excessive computation time. Moreover, the recovered schedule may deviate prohibitively from the ongoing schedule. This paper studies two methods how to modify a schedule in response to a machine breakdown: right-shift of affected activities and simple temporal network recovery. The importance is put on the speed of the rescheduling procedures as well as on the minimum deviation from the original schedule. In addition, this paper models the problem as a Mixed Integer Program and compares the proposed algorithms to the model using the mosek optimizer. The scheduling model is motivated by the FlowOpt project, which is based on Temporal Networks with Alternatives and supports simple temporal constraints between the activities.

Keywords: Schedule updates · Rescheduling · Predictive-reactive scheduling · Constraint satisfaction · Resource failure

1 Introduction

Scheduling is a decision-making process of which the aim is to allocate limited resources to activities so as to optimize certain objectives. In a manufacturing environment, developing a detailed schedule of the activities to be performed helps maintain efficiency and control of operations.

In the real world, however, manufacturing systems face uncertainty due to unexpected events occurring on the shop floor. Machines break down, operations take longer than anticipated, personnel do not perform as expected, urgent orders arrive, others are cancelled, etc. These disturbances render the ongoing schedule infeasible. In such case, a simple approach is to collect the data from the shop floor when the disruption occurs and to generate a new schedule from scratch. Gathering the information and total rescheduling involve excessive amount of time which may lead to failure of the scheduling mechanism and thus have far-reaching consequences.

© Springer International Publishing Switzerland 2015
B. Duval et al. (Eds.): ICAART 2015, LNAI 9494, pp. 185–206, 2015.
DOI: 10.1007/978-3-319-27947-3_10

For these reasons, reactive scheduling, which may be understood as the continuous correction of precomputed predictive schedules, is becoming more and more important. On the one hand, reactive scheduling has certain things in common with some predictive scheduling approaches, such as iterative improvement of some initial schedule. On the other hand, the major difference between reactive and predictive scheduling is the on-line nature and associated real-time execution requirements. The schedule update must be accomplished before the running schedule becomes invalid, and this time window may be very small in a complex manufacturing environment.

In this work we take the scheduling model from the FlowOpt project [1]. Simply said, a schedule consists of activities, resources, and constraints. Activities require resources to process them, and all resources may perform at most one activity at a time. Possible positions of activities in time are restricted by simple temporal constraints.

The aim of this work is to propose a technique to recover a schedule from machine breakdown. The intention is to find a feasible schedule as similar to the original one as possible, and as fast as possible. The paper proposes two methods. The Right Shift Affected algorithm reallocates activities from the failed resource to available resources and then it keeps repairing violated constraints until the feasible schedule is obtained. The STN-recovery algorithm retracts a certain subset of activities from resources and then it allocates one activity after another in suitable order in such a way that no constraints are violated. The major innovation is support for simple temporal constraints [2] rather than assuming precedence constraints only. Further, we propose how the problem may be modelled as a Mixed Integer Program and solve the model using the mosek optimizer [3].

We first survey briefly the closely related works on which our approaches are based. Section 3 then explains the problem tackled in this work. The suggested methods are described in Sects. 4, 5, and 6. The experimental results are given in Sect. 7, and the final part points out possible future work.

2   Related Works

The field of rescheduling (predictive-reactive scheduling) has been addressed in a number of works, as surveyed for instance in [4–6]. However, the algorithms discussed in the scheduling literature deal with scheduling problems that do not consider temporal constraints (minimal and maximal time lags) but usually only precedences. To the best of our knowledge, there is no algorithm that could be straightforwardly used for the problem with simple temporal constraints studied in this paper. Hence, we suggest exploiting and integrating some known techniques to tackle this type of problem.

The fundamental inspiration comes from *heuristic-based* approaches, which do not guarantee to find an optimal solution, but respond in a short time. The simplest schedule repair technique is the *right shift rescheduling* [7]. This technique shifts the operations globally to the right on the time axis in order to cope with disruptions. When it arises from machine breakdown, the method introduces gaps in the schedule, during which the machines are idle. It is obvious that this approach results in schedules of bad quality, and can be used only for environments involving minor disruptions.

The shortcomings of total rescheduling and right shift rescheduling gave rise to another approach: *affected operation rescheduling*, also referred to as partial schedule repair [8]. The idea of this algorithm is to reschedule only the operations directly and indirectly affected by the disruption in order to minimize the deviation from the initial schedule.

The *Repair-DTP* algorithm proposed in [9] tackles a problem very similar to ours, however, it is designed to correct violated constraints in manually edited schedules. The model involves precedence constraints and synchronization constraints, but excludes minimum and maximum time lags. Nonetheless, in order to reduce searching space, the Repair-DTP algorithm employs *Simple Temporal Networks* (STN) [2] and *Incremental Full Path Consistency* (IFPC) algorithm [10], which incrementally maintains the *All Pairs Shortest Path* (APSP) property. If a feasible correction exists, the algorithm tries to find the most similar schedule to the initial one through only shifting activities in time. Since the Repair-DTP algorithm does not try changes in resource selection, it cannot be used to deal with machine failure. Moreover, the main shortcoming of the algorithm is searching through disjunctions, introduced by hierarchical nature of the model and by resource unarity. This leads to excessive (exponentially growing) amount of temporal networks that are inspected, which requires unacceptable amount of time.

In the methods proposed further, apart from STN and IFPC algorithm, some widely used search techniques from the field of *Constraint Satisfaction* [11] are employed, namely *Conflict-directed Backjumping with Backmarking* [12].

3   Problem Definition

3.1   Scheduling Problem

Scheduling problem P is a triplet of three sets: *Activities*, *Constraints*, and *Resources*.

- *Activities* = {all activities in P}
- *Constraints* = {all temporal constraints in P}
- *Resources* = {all available resources in P}

Each activity A is specified by its start time $Start(A)$ and end time $End(A)$, which we will look for, and fixed duration $Duration(A)$, which is part of the problem specification. All these numbers are nonnegative integers. Since we do not allow preemptions (interruptibility of activities), $Start(A) + Duration(A) = End(A)$ holds.

Temporal Constraints. Constraints determine mutual position in time of two distinct activities. Constraint $C \in Constraints$ is a triplet (A_i, A_j, w), where $A_i, A_j \in Activities$, $w \in \mathbb{Z}$, and the semantics is following.

$$Start(A_j) - Start(A_i) \leq w \tag{1}$$

Now, some terminology from the graph theory deserves to be clarified in terms of the scheduling model. Activities A_i and A_j are called *adjacent* if there exists a constraint (A_i, A_j, w) or (A_j, A_i, w) for any $w \in \mathbb{Z}$.

Two activities A_i and A_j are *connected* if there exists a sequence of activities $A_i, A_{i+1}, ..., A_{j-1}, A_j$ such that A_i and A_{i+1} are adjacent, A_{i+1} and A_{i+2} are adjacent, ..., A_{j-1} and A_j are adjacent. A *connected component* is a maximal (in terms of inclusion) subset of activities such that all activities from the subset are connected. Each activity as well as each constraint belongs to exactly one connected component.

Resource Constraints. Let $A \in Activities$, then the set of resources that may process activity A is denoted $Resources(A)$. The set $Resources(A)$ is often referred to as a resource group.

Each activity needs to be allocated to exactly one resource from its resource group. Let $A \in Activities$, then a resource $R \in Resources(A)$ is *selected* if resource R is scheduled to process activity A, which we denote *Selected Resource*$(A) = R$.

Each activity must have a selected resource to make a schedule feasible. Formally:

$$\forall A \in Activities : SelectedResource(A) \neq null$$

All resources in a schedule are unary, which means that they cannot execute more activities simultaneously. Therefore, in a feasible schedule for all activities $A_i \neq A_j$ the following holds.

$$SelectedResource(A_i) = SelectedResource(A_j)$$
$$\Rightarrow End(A_i) \leq Start(A_j) \vee End(A_j) \leq Start(A_i) \tag{2}$$

A Special Case. Real-life scheduling problems are usually designed in such a way that there are subsets of resources that share certain capabilities and which then constitute resource groups of activities. This observation may make some models easier to solve.

The resource groups of a scheduling problem are *equivalent* if one and only one of the following conditions holds for any two resource groups $Resources(A_1)$ and $Resources(A_2)$ of two distinct activities A_1 and A_2.

- $Resources(A_1) = Resources(A_2)$.
- $Resources(A_1) \cap Resources(A_2) = \emptyset$.

If the resource groups are not equivalent, they are called *arbitrary*.

Motivated by the nature of real-life scheduling problems and their need for speed, the proposed algorithms anticipate that the resource groups are equivalent.

3.2 Schedule

A schedule S (sometimes referred to as a resulting schedule or a solution) is acquired by allocating activities in time and on resources. Allocation of activities in time means assigning particular values to the variables $Start(A)$ for each $A \in Activities$. Allocation of activities on resources means selecting a particular resource ($SelectedResource(A)$) from the resource group ($Resources(A)$) of each activity $A \in Activities$.

To make a schedule *feasible*, the allocation must be conducted in such a way that all the temporal constraints (1) as well as all the resource constraints (2) in the model are satisfied.

3.3 Rescheduling Problem

The problem we generally deal with is that we are given a particular instance of the scheduling problem along with a feasible schedule, and also with a change in the problem specification. The aim is to find another schedule that is feasible in terms of the new problem definition. The feasible schedule we are given is referred to as an original schedule or an ongoing schedule.

The machine breakdown, which is also referred to as a machine or resource failure, may happen in the manufacturing system at any point in time, say t_f, and means that a particular resource cannot be used anymore, i.e., for all $t \geq t_f$. This makes further questions arise, e.g., whether the activities that were being processed at time t_f are devastated and thus must be performed from the beginning, whether their predecessors must be also re-executed if there are only solutions violating temporal constraints, and many others.

For the sake of simplicity, let us assume that a resource fails at the beginning of the time horizon (at time point $t = 0$), i.e., right before the schedule execution begins. The resource that fails is in what follows also referred to as a forbidden resource. Formally, let S_0 be the schedule to be executed and R_f be the failed resource; the aim is to find a feasible schedule S_1, such that R_f is not used at any point in time $t \geq 0$. S_1 is referred to as a recovered schedule. The intention is to find S_1 as fast as possible and, regardless of the initial objectives, the more similar to S_0, the better. For this purpose we need to evaluate the modification distance.

Let us denote $Start_S(A)$ the start time of activity A in schedule S. In what follows we distinguish the following distance functions.

$$f_1 = \sum_{A \in Activities} |Start_{S_1}(A) - Start_{S_0}(A)|$$

$$f_2 = |\{A \in Activities \mid Start_{S_1}(A) \neq Start_{S_0}(A)\}|$$

$$f_3 = \max_{A \in Activities} |Start_{S_1}(A) - Start_{S_0}(A)|.$$

4 Right Shift Affected

The Right Shift Affected algorithm is a greedy algorithm to tackle the machine breakdown disruption. For each $A \in Activities$, it is assumed throughout that the forbidden resource is deleted from the resource group of activity A, i.e., $Resources(A) = Resources(A) \setminus \{ForbiddenResource\}$.

The algorithm is aimed at moving as few activities as possible, i.e., optimizing the distance function f_2. The idea is to reallocate activities from the forbidden resource and then keep reallocating activities that violate some constraint until the schedule is feasible.

How to move (reallocate) the activities, how to repair the constraints, and in what order to pick the activities to repair the constraints is described next.

4.1   Reallocating Activities

Activities are reallocated as follows. Suppose the algorithm wants to repair a constraint in such a way that an activity A should be reallocated to a time point t. The natural idea was to reallocate the activity A exactly to the time point t even if there is no resource available for the required $Duration(A)$. Then, when a repair function verifies constraints, it would have to verify the resource constraints too and then repair according to the resource constraint violation. Unfortunately, there always turned out to be a model for which this method gets stuck in an infinite loop, regardless of the way the constraints are repaired and the sequence of activities to be repaired.

Consequently, the algorithm always allocates activity A in such a way that it does not violate any resource constraint. This is achieved through seeking a time point t^* (which is greater or equal to time point t) where activity A can be allocated without violating the resource constraints. Formally, when the algorithm desires to allocate activity A to time point t, then activity A is allocated to time point t^*, such that $t^* \geq t$ and $\forall t' : t' \geq t \wedge t' < t^*$ activity A cannot be allocated in t' without overlapping some other activity on any resource from $Resources(A)$.

Checking Resource Availability. In order to express whether or not a resource is free at a specified time interval, let us first define $Impedimentary$ (A, R, t) as the set of activities that preclude activity A from being allocated on resource R at time t.

$$Impedimentary(A, R, t) = \{A' \mid A' \in Activities \wedge R = SelectedResource(A')$$
$$\wedge(t < End(A') \leq t + Duration(A) \vee t \leq Start(A') < t + Duration(A))\}$$

Now we can define a set of resources where activity A can be allocated at time t as such:

$$AvailableResources(A, t) = \{R \mid R \in Resources(A)$$
$$\wedge Impedimentary(A, R, t) = \emptyset\}$$

Another question is which resource the algorithm should select if there are more resources available. Since the resource groups in the model are expected to be equivalent, it seems useful to pick the resource on which the activity best fits in terms of surrounding gaps. Therefore, the following heuristic is used.

Earliest Succeeding Start Latest Previous End (ESSLPE) Rule. Suppose activity A is about to be allocated at time t. The algorithm picks the resource with the earliest (closest) occupied time after the time point $t+Duration$ (A) (= earliest succeeding start). When there are more resources with the same earliest succeeding start, then the algorithm picks the resource with the latest (closest) occupied time before the time point t (= latest previous end) with ties breaking arbitrarily. Consequently, a resource that has at least some activity to process is always preferred to an empty resource.

Reallocation. The procedure `ReallocateActivity` (see Algorithm 1) obtains two parameters: an activity to allocate (A) and a time point where it is desired to allocate the activity (t). Seeking for an available resource starts at time t, but the activity is ultimately allocated to the time point t^*, where an available resource is found.

Algorithm 1. Reallocating an activity.

---

    function REALLOCATEACTIVITY(Activity A, TimePoint t)
        $SelectedResource(A) \leftarrow$ null
        $Start(A) \leftarrow$ null
        $t^* \leftarrow \min_{t' \geq t}\{t' \mid AvailableResources(A, t') \neq \emptyset\}$
        $Start(A) \leftarrow t^*$
        $SelectedResource(A) \leftarrow$ by ESSLPE rule from $AvailableResources(A, t^*)$
    end function

4.2 Constraint Repair

The violated constraints are repaired as follows. When a temporal constraint between activities A_1 and A_2 of weight w is violated, it means that the distance between $Start(A_1)$ and $Start(A_2)$ is greater than allowed. Then the algorithm seeks for possible allocation of A_1 from the minimal time point that satisfies the constraint rightwards.

Here is where the title of the algorithm comes from. It repairs temporal constraints via moving activities to the right, which, of course, may cause violation of other temporal constraints. An important property is that when the algorithm picks an activity to be repaired, then it iterates over all temporal constraints associated with the activity being repaired until the activity does not violate any associated constraint.

Regardless of the order, in which the activities are selected to be repaired, the entire `RightShiftAffected` algorithm works as follows (see Algorithm 2). First, it goes through all activities in the model and checks whether the activity uses the forbidden resource. In the positive case, the activity is reallocated through the `ReallocateActivity` procedure (seeking for an available resource starts at the original start time of the activity), and the activity is added to the set *affected*. Now, none of the activities uses the forbidden resource and the set *affected* contains activities that have been reallocated and therefore must be checked for temporal constraint violation.

Next, the algorithm takes an activity from the set *affected* and proceeds to repair all violated temporal constraints associated with the activity in question. It repairs the constraints, as described, through moving activities to the right, so that if another activity is moved, it is added into the set *affected* because it must be then checked for constraint violation. Recall that `ReallocateActivity` procedure always allocates an activity such that it does not violate any resource constraint, so that only temporal constraints are checked here. If the activity has been successfully healed, which means that the activity does not violate any constraint, the algorithm proceeds to another one from *affected*.

As far as the order of taking activities from *affected* is concerned, the best heuristic with respect to all conceivable performance measures turned out to be picking the rightmost activity, i.e., the activity with the maximum $Start(A)$. The explanation is that shifting the rightmost activities rightwards makes free

---

Algorithm 2. Right Shift Affected.

---
function RIGHTSHIFTAFFECTED
    affected $\leftarrow \emptyset$
    for all $A \in Activities$ **do**
        if $SelectedResource(A) = ForbiddenResource$ **then**
            REALLOCATEACTIVITY$(A, Start(A))$
            affected $\leftarrow$ *affected* $\cup \{A\}$
        end if
    end for
    while *affected* $\neq \emptyset$ **do**
        $A \leftarrow PopFrom(affected)$
        while $(A_1, A_2, w) \in ViolatedConstraints(A)$ **do**
            REALLOCATEACTIVITY$(A_1, Start(A_2) - w)$
            if $A_1 \neq A$ **then**
                affected $\leftarrow$ *affected* $\cup \{A_1\}$
            end if
        end while
    end while
end function

---

space for shifting the activities allocated more on the left, which would otherwise have to creep over one another.

Termination. The algorithm successfully found a feasible schedule recovery for all input models that were assuredly solvable (which is guaranteed when there are more resources in each resource group than the number of activities in one connected component). However, the question whether the algorithm always ends and finds the solution, provided the schedule is recoverable, is still open.

If there is no feasible schedule recovery, the algorithm keeps repairing and never terminates. This is obviously the main shortcoming of the algorithm. One possible way to detect unrecoverability of the schedule is by passing and checking a time limit. Another way is to check where an activity is being allocated, and if the activity is allocated at a time point exceeding a certain threshold, it may be considered as an unsuccessful finding of a schedule.

5   STN-recovery

The STN-recovery is a bit more sophisticated algorithm to tackle the machine breakdown. This algorithm anticipates that moving a large number of activities by small time is preferable to moving activities a lot in time. The basic idea is to deallocate some set of already scheduled activities and then allocate them back again. This is what is now meant by reallocation.

The point of the algorithm is to allocate connected components one after another through Conflict-directed Backjumping. The allocation of an activity is carried out such that the start time of an activity is continuously incremented until an available resource at that time is found, or until the maximal possible value of the start time (which is determined with respect to the start times of already allocated activities) is exceeded. In the former case the algorithm proceeds to allocate the next activity, in the latter case the algorithm goes back to reallocate some previous activity. Since this allocation process might involve excessive computational burden, it is useful to prune the search space based on the fact that a resource failure leads only to deterioration of the schedule in the original optimization objective. Moreover, the group of resources where the broken down resource belongs is now likely to make a bottleneck. This assumption is used in such a way that the activities are reallocated from the broken down resource to available resources and then the activities are shifted so as they do not overlap each another – thus the minimal potential start times for allocation are obtained – and then the reallocation process can begin.

Firstly, the skeleton of the algorithm is given, and next, its particular steps are described in more details.

Skeleton of STN-recovery

The STN (including the global predecessor) with the APSP property is supposed to have already been computed from the temporal constraints in the model; the resource constraints are not involved in the STN. Recall that the APSP property of the STN provides us the two-dimensional array w, of which the values say that $Start(A_j) - Start(A_i) \leq w[i,j]$, where $A_i, A_j \in Activities$.

STN-recovery itself consists of the following six steps.

1. Find activities allocated to the forbidden resource and change their resource selection from the forbidden resource to an available resource, picking the resource with the lowest usage, while keeping the start times of the activities unchanged. Now some activities allocated on the same resource may overlap.

2. For each resource (to which some activity has been added in step 1) shift the activities that overlap (to the right) so as they do not overlap, and add them into the set *affected*. Include in *affected* also activities that were not actually shifted but are allocated on the right of those shifted.
3. For the sake of pruning the search space of the forthcoming allocation search, add STN constraints between the global predecessor and each activity in *affected* so as to enforce that they can only start at the time they are currently allocated or later. Update the STN via Incremental Full Path Consistency [10] to preserve the APSP property.
4. For each activity A in *affected*, acquire the connected component the activity A belongs to, and for all activities in all acquired connected components compute the values from which the allocation of the activity in the last step will begin ($= MinStart$), which is the maximum of (i) its current start time and (ii) its minimal distance from the global predecessor resulting from the STN.
5. Deallocate (retract from resources) all activities in all connected components acquired in step 4.
6. Take the leftmost (according to the *MinStart* values) non-allocated component C and allocate all activities in C starting with its leftmost activity using Conflict-directed Backjumping with Backmarking. The activities within a connected component are allocated in the increasing order of their *MinStart* values. Repeat this step until all connected components are allocated.

The skeleton of the algorithm is depicted in Algorithm 3.

Algorithm 3. STN-recovery.

Require: The STN with the APSP property
   function STN-RECOVERY
      for all $A \in Activities$ **do**
         if $SelectedResource(A) = ForbiddenResource$ **then**
            SWAPFORBIDDENSELECTION(A)
         end if
      end for
      affected ← SHIFTONRESOURCES
      for all $A_i \in affected$ **do**
         IFPC(i, 0, $-Start(A_i)$)
      end for
      components ← ACQUIRECOMPONENTS(*affected*)
      DEALLOCATECOMPONENTS(*components*)
      while *components* $\neq \emptyset$ **do**
         C ← GETLEFTMOSTCOMPONENT(*components*)
         ALLOCATECOMPONENT(C)
         components ← *components* $\setminus \{C\}$
      end while
   end function

5.1   Swapping Resource Selections

In the first step, the algorithm goes through all activities in the model and checks whether the activity is scheduled to be processed on the forbidden resource. In the positive case, the function SwapForbiddenSelection(Activity A) changes resource selection of activity A to some allowed resource.

It is not important which resource is selected because the activity is most likely going to be reallocated in the later steps. Nevertheless, the algorithm picks the resource with the lowest usage, which is the sum of the durations of the activities that are allocated to the resource in question.

Formally, let us first denote the set of activities that use resource R as such.

$$ResourceActivities(R) = \{A \in Activities \mid SelectedResource(A) = R\}$$

The usage of resource R can be written as follows.

$$Usage(R) = \sum_{A \in ResourceActivities(R)} Duration(A)$$

Then picking the resource with the lowest usage means this:

$$SelectedResource(A) = \arg\min_{R \in Resources(A)} (Usage(R))$$

At this time being, some activities may violate resource constraints.

5.2   Shifting Activities

In the second step, the algorithm repairs the violated resource constraints. It visits the resources one after another and shifts activities that overlap to the right. Since the original schedule is supposed to have been feasible, only the resources where some activities were added should be revised.

Procedure ShiftOnResources sweeps over the activities and conducts the shifting as follows. If activity A_0 overlaps activity A_1 on a resource, the activity with the later start time, say A_1, is set its start time to the end time of A_0. This shift may cause activity A_1 to overlap next activity, which is then set to start at the end of activity A_1 and so forth. The order of activities on the resource is preserved. All activities from the first activity that has been shifted up to the last activity (in terms of start times), even if some have not been shifted, are added to the set *affected*.

Formally, let $begin(R)$ be the start time of the first (earliest) activity that overlaps with another activity on resource R.

$$begin(R) \leftarrow \min_{A \in ResourceActivities(R)} \{Start(A) \mid \exists B \in ResourceActivities(R),$$

$$B \neq A, Start(A) \leq Start(B) < End(A)\}$$

Further, let us denote R^i the i-th earliest activity allocated on resource R, which means that the following holds.

$$1 \leq i < j \leq |ResourceActivities(R)| \Rightarrow Start(R^i) \leq Start(R^j)$$

The activities on resource R are consecutively (from the leftmost activity) shifted such that:

$$Start(R^i) \leftarrow \max\{Start(R^i), End(R^{i-1})\}$$

Finally, the activities are added to the set *affected* as follows.

$$affected \leftarrow \{A \in Activities \mid Start(A) > begin(SelectedResource(A))\}$$

This shifting may violate a large number of temporal constraints. The activities in the set *affected* are going to be reallocated in the forthcoming steps. The reason why the set *affected* includes the activities that have not been shifted, but are allocated on the right of the shifted activities, is, that they would otherwise preclude other activities from allocation.

5.3 Updating STN

In this step, the constraints determining the minimal distance of an activity from the global predecessor are added to the STN so as to modify the *MinStart* values of activities to be reallocated, according to the start time values set in the previous shifting step. The IFPC algorithm is used because modifying the minimal start time of an activity affects the minimal start times of other activities from the same connected component.

Precisely, for each $A_i \in$ *affected*, add to the STN via IFPC algorithm the constraint $(A_i, A_0, -Start(A_i))$, where A_0 denotes the global predecessor.

The point of adding this constraints is to reasonably maintain similarity to the original schedule, along with adequate pruning of the search space of the upcoming reallocation process.

5.4 Components Acquirement

There is still a question which and in what order the activities should be reallocated. Because shifting one activity is likely to violate temporal constraints emanating from or to the activity, it is necessary to reallocate the entire connected component. Therefore, procedure `AcquireComponents(affected)` acquires the connected component that each activity $A \in$ *affected* belongs to, and the acquired connected component is added to the set *components*. After this step, *components* $= \{C_1, ...C_k\}$, where C_z for $z = 1, ..., k$ is a connected component.

In addition, for each activity, the *MinStart* value, which is the maximum of the current start time and of the minimal potential start time following from the STN (computed via IFPC in the previous step), is computed. Precisely, for each $C_z \in$ *components* and for each $A_i \in C_z$, assign:

$$MinStart(A_i) = \max\{Start(A_i), -w[i,0]\}$$

As to the order for upcoming allocation, it is suitable to allocate activities in the increasing order of the $MinStart$ values. The activity in a connected component with the lowest $MinStart$ value is referred to as the leftmost activity. The leftmost connected component is the connected component of which the leftmost activity has the lowest $MinStart$ value among all connected components. The algorithm always selects for allocation the leftmost component that has not yet been allocated.

5.5   Deallocation

Since the best way for allocating activities turned out to be the way without violating resource constraints, it is necessary to deallocate all activities in the connected components acquired in the previous step. Otherwise they would preclude other activities from allocation. Procedure `DeallocateComponent(components)` deallocates activities from each connected component $C \in components$, which means that for each $A \in C$: $Start(A) = null$ and $SelectedResource(A) = null$. After this (fifth) step, all activities from $components$ are deallocated.

5.6   Allocation

Allocating an activity again means searching for the time point when there is an available resource for the required duration. The resources are selected according to the ESSLPE rule described in 4.1.

In order to allocate a connected component, Conflict-directed Backjumping with Backmarking is used (see Algorithm 4). When an activity cannot be successfully allocated, it is necessary to jump back to the activity that is causing the conflict. For keeping the information which activity is conflicting with the activity being allocated, the conflict set for each activity is remembered. For this purpose, $cs[i]$ is a set of activities conflicting with A_i.

The activities are going to be allocated in the increasing order of their indexes that are determined according to their $MinStart$ values. Thus we can anticipate that the connected component to be allocated, which is passed as a parameter, consists of activities $A_1, ..., A_n$. When two activities are compared, i.e., $A_j < A_i$, it means that their indexes are compared $(j < i)$.

There are two possible causes why an activity cannot be allocated: a temporal conflict and a resource conflict.

Temporal Conflicts. Temporal conflicts are handled in procedure Update Bounds (Activity A) (see Algorithm 5), which is called before activity A_i is going to be allocated (line 6). In this procedure, the bounds of possible time allocation for activity A_i are computed according to the STN and start times of already allocated activities.

The lower bound of an activity is initially set to the $MinStart$ value acquired in the previous steps. Then the procedure goes through the already allocated

---

Algorithm 4. Allocating entire connected component.

```
 1: function ALLOCATECOMPONENT(Activities A₁, ..., Aₙ)
 2:     i ← 1
 3:     while i ≤ n do
 4:         newVal ← newVals[i]                                          ▷ initially 0
 5:         if newVal = 0 then
 6:             UPDATEBOUNDS(Aᵢ)
 7:             newVal ← LowerBound(Aᵢ)
 8:         end if
 9:         while SelectedResource(Aᵢ) = null & newVal ≤ UpperBound(Aᵢ) do
10:             if
    newVal ∈ Keys(Mark[i]) & max(Mark[i][newVal]) < BackTo[i][newVal] then
11:                 cs[i] ← cs[i] ∪ Mark[i][newVal]
12:                 newVal ← newVal + 1
13:                 continue
14:             end if
15:             BackTo[i][newVal] ← Aᵢ
16:             newConflicts ← ∅
17:             for all R ∈ Resources(Aᵢ) do
18:
    newConflicts ← newConflicts ∪ Min*(Impedimentary(Aᵢ, R, newVal))
19:             end for
20:             if AvailableResources(Aᵢ, newVal) ≠ ∅ then
21:                 SelectedResource(Aᵢ) ← by ESSLPE rule from
    AvailableResources(Aᵢ, newVal)
22:                 Start(Aᵢ) ← newVal
23:                                                          ▷ newVal can be tried again
24:                 Keys(Mark[i]) ← Keys(Mark[i]) \ {newVal}
25:             else
26:                 Keys(Mark[i]) ← Keys(Mark[i]) ∪ {newVal}
27:                 Mark[i][newVal] ← newConflicts
28:             end if
29:             cs[i] ← cs[i] ∪ newConflicts
30:             newVal ← newVal + 1
31:         end while
32:         if SelectedResource(Aᵢ) = null then
33:             Aⱼ ← max(cs[i])
34:             cs[j] ← cs[j] ∪ cs[i] \ {Aⱼ}
35:             for k ← j + 1 to n do
36:                 for all key ∈ Keys(BackTo[k]) do
37:                     BackTo[k][key] ← min(BackTo[k][key], Aⱼ)
38:                 end for
39:             end for
40:             while i > j do                                          ▷ jump back to j
41:                 newVals[i] ← 0
42:                 i ← i − 1
43:                 SelectedResource(Aᵢ) ← null
44:                 Start(Aᵢ) ← null
45:             end while
46:         else
47:             newVals[i] ← newVal
48:             i ← i + 1
49:         end if
50:     end while
51: end function
```

activities within the connected component in the same order as they have been allocated and updates bounds of A_i. Precisely, for each $k < i$, if $Start(A_k)$ + "minimal distance from $Start(A_k)$ to $Start(A_i)$" is greater than the current lower bound, then increase the lower bound, and add A_k to the conflict set of A_i. Similarly, if $Start(A_k)$ + "maximal distance from $Start(A_k)$ to $Start(A_i)$" is smaller than the current upper bound, then decrease the upper bound, and add A_k to the conflict set of A_i. The reason why activity A_k is added to the conflict set is that changing the start time of A_k creates (straight away or after a number of steps) some new possible start time for A_i.

Resource Conflicts. As far as resource conflicts are concerned, recall that $Impedimentary(A_i, R, t)$, formally introduced in Sect. 4.1, is a set of activities that preclude activity A_i from selecting resource R at time t. To make it possible to allocate activity A_i on resource R at time t, all activities from the set $Impedimentary(A_i, R, t)$ would have to be reallocated. Hence, among the activities in $Impedimentary(A_i, R, t)$, the activity that has been the least recently allocated (from the connected component being allocated) is added to the conflict set of activity A_i. But if there is an activity in $Impedimentary(A_i, R, t)$ from another connected component, which means it cannot be deallocated, then no activity is added to the conflict set.

This is exactly what Min^* does (at line 18). Formally, let C be the connected component being allocated. If $Impedimentary(A_i, R, t) \subseteq C$, then:

$$Min^*(Impedimentary(A_i, R, t)) = \underset{A_k \in Impedimentary(A_i, R, t)}{\arg\min} \{k\}$$

Otherwise $Min^*(Impedimentary(A_i, R, t)) = \emptyset$.

For illustration, when the algorithm is allocating activity A_7 and there are activities A_2, A_4, and A_6 inhibiting on a resource, then activity A_2 is added to the conflict set. If there is an activity from different, already allocated component, then no activity is added to the conflict set.

Further, recall $AvailableResources(A_i, t)$ is a subset of available resources from which the resource according to the ESSLPE rule is selected. Regardless of the result of the search for an available resource, the conflicting activities are merged into the conflict set of the activity being allocated (line 29).

Backjump. When the algorithm is about to conduct a backjump (starting at line 32), which happens when all possible start times of A_i have been tried, the most recently allocated activity from the conflict set of A_i is found (line 33). Let us denote this activity as A_j. Next, before deallocating activities that are jumped over, the activities from the conflict set of A_i except activity A_j are added to the conflict set of A_j.

Backmarking. The backmarking technique is implemented as follows. Firstly, the time horizon is infinite so that the structures $BackTo$ and $Mark$ cannot be

---

Algorithm 5. Updating lower and upper bounds.

function UPDATEBOUNDS(Activitiy A_i)
    $cs[i] \leftarrow \emptyset$ $\triangleright$ clear conflict set
    $LowerBound(A_i) \leftarrow MinStart(A_i)$
    $UpperBound(A_i) \leftarrow \infty$
    for $k \leftarrow 1$ **to** $i-1$ **do**
        $newValue \leftarrow Start(A_k) - w[i,k]$
        if $LowerBound(A_i) < newValue$ **then**
            $LowerBound(A_i) \leftarrow newValue$
            $cs[i] \leftarrow cs[i] \cup \{A_k\}$
        end if
        $newValue \leftarrow Start(A_k) + w[k,i]$
        if $UpperBound(A_i) > newValue$ **then**
            $UpperBound(A_i) \leftarrow newValue$
            $cs[i] \leftarrow cs[i] \cup \{A_k\}$
        end if
    end for
end function

---

simple two-dimensional arrays but arrays of dictionaries. Precisely, $BackTo$ is an array of size n, $BackTo[i]$ is a dictionary, where keys are the (attempted) start times of the activity, and values are activities, i.e., $BackTo[i][newVal]$ is the lowest-indexed activity whose instantiation has changed since activity A_i was last tried to be allocated at time $newVal$.

As to the structure $Mark$, there is one difference. Notice that when the algorithm cannot find an available resource for activity A_i at time $newVal$, not only one, but a number of activities may be added to the conflict set of A_i. Consequently $Mark[i][newVal]$ is a set of activities, of which at least one must be reallocated in order to make activity A_i allocatable at time $newVal$. Therefore, when values $BackTo$ and $Mark$ are to be compared, it is firstly checked, whether there is $newVal$ among the keys of $Mark[i]$, and in the positive case, $\max(Mark[i][newVal])$ and $BackTo[i][newVal]$ are compared (see line 10).

If $\max(Mark[i][newVal]) < BackTo[i][newVal]$, it means that none of the conflicting activities has been re-instantiated and thus it makes no sense to look for an available resource. However, before proceeding to the next value of $newVal$, it is necessary to merge the conflicting activities to the current conflict set (line 11) as if the search for an available resource was conducted – this is the reason why $Mark[i][newVal]$ must store the set of activities (and not just the most recent activity).

Oppositely, if $newVal$ is not presented among the keys of $Mark[i]$ or $\max(Mark[i][newVal]) \geq BackTo[i][newVal]$, the algorithm does look for an available resource. If activity A_i is successfully allocated, the key $newVal$ is removed from $Mark[i]$ (line 24), otherwise $Mark[i][newVal]$ stores the conflicting activities (line 27).

Termination. Notice that the algorithm does not check for the recoverability of the disrupted ongoing schedule, which means that if there is no feasible solution, the procedure `AllocateComponent(Component C)` never terminates. This can be solved by giving it a limited time (cut-off limit), or by detecting that the method got stuck in a loop, which may be proven for example when it tries to allocate an activity in time greater than the lower bound of makespan (which may be the sum of the durations of all activities and of all minimal distances between the activities in the problem).

6 Rescheduling as a Mixed Integer Program

The rescheduling problem can be modelled as a Mixed Integer Programming (MIP) problem as follows. Let the scheduling problem have n activities and m resources, the start time of activity i in the original schedule be denoted $\bar{s}_i$ and its duration p_i. Then we introduce variables $s_i > 0$ $(1 \leq i \leq n)$ for new start times, and binary variables $r_{ij}, 1 \leq i \leq n, 1 \leq j \leq m$ where value 1 means that activity i is scheduled to resource j and value 0 is used otherwise. If activity i cannot be processed on resource j, then r_{ij} is set to 0. The objectives are described further because they differ for each of the defined distance functions.

For each temporal constraint (A_{i_1}, A_{i_2}, w) the following constraints are added:

$$s_{i_2} - s_{i_1} \leq w$$

In order to enforce that each resource can perform at most one activity at any time, the following constraints are used, for all $1 \leq i_1 < i_2 \leq n, 1 \leq j \leq m$:

$$s_{i_2} + p_{i_2} \leq s_{i_1} \qquad + b_{i_1,i_2,j} \cdot M + (1 - r_{i_1,j}) \cdot M + (1 - r_{i_2,j}) \cdot M$$
$$s_{i_1} + p_{i_1} \leq s_{i_2} \qquad + (1 - b_{i_1,i_2,j}) \cdot M + (1 - r_{i_1,j}) \cdot M + (1 - r_{i_2,j}) \cdot M$$

Note that M is some big enough constant, e.g., the lower bound of makespan, and $b_{i_1,i_2,j}$ are binary variables ensuring that activity i_1 is either followed or preceded by activity i_2, provided that $r_{i_1} = r_{i_2} = 1$. Finally, selecting exactly one resource for each activity is achieved through adding the following constraints, for all $1 \leq i \leq n$:

$$\sum_{j=1}^{m} r_{ij} = 1$$

In order to avoid absolute values in the objective functions, every start time s_i is replaced by $\bar{s}_i + shr_i - shl_i$, where $shr_i > 0$ are continuous variables for the time shift of activity i to the right and $shl_i > 0$ denotes the shift to the left.

Let us denote the model just described as $MIP0$. This model corresponds to rescheduling from scratch. Now, recall that the first five steps of the STN-recovery algorithm obtain and unschedule a set of activities that are to be allocated in the last (sixth) step, while the other activities remain untouched. Suppose that each activity i that is to remain untouched is fixed so that $shr_i = shl_i = 0$ and $r_{ij} = 1$ for resource j to which activity i is allocated. Let us refer to this model as $MIP1$. The last open question is how to model the objectives.

Assume the intention is to find a recovered schedule minimizing the total sum of shifts (distance function f_1). Then the objective is the following:

$$\min \sum_{i=1}^{n} shr_i + shl_i$$

If the optimization objective is the total number of moved activities (distance function f_2), then the objective is

$$\min \sum_{i=1}^{n} \widehat{sh_i},$$

where $\widehat{sh_i}$ are binary variables indicating that the start time of activity i has changed. This is modelled using the following constraints for all $1 \leq i \leq n$:

$$shr_i + shl_i \leq \widehat{sh_i} \cdot M$$

In case of minimizing the biggest time shift (distance function f_3) the objective is $\min U$, where U is a new continuous variable describing the maximal time shift. Thus these constraints must be added:

$$shr_i + shl_i \leq U$$

In the following experiments, the models are referred to as $MIP0f1$, $MIP0$ $f2$, and $MIP0f3$ (respectively $MIP1f1$, $MIP1f2$, and $MIP1f3$).

7   Experimental Results

The STN-recovery algorithm is designed to move a lot of activities by a small amount of time, which means that it should not be used when minimizing the number of shifted activities (objective f_2). On the other hand, the algorithm should perform well in minimizing the biggest shift of an activity (objective f_3). On the contrary, the Right Shift Affected algorithm intents to affect only the necessary subset of activities, making it better when minimizing the objective f_2. Oppositely, if the alternative resources for the broken-down resource make a bottleneck, the affected activities (and subsequently all connected components with them) are moved to the end of the schedule horizon. This is expected to yield a poor performance in the objective f_3, which is unacceptable when the original schedule objective is related to lateness or tardiness. The distance functions f_2 and f_3 are expected to grow linearly with the increasing number of activities in the model for both the algorithms.

To support the above hypotheses we performed experiments with randomly generated problems composed of 6 resources in each of two resource groups. Each connected component consists of 5 activities and up to 10 temporal constraints (some may be redundant). The values of x-axes in the following figures are the number of connected components in the model. Having more resources in a

group than the number of activities in a component ensures recoverability from
a resource failure.

To justify the claims from the introduction, the comparison also includes
what we refer to as $STN0$ that is the sixth step of STN-recovery itself and thus
corresponds to the rescheduling from scratch. The STN-recovery algorithm as
described in Sect. 5 is referred to as $STN1$.

Further, the MIP models are included in the comparison. The experiments
were conducted using the mosek optimizer [3] with the following settings. If an
optimal solution is not found in 10 s, the engine outputs the first integer feasible
solution found. All the algorithms were running on Intel(R) Core(TM) i7-2600K
CPU @ 3.40 GHz, 3701 Mhz, kernels: 4, logical processors: 8; RAM: 8,00 GB.

Briefly speaking, the experimental results confirmed the hypotheses. The
Right Shift Affected algorithm is better when optimizing the distance function f_2
(Fig. 2), but the STN-recovery algorithm is better when optimizing the distance
function f_3 (Fig. 3). The function f_1 (which is the total sum of shifts) is depicted
in Fig. 1. Since the MIP models terminated only for smaller instances of the
problem, we include one figure with and one figure without the MIP models for
each of the performance measures.

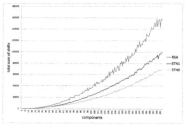

(a) Comparison for Right Shift Affected and STN-recovery.

(b) Comparison including MIP models.

Fig. 1. Distance function f1 – the total sum of shifts.

The Right Shift Affected algorithm is somewhat faster than STN-recovery
(Fig. 4), however, STN-recovery has the following advantage. The algorithm
always allocates the leftmost connected component that has not been allocated
yet, therefore, when the algorithm is allocating the connected component with
the leftmost activity that has the *MinStart* value t, the schedule is not going
to be modified before time point t. This allows the system to keep executing an
ongoing schedule even if it has not been completely recovered yet.

The dependencies on the density of constraints showed no tendency. However, one might wonder how the algorithms perform as the size of connected
components increases. For this reason, we performed experiments with problems composed of 20 resources in one resource group. Each problem contains 10
connected components, and the number of activities in each component is now

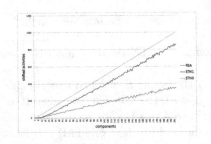

(a) Comparison for Right Shift Affected and STN-

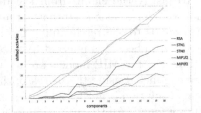

(b) Comparison including MIP models.

Fig. 2. Distance function f2 – the number of shifted activities.

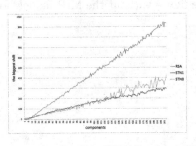

(a) Comparison for Right Shift Affected and STN-recovery.

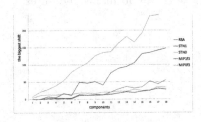

(b) Comparison including MIP models.

Fig. 3. Distance function f3 – the biggest shift of an activity.

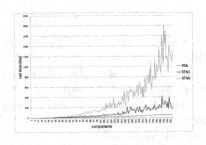

(a) Comparison for Right Shift Affected and STN-recovery.

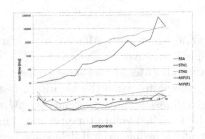

(b) Comparison including MIP models (logarithmic scale).

Fig. 4. Run times for the algorithms in milliseconds.

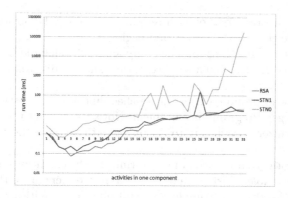

Fig. 5. Run times for the algorithms in milliseconds dependent on the number of activities in one connected component (logarithmic scale).

increasing. This is depicted in Fig. 5. The MIP models are not included in the figure because they terminated in reasonable time only for the components of size 4.

The experiments confirm the claims that fixing some activities may help find more similar schedules faster, which holds for STN-recovery as well as for the MIP models. We also observed behavior of other levels of pruning the search space for the MIP models, namely allowing shifting of activities only to the right and allowing shifting only beyond the $MinStart$ values obtained from the first five steps of STN-recovery, but the results were even worse than $MIP0$. Generally speaking, the MIP models as described in Sect. 6 turned out to be inapplicable to the type of problems tackled in this paper.

8 Conclusions

This paper proposed two different methods to handle a resource failure, i.e., a disruption when a resource suddenly cannot be used anymore by any activity, which may occur during a schedule execution.

The first method takes the activities that were to be processed on a broken machine, reallocates them, and then it keeps repairing violated constraints until it gets a feasible schedule. This approach is suitable when it is desired to move as few activities as possible; however, the question whether the algorithm always ends is still open. The second method deallocates a subset of activities and then it allocates them back through Conflict-directed Backjumping with Backmarking. This approach is useful when the intention is to shift activities by a short time distance, regardless of the number of moved activities.

The main shortcoming is that if there is no feasible recovery of the ongoing schedule, neither of the methods is able to quickly and securely report it. In real-life environments, however, the schedule recoverability from the breakdown of any particular machine is often known (for instance the minimum required number of available resources of each resource group may be obvious) or can be computed before the schedule execution begins.

Both suggested algorithms may be easily adapted to handle the models with arbitrary resource groups, and also to cope with another disturbance – hot order arrival [13].

This paper also proposed how the rescheduling problem may be modelled as a Mixed Integer Programming problem. However, solving the models using the mosek optimizer turned out to be uncompetitive with the two suggested algorithms.

Further investigation is needed for determining the conditions under which a schedule is recoverable. Next, it may be of interest to generalize the algorithms for models that involve for example interruptibility of activities, various speeds of resources, setup times of resources or calendars of availabilities of resources.

Acknowledgements. This research is partially supported by SVV project number 260 224 and by the Czech Science Foundation under the project P103-15-19877S.

References

1. Barták, R., Jaška, M., Novák, L., Rovenský, V., Skalický, T., Cully, M., Sheahan, C., Thanh-Tung, D.: Flowopt: Bridging the gap between optimization technology and manufacturing planners. In: De Raedt, L., et al. (eds.) Proceedings of 20th European Conference on Artificial Intelligence (ECAI 2012), pp. 1003–1004. IOS Press (2012)
2. Dechter, R., Meiri, I., Pearl, J.: Temporal constraint networks. Artif. Intell. **49**, 61–95 (1991)
3. Andersen, E.D., Andersen, K.D.: The mosek interior point optimizer for linear programming: an implementation of the homogeneous algorithm. In: Frenk, H., Roos, K., Terlaky, T., Zhang, S. (eds.) High Performance Optimization, pp. 197–232. Springer, USA (2000)
4. Raheja, A.S., Subramaniam, V.: Reactive recovery of job shop schedules - a review. Int. J. Adv. Manuf. Technol. **19**, 756–763 (2002)
5. Vieira, G., Herrmann, J., Lin, E.: Rescheduling manufacturing systems: a framework of strategies, policies, and methods. J. Sched. **6**, 39–62 (2003)
6. Ouelhadj, D., Petrovic, S.: A survey of dynamic scheduling in manufacturing systems. J. Sched. **12**, 417–431 (2009)
7. Abumaizar, R.J., Svestka, J.A.: Rescheduling job shops under random disruptions. Int. J. Prod. Res. **35**, 2065–2082 (1997)
8. Smith, S.F.: Reactive scheduling systems. In: Brown, D., Scherer, W. (eds.) Intelligent Scheduling Systems, pp. 155–192. Springer, USA (1995)
9. Skalický, T.: Interactive scheduling and visualisation. Master's thesis, Charles University in Prague (2011)
10. Planken, L.R.: New algorithms for the simple temporal problem. Ph.D. thesis, TU Delft, Delft University of Technology (2008)
11. Brailsford, S.C., Potts, C.N., Smith, B.M.: Constraint satisfaction problems: algorithms and applications. Eur. J. Oper. Res. **119**, 557–581 (1999)
12. Kondrak, G., Van Beek, P.: A theoretical evaluation of selected backtracking algorithms. Artif. Intell. **89**, 365–387 (1997)
13. Vlk, M.: Dynamic scheduling. Master's thesis, Charles University in Prague (2014)

From Information Assistance to Cognitive Automation: A Smart Assembly Use Case

Mario Aehnelt[1]([⊠]) and Sebastian Bader[2]

[1] Fraunhofer IGD, Joachim-Jungius-Str. 11, 18059 Rostock, Germany
mario.aehnelt@igd-r.fraunhofer.de
[2] MMIS, University of Rostock, Albert-Einstein-Str. 22, 18059 Rostock, Germany
sebastian.bader@uni-rostock.de

Abstract. Information assistance helps in many application domains to structure, guide and control human work processes. However, it lacks a formalisation and automated processing of background knowledge which vice versa is required to provide ad-hoc assistance. In this paper, we describe our conceptual and technical work towards this cognitive automation. We focus here on including contextual background knowledge to raise the worker's awareness, guide, and monitor assembly activities. We present cognitive architectures as missing link between highly sophisticated manufacturing data systems and implicitly available contextual knowledge on work procedures and concepts of the work domain. Our work is illustrated with examples in SWI-Prolog and the Soar cognitive architecture which is part of the Plant@Hand assembly assistance system.

1 Introduction

Evaluations show that people with a detailed work plan complete their tasks faster than without it, even if they did not carry out the planning themselves [12]. This is a key motivation for intelligent systems which assist the worker by creating work plans autonomously and guide him through single work procedures aiming to improve both efficiency and effectiveness of his work. Such intelligent systems will help in manufacturing to ensure a high product quality even when working with insufficiently qualified personnel. They inform the worker about current and upcoming tasks, provide him with detailed knowledge on assembly procedures, or monitor correct work order execution.

Although manufacturing industries already use powerful data management systems that support the planning, execution and monitoring of production processes, there is still a lack of methods and technologies which bring intelligent assistance to the shop floor. Basically, it lacks an automated processing of the lion's share of domain dependent background knowledge. It is hidden in work related standards, regulations, guidelines or simply maintained by experts, thus not available for the average worker.

Our research specifically addresses information assistance for assembly stations at the manufacturing shop floor. Although *smart factories* establish digitalisation and automation to streamline manufacturing processes and quality, there

© Springer International Publishing Switzerland 2015
B. Duval et al. (Eds.): ICAART 2015, LNAI 9494, pp. 207–222, 2015.
DOI: 10.1007/978-3-319-27947-3_11

is still the need for manual assembly operations [19]. Here, it requires systematic information assistance in order to manage the complexity and heterogeneity of extremely small lot sizes. This research can be understood as technical perspective on the *cognitive automation* of manual work processes as introduced by [8].

Throughout this paper we focus on smart factories in which individually customised products are assembled by humans. In particular, we assume a lot size of one. This implies, that basically every product is unique and required new construction plans. In contrast to larger lot sizes or series production, it is not profitable to invest much into product-specific assistance systems. Therefore, we need to derive useful assistance systems from existing information sources.

This paper is organised as follows: First, we discuss different types of assistance within the focus of manual assembly processes. Sects. 3 and 4 describe how to detect important situations and how to provide assistance, respectively. In Sect. 5 we show how cognitive architectures can be used to formalize and process the missing background knowledge. We conclude our work with Sect. 7.

2   Required Assistance

Below we discuss use cases in which different types of assistance are required to support manual assembly processes. But first we give a short introduction to assembly work activities.

The assembly of machines and technical systems is an essential part of production. It consumes up to 40 % of costs and even 70 % of production time. During an assembly single machine parts are joined to first-order assemblies (*pre-assembly*), then to assemblies of higher order (*intermediate assembly*) and finally to an end product (*final assembly*). The German VDI guideline 2860 [9] further differentiates between *primary assembly*, which includes the main joining operations as defined with the DIN 8580 [7], and *secondary assembly*, including all additional assembly activities like handling, adjustment and control of parts, material, tools, and machines. Assembly operations such as joining directly refer to physical activities of the worker. A more detailed description of the manual operations as well as of the physical work environment can, for example, be found in [2].

Traditionally, a worker is equipped with work orders describing the work to be done on an abstract level. It strongly depends on his individual knowledge and experiences to interpret the given information correctly. Information assistance, especially in complex and continuously changing assembly work processes, improves the quality of work by ensuring an immediate transfer of required work information to the workplace and back to planning systems for example. Here, we differentiate between five general types of information assistance:

- *Raising Awareness*: The worker requires up-to-the-minute knowledge about his direct and relevant work environment in order to align his own activities accordingly. Knowing early enough the malfunction or breakdown of a machine, which produces parts for his own assembly, influences his situational decisions and activities. Thus, information assistance needs to make the worker aware of relevant states, events and occurrences within the work environment which have an influence on the planning and execution of the worker's tasks.

- *Guiding*: The worker requires orientation with respect to his current and upcoming assembly tasks. This needs to be given through operational guidance which filters available information for each specific work step, in order to reduce the parallel information load to a required minimum. Knowing the exact joining procedure beforehand does not reduce the risk of failures, especially in complex assembly cases. Thus, information assistance needs to split complex procedures into smaller but easier understandable parts, used to guide the worker step-by-step through the assembly.

- *Monitoring*: In the first place, monitoring the assembly process has a practical value. It allows a detailed comparison as well as re-calculation of planned and real time figures. Additionally, it enables the early identification of quality issues or interruptions. Information assistance needs to collect required data from the workplace which supports the continuously production re-planning. It also needs to control the correct execution of assembly procedures to avoid reworking in case of wrong assembly orders, skipped parts or incorrect tool usage.

- *Documenting*: When it comes to quality issues or even complaints, information assistance needs to support tracking back these issues to their roots, which requires a parallel documentation of assembly tasks. However, this kind of documentation can also be helpful to evaluate assembly procedures finding examples of best practice or expert knowledge inherited within individual work processes.

- *Guarding*: The physical and cognitive loads at the assembly workplace vary from situation to situation. Information assistance needs to guard the worker from overload by balancing the load levels within healthy borders or by visualising it.

Based on the use cases introduced above, we discuss the current state of the art in assistance for manual assembly tasks. Smart assistance is no novelty in manufacturing. The growing complexity of todays' mass customized products leads there to increased cognitive loads resulting in rising assembly error rates. Fast-Berglund et al. [8] showed that up to 60 % of a manual assembly is based on the worker's own knowledge and experience. Smart assistance systems can automate here the decision making as well as information processing thus decreasing the individual cognitive load and human failure.

Korn et al. [13] demonstrate here an interesting approach towards combining work assistance and training when addressing physical and cognitive impaired workers. They use the concept of *gamification* to steer the worker's motivation and control the cognitive balancing of work tasks.

However, we find there a majority of specialised and single task solutions focussing on quality assurance and information transfer [6]. Other research deals with concepts for smart factories which automate the planning and execution of manufacturing processes in autonomously working factories. Focussing on the automation of robot cells Mayer et al. proposed the usage of intelligent systems to resemble human decision making and problem solving for complex assembly tasks [17]. They introduce the *cognitive control unit* (CCU) which ensures the numerical planning of robot behaviour backed by a cognitive architecture. Cognitive architectures can be understood as a mean to implement intelligent and autonomous behaviour in assistance applications. They have proven capable of supporting complex problem solving tasks. A recent example is the simulation of mission management for unmanned aircrafts [10].

Our own work contributes to the growing demand of information assistance for manual work operations in manufacturing which underlies human flexibility and failures as motivated by [5]. In particular, we focus on assistance that can be generated automatically from existing knowledge sources. This allows to use the approach also for small lot sizes.

3   Detecting Situations

To actually provide assistance, we first need to recognize situations in which this is necessary. We will discuss the recognition process only briefly, because we simply utilize an approach presented at ICAART 2014. Therefore, we only review some ideas presented in [5]. Based on a formalization of assembly tasks, using so-called task models, a Hidden Markov Model (HMM) is synthesized. The resulting HMM is used to filter sensor data and compute a probability distribution over the current state of the process. As sensory inputs only the processed building blocks are used and the accuracy is analysed with respect to different sensor errors. Here, we use a similar approach, but instead of using the single building blocks as sensory inputs, we also utilize the tools used for the assembly. Figure 1 shows such an enhanced task model, stating that a *wire-spool* is built from 5 *wires* and some *tin-solder*. The parts are joined by *soldering* them using a *soldering-iron*.

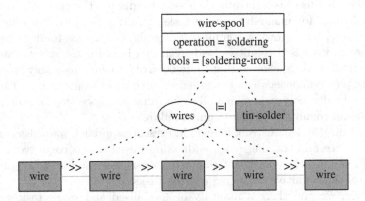

Fig. 1. A simple task model stating that a wire-spool is build from 5 wires and tin-solder. In addition, the top-most node contains the joining operation (*soldering*) and the tools to be used (*soldering-iron*).

To raise awareness for important state changes in the environment as well as for guiding the worker, the current state of the assembly process needs to be determined. For this, we rely on the results reported in [5], indicating that this is indeed feasible. Based on our annotated models, we believe that the results should be even better, but a detailed analysis is subject to future work.

To detect assembly errors or deviations from the usual procedure is harder to track. In [5], the authors describe how the system reacts with respect to different types of sensor errors (missing and repeated readings).

But here, we need to detect actual assembly errors, which has not been tackled before. As the task model describes valid construction paths only, the resulting HMM will always compute a probability distribution over valid paths. Therefore, an assembly error is not directly observable. To track assembly errors nonetheless, we analyse the development of the probability distribution over states. Because valid paths result in rather crisp probability distributions (i.e., one path has a very high probability while all others a low one), errors result in a higher entropy of the distribution. Based on this insight, we are able to detect situations in which an error occurred.

4   Providing Assistance

Information assistance at the assembly workplace aims at the continuous information exchange between leading manufacturing data systems (enterprise resource planning, manufacturing execution, etc.) and the worker in order to support efficient working and to avoid interruptions, failures or quality related issues.

To keep argumentation and presentation simple, we assume that the state of the world is known exactly. The system described here, has been implemented in SWI-Prolog[1]. The state of the world is described as static and dynamic facts shown in Listings 1.1 and 1.2, respectively.

```
produces('WireMachine', wire).
task(wire—spool,        % goal
  soldering ,           % operation
  [soldering —iron],    % tools
  [tin—solder, 5*wire]). % parts
```

Listing 1.1. tatic background information describing that a WireMachine produces wires and that a wire-spool is assembled by soldering wires using a soldering-iron. The task corresponds to the task-model shown in Fig. 1.

---

[1] http://www.swi-prolog.org.

```
storage(wire, 3).
assembles(worker1, wire—spool).
broken('WireMachine', 'no copper available').
knows(worker1, howTo(soldering)).
```

Listing 1.2. Dynamic background information describing that 3 wires are available, worker1 assembles a wire-spool, and that the wire machine is broken.

Below, we work out information which helps to provide awareness on the assembly situation, guides the worker through an assembly, and finally monitors his work and results.

4.1   Raising Awareness

Situational awareness with respect to his work environment helps the worker to orientate within complex processes and to align his own activities accordingly [11]. It can be understood as inherent information demand of carrying out and completing work tasks.

```
informationDemand(InfoType, Person, Info) :—
% Person assembles a given item ..
assembles(Person, Item),
% ... containing a Part with a given Quantity
isPartOf(Part, Item, Quantity),
% The Machine producing the Part ...
produces(Machine, Part),
% ... is broken for a given Reason
broken(Machine, Reason),
% The Quantity is larger than the StoredQuantity
storage(Part, SQ), Quantity > SQ,

InfoType = awareness(stateOf(Machine)),
Info = brokenMachine(Machine, Part, SQ).
```

Listing 1.3. Specification of an information demand to raise awareness with respect to a broken machine. The predicate `isPartOf` allows to access sup-parts as defined through the task model.

All changes of the virtual or physical work environment which influence the ongoing or upcoming assembly tasks need to made aware to the worker. This includes, for example:

– *planned tasks* which can change in time and priority,
– *missing material, tool or information* which are required but not available for assembly, or
– *deviations* from normal procedures, orders and qualities.

> **Type:** *awareness(stateOf(WireMachine))*
> **User:** *worker1*
> **Info:** *We are running low on wire, because WireMachine is broken and only 3 items are left in storage.*
> **Explanation:** *It is assumed that* worker1 *assembles* wire-spool. *Item* wire *is needed 5 times to assemble a* wire-spool. WireMachine *produces* wire. *It is assumed that* WireMachine *is broken, because* no copper available. *It is assumed that 3 items of* wire *are left in storage.* Worker1 *should be aware of the state of* WireMachine.

Fig. 2. Infomessage and explanation generated for the information demand specified in Listing 1.3.

Depending on the information impact as well as urgency, assistance needs to help perceiving it embedded in the ongoing work flow.

After evaluating the information demand as specified in Listing 1.3 with respect to the current state of the world, InfoType is unified with awareness(stateOf ('WireMachine')) and Info with brokenMachine('Wire Machine', wire, 3). In addition, all premises are known. This allows to generate the output shown in Fig. 2. A simple verbalisation engine is used to translate the predicates (e.g., shown in bold font in Listing 1.3) instantiated while computing the information demand into english sentences. Predicates corresponding to dynamic facts are verbalised as assumptions.

4.2 Guiding

Similar to formal education processes, information assistance in form of guiding can be understood as an informal way of mediating and learning facts (*what*), procedures (*how*) and concepts (*why*) required for a specific assembly task. The shaping and depth of guidance varies depending on a specific assistance objective to be supported [3]. In a first step the worker is required to *remember, understand* and *apply* the given information in order to prepare and execute his assembly task correctly. Thus, information assistance has to collect and visualise:

- *bills of material* which identify the material to be used for an assembly step,
- *bills of tools* which lists the tools and machines to be used for joining procedures,
- *procedures* which describe the correct handling, adjusting, joining, and controlling of materials and tools including safety relevant information, and
- *planned figures* which detail the expected assembly times and results.

As motivated in Sect. 2, it is important to split complex assembly procedures into smaller instructions (*steps*), reducing thus cognitive loads for the worker and giving them a clear work structure [12]. Showing then the required information parallel to the ongoing work process for each step only, helps to achieve the three assistance objectives.

Similar to the information demand specified in Listing 1.3, it is possible to formalise guiding knowledge. This includes for example the tool to be used for the current assembly operation as shown in Listing 1.4. Figure 3 shows the resulting output after verbalising the predicates.

```
informationDemand(InfoType, Person, Info) :–
  % Person assembles a item
  assembles(Person, Item),
  % get Join–Operation from task model
  task(Item, JoinOp, Tools, Parts),

  InfoType = guiding(JoinOp),
  Info = currJoinOp(Person, Item, JoinOp, Tools).
```

Listing 1.4. Specification of an information demand with respect to the current type of join operation and the tools to be used.

```
Type: guiding(JoinOp)
User: worker1
Info: You should soldering the wire-spool using soldering-iron.
Explanation: It is assumed that worker1 assembles wire-spool. Item wire-spool is assembled
    via soldering, using a soldering-iron.
```

Fig. 3. Infomessage and explanation generated for the information demand specified in Listing 1.4.

Similar specifications can be used to refer to the items to be used. For complex assembly tasks, many different types of joining operations have to be performed by the worker. Usually, not every worker has the same in-depth training for all of them. Therefore, more background knowledge should be provided for unknown operations. This can be formalised as shown in Listing 1.5.

```
informationDemand(InfoType, Person, Info) :–
  % Person assembles a given part
  assembles(Person, Part),
  % get information from task model
  task(Part, JoinOp, Tools, _Children),
  % if there is a description D of the op ...
  bgInfo(joinOp(JoinOp), description(D)),
  % ... and the person does not know it
  not( knows(Person, howTo(JoinOp)) ),

  InfoType = bgInfo(joinOp(JoinOp))
  Info = bgInfo(joinOp(JoinOp), description(D)).
```

Listing 1.5. Specification of an information demand with respect to missing background knowledge.

Assuming knows(worker1, howTo(soldering)) to be true, and false for worker2, results in different information assistance for both.

4.3 Monitoring

Monitoring the ongoing assembly activities of the worker establishes a feedback channel to the information assistance system. It requires a close observation of work progress, rejects, and issues for practical reasons. Manufacturing execution systems need this information to allow a detailed planning of production processes. For situation recognition we require more detailed knowledge from monitoring: the *material* taken as well as *tools* picked up and their *configuration*, which enables us to draw conclusions on the current assembly step executed and possible deviations in comparison to the provided instructions.

5 Using Soar to Provide Assistance

The previous sections showed conceptual and technical considerations with respect to acquiring knowledge on actual assembly situations as well as to providing information assistance at the assembly workplace. Although, a vast amount of required information can already be found in manufacturing data management systems, the major share of procedural and conceptual knowledge is not yet formalised in systems which allow their automated processing (see Fig. 4). We find work instructions, standards, or assembly guidelines normally written in natural language within accompanying documents. However, there has already been research to distinguish between the semantic meaning of instructions and their visual representation [16] based on controlled vocabularies which allows for automation. They still require a manual authoring of instructions for each assembly process individually. What we require in contrast for guiding for example, is an abstract formalisation of assembly procedures in general which is filled at runtime with factual knowledge about the specific product or situation.

Cognitive architectures are a mean to bridge the gap between common assembly descriptions, that we find in VDI 2860 or DIN 8580, and reusable procedural knowledge in information assistance systems. Below, we summarize our approach of utilising the cognitive architecture *Soar* for assisting the worker during assembly.

5.1 Cognitive Architectures

Cognitive architectures can be traced back to Newell's early hypothesis that any artificial intelligence is based on a symbol system and related rules [18]. As of today, a cognitive architecture describes the *mental structure* for human information processing, the *representation* and *organization* of information within these structures as well as the *functional processing* required to acquire, use, and modify information [15]. Hence, they allow modelling and implementing intelligent behaviour in smart applications and environments. We also need it for providing assistance as described in Sect. 2. In our own work we use the cognitive architecture Soar (*state, operator and result*) for:

- *situation detection* based on observations of the physical work environment and following reasoning,

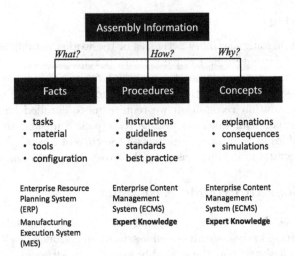

Fig. 4. Required information is contained in different enterprise resources. Partly it is individual expert knowledge which is not externalised in any management system.

- the *formalisation and processing* of contextual background knowledge (e.g. procedures, explanations),
- *interactions* with the worker as well as the physical environment to provide assistance by raising awareness and guiding for example, and for
- additionally *learning* assembly related practices from observation.

In general, processes in Soar are related to the gradual alternation of information and states in working or long-term memory [14]. Here, a situation is formalized as a state in working memory, which is modified by evaluating and applying *operators* until an intended final state is reached. The operator definition consists of required conditions and actions on the working memory. It inherits procedural and conceptual knowledge from the corresponding knowledge domain. New operators can also be derived by observation of decision making processes (*chunking*) and through learning processes.

First examples on how we use Soar to provide assembly assistance are illustrated below.

5.2   Situation Detection

In Soar we represent the individual situations of the work environment during an assembly by *states*. Each state identifies a different condition of elements within the Soar working memory, which finally holds a virtual copy of the physical environment. Thus, we transfer the state of real objects, e.g. tools, the material stack, or even the workplace, into logical *objects* and their *attributes* in working memory. Soar connects then to sensors which allow the observation of individual object states and events, e.g. the usage of a tool, in order to update attributes of the related working memory object. The working memory is so the basis of all reasoning on discrete states of the work environment.

In Listing 1.6 we illustrate the usage of Soar's state operator mechanism for a specific soldering situation. It consists of two parts, an operator proposal rule and an application rule. The first one defines the pre-condition of a state described by working memory objects and their attributes. In our example it requires at least two materials or parts and a soldering iron in order to start a soldering operation. If the current state of the working memory matches these conditions, the operator *join-part* becomes candidate in following decision making.

Soar evaluates the likelihood of each operator based on the current state of objects in working memory and all candidate proposal rule definitions. It uses contextual knowledge (see Sect. 5.3) to compare and select candidate operators during decision making.

```
# parts can only be soldered if there are at least
# two parts taken, a soldering iron and solder to
# support the joining operation
sp {propose*soldering−parts
   (state <s> ^name assemble)
   (<s> ^count_taken > 1)
   (<s> ^iron_taken <=> yes)
   (<s> ^solder_taken <=> yes)
-->
   (<s> ^operator <o> + =)
   (<o> ^name soldering−parts )                    }

# soldering parts reduces the taken parts to a
# single compound part and consumes solder
sp {apply*soldering−parts
   (state <s> ^operator.name soldering−parts)
   (<s> ^count_taken <t>)
   (<s> ^solder_taken <m>)
-->
   (<s> ^name soldering)
   (<s> ^count_taken 1)
   (<s> ^count_taken <t> −)
   (<s> ^solder_taken <m> −)                    }
```

Listing 1.6. Definition of operator and production rules in Soar for joining assembly step.

With applying finally the operator *soldering-parts* the working memory state is changed by modifying single memory objects, e.g. by reducing the amount of available parts.

5.3   Contextual Knowledge

One of Soar's strengths lays in its interaction between working and long-term memory. While the working memory holds information about the current condition of logical objects (see Sect. 5.2), the long-term memory represents the contextual knowledge which is required to select and apply an operator. Here, we find five different knowledge types in Soar: knowledge which qualifies an operator for a situation, knowledge to compare operators, knowledge to select a single one, knowledge to change the working memory, and knowledge to elaborate a state. All types contain contextual knowledge of the application work domain, in our case of assembly activities as formulated in VDI 2860 and DIN 8580.

In Listing 1.7 we encode this assembly knowledge to define the sequential order of single work steps and their requirements. In this example, we require further solder material prior to collecting the soldering iron, which will be defined by additional preference operators, such as $+$, $>$, $<$, or $!$.

```
# soldering parts requires additional solder
# material which need to be taken first
sp {propose*take-solder
   (state <s> ^name assemble)
   (<s> ^iron_taken <=> yes - ^solder_taken)
-->
   (<s> ^operator <o1> + ; <o1> > <o2>)
   (<o1> ^name take-solder)
   (<o2> ^name take-iron)                    }
```

Listing 1.7. Contextual knowledge of the work domain is encoded in Soar's production rules.

In this way, we were able to transfer the relevant assembly process logic into Soar operators. They help us guiding the worker with small sized assembly instructions as required for an automated information assistance.

5.4   Interaction

We also use Soar to establish an interaction between information assistance system and the worker as well as vice versa. As described in Sect. 4 we aim to raise the worker's awareness with respect to relevant information on his ongoing assembly process, guide him step by step through the assembly, and monitor his work activities. It finally requires the interaction to inform him and collect data from him. This can also be formalised by operator rules.

```
# provide information assistance once the worker
# is not informed on his following work step
sp {propose*inform
   (state <s> ^type state)
   (<s> ^name <n> - ^is_informed)
-->
   (<s> ^operator <o1> !)
   (<o1> ^name inform)                    }
```

Listing 1.8. Information assistance is modeled as operators in Soar.

Listing 1.8 shows the proposal rule of an *inform* operator which will provide the worker with instructions for his next assembly steps. In a similar manner we define operators for raising awareness for example.

6   Industrial Application in Plant@Hand

The proposed approach is part of the continuously development of the *Plant@-Hand* assembly assistance system which we already introduced in previous works [1,4]. We used here *Soar* as cognitive architecture which enables us now to analyze the specific work situation and to provide cognitive automation for the worker. The whole system is developed to provide mobile information assistance for the assembly part of the manufacturing shop floor.

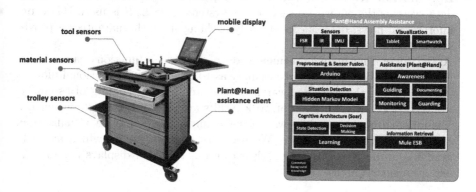

Fig. 5. Hardware and software components of the industrial *Plant@Hand smart assembly trolley* prototype.

The assembly of partly large and complex special units requires from the worker a high degree of flexibility and mobility. Components need to be assembled in varying complexities at different locations of the special unit. This makes it difficult to instrument the work environment with activity recognizing sensors. An instrumentation of the worker is also limited due to safety reasons. Because of this challenging conditions we use a standard mobile workshop trolley (see Fig. 5) as technical basis for our assembly assistance application. Such a unit is normally used to store and transport tools as well as material during an assembly. The trolley provides shelves and drawers for different sorts of assembly tools or small to medium sized work materials. All hardware and software components of the *Plant@Hand* assembly assistance system are built into the mobile workshop trolley:

– **Sensors:** We use different sensor types to monitor the ongoing assembly activities of the worker. *Force sensitive resistors* (FSR), *infrared sensors* (IR) and *RFID sensors* provide data on material and tool usage, e.g. the removal of screws from a material container. *Inertial measurement units* (IMU) give us information on the trolley movements.

- **Preprocessing and Sensor Fusion:** An *Arduino Uno* board is used to make a first preprocessing (filtering) and fusion of incoming sensor data. It generates activity events for interpretation in the cognitive architecture.
- **Situation Detection:** For the recognition of different situations, we are currently using a simple forward filtering algorithm for HMMs.
- **Cognitive Architecture:** The cognitive architecture *Soar* provides the functional subcomponents for state detection based on the previously computed most likely work situation, followed by decision making on required assistance actions and information to be provided as well as machine learning from observed activities. It also allows the implementation of adaptive and smart learning support.
- **Information Retrieval:** For the connection with external manufacturing data systems the enterprise service bus system *Mule ESB* is used. Based on information flows, data is continuously exchanged which guarantees a provision of the latest information.
- **Assistance:** The main implementation of assistance functions can still be found within the *Plant@Hand* assembly assistance system. Functional blocks, such as raising the workers awareness, the step-by-step guiding of assembly works, or the documentation of work results are part of the assistance client.
- **Visualisation:** The mobile workplace requires also a mobile visualisation of information for the worker. We use here mobile displays which are still available during the assembly task execution. Provided displays are tablets and even smartwatches.

We use the described technical setup in our experiments on integrating cognitive automation and information assistance under industrial work conditions.

7   Conclusions

In this paper we showed how to provide information assistance for a smart assembly station. After defining different types of information demands, we briefly discussed a possibility to detect situations in which assistance is needed. Then we showed how assistance can be provided using a crisp state of the world and logical specifications of the information demand (using an implementation in SWI Prolog). Even though, most information can already be found in manufacturing data management systems, the majority of procedural and conceptual knowledge is not yet formalised. To bridge this gap we use the Soar architecture.

Although the concept of cognitive architectures is not new to implementing systems with intelligent behaviour, it is still rarely used to make the contextual background knowledge from an application domain accessible for complex problem solving tasks. Our approach shows on both, conceptual as well as technical level, the usage of an cognitive architecture for supporting information assistance and thus the cognitive automation on the manufacturing shop floor. It illustrates the role of logical modelling and the transfer of implicit and barely formalised knowledge into predicate logic and state operators.

However, one of the next required steps is to learn new procedures and novel connections from observation of real assembly activities. Here it is promising to start with a basic guidance skeleton and detail the missing assembly steps by tracking, interpreting, and learning from work procedures of assembly experts. In addition, we are working on an experimental evaluation of the ideas. This includes the collection of real sensor data and the formalisation of real-world examples. And finally we will work on an automated transfer of real existing knowledge into an assistance system.

Acknowledgements. This research has been supported by the German Federal State of Mecklenburg-Western Pomerania and the European Social Fund under grant ESF/ IV-BM-B35-0006/12.

References

1. Aehnelt, M., Bader, S.: Information assistance for smart assembly stations. In: Loiseau, S., Filipe, J., Duval, B., van den Herik, J. (eds.) Proceedings of the 7th International Conference on Agents and Artificial Intelligence (ICAART 2015), vol. 2, pp. 143–150. SciTePress, Lisbon (2015). http://dx.doi.org/10.5220/0005216501430150
2. Aehnelt, M., Gutzeit, E., Urban, B.: Using activity recognition for the tracking of assembly processes: challenges and requirements. In: Bieber, G., Aehnelt, M., Urban, B. (eds.) WOAR 2014, pp. 12–21. Fraunhofer-Verlag, Stuttgart (2014)
3. Aehnelt, M., Urban, B.: Follow-Me: smartwatch assistance on the shop floor. In: Nah, F.F.-H. (ed.) HCIB 2014. LNCS, vol. 8527, pp. 279–287. Springer, Heidelberg (2014)
4. Aehnelt, M., Urban, B.: The knowledge gap: providing situation-aware information assistance on the shop floor. In: Proceedings of the 17th International Conference on Human-Computer Interaction, 2–7 August 2015, Los Angeles, USA (2015)
5. Bader, S., Aehnelt, M.: Tracking assembly processes and providing assistance in smart factories. In: Proceedings of the 6th International Conference on Agents and Artificial Intelligence (ICAART) (2014)
6. Berndt, D., Sauer, S.: Visuelle assistenzsysteme in der montage verhindern ausfälle. MM MaschinenMarkt **19**, 46–49 (2012)
7. DIN Deutsches Institut für Normung e.V.: Din 8580 manufacturing processes - terms and definitions, division (2003)
8. Fast-Berglund, Å., Fässberg, T., Hellman, F., Davidsson, A., Stahre, J.: Relations between complexity, quality and cognitive automation in mixed-model assembly. J. Manuf. Syst. **32**(3), 449–455 (2013)
9. German Engineers' Association: Vdi 2860:1990–05 assembly and handling; handling functions, handling units; terminology, definitions and symbols (1990)
10. Gunetti, P., Dodd, T., Thompson, H.: Simulation of a soar-based autonomous mission management system for unmanned aircraft. J. Aerosp. Inf. Syst. **10**(2), 53–70 (2013)
11. Gutwin, C., Greenberg, S.: A descriptive framework of workspace awareness for real-time groupware. Comput. Support. Coop. Work (CSCW) **11**(3), 411–446 (2002)

12. Kokkalis, N., Köhn, T., Huebner, J., Lee, M., Schulze, F., Klemmer, S.R.: Taskgenies: automatically providing action plans helps people complete tasks. ACM Trans. Comput. Human Interact. **20**(5), 1–25 (2013)
13. Korn, O., Funk, M., Schmidt, A.: Assistive systems for the workplace. In: Theng, L.B. (ed.) Assistive Technologies for Physical and Cognitive Disabilities, pp. 121–135. IGI Global, Duisburg (2015)
14. Laird, J.E.: The soar cognitive architecture. Artif. Intell. Simul. Behav. Q. **134**, 1–4 (2012)
15. Langley, P., Laird, J.E., Rogers, S.: Cognitive architectures: research issues and challenges. Cogn. Syst. Res. **10**(2), 141–160 (2008)
16. Mader, S., Urban, B.: Creating instructional content for augmented reality based on controlled natural language concepts. In: Proceedings of 20th International Conference on Artificial Reality and Telexistence (ICAT 2010) (2010)
17. Mayer, M.P., Odenthal, B., Wagels, C., Kuz, S., Kausch, B., Schlick, C.M.: Cognitive engineering of automated assembly processes. In: Harris, D. (ed.) Engin. Psychol. and Cog. Ergonomics, HCII 2011. LNCS, vol. 6781, pp. 313–321. Springer, Heidelberg (2011)
18. Newell, A.: Physical symbol systems*. Cogn. Sci. **4**(2), 135–183 (1980). http://dx.doi.org/10.1207/s15516709cog0402_2
19. Würtz, G., Kölmel, B.: Integrated engineering – a SME-suitable model for business and information systems engineering (BISE) towards the smart factory. In: Camarinha-Matos, L.M., Xu, L., Afsarmanesh, H. (eds.) Collaborative Networks in the Internet of Services. IFIP AICT, vol. 380, pp. 494–502. Springer, Heidelberg (2012)

A Heuristic for Constrained Set Partitioning in the Light of Heterogeneous Objectives

Gerrit Anders[✉], Florian Siefert, and Wolfgang Reif

Institute for Software and Systems Engineering, University of Augsburg,
Augsburg, Germany
{anders,siefert,reif}@informatik.uni-augsburg.de

Abstract. The set partitioning problem (SPP) is at the heart of the formation of several organizational structures in multi-agent systems. Essentially, such structures can improve scalability and enable cooperation between agents with limited resources and capabilities. We present a discrete Particle Swarm Optimizer that solves the NP-hard SPP in the presence of partitioning constraints which restrict valid partitionings in terms of acceptable ranges for the number and the size of partitions. To be applicable to a broad range of applications, our algorithm relies on basic set operations to come to a solution and is thus independent of the characteristics of a specific objective function. Among other things, it can be used for coalition structure generation, strict partitioning clustering, anticlustering, and, combined with an additional control loop, even for the creation of hierarchical partitionings. Our evaluation confirms that it finds high-quality solutions in different scenarios and for various objectives in short time.

Keywords: Set partitioning problem · Clustering · Anticlustering · Particle swarm optimization · Evolutionary computing

1 Introduction and Related Work

In numerous multi-agent systems (MAS), a crucial step is to establish an organizational structure that supports the agents' and the system's objectives [14]. Among other things, these structures allow agents to benefit from the capabilities of others, thereby increasing their own value of participating in the system. In large-scale systems, organizations are also a way of dealing with complexity and scalability issues, which is often accomplished by hierarchy formation [28].

In many cases, these organizations are based on structures that can be described as a *partitioning*. In the *set partitioning problem* (SPP) (cf. [10]), a set $\mathfrak{A} = \{a_1, \ldots, a_n\}$ of $n > 1$ agents a_i is partitioned into non-empty and pairwise disjoint subsets, called *partitions*, that together constitute a partitioning

This research is partly sponsored by the research unit *OC-Trust* (FOR 1085) of the German Research Foundation.

B. Duval et al. (Eds.): ICAART 2015, LNAI 9494, pp. 223–244, 2015.
DOI: 10.1007/978-3-319-27947-3_12

at minimal cost. Feasible, i.e., valid, partitions $\mathfrak{B} = \{b_1, \ldots, b_m\}$ are predefined and finding the optimal partitioning is NP-hard. In this paper, we assume that feasible partitions are only constrained in terms of a minimum s_{min} and maximum s_{max} size. This will often result in a very large number of feasible partitions. The so-called *complete SPP* (cf. [20]) constitutes the unbounded case in which the number of feasible partitions m grows exponentially with n since there are $m = 2^n - 1$ partitions. In this situation, the size of the search space, i.e., the number of possible partitionings, is given by the nth *Bell number* $\mathcal{B}_n$ (e.g., $\mathcal{B}_{50} \approx 1.86 \cdot 10^{47}$), which is defined by *Dobiński's formula* $\mathcal{B}_n = \frac{1}{e} \cdot \sum_{k=0}^{\infty} \frac{k^n}{k!}$ [8]. Note that even in a system in which the set of agents $\mathfrak{A}$ is not subject to change over time, it would not be suitable to pre-calculate all feasible partitions in advance (for $n = 50$ and the complete SPP, this needs more than one week on our Xeon machine), not to mention the possible partitionings. To differentiate this specific problem from the original SPP more clearly, we will refer to it as the *partitioning problem* (PP). In contrast to the SPP's original definition – in which the costs of having a partition b_j included are additive and predefined –, we further allow a more flexible objective function in the PP: We only presume an application-specific metric that evaluates if a partitioning, i.e., a combination of partitions, is fit for purpose. If the metric aims at partitions featuring similar properties (e.g., if the agents represent real numbers, partitions with a similar sum of their members), we speak of *homogeneous partitioning*. Note that many instances of homogeneous partitioning are not supported by the original SPP due to its restriction to additive and predefined costs of partitions. If the metric specifies to group similar or dissimilar agents, the PP is equivalent to *strict partitioning clustering (with outliers[1])* or *anticlustering[2]* (cf. [27,29]), respectively. If the metric defines how well agents can work together on a common task, the PP is equivalent to *coalition structure generation* (cf. [26]). Of course, one can also think of a combination of these heterogeneous objectives.

If an algorithm solves the PP by representing each agent $a_i \in \mathfrak{A}$ by a vector $\boldsymbol{g}_i$ of those attributes of a_i that are relevant to solve the PP, it actually has to solve a *multiset partitioning problem* (MPP) for the multiset $\mathfrak{G} = \{g_1, \ldots, g_n\}$. That is because we might have $\boldsymbol{g}_i = \boldsymbol{g}_j$ for two agents $a_i \neq a_j$. In the MPP, the multiset sum $\biguplus_{K \in \mathcal{P}} K$ of all partitions K (here, non-empty multisets) in the partitioning $\mathcal{P}$ must equal $\mathfrak{G}$. In this paper, we assume heterogeneous agents so that all vectors $\boldsymbol{g}_i$ are different (i.e., $\forall a_i, a_j \in \mathfrak{A} : a_i \neq a_j \to \boldsymbol{g}_i \neq \boldsymbol{g}_j$). Hence, $\mathfrak{G}$ is a set and the problem is reduced to a PP.

Algorithms for the solution of the PP in MAS have a broad area of application, e.g., in sensor networks, power management systems, manufacturing systems, communication systems, or e-commerce: In [30], a highly decentralized algorithm is used to assign each sensor node a cluster head within its communication radius and to allow all cluster heads to communicate with each other.

---

[1] Supported by a separate partition that holds all outliers.

[2] While clustering dissimilar elements leads to partitions whose mean values correspond to the mean of all elements in the system, homogeneous partitioning is not limited to this specific property and does not necessarily group dissimilar elements.

Anders et al. [5] present a decentralized graph-based algorithm, called SPADA, that allows power plants to self-organize into virtual power plants in order to lower the time needed to create power plant schedules. In [3], existing organizational structures are exploited in form of input/output relations between agents to guide a decentralized coalition formation that reconfigures a production cell. Al Faruque et al. [1] show an agent-based clustering approach for networks on chip that is used to map tasks to processing elements. In [9], costumers of e-commerce websites are categorized into different profiles on the basis of global knowledge.

Some algorithms that solve instances of the PP, e.g., those formulated and solved as a linear programming problem, require global system knowledge but yield optimal solutions (cf. [24]). Because of the PP's complexity they are often designed as anytime algorithms or distribute the entire search space among the agents to be able to calculate the utility of all possible partitions and pick the best one after a global announcement (cf. [26]). Other approaches, such as [5] or [23], rely on local knowledge and solve the PP in a completely decentralized fashion. While such strong self-organization approaches can deal with very large systems [12], the lack of regional or global knowledge is sometimes reflected in the solutions' quality.

Usually, algorithms that solve the PP are either (1) specialized to a particular problem in a certain domain, (2) depend on the properties of a specific objective function, or are (3) very restrictive with regard to the possibility to specify mandatory characteristics of the resulting partitioning's structure in the form of the number and the size of partitions. These attributes limit the algorithms' applicability. As for point (2), many algorithms – especially those addressing the original SPP – are specialized to certain objective functions, e.g., those in which the quality of partitions is additive and can thus be assessed independently of each other. The well-known k-means [21] or k-medoids [16] clustering algorithms, for instance, assign elements to clusters in a way that minimizes (or, in case of anticlustering, maximizes) the sum of the distances between the elements and their cluster center. These algorithms are not able to a establish certain homogeneous partitionings, such as our previous example of creating partitions with a similar sum of assigned real numbers. With respect to point (3), most algorithms either do not allow to characterize valid partitionings at all (cf. [23]) or the user or the agents have to be very specific. Using the k-means clustering algorithm, for example, the user has to specify the number of partitions k exactly. Because a suitable exact number of partitions is often not known (further drawbacks of k-means, such as the formation of partitions of similar size, are discussed in [7]), there are different approaches that extend the k-means algorithm by the possibility to automatically find a suitable number of partitions for a given data set, such as the x-means algorithm [15]. In contrast to these approaches, we want to allow the user or the system itself to specify suitable *ranges* for the number and the size of partitions, i.e., the minimum n_{min} and the maximum n_{max} number of partitions *as well as* their minimum s_{min} and maximum s_{max} size. These partitioning constraints allow, e.g., to define appropriate sizes of subsystems in the context of compartmentalization in MAS. As mentioned at the beginning of this section, compartmentalization is a means to decompose the complexity of a system's task. In [28], e.g., the partitioning of power plants into virtual power plants decreases the time needed to calculate schedules for them, a task whose complexity depends on the number of power plants involved. In this example, it is required that the size of each virtual power plant is not less than two and below a certain threshold restricting the maximum time needed for schedule creation.

In this paper, we present *PSOPP*, a discrete **P***article* **S***warm* **O***ptimizer for the* **P***artitioning* **P***roblem*. PSOPP is based on *Particle Swarm Optimization* (PSO) [17], a biologically-inspired computational method and metaheuristic for optimization in large search spaces. The application of a metaheuristic is suitable because of the PP's complexity. For this reason, a plethora of metaheuristics solving related problems can be found in the body of literature: In [10], a genetic algorithm (GA) is used to solve the original SPP, meaning that the GA needs a pre-calculated set of feasible partitions. As discussed before, we want to avoid this in our approach. In theory, their GA could also be extended to respect prescribed ranges for the number of partitions by so-called *base constraints*. However, since their GA allows the generation of invalid interim solutions, it would not benefit from a reduced search space and require additional heuristics for their correction to valid candidate solutions. Using PSO for data clustering has been proposed in [22], where each particle represents a complete solution of the clustering. In [2], the authors present an evolutionary PSO algorithm in which a new generation of particles can replace those contributing to a bad solution to be able to leave local optima. Importantly, their particles represent partial solutions, comprising a single centroid and assigned elements, instead of a complete solution.

As opposed to these and the other afore-mentioned approaches, PSOPP (1) solves the PP in a general manner and (2) allows to specify and efficiently deal with suitable ranges for the number as well as the size of partitions. Our central idea – which could also be applied to other metaheuristics – is to use basic set operations to come to a solution. The reason for using these operations is that they make no assumptions about the objective function assessing the quality of candidate solutions and steering the search for them. As this enables optimization in the light of heterogeneous objectives, PSOPP can be customized to a specific application by devising an appropriate fitness function. Because we define PSOPP's operations in a way that their application always maintains solution correctness, it combs through a search space that only contains correct solutions, which is advantageous for its performance. Moreover, given that PSOPP is initialized with a correct candidate solution, it is an anytime algorithm. Due to these characteristics, PSOPP can be applied to many different applications in which solving the PP is relevant and global knowledge is available. In conjunction with the control loop presented in [28], it can be used to establish self-organizing hierarchical system structures that overcome the drawbacks of strictly weak self-organization [12].

This paper is a substantially revised version of [4] and emphasizes PSOPP's ability to solve the PP in case of clustering, anticlustering, and homogeneous partitioning. Its remainder is structured as follows: In Sect. 2, we give an introduction to the principle of PSO and some of its variants for combinatorial optimization. In Sect. 3, we present our algorithm, PSOPP. Section 4 outlines evaluation results showing that PSOPP efficiently solves the PP in various scenarios. Finally, we conclude the paper and give an outlook on future work in Sect. 5.

2 Particle Swarm Optimization

PSO is a search heuristic for optimization problems. Its principle is based on the flocking behavior of birds or schools of fish. Before we present a special form of PSO that is applicable to discrete optimization problems, such as the PP, in Sect. 2.2, we explain the basic idea of PSO in Sect. 2.1.

2.1 General Definition

In the original definition of PSO [17], a swarm of *particles* moves around in an n-dimensional continuous search space in order to find nearly optimal solutions by iteratively improving *candidate solutions* of the optimization problem. Such a candidate solution is represented by a particle's position in the search space. Its quality is rated by a fitness function that corresponds to the "objective function" and the "metric" used in the PP's definition in Sect. 1: the higher the fitness, the better the solution. To be able to improve the quality of its solution over time in a target-oriented manner, each particle Π_i is aware of *its best found solution* $\mathcal{B}_i$ and the *best found solution* $\mathcal{B}_{\mathcal{N}_i}$ *in its neighborhood* $\mathcal{N}_i$. If a particle's neighborhood consists of all particles, $\mathcal{B}_{\mathcal{N}_i}$ corresponds to the *global best found solution* $\mathcal{B}$.

Initially, particles usually start at random positions. In each iteration, the particles update their positions and best found solutions. The algorithm terminates, e.g., after a certain amount of iterations or if the particles converge to a (local) optimum. Its outcome is the global best found solution $\mathcal{B}$. In detail, a particle Π_i determines its *position* $x_i(t+1)$ for the next iteration $t+1$ on the basis of its current position $x_i(t)$ and its updated *velocity* $v_i(t+1)$:

$$x_i(t+1) = x_i(t) + v_i(t+1) \tag{1}$$

$$v_i(t+1) = \omega \cdot v_i(t) + c_1 \cdot r_1 \cdot (\mathcal{B}_i - x_i(t)) + c_2 \cdot r_2 \cdot (\mathcal{B}_{\mathcal{N}_i} - x_i(t)) \tag{2}$$

$$\text{with } \omega, c_1, c_2 \in \mathbb{R}_0^+, \ r_1, r_2 \in [0,1], \text{ and } \forall t : x_i(t), v_i(t), \mathcal{B}_i, \mathcal{B}_{\mathcal{N}_i} \in \mathbb{R}^n$$

Since $v_i(t+1)$ depends on the current velocity $v_i(t)$, it embodies a certain *inertia* for the purpose of exploration. To search in promising regions of the search space, a particle's motion is further influenced by its best found solution $\mathcal{B}_i$ and the best found solution $\mathcal{B}_{\mathcal{N}_i}$ in its neighborhood. As there is always a trade-off between exploration and exploitation, the constants ω, c_1, and c_2 allow to establish an appropriate balance between the particle's inertia and its attraction towards $\mathcal{B}_i$ and $\mathcal{B}_{\mathcal{N}_i}$. The random numbers r_1 and r_2 are regenerated in every iteration.

2.2   Discrete Particle Swarm Optimization

PSO as defined in Sect. 2.1 is not applicable to discrete, e.g., combinatorial, optimization problems, such as the PP. Kennedy et al. [18] solve this dilemma for n-dimensional binary search spaces by introducing *Discrete PSO* (DPSO) in which the positions $x_i(t)$, $\mathcal{B}_i$, and $\mathcal{B}_{\mathcal{N}_i}$ are values of the domain $\{0,1\}^n$. While the domain and the definition of the velocity $v_i(t+1) \in \mathbb{R}^n$ are not modified (see Eq. 2), the semantics of the velocity changes. In contrast to the original definition, each component $(v_i(t+1))_j \in \mathbb{R}$ of the vector $v_i(t+1)$ represents a probability that the jth component of the particle's position $x_i(t+1)$ is either 0 or 1. Equation 1 therefore becomes invalid.

Another DPSO approach, which is called *Jumping PSO* (JPSO) [13], omits the concept of the velocity as defined in [17]. In simplified terms, JPSO redefines the motion of particles by replacing the linear combinations in Eqs. 1 and 2 by an "either-or" operation that makes them "jump" through the search space:

$$x_i(t+1) = \begin{cases} rdm(x_i(t)) & \text{if } r_i \leq c_{rdm} \\ appr(x_i(t), \mathcal{B}_i) & \text{if } c_{rdm} < r_i \leq c_{\mathcal{B}_i}^* \\ appr(x_i(t), \mathcal{B}_{\mathcal{N}_i}) & \text{if } c_{\mathcal{B}_i}^* < r_i \leq c_{\mathcal{B}_{\mathcal{N}_i}}^* \\ appr(x_i(t), \mathcal{B}) & \text{otherwise} \end{cases} \tag{3}$$

$$c_{rdm}, c_{\mathcal{B}_i}, c_{\mathcal{B}_{\mathcal{N}_i}}, c_{\mathcal{B}} \in [0,1], \; c_{rdm} + c_{\mathcal{B}_i} + c_{\mathcal{B}_{\mathcal{N}_i}} + c_{\mathcal{B}} = 1,$$

$$r_i \in [0,1], \; c_{\mathcal{B}_i}^* = c_{rdm} + c_{\mathcal{B}_i}, \text{ and } c_{\mathcal{B}_{\mathcal{N}_i}}^* = c_{rdm} + c_{\mathcal{B}_i} + c_{\mathcal{B}_{\mathcal{N}_i}}$$

Equation 3 states that a particle Π_i either makes a random move $rdm(x_i(t))$ with a probability of c_{rdm} or approaches $appr(x_i(t), \beta)$ a specific candidate solution $\beta \in \{\mathcal{B}_i, \mathcal{B}_{\mathcal{N}_i}, \mathcal{B}\}$ with a probability of $c_{\mathcal{B}_i}$, $c_{\mathcal{B}_{\mathcal{N}_i}}$, or $c_{\mathcal{B}}$, respectively. In each iteration, this direction is determined by a random number r_i that is generated individually for each particle. Similarly to Eq. 2, the constants $c_{rdm}, c_{\mathcal{B}_i}, c_{\mathcal{B}_{\mathcal{N}_i}}$, and $c_{\mathcal{B}}$ stipulate the particles' attitude towards exploration and exploitation. The idea of JPSO has been successfully applied to a number of high dimensional combinatorial problems (see, e.g., [11,25]).

3   The Particle Swarm Optimizer for Solving the Partitioning Problem

As for our algorithm, *PSOPP*, each particle embodies a solution of the PP, i.e., a partitioning of the set of elements $\mathfrak{G}$. PSOPP is inspired by DPSO's derivative JPSO (see Sect. 2.2). The motion of particles is thus not subject to inertia, i.e., $x_i(t+1)$ does not depend on the modifications made to move from $x_i(t-1)$ to $x_i(t)$. In PSOPP, a particle's motion is influenced by its best found solution $\mathcal{B}_i$ and the best found solution $\mathcal{B}_{\mathcal{N}_i}$ in its neighborhood $\mathcal{N}_i$. This complies with the general definition of PSO outlined in Sect. 2.1. While we could easily extend PSOPP such that its particles' motion is additionally influenced by the global best solution $\mathcal{B}$ – as is the case with JPSO (see Sect. 2.2) –, we deliberately omit this feature for the sake of simplicity. With respect to the definition of JPSO's behavior in Eq. 3, this corresponds to a probability of $c_{\mathcal{B}} = 0$.

3.1   Constraining Valid Solutions

As stated in Sect. 1, PSOPP allows to specify mandatory characteristics of a solution, i.e., partitioning, in terms of the minimum n_{min} and the maximum n_{max} number of partitions ($1 \leq n_{min} \leq n_{max} \leq |\mathfrak{G}|$) as well as their minimum s_{min} and maximum s_{max} size ($1 \leq s_{min} \leq s_{max} \leq |\mathfrak{G}|$). These boundaries represent hard constraints that we call *partitioning constraints* in the following. Obviously, as the possible number and size of partitions are interconnected, one has to make sure that the problem is not overconstrained. In case of $\mathfrak{G} = \{g_1, g_2, g_3\}$, e.g., there is no valid solution if we set n_{min} and s_{min} to 2. Either n_{min} or s_{min} would have to be relaxed, i.e., set to 1. Because we define PSOPP's operations for the particles' motion in a way that always preserves the correctness of candidate solutions with respect to the constraints, partitionings that do not meet them are not represented in the search space. As we show in our evaluation in Sect. 4, suitable boundaries can thus lower the time needed to find high-quality solutions.

3.2   The Algorithm's Basic Procedure

Having defined valid partitionings by means of $n_{min}, n_{max}, s_{min}, s_{max}$ as well as the particles' attitude towards exploration and exploitation by fixing the constants $c_{rdm}, c_{\mathcal{B}_i}, c_{\mathcal{B}_{\mathcal{N}_i}}$, PSOPP creates a predefined and invariant number of particles at random or predetermined positions. The latter is especially suitable when a reorganization of an existing system structure has to take place: If the current structure does not contradict the partitioning constraints, it can be used as a starting point for the self-organization process. Mixing predefined and randomly generated initial partitionings allows to hold up diversity. When searching for an initial system structure, particles are created at random positions.

The position $x_i(t)$ of each particle Π_i represents a partitioning $\mathcal{P}$ (hereinafter, we use $\mathcal{P}$ synonymous for $x_i(t)$) that consists of $n_{min} \leq |\mathcal{P}| \leq n_{max}$ partitions. Every partition $K \in \mathcal{P}$ comprises $s_{min} \leq |K| \leq s_{max}$ elements. All particles concurrently explore the search space in search of better solutions by modifying their current positions (at random or by approaching other solutions) as long as a specific termination criterion is not met. For this purpose, in each iteration, a particle Π_i performs the following actions that are also depicted in Fig. 1:

Fig. 1. Actions performed by particles in each iteration.

1. Evaluate the fitness $f(\mathcal{P})$ of the represented partitioning $\mathcal{P}$.
2. If the particle's fitness $f(\mathcal{P})$ is higher than the fitness $f(\mathcal{B}_i)$ of its best found solution $\mathcal{B}_i$, set $\mathcal{B}_i$ to $\mathcal{P}$. Further, inform all other particles Π_j that contain Π_i in their neighborhood $\mathcal{N}_j$ about the improvement so that they can update $\mathcal{B}_{\mathcal{N}_j}$, i.e., the best found solution in their neighborhood.
3. Update the best found solution $\mathcal{B}_{\mathcal{N}_i}$ in the particle's neighborhood $\mathcal{N}_i$.
4. Stop if the termination criterion is met.
5. Otherwise, opt for the direction in which to move by generating the random number $r_i \in [0,1]$ on the basis of a uniform distribution (see Eq. 3), i.e., choose whether a random move or an approach operation should be applied. In case of an approach operation, r_i also determines whether $\mathcal{B}_i$ or $\mathcal{B}_{\mathcal{N}_i}$ should be approached (see Eq. 3).
6. Determine the new position $\mathcal{P}'$ by applying the selected move operation to $\mathcal{P}$.

Once all particles terminated, PSOPP returns the best found solution $\mathcal{B}$. Possible termination criteria are, e.g., a predefined amount of time, a predefined number of iterations (i.e., moves through the search space), a predefined threshold for the minimum fitness value, or a combination of these criteria.

3.3 Similarity of Partitionings

The purpose of an approach operation is to increase the *similarity* of two partitionings $\mathcal{P}$ and $\mathcal{Q}$ by assimilating characteristics from $\mathcal{Q}$ into $\mathcal{P}$. With regard to the search space, the intention is that the particle representing $\mathcal{P}$ might find better solutions in the neighborhood of $\mathcal{Q}$. In this section, we define the *similarity* of partitionings on the basis of a definition by [19]. Note that the similarity does not give an indication of how many operations/moves are necessary to transfer one partitioning into another (i.e., to move from one position to another). Instead, it compares partitionings with regard to their composition. According to [19], the similarity of two partitionings $\mathcal{P}, \mathcal{Q}$ is based on the definitions of a *refinement* and the *intersection* of two partitionings.

Definition (Refinement). *Partitioning $\mathcal{P}$ is a **refinement** $ref(\mathcal{P}, \mathcal{Q})$ of partitioning $\mathcal{Q}$ if and only if all partitions $K \in \mathcal{P}$ are subsets of partitions $L \in \mathcal{Q}$:*

$$ref(\mathcal{P}, \mathcal{Q}) :\Leftrightarrow \forall K \in \mathcal{P} : \exists L \in \mathcal{Q} : K \subseteq L \tag{4}$$

Hence, if $\mathcal{P}$ is a refinement of $\mathcal{Q}$, $\mathcal{P}$ does not contain less partitions than $\mathcal{Q}$ (i.e., $|\mathcal{P}| \geq |\mathcal{Q}|$). For instance, $\mathcal{P} = \{\{g_1, g_2\}, \{g_3\}, \{g_4\}\}$ is a refinement of $\mathcal{Q} = \{\{g_1, g_2, g_3\}, \{g_4\}\}$, whereas $\mathcal{R} = \{\{g_1, g_2, g_4\}, \{g_3\}\}$ is not.

Definition (Intersection of Partitionings). *The **intersection** $\mathcal{P} \cap \mathcal{Q}$ of two partitionings $\mathcal{P}, \mathcal{Q}$ is the set of all non-empty intersections of partitions in $\mathcal{P}$ and $\mathcal{Q}$:*

$$\mathcal{P} \cap \mathcal{Q} :\Leftrightarrow \{K \cap L \mid K \in \mathcal{P} \wedge L \in \mathcal{Q} \wedge K \cap L \neq \emptyset\}$$

Note that the intersection $\mathcal{P} \cap \mathcal{Q}$ is always a refinement of $\mathcal{P}$ and $\mathcal{Q}$. For example, the intersection $\mathcal{S} \cap \mathcal{Q} = \{\{g_1, g_2\}, \{g_3\}, \{g_4\}\}$, which equals $\mathcal{P}$ in the example above, is a refinement of $\mathcal{S} = \{\{g_1, g_2\}, \{g_3, g_4\}\}$ and $\mathcal{Q} = \{\{g_1, g_2, g_3\}, \{g_4\}\}$.

Definition (Similarity of Partitionings). *The **similarity** $sim(\mathcal{P}, \mathcal{Q}) \in \,]0, 1]$ of two non-empty partitionings $\mathcal{P}, \mathcal{Q}$ is directly proportional to the ratio of the sum of their cardinalities to the cardinality of their intersection:*

$$sim(\mathcal{P}, \mathcal{Q}) := \frac{|\mathcal{P}| + |\mathcal{Q}|}{2 \cdot |\mathcal{P} \cap \mathcal{Q}|} \tag{5}$$

According to this definition, the similarity decreases with the cardinality of the intersection $\mathcal{P} \cap \mathcal{Q}$. So the more elements are in the same partitions in $\mathcal{P}$ and $\mathcal{Q}$ (i.e., the more elements constitute the *partitions'* intersection), the smaller $|\mathcal{P} \cap \mathcal{Q}|$ and thus the more similar the partitionings. In other words, the intersection $\mathcal{P} \cap \mathcal{Q}$, which is a refinement of $\mathcal{P}$ and $\mathcal{Q}$, should be as similar as possible to $\mathcal{P}$ and $\mathcal{Q}$. Hence, $sim(\mathcal{P}, \mathcal{Q}) = 1$ if and only if $\mathcal{P} = \mathcal{Q}$, because then $\mathcal{P} \cap \mathcal{Q} = \mathcal{P} = \mathcal{Q}$. Regarding the two examples above, $sim(\mathcal{S}, \mathcal{Q}) = \frac{2+2}{2\cdot3} = \frac{4}{6}$ is smaller than $sim(\mathcal{P}, \mathcal{Q}) = \frac{3+2}{2\cdot3} = \frac{5}{6}$ since $\mathcal{P}$ is a refinement of $\mathcal{Q}$. While not required, this definition of similarity does not allow to compare two similarity values $sim(\mathcal{P}, \mathcal{Q})$ and $sim(\mathcal{R}, \mathcal{S})$ if they stem from four different partitionings.

Based on these definitions, we show that the operations enabling particles to approach each other always increase the similarity of the represented partitionings (see Sect. 3.5). Before we explain these operations in detail, we introduce the basic operations by means of random moves in the search space.

3.4   Random Moves in the Search Space

The motion of particles is a key factor in PSO because it is the only measure to find better candidate solutions. As a solution of the PP is a partitioning (that is a set of sets), the motion of particles in the search space can be realized by the two set operations *split* and *join* [6]. In each iteration, each PSOPP particle makes exactly one move, either in a random direction or by approaching a specific position in the search space in a target-oriented manner (see Sect. 3.5). The corresponding operator is randomly selected. In this section, we concentrate on *random moves*, i.e., operators that modify the represented partitioning at random. In case the selected operator cannot be applied without violating a constraint, another operator is chosen. Because of the partitioning constraints, there are situations in which neither the split nor the join operator can be applied. For such situations, we introduce an additional *exchange* operation.

Unless otherwise stated, we use $\mathcal{P}_* = \{\{g_1, g_2, g_4, g_5\}, \{g_3, g_6\}, \{g_7, g_8\}\}$ with partitions $K_* = \{g_1, g_2, g_4, g_5\}$, $L_* = \{g_3, g_6\}$, and $M_* = \{g_7, g_8\}\}$, $s_{min} = n_{min} = 2$, and $s_{max} = n_{max} = 4$ to illustrate the operators' application.

Random Split. The split operation divides a *randomly splitable partition* $K \in \mathcal{P}$ into two new non-empty disjoint partitions L, M such that $K = L \cup M$. For the resulting partitioning $\mathcal{P}'$, we have $\mathcal{P}' = (\mathcal{P} \setminus \{K\}) \cup \{L, M\}$. Note that the split operation can only be applied if the partition K is big enough, i.e., if $|K| \geq 2 \cdot s_{min}$. That is because the resulting partitions L and M both have to fulfill the minimum size constraint, i.e., $|L|, |M| \geq s_{min}$. Furthermore, the split operation can only be applied if the number of partitions $|\mathcal{P}|$ in the original partitioning $\mathcal{P}$ is below the maximum number of partitions n_{max} since it increases the number of partitions $|\mathcal{P}'|$ of the resulting partitioning $\mathcal{P}'$ compared to $\mathcal{P}$ by one (i.e., $|\mathcal{P}'| = |\mathcal{P}|+1$). That way, it is ensured that $\mathcal{P}'$ also complies with n_{max}. Summarizing, the set of *randomly splitable partitions* $\sigma_{rdm}(\mathcal{P})$ is defined as:

$$\sigma_{rdm}(\mathcal{P}) :\Leftrightarrow \{K \mid K \in \mathcal{P} \wedge |K| \geq 2 \cdot s_{min} \wedge |\mathcal{P}| < n_{max}\}$$

In our example $\mathcal{P}_*$, only $K_* = \{g_1, g_2, g_4, g_5\}$ is randomly splitable, resulting, e.g., in a partitioning $\mathcal{P}_*' = \{\{g_1, g_2\}, \{g_4, g_5\}, \{g_3, g_6\}, \{g_7, g_8\}\}$.

Random Join. The join operation merges a *randomly joinable partition* $K \in \mathcal{P}$ and a *randomly joinable counterpart* $L \in \mathcal{P}$ (with $K \neq L$) into a single new partition M such that $K \cup L = M$. For the resulting partitioning $\mathcal{P}'$, we have $\mathcal{P}' = (\mathcal{P} \setminus \{K, L\}) \cup \{K \cup L\}$. Because M has to satisfy the maximum size constraint, L must be a partition that can be integrated into K without exceeding the maximum allowed size, i.e., $|K| + |L| \leq s_{max}$. Since the join operator decreases the number of partitions in the resulting partitioning $\mathcal{P}'$ by one, the operator can only be applied if $\mathcal{P}$ features a sufficient number of partitions, i.e., if $|\mathcal{P}| > n_{min}$. Otherwise, $\mathcal{P}'$ would violate the minimum number of partitions constraint. Summarizing, the sets of *randomly joinable partitions* $\iota_{rdm}(\mathcal{P})$ and *randomly joinable counterparts* $\iota_{rdm}^{\leftrightarrow}(K, \mathcal{P})$ are defined as follows:

$$\iota_{rdm}(\mathcal{P}) :\Leftrightarrow \{K \mid K \in \mathcal{P} \wedge \iota_{rdm}^{\leftrightarrow}(K, \mathcal{P}) \neq \emptyset \wedge |\mathcal{P}| > n_{min}\}$$

$$\iota_{rdm}^{\leftrightarrow}(K, \mathcal{P}) :\Leftrightarrow \{L \mid L \in \mathcal{P} \wedge |K| + |L| \leq s_{max} \wedge K \neq L\}$$

With regard to our example $\mathcal{P}_*$, randomly joinable partitions are $L_* = \{g_3, g_6\}$ and $M_* = \{g_7, g_8\}$ with randomly joinable counterparts $\{M_*\}$ and $\{L_*\}$, respectively. Merging L_* and M_* yields $\mathcal{P}_*' = \{\{g_1, g_2, g_4, g_5\}, \{g_3, g_6, g_7, g_8\}\}$.

Random Exchange. Obviously, there are situations in which neither the split nor the join operator can be applied (particles must not violate the constraints temporarily since the search space only contains valid solutions). For example, if $s_{min} = s_{max}$ or $n_{min} = n_{max}$, not a single particle is able to make a move using the split or the join operation. But even if $s_{min} \neq s_{max}$ and $n_{min} \neq n_{max}$, specific combinations of $s_{min}, s_{max}, n_{min}$, and n_{max} can cause individual particles to freeze: For instance, consider a partitioning $\mathcal{P} = \{\{g_1, g_2, g_3\}, \{g_4, g_5, g_6\}\}$ with $s_{min} = 2$, $s_{max} = 4$, $n_{min} = 2$, and $n_{max} = 3$. To prevent the particles from becoming jammed, we additionally introduce an *exchange* operator that atomically swaps some of the elements of two partitions.

The exchange operation interchanges the proper subset $\hat{K} \subset K$ (with $\hat{K} \neq \emptyset$) and the subset $\hat{L} \subseteq L$ ($\hat{L}$ is allowed to be the empty set $\emptyset$) between a *randomly exchangeable partition* $K \in \mathcal{P}$ and a *randomly exchangeable counterpart* $L \in \mathcal{P}$. Using the non-empty proper subset $\hat{K}$ of K avoids that the operation has no effect at all (as would be the case if all or no elements of K were integrated into L and vice versa). We deliberately allow $\hat{L}$ to be empty in order to handle situations as given in the example above: Regarding partitioning $\mathcal{P} = \{\{g_1, g_2, g_3\}, \{g_4, g_5, g_6\}\}$, we can simply move $\hat{K} = \{g_3\}$ from

$K = \{g_1, g_2, g_3\}$ into $L = \{g_4, g_5, g_6\}$. If we did not allow $\hat{L} = \emptyset$, we would have to perform multiple consecutive exchange operations to achieve the same result. With respect to the example, we would need two operations, e.g., by exchanging $\{g_2, g_3\}$ and $\{g_4\}$, and finally $\{g_4\}$ and $\{g_2\}$.

Basically, the exchange operation corresponds to a join that is followed by a split. Since $\hat{K}$ is a non-empty proper subset of K, as the split operation, it yields two non-empty partitions. Because an exchange between two partitions of size one would contradict this characteristic or not have any effect, we define the sets of *randomly exchangeable partitions* $\epsilon_{rdm}(\mathcal{P})$ and *randomly exchangeable counterparts* $\epsilon_{rdm}^{\leftrightarrow}(K, \mathcal{P})$ as:

$$\epsilon_{rdm}(\mathcal{P}) :\Leftrightarrow \{K \mid K \in \mathcal{P} \wedge |K| > 1\}$$

$$\epsilon_{rdm}^{\leftrightarrow}(K, \mathcal{P}) :\Leftrightarrow \mathcal{P} \setminus \{K\}$$

When integrating an arbitrary non-empty proper subset $\hat{K} \subset K$ into L, $\hat{K}$ as well as the subset $\hat{L} \subseteq L$ that is integrated into K must be specified in a way that the condition $|K'|, |L'| \in [s_{min}, s_{max}]$ holds for the resulting partitions K', L'. More precisely, while the size of $\hat{K}$ is randomly chosen between 1 and $|K| - 1$ to ensure that $\hat{K}$ is a non-empty proper subset of K, valid cardinalities of $\hat{L}$ are subject to $|\hat{K}|$. In detail, $|\hat{L}| \leq min\{|L|, min\{(|L| + |\hat{K}|) - s_{min}, s_{max} - (|K| - |\hat{K}|)\}\}$ and $|\hat{L}| \geq max\{max\{0, s_{min} - (|K| - |\hat{K}|)\}, (|L| + |\hat{K}|) - s_{max}\}$ must hold for the randomly determined set $\hat{L}$ to guarantee that the resulting partitioning $\mathcal{P}' = (\mathcal{P} \setminus \{K, L\}) \cup \{(K \setminus \hat{K}) \cup \hat{L}, (L \setminus \hat{L}) \cup \hat{K}\}$ respects s_{min} and s_{max}. In our example $\mathcal{P}_*$, we can, e.g., exchange $\hat{K}_* = \{g_1, g_2, g_5\}$ and $\hat{M}_* = \{g_7\}$ between K_* and M_*, resulting in $\mathcal{P}_*' = \{\{g_4, g_7\}, \{g_3, g_6\}, \{g_1, g_2, g_5, g_8\}\}$.

There are two situations that obstruct the application of the random exchange operator: First, if all partitions are singletons (i.e., if $|\mathcal{P}| = |\mathfrak{G}|$), there is no randomly exchangeable partition, i.e., $\epsilon_{rdm}(\mathcal{P}) = \emptyset$. In such a case, a particle can use the random join operator to change its position if $n_{min} < |\mathfrak{G}|$ and $s_{max} \geq 2$. Second, if there is only a single partition, the set of randomly exchangeable counterparts $\epsilon_{rdm}^{\leftrightarrow}(K, \mathcal{P})$ is empty. Here, the random split operator can be used if $|\mathfrak{G}| \geq 2 \cdot s_{min}$ and $n_{max} \geq 2$.

The three operations split, join, and exchange allow to create new or dissolve existing partitions or to swap elements between them while maintaining the properties of a partitioning and complying with the partitioning constraints (see Sect. 3.1). In this section, we focused on random moves, where we cannot make any statement with regard to the change in similarity to another partitioning. In the next section, we explain how particles use the basic split, join, and exchange operators to approach a specific position in the search space.

3.5 Approach of Other Particles

When a particle Π_i approaches $\mathcal{B}_i$ or $\mathcal{B}_{\mathcal{N}_i}$, we ensure that the similarity of the modified partitioning $\mathcal{P}$ and the approached partitioning $\mathcal{Q} \in \{\mathcal{B}_i, \mathcal{B}_{\mathcal{N}_i}\}$ is increased. Recalling the definition of the similarity (see Eq. 5), this can, among other possibilities, be achieved by increasing $|\mathcal{P}|$, i.e., the number of partitions in $\mathcal{P}$, without changing $|\mathcal{P} \cap \mathcal{Q}|$ at all, or decreasing $|\mathcal{P} \cap \mathcal{Q}|$ (note that a decrease of $|\mathcal{P} \cap \mathcal{Q}|$ might come along with a decrease of $|\mathcal{P}|$). The former is obtained by splitting a partition containing elements that are members of two or more partitions in $\mathcal{Q}$, whereas a join or exchange achieves the latter by merging elements that reside in a single partition in $\mathcal{Q}$ but are spread over multiple partitions in $\mathcal{P}$. In contrast to random moves, the applicability of the approach operations does not only depend on $\mathcal{P}$'s cardinality and the size of its partitions but also on $\mathcal{P}$'s and $\mathcal{Q}$'s composition. Obviously, an approach is not possible if $\mathcal{P} = \mathcal{Q}$.

Unless otherwise stated, we assume $\mathcal{P}_* = \{\{g_1, g_2, g_4, g_5\}, \{g_3, g_6\}, \{g_7, g_8\}\}$ to approach $\mathcal{Q}_* = \{\{g_1, g_2\}, \{g_4, g_6, g_7\}, \{g_3, g_5, g_8\}\}$ with $s_{min} = n_{min} = 2$ and $s_{max} = n_{max} = 4$ to illustrate the operators' application in our examples.

Approach Split. Analogously to the definition of $\sigma_{rdm}(\mathcal{P})$, this operator can only be applied if $|\mathcal{P}| < n_{max}$. Furthermore, a partition K must fulfill $|K| \geq 2 \cdot s_{min}$ to be contained in the set of *splitable partitions* $\sigma(\mathcal{P}, \mathcal{Q})$. Here, this property results from the definition of *extractable subsets* $\sigma^\uparrow(K, \mathcal{P}, \mathcal{Q})$:

$$\sigma(\mathcal{P}, \mathcal{Q}) :\Leftrightarrow \{K \mid K \in \mathcal{P} \wedge \sigma^\uparrow(K, \mathcal{P}, \mathcal{Q}) \neq \emptyset \wedge |\mathcal{P}| < n_{max}\}$$

$$\sigma^\uparrow(K, \mathcal{P}, \mathcal{Q}) :\Leftrightarrow \{L \mid L \in (\mathcal{P} \cap \mathcal{Q}) \wedge L \subset K \wedge |K \setminus L| \geq s_{min} \wedge |L| \geq s_{min}\}$$

An extractable subset $L \in \sigma^\uparrow(K, \mathcal{P}, \mathcal{Q})$ is a *proper* subset of $K \in \mathcal{P}$, i.e., with respect to $\mathcal{Q}$, K contains further elements that are not contained in the same partition as the elements in L. Hence, the split operator cannot be applied to approach another particle if all partitions in $\mathcal{P}$ are subsets of partitions in $\mathcal{Q}$, i.e., if $\mathcal{P}$ is a refinement of $\mathcal{Q}$ (see Eq. 4). For the resulting partitioning, we have $\mathcal{P}' = (\mathcal{P} \setminus \{K\}) \cup \{K \setminus L, L\}$. Extracting the set L from K increases the similarity between $\mathcal{P}$ and $\mathcal{Q}$ because $|\mathcal{P}'| = |\mathcal{P}| + 1$, $\mathcal{Q}$ is not changed, and $\mathcal{P}' \cap \mathcal{Q} = \mathcal{P} \cap \mathcal{Q}$, i.e., the intersection of the partitionings does not change either. With regard to $\mathcal{P}_*$ and $\mathcal{Q}_*$, $K_* = \{g_1, g_2, g_4, g_5\}$ is the only splitable partition with extractable subset $N_* = \{g_1, g_2\}$ (N_* is the only element of $\sigma^\uparrow(K_*, \mathcal{P}_*, \mathcal{Q}_*)$). A split results in $\mathcal{P}_*' = \{\{g_1, g_2\}, \{g_4, g_5\}, \{g_3, g_6\}, \{g_7, g_8\}\}$.

Approach Join. As before, a join can only be applied if $|\mathcal{P}| > n_{min}$. Similarly to the definition of *randomly* joinable partitions, *joinable partitions* $\iota(\mathcal{P}, \mathcal{Q})$ are those partitions for which *joinable counterparts* $\iota^\leftrightarrows(K, \mathcal{P}, \mathcal{Q})$ exist:

$$\iota(\mathcal{P}, \mathcal{Q}) :\Leftrightarrow \{K \mid K \in \mathcal{P} \wedge \iota^\leftrightarrows(K, \mathcal{P}, \mathcal{Q}) \neq \emptyset \wedge |\mathcal{P}| > n_{min}\}$$

$$\iota^\leftrightarrows(K, \mathcal{P}, \mathcal{Q}) :\Leftrightarrow \{L \mid L \in \mathcal{P} \wedge |K| + |L| \leq s_{max}$$
$$\wedge \underbrace{K \neq L \wedge \exists M \in \mathcal{Q} : (M \cap K \neq \emptyset \wedge M \cap L \neq \emptyset)}_{C}\}$$

Please note that the definition of joinable counterparts $\iota^\leftrightarrows(K, \mathcal{P}, \mathcal{Q})$ is very similar to the definition of *randomly* joinable counterparts $\iota_{rdm}^\leftrightarrows(K, \mathcal{P})$. To ensure that $\mathcal{P}$ approaches $\mathcal{Q}$, we introduce an additional condition C that implies $M \nsubseteq K$ because M does not only contain elements of K but also of L (with $M \in \mathcal{Q}$ and

$K, L \in \mathcal{P}$). That way, we bring together elements that are in a single partition in $\mathcal{Q}$ but spread over two or more partitions K, L in $\mathcal{P}$. Note that $\mathcal{Q}$ cannot be approached by a join if all partitions in $\mathcal{P}$ are supersets of partitions in $\mathcal{Q}$, i.e., if $\mathcal{Q}$ is a refinement of $\mathcal{P}$ (see Eq. 4). In such a situation, condition C cannot be satisfied. For the resulting partitioning, we have $\mathcal{P}' = (\mathcal{P} \setminus \{K, L\}) \cup \{K \cup L\}$. The similarity between $\mathcal{P}$ and $\mathcal{Q}$ is increased because $|\mathcal{P}'| = |\mathcal{P}| - 1$, $\mathcal{Q}$ is not changed, and $|\mathcal{P}' \cap \mathcal{Q}| \leq |\mathcal{P} \cap \mathcal{Q}| - 1$. Note that we have to write "$\leq$" since K and L might both contain elements that are contained in a further partition $M' \in \mathcal{Q}$ with $M' \neq M$. With regard to $\mathcal{P}_*$ and $\mathcal{Q}_*$, $L_* = \{g_3, g_6\}$ and $M_* = \{g_7, g_8\}$ are joinable partitions with counterparts M_* and L_*, respectively. A join results in $\mathcal{P}_*{'} = \{\{g_1, g_2, g_4, g_5\}, \{g_3, g_6, g_7, g_8\}\}$.

Approach Exchange. If neither a split nor a join can be used to approach a partitioning $\mathcal{Q} \neq \mathcal{P}$, PSOPP falls back on the exchange operator that swaps one or more elements between a partition K contained in the set of *exchangeable partitions* $\epsilon(\mathcal{P}, \mathcal{Q})$ and one of K's *exchangeable counterparts* $\epsilon^{\leftrightarrow}(K, \mathcal{P}, \mathcal{Q})$:

$$\epsilon(\mathcal{P}, \mathcal{Q}) :\Leftrightarrow \{K \mid K \in \mathcal{P} \land \epsilon^{\leftrightarrow}(K, \mathcal{P}, \mathcal{Q}) \neq \emptyset\}$$

$$\epsilon^{\leftrightarrow}(K, \mathcal{P}, \mathcal{Q}) :\Leftrightarrow \Big\{ L \mid L \in \mathcal{P} \land K \neq L \land \exists M \in \mathcal{Q} : \exists \hat{K} \subset K : \quad (6)$$
$$\Big(\hat{K} \cap M \neq \emptyset \land L \cap M \neq \emptyset \land \hat{K} \in 2^{\mathcal{P} \cap \mathcal{Q}} \land \Big(\exists \hat{L} \subset L : \hat{L} \cap M = \emptyset \land \hat{L} \in 2^{\mathcal{P} \cap \mathcal{Q}}$$
$$\land s_{min} \leq |(K \setminus \hat{K}) \cup \hat{L}| \leq s_{max} \land s_{min} \leq |(L \setminus \hat{L}) \cup \hat{K}| \leq s_{max} \Big) \Big) \Big\}$$

Note that $\hat{K} \cap M \neq \emptyset \land L \cap M \neq \emptyset$ implies that $K \in \mathcal{P}$ as well as $L \in \mathcal{P}$ contain elements that belong to the same partition $M \in \mathcal{Q}$. The goal of the exchange operation is to bring these elements together. Also note that $\hat{L} \subset L$ might be an empty set $\emptyset$, whereas $\hat{K} \subset K$ is always non-empty. The latter causes $|\mathcal{P}|$ to be left unchanged. The condition $\hat{L} \subset L$ is implied by $L \cap M \neq \emptyset \land \hat{L} \cap M = \emptyset$. The reader can convince herself that excluding $\hat{L} = L$ does not restrict the applicability of the operator because the forbidden exchange of $\hat{K}$ and $\hat{L} = L$ can be realized by swapping $K \setminus \hat{K}$ and $L \setminus \hat{L} = \emptyset$.

Integrating $\hat{K}$ into L and $\hat{L}$ into K increases the similarity of $\mathcal{P}$ and $\mathcal{Q}$ by leaving $|\mathcal{P}|$ and $|\mathcal{Q}|$ unchanged and reducing $|\mathcal{P} \cap \mathcal{Q}|$ by ≥ 1. On the one hand, $\hat{L} \cap M = \emptyset$, $\hat{K} \cap M \neq \emptyset$, and $\hat{K} \in 2^{\mathcal{P} \cap \mathcal{Q}}$ ($2^{\mathcal{P} \cap \mathcal{Q}}$ denotes the power set of $\mathcal{P} \cap \mathcal{Q}$) ensure that we not only merge elements of M but also reduce the number of partitions containing elements of M by one. On the other hand, $\hat{L} \in 2^{\mathcal{P} \cap \mathcal{Q}}$ assures that we do not spread a set of elements $V \in (\mathcal{P} \cap \mathcal{Q})$ (V is thus contained in a single partition in $\mathcal{P}$ and $\mathcal{Q}$) over K and L by merging $\hat{L}$ into K. This has to be avoided because it would decrease the similarity of $\mathcal{P}$ and $\mathcal{Q}$. The conditions $s_{min} \leq |(K \setminus \hat{K}) \cup \hat{L}| \leq s_{max}$ and $s_{min} \leq |(L \setminus \hat{L}) \cup \hat{K}| \leq s_{max}$ restrict the size of the resulting partitions to the allowed range.

For the resulting partitioning, we have $\mathcal{P}' = (\mathcal{P} \setminus \{K, L\}) \cup \{(K \setminus \hat{K}) \cup \hat{L}, (L \setminus \hat{L}) \cup \hat{K}\}$. The similarity between $\mathcal{P}$ and $\mathcal{Q}$ is increased because $|\mathcal{P}'| = |\mathcal{P}|$, $\mathcal{Q}$ is not changed, and $|\mathcal{P}' \cap \mathcal{Q}| \leq |\mathcal{P} \cap \mathcal{Q}| - 1$. With regard to $\mathcal{P}_*$ and $\mathcal{Q}_*$, for instance, $K_* = \{g_1, g_2, g_4, g_5\}$ is an exchangeable partition with exchangeable counterparts $L_* = \{g_3, g_6\}$ and $M_* = \{g_7, g_8\}$. For example, we can exchange $\hat{K}_* = \{g_4\}$ and $\hat{L}_* = \emptyset$ between K_* and L_* by which we obtain $\mathcal{P}_*' = \{\{g_1, g_2, g_5\}, \{g_3, g_4, g_6\}, \{g_7, g_8\}\}$.

However, there are situations in which the exchange operator cannot be applied: For example, consider a partitioning $\mathcal{Q} = \{N, O, P\}$, where each partition has a cardinality of 100 and $s_{min} = s_{max} = 100$. A partitioning $\mathcal{P} = \{K, L, M\}$ cannot approach $\mathcal{Q}$, e.g., if K contains 39, 27, and 34, L contains 25, 40, and 35, and M contains 36, 33, and 31 elements of N, O, and P, respectively. In such situations, one might relax the constraint $\hat{L} \in 2^{\mathcal{P} \cap \mathcal{Q}}$ in Eq. 6 to $\hat{L} = U \cup V$, where $U \in 2^{\mathcal{P} \cap \mathcal{Q}}$ and $V \subset W \in (\mathcal{P} \cap \mathcal{Q})$. While this relaxation allows to apply the operator in each situation, it only guarantees to *not decrease* the similarity of $\mathcal{P}$ and $\mathcal{Q}$ because we spread the elements of W over two partitions.

4   Evaluation

In our evaluation, we analyze PSOPP's behavior in various scenarios: We (1) investigate the influence of the numbers of elements $|\mathfrak{G}|$ on its performance with regard to the quality of the result and the number of moves particles perform, (2) examine PSOPP's convergence, (3) compare its behavior with less and more constrained partitionings on the basis of the partitioning constraints introduced in Sect. 3.1, (4) make these investigations for strict partitioning clustering (C), anticlustering (AC), two instances of homogeneous partitioning[3] (HPm, HPs), as well as different combinations of these objectives, and (5) compare our results to those achieved with an x-means implementation[4] as, to the best of our knowledge, there is no other renowned algorithm supporting more of our partitioning constraints out of the box. For a comparison with IBM ILOG CPLEX[5] demonstrating the need for metaheuristics, we refer the interested reader to [4].

For evaluation, we used a Java implementation of PSOPP. Each particle runs in its own thread, which allows for the parallel examination of the search space. Because preceding evaluations in [4] showed that PSOPP achieves good results with a relatively small number of particles, we used particle neighborhoods $\mathcal{N}_i$ that contain all particles in the system. As mentioned in Sect. 2.1, $\mathcal{B}_{\mathcal{N}_i}$ thus corresponds to $\mathcal{B}$. In each setting, PSOPP solved the PP for a set of elements $\mathfrak{G} = \{0, 1, 2, \ldots, n-1\}$, where $n = |\mathfrak{G}|$ is the number of elements to partition.

As stated above, we performed evaluations for the objectives C, AC, HPm, and HPs (see Sect. 1). To group similar elements in case of C, the sum of the squared Euclidean distances between the elements and their cluster center (this corresponds to the "classic" k-means distance measure) is to be minimized. For AC, PSOPP *maximizes*, in accordance with [27], the sum of the squared Euclidean distances to form partitions consisting of dissimilar elements. To establish homogeneous partitionings in case of HPm and HPs, we calculate a value p_K for all partitions $K \in \mathcal{P}$. As the goal is to form similar partitions, the standard deviation of the values p_K should be minimized. For HPm, p_K is the

---

[3] Note that we refer to "homogeneous partitioning" as "anticlustering" in [4].

[4] Weka, Version 3.6: http://weka.sourceforge.net.

[5] http://www-01.ibm.com/software/commerce/optimization/cplex-optimizer/.

mean of the elements contained in K. In case of HPs, p_K represents the sum of the elements in K. Hereinafter, we call the values of the aggregated squared Euclidean distances or standard deviations *raw values* v. For better comparability, we normalize the raw values to the interval $[0, 1]$. This is achieved by the fitness function $\mathcal{F}_o(v) = 1.0 - \frac{b_o - v}{b_o - w_o}$, which yields a fitness value for a specific raw value v. It is based on identified worst w_o and best b_o values of v for objective $o \in \{C, AC, HPm, HPs\}$.[6] For all objectives, PSOPP's goal is to maximize the fitness since the higher the fitness, the better the solution.

Where not otherwise stated, we used a time limit of 10 s as termination criterion and performed 500 simulation runs for each evaluation scenario. All presented results are average values; values σ denote standard deviations. Further, apart from $s_{min} = 2$ (i.e., each partition has to be composed of more than one element) and $n_{min} = 2$, which prevents the "grand coalition", we did not restrict valid partitionings (i.e., $s_{max} = n$, $n_{max} = \frac{n}{2}$). As discussed in Sect. 1, such restrictions enable hierarchical decomposition. The influence of restrictions on PSOPP's behavior is examined in a separate evaluation scenario.

In previous work [4], we identified suitable parameters sets $c_{rdm}, c_{\mathcal{B}_i}, c_{\mathcal{B}_{N_i}}$ for C and HPm on the basis of different numbers of elements $n \in \{100, 500, 1000\}$. For our extended evaluation, we used the same procedure to identify these parameters for AC and HPs as well. It turned out that $c_{rdm} = 0.3, c_{\mathcal{B}_i} = 0.0$, and $c_{\mathcal{B}} = 0.7$ are useful parameters for C, AC, as well as HPs, and that $c_{rdm} = 0.2, c_{\mathcal{B}_i} = 0.7$, and $c_{\mathcal{B}} = 0.1$ are suitable parameters for HPm. For all objectives, we observed a plateau of moderate to good fitness values for $0.0 < c_{rdm} < 0.5$, indicating the trade-off between exploration and exploitation. In particular for C, approaching $\mathcal{B}$ is far more important than for HPm and especially AC. We assume that the fitness landscapes of HPm and AC contain more spikes that are worth to be explored by the particles individually, while C requires all particles to work together in order to improve a specific candidate solution (less but more prominent spikes in the fitness landscape). HPs yielded high-quality results for almost every investigated parametrization.

We further noticed in [4] that the total no. of moves only shows slight increases for $\#P > 4$. In most cases, the coefficient of variation of the no. of moves per particle increases significantly with $\#P > 4$, meaning that some particles made many and others only few moves (the threshold of 4 can be attributed to our 4-core Xeon machines). This characteristic together with a remarkable drop of the average no. of moves per particle results in lower fitness values if the problem being solved requires a systematic exploration of the search space, as is the case with C. Summarizing, there is certainly a trade-off between the average no. of moves per particle and the provision of diversity through a larger no. of particles that represent and improve different candidate solutions. Due to these observations, we used $\#P = 4$ in our experiments.

---

[6] For HPm and HPs, we used PSOPP to empirically identify w_o/b_o by minimizing/maximizing the corresponding objective's fitness and taking the worst/best value of v from 500 runs. For C and AC, we calculated w_o and b_o as described in our discussion entitled "Influence of Partitioning Constraints".

Table 1. Selected results for the objectives C, AC, HPm, and HPs obtained with PSOPP and RDM using a time limit of 10 s for different values of the number of elements. All values are averages over 500 runs. Parentheses contain standard deviations.

#Elements	objective C				objective AC		objective HPm		objective HPs	
	250	500	1000	2000	1000	3000	1000	4000	100	4000
w_o	1.30E6	1.04E7	8.33E7	6.67E8	250.00	750.00	499.00	1998.50	3498.76	5.66E6
b_o	62.50	125.00	250.00	500.00	8.33E7	2.25E9	0.00	0.00	0.00	263.60
RDM										
v	4.35E5 (1.50E4)	4.08E6 (9.90E4)	3.59E7 (6.51E5)	3.08E8 (4.39E6)	7.55E7 (6.70E6)	2.04E9 (1.85E8)	82.92 (40.67)	350.73 (171.56)	26.76 (1.45)	1698.47 (32.87)
$\mathcal{F}_{(v)}$	0.67 (0.01)	0.61 (0.01)	0.57 (0.01)	0.54 (0.01)	0.91 (0.08)	0.91 (0.08)	0.83 (0.08)	0.82 (0.09)	0.99 (0.00)	1.00 (0.00)
PSOPP										
v	72.66 (4.15)	1423.44 (184.13)	2.51E5 (3.49E4)	7.66E7 (7.36E6)	8.33E7 (0.00)	2.25E9 (0.11)	0.00 (0.00)	75.53 (145.05)	0.66 (0.16)	1671.94 (131.18)
$\mathcal{F}_{(v)}$	1.00 (0.00)	1.00 (0.00)	1.00 (0.00)	0.89 (0.01)	1.00 (0.00)	1.00 (0.00)	1.00 (0.00)	0.96 (0.07)	1.00 (0.00)	1.00 (0.00)
#Partitions	121.33 (1.43)	242.65 (2.25)	481.48 (6.01)	939.75 (23.44)	2.00 (0.00)	2.00 (0.00)	2.00 (0.09)	192.31 (351.88)	38.95 (6.08)	1716.53 (227.18)
Partition Size	2.06 (0.24)	2.06 (0.24)	2.08 (0.27)	2.13 (0.34)	500.00 (312.22)	1500.00 (879.04)	499.00 (336.64)	20.80 (198.85)	2.57 (1.47)	2.33 (0.70)
#Total Moves [in 1000]	985.52 (32.24)	482.67 (18.95)	187.05 (9.33)	52.95 (5.27)	214.15 (12.98)	78.19 (3.04)	206.20 (29.37)	39.37 (17.11)	1733.64 (216.73)	36.39 (12.08)
#Rdm. Moves [in 1000]	459.54 (14.87)	222.73 (8.72)	82.97 (4.14)	20.19 (1.90)	90.29 (4.48)	31.43 (1.14)	78.84 (7.61)	15.31 (5.83)	767.87 (95.98)	11.73 (3.84)
#Appr. Moves [in 1000]	525.98 (17.43)	259.94 (10.27)	104.08 (5.23)	32.76 (3.39)	123.87 (8.52)	46.76 (2.29)	127.36 (21.96)	24.05 (11.33)	965.77 (122.44)	24.66 (8.25)
#Moves per Particle [in1000]	246.38 (8.20)	120.67 (4.84)	46.76 (2.43)	13.24 (1.95)	53.54 (3.30)	19.55 (1.01)	51.55 (9.40)	9.84 (8.26)	433.41 (54.27)	9.10 (4.55)

To appraise PSOPP's performance, we performed all experiments with an additional parametrization of $c_{rdm} = 1.0, c_{\mathcal{B}_i} = 0.0, c_{\mathcal{B}} = 0.0$, and $\#P = 4$, which is similar to a random search. In the following, we refer to this procedure as RDM.

Influence of the Number of Elements to Partition. We evaluated the influence of n for the set of problem sizes $\mathfrak{N} = \{100, 250, 500, 1000, 2000, 3000, 4000\}$. As shown in Table 1, an increase of n comes along with a decrease in the no. of moves particles make in the search space in C, AC, HPm, as well as HPs. Evidently, that is because the application of move operators (especially the approach operators) needs more time. Because the size of the search space grows significantly with n (see Sect. 1), it is not surprising that the achieved fitness drops with greater n: While PSOPP obtains very convincing results for $n \leq 1000$ in case of C, we need a higher time limit (i.e., more than 10 s) for $n \geq 2000$ (see convergence evaluation). Nevertheless, PSOPP notices that it is a good idea to establish small partitions of size two for all n. In HPm and AC, PSOPP scales much better with n. Even for $n = 4000$, the obtained fitness of 0.96 ($\sigma = 0.07$) for HPm and 1.00 ($\sigma = 0.02$) for AC is still very close to the optimum in all runs. For $n \leq 1000$, PSOPP achieves optimal results in all HPm and AC runs by establishing an appropriate partitioning consisting of two big partitions. With regard to RDM, the obtained fitness values are remarkably lower for $n \leq 2000$ than those of PSOPP in case of C, but, although the fitness decreases, the gap narrows clearly with increasing n (from 0.43 for $n = 1000$ to 0.04 for $n = 4000$), which emphasizes the need for higher time limits. As for HPm and AC, RDM's average fitness values only show slight variations with n (on average, RDM yields 0.83 for HPm and 0.91 for AC, both with $\sigma = 0.01$) and are – while still being

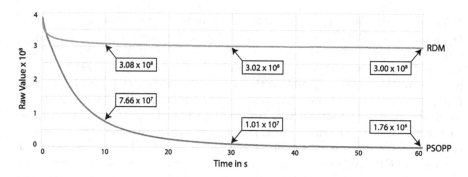

Fig. 2. PSOPP's convergence with regard to raw values for $n = 2000$, $\#P = 4$, and a time limit of 60 s in case of objective C (average of 500 runs).

significantly smaller – closer to PSOPP's fitness (on average, 0.99 for HPm and 1.00 for AC, both with $\sigma = 0.01$) than in case of C. Hence, C appears to be more difficult than HPm, which, in turn, seems more difficult than AC. HPs appears to be the easiest of our problems, which already aroused suspicion in the course of the search for appropriate parameters: Surprisingly, not only PSOPP but also RDM reaches a fitness of 1.00 for all $n \geq 250$. With regard to raw values v, PSOPP outperforms RDM by an average of 190.87 ($\sigma = 147.60$) over all $n \in \mathfrak{N}$. When minimizing instead of maximizing the fitness of HPs, the problem turns out to be much more complex: While PSOPP reaches an almost optimal average fitness value of 0.01 ($\sigma = 0.02$), RDM only yields an average of 0.94 ($\sigma = 0.06$) over all $n \in \mathfrak{N}$.

Convergence. For the evaluation of PSOPP's convergence, we ran experiments for additional time limits of 30 s and 60 s for all $n \in \mathfrak{N}$. Especially objective C benefits from higher time limits in case of $n \geq 2000$: On average, the fitness is 23.49 % ($\sigma = 8.70$ %) and 36.14 % (16.97 %) higher after 30 s and 60 s, respectively, compared to a limited runtime of 10 s. The total no. of moves increased up to an average of 361.51 % ($\sigma = 214.19$ %) after 60 s. In HPm and $n \geq 2000$, PSOPP already yields high-quality results after 10 s. The fitness therefore only improves by 1.57 % ($\sigma = 1.43$ %) and 1.73 % ($\sigma = 1.64$ %) after 30 s and 60 s, respectively, while the total no. of moves grows by 611.48 % ($\sigma = 110.75$ %) in case of a maximum runtime of 60 s. After 60 s, PSOPP achieves optimal fitness values for HPm in all runs. We observe a similar behavior in case of AC and $n \geq 2000$: The fitness can only increase by 0.12 % ($\sigma = 0.17$ %) until reaching optimal values after 30 s, while the total no. of moves increases up to 456.56 % ($\sigma = 10.15$ %). In case of HPs, the average increase of the total no. of moves by 509.39 % ($\sigma = 154.26$ %) does not have a significant effect on the fitness values since they are already at a very high level after 10 s. Figure 2 illustrates PSOPP's convergence in terms of the mean development of the raw value v for objective C over a time frame of 60 s.

Influence of Partitioning Constraints. To examine the influence of constrained partitionings on PSOPP's behavior, we additionally used $n_{max} = \frac{n}{2}$, $n_{min} = 0.98 \cdot n_{max}$, $s_{min} = 2$, and $s_{max} = n - (n_{min} - 1) \cdot s_{min}$ for C and HPs, and $n_{min} = 2$, $n_{max} = n \cdot 0.02$, $s_{min} = \frac{n}{n_{max}}$, and $s_{max} = \frac{n}{n_{min}}$ for AC and HPm. These parametrizations are compatible with the average number and size of partitions PSOPP found in the other evaluation scenarios (see Table 1): In C, it is preferred to create partitions that contain two very similar elements (e.g., a partition containing i and $i+1$), whereas it is preferred to group two dissimilar elements i and $(n-1)-i$ with sum $n-1$ in order to equalize the sum of the elements of each partition in HPs. AC also favors to group such dissimilar elements to maximize the sum of the squared Euclidean distances. In our experiments, AC establishes two big partitions that contain pairs $(i, (n-1)-i)$. Since both partitions have a mean of $\frac{n-1}{2}$, optimal results of HPm can be achieved analogously to AC. For $n \geq 2000$, we observed that the new restrictions allow PSOPP to improve the fitness by an average of 5.66 % ($\sigma = 4.04$ %) in case of C, and 1.73 % ($\sigma = 1.64$ %) in case of HPm. Hence, these restrictions allowed PSOPP to achieve an optimal fitness even for $n \geq 2000$ in all HPm runs. While this improvement is accompanied by a slight average decline of the total no. of moves by 1.35 % ($\sigma = 9.17$ %) in C, the total no. of moves significantly increases by 44.39 % ($\sigma = 26.19$ %) in HPm. Restrictions also have a positive effect on AC: For $n = 4000$, the increase of the total no. of moves by 9.93 % comes along with the ability to gain optimal fitness values in all runs. In HPs, the average raw value over all $n \in \mathfrak{N}$ can be decreased by 45.12 ($\sigma = 76.80$), although the total no. of moves drops considerably by 19.44 % ($\sigma = 12.17$ %). As opposed to the other objectives, the fitness does not change. Summarizing, this shows that PSOPP cannot only deal with constrained partitionings but also benefits from them, especially if n is large. While the former is not to be taken for granted (as outlined in Sect. 1, to the best of our knowledge, there is no partitioning algorithm that supports all of these constraints out of the box), the latter is mainly because the partitioning constraints reduce the size of the search space. Where appropriate, restricting the search space is thus an alternative to raising the time limit.

Comparison with x-means. Unlike PSOPP, which solves the PP in a *general manner*, x-means is specialized to problems where the costs of partitions can be assessed independently of each other. Therefore, x-means is *not* compatible with our homogeneous partitioning problems HPm and HPs. Moreover, PSOPP allows to restrict valid partition sizes, which is not possible in x-means. Because it is not obvious how to extend x-means by this feature, we used $s_{min} = 1$ to compare PSOPP to x-means. For these experiments, we used objective C and performed 100 x-means runs for each $n \in \mathfrak{N}$. In this situation, the highly specialized x-means obtains an average fitness of 1.00 ($\sigma = 0.00$) over all $n \in \mathfrak{N}$ (here, $b_C = 0.00$). With regard to the fitness $\mathcal{F}_C(v)$, PSOPP can keep up with x-means until $n = 1000$. As for raw values v, after 10 s, PSOPP obtains an average of 30.57 ($\sigma = 1.29$) for $n = 100$ and 101.11 ($\sigma = 5.94$) for $n = 250$, compared to 38.00 ($\sigma = 0.00$) and 68.00 ($\sigma = 0.00$) in case of x-means. For $n \geq 500$, we have to admit that x-means performs much better in terms of raw

Table 2. The avg. $\bar{r}_n$ and the max. $\hat{r}_n$ time PSOPP needed to find optimal solutions in its $500 \cdot 99\% = 495$ best runs, and the avg. raw value v x-means obtained in its $100 \cdot 99\% = 99$ best runs limited by the time $\hat{r}_n$ PSOPP needed to find the optimum for C $(s_{min} = n_{min} = 1, s_{max} = n_{max} = n)$. Parentheses contain standard deviations.

	PSOPP						x-means
	objective HPm		objective AC		objective C		objective C
#Elements	$\bar{r}_n$ [in s]	$\hat{r}_n$ [in s]	$\bar{r}_n$ [in s]	$\hat{r}_n$ [in s]	$\bar{r}_n$ [in s]	$\hat{r}_n$ [in s]	v
100	0.02 (0.02)	0.16	0.07 (0.01)	0.09	0.01 (0.01)	0.08	18.00 (0.00)
250	0.06 (0.05)	0.36	0.02 (0.02)	0.16	0.02 (0.03)	0.27	63.43 (24.22)
500	0.21 (0.21)	0.98	0.06 (0.07)	0.31	0.08 (0.08)	0.58	604.00 (0.00)
1000	1.11 (1.10)	4.88	0.29 (0.31)	1.51	0.41 (0.31)	1.28	5040.00 (0.00)
2000	7.95 (8.39)	34.01	1.28 (1.68)	9.20	2.85 (2.22)	8.53	10080.00 (0.00)
3000	28.26 (33.64)	148.02	4.18 (5.47)	27.21	9.47 (7.78)	29.80	8420.00 (0.00)
4000	73.49 (92.60)	388.23	9.44 (14.40)	77.16	21.98 (17.31)	69.01	20160.00 (0.00)

values than PSOPP. In case of $n = 500$, x-means reaches a raw value of 142.00 on average ($\sigma = 0.00$), whereas PSOPP yields 1837.05 ($\sigma = 274.50$). A comparable value of 227.52 ($\sigma = 12.31$) is achieved after 60 s. However, we observed that PSOPP outperforms x-means when we do not constrain valid partitionings at all (here, $s_{min} = n_{min} = 1$ and $s_{max} = n_{max} = n$). Table 2 depicts the average $\bar{r}_n$ and the maximal $\hat{r}_n$ time the $500 \cdot 99\% = 495$ best runs of PSOPP needed to find optimal solutions in case of C, AC, and HPm for all $n \in \mathfrak{N}$ (please note the approximately cubic growth of $\bar{r}_n$ and $\hat{r}_n$ with n). In contrast to PSOPP, whose 495 best runs always yielded optimal raw values of 0.00 after $\hat{r}_n$ seconds in C, x-means was not able to find optimal solutions. The average raw values obtained by x-means after $\hat{r}_n$ seconds are also depicted in Table 2 (analogously to PSOPP, these data are based on the $100 \cdot 99\% = 99$ best runs of x-means).

Optimization of Multiple Heterogeneous Objectives. Finally, we analyzed in which way the combination of our objectives C, AC, HPm, and HPs influences PSOPP's ability to obtain high-quality results. For this purpose, we regarded the two three-dimensional combinations C-HPm-HPs and AC-HPm-HPs, as well as the four-dimensional case C-AC-HPm-HPs. In these multi-objective optimizations, we used an a priori prioritization by taking the average of the fitness values of the corresponding optimization criteria to assess the quality of a candidate solution (each criteria was thus equally weighted). Our parameter search yielded $c_{rdm} = 0.2, c_{\mathcal{B}_i} = 0.1$, and $c_{\mathcal{B}} = 0.7$ for AC-HPm-HPs, and $c_{rdm} = 0.2, c_{\mathcal{B}_i} = 0.0$, and $c_{\mathcal{B}} = 0.8$ for C-HPm-HPs as well as C-AC-HPm-HPs. In tune with our previous observations, the valuation of the different parameter sets was mainly influenced, if not dominated, by C in C-HPm-HPs and C-AC-HPm-HPs, and by HPm in AC-HPm-HPs. In all cases, there is a conspicuous need for a systematic exploration of the search space, indicated by the high values of $c_{\mathcal{B}}$. As for AC-HPm-HPs, the average fitness achieved for a tuple (o, n) (with $o \in$ {HPm, HPs, AC} and $n \in \mathfrak{N}$) did not drop by more than 0.92 %, compared to optimizing for a single objective. Overall, PSOPP achieves an average fitness of 1.00 ($\sigma = 0.01$), compared to 0.90 ($\sigma = 0.00$) in case of RDM. In scenario C-HPm-HPs, the decrease in fitness ranges between 1.55 % and 12.50 % for C (with an average of 5.88 % and $\sigma = 4.17$ %). However, the fitness of HPm pays tribute to this relatively small reduction, in particular for large $n \geq 2000$. The drop of HPm's fitness ranges between 1.72 % and 31.85 % (with an average of 13.58 % and $\sigma = 13.36$ %). Again, the fitness of HPs remains at high levels and does not diminish by more than 0.77 %. Over all $n \in \mathfrak{N}$, PSOPP achieves an average fitness of 0.89 ($\sigma = 0.11$), compared to 0.73 ($\sigma = 0.04$) in case of RDM. Regarding the four-dimensional case C-AC-HPm-HPs, the decline in HPm's fitness is much lower and ranges between 1.13 % and 8.32 % (with an average of 3.73 % and $\sigma = 2.82$ %). We ascribe this to the related AC problem that is also solved in this scenario. As a result, HPm and AC weigh more than C. With respect to AC, the fitness values diminish by at least 0.34 % and at most 5.25 % (with an average of 1.86 % and $\sigma = 1.92$ %). This comes at the price of a significant decrease in C's fitness, which ranges between 4.92 % and 50.45 % (with an average of 21.35 % and $\sigma = 16.63$ %). Due to the supposed high density of high-quality results for HPs, its maximum decline in fitness is only 0.91 %. Overall, PSOPP achieves an average fitness of 0.91 ($\sigma = 0.08$), compared to 0.72 ($\sigma = 0.02$) in case of RDM. While one might have to adjust the weights of the different optimization criteria to the needs of a specific application, these experiments highlight PSOPP's ability to solve the PP in the context of multiple heterogeneous objectives.

5 Conclusion and Future Work

In this paper, we introduced PSOPP, a discrete Particle Swarm Optimizer that solves the partitioning problem (PP) outlined in Sect. 1. In contrast to the majority of other approaches, PSOPP solves the PP in a general manner, i.e., independently of the characteristics of a specific objective function. To this end, it uses the basic set operations split, join, and exchange to explore the search space. As a result, PSOPP can be applied to diverse problems in various domains (see Sect. 1 for examples) by defining an appropriate fitness function that evaluates the quality of candidate solutions. Possible problems comprise strict partitioning clustering (with outliers), anticlustering, homogeneous partitioning, and coalition structure generation, among others. Moreover, PSOPP allows to specify valid partitionings in terms of a minimum and maximum number and size of partitions. These properties clearly distinguish PSOPP from other partitioning methods. Our evaluation shows that it finds high-quality solutions respecting prescribed partitioning constraints in different evaluation scenarios with a low number of particles.

In this paper, we assumed that PSOPP partitions a *set* of elements (see Sect. 1). In future work, we will revise the definition of the similarity of partitionings and adjust PSOPP's approach operations so that it can solve multiset partitioning problems. In this context, we want to examine which influence these changes have on PSOPP's performance. With regard to multi-objective optimization, we will extend PSOPP to gather solutions lying on a pareto frontier.

References

1. Al Faruque, M.A., Krist, R., Henkel, J.: ADAM: run-time agent-based distributed application mapping for on-chip communication. In: Proceedings of the 45th Annual Design Automation Conference, pp. 760–765. ACM (2008). http://doi.acm.org/10.1145/1391469.1391664

2. Alam, S., Dobbie, G., Riddle, P.: An evolutionary particle swarm optimization algorithm for data clustering. In: IEEE Swarm Intelligence Symposium, pp. 1–6, September 2008

3. Anders, G., Seebach, H., Nafz, F., Steghöfer, J.P., Reif, W.: Decentralized reconfiguration for self-organizing resource-flow systems based on local knowledge. In: 8th IEEE International Conference and Workshops on Engineering of Autonomic and Autonomous Systems (EASe), pp. 20–31 (2011)

4. Anders, G., Siefert, F., Reif, W.: A particle swarm optimizer for solving the set partitioning problem in the presence of partitioning constraints. In: Proceedings of the 7th International Conference Agents and Artificial Intelligence (ICAART 2015), pp. 151–163. SciTePress (2015)

5. Anders, G., Siefert, F., Steghöfer, J.-P., Reif, W.: A decentralized multi-agent algorithm for the set partitioning problem. In: Rahwan, I., Wobcke, W., Sen, S., Sugawara, T. (eds.) PRIMA 2012. LNCS, vol. 7455, pp. 107–121. Springer, Heidelberg (2012)

6. Apt, K.R., Witzel, A.: A generic approach to coalition formation. In: Proceedings of the International Workshop on Computational Social Choice COMSOC, vol. 11, no. 3 (2007). http://arxiv.org/abs/0709.0435

7. Äyrämö, S., Kärkkäinen, T.: Introduction to partitioning-based clustering methods with a robust example. Technical report, Reports of the Department of Mathematical Information Technology, Series C. Software and Computational Engineering of the University of Jyväskylä (2006)

8. Bender, C., Brody, D., Meister, B.: Quantum field theory of partitions. J. Math. Phys. **40**, 3239 (1999)

9. Buccafurri, F., Rosaci, D., Sarné, G.M.L., Ursino, D.: An agent-based hierarchical clustering approach for e-commerce environments. In: Bauknecht, K., Tjoa, A.M., Quirchmayr, G. (eds.) EC-Web 2002. LNCS, vol. 2455, pp. 109–118. Springer, Heidelberg (2002). http://dx.doi.org/10.1007/3-540-45705-4_12

10. Chu, P., Beasley, J.: Constraint handling in genetic algorithms: the set partitioning problem. J. Heuristics **4**(4), 323–357 (1998). http://dx.doi.org/10.1023/A3A1008668508685

11. Consoli, S., Moreno-Pérez, J., Darby-Dowman, K., Mladenović, N.: Discrete particle swarm optimization for the minimum labelling steiner tree problem. Natural Comput. **9**(1), 29–46 (2010)

12. Di Marzo Serugendo, G., Gleizes, M.P., Karageorgos, A.: Self-organization in multi-agent systems. Knowl. Eng. Rev. **20**, 165–189 (2005). http://journals.cambridge.org/article_S0269888905000494

13. Garcia, F., Perez, J.: Jumping frogs optimization: a new swarm method for discrete optimization. Technical report 3, Documentos de Trabajo del DEIOC, Department of Statistics, O.R. and Computing, University of La Laguna, Tenerife, Spain (2008)

14. Horling, B., Lesser, V.: A survey of multi-agent organizational paradigms. Knowl. Eng. Rev. **19**(04), 281–316 (2004)

15. Ishioka, T.: An expansion of x-means for automatically determining the optimal number of clusters. In: Proceedings of International Conference on Computational Intelligence, pp. 91–96 (2005)

16. Kaufman, L., Rousseeuw, P.: Clustering by Means of Medoids. North-Holland, Amsterdam (1987)

17. Kennedy, J., Eberhart, R.: Particle swarm optimization. In: Proceedings of the IEEE International Conference on Neural Networks, vol. 4, pp. 1942–1948, November/December 1995

18. Kennedy, J., Eberhart, R.: A discrete binary version of the particle swarm algorithm. In: IEEE International Conference on Systems, Man, and Cybernetics, Computational Cybernetics and Simulation, vol. 5, pp. 4104–4108, October 1997

19. Kudo, Y., Murai, T.: On a criterion of similarity between partitions based on rough set theory. In: Sakai, H., Chakraborty, M.K., Hassanien, A.E., Ślęzak, D., Zhu, W. (eds.) RSFDGrC 2009. LNCS, vol. 5908, pp. 101–108. Springer, Heidelberg (2009). http://dx.doi.org/10.1007/978-3-642-10646-0_12

20. Lamarche-Perrin, R., Demazeau, Y., Vincent, J. M.: A generic algorithmic framework to solve special versions of the set partitioning problem. In: 2014 IEEE 26th International Conference on Tools with Artificial Intelligence (ICTAI), pp. 891–897, November 2014

21. MacQueen, J.: Some methods for classification and analysis of multivariate observations (1967)

22. Van der Merwe, D., Engelbrecht, A.P.: Data clustering using particle swarm optimization. In: The 2003 Congress on Evolutionary Computation, vol. 1, pp. 215–220. IEEE (2003)

23. Ogston, E., Overeinder, B., Steen, M.V., Brazier, F.: A method for decentralized clustering in large multi-agent systems. In: Proceedings of the 2nd International Joint Conference on Autonomous Agents and Multiagent Systems, pp. 789–796 (2003)

24. Rahwan, T., Ramchurn, S.D., Jennings, N.R., Giovannucci, A.: An anytime algorithm for optimal coalition structure generation. J. Artif. Intell. Res. **34**, 521–567 (2009)

25. Seren, C.: A hybrid jumping particle swarm optimization method for high dimensional unconstrained discrete problems. In: 2011 IEEE Congress on Evolutionary Computation, pp. 1649–1656 (2011)

26. Shehory, O., Kraus, S.: Methods for task allocation via agent coalition formation. Artif. Intell. **101**(1–2), 165–200 (1998)

27. Späth, H.: Anticlustering: maximizing the variance criterion. Control Cybern. **15**(2), 213–218 (1986)

28. Steghöfer, J.P., Behrmann, P., Anders, G., Siefert, F., Reif, W.: HiSPADA: self-organising hierarchies for large-scale multi-agent systems. In: Proceedings of the Ninth International Conference on Autonomic and Autonomous Systems (ICAS). IARIA (2013)

29. Valev, V.: Set partition principles revisited. In: Amin, A., Pudil, P., Dori, D. (eds.) SPR 1998 and SSPR 1998. LNCS, vol. 1451, pp. 875–881. Springer, Heidelberg (1998)

30. Younis, O., Fahmy, S.: HEED: a hybrid, energy-efficient, distributed clustering approach for ad hoc sensor networks. IEEE Trans. Mob. Comput. **3**, 366–379 (2004)

Using Process Calculi for Plan Verification in Multiagent Planning

Jan Jakubův[(✉)], Jan Tožička, and Antonín Komenda

CTU in Prague FEE Department of Computer Science, Agent Technology Center,
Karlovo Náměstí 13, 121 35 Prague 2, Czech Republic
{jan.jakubuv,jan.tozicka,antonin.komenda}@agents.fel.cvut.cz

Abstract. Multiagent planning is a coordination technique used for deliberative acting of a team of agents. One of vital planning techniques uses declarative description of agents' plans based on Finite State Machines and their later coordination by intersection of such machines with successive verification of the resulting joint plans.

In this work, we firstly introduce a method of multiagent planning which makes use of projections of other agent actions in order to iteratively search for a skeleton of a multiagent plan. Secondly, we describe integration of the static analysis provided by process calculi type systems for approximate verification of exchanged local plans. Furthermore, we introduce an alternative method to accomplish the above verification by a classical planner. Finally, we compare our approach with current state-of-the-art planner on an extensive benchmark set.

Keywords: Multiagent planning · Action landmarks · Plan verification · Process calculi · Type systems · Delete relaxation

1 Introduction

Intelligent agents requested to act together in a team require to some extent an ability to plan their actions in advance. If the agents prepare complete plans towards their goals, the problem they have to solve is a form of multiagent planning.

Similarly to classical planning, our multiagent planning approach assumes STRIPS [3] actions, which are deterministic and described by precondition and effects on the environment they are executed in. Thereby, the action state progression follows the STRIPS principles as well.

Although the action model is STRIPS, the complete multiagent planning model is subsequent to a recent extension of STRIPS by Brafman & Domshlak called MA-STRIPS [2]. In MA-STRIPS, the agents are cooperative with common goals and the resulting multiagent plan prescribes their coordinated acting from the initial state of the environment towards the goals. The agents are heterogeneous with different capabilities described by their STRIPS actions. Straightforwardly, their actions define parts of the environment they can affect and this

© Springer International Publishing Switzerland 2015
B. Duval et al. (Eds.): ICAART 2015, LNAI 9494, pp. 245–261, 2015.
DOI: 10.1007/978-3-319-27947-3_13

gives rise to their local planning problems. Conveniently, this (partial) "separation of concerns" helps to increase efficiency of the planning process and provides intrinsic separation of public information the agents have to share and internal facts, which can be kept private.

The multiagent planning approach proposed in this work extends recent works by Tožička, et al. on representation of multiagent plans in form of Finite State Machines and their merging [11] and plan generation using diverse planning with homotopy class constraints with testing of usability of partial plans among the agents by compilation into planning landmarks [10].

In this work, we initially propose to use a projections of actions [7] directly for multiagent planning, which was in the literature used so far only in relaxation heuristic estimations [8]. The main improvement is based on integration of theory and analysis provided by process calculi and their type systems. Concretely, we use generic process calculi type system scheme POLY* [5,6] for approximate verification of foreign plans received from other agents, which prospectively increases efficiency of search for coordinated multiagent plans. Finally, we compare our approach with current state-of-the-art planner FMAP [9] on an extensive benchmark set.

2   Multiagent Planning

We consider a number of *cooperative* and *coordinated* agents featuring distinct sets of capabilities (actions) which concurrently plan and execute their local plans in order to achieve a joint goal. The environment wherein the agents act is *classical* with *deterministic* actions. The following formal preliminaries restate the MA-STRIPS problem [2] required for the following sections.

2.1   Planning Problem

An MA-STRIPS planning problem Π is a quadruple $\Pi = \langle P, \{A_i\}_{i=1}^n, I, G \rangle$, where P is a set of facts, A_i is the set of actions of i-th agent, $I \subseteq P$ is an initial state, and $G \subseteq P$ is a set of conditions on the goal states. Given Π, we use A to denote all the actions from Π, that is, $A = \bigcup_{i=1}^n A_i$.

An *action* an agent can perform is a triple of subsets of P which in turn denote the set of *preconditions*, the set of *add effects*, and the set of *delete effects*. Selector functions $\mathsf{pre}(a)$, $\mathsf{add}(a)$, and $\mathsf{del}(a)$ are defined so that $a = \langle \mathsf{pre}(a), \mathsf{add}(a), \mathsf{del}(a) \rangle$. Moreover let $\mathsf{eff}(a) = \mathsf{add}(a) \cup \mathsf{del}(a)$.

An *agent* is identified with its capabilities, that is, an agent $\alpha = A_i = \{a_1, \ldots, a_m\}$ is characterized by a finite repertoire of actions it can perform in the environment. We use metavariables α and β to range over agents from Π. A *planning state* s is a finite set of facts and we say that fact p holds in s iff $p \in s$. When $\mathsf{pre}(a) \subseteq s$ then *state progression* function γ is defined classically as $\gamma(s, a) = (s \setminus \mathsf{del}(a)) \cup \mathsf{add}(a)$.

2.2   Public and Internal Classification

In multiagent planning each fact is classified either as *public* or as *internal* out of computational or privacy concerns. MA-STRIPS specifies this classification as follows. A fact is *public* when it is mentioned by actions of at least two different agents. A fact is *internal for* α when it is not public but mentioned by some action of α. A fact is *relevant for* α when it is either public or internal for α. Relevant facts contain all the facts which agent α needs to understand, because other facts are internal for other agents and thus not directly concerns α. Given Π, the set pub of public facts, and sets int(α) and rel(α) of facts internal and relevant for α are formally defined as follows. Let facts(a) = pre(a) $\cup$ add(a) $\cup$ del(a) and similarly facts(α) = $\bigcup_{a \in \alpha}$ facts(a).

$$\mathsf{pub} = \bigcup_{\alpha \neq \beta}(\mathsf{facts}(\alpha) \cap \mathsf{facts}(\beta))$$
$$\mathsf{int}(\alpha) = \mathsf{facts}(\alpha) \setminus \mathsf{pub}$$
$$\mathsf{rel}(\alpha) = \mathsf{pub} \cup \mathsf{int}(\alpha)$$

It is possible to extend the set of public facts to contain additionally some facts that would be internal by the above definition. It is common in literature [7] to require that all the goals are public. Then pub is defined as the minimal superset of the intersection from the definition that satisfies $G \subseteq$ pub. In the rest of this paper we suppose $G \subseteq$ pub and also another simplification common in literature [2] which says that A_i are pairwise disjoint[1].

MA-STRIPS further extends this classification of facts to actions as follows. An action is *public* when it has a public effect (that is, eff(a)$\cap$pub $\neq \emptyset$), otherwise it is *internal*. Strictly speaking, MA-STRIPS defines an action as public whenever it mentions a public fact even in a precondition (that is, when facts(a)$\cap$pub $\neq \emptyset$). However, as our approach does not rely on synchronization on public preconditions, we can consider actions with only public preconditions as internal. For our approach it is enough to know that internal actions do not *modify* public state.

2.3   Local Planning Problems

In MA-STRIPS model, agent actions are supposed to manipulate a shared global state when executed. In our approach to multiagent planning, a *local planning problem* is constructed for every agent α. Each local planning problem for α is a classical STRIPS problem where agent α has its own internal copy of the global state and where each agent is equipped with information about public actions of other agents. These local planning problems allow us to divide an MA-STRIPS problem to several STRIPS problems which can be solved separately by a classical planner. This paper describes a way to find a solution of an MA-STRIPS problem

---

[1] These two conditions rules out *private goals* and *joint actions*. Any MA-STRIPS problem which does not satisfy the two conditions can be translated to an equivalent problem which satisfies them. However, a solution that would take advantage of private goals and joint actions is left for future research.

but it does not address the question of *execution* of a plan in some real-world environment.

The *projection* $F \triangleright \alpha$ *of* an arbitrary set $F \subseteq P$ of facts to agent α is the restriction of F to the facts relevant for α, that is, $F \triangleright \alpha = F \cap \mathsf{rel}(\alpha)$. Projection removes from F facts not relevant for α and thus it represents F as understood by agent α. The *projection* $a \triangleright \alpha$ *of* action a to agent α removes from a facts not relevant for α, again representing a as seen by α.

$$a \triangleright \alpha = \langle \mathsf{pre}(a) \triangleright \alpha, \ \mathsf{add}(a) \triangleright \alpha, \ \mathsf{del}(a) \triangleright \alpha \rangle$$

Note that $a \triangleright \alpha = a$ when $a \in \alpha$. Hence projection to α alters only actions of other agents.

In the multiagent planning approach presented in this paper, every agent α is from the beginning equipped with projections of other agents public actions. These projections, which we call *external actions*, describe how agent α sees effects of public actions of other agents. Given Π, the set $\mathsf{ext}(\alpha)$ of external actions of agent α is defined as follows.

$$\mathsf{ext}(\alpha) = \{a \triangleright \alpha : a \text{ is a public action of } \beta \neq \alpha\}$$

Recall that A denotes the set of all the actions from Π. The set $A \triangleright \alpha$ contains actions of α plus external actions it is defined as follows.

$$A \triangleright \alpha = \alpha \cup \mathsf{ext}(\alpha)$$

Now it is easy to define a *local planning problem* $\Pi \triangleright \alpha$ of agent α also called *projection of* Π *to* α.

$$\Pi \triangleright \alpha = \langle P \triangleright \alpha, \ A \triangleright \alpha, \ I \triangleright \alpha, \ G \rangle.$$

2.4 Plans and Extensibility

We would like to solve agent local problems separately and compose local solutions to a global solution of Π. However, not all local solutions can be easily composed to a solution of Π. Concepts of *public plans* and *extensibility* helps us to recognize local solutions which are conductive to this aim.

A *plan* π is a sequence of actions $\langle a_1, \ldots, a_k \rangle$. A plan π defines an order in which the actions are executed by their unique owner agents. It is supposed that independent actions can be executed in parallel. A *solution* of Π is a plan π whose execution transforms the initial state I to subset of G. A *local solution* is a solution of a local planning problem. Let $\mathsf{sols}(\Pi)$ and $\mathsf{sols}(\Pi \triangleright \alpha)$ denote the set of all solutions of a given problem.

A *public plan* σ is a plan that contains only public actions. A public plan can be seen as a solution outline that captures execution order of public actions while ignoring agents internal actions. In order to avoid confusions between public and external versions of the same action, we suppose that actions are annotated with unique *ids* which are preserved under projection. From now on we consider public plans to be sequences of public action *ids*.

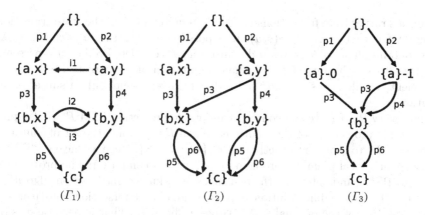

Fig. 1. Example of computing PSM public projection [11]. We suppose a context where pn are public and in internal actions, and where a, b, c are public and x, y internal facts.

Let operator $\cdot^\star$ construct a public plan from plan π, that is, let $\pi^\star$ be the sequence of all public action *ids* from π preserving their order. A public plan σ is called *extensible* iff it be can extended to a solution of Π by insertion of internal actions of any agent, that is, iff there is $\pi \in \text{sols}(\Pi)$ such that $\pi^\star = \sigma$. A public plan is called α-*extensible* iff it can be extended to a local solution of $\Pi \triangleright \alpha$ by insertion of internal actions of α, that is, iff there is agent α's plan $\pi_\alpha \in \text{sols}(\Pi \triangleright \alpha)$ such that $\pi_\alpha^\star = \sigma$.

The following proposition states the correctness of the used approach to multiagent planning. Its direct consequence is that to find a solution of Π it is enough to find a local solution $\pi_\alpha \in \text{sols}(\Pi \triangleright \alpha)$ which is β-extensible for every other agent β. A constructive proof can be found in [10].

Proposition 1. *Let public plan σ of Π be given. Public plan σ is extensible if and only if σ is α-extensible for every agent α.*

3   Planning State Machines

This section briefly restates the previous work by [11] our work is based on, while its extensions, which are the main contributions of this paper, are described in following sections. We use nondeterministic finite state machines (NFS) [4] as a compact representation of a set of solutions of a STRIPS problem. We call an NFS that represents a set of solutions a *planning state machine* (PSM).

A *planning state machine (PSM)* of a STRIPS problem $\Pi = \langle P, A, I, G \rangle$ is a NFS $\Gamma = \langle A, S, I, \delta, F \rangle$ where the alphabet A is the set of actions of Π, states from S are subsets of P, the state transition function δ resembles the classical STRIPS state progression function γ, and $F \subseteq S$ contains all the states that satisfies goal G. To avoid confusions, we suppose that alphabet A contains unique action *ids* rather than full actions. The only requirement[2] on the state transition function δ is that $\delta(s,a) = \gamma(s,a)$. It is possible to construct a *complete* PSM that contains all possible states and transitions. A complete PSM of Π represents exactly all the solutions of Π. As the computation of a complete PSM can be inefficient, we also consider *partial* PSMs which represents only a subset of all solutions.

For every PSM Γ we can construct its public projection PSM $\Gamma^\star$ that represents public projections of the solutions. When Γ represents the set of solutions S we want $\Gamma^\star$ to represent exactly the set $\{\pi^\star : \pi \in S\}$. Once we have a PSM for every agent's local planning problem $\Pi \triangleright \alpha$, we can compute public projections of these PSMs and intersect them using a well-known intersection algorithm for NFS [4]. Any public solution σ in a non-empty intersection constitutes a public solution of the original MA-STRIPS problem Π. That is because σ is α-extensible for every α (as it comes from the intersection) and thus extensible by Proposition 1.

Figure 1 provides an example PSM Γ_1 demonstrating PSM public projection algorithm. First, PSM Γ_2 is obtained from the input Γ_1 by renaming internal actions to ϵ-transitions and eliminating them by the intersection algorithm [4]. Second, the public projection Γ_3 of Γ_1 is obtained from Γ_2 by projecting states (removing internal facts) and by unification of states with equal public projection. Hence $\Gamma_1^\star = \Gamma_3$. When two states with equal public projection differ in outgoing edges then they can not be unified and an integer *mark* is introduced to distinguish them. Note that if the two states {a}-0 and {a}-1 were unified in Γ_3, then the resulting PSM would also represent a public plan $\langle \mathsf{p1}, \mathsf{p4}, \mathsf{p5} \rangle$ which does not correspond to any plan from Γ_1.

Algorithm 1 provides an overview of a distributed algorithm [11] to find a solution of an MA-STRIPS problem. We suppose that every agent α executes `PsmPlanDistributed` in a separate process, possibly on a separate machine. We suppose that agent processes can communicate with each other by sending structured messages. Every agent α starts with an empty PSM Γ_α which contains only the initial state of $\Pi \triangleright \alpha$. In every loop iteration, every agent generates a new plan of its local problem $\Pi \triangleright \alpha$ and it adds this plan to Γ_α. Then public projection $\Gamma_\alpha^\star$ is computed and exchanged with other agents. The easiest way to implement PSM projections exchange is when every agent sends its projection to every other agent. The projections can also be exchanged in a round-robin manner. The loop in the algorithm continues until the intersection $\bigcap_\beta (\Gamma_\beta^\star)$ is not empty. The operation written in **bold italics** is an optional extension described in Sect. 5.

---

[2] Although a PSM as defined here suggests a deterministic finite state machine, a non-deterministic transitions can be introduced by public projection defined later. Thus we prefer to work with non-deterministic machines from the beginning.

Algorithm 1. Distributed algorithm to find a solution of MA-STRIPS problem Π.

Function PsmPlanDistributed($\Pi \triangleright \alpha$) **is**

    $\Gamma_\alpha \leftarrow$ empty PSM (initial state of $\Pi \triangleright \alpha$);

    loop

        generate a new plan π_α of $\Pi \triangleright \alpha$;

        analyse plan π_α *(Sec. 5)*;

        extend Γ_α with π_α;

        compute public projection Γ_α^* of Γ_α;

        exchange PSM public projections;

        if intersection $\bigcap_\beta (\Gamma_\beta^{\text{pub}}) \neq \emptyset$ **then**

            return the intersection;

        end

        create landmarks from plans;

    end

end

By a new plan in the first step we mean a plan that was not generated in any of the previous iterations. To achieve this we have modified an existing planner FastDownward[3] so that it is able to generate a plan which differs from plans provided as an input. This extension is inspired by diverse planning with homotopy class constraints [1]. Homotopy classes of plans are naturally defined by their public projections, that is, two plans belong to same homotopy class iff they have equal public projection.

In the last step of the loop, other agents plans are incorporated into the local planning problem $\Pi \triangleright \alpha$ using the principle of *prioritizing actions* and *soft-landmarks*. Prioritizing actions are implemented using action costs so that internal actions are preferred to public actions, and α's public actions are preferred to other agent actions. When agent α finds a new local solution it sends its public projection to all the other agents. Other agents then extend their local problem $\Pi \triangleright \beta$ to contain duplicated landmark actions from the received plan. These landmark actions have significantly decreased cost and they are interlinked using additional facts to ensure they are used in the order suggested by the public plan. See [10] for details.

4   Planning Calculus

In this section we show how classical planning can be expressed as a process calculus. Furthermore we show how to use existing process calculi type systems for static analysis of classical planning problems and how to use this static analysis for approximation of planning problem solvability. In the next section, this static analysis will be incorporated into the multiagent planning algorithm from the previous section (Algorithm 1).

---

[3] http://www.fast-downward.org/.

4.1   Planning as Process Calculus

A typical *process calculus* is defined by a set of *processes* together with a binary *rewriting relation* ($\rightarrow$) on these processes. Processes describe possible system states while the rewriting relation describes possible transitions between states. Hence $Q_0 \rightarrow Q_1$ means that the system can be transformed (in one step) from the state described by Q_0 to state Q_1.

Process calculi are usually used to model concurrent environments where several units (processes) engage in activity at the same time. Processes usually take form of programs and thus system states are identified with programs currently running in the system, while rewriting relation captures program evaluation.

Processes are usually constructed from atomic processes using standard operators. In this paper, we will use only the *parallel composition* operator ("$|$"). Process "$Q_0 | Q_1$" describes a system where processes Q_0 and Q_1 are running in parallel. We will also use standard *null* or *inactive* process denoted "0". Parallel composition is considered commutative and associative with 0 being an identity element (that is, $Q | 0 = Q$).

Given a STRIPS problem Π with set of facts P, we use facts $p \in P$ as atomic processes. Hence our processes correspond to planning states while the rewriting relation emulates action application by adjusting state (process) appropriately. The set of our processes is generated by the following grammar.

$$Q ::= 0 \mid p \mid (Q_0 \mid Q_1)$$

That is, null process 0 is a process, every fact p is a process, and other processes can be constructed using parallel composition. Function $\lceil s \rceil$ encodes a state as a process.

$$\lceil \{p_1, p_2, \ldots, p_n\} \rceil = p_1 \mid p_2 \mid \cdots \mid p_n \mid 0$$

Furthermore, to simplify the presentation we consider processes to be equal modulo fact duplications (that is, "$(p \mid p) = p$" and so on).

The rewriting relation $\rightarrow$ is the minimal relation which satisfies the following rules.

$$\frac{a \in A}{\lceil \mathsf{pre}(a) \rceil \rightarrow \lceil \gamma(\mathsf{pre}(a), a) \rceil} \qquad \frac{Q_0 \rightarrow Q_1}{Q_0 \mid Q_2 \rightarrow Q_1 \mid Q_2}$$

Recall that the state progression function γ for action a applied to the state $\mathsf{pre}(a)$ is defined as follows.

$$\gamma(\mathsf{pre}(a), a) = (\mathsf{pre}(a) \setminus \mathsf{del}(a)) \cup \mathsf{add}(a)$$

Hence the first rule says that, for every action a, the process $\lceil \mathsf{pre}(a) \rceil$ can be rewritten to the process $\lceil \mathsf{pre}(a) \rceil$ with delete effects removed and add effects added. The second rule is a context rule which allows us to apply rewriting in the presence of additional facts. The following formally states that the rewriting relation $\rightarrow$ correctly captures planning action execution.

Proposition 2. *Let $\Pi = \langle P, A, I, G \rangle$ be a classical* STRIPS *problem such that* $\mathsf{del}(a) \subseteq \mathsf{pre}(a)$ *for every action $a \in A$. For any two planning states s_0 and s_1 the following holds.*

$$\lceil s_0 \rceil \to \lceil s_1 \rceil \quad \text{iff} \quad \exists a \in A : \gamma(s_0, a) = s_1$$

The requirement that every action deletes only facts mentioned in its preconditions ($\mathsf{del}(a) \subseteq \mathsf{pre}(a)$) is necessary because the right-hand side of a rewriting rule can refer only to processes mentioned on the left-hand side. This requirement simplifies formal presentation while it does not restrict usability because problems not fulfilling the requirement can be translated[4] to equivalent problems which do so. Moreover, it is usually satisfied in practice.

4.2 Planning Calculus Type System

In this section we show how to use existing process calculi type systems for static analysis of planning problems. Type systems for processes calculi are used to prove various properties of processes. A type system is usually handcrafted for a specific calculus and thus we can not use an arbitrary type system for our planning process calculus. However, there is a generic process calculi type system scheme POLY✶ [6] which works for many calculi including ours. Furthermore, POLY✶ has already been successfully used for static analysis [5].

A detailed description of POLY✶ is beyond the scope of this paper and thus we provide only a necessary background. POLY✶ provides a syntax to describe rewriting rule axioms. Here we just state that rewriting rules from the previous section can be easily described in this syntax. Once rewriting rules are given, POLY✶ automatically derives syntax of types together with a type system for the given calculus. Furthermore, an effective type inference algorithm is provided to compute a principal (most general) type of an arbitrary process.

For our purposes, it is enough to state that a POLY✶ type τ for our planning process calculus can be understood as a set of facts. POLY✶ defines a *typing relation*, written $\vdash Q : \tau$, which states that Q has type τ. The most important property of the typing relation is *subject reduction* which ensures that types are preserved under rewriting, that is, when $\vdash Q_0 : \tau$ and $Q_0 \to Q_1$ then $\vdash Q_1 : \tau$. Another property that interests us is that whenever $\vdash Q : \tau$ then τ contains all the facts mentioned in Q. In particular, $\vdash \lceil s \rceil : \tau$ implies $s \subseteq \tau$ for any state s.

The previous paragraph suggests the following procedure. Given a STRIPS problem $\Pi = \langle P, A, I, G \rangle$, we can use POLY✶ to compute the principal type τ of the initial state process $\lceil I \rceil$. Hence $\vdash \lceil I \rceil : \tau$. Because types are preserved under rewriting, we know that whenever $\lceil I \rceil$ rewrites using an arbitrary many applications of $\to$ to some process Q, then also $\vdash Q : \tau$. In other words, whatever state s is reachable from I, we know that $s \subseteq \tau$. Hence when $G \not\subseteq \tau$ then Π is not solvable. The opposite implication, which would also allow us to recognize

---

[4] Briefly, for a delete effect $p \notin \mathsf{pre}(a)$, we can introduce a new fact p^- complementary to p and then provide two rewriting rule axioms for a; the first applies in states where p holds while the second in states where p^- holds.

solvable problems, does not generally hold because POLY* type τ only over-approximates all reachable states.

In this way we can use POLY* types to recognize some unsolvable problems. We instantiate POLY* by translating actions to rewriting rules, and we use POLY* to compute the principal type τ of $\lceil I \rceil$. When $G \not\subseteq \tau$ then the problem is clearly unsolvable. Otherwise we can not conclude anything. This is the price we pay for effectiveness as POLY* types can be computed in polynomial time while planning is PSPACE-complete.

Our experiments have shown that POLY* type analysis is essentially equivalent to computing a planning graph with the delete effect relaxation. The POLY* type contains exactly the same facts as the last layer of a relaxed planning graph. A possible extensions of POLY* analysis that would give more precise results than relaxed planning graphs are left for future research. One of the advantages of using POLY* over relaxed planning graphs is in that we can rely on its already proved formal properties (subject reduction, principal typings) and that there is no need to implement equivalent methods because an effective type inference algorithm is already implemented.

5   PSM with Plan Analysis

This section describes improvements from the basic version of Algorithm 1 denoted in **_bold italics_** in the algorithm. We introduce two different methods (PSM+ and PSM*) to incorporate the static analysis from the previous section into our PSM-based planner (Algorithm 1). The static analysis is used to analyze plans at the second line of the loop in the algorithm. Section 5.1 describes an encoding of an α-extensibility check into a planning problem, which is a technique shared by both the methods. It basically restates our previous work [10] required for the understanding of the next sections. Sections 5.2 and 5.3 describe in turn the methods PSM+ and PSM*.

5.1   Plan Extensibility as Planning

First we describe how the static analysis from the previous section can be used to approximate α-extensibility of public plan σ. This is done by running the static analysis on a classical planning problem Π_σ constructed as follows. Problem Π_σ is similar to $\Pi \triangleright \alpha$ but it contains only a subset of its actions. Concretely, Π_σ contains all the internal actions of α but only those public or external actions which are mentioned in σ. Furthermore, actions from σ are interlinked using additional facts to ensure they are executed in the order suggested by σ. Formally, let a_i be the action from $A \triangleright \alpha$ which corresponds to the i-th action in σ. Let $mark_0, \ldots, mark_n$ be additional facts (n is the length of σ). Then Π_σ contains the following action b_i.

$$b_i = \langle\ \mathsf{pre}(a_i)\ \cup\ \{mark_{i-1}\},$$
$$\mathsf{add}(a_i)\ \cup\ \{mark_i\},$$
$$\mathsf{del}(a_i)\ \cup\ \{mark_{i-1}\}\ \rangle$$

Finally $mark_0$ is added to the initial state of Π_σ and $mark_n$ is added to the goal state. When action b_i is used, the mark is increased which enables action b_{i+1}. In the end we want all b_i's to be used, possibly interleaved with some α-internal actions which are just added to Π_σ without any additional changes. It can be proved that Π_σ is solvable iff σ is α-extensible [10].

5.2 Simplified Plan Analysis (PSM+)

The previous section suggests the following plan verification procedure. When agent α generates a new plan π_α, it sends its public projection $\pi_\alpha^\star$ to all the other agents. Once other agent β receives $\pi_\alpha^\star$, it uses the static analysis to check whether $\pi_\alpha^\star$ is β-extensible. That is, agent β constructs Π_σ (for $\sigma = \pi_\alpha^\star$) and executes the POLY$\star$ analysis yielding the type τ. When $G \not\subseteq \tau$ then agent β informs α that $\pi_\alpha^\star$ is not β-extensible. Otherwise agent β returns an unknown status back to agent α.

Once the initiator agent α receives back results from all the other agents it simply checks whether $\pi_\alpha^\star$ was *rejected* by, that is, found not β-extensible for, at least one agent. When the plan is rejected by at least one agent, then agent α simply drops the plan and directly continues with the next loop iteration by generating another plan. Optionally, agent α can incorporate plans generated by other agents as landmarks (last operation in the loop) provided these plans were not rejected.

We have mentioned above that the results of POLY$\star$ analysis are equivalent to computing a planning graph with delete effect relaxation. This gives us an alternative approach to implement plan verification in the PSM+ variant. When verifying a public plan $\pi_\alpha^\star$ of agent α by agent β, agent β computes Π_σ as above. However, instead of using POLY$\star$ to compute the principal type, agent β can apply delete relaxation to the verification problem Π_σ and launch a classical planner to solve it. When the delete relaxation of Π_σ is found unsolvable, then agent β informs α that $\pi_\alpha^\star$ is not β-extensible. Otherwise agent β returns an unknown status back to agent α. We have implemented both verification variants of PSM+ in order to evaluate effectiveness of POLY$\star$ type inference engine when compared to a state-of-the-art classical planner FastDownward. The results of this evaluation are presented in Sect. 6.

5.3 Partial Plan Reuse (PSM$\star$)

Experiments with PSM+ showed that plan analysis had increased the number of solved problems when compared to the basic variant PSM without any plan analysis. However, there were some problems solved by PSM which were no longer solved by PSM+. A more detailed analysis revealed that in some cases a useful landmark was created from the beginning of a plan that was rejected in PSM+. This is because it can happen that a rejected plan is correct up to some point. The method introduced in this section tries to find a usable plan prefix and use it as a landmark.

The procedure starts as in the previous section, that is, agent α generates a new plan π_α and sends its public projection $\pi_\alpha^\star$ to all the other agents. Once Π_σ is constructed by other agent β, the POLY$\star$ analysis of Π_σ is executed yielding the type τ. When the last mark $mark_n$ is not in τ, not only we know that σ is surely not β-extensible, but the maximum mark present in τ gives us other insight into σ. Hence type τ is examined and the maximum i such that $mark_i \in \tau$ is found. From that we can conclude that it is not possible for β to follow the public plan σ to a state where the $(i+1)$-th action of σ can be executed. Hence this maximum i is returned as a result of β's analysis of σ back to agent α.

Finally, agent α collects analysis results from all the other agents and computes their minimum j. Plan σ is then stripped so that only the first j actions remain in it. This stripped plan is then sent to the other agents to be used as a landmark and to guide future plan search.

With the previous variant PSM+, we have introduced an alternative method of verification which uses a classical planner instead of the POLY$\star$ type inference engine. This alternative verification method is not directly adaptable to variant PSM$\star$ because a classical planner does not provide additional information when a problem is found unsolvable. Hence it is not straightforward to extract the first unreachable mark as it would require modifications in planner implementation. Hence in the case of variant PSM$\star$, the results of POLY$\star$ analysis provide more information than the analysis implemented using a classical planner.

6   Experimental Results

We have performed a set of experiments to evaluate an impact of plan verification on a PSM-based planner and also to compare our planners with another state-of-the-art multiagent planner[5]. We have decided to compare our approach with FMAP [9] which uses well defined problems taken from International Planning Competition (IPC) problems. FMAP classifies facts as public or internal using a manual selection of public predicate names. In practice, FMAP public facts are a superset of MA-STRIPS public facts and thus FMAP classification is compatible with our algorithms. In our experiments we use exactly the same input files as the authors of FMAP used during its evaluation[6], and we also use the same time limit of 30 min for each problem. The binary and source codes of our PSM-based planner are available on demand. Please contact us by email in order to obtain them.

The first four number columns in Table 1 show an overall coverage of solved problems. We can see that the FMAP has better results in most of the domains and also in the overall coverage. Nevertheless PSM+ performed better in two tightly-coupled domains as it was able to solve all the *Openstacks* problems and two additional *Woodworking* problems over FMAP. We can see that PSM$\star$

---

[5] All the tests were performed on a single PC, CPU Intel i7 3.40 GHz with 8 cores, and memory limited to 8GB RAM.

[6] We would like to thank the authors of FMAP for a kind support with their planner.

Table 1. First four number columns show the number of problems solved by the compared planners. Last two columns show the percentage of time spent by plan verification in PSM+ variant with the verification done by POLY★ and by FastDownward (FD).

Domain	FMAP	PSM	PSM+	PSM★	POLY★	FD
Blocksworld (34)	19	**27**	26	26	**3.53**	5.48
Driverlog (20)	**15**	10	9	14	**9.24**	11.87
Elevators (30)	**30**	1	3	4	**8.93**	10.41
Logistics (20)	**10**	0	0	0	0	0
Openstacks (30)	23	**30**	**30**	**30**	**16.58**	17.48
Rovers (20)	**19**	7	14	14	13.91	**10.96**
Satellite (20)	**16**	6	13	9	**7.92**	8.80
Woodworking (30)	22	**27**	**27**	**27**	**9.45**	10.57
Zenotravel (20)	**18**	17	17	17	**9.33**	11.73
Total (224)	**172**	125	139	141	**10.24 %**	11.29 %

outperforms PSM+ in *Driverlog* and *Elevators* domains but it loses in *Satellite* domain. Moreover, there were eight other differences in individual problems, where half of them in each domain were in favor of each method and thus these differences are not reflected in the table. The results show that a possible enhancement of POLY★ verification could bring even higher coverage. This will be part of our future research. Also note that PSM★ is strictly better in coverage[7] than the basic variant PSM.

The last two columns in Table 1 evaluate effectiveness of the two verification methods for variant PSM+ described in Sect. 5.2. Experiments reveled, that both the verification methods in variant PSM+ led to exactly the same sets of solved problems and varied only in run times. The numbers show an average percentage of runtime used for plan verification. We see that POLY★ runs faster than FastDownward except for the *Rovers* domain which is caused probably by a great number of internal actions. As the plan verification by a classical planner can be used only by variant PSM+, it makes POLY★ a suitable tool for plan verification. Furthermore, the table shows that plan verification in general is easier than local problem solving.

For a more detailed analysis of PSM variants we have chosen three domains with the highest coverage. The left table in Table 2 shows an average number of iterations and run times needed to find a solution for problems which were solved by all the three variants. Sequential times show how long it would take if all the agents share a single CPU, while the parallel time correspond to a

---

[7] However, there were still two individual problems which were solved by PSM but not by PSM★. As this happens relatively rarely, it is left for future research to find out whether this is because of the approximation in POLY★ analysis or whether it can happen that in some cases a useful landmark is constructed from a rejected plan part.

Table 2. (**Left**) Performance cost of PSM extended with plan verification. The table shows average values for all the solved problems. Run times are in seconds. (**Right**) Comparison of run times on selected problems solved by all the planners. Times are in seconds, PSM times correspond to parallel times, and PSM variants have number of iterations in parenthesis.

	PSM	PSM+	PSM∗
Driverlog			
Iterations	3.4	2	2.3
Sequential time	23.5	9.6	12.1
Parallel time	9.7	4.5	5.6
Openstacks			
Iterations	1	1	1
Sequential time	2.6	7.1	7.1
Parallel time	1.3	4.4	4.4
Woodworking			
Iterations	1.4	1.3	1.3
Sequential time	79.1	84.1	84.0
Parallel time	20.3	21.7	21.6

	FMAP	PSM	PSM+	PSM∗
Driverlog				
p-01	**0.6**	2.2 (2)	2.3 (2)	2.3 (2)
p-05	**1.8**	34.1 (9)	4.0 (2)	6.5 (3)
p-08	11.9	11.6 (3)	**5.4** (2)	6.2 (2)
p-10	2.1	**3.0** (2)	4.2 (2)	4.6 (2)
p-13	16.2	14.3 (3)	**8.7** (2)	14.8 (3)
Openstacks				
p-01	1.4	**1.2** (1)	1.3 (1)	1.3 (1)
p-06	9.7	**1.1** (1)	1.7 (1)	1.7 (1)
p-11	51.0	**1.2** (1)	2.3 (1)	2.3 (1)
p-16	171.0	**1.2** (1)	4.3 (1)	4.5 (1)
p-21	497.0	**1.4** (1)	6.7 (1)	6.5 (1)
Woodworking				
p-01	**2.7**	4.7 (2)	5.6 (2)	5.6 (2)
p-06	200.3	**30.1** (2)	33.7 (2)	33.8 (2)
p-11	1.9	**1.8** (1)	2.3 (1)	2.3 (1)
p-21	**0.4**	1.3 (1)	1.5 (1)	1.5 (1)

situation where each agent is equipped with its own CPU. The results show that in *Driverlog* domain the number of iterations decreased which also caused a decrease in run times. PSM+ achieved the best results for this domain. All problems of *Openstacks* domain have been solved during the first iteration even by the simplest version PSM. Therefore run times needed by the other versions are higher because of the time needed for the verification. Only a tiny decrease of iteration count in *Woodworking* domain could not outweigh the price for verification and thus the versions with plan verification are a bit slower than PSM. A slight increase of run time in PSM∗ over PSM+ is caused by additional landmarks which come from plans which were completely rejected by PSM+.

The right table in Table 2 compares run times needed to solve selected tasks solvable by all the planners. We can see that PSM-variants are able to find solution faster than FMAP in the case of complex problems.

The left graph in Fig. 2 compares times needed for planning and plan verification in PSM∗. It shows that the time needed for verification in PSM∗ is much smaller than the time needed for agent internal planning. The graph is constructed as follows. The x-axis in the graph shows total time needed to solve a problem, that is, planning together with verification. For each problem, planning and verification times are depicted as two values in the same column whose

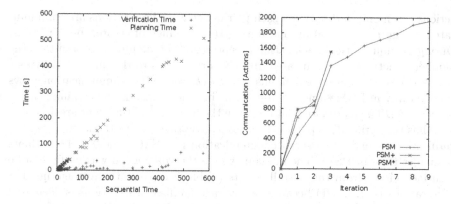

Fig. 2. (Left) Verification and planning times in PSM✶. **(Right)** Amount of communication during solving of *Driverlog05*.

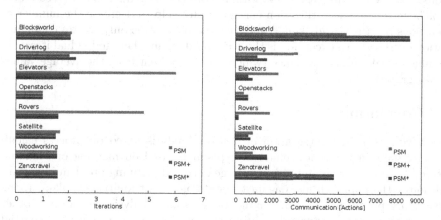

Fig. 3. An average number of iterations (left) and an average amount of communication (right) for each domain in PSM, PSM+, and PSM✶ variants.

x-coordinate correspond to the total sequential time. Thus the sum of the two values in each column is always equal to the x-coordinate of the column.

The right graph in Fig. 2 shows amount of communication among the agents in a single selected problem (*Driverlog05*). This problem was chosen because it was solved by all the approaches but not in a trivial manner (in the first or second iteration). Each curve ends in the column that corresponds to the last iteration. We can see that the verification creates communication overhead in individual iterations but the total communication is smaller with verification because the number of iterations is decreased.

Graphs in Fig. 3 show, for each domain, an average number of iterations and an average amount of communication among all the agents measured in actions. The average values are computed only for the problems solved by all PSM, PSM+ and PSM✶ variants. The communication is measured as the number of actions communicated between each pair of agents. These actions are communicated during the verification and during the exchange of created public PSMs. During communication, each action is represented by its unique id and thus the number of actions communicated directly corresponds to the number of bytes.

We can see that in some domains (e.g. *Blocksworld*) the communication grows substantially in PSM∗ and PSM+, while in other domains the communication is decreased. The reason for that is that in the first case all the plans are accepted and thus the verification process brings no advantage. In the domains where the verification helped, the overall communication in PSM+ and PSM∗ variants is smaller than in PSM. The domains where the verification was useful can be identified either from the overall results (Table 1) or from the average number of iterations (Fig. 3, left) because the average number of iterations is decreased by success of the verification process (see domains *Driverlog, Elevators, Rovers*). In the domains where all the solved problems were solved in first few iterations even by the simplest PSM variant (*Blocksworld, Openstacks, Woodworking, Zenotravel*), the verification can not really help to decrease the number of iterations (as it is already small) and thus the verification only creates communication overhead. An exception is the *Satellite* domain where individual iteration numbers have a higher variance (which is not apparent from the average values in the graph).

7   Conclusions

We have shown how integration of a static analysis based on process calculi type systems in validation phase of a planner based on merging of Planning State Machines strictly improves coverage of solved planning problem instances. Although the approach loses against a state-of-the-art multiagent planner, the results are promising. Moreover usage of the static analysis can improve other multiagent planning approaches using cooperation by coordination of partial agents' plans. We have argued that it is feasible to use POLY∗ for plan verification even though the same analysis can be, in some cases, done using a classical planner.

Furthermore, we have also extended our approach with a new heuristic with notable improvements. This new heuristic will be part of our future research. In future research, we want also to focus on more precise static analysis by POLY∗ and therefore hypothetically less approximate test of the extensibility of partial plans.

Acknowledgements. This research was supported by the Czech Science Foundation (grant no. 13-22125S).

References

1. Bhattacharya, S., Kumar, V., Likhachev, M.: Search-based path planning with homotopy class constraints. In: Felner, A., Sturtevant, N.R. (eds.) SOCS. AAAI Press, Menlo Park (2010)

2. Brafman, R., Domshlak, C.: From one to many: planning for loosely coupled multi-agent systems. In: Proceedings of ICAPS 2008, vol. 8, pp. 28–35 (2008)
3. Fikes, R., Nilsson, N.: STRIPS: a new approach to the application of theorem proving to problem solving. In: Proceedings of the 2nd International Joint Conference on Artificial Intelligence, pp. 608–620 (1971)
4. Hopcroft, J.E., Motwani, R., Ullman, J.D.: Introduction to Automata Theory, Languages, and Computation, 3rd edn. Addison-Wesley Longman Publishing Co., Inc., Boston (2006)
5. Jakubův, J., Wells, J.B.: Expressiveness of generic process shape types. In: Wirsing, M., Hofmann, M., Rauschmayer, A. (eds.) TGC 2010. LNCS, vol. 6084, pp. 103–119. Springer, Heidelberg (2010)
6. Makholm, H., Wells, J.B.: Instant polymorphic type systems for mobile process calculi: just add reduction rules and close. In: Sagiv, M. (ed.) ESOP 2005. LNCS, vol. 3444, pp. 389–407. Springer, Heidelberg (2005)
7. Nissim, R., Brafman, R. I.: Multi-agent A* for parallel and distributed systems. In: Proceedings of AAMAS 2012, Richland, SC, pp. 1265–1266 (2012). http://dl.acm.org/citation.cfm?id=2343896.2343955
8. Štolba, M., Komenda, A.: Relaxation heuristics for multiagent planning. In: Proceedings of ICAPS 2014 (2014)
9. Torreño, A., Onaindia, E., Sapena, S.: Fmap: distributed cooperative multi-agent planning. Appl. Intell. **41**(2), 606–626 (2014). http://dx.doi.org/10.1007/s10489-014-0540-2
10. Tožička, J., Jakubův, J., Durkota, K., Komenda, A., Pěchouček, M.: Multiagent planning supported by plan diversity metrics and landmark actions. In: Proceedings ICAART 2014 (2014)
11. Tožička, J., Jakubův, J., Komenda, A.: Generating multi-agent plans by distributed intersection of finite state machines. In: Proceedings ECAI 2014, pp. 1111–1112 (2014)

Speeding up Planning in Multiagent Settings Using CPU-GPU Architectures

Fadel Adoe$^{(\boxtimes)}$, Yingke Chen, and Prashant Doshi

THINC Lab, Department of Computer Science, University of Georgia,
Athens, GA, USA
{fad777,ykchen,pdoshi}@uga.edu

Abstract. Planning under uncertainty in multiagent settings is highly intractable because of history and plan space complexities. Probabilistic graphical models exploit the structure of the problem domain to mitigate the computational burden. In this article, we introduce the first parallelization of planning in multiagent settings on a CPU-GPU heterogeneous system. In particular, we focus on the algorithm for exactly solving *interactive dynamic influence diagrams*, which is a recognized graphical models for multiagent planning. Beyond parallelizing the standard Bayesian inference and the computation of decisions' expected utilities, we also solve the other agents behavioral models in a parallel manner. The GPU-based approach provides significant speedup on two benchmark problems.

Keywords: GPU · Multiagent systems · Planning · Speed up

1 Introduction

Planning under uncertainty in multiagent settings is a very hard problem because it involves reasoning about the actions and observations of multiple agents simultaneously. In order to formally study this problem, the approach is to generalize single-agent planning frameworks such as the partially observable Markov decision process (POMDP) [15] to multiagent settings. This has led to the decentralized POMDP [2] for multiagent planning in cooperative settings and the interactive POMDP [7] for individual planning in cooperative or non-cooperative multiagent settings. A measure of the involved computational complexity is available by noting that the problem of solving a decentralized POMDP exactly for a finite number of steps is NEXP complete [1].

Some of the complexity of multiagent planning may be mitigated by exploiting the structure in the problem domain. Often, the state of the problem can be *factored* into random variables and the conditional independence between the variables may be naturally exploited by representing the planning problem using probabilistic graphical models. An example of such a model is the *interactive dynamic influence diagram* (I-DID) [5] that generalizes the well-known DID [8], which may be viewed as a graphical counterpart of POMDP, to multiagents

© Springer International Publishing Switzerland 2015
B. Duval et al. (Eds.): ICAART 2015, LNAI 9494, pp. 262–283, 2015.
DOI: 10.1007/978-3-319-27947-3_14

settings in the same way that an interactive POMDP generalizes the POMDP. In addition to modeling the problem structure, graphical models provide an intuitive language for representing the planning problem thereby serving as an important tool to enable multiagent planning.[1]

Emerging applications in automated vehicles that communicate [12], integration with the belief-desire-intention framework [4], and for ad hoc teamwork [3] motivate improved solutions of I-DIDs. While techniques exist for introducing further efficiency into solving I-DIDs [19], we may also explore parallelizing its solution algorithm on new high-performance computing architectures such as those utilizing graphic processing units (GPU). A GPU consists of an array of streaming multiprocessors (SM) connected to a shared memory. Each SM typically consists of a set of streaming processors. Consequently, a GPU supplements the CPU by enabling massive parallelization of simple computations that do not require excessive memory.

In addition to the usual chance, decision and utility nodes, I-DIDs include a new type of node called the model node and a new link called the policy link between the model node and a chance node that represents the distribution over the other agent's actions given its model. The algorithm for solving an I-DID expands a given two-time slice I-DID over multiple steps and collapses the I-DID into a flat DID. We may then use the standard sum-max-sum rule and a generalized variable elimination algorithm for IDs [10] to compute the maximum expected utilities of actions at each decision node to solve the I-DID. Multiple models in the model node are recursively solved in an analogous manner.

Our contribution in this article is ways of parallelizing multiple steps of the algorithm for exactly solving I-DIDs on CPU-GPU architectures. This promotes significantly faster planning on benchmark and large multiagent problems up to an order of magnitude in comparison to the run-time performance of the existing algorithm. Our approach is to parallelize three steps of this algorithm: (*i*) At a higher level, we distribute the solving of the multiple candidate models of the other agents among GPUs and obtain the solutions in parallel. (*ii*) The four operations involved in the sum-max-sum rule: max-marginalization (of decisions), sum-marginalization (of chance variables), factor-product (of probabilities and utilities) and factor-addition (of utilities) are parallelized on the GPU. (*iii*) Probability factors in the variable elimination could be large joints of the Bayesian network at each time slice, and we parallelize the message passing performed on a junction tree during the inference, on the GPU.

We evaluate the parallelized I-DID solution algorithm on two benchmark planning domains, and show more than an order of magnitude in speed up on some of the problems compared to the previous algorithm. To further speed up the solution algorithm, the algorithm extends to use two GPUs with MPI in the same system to solve the lower level models independently. This extension considerably increased the speed up factor. We evaluate on planning domains that differ in size of the state, action and observation spaces, and extend the planning

---

[1] A GUI-based software application called Netus is freely available from http://tinyurl.com/mwrtlvg for designing I-DIDs.

over longer horizons. In addition, we study the properties of our algorithm by allocating it increasing concurrency on the GPU and show that it's run time improves up to a point beyond which the gains are lost.

The rest of the article is organized as follows. Section 2 provides preliminaries about the I-DID and concepts of GPU-based programming. Section 3 reviews related work. Section 4 proposes a GPU-based approach to exactly solve the I-DID in parallel. Section 6 theoretically analyze the speed up. Section 7 demonstrates the speed up by the proposed approach on two problems. Section 8 concludes this article.

2 Background

In this section, we briefly review the probabilistic graphical model, DID, and its generalization to multiagent settings, I-DID. General principles behind GPU-based programming are also briefly described.

2.1 Dynamic Influence Diagram

A DID, $\mathcal{D}$, is a directed acyclic graph over a set of nodes: chance nodes $\mathbf{C}$ (ellipses), representing random variables; decision nodes $\mathbf{D}$ (rectangles), modeling the action choices; utility nodes $\mathbf{U}$ (diamonds), representing rewards based on chance and decision node values, and a set of arcs representing dependencies. Conditional probability distributions, $\mathbf{P}$, and utility functions, $\mathbf{R}$, are associated with the chance and utility nodes, respectively. In rest of the article, nodes and variables are used interchangeably.

The domain of a variable Q, denoted as $dom(Q)$, contains its possible values. The parent of Q, denoted as Pa_Q, is a set of variables having direct arcs incident on Q. The domain of Pa_Q, $dom(Pa_Q)$, is the Cartesian product of the individual domains: $dom(Pa_Q) = \prod_{Z \in Pa_Q} dom(Z)$, and a value of this domain is denoted as, pa_Q. A probability factor, $\phi(Q) = P(Q|Pa_Q)$, which defines conditional probability distribution given instantiation of parent variables, is attached to each chance variable $Q \in \mathbf{C}$. We use Ch_Q to denote Q's children. A utility factor, $\psi(U) = R(Pa_U)$, where R returns real-valued rewards, is associated with each utility node, $U \in \mathbf{U}$. The variables involved in a probability or utility factor become the domain of this factor, for example, $dom(\phi(Q)) = \{Q\} \cup Pa_Q$.

A policy for decision node, $D_i \in \mathbf{D}$, is a mapping, $\delta_i : dom(Pa_{D_i}) \rightarrow dom(D_i)$, i.e., $\delta_i(pa_{D_i}) = d_i$. A policy for the decision problem is a sequence of policies for all the decision nodes. The solution of a DID is a strategy that maximizes the expected value $MEU(\mathcal{D})$, computed using the *sum-max-sum rule* [10]:

$$\sum_{I_0} \max_{D_1} \sum_{I_1} \dots \max_{D_n} \sum_{I_n} (\prod_{Q_i \in \mathbf{C}} P(Q_i|Pa_{Q_i}) \cdot \sum_{\mathbf{C}, \mathbf{D}} R(\mathbf{C}, \mathbf{D}))$$

where $I_0, I_1, \dots, I_{n-1}$ is the set of chance variables incident on the decision nodes, $D_1, D_2, \dots, D_n$, thereby forming the information sets.

The MEU may be computed by repeatedly eliminating variables. Let Φ and Ψ be the set of probability and utility factors, respectively. Given variable Q, the probability and utility factors having Q in their domain are denoted as Φ_Q and Ψ_Q, respectively. After Q is eliminated, the factor sets are updated as follows:

$$\Phi = (\Phi \setminus \Phi_Q) \cup \{\phi_{\setminus Q}\} \text{ and } \Psi = (\Psi \setminus \Psi_Q) \cup \{\psi_{\setminus Q}/\phi_{\setminus Q}\}.$$

Here, $\phi_{\setminus Q} = \sum_Q \prod \Phi_Q$ and $\psi_{\setminus Q} = \sum_Q \prod \Phi_Q (\sum \Psi_Q)$ when Q is a chance variable; if Q is a decision variable, then, $\phi_{\setminus Q} = \max_Q \prod \Phi_Q$ and $\psi_{\setminus Q} = \max_Q \prod \Phi_Q (\sum \Psi_Q)$.

2.2 Interactive DID

Interactive DID (I-DID) [5] models an individual agent's planning (sequential decision making) in a multiagent setting. In a I-DID, other agents' candidate behaviors are modeled as they impact the common states and rewards during the subject agent's decision-making process. Simultaneously, other agents also reason about the subject agent's possible actions in their decision making. This recursive modeling is encoded in an auxiliary data item called the model node $M_{j,l-1}^t$ which contains models of the other agent, say j of level $l-1$ and chance node A_j which represents the distribution over j's actions. The link between $M_{j,l-1}^t$ and A_j^t, named as policy link, indicates that the other agent's predicted action is based on its models. The models can be DIDs, I-DIDs or simply probability distributions over actions. The link between $M_{j,l-1}^t$ and $M_{j,l-1}^{t+1}$, called model update link, represents the update of j's model over time.

Example 1 (Multiagent tiger problem [7]). Consider two agents standing in front of two closed doors with a tiger or some gold behind each door. If an agent opens a door with a tiger behind it, it receives a penalty, otherwise a reward. Agents can listen for growls to gain information about the tiger's location as well as hear creaks if the other agent opens a door. But, listening is not accurate. When the agent receives a reward or penalty, the game is reset. There is another agent j with the same character sharing the environment with agent i without noticing the existence of agent i. They receives reward or penalty together, therefore agent i needs to take into account agent j's behavior. A two time-slice I-DID for agent i situated in the multiagent tiger problem is depicted in Fig. 1.

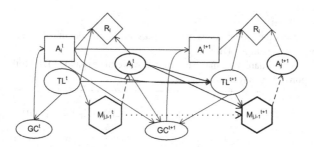

Fig. 1. A two time-slice I-DID for agent i in the tiger problem. Policy links are marked as dash lines, while model update links are marked as dotted lines. TL stands for '*Tiger Location*' and GC stands for '*Growl&Creak*'.

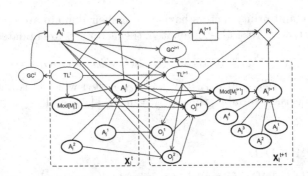

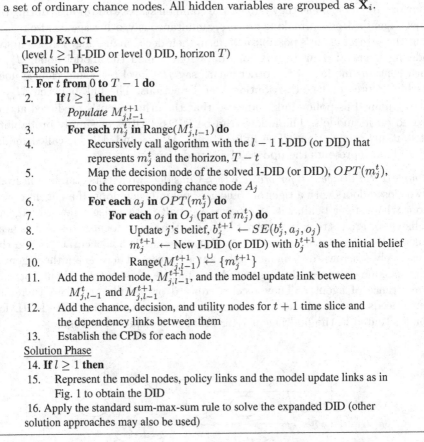

Fig. 2. The flat two time-slice DIDs for the tiger problem. Model nodes are replaced by a set of ordinary chance nodes. All hidden variables are grouped as $\mathbf{X}_i$.

I-DID EXACT

(level $l \geq 1$ I-DID or level 0 DID, horizon T)

Expansion Phase

1. **For** t **from** 0 **to** $T - 1$ **do**
2.   **If** $l \geq 1$ **then**
          Populate $M_{j,l-1}^{t+1}$
3.   **For each** m_j^t **in** Range($M_{j,l-1}^t$) **do**
4.   Recursively call algorithm with the $l - 1$ I-DID (or DID) that
             represents m_j^t and the horizon, $T - t$
5.   Map the decision node of the solved I-DID (or DID), $OPT(m_j^t)$,
             to the corresponding chance node A_j
6.   **For each** a_j **in** $OPT(m_j^t)$ **do**
7.   **For each** o_j **in** O_j (part of m_j^t) **do**
8.   Update j's belief, $b_j^{t+1} \leftarrow SE(b_j^t, a_j, o_j)$
9. $m_j^{t+1} \leftarrow$ New I-DID (or DID) with b_j^{t+1} as the initial belief
10.   Range($M_{j,l-1}^{t+1}$) $\overset{\cup}{\leftarrow} \{m_j^{t+1}\}$
11.   Add the model node, $M_{j,l-1}^{t+1}$, and the model update link between
          $M_{j,l-1}^t$ and $M_{j,l-1}^{t+1}$
12.   Add the chance, decision, and utility nodes for $t + 1$ time slice and
        the dependency links between them
13.   Establish the CPDs for each node

Solution Phase

14. **If** $l \geq 1$ **then**
15.   Represent the model nodes, policy links and the model update links as in
         Fig. 1 to obtain the DID
16. Apply the standard sum-max-sum rule to solve the expanded DID (other
solution approaches may also be used)

Fig. 3. Algorithm for exactly solving a level $l \geq 1$ I-DID or level 0 DID expanded over T time steps.

Solving an I-DID (shown in Fig. 3) requires solving the lower-level models, and this recursive procedure ends at level 0 where the I-DID reduces to a DID (Line 4). The policies from solving lower-level models are used to expand the next higher-level I-DID (Line 5–10). We may then replace the model nodes, policy and the model update links with regular chance nodes and dependency links. States of the nodes and parameters of the links are specified according to the obtained policies (Line 11–13). Subsequently, an I-DID becomes a regular DID, whose MEU is obtained (Line 15). Doshi and Zeng [5] provide more details about I-DIDs including an algorithm for solving it optimally.

Example 2. The I-DID shown in Fig. 1 is expanded as shown in Fig. 2. *GC* denotes a chance variable for observations of Growl&Creak, and the remaining chance nodes are grouped and denoted by $\mathbf{X}_i$ for convenience. The MEU is calculated as follows.

$$MEU[\mathcal{D}] = \sum_{\mathbf{X}_i^t} \max_{A_i^t} \sum_{GC^t} P(\mathbf{X}_i^t) P(GC^t | \mathbf{X}_i^t) \sum_{\mathbf{X}_i^{t+1}} \max_{A_i^{t+1}}$$
$$\sum_{GC^{t+1}} P(\mathbf{X}_i^{t+1} | \mathbf{X}_i^t, A_i^t) P(GC^{t+1} | \mathbf{X}_i^{t+1}) [R_i^t(A_i^t, \mathbf{X}_i^t) + R_i^{t+1}(A_i^{t+1}, \mathbf{X}_i^{t+1})]$$
$$(1)$$

2.3 CPU-GPU Architecture

Graphics processing units (GPUs) were originally designed for rendering computer graphics. In a GPU, there are a number of streaming multiprocesssors (SM), each containing a set of stream processors, registers and shared local memory (SMEM). At run time, a set of parallelized computation tasks referred to as a thread block are executed on a SM and distributed across the processors. In order to achieve good performance, it is crucial to map algorithms to the GPU architecture efficiently, which is optimized for high throughput. For example, designs that favor coalesced memory access are cost-effective. In the past decade, general purpose computing on the GPU has increased with a focus on bridging the gap between GPUs and CPUs by letting GPUs handle the most intensive computing while still leaving controlling tasks to CPU. CUDA provided by NVIDIA is a general-purpose parallel computing programming model for NVIDIA's GPUs. CUDA abstracts most operational details of GPU and alleviates the developer from the technical burden of GPU-oriented programming. An important component of a CUDA program is a *kernel*, which is a function that executes in parallel on a thread block.

3 Related Work

Multiple frameworks formalize planning under uncertainty in settings shared with other agents who may have similar or conflicting objectives. A recognized framework in this regard is the interactive POMDP [7] that facilitates the study of planning in partially observable multiagent settings where other agents may be cooperative or non-cooperative. I-DIDs [5] are a graphical counterpart of interactive POMDPs and have the advantage of a representation that explicates the embedded domain structure by decomposing the state space into variables and relationships between the variables.

I-DIDs contribute to a promising line of research on graphical models for multiagent decision making and planning, which includes multiagent influence diagrams (MAID) [11], networks of influence diagrams (NID) [6], and limited memory influence diagram based players [16]. I-DIDs differ from MAIDs and NIDs by offering a subjective perspective to the interaction and solutions not limited to equilibria, by ascribing other agents with a distribution of non-equilibrium behaviors as well. Importantly, I-DIDs offer solutions over extended time interactions, where agents act and update their beliefs over others' models which are themselves dynamic.

Previous uses of CPU-GPU heterogeneous systems in the context of graphical models focus on speeding up exact inference in Bayesian networks due to parallelization [9,17,18]. For example, Jeon et al. [9] report speedup factors in the range from 5 to 12 for both marginal and most probable inference in junction trees. *In comparison, we elevate the problem from performing inference in junction trees to finding optimal policies in I-DIDs and DIDs.* As solving I-DIDs requires performing inference on the underlying Bayesian network in each time slice, our approach also parallelizes exact inference using junction trees in a manner similar to previous work [20]. Additionally, we provide a fast method for evaluating the sum-max-sum rule for DIDs by parallelizing component operations such as sum-marginalization and others on a GPU.

4   Parallelized Planning Approach

Our approach revises the algorithm, I-DID Exact, presented in Fig. 3 by parallelizing two component steps for utilization on a CPU-GPU heterogeneous computing architecture and through leveraging some of the recent advances in parallelizing inference in Bayesian networks.

4.1   Parallelizing Solving Models in the I-DID

As we mentioned previously, models in $\mathcal{M}_{j,l-1}$, which is part of a level l I-DID, could be simple probability distributions, DIDs or I-DIDs with models in a level 1 I-DID being DIDs or probability distributions. These candidate models are differing hypotheses of the other agent's behavior, not linked, and therefore may be solved independently in parallel.

Consequently, we may distribute the solution of multiple models on the multiple GPU units. If we allocate one GPU unit to each I-DID, we may obtain a speed up factor that is about the same as the number of GPU units in the computing platform.

4.2   Parallelizing Sum-Max-Sum Rule for MEU

A solution of the sum-max-sum rule mentioned in Sect. 2 gives the maximum expected utility of the flat DID that results from transforming the I-DID. The temporal structure of the DID provides an ordering of the chance, decision and utility variables that is utilized by generalized variable elimination for IDs to compute the MEU. In our two-time slice DID for the multiagent tiger problem, the elimination ordering is: $\mathbf{X}^{t+1}$, $\mathbf{Y}^{t+1}$, A_i^{t+1}, $\mathbf{X}^t$, $\mathbf{Y}^t$, A_i^t, where $\mathbf{X}$ and $\mathbf{Y}$ are the sets of hidden variables and those in the information set of a decision variable in each time slice, respectively. The sum-max-sum rule does not specify an ordering between the variables $\mathbf{X}$ and $\mathbf{Y}$.

Memory-Efficient Variable Elimination for DIDs. In order to efficiently use the CPU-GPU memory, we design the variable elimination memory efficiently. Specifically, instead of keeping the entire DID in memory while performing variable elimination, we lazily bring the minimal set of the other variables and their factors that are needed in order to eliminate the variable in question. We refer to this set of variables as a *cover set*. We first revisit the definition of a Markov blanket of a variable.

Definition 1 (Markov Blanket, [13]). *The Markov blanket of a random variable Q, denoted as $MB(Q)$, is the minimal set of variables that makes Q conditionally independent of all other variables given $MB(Q)$. Formally, Q is conditionally independent of all other variables in the network given its parents, children, and children's parents.*

Definition 2 (Cover Set). *The cover set of a random variable, Q, denoted by $CS(Q)$ is defined as:*

$$CS(Q) = \{Q\} \cup MB(Q).$$

Notice that the cover set of Q consists of itself and its Markov blanket. Furthermore, we make the following straightforward observation:

Observation 1. $CS(Q)$ is exactly identical to the union of the domains of the factor of Q and the factors of the children of Q,

$$CS(Q) = dom(\phi_Q) \bigcup_{Z \in Ch_Q} dom(\phi_Z)$$

Let $\mathbf{X}$ be the set of variables in the elimination order that precedes Q. As the cover sets of variables in $\mathbf{X}$ would be in memory already, we define an *incremental cover set* below that is the set of all variables in the cover set less all those variables contained in the cover sets of the variables preceding Q in the elimination ordering.

Definition 3 (Incremental Cover Set). *The incremental cover set of a random variable, Q, denoted by $ICS(Q)$ is defined as:*

$$ICS(Q) = \{Q\} \cup MB(Q) \setminus \bigcup_{X \in \mathbf{X}} CS(X),$$

where $\mathbf{X}$ are the variables that preceded Q in the elimination ordering.

Factors related to variables in $ICS(Q)$ need to be additionally fetched into memory because the latter cover sets are already in memory and overlapping variables need not be fetched. Lemma 1 provides a simple way to determine the incremental cover set.

Lemma 1. *As variable elimination proceeds, let $\boldsymbol{F}_Q$ be the set of all factors not previously loaded in memory with Q in each of their domains. Then, the union of all variables in the domains of $\boldsymbol{F}_Q$, denoted as Δ_Q forms the incremental cover set of Q.*

Proof. For the *base case*, let Q be the first variable to be eliminated. The union of domains of all factors with Q in their domains is: $\Delta_Q = dom(\phi_1(\mathbf{X}_1)) \cup dom(\phi_2(\mathbf{X}_2)) \cup \ldots dom(\phi_n(X_n))$. We will show that $\forall y \in \mathbf{X}_i$, $y \in MB(Q)$ or $y = Q$ for $i \in [1, n]$. Suppose that $\exists y \in \mathbf{X}_i$ and $y \notin MB(Q)$ and $y \neq Q$. Given the definition of the Markov blanket, y is not a child of Q or parent of a child of Q. Therefore, from Observation 1, the corresponding factor, ϕ_i, cannot contain Q in its domain. This is a contradiction and no such y exists. Therefore, $\forall y \in \mathbf{X}_i$, $y \in MB(Q)$ or y is Q.

Let Q_k be the kth variable to be eliminated. As the *inductive hypothesis*, $\Delta_{Q_k} = \{Q_k\} \cup MB(Q_k) \setminus \bigcup_{X \in \mathbf{X}} CS(X)$. For the *inductive step*, let Q_{k+1} be the next variable to be eliminated. Notice that

$$\Delta_{Q_k} = \Delta_{Q_{k+1}} \cup CS(Q_k) \cup dom(\Phi_{Q_k \setminus Q_{k+1}}) \setminus dom(\Phi_{Q_{k+1} \setminus Q_k})$$

where $\Phi_{Q_k \setminus Q_{k+1}}$ are the factors with Q_k in their domains and not Q_{k+1} – these would be absent from $\Delta_{Q_{k+1}}$ – and $\Phi_{Q_{k+1} \setminus Q_k}$ are the factors with Q_{k+1} and not Q_k in their domains.
We may rewrite the above as:

$$\begin{aligned}\Delta_{Q_{k+1}} &= \Delta_{Q_k} \cup dom(\Phi_{Q_{k+1} \setminus Q_k}) \setminus dom(\Phi_{Q_k \setminus Q_{k+1}}) \setminus CS(Q_k) \\ &= dom(\Phi_{Q_{k+1} \setminus Q_k}) \cup \Delta_{Q_k} \setminus dom(\Phi_{Q_k \setminus Q_{k+1}}) \setminus CS(Q_k)\end{aligned}$$

As Δ_{Q_k} denotes the domains of all factors with Q_k and additionally, with Q_{k+1} being present or absent, $\Delta_{Q_k} = dom(\Phi_{Q_k, Q_{k+1}}) \cup dom(\Phi_{Q_k \setminus Q_{k+1}}) \setminus \bigcup_{X \in \mathbf{X}} CS (X)$. Using this in the above equation,

$$\begin{aligned}\Delta_{Q_{k+1}} &= dom(\Phi_{Q_{k+1} \setminus Q_k}) \cup dom(\Phi_{Q_k, Q_{k+1}}) \cup dom(\Phi_{Q_k \setminus Q_{k+1}}) \setminus dom(\Phi_{Q_k \setminus Q_{k+1}}) \\ &\quad \setminus \bigcup_{X \in \mathbf{X}} CS(X) \setminus CS(Q_k) \\ &= dom(\Phi_{Q_{k+1} \setminus Q_k}) \cup dom(\Phi_{Q_k, Q_{k+1}}) \setminus \bigcup_{X \in \mathbf{X}} CS(X) \setminus CS(Q_k) \\ &= dom(\Phi_{Q_{k+1}}) \setminus \bigcup_{X \in \mathbf{X} \cup Q_k} CS(X)\end{aligned}$$

We may apply a proof similar to that in the base case to the first term above. Therefore,

$$\Delta_{Q_{k+1}} = \{Q_{k+1}\} \cup MB(Q_{k+1}) \setminus \bigcup_{X \in \mathbf{X} \cup Q_k} CS(X) = ICS(Q_{k+1})$$

Next, we establish the benefits and correctness of solely considering the cover set of Q in Theorem 1. We define the joint probability distribution of the variables in the cover set first.

Definition 4 (Factored Joint Probability Distribution of Cover Set). *The factored joint probability distribution for a cover set of a random variable, Q, is defined as:*

$$P(Q|Pa_Q) \prod_{Z \in Ch_Q} P(Z|Pa_Z)$$

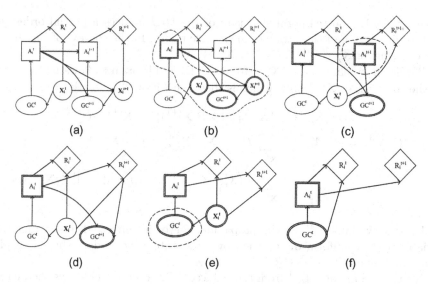

Fig. 4. An illustration of variable elimination for DIDs. The incremental cover set for each variable is marked using a dashed line. In $(a-f)$, the DID is progressively reduced following the elimination order: $\{\mathbf{X}_i^{t+1}, A_i^{t+1}, GC^{t+1}, \mathbf{X}_i^{t}\}$.

Theorem 1. *Let Φ_Q (Ψ_Q) be a set of relevant probability (or utility) factors required to compute the new factor ϕ_Q (ψ_Q) for eliminating variable Q. All the variables in the domain of Φ_Q (Ψ_Q) exactly comprise the cover set of Q, $CS(Q)$.*

Proof. The set of relevant probability factors Φ_Q can be separated into two categories: $P(Q|Pa_Q)$ and $P(X|Pa_X)$ where $X \in Ch_Q$. Consequently, the variable in domains of factors in Φ_Q are included in $Pa_Q \cup Ch_Q \bigcup_{Z \in Ch_Q} Pa_Z \cup \{Q\}$, which is the cover set of Q by definition.

Assume there exists a variable $Y \neq Q$, $Y \in CS(Q)$ and Y does not appear in either $P(Q|Pa_Q)$ or $P(X|Pa_X)$ where $X \in Ch_Q$. In other words, $Y \notin Pa_Q$, $Y \notin Ch_Q$ and $Y \notin \bigcup_{Z \in Ch_Q} Pa_Z$. Consequently, $Y \notin MB(Q)$. As $Y \neq Q$, therefore $Y \notin CS(Q)$, but this is a contradiction. Therefore, all variables in $CS(Q)$ appear in the relevant factors. A similar argument is applicable to the utility factors Ψ_Q.

Thus, the cover set of a variable, Q, locally identifies those variables whose factors change on eliminating Q. These factors contain Q in their domains. The alternative is a naive global method that searches over all factors and identifies those with Q in their domains. We illustrate the use of the cover set in eliminating chance and decision variables in the context of the multiagent tiger problem below.

Example 3 (Variable Elimination Using Cover Set). The two-time slice flat DID is shown in Fig. 4(a). For clarity, the hidden chance variables in each time slice are replaced with $\mathbf{X}_i$ thereby compacting the DID. The MEU for the DID is given by Eq. 1. The temporal structure of the DID induces a partial ordering for the elimination of the variables in the rule above. In the context of Fig. 4(a), this ordering is: $\mathbf{X}_i^{t+1}$, A_i^{t+1}, GC^{t+1}, $\mathbf{X}_i^t$, A_i^t, GC^t.

We begin by eliminating $\mathbf{X}_i^{t+1}$ from the DID. Theorem 1 allows us to focus on the cover set of $\mathbf{X}_i^{t+1}$ only, which is shown in Fig. 4(b).

$$CS(\mathbf{X}_i^{t+1}) \leftarrow \{\mathbf{X}_i^{t+1}\} \bigcup MB(\mathbf{X}_i^{t+1})\} = \{\mathbf{X}_i^{t+1}, GC^{t+1}, \mathbf{X}_i^t, A_i^t\}$$

$$\psi_1(GC^{t+1}, \mathbf{X}_i^t, A_i^t, A_i^{t+1}) = \sum_{\mathbf{X}_i^{t+1}} P(CS(\mathbf{X}_i^{t+1})) R_i^{t+1}(A_i^{t+1}, \mathbf{X}_i^{t+1})$$

$$= \sum_{\mathbf{X}_i^{t+1}} P(\mathbf{X}_i^{t+1}, GC^{t+1} | \mathbf{X}_i^t, A_i^t) \times R_i^{t+1}(A_i^{t+1}, \mathbf{X}_i^{t+1})$$

Decision variable, A_i^t, in the probability factor is converted into a random variable with a uniform distribution over its states. We update the set of all utility factors as: $\Psi \leftarrow \{\psi_1(GC^{t+1}, \mathbf{X}_i^t, A_i^t, A_i^{t+1})\}$.

Next, we eliminate A_i^{t+1} from the reduced DID. Figure 4(c) shows the incremental cover set of A_i^{t+1} with the dashed loop: A_i^{t+1} and its factors additionally need to be fetched into memory.

$$CS(A_i^{t+1}) \leftarrow \{A_i^{t+1}, GC^{t+1}, A_i^t\}$$

$$\psi_2(GC^{t+1}, \mathbf{X}_i^t, A_i^t) = \max_{A_i^{t+1}} \psi_1(GC^{t+1}, \mathbf{X}_i^t, A_i^t, A_i^{t+1})$$

The set of utility factors updates to $\Psi \leftarrow \{\psi_2(GC^{t+1}, \mathbf{X}_i^t, A_i^t)\}$.

The DID reduces to the one shown in Fig. 4(d), from which we now eliminate GC^{t+1}. The incremental cover set of this variable is empty as all the variables in its cover set were utilized previously and preexist in memory.

$$CS(GC^{t+1}) \leftarrow \{GC^{t+1}, A_i^t\}$$

$$\psi_3(\mathbf{X}_i^t, A_i^t) = \sum_{GC^{t+1}} P(GC^{t+1} | A_i^t) \, \psi_2(GC^{t+1}, \mathbf{X}_i^t, A_i^t)$$

The set of utility factors now becomes: $\Psi \leftarrow \{\psi_3(\mathbf{X}_i^t, A_i^t)\}$.

Finally, we eliminate $\mathbf{X}_i^t$ and GC^t after fetching GC^t (and its factors) into memory.

$$CS(\mathbf{X}_i^t) \leftarrow \{\mathbf{X}_i^t, GC^t\}$$

$$\psi_4(A_i^t, GC^t) = \sum_{\mathbf{X}_i^t} P(GC^t | \mathbf{X}_i^t) \, [R_i^t(\mathbf{X}_i^t, A_i^t) + \psi_3(\mathbf{X}_i^t, A_i^t)]$$

The utility factor set becomes $\Psi \leftarrow \{\psi_4(A_i^t, GC^t)\}$.

Maximizing over A_i^t and sum marginalization of GC^t will yield an empty factor set and the decision that maximizes the expected utility of the DID.

Speeding up Factor Operations Using GPU. We perform the product operation between probability and utility factors in parallel on a GPU.

The operation is a pointwise product of the entries in factors. When there are common variables, only entries with the same value of the common variables is multiplied. For convenience, we denote $R_i^t(\mathbf{X}_i^t, A_i^t) + \psi_3(\mathbf{X}_i^t, A_i^t)$ simply as $\psi_3'(\mathbf{X}_i^t, A_i^t)$.

In order to parallelize the factor product, indices of entries to be multiplied in the factors are needed. Previous parallelization of inference in Bayesian networks sought to minimize the size of the index mapping table for GPUs [9] due to the SM memory limitation. The entire mapping table was decomposed into smaller ones each giving the mapped indices of the entries in the second factor for each non-common variable in the first factor. Our utility factor product follows the similar principle of message passing for belief propagation in junction trees.

Entries in a factor are indexed according to variables as $index = \sum_{Q \in dom(\psi)} state_Q \times stride_Q$. The stride of a variable X_i in a factor, $P(X_0, \ldots, X_n)$ is defined as $stride_{X_0} = 1$ and $stride_{X_i} = stride_{X_{i-1}} \cdot |dom(X_{i-1})|$, for $i \in [1, n]$. We also define an entry's state vector as $\langle state_1, \ldots, state_n \rangle$. Here, $n = |dom(\mathbf{X}_i^t)||dom(GC^t)|$, and $state_Q = \lfloor \frac{index}{stride_Q} \rfloor \mod |dom(Q)|$. A tag for an entry is the portion of the state vector pertaining to common variables.

A thread in a SM is allocated to finding the entries of the second factor with which we may multiply a probability value in the first factor as we show in Fig. 5. We allocate as many threads as the number of distinct entries in the first factor until no more threads are available, in which case multiple entries may be assigned to the same thread. Indices for the entries whose tags match the tag of the subject entry in the first factor are obtained and the corresponding products are performed. Because the index is needed repeatedly, it is beneficial to investigate efficient ways of computing it. Notice that the $index$ values can be computed as: $index = \sum_{Q \in c.\ v.} state_Q \times stride_Q + \sum_{Q \in dom(\psi)/c.\ v.} state_Q \times stride_Q$, here c.v. stands for common variables.

As a particular thread must find entries with the same tag, we compute the first summation in the above equation once, cache it and then reuse it in finding the indices of the other entries. As illustrated in Fig. 5(a), each thread saves on computing the first summation two times because the noncommon variable, A_i^t, has three states, thereby saving $\mathcal{O}(|\mathbf{X}_i^t|)$ each time which gets substantial in the context of factor products that have a large number of common variables.

Factor products in the sum-max-sum rule are usually followed by sum marginalization operations. For example, the last variable elimination shown in Fig. 4 marginalizes the set of variables in $\mathbf{X}_i^t$ that includes tiger_location^t, A_j^t, $Mod[M_j^t]$, among others, from the factor, $P(\mathbf{X}_i^t, GC^t) \times \psi_3'(\mathbf{X}_i^t, A_i^t)$. Let us denote the resulting product factor as, $\psi_{34}(\mathbf{X}_i^t, GC^t, A_i^t)$. For illustration purposes, let us focus on marginalizing a single variable, $A_j^t \in \mathbf{X}_i^t$ from $\psi_{34}(\mathbf{X}_i^t, GC^t, A_i^t)$.

We parallelize and speed up sum-marginalization by allowing a separate thread to sum those entries in the factor that correspond to the different values of A_j^t while keeping the other variable values fixed [20] (Fig. 5(b)).

Parallelizing Message Passing in the BN. Probability factors utilized during variable elimination for computing the MEU of the flat DID often involve

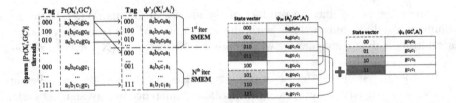

Fig. 5. (a) The index mapping table. We assume that all variables are binary. SMEM denotes shared memory. (b) Four threads are used to produce the entries in the four rows of the resulting factor, ψ_4, on the right.

joint probability distributions. For example, the factor $P(\mathbf{X}_i^t, GC^t)$ utilized in the elimination of $\mathbf{X}_i^t$ is the joint distribution over the multiple variables in $\mathbf{X}_i^t$ and GC^t. We may efficiently compute the probability factor tables by forming a junction tree of the Bayesian network in each time slice, and computing the joints using message passing [20].

Analogously to the operations involved in variable elimination, message passing in a junction tree involves sum-marginalization and factor products. However, the typical order of these operations in message passing is the reverse of those in the sum-max-sum rule: we perform marginalizations first followed by factor products. These operations are part of the marginalization and scattering steps that constitute message passing.

We parallelize message passing in junction trees to efficiently compute the probability factors. Both sum-marginalizations and factor products are performed on a CPU-GPU heterogeneous system by utilizing multiple threads in a SM each of which computes the relevant index mapping tables *online* and performs the products as we described previously in Fig. 5(a) and (b). This is similar to the approach of Zheng et al. [20] that decomposes the whole index mapping table into smaller components that are relevant to each thread. However, the latter precomputes tables while forming the junction trees and stores them in memory.

5   Algorithm Design

The expansion phase of the I-DID EXACT algorithm in Fig. 3 is multi-threaded in order to solve the models in $\mathcal{M}_j^{t-1}$ in parallel. We utilize as many threads as the number of GPUs in the system. The MEU of a flat DID is computed using the sum-max-sum rule. Factor product and sum-marginalization operations are parallelized by wrapping them in a GPU kernel function. This launches one or more blocks of threads for performing the products and sums of probabilities and utilities. The task of solving the lower level models are fairly partitioned among the two processors each linked to a GPU.

For the message passing performed on the junction tree, a CPU routine call selects the relevant cliques, which are nodes in the junction tree, for processing. It computes the required parameters for cliques involved in the current

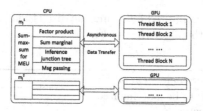

Fig. 6. An abstract view of the parallelization of MEU computation for solving a DID. Lower-level models are distributed across a multiprocesssor CPU-GPU system using MPI.

Algorithm 1. Factor Product on GPU.

Require: probability factor ϕ and utility factor ψ
Ensure: product factor ψ'
1: *tid* is the thread id
2: *numIter* is the number of iterations
3: *workSize* is the number of products per thread
4: **for** $i \leftarrow 1$ to *numIter* **parallel do**
5:     *begLoadIdx* ← begin offset
6:     *endLoadIdx* ← end offset
7:     $SMEM \leftarrow \psi[begLoadIdx...endLoadIdx]$
8:     **for** $j \leftarrow 1$ to *workSize* **parallel do**
9:         *iidx* is the input index
10:       *oidx* is the output index
11:       $\psi'[oidx] \leftarrow \phi[tid] * SMEM[iidx]$
12:     **end for**
13: **end for**

---

communication, and asynchronously transmits the result to the GPU. After all parameters are computed, a GPU block of threads is launched to compute and propagate the message to a recipient clique.

Before running the algorithm, CUDA requires the kernel to be appropriately configured: in terms of grid size and shape, shared memory and registers utilization. We note three choices: (1) fixing thread block size in order to utilize more registers; (2) minimizing the number of registers to possibly achieve high occupancy; and (3) finding shared memory size per block to minimize global memory accesses. Quick experimentation revealed that for both the factor operations and the message passing algorithm, fixing the number of registers to 32 and using shared memory chunk size of 512 were suitable. For effective allocation of memory, we allocate large chunks of memory at program start, and all GPU memory allocation requests use one of these chunks of memory. If more memory is requested than chunks available, a chunk is reallocated to possibly accommodate the request.

Algorithms 1 and 2 provide the steps for performing the factor product and the sum-marginalization, respectively, on the GPU. In Algorithm 1, the utility factor is divided and loaded into shared memory. The input and output indices in both algorithms are computed following the discussion in Sect. 4.1.2. We show the abstract design of the algorithm in Fig. 6.

Algorithm 2. Sum-marginalization on GPU.

Require: ψ which needs to be marginalized
Ensure: the resulting factor ψ'
1: tid is the thread id
2: $workSize$ is the number of additions per thread
3: $sum \leftarrow 0$
4: **for** $j \leftarrow 1$ to $workSize$ **parallel do**
5:     $iidx \leftarrow$ index to ψ
6:     $sum \leftarrow sum + \psi[iidx]$
7: **end for**
8: $oidx \leftarrow$ output index to ψ'
9: $\psi'[oidx] \leftarrow sum$

---

6   Theoretical Analysis of Speed up

We theoretically analyze the speed up resulting from parallelizing the factor product, sum-marginalization and factor sum operations that are involved in computing the MEU. Let ϕ_Q and ψ_Q be some probability and utility factors involving chance variable, Q, respectively, and $\mathcal{S}_{\phi_Q\psi_Q}$ denote the set of variables in common between the domains of the two factors. Then, $dom(\psi_Q) - \mathcal{S}_{\phi_Q\psi_Q}$ is the set of variables in ψ that are not in ϕ. In multiplying the two factors, the number of independent products are:

$$\mathcal{FP}_{\phi_Q\psi_Q} = \begin{cases} |\phi_Q||\psi_Q|/|\mathcal{S}_{\phi_Q\psi_Q}| & \text{if } |\mathcal{S}_{\phi_Q\psi_Q}| > 0; \\ |\phi_Q||\psi_Q| & \text{otherwise.} \end{cases}$$

Our approach parallelizes the above factor product using $|\phi_Q|$ threads, with each thread performing $\frac{|\psi_Q|}{|\mathcal{S}_{\phi_Q\psi_Q}|}$ products if $|\mathcal{S}_{\phi_Q\psi_Q}| > 0$ otherwise $|\psi_Q|$. Analogously, the number of independent sums are:

$$\mathcal{FS}_{\psi'_Q\psi_Q} = \begin{cases} |\psi'_Q||\psi_Q|/|\mathcal{S}_{\psi'_Q\psi_Q}| & \text{if } |\mathcal{S}_{\psi'_Q\psi_Q}| > 0; \\ |\psi'_Q||\psi_Q| & \text{otherwise.} \end{cases}$$

For marginalization of a utility factor ψ_Q over a random variable Q in its domain, the number of independent maximizations are $|\psi_Q|/|dom(Q)|$, where $dom(Q)$ gives the number of states of the variable, Q. We assign a thread to each independent maximization.

Let $\mathbf{C}$, $\mathbf{D}$ and $\mathbf{U}$ denote the sets of decision, chance and utility variables respectively in the DID. We begin by establishing the time complexity of evaluating the sum-max-sum rule serially on a flat DID. Overall, this requires summing utility factors, whose complexity is $\sum_{Q \in \mathbf{U}} \mathcal{FS}_{\psi'_Q\psi_Q} = \mathcal{O}(|\mathbf{U}||\psi'_Q||\psi_Q|/|\mathcal{S}_{\psi'_Q\psi_Q}|)$;

performing as many factor products as there are chance variables, whose time complexity is $\sum_{Q \in C} \mathcal{FP}_{\phi_Q \psi_Q} = \mathcal{O}(|\mathbf{C}||\phi_Q||\psi_Q|/|\mathcal{S}_{\phi_Q \psi_Q}|)$; sum-marginalization of the chance variables in probability factors with complexity, $\mathcal{O}(|\mathbf{C}||\phi_Q|)$; and the maximization over the decision variables, whose complexity is $\mathcal{O}(|\mathbf{D}||\psi_{D^*}|)$. The total complexity for the serial computation is

$$\mathcal{O}((|\mathbf{U}|\frac{|\psi_Q'||\psi_Q|}{|\overline{\mathcal{S}}_{\psi_Q' \psi_Q}|}) + |\mathbf{C}||\phi_Q|(\frac{|\psi_Q|}{|\overline{\mathcal{S}}_{\phi_Q \psi_Q}|} + 1) + |\mathbf{D}||\psi_{\overline{D}}|).$$

Here, ψ' denotes an expected utility; $\overline{\mathcal{S}}_{\phi_Q \psi_Q}, \overline{\mathcal{S}}_{\phi_Q \psi_Q}$ are the smallest sets of shared variables between probability and utility factors respectively; $\overline{D}$ is the decision variable with the largest utility factor to maximize over.

Each parallelized utility sum operation has a theoretical time of $\mathcal{FS}_{\psi_Q' \psi_Q} |\psi_Q|$; the parallelized factor product requires a time of $\mathcal{FS}_{\phi_Q \psi_Q} |\phi_Q|$; the parallelized sum-marginalization requires a time of $|\phi_Q|/|dom(Q)|$; and the parallelized max-marginalization requires a time of $|\psi_D|/|dom(D)|$ units. Consequently, the total complexity for the parallel computation is:

$$\mathcal{O}(\kappa + (|\mathbf{U}|\frac{|\psi_Q|}{|\overline{\mathcal{S}}_{\psi_Q' \psi_Q}|}) + |\mathbf{C}|(\frac{|\psi_Q|}{|\overline{\mathcal{S}}_{\phi_Q \psi_Q}|} + 1) + \frac{|\mathbf{D}||\psi_{\overline{D}}|}{|dom(\underline{D})|})$$

where $\underline{D}$ is the decision variable with the smallest domain size and κ, which is a function of the size of the network, is the total cost for kernel invocations and memory latency in the GPU.

Lemma 2 (Speed Up). *The speed up of evaluating the sum-max-sum rule for a flat DID with set, $\mathbf{C}$, of chance variables, $\mathbf{D}$ of decision variables, and $\mathbf{U}$ of utility variables is upper bounded by:*

$$\frac{(|\mathbf{U}|\frac{|\psi_Q'||\psi_Q|}{|\overline{\mathcal{S}}_{\psi_Q' \psi_Q}|}) + |\mathbf{C}||\phi_Q|(\frac{|\psi_Q|}{|\overline{\mathcal{S}}_{\phi_Q \psi_Q}|} + 1) + |\mathbf{D}||\psi_{\overline{D}}|}{\kappa + (|\mathbf{U}|\frac{|\psi_Q|}{|\overline{\mathcal{S}}_{\psi_Q' \psi_Q}|}) + |\mathbf{C}|(\frac{|\psi_Q|}{|\overline{\mathcal{S}}_{\phi_Q \psi_Q}|} + 1) + \frac{|\mathbf{D}||\psi_{\overline{D}}|}{|dom(\underline{D})|}}$$

where ψ' denotes an expected utility; $\overline{\mathcal{S}}_{\phi_Q \psi_Q}, \overline{\mathcal{S}}_{\phi_Q \psi_Q}$ are the smallest sets of shared variables between probability and utility factors respectively; $\overline{D}$ is the decision variable with the largest utility factor to maximize over; $\underline{D}$ is the decision variable with the smallest domain size and κ, which is a function of the size of the network, is the total cost for kernel invocations and memory latency in the GPU.

Next, we formulate the speed up due to solving $|M_j|$ level 0 models (DIDs) across P GPUs.

Theorem 2 (Speed up). *The speed up of solving a level 1 I-DID on multiple GPUs is upper bounded by:*

$$\frac{T_s|M_j| + Exp + T_s'}{\frac{T_p}{P}|M_j| + Exp + T_p'}$$

where T_s, T_p are the serial and parallel run times respectively for evaluating a lower level model. In our context, T_s and T_p are the numerator and the denominator of the expression in Lemma 2 respectively. Exp, which remains unchanged under parallelization, is the time taken for expanding the I-DID into a flat DID. T_s', T_p' are the run times for evaluating the resulting DID after expanding the I-DID. $|M_j|$ is the number of level 0 models ascribed by the subject agent to the other agent and P is the number of GPUs.

7   Experiments

In this section we empirically evaluate the performance and scalability of Parallelized I-DID Exact on different networks against its serial implementation I-DID Exact. Experiments were performed on a desktop with four Intel quad-core CPUs (3.10 GHz), 16 GB RAM and two NVIDIA Geforce GTX480 graphics card with 480 cores, 1.5 GB global memory and 64KB of shared memory for each SM.

Besides the tiger problem ($|S|=2$, $|A_i|=|A_j|=3$, $|\Omega_i|=6$ and $|\Omega_j|=2$), we also evaluated the proposed approach on a larger problem domain: the two-agent unmanned aerial vehicle (UAV) interception problem ($|S_i|=25$, $|S_j|=9$, $|A_i|=|A_j|=5$, $|\Omega_i|=|\Omega_j|=5$). In this problem, there is a UAV and a fugitive with noisy sensors and unreliable actuators locating in a 3×3 grid. The fugitive j plans to reach the safe house while avoiding detection by the hostile UAV i [19].

7.1   Performance Evaluation

For the Tiger problem, different numbers of (10, 50, and 100) level 0 DIDs with the number of planning horizons from 6 to 9 are solved and used to expand the level 1 I-DIDs of 3 to 5 horizons. The average factor sizes increases along with the number of horizons. For the single (multiple) GPU implementation, the mean speed up ranges between 6 (14) and slightly greater than 10 (23), with I-DIDs of longer horizon demonstrating greater speed up in their solution. We also observe *super-linear* speed up when two GPUs on the same system are used. Our investigations into this phenomena reveal that the super-linear speed up can be attributed to the computations that occur on the CPU and is most likely due to the fast caching and retrieval of the common components in the models. Due to the complexity of the UAV domain and limited global memory, the current implementation solves the problem optimally up to horizon 3. However, parallelized I-DID Exact (with or without parallelized candidate model solving) still provides promising speedups. Problems with larger factors, which contain more common variables, show greater speedups.

All experiment results are summarized in Tables 1 and 2. The I-DIDs for the different problem domains unrolled to different look ahead (T_1) with different number of level 0 models (the column $|M_j|$) at different look aheads (T_0) were used to evaluate the performance of the proposed algorithm. The average sizes of factors processed during variable elimination, including probability and utility factors, of level 0 and level 1 models are listed in columns titled by $|\overline{\phi}|$ and $|\overline{\psi}|$.

Table 1. Run times, factor sizes and speed ups for the multiagent tiger problem. $|M_j|$ denotes the number of level 0 models. $\overline{|\phi|}$ and $\overline{|\psi|}$ are the round average sizes of probability and utility factors in the models $(\times 10^3)$, respectively. Columns titled by CPU, GPU and GPU+MPI denote the running times for the serial (CPU only), single GPU, and two GPUs implementations respectively. The speedups are listed in the last two columns. SpUP denotes the speedup using single GPU and SpUP_MPI represents the speedup using two GPUs with MPI.

$|M_j|$	Level 1			Level 0			Time (seconds)			SpUP	SpUP_MPI
	T_1	$\overline{|\phi|}$	$\overline{|\psi|}$	T_0	$\overline{|\phi|}$	$\overline{|\psi|}$	CPU	GPU	GPU+MPI		
10	3	1959	2237	6	2192	1703	3.1	0.5	0.2	6.2	14.2
				7	11126	8620	17.8	1.9	0.9	9.2	20.5
				8	58835	45556	106	10.2	4.7	10.4	22.5
				9	306284	237130	644	60.0	27.8	10.8	23.2
	4	38376	44998	6	2192	1703	5.6	0.8	0.5	7.3	11.6
				7	11126	8620	20.3	2.2	1.1	9.3	17.9
				8	58835	45556	108	10.5	5.0	10.3	21.9
				9	306284	237130	647	60.0	28.1	10.8	23.0
	5	600493	655141	6	2192	1703	50.0	5.1	4.9	9.8	10.2
				7	11126	8620	64.7	6.5	5.5	10.0	11.7
				8	58835	45556	153	14.7	9.4	10.4	16.3
				9	306284	237130	691	64.3	32.5	10.7	21.2
50	3	5449	5307	6	2192	1703	13.7	1.8	0.9	7.5	15.7
				7	11126	8620	80.5	8.2	4.1	9.8	19.5
				8	58835	45556	481	46.0	23.2	10.5	20.7
				9	306284	237130	2930	272	140	10.8	21.0
	4	63225	65249	6	2192	1703	16.1	2.1	1.1	7.7	14.4
				7	11126	8620	83.0	8.5	4.4	9.8	18.9
				8	58835	45556	484	45.9	23.5	10.5	20.5
				9	306284	237130	2931	272	139	10.7	21.1
	5	672794	683530	6	2192	1703	60.5	6.44	5.7	9.4	10.9
		879830	910980	7	11126	8620	127	12.7	8.8	10.0	14.5
				8	58835	45556	528	50.6	27.9	10.4	18.9
				9	306284	237130	2972	277	144	10.7	20.7
100	3	5546	5322	6	2192	1703	27.4	3.6	1.7	7.7	16.1
				7	11126	8620	162.5	16.3	8.2	9.9	19.8
				8	58835	45556	971	92.8	46.3	10.4	20.9
				9	306284	237130	5937	573	285	10.3	20.8
	4	63294	65260	6	2192	1703	29.9	3.8	2.0	7.8	15.3
				7	11126	8620	164.9	16.7	8.4	9.8	19.5
				8	58835	45556	974	92.4	46.6	10.5	20.9
				9	306284	237130	5937	569	285	10.7	20.8
	5	672848	683538	6	2192	1703	74.3	8.1	6.37	9.2	11.6
		879884	910989	7	11126	8620	209	21.0	12.9	9.9	16.2
				8	58835	45556	1018	96.8	51.0	10.5	20.0
				9	306284	237130	5975	575	288	10.4	20.7

Table 2. Run times, factor sizes and speed ups for the multiagent UAV problem. Columns have similar meanings.

$|M_j|$	Level 1			Level 0			Time (seconds)				
	T_1	$|\phi|$	$|\psi|$	T_0	$|\phi|$	$|\psi|$	CPU	GPU	GPU+MPI	SpUP	SpUP_MPI
10	3	104223	75120	3	1235	1029	16.6	2.2	2.1	**7.5**	**8.0**
				4	20237	9467	24.4	3.2	2.5	**7.7**	**9.6**
				5	392043	170405	239	27.6	13.5	**8.7**	**17.7**
25	3	106410	75270	3	1235	1029	16.9	2.3	2.1	**7.4**	**8.0**
				4	20237	9467	32.6	4.2	3.2	**7.7**	**10.3**
				5	392043	170405	462	55.6	28.6	**8.8**	**16.2**
50	3	209573	117520	3	1235	1029	17.5	2.4	2.2	**7.3**	**8.0**
		212260	117695	4	20237	9467	46.6	6.0	4.1	**7.7**	**11.5**
		153348	81195	5	392043	170405	845	99.3	51.0	**8.5**	**16.6**

Columns labeled by CPU, GPU and GPU+MPI contain the total running times, which include the time for solving level 0 models, expanding the level 1 I-DIDs into flat DIDs, and solving the resulting level 1 models. The speedup is indicated in the last two columns titled with SpUP and SpUP_MPI. As observed, the benefits of parallelizing the computation of MEU and having multiple GPUs to solve lower level models are demonstrated.

As suggested in Theorem 2, the theoretical speedup, for these two domains are $70/(\kappa+22)$ and $450/(\kappa+28)$, respectively, where κ is the total cost for kernel invocations and memory latency in the GPU. As the tiger problem is a small domain, the cost of data transmission is negligible, and the lower bound can be seen as approximately 4. However for the larger UAV problem, a comparison with the reported empirical speedup shows that κ is not negligible.

Figure 7 shows the speedup for the Tiger and the UAV domain with different problem sizes. Overall, the speed up in planning optimally increases as the sizes of the level 1 and level 0 planning problems increase. Varying the number of candidate models (DIDs) ascribed to the other agent did not significantly impact the speedup. This is expected as the lower-level models are solved independently. However, the parallelization of their solutions on two GPUs with MPI increased the speedup factor considerably. Note that the overall speedup decreases when level 0 models are solved in parallel given level 1 models of increasing horizon. The reason is that the expanded level 1 models are solved by single GPU.

7.2 Optimizing Thread Block Size

By parallelizing the computation on the GPU, we observed around an order of magnitude speedup through the performed experiments. As computation tasks are organized as a set of thread blocks and executed on SMs, the number of thread blocks determines the overall performance. Generally speaking, more thread blocks will increase the degree of parallelization with higher synchronization cost. Automatically calculating the optimal thread-block sizes [14],

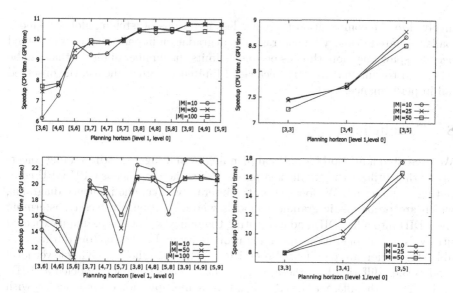

Fig. 7. The speedup for the multiagent tiger problem (the first column) and the UAV problem (the second column) given different amount of level 0 models and number of decision horizons. Results shown in figures in the first row are obtained by using single GPU, while the ones in the second row are obtained by using multiple GPUs.

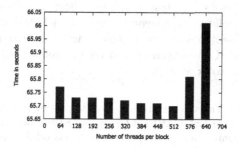

Fig. 8. The running time of the multiagent tiger problem given different GPU's thread block sizes.

which is domain dependent, is beneficial but computationally expensive. The expense may be amortized over multiple runs. But, because we solve I-DIDs just once for a domain, this expense cannot be amortized and significantly adds to the run time. As a trade-off, we empirically search for a block size that optimizes the solution for many problem domains following the CUDA optimization heuristics.

We evaluated the performance of Parallelized I-DID Exact as the number of threads in each block is increased from 64 to 640, on a level 1 I-DID of horizon 3 and 10 lower-level DIDs as candidate models. The impact of different blocks sizes on run time is shown in Fig. 8. As observed, the block size of 512 gives the best performance in terms of running time. The upside is that as more threads are involved in the computation there are less iterations of fetching global memory loads to shared memory. In contrast, the degradation in performance is expected because spawning more threads per block limits the number of blocks that can be scheduled to run concurrently because of limited resources, hence, the observed fall in performance.

8   Conclusion

We presented a method for optimal planning in multiagent settings under uncertainty that utilizes the parallelism provided by a heterogeneous CPU-GPU computing architecture. We focused on the interactive dynamic influence diagrams, which are probabilistic graphical models whose solution involves transforming the I-DID into a flat DID and computing the policy with the maximum expected utility. Not only operations involving probability and utility factors during variable elimination are parallelized on GPUs, we also parallelize solving lower level models (i.e., differing hypotheses of the other agent's behavior modeled as DIDs or I-DIDs with different initial beliefs) on a multiple processor machine with multiple GPUs using MPI. Specifically, two processors each with its own GPU were used to solve the lower level models in parallel.

We demonstrate speed ups close to an order of magnitude on multiple problem domains for large numbers of models and long horizons. To the best of our knowledge, these are the fastest run times reported so far for exactly solving I-DIDs and other related frameworks such as I-POMDPs for multiagent planning, and represent a significant step forward in making these complex frameworks practical. Comparisons based on different types of GPUs will be our immediate future work as well.

Acknowledgements. This research is supported in part by an ONR Grant, #N00014 1310870, and in part by an NSF CAREER Grant, #IIS-0845036. We thank Alex Koslov for making his implementation of a parallel Bayesian network inference algorithm available to us for reference.

References

1. Bernstein, D.S., Givan, R., Immerman, N., Zilberstein, S.: The complexity of decentralized control of markov decision processes. Math. Oper. Res. **27**(4), 819–840 (2002)
2. Berstein, D.S., Hansen, E.A., Zilberstein, S.: Bounded policy iteration for decentralized POMDPs. In: IJCAI, pp. 1287–1292 (2005)
3. Chandrasekaran, M., Doshi, P., Zeng, Y., Chen, Y.: Team behavior in interactive dynamic influence diagrams with applications to ad hoc teams. In: AAMAS, pp. 1559–1560 (2014)
4. Chen, Y., Hong, J., Liu, W., Godo, L., Sierra, C., Loughlin, M.: Incorporating PGMs into a BDI architecture. In: Boella, G., Elkind, E., Savarimuthu, B.T.R., Dignum, F., Purvis, M.K. (eds.) PRIMA 2013. LNCS, vol. 8291, pp. 54–69. Springer, Heidelberg (2013)

5. Doshi, P., Zeng, Y., Chen, Q.: Graphical models for interactive POMDPs: representations and solutions. JAAMAS **18**(3), 376–416 (2009)
6. Gal, K., Pfeffer, A.: Networks of influence diagrams: a formalism for representing agents' beliefs and decision-making processes. JAIR **33**, 109–147 (2008)
7. Gmytrasiewicz, P.J., Doshi, P.: A framework for sequential planning in multiagent settings. JAIR **24**, 49–79 (2005)
8. Howard, R.A., Matheson, J.E.: Influence diagrams. In: Howard, R.A., Matheson, J.E. (eds.) The Principles and Applications of Decision Analysis. Strategic Decisions Group, Menlo Park (1984)
9. Jeon, H., Xia, Y., Prasanna, K.V.: Parallel exact inference on a cpu-gpgpu heterogenous system. In: ICPP, pp. 61–70 (2010)
10. Koller, D., Friedman, N.: Probabilistic Graphical Models: Principles and Techniques. MIT Press, Cambridge (2009)
11. Koller, D., Milch, B.: Multi-agent influence diagrams for representing and solving games. In: IJCAI, pp. 1027–1034 (2001)
12. Luo, J., Yin, H., Li, B., Wu, C.: Path planning for automated guided vehicles system via I-DIDs with communication. In: ICCA, pp. 755–759 (2011)
13. Pearl, J.: Probabilistic Reasoning in Intelligent Systems: Networks of Plausible Inference. Morgan Kaufmann, Berlin (1998)
14. Sano, Y., Kadono, Y., Fukuta, N.: A performance optimization support framework for gpu-based traffic simulations with negotiating agents. In: ACAN (2014)
15. Smallwood, R., Sondik, E.: The optimal control of partially observable markov decision processes over a finite horizon. Oper. Res. **21**, 1071–1088 (1973)
16. Søndberg-Jeppesen, N., Jensen, F. V., Zeng, Y.: Opponent modeling in a PGM framework. In: AAMAS, pp. 1149–1150 (2013)
17. Kozlov, A.V., Singh, J.P.: A parallel Lauritzen-Spiegelhalter algorithm for probabilistic inference. In: Supercomputing, pp. 320–329 (1994)
18. Xia, Y., Prasanna, K.V.: Parallel exact inference on the cell broadband engine processor. In: SC, pp. 1–12 (2008)
19. Zeng, Y., Doshi, P.: Exploiting model equivalences for solving interactive dynamic influence diagrams. JAIR **43**, 211–255 (2012)
20. Zheng, L., Mengshoel, O.J., Chong, J.: Belief propagation by message passing in junction trees: computing each message faster using gpu parallelization. In: UAI (2011)

LS²C - A Platform for Norm Controlled Social Computers

Flavio S. Correa da Silva[1]([✉]), David S. Robertson[2],
and Wamberto W. Vasconcelos[3]

[1] Department of Computer Science, University of Sao Paulo, São Paulo, Brazil
fcs@ime.usp.br
[2] School of Informatics, University of Edinburgh, Edinburgh, UK
dr@inf.ed.ac.uk
[3] Department of Computing Science, University of Aberdeen, Aberdeen, UK
w.w.vasconcelos@abdn.ac.uk

Abstract. Social computers have been characterised as goal oriented socio-technical systems comprised of humans as well as computational devices. Such systems can be found *in natura* in a variety of scenarios, as well as designed to tackle specific issues of social and economic relevance. In the present article we introduce the *Lightweight Situated Social Calculus* (*LS²C*) as a language to design norm controlled executable specifications of interaction protocols for social computers. Additionally, we describe a platform to process these specifications, giving them a computational realisation. We argue that *LS²C* can be used to design, implement and execute algorithms in social computers.

Keywords: Interaction models · Social computers · Social interaction protocols

1 Introduction

Social computers have been characterised as socio-technical systems that bring together the innate problem solving, action and information gathering powers of humans and the environments in which they live and of computational devices, in order to tackle large scale social and economic problems [15]:

- The "hardware" of a social computer is supplied by humans (taken as individuals as well as collectively in the form of human-powered institutions) and the environment where these humans live, including all relevant artifacts which can be natural or man-made, as well as computational devices.
- The "software" of a social computer is comprised of human capabilities, organisational and social rules and norms, social conventions, as well as computer software.

This work has been partially supported by FAPESP and CNPq. This article is a revised and extended version of the article *LS²C – A Platform to Design, Implement and Execute Social Computations*, presented at ICAART 2015 [7].

© Springer International Publishing Switzerland 2015
B. Duval et al. (Eds.): ICAART 2015, LNAI 9494, pp. 284–297, 2015.
DOI: 10.1007/978-3-319-27947-3_15

- The "algorithms" in social computer are defined by socially accepted goals and corresponding actions which can be taken to achieve local as well as global goals.
- Finally, the "processing" of algorithms in social computers are collective, decentralised, goal-oriented actions whose emergent results can be iteratively evaluated and steered towards active goals.

A social computer is not programmed the same way as conventional computational devices. Social computers are evolving social systems, whose components (i.e. their "hardware", "software", "algorithms" and "processing") are dynamically and evolutionarily designed together with their goals and available resources. The analysis and design of social computers require novel methodological practices, blending existing techniques and experiences from applied social sciences and computational sciences [6].

The design of a social computer requires participatory definition of goals, elicitation of resources and coordination of actions. Appropriate methodologies for such activities can be borrowed from or inspired by existing practices of Participatory Action Research [2], in which the goals and the resources to reach these goals are defined collectively by the members of the community who shall be directly interested in these goals and ready to work to reach them.

In order to design, implement, and continuously monitor and steer the behaviour of social computers, specialised languages are required to build specifications, and corresponding computational platforms are required to support, manage and provide a computational realisation of social computers. An essential aspect to be represented in such languages is interaction between actors in social computers, so that the internal behaviour of these actors can be abstracted and the resulting systems can be analysed as a whole. Additionally, since these languages should be used to communicate specifications as well as processing results to participants in social computers (i.e. humans who behave as actors in social computers), they should be concise and simple to understand. Finally, in order to build social computers whose behaviour can be verified with respect to desired requirements and attributes, these languages should have a formal underpinning and the corresponding specifications and processing results should be formally verifiable.

Social computers can be found *in natura* or designed to tackle specific issues of social and economic relevance. Designed social computers contain rules that specify their general behaviour, which are built in the form of normative systems. Normative systems can be fixed or evolving, and they can steer the behaviour of the system according to norm management procedures that can be centralised or distributed across the social computer.

In the present article we present the ongoing development of a language and a platform for norm controlled social computers. The proposed language and companion computational platform – coined the *Lightweight Situated Social Calculus* (LS^2C) is a fusion of two previously existing languages, respectively the *Lightweight Social Calculus (LSC)* and the *JamSession platform*.

In Sect. 2 we present some related work and the preliminary concepts that have guided the development of the LS^2C language and platform. In Sect. 3 we introduce in detail the LS^2C language. In Sect. 4 we briefly describe the platform in which this language shall be used. In Sect. 5 we illustrate how this platform can be used in practice. Finally, in Sect. 6 we present some conclusions and proposed future work.

2   Preliminary Concepts and Related Work

The LS^2C platform is a fusion of the *Lightweight Social Calculus (LSC)* and the *JamSession platform*. LSC, in turn, is an extension of the *Lightweight Coordination Calculus (LCC)*. In the following paragraphs we briefly introduce these languages and platforms.

The *LCC* is an executable specification language grounded on the notions of process algebras and initially proposed for the specification and processing of interaction models for distributed software components [24]. It has been extended in a variety of ways, e.g. for contextual reasoning about distributed software systems [27], for the specification and execution of choreographies for web services [1] and, more recently, for the specification of social computers, under the name of *Lightweight Social Calculus – LSC* [22]. It has also been successfully implemented using the logic programming language *Prolog*, the object oriented programming language *Java* and the object-functional programming language *Scala*.

LCC and its variations – particularly *LSC* – fulfill most of the requirements to be a language for the specification, implementation and execution of algorithms in social computers. *LSC* is a compact formal language that can be used to specify and to mediate ongoing social interaction protocols. The syntax of *LSC* (as well as all other variations of *LCC*), however, can lead to lengthy specifications which can be difficult for human reading and understanding. Moreover, the extension of *LCC* to manage contexts (coined *Ambient LCC* [27]) departs from the lightweight approach and becomes more complex than the other variations of *LCC*, resulting in a not so concise and effective platform for the specification and execution of interaction protocols by human system designers.

The explicit management of contexts can be a powerful technique to help in the analysis and design of social interactions, given that many of these interactions are context-dependent (e.g. business negotiations must occur in adequately equipped meeting rooms, to ensure privacy and the availability of required communication resources; healthcare must occur in hospitals and clinics, to ensure the availability of required specialised equipment and personnel; bank transactions must occur over the appropriate counters; the automated interactions among communicating portable devices in an Internet of Things scenario must be context sensitive to ensure privacy and reliability of interactions; and so on).

Contexts are also an expressive and convenient way to design and implement norms and norm management systems, in the form of contextual rules that steer the behaviour of a social computer. Therefore, a useful feature in a language for social computers is the explicit representation and management of contexts, which can be abstracted as *locations* in which certain interactions are allowed to occur.

The *JamSession platform* is a language developed for purposes similar to those of *LSC*. It was initially conceived as an executable specification language to manage the interactions between human controlled and synthetic characters in *Second Life*-style virtual worlds and multiplayer computer games, and later employed to mediate business interactions between organisations in cross-organisational workflows [4,5]. A simplified prototype of *JamSession* has been implemented in *Prolog*, and a cloud-based prototype of *JamSession* has been implemented using the functional language *F*♯, based on which sample demos of applications have been developed [8]. The fundamental concept in *JamSession* is the notion of *situated interaction protocols*, which determine how and where actors can interact with each other and with the environment. The semantics of situated interaction protocols can be formally characterised in terms of Nested Petri Nets, which are an extension of coloured Petri nets to handle recursion [12]. Nested Petri Nets, in turn, can be translated into the specification language Promela and verified using the model checker SPIN with respect to properties of their operational behaviour (such as liveness and termination) [13].

There have been initiatives by other authors to analyse social interactions based on formal languages capable of capturing the dynamics of interactions, in many cases grounded on the notions of dynamic modal logics, preference logics and public announcement logics [3,16,26,28]. Our work distinguishes from these initiatives at least in two senses:

1. We focus on systems *design* as well as analysis, whereas those initiatives focus primarily on analysis of existing social networks grounded on formal theories.
2. Since we are interested in the design of systems for goal-oriented social interactions, we have taken into account scalability and computational performance issues, as well as interaction design issues. Previously existing initiatives have mostly focused on theoretical issues, accounting for computational and system level performance as secondary issues. Scalability in *LS^{2}C* shall be ensured by the appropriate use of asynchronous state management based on *Linda*-style tuple spaces [14], following the implementation practices used in *JamSession*.

3   The *LS^{2}C* Language

The *Lightweight Situated Social Calculus LS^{2}C* is based on the notion of *situated social interactions*, in which situations are used to represent the notion of contexts and, therefore, of normative systems.

A situated social interaction is comprised of actions which are permitted to occur if performed by specific agents at specific locations, together with messages exchanged among agents in order to enable and trigger further actions, and with migrations of agents across locations that occur in order to enable agents to dynamically update their roles in a social computer and, as a consequence, adjust their capabilities.

In LS^2C , locations are an abstraction used to represent a variety of concepts, such as:

- Actual physical locations, e.g. the counter in a bank where financial transactions are permitted to occur.
- Contextual information, e.g. characterising the collective acceptance of interaction protocols by agents in a business transaction (buy, sell, legal procedures, and so on) so that it is common knowledge that the transaction can be carried out as long as all actions in all protocols – the "setting" for the transaction – are fulfilled.

Locations are represented as nodes in a directed graph, in which edges represent accessibility relations, characterising allowed transitions between locations or contexts. We denote the set of nodes in a graph of locations as $S = \{s_1, ..., s_r\}$[1].
Each location can host an unlimited number of agents. An agent is capable of:

- Moving between directly connected locations.
- Performing allowed actions while in specific locations.
- Reading, writing or deleting messages in locations.

We have a set of agents $A = \{a_1, ..., a_m\}$ whose behaviour is constrained and determined by each role that they adopt, according to each location to which they move. Actions and message types are available only to agents bearing specific roles at specific locations. The positioning of agents in locations is the way to control the processing of algorithms in social computers represented using LS^2C.

Actions can be enabled by and influence or transform objects that can be found in the environment. We have a set of objects $B = \{b_1, ..., b_n\}$, which are subject to the actions of agents. Objects can be physical objects as well as their digital counterparts.

We build mappings pointing to agents and objects, so that we can refer to them indirectly through built connections between them (such as *FatherOf(X)* to refer to an agent by naming another agent). For this reason, we also include in the language a set F of n-ary functions, $0 < n < \infty$, such that if $f \in F$ has arity j, it can be used to build or point to an element of $A \cup B$ given j elements of $A \cup B \cup S$. In other words, $f : (A \cup B \cup S)^j \mapsto A \cup B$.

In order to be able to build terms as in first order logics, we also include a countable set of variables $X = \{x_1, ...\}$. Every formula built in this calculus is assumed to be existentially closed, i.e. free variables are implicitly bound to existential quantifiers.

We build relations involving agents and objects, representing information that can be known by agents and action statements. We have three sets of n-ary predicates to represent each of these relation types:

- P : set of n-ary knowledge predicates, $0 \leq n < \infty$.
- Q : set of n-ary action predicates, $0 \leq n < \infty$.

---

[1] We abuse notation and also refer to the graph of locations itself as S.

– $\mathcal{R}$: set of n-ary protocol names, $0 \leq n < \infty$.

Predicates are prefixed by modal operators as follows, in which $p \in \mathcal{P}, q \in \mathcal{Q}, r \in \mathcal{R}, s \in \mathcal{S}$ and $a \in \mathcal{A}$:

– $[k]^s_a p$ denotes a knowledge modality – agent a knows fact $p \in \mathcal{P}$ at location s.
– $[e]^s_a q$ denotes an engagement modality – agent a performs action $q \in \mathcal{Q}$ at location s.
– $[i]^s q$ denotes a location-specific computation modality – action $q \in \mathcal{Q}$ is processed at location s.
– $[i]^s r$ denotes a location-specific interaction protocol – protocol $r \in \mathcal{R}$ can be started from location s.

In order to avoid unnecessary complications in our proposed language, we allow modal operators to only prefix a single predicate, i.e. no nesting of modalities is allowed, nor it is allowed to have a modality prefixing arbitrary formulae.

Communicative actions are defined as follows, in which $p \in \mathcal{P}, a, a' \in \mathcal{A}$ and $s, s' \in \mathcal{S}$:

– *null*: a void message.
– $[e]^s_a write(p, a')$: agent a writes message in location s, which is then stored as predicate p known by agent a' in s, i.e. $[k]^s_{a'} p$. In other words, agent a tells p to a' in s.
– $[e]^s_a del(p, a')$: agent a deletes message which was previously stored in location s as predicate p known by a' in s, i.e. the piece of knowledge $[k]^s_{a'} p$ is retracted from location s.

In order to continue with the definition of LS^2C , we need to define two connectives:

– Non-commutative conjunction: given two existentially closed formulae φ and ψ, the conjunction $\varphi \wedge \psi$ is evaluated as $\top$ if:
  1. φ is evaluated as $\top$ *AND*
  2. the variable bindings performed during the evaluation of φ are used to bind the values of variables in ψ, producing the instatiated formula $\hat{\psi}$ *AND*
  3. $\hat{\psi}$ is also evaluated as $\top$.
  Otherwise, the conjunction $\varphi \wedge \psi$ is $\bot$.
– Non-commutative disjunction: given two existentially closed formulae φ and ψ, the disjunction $\varphi \vee \psi$ is evaluated as $\top$ if:
  1. φ is evaluated as $\top$, in which case ψ is never evaluated *OR*
  2. φ is evaluated as $\bot$, and ψ is evaluated as $\top$. In this case, the variable bindings performed during the evaluation of φ are not used to bind the values of variables in ψ.
  Otherwise, the disjunction $\varphi \vee \psi$ is $\bot$.

We define an atomic event AE as one of the following expressions, in which $p \in \mathcal{P}, q \in \mathcal{Q}, r \in \mathcal{R}, a \in \mathcal{A}$ and $s, s_i, s_j \in \mathcal{S}$:

– $[k]^s_a p$.

- $[e]^s_a q$.
- $[i]^s q$.
- $[i]^s r$.
- $[i]^{s_i \to s_j}_a mv$, in which the special predicate mv is used to state that agent a is being moved from location s_i to location s_j.
- a communicative action M.

We define an event E as a conjunction of atomic events, i.e. $E = \wedge_i AE_i$.

Finally, we define an interaction protocol as a pair $\langle [i]^s r, \vee_i E_i \rangle$, in which $[i]^s r$ is a location-specific interaction protocol and $\vee_i E_i$ is a non-commutative disjunction of events.

The interaction protocol $\langle [i]^s r, \vee_i E_i \rangle$ is triggered by a formula that unifies with the left hand side expression $[i]^s r$. Variable bindings are applied to the right hand side expression $\vee_i E_i$, which is then computed. Each event E_i is an alternative course of actions that can be tested. If one of the events E_i returns $\top$, then the interaction protocol succeeds and the corresponding variable bindings are presented. If all alternatives in $\vee E_i$ return $\bot$, then the interaction protocol fails and variable bindings are discarded.

It should be observed that, since location-specific interaction protocol expressions $[i]^{s_i} r_i$ can occur as atomic events in the right hand side of interaction protocols, recursive interaction protocols are allowed in LS^2C.

LS^2C is a coordination language. Knowledge is encoded in the platform using communicative actions that update knowledge predicates $p \in \mathcal{P}$, and action predicates are expected to be evaluated by external actors, which can include human as well as computational agents.

4   The LS^2C Platform

We are working on a robust implementation for the LS^2C language, benefitting from existing implementations of LSC and of *JamSession*, that shall be freely deployed as the LS^2C *platform*. In this software platform, the graph of locations, the list of pairs $\langle s, a \rangle, s \in \mathcal{S}, a \in \mathcal{A}$ for each predicate indicating where and by whom it can be evaluated, and the state of each location are managed in a centralised cloud server.

Interaction protocols are stored in distributed hosts. The processing of these protocols may require human intervention, this way characterising the LS^2C *Platform* as a tool to support and manage social interactions. The physical location where interaction protocols can be found is stored in the centralised cloud server as an address catalog. This catalog can be rearranged locally according to private ranking criteria, defined by priority policies used in different sites which can be used to rank interaction protocols.

The locations of agents are also managed in the centralised server, characterising the notions of *virtual worlds* as featured in the *JamSession* literature [4] and *mirror worlds* as featured in the LSC literature [22].

The definitions of predicates – including action predicates, which can capture the input-output expected behaviour of human actions – are stored in the distributed hosts. The locations of interaction protocols and their corresponding predicates are stored in the centralised server.

The architecture of the LS^2C Platform is depicted in Fig. 1.

Protocols can be triggered concurrently and asynchronously by several users. As a consequence, the verification of properties related to distribution and concurrency is important to ensure an expected behaviour in a system whose interactions are specified using LS^2C. We are working on the characterisation of LS^2C protocols using Nested Petri Nets, based on our experience using the same formalism to characterise *JamSession* protocols. Nested Petri Nets can be used to formally verify properties such as fairness, liveness and termination. Given that Nested Petri Nets can also be translated as Promela programs to be verified using the model checker SPIN [13], we will be able to verify such properties also for LS^2C social interaction protocols.

Similarly to LCC and to what can be observed in business process modeling [5,24], social interaction protocols can be considered at specification time and at run time. Specification time refers to the design of social computers, while run time can refer to the *a posteriori* analysis of the actual execution of algorithms in social computers, in which e.g. specific protocols are used to enact concrete interactions. Such analysis can reveal social network properties involving interacting peers, such as centrality of a location, and cohesiveness and density of location-related interactions [17], whose interpretation can be relevant to understand features of specific domains.

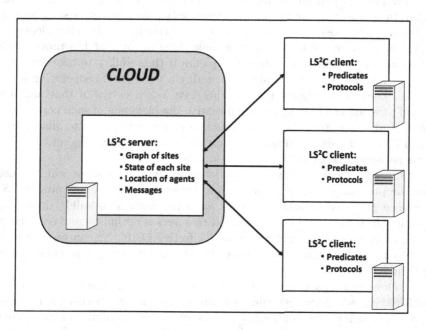

Fig. 1. The architecture of the LS^2C Platform.

5   An Example – LS^2C for S^3

In this section we mention some potential applications for the LS^2C platform, and sketch how some interaction protocols can be encoded for one of these applications.

The LS^2C platform has been conceived to design and implement social computers in which situated interactions are most relevant. Social computers of this sort can be found in *urban computing* and in *smart city* environments, which are urban landscapes augmented with digital communication and processing devices and applications [18,19,25,29].

Urban computing refers to requesting citizens to carry (most likely within their smartphones) software applications that track their activities, interact with them and provide information to service managers, so that the quality of service provisioning can be improved in issues such as traffic monitoring, public transportation and emergency relief.

Smart cities are urban settings which have been augmented with ubiquitous computing devices, in such way that existing services can become more effective and novel services can be offered to citizens, businesses and governments. A representative example of what can be achieved under the concept of smart cities is the structuring of effective business clusters supported by digital services, which enable economic sustainability and the creation of jobs in cities. In the following paragraphs we detail this possibility.

An important well known factor for regional economic development is innovation. Innovative entrepreneurship is frequently associated with start-up companies, which in most cases are small companies which hold deep knowledge and skills over a narrow and specialised domain. One factor that has proven to be influential for the survival of these companies is their ability to cooperate with other companies, possibly forming or entering a network of cooperating organisations. Local and regional governments have taken notice of that and have created programmes to support and incentive the blooming of such networks, as well as studied how these networks should be structured in order to minimise the risk of failure of participating companies and maximise the economic efficiency of the networks [11,20,21,23].

Business clusters are emergent agglomerations of companies which benefit from the proximity of each other to grow. Smart Specialisation Strategies (S^3) have been proposed recently as means for policy makers to build "smart clusters", in which the use of knowledge and resources is optimised and cooperation among companies is brought to be most effective [9,10]. S^3 can be seen as an effort to design business clusters, instead of simply providing appropriate means for them to emerge.

Business relations are partially constrained by rationality rules (such as profit maximisation and risk minimisation) and by general norms (such as legal constraints on business contracts). On the other hand, companies are human-powered and human controlled institutions, and therefore – especially small companies – are influenced by human decision making, which takes into account rules beyond those that can be captured by simplified models of pure rationality

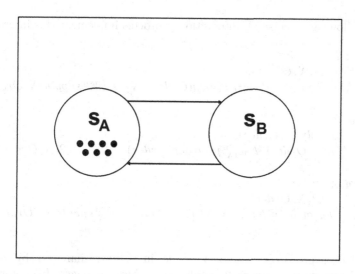

Fig. 2. The two locations and corresponding agents for the customer-supplier example.

(e.g. brand fidelity, intuition driven trust relations, aesthetic considerations and cultural affinity) as well as social norms (such as socially defined ethical rules). Company relations are diversified and include customer-supplier relations as well as cooperative relations involving similar companies [20,21,23]. Hence, we suggest that business networks can be treated as social computers, and that the *LS²C Platform* can be a useful tool to design, implement, run, monitor and iteratively refine Smart Specialisation Strategies.

In order to illustrate how this can be done, we show a simplified version of interaction rules that could be relevant in a customer-supplier relationship involving two companies. In this example, company **A** asks company **B** to provide a service that is required to carry on production activities within company **A**[2].

Company **A** may wish to minimise risk in its operations by limiting the number of open requests sent to company **B** to a fixed value N: once **A** has sent N requests to **B**, it will only send a new request after **B** has fulfilled at least one of the queued requests.

In order to model this small example, the graph consists of two locations s_A and s_B, and edges connecting these two locations in both directions (Fig. 2). Agents, in this example, represent orders: when company **A** places an order, an agent is sent from s_A to s_B, and when this order is delivered by company **B** the agent is sent back from s_B to s_A. In Fig. 2 we depict agents as black dots. In that figure, company **A** accepts to have seven simultaneous open orders at most (i.e. $N = 7$), as shown by the seven agents that are inside s_A.

---

[2] This example is borrowed and adapted from [5] and from [7]. Evidently, we are exhibiting only a very small fraction of a model for S^3 using this example. Our goal is simply to illustrate how rules that could be used to model a S^3 would look like.

The following three small interaction protocols implement this interaction[3]:

- *Protocol 1:*
  1. $\langle [i]^{s_A} req1(X, Order),$
  2. $[i]_X^{s_A \rightarrow s_B} mv \;\wedge\; [e]_X^{s_B} write(msg(Order), X) \;\wedge\; [i]^{s_B} supply(X, Order)$
  3. $\rangle.$
- *Protocol 2:*
  1. $\langle [i]^{s_B} supply(X, Order),$
  2. $[k]_X^{s_B} msg(Order) \;\wedge\; [e]_X^{s_B} prOrder(Order) \;\wedge\; [i]^{s_B} req2(X, Order)$
  3. $\rangle.$
- *Protocol 3:*
  1. $\langle [i]^{s_B} req2(X, Order),$
  2. $[e]_X^{s_B} del(msg(Order), X) \;\wedge\; [i]_X^{s_B \rightarrow s_A} mv \;\wedge\; [e]_X^{s_A} endOrder(Order)$
  3. $\rangle.$

Interaction protocols 1 and 3 reside in a host managed by company **A**, and interaction protocol 2 resides in a host managed by company **B**. $[i]^{s_A} req1(X, Order)$ triggers the interactions, by asking an agent X in location s_A to start interaction $req1$, in which order $Order$ will be requested to company **B**. This is performed by moving the agent to location s_B, where it registers the order and triggers protocol 2.

By pattern matching on the right hand side of protocol 2, the message stored in location s_B containing the specification of the order is verified as being part of the knowledge of X while in s_B, based on which the order is processed (by triggering the action predicate $prOrder$) and finally protocol 3 is triggered.

By pattern matching on the right hand side of protocol 3, the message is deleted and the agent is moved back to location s_A, then the order is properly delivered (using the action predicate $endOrder$).

This is a simplified example, in which success/failure verifications of performed operations and security issues are not taken into account. Additional features can be implemented by extending these protocols and/or by adding special purpose protocols, towards the design of interaction rules that can specify and characterise successful relations between companies in a supply chain.

Other protocols can be designed to compete with these protocols, and protocols can also be designed to characterise cooperative behaviour of suppliers to provide combined services to customers, towards the design of interaction rules that can specify and characterise relations between companies in a network. Hence, the relations involving companies in a netchain, i.e. a network of relations mixing supply chains and cooperative/competitive relations [20] can be designed.

Based on theoretical analysis of properties of the interaction protocols, as well as empirical analysis of actual relations that can result from the use of these protocols, iterative refinements and adjustments can be made.

---

[3] We adopt the Prolog convention that variables begin with capital letters, and all other terms begin with small letters.

6   Conclusion and Future Work

In this article we have introduced the LS^2C platform to design, implement and execute algorithms in social computers, and sketched how it can be used to model and support a complex system of economic relevance, namely the organisation of companies in a business cluster according to S^3.

A platform for social computers should present features such as:

- The possibility to empower domain experts and end users to build specifications and execute them,
- Technology-agnosticism, meaning that implementations can be built based on various and diverse software platforms, operating systems and programming languages,
- Explicit account of participants in social interactions and their possible behaviours,
- Resources for the design of interaction protocols as well as for the analysis of existing protocols, including formal analysis based on algebraic and logical concepts.

We are currently working on the design and implementation of the LS^2C platform as a framework (in the software engineering sense) of LCC/LSC protocols. Since it inherits features and properties of LCC/LSC as well as of $JamSession$, we claim that this platform addresses all these features.

The specification of social interactions as characterised in the LS^2C platform can be used at least in three different ways:

1. As a design tool to specify desired features of interaction protocols in a decentralised way,
2. As a platform for the execution of algorithms in social computers, and
3. As a tool to reason about specifications, including strategic reasoning (e.g., given alternative protocols that can be built, what is best for me/my company?), whereby participants may try out certain behaviours "in vitro" before these can be actually enacted.

LSC has been combined with an existing social network platform [22], and $JamSession$ has been combined with an existing workflow management platform [8]. We envisage that a full LS^2C Platform can be implemented as the combination of a novel implementation of the LS^2C language, a workflow management system (e.g. Bonita[4]) and a social network platform (e.g. elgg[5] or eXo[6]). The implementation of the LS^2C language shall benefit from previous experience implementing LSC and $JamSession$.

We are particularly interested in the characterisation of Smart Specialisation Strategies (S^3) as a discipline to steer the emergency of networks of social interactions involving human-powered agencies aiming at regional economic efficacy.

---

[4] http://www.bonitasoft.com/.
[5] http://elgg.org/.
[6] http://www.exoplatform.com/.

We believe that this approach can be appropriate to implement S^3 effectively, and that the LS^2C platform can be useful to support the design and operation of business clusters following S^3. In future work, we shall explore these views, hopefully through the analysis of empirical data resulting from the actual structuring of clusters of innovation as goal-oriented social interaction networks.

References

1. Bai, X., Klein, E., Robertson, D.: Choreographing web services with semantically enhanced scripting. In: Web Intelligence and Intelligent Agent Technology, pp. 583–587 (2012)
2. Chevalier, J.M., Buckles, D.J.: Participatory Action Research: Theory and Methods for Engaged Inquiry. Routledge, USA (2013)
3. Christoff, Z., Hansen, J.U.: A two-tiered formalization of social influence. In: Grossi, D., Roy, O., Huang, H. (eds.) LORI. LNCS, vol. 8196, pp. 68–81. Springer, Heidelberg (2013)
4. Correa da Silva, F.S.: Knowledge-based interaction protocols for intelligent interactive environments. Knowl. Inf. Syst. **30**, 1–24 (2011)
5. da Silva, F.S.C., Venero, M.L.F., David, D.M., Saleem, M., Chung, P.W.H.: Interaction protocols for cross-organisational workflows. Knowledge Based Systems **37**, 1–16 (2012)
6. da Silva, F.S.C., Robertson, D., Vasconcelos, W.: Experimental interaction science. Artificial Intelligence and Simulation of Behaviour - Annual Convention 2013: Workshop on Social Coordination - Principles, Artifacts and Theories (2013)
7. da Silva, F.S.C., Robertson, D.S., Vasconcelos, W.W.: Ls2c - a platform to design, implement and execute social computations. In: International Conference on Agents and Artificial Intelligence 2015, (2015)
8. David, D.M.: Protocolos de interacao baseados em conhecimento: implementacao da plataforma JamSession (in Portuguese), MSc dissertation. University of Sao Paulo, Brazil (2012)
9. European Comission, E.U.: The role of clusters in smart specialisation strategies. European Union, Brussels (2013)
10. European Commission, E.U.: Guide to Research and Innovation Strategies for Smart Specialisation. European Union, Brussels (2012)
11. Feldman, M.P., Audretsch, D.B.: Innovation in cities: science-based diversity, specialization and localized competition. Eur. Econ. Rev. **43**, 409–429 (1999)
12. Venero, M.L.F., da Silva, F.S.C.: Modelling and simulating interaction protocols using nested petri nets. In: Workshop on Formal Methods in the Development of Software (2013)
13. Venero, M.L.F., da Silva, F.S.C.: On the use of SPIN for studying the behavior of nested petri nets. In: 16th Brazilian Symposium on Formal Methods (2013)
14. Gelernter, D.: Generative communication in linda. ACM Trans. Program. Lang. Syst. **7**, 80–112 (1985)
15. Giunchiglia, F., Robertson, D.S.: The social computer - combining machine and human computation. University of Trento Technical report, DISI-10-036 (2010)
16. Hansen, J.U.: Reasoning about opinion dynamics in social networks. In: Proceedings of the Eleventh Conference on Logic and the Foundations of Game and Decision Theory (LOFT 11) (2014)

17. Jackson, M.O.: Social and Economic Networks. Princeton University Press, USA (2008)
18. Jiang, S., Fiore, G.A., Yang, Y., Ferreira Jr, J., Frazzoli, E., Gonzalez, M.C.: A review of urban computing for mobile phone traces: current methods, challenges and opportunities. In: Urban Computing (2013)
19. Komninos, N.: The architecture of intelligent cities: integrating human, collective, and artificial intelligence to enhance knowledge and innovation. In: Intelligent Environments (2006)
20. Lazzarini, S.G., Haddad, F.R., Cook, M.: Integrating supply chain and network analyses: the study of netchains. J. Chain Netw. Sci. 1(1), 7–22 (2001)
21. Mesquita, L.M., Lazzarini, S.G.: Horizontal and vertical relationships in developing economies: implications for smes access to global markets. Acad. Manag. J. **51**(2), 359–380 (2007)
22. Murray-Rust, D., Robertson, D.: LSCitter: building social machines by augmenting existing social networks with interaction models. In: International World Wide Web Conference Committee (2014)
23. Pedrozo, E.A., Pereira, B.A.D.: Empreendedorismo coletivo e possivel? uma analise do processo de constituicao de relacionamentos cooperativos em rede. Revista de Administracao (in Portuguese), 12(4) (2006)
24. Robertson, D.: Multi-agent coordination as distributed logic programming. In: Demoen, B., Lifschitz, V. (eds.) ICLP 2004. LNCS, vol. 3132, pp. 416–430. Springer, Heidelberg (2004)
25. Schaffers, H., Komninos, N., Pallot, M., Trousse, B., Nilsson, M., Oliveira, A.: Smart cities and the future internet: towards cooperation frameworks for open innovation. In: Domingue, J., et al. (eds.) Future Internet Assembly, pp. 431–446. Springer, Heidelberg (2011)
26. Seligman, J., Liu, F., Girard, P.: Logic in the community. In: Banerjee, M., Seth, A. (eds.) Logic and Its Applications. LNCS, vol. 6521, pp. 178–188. Springer, Heidelberg (2011)
27. Sindhu, J., Perreau De Pinninck, A., Robertson, D., Sierra, C., Walton, C.: Interaction model language definition. Open Knowledge Project - Technical reports, UK (2006)
28. Zhen, L., Seligman, J.: A logical model of the dynamics of peer pressure. In: Proceedings of the 7th Workshop on Methods for Modalities (M4M2011) and the 4th Workshop on Logical Aspects of Multi-Agent Systems (LAMAS2011), Electronic Notes in Theoretical Computer Science, vol. 278, pp. 275–288 (2011)
29. Zheng, Y., Liu, Y., Yuan, J., Xie, X.: Urban computing with taxicabs. In: UbiComp (2011)

Construction of a Planar PLCA Expression: A Qualitative Treatment of Spatial Data

Kazuko Takahashi[(⊠)], Mizuki Goto, and Hiroyoshi Miwa

School of Science and Technology, Kwansei Gakuin University,
2-1, Gakuen, Sanda 669-1337, Japan
{ktaka,miwa}@kwansei.ac.jp, izconnect705@gmail.com

Abstract. Qualitative spatial reasoning (QSR) is a method of representing spatial data by extracting necessary information depending on a user's purpose, and allowing reasoning on this representation. Although many studies have examined QSR, little work has been carried out from the viewpoint of computational models, which are necessary for practical use in an implemented system. This paper presents a computational model of a qualitative spatial representation and shows the correspondence of an image and its symbolic expression. Specifically, we take PLCA as a framework of QSR, which represents a figure using the objects used to construct it, i.e., points, lines, circuits, and areas, as well as the relationships among them, without using numerical data. We describe a method of constructing a PLCA expression inductively, and prove that the defined class coincides with a subclass of PLCA that can be realized on a two-dimensional plane. Part of the proof is implemented using the proof assistant Coq.

Keywords: Qualitative spatial reasoning · Formalization · PLCA · Planarity

1 Introduction

With the advances in computer performance, we often need to deal with large amounts of static or dynamic image data. Image data are usually represented in raster or vector form using coordinates, which require much time and memory, if we reason on these data. Fortunately, a user's purpose may be met without using precise data. For example, it is sometimes sufficient to know a relative direction or positional relationships between landmarks during route navigation, or it is sometimes sufficient to grasp qualitative change, such as the fact that connected objects can be disconnected to separate them, when extracting events from a sequence of video frames. Qualitative reasoning or qualitative physics is a method that has long been studied in artificial intelligence (AI) [9]. It reasons about contiguous aspects of the physical world without using numerical data. Qualitative spatial reasoning (QSR) is a method of representing spatial data by

M. Goto—Currently, JFE Advantech Co., Ltd.

© Springer International Publishing Switzerland 2015
B. Duval et al. (Eds.): ICAART 2015, LNAI 9494, pp. 298–315, 2015.
DOI: 10.1007/978-3-319-27947-3_16

extracting their topological, mereological, or geometric properties depending on the application [5,14,16,19]. Various proposed systems for doing this depend on focal aspects such as the relative positional relations or relative sizes of objects and orientations.

Studies have ranged from theoretical work to practical applications, including simulations using geographic information systems, query-answering systems for spatial databases, and navigation in mobile robots. The qualitative treatment not only reduces computational complexity but also reflects human cognition and reasoning using common-sense knowledge. Moreover, it gives clear semantics, as it uses symbolic data. Typically, these representations adopt logical expressions, which enable us to perform mechanical reasoning on symbols.

To certify a QSR system, we must prove that an expression correctly represents the properties of the image data and that there is a corresponding image for a given expression. Although many studies have examined QSR in artificial intelligence [3,8,10,17,18], little work has been carried out from the viewpoint of computational models. For representations, most studies claim expressive power for spatial knowledge but do not refer to the class the expression stands for. Hence, we do not know whether a proposed expression is valid or reliable. Therefore, it is necessary to clarify the extent to which the expression is effective if we are to implement a system based on the expression. For reasoning, most research has focused on the consistency check, that is, whether there exist a space that can satisfy all of the given relationships among spatial objects and efficient algorithms for solving this problem. However, there has been no discussion of how to construct such a consistent set. Practical use of an implemented system requires rigorous proof for the correspondence of the real figure and a symbolic expression. Mechanical proving with a proof assistant is an effective approach for this purpose.

In this paper, we describe a computational model of a qualitative representation.

Takahashi et al. have proposed a framework for qualitative spatial reasoning, $PLCA^1$ [20,21], which focuses on the patterns of connections between regions. This method distinguishes patterns in which regions are connected in different ways, for example, by a single point, by two points, by a line and so on. For example, in Fig. 1(a), (b) and (c) are regarded as the same, while 1(d) and 1(e) and these figures are regarded to be different. PLCA expressions represent the properties of spatial data by describing the constituent objects, and the relationships between them, without considering attributes such as the size, direction, or shape.

Takahashi et al. have described the conditions for planarity of a given PLCA expression [22], that is, an existence of the corresponding figure on a two-dimensional plane, and given a proof for this; however, they have not discussed the construction of such a planar PLCA expression.

---

[1] The name of PLCA is originated from an acronym for Point (P), Line (L), Circuit (C) and Area (A).

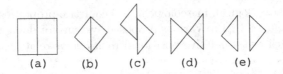

Fig. 1. Classification of figures in PLCA. (a)–(c) Regions connected by a line, (d) regions connected by a point, and (e) regions that are not connected.

In this paper, we describe the construction of a planar PLCA expression inductively, and prove that the resulting class coincides with that of the planar PLCA. The part of this proof is implemented using a proof assistant Coq [2].

The remainder of this paper is organized as follows. In Sect. 2, we describe a PLCA expression. In Sect. 3, we describe the inductive construction of a PLCA expression. In Sect. 4, we prove that the constructed class coincides with that of planar PLCA. In Sect. 5 we compare our work with the related work, and Sect. 6 concludes the paper.

2 PLCA

2.1 Target Figure

The target figure of PLCA is considered as a region segmentation of a finite space. In addition, PLCA admits regions with holes, and regards a hole itself to be a region. It does not admit isolated lines or points, because a region cannot be properly defined. Here, we describe a target figure using a simple closed curve [15].

Definition 1 (Simple Closed Curve). *A non-self-intersecting continuous loop in a plane is called a* simple closed curve *or a* Jordan curve.

The following is the well-known theorem on a simple closed curve.

Theorem 1. *Every simple closed curve divides the plane into an interior region bounded by the curve and an exterior region containing all of the nearby and far away exterior points.*

Formally, our target figure is a finite region on a two-dimensional plane, divided into a finite set of subregions of which each boundary is a simple closed curve. In Fig. 2(a) and (b) are target figures, whereas 2(c) and 2(d) are not.

2.2 PLCA Expression

A PLCA expression is defined as a five-tuple, $\langle P, L, C, A, outermost \rangle$, where P is a set of points, $L \subseteq P^2$, $C \subseteq L^n$ $(n \geq 3)$, $A \subseteq C^m$ $(m \geq 1)$, $outermost \in C$.

In PLCA, there are four basic types of object: points P, lines L, circuits C and areas A. An element $l \in L$ is defined as a pair of points p_1 and p_2,

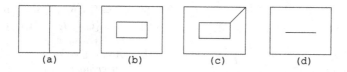

Fig. 2. Examples of (a) and (b) target figures, and (c) and (d) non-target figures.

and denoted by $l.points = [p_1, p_2]$, where p_1 and p_2 are distinct. Intuitively, a line is an edge between points. No two lines are allowed to cross. A line has an inherent orientation. When $l.points = [p_1, p_2]$, l^+ and l^- mean $[p_1, p_2]$ and $[p_2, p_1]$, respectively. They are called *directed lines*. l^* denotes either l^+ or l^- and l^{*re} denotes the line with the inverse orientation of l^*.

An element $c \in C$ is defined as a list of directed lines and denoted by $c.lines = [l_0^*, \ldots, l_n^*]$, where $l_i^* \neq l_j^*$ if $i \neq j$ $(0 \leq i, j \leq n)$, $l_i^* = [p_i, p_{i+1}](0 \leq i \leq n)$ and $p_{n+1} = p_0$. If $p \in l.points \land l^* \in c.lines$, it is said that p *is on* c. A circuit has a cyclic structure, that is, $[l_0^*, \ldots, l_n^*]$ and $[l_j^*, \ldots, l_n^*, l_0^*, \ldots, l_{j-1}^*]$ represent the same circuit for any j $(0 \leq j \leq n)$. Intuitively, a circuit is the boundary between an area and its adjacent areas.

An element $a \in A$ is defined as a set of circuits and denoted by $a.circuits = \{c_0, \ldots, c_n\}$, where any pair of circuits c_i and c_j $(0 \leq i \neq j \leq n)$ cannot share a point. Intuitively, an area is a connected region which consists of exactly one piece encircled by a single closed curve.

In addition, *outermost* is a specific circuit in the outermost side of the figure.

Example 1. Figure 3 shows an example of a target figure and its PLCA expression $\langle P, L, C, A, outermost \rangle$.

2.3 Basic Concepts of PLCA Expressions

For $c_1, c_2 \in C$, we introduce two new predicates lc and pc to indicate that two circuits share line(s) and point(s), respectively.

$$lc(c_1, c_2) \overset{\text{def}}{=} \exists l \in L; (l^* \in c_1.lines) \land (l^{*re} \in c_2.lines)$$

$$pc(c_1, c_2) \overset{\text{def}}{=} \exists p \in P; (p \in l_1.points) \land (p \in l_2.points) \land (l_1^+ \in c_1.lines)$$
$$\land (l_2^- \in c_2.lines).$$

If $lc(c_1, c_2)$, then either $pc(c_1, c_2)$ or $pc(c_2, c_1)$ holds. For any pair of circuits $c_1, c_2 \in C$, if $c_1, c_2 \in a.circuits$, then $\neg pc(c_1, c_2)$ holds from the definition of Area.

For a circuit c, we define a corresponding circuit-segment.

Definition 2 (Circuit-Segment). *Let* $c.lines = [l_0^*, \ldots, l_n^*]$. *A sequence* $cs = [m_0^*, \ldots, m_k^*]$ $(0 \leq k \leq n)$, *where* $m_i^* = l_{(i+j) \bmod n}^*$ $(0 \leq j \leq n-1)$ *is said to be a circuit-segment of* c, *and denoted by* $cs \sqsubseteq c$.

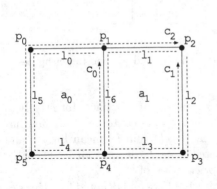

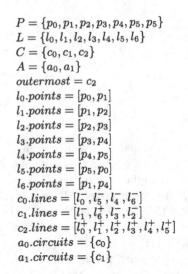

$P = \{p_0, p_1, p_2, p_3, p_4, p_5, p_5\}$

$L = \{l_0, l_1, l_2, l_3, l_4, l_5, l_6\}$

$C = \{c_0, c_1, c_2\}$

$A = \{a_0, a_1\}$

$outermost = c_2$

$l_0.points = [p_0, p_1]$

$l_1.points = [p_1, p_2]$

$l_2.points = [p_2, p_3]$

$l_3.points = [p_3, p_4]$

$l_4.points = [p_4, p_5]$

$l_5.points = [p_5, p_0]$

$l_6.points = [p_1, p_4]$

$c_0.lines = [l_0^-, l_5^-, l_4^-, l_6^-]$

$c_1.lines = [l_1^-, l_6^+, l_3^-, l_2^-]$

$c_2.lines = [l_0^+, l_1^+, l_2^+, l_3^+, l_4^+, l_5^+]$

$a_0.circuits = \{c_0\}$

$a_1.circuits = \{c_1\}$

Fig. 3. An example of a target figure and its PLCA expression.

For a circuit-segment $cs = [m_0^*, \ldots, m_k^*]$, we define its inverse as $inv(cs) = [m_k^{*re}, \ldots, m_0^{*re}]$.

Example 2. In Example 1, $[l_0^-, l_5^-]$, $[l_4^-, l_6^-, l_0^-]$, $[l_0^-, l_5^-, l_4^-, l_6^-]$ are some circuit-segments of c_0. Furthermore, $inv([l_0^-, l_5^-])$ is $[l_5^+, l_0^+]$.

For a pair of circuits c_1 and c_2, $S_{scs}(c_1, c_2)$ represents a set of their shared circuit-segments, that is, $S_{scs}(c_1, c_2) = \{cs \mid cs \sqsubseteq c_1, inv(cs) \sqsubseteq c_2\}$. For any $cs \in S_{scs}(c_1, c_2)$, $inv(cs) \in S_{scs}(c_2, c_1)$ holds.

Definition 3 (MSCS). *An element $cs \in S_{scs}(c_1, c_2)$ is said to be a maximal shared circuit-segment of c_1 and c_2 if there does not exist $cs' \in S_{scs}(c_1, c_2)$ such that cs is a subsequence of cs'. A set of maximal shared circuit-segments of c_1 and c_2 is denoted by $S_{MSCS}(c_1, c_2)$.*

When $S_{MSCS}(c_1, c_2) = \{c_1.lines\}$, c_1 and c_2 are the inner and the outer circuits of a simple closed curve, respectively. Note that if $pc(c_1, c_2) \wedge \neg lc(c_1, c_2)$, then $S_{MSCS}(c_1, c_2) = \{\}$.

Example 3. In Fig. 4, $S_{scs}(c_0, c_1) = \{[], [l_0^+], [l_1^+], [l_2^+], [l_3^+], [l_0^+, l_1^+], [l_2^+, l_3^+]\}$. Furthermore, $S_{MSCS}(c_0, c_1) = \{[l_0^+, l_1^+], [l_2^+, l_3^+]\}$ and $S_{MSCS}(c_1, c_0) = \{[l_1^-, l_0^-], [l_3^-, l_2^-]\}$.

Here, we introduce a new type *Path*. An instance *path* of type *Path* is defined as a list of directed lines $[l_0^*, \ldots, l_n^*]$, where $l_i^* = [p_i, p_{i+1}]$ and $p_i \neq p_j$ if $i \neq j$ $(0 \leq i, j \leq n)$. It is represented by quad-ruple of the starting point, ending point, list of inner points and list of inner lines. For *path*, *start(path)*, *end(path)*, *inner_points(path)* and *inner_lines(path)* show the starting point,

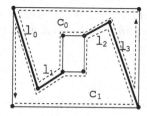

Fig. 4. Shared circuit-segments of c_0 and c_1.

ending point, list of inner points and list of inner lines, respectively. The length of *inner_lines(path)*, which may be 0, is said to be the *length of the path*. Clearly, any circuit-segment is a *Path*. *Path* is used to construct a new circuit.

2.4 Consistency

A consistent PLCA expression does not allow an isolated point or an isolated line, and all of the objects should be correctly defined by the incidence relations. For any point, there exists at least one line that contains it. For any line, there exist exactly two distinct circuits that contain it and its inverse direction, respectively. For any circuit, there exists exactly one area that contains it. The *outermost* is not included in any area. The consistency is formally defined as follows.

Definition 4 (PLCA Consistency).

- **[Consistency of Point-Line]**
    $\forall p \in P(\exists l \in L; p \in l.points)$
    $\forall l \in L(\forall p \in l.points; p \in P)$
- **[Consistency of Line-Circuit]**
    $\forall l \in L(\exists c, c' \in C; l^{+} \in c.lines \wedge l^{-} \in c'.lines)$
    $\forall c \in C(\forall l^{*} \in c.lines; l \in L)$
    $\forall l \in L(l^{*} \in c_1.lines, l^{*} \in c_2.lines \rightarrow c_1 = c_2)$
- **[Consistency of Circuit-Area]**
    $\forall c \in C(\exists a \in A; c \in a.circuits)$
    $\forall a \in A(\forall c \in a.areas; c \in C)$
    $\forall c \in C(c \in a_1.circuits, c \in a_2.circuits \rightarrow a_1 = a_2)$
- **[Independence of outermost]**
    $\neg \exists a \in A; outermost \in a.cuicuit.$

2.5 PLCA-connectedness

Intuitively, PLCA-connectedness guarantees that no objects are separated, including the *outermost*. In other words, for any pair of objects, there exists a trail from one object to the other via further objects.

Definition 5 (d-pcon). *Let* $e = \langle P, L, C, A, outermost \rangle$ *be a PLCA expression. For a pair of objects of* e*, the binary relation d-pcon on* $P \cup L \cup C \cup A$ *is defined as follows.*

1. *d-pcon(p, l) iff $p \in l$.points.*
2. *d-pcon(l, c) iff $l \in c$.lines.*
3. *d-pcon(c, a) iff $c \in a$.circuits.*

Definition 6 (pcon). *Let* α*,* β *and* γ *be objects of a PLCA expression.*

1. *If d-pcon(α, β), then pcon(α, β).*
2. *If pcon(α, β), then pcon(β, α).*
3. *If pcon(α, β) and pcon(β, γ), then pcon(α, γ).*

Definition 7 (PLCA-Connected). *A PLCA expression* e *is said to be PLCA-connected iff pcon(α, β) holds for any pair of objects* α *and* β *of* e*.*

2.6   PLCA-Euler

Intuitively, PLCA-Euler guarantees that a PLCA expression can be embedded in a two-dimensional plane so that the orientation of each circuit can be correctly defined.

Definition 8 (PLCA-Euler). *For a PLCA expression* $\langle P, L, C, A, outermost \rangle$*, if* $|P| - |L| - |C| + 2|A| = 0$*, then it is said to be PLCA-Euler.*

Takahashi et al. have derived this equation from Euler's formula on a connected planar graph [22].

2.7   Planar PLCA Expression

Takahashi et al. have given a proof of the following theorem on the planarity of a PLCA expression [22].

Theorem 2. *For a consistent, connected PLCA expression, it is PLCA-Euler iff there exists a corresponding target figure on a two-dimensional plane.*

Planar PLCA is defined as follows.

Definition 9 (Planar PLCA). *For a PLCA expression, if it is consistent, PLCA-connected and PLCA-Euler, then it is said to be planar PLCA[2].*

For example, the PLCA expression in Example 1 is planar.

The following lemmas hold for a planer PLCA expression, and are used in the subsequent proof for the realizability of an inductively constructed PLCA.

---

[2] Strictly, the original PLCA admits a curved line, and multiple lines between the same pair of points. If we admit only straight lines, we convert a PLCA expression in the original definition by adding the same number of points and lines, and this conversion does not affect the condition for planarity or the proof thereof.

Lemma 1. *For a planar PLCA expression, there exists an area that has a single circuit.*

Proof. Let $\langle P, L, C, A, outermost \rangle$ be a planar PLCA expression. Assume that for any area $a \in A$, $|a.circuits| \geq 2$ holds.

Set $k = 0$ and c_k be *outermost*. Take c such that $lc(c_k, c)$ holds. Take an area a_k such that $c \in a_k.circuits$ holds. Let $a_k.circuits$ be $\{c, c_{k_1}, \ldots, c_{k_n}\}$. Note that $\neg pc(c, c_{k_i})$ holds for all i from the definition of Area. Take an arbitrary c_{k_i} ($c_{k_i} \neq c$) and let c_{k+1} be c_{k_i} Increment k and repeat this procedure, then we can take an infinite sequence of circuits $SeqC = c_0, c_1, \ldots$.

Figure 5 illustrates each step of this procedure. Take c_0 as an *outermost* and c such that $lc(c_0, c)$ holds. Take an area a_0 such that $c \in a_0.circuits$ holds (Fig. 5(a)). There are three circuits in $a_0.circuits$ other than c. Take an arbitrary circuit among them and set it as c_1; take c such that $lc(c_1, c)$ holds. Take an area a_1 such that $c \in a_1.circuits$ holds (Fig. 5(b)). There is one circuit in $a_1.circuits$ other than c. Take this circuit and set it as c_2; take c such that $lc(c_2, c)$ holds. Take an area a_2 such that $c \in a_2.circuits$ holds (Fig. 5(c)). We continue this procedure.

Since each circuit is a simple closed curve, c_i and c_{i+2} are circuits in the exterior region and interior region of c_i, respectively, by Theorem 1. Therefore, $\neg pc(c_i, c_{i+2})$ holds for each i, On the other hand, the number of circuits is finite. Therefore, we cannot take an infinite sequence of circuits $SeqC$. Hence, there exists an area $a \in A$ such that $|a.circuits| = 1$. ∎

Lemma 2. *For any circuit c of a planar PLCA expression, there exists a circuit that has only one maximal shared circuit-segment with c.*

Proof. Let $\langle P, L, C, A, outermost \rangle$ be a planar PLCA, and $c \in C$ be an arbitrary circuit. There should be a circuit $c' \in C$, such that $|S_{MSCS}(c, c')| \neq 0$ holds, by the consistency of Line-Circuit. We take such a circuit c'. Assume that $|S_{MSCS}(c, c')| \geq 2$. Let $S_{MSCS}(c, c') = \{cs_1, cs_2\}$ without losing generality (Fig. 6). Circuit-segments cs_1 and cs_2 do not share a point. Since cs_1 and cs_2 are considered to be paths, we can take their starting points and ending points: $start(cs_1) = p, end(cs_1) = q, start(cs_2) = r, end(cs_2) = s$. Then there exists $cs \sqsubseteq c$ such that $start(cs) = q, end(cs) = r$, and each line in cs is not included in $c'.lines$. Here, p, q, r and s are distinct with each other. Since c' is a circuit, there exists cs'; $cs' \sqsubseteq c'$, $start(cs') = r, end(cs') = q$. On the other hand, from the consistency of Line-Circuit, there exists c_0; $inv(cs) \sqsubseteq c_0$, $start(inv(cs)) = r, end(inv(cs)) = q$. Then, circuit c_0 is defined by appending two circuit-segments $inv(cs')$ and $inv(cs)$. Therefore, $S_{scs}(c, c_0) = \{cs\}$. It follows that $|S_{MSCS}(c, c_0)| = 1$, which is a contradiction. ∎

3   Construction of PLCA

Theorem 2 gives the conditions for planarity of a given PLCA expression. The next issue to address is how to construct such an expression.

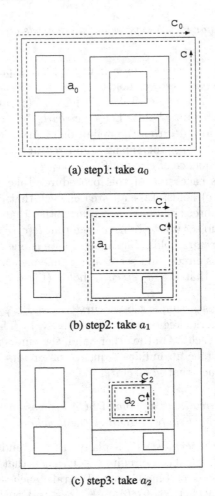

(a) step1: take a_0

(b) step2: take a_1

(c) step3: take a_2

Fig. 5. Existence of an area with a single circuit.

We can construct a PLCA expression of elements P, L, C and A in this order, for example. In this approach, we must check all of the constraints on the objects carefully during each stage. For example, we must make a circuit so that there exist exactly two distinct circuits: one that contains a line, and the other that contains the line in its inverse direction. If this is not satisfied, we must backtrack to construct these lines. This not only requires time, but it is also very difficult to prove that the resulting structure is a planar PLCA expression.

Therefore, we take a different approach, in which we begin with *outermost* and construct a PLCA expression inductively.

We define a class for PLCA expressions using the following three constructors: *single_loop*, *add_loop* and *add_path*. A constructor *single_loop* corresponds to the base case, and the other two correspond to operations that construct a

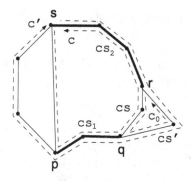

Fig. 6. Existence of an area with a single maximal shared circuit-segments. (Relationships of circuit-segments: $cs_1, cs_2, cs \sqsubseteq c$, $inv(cs_1), inv(cs_2), cs' \sqsubseteq c'$ $inv(cs), inv(cs') \sqsubseteq c_0$, $start(cs_1) = p, end(cs_1) = q$, $start(cs_2) = r, end(cs_2) = s$. $start(cs) = q, end(cs) = r$, $start(cs') = r, end(cs') = q$.)

new PLCA expression by dividing an existing area in a current PLCA expression using a path. An arbitrary path, the length of which is more than one is introduced, makes a new circuit using it. Points and lines contained in the path are added simultaneously, and the area is divided into two areas.

We must add objects of four different types simultaneously during an induction step because the objects of a PLCA expression are mutually related. We take the number of areas as a measure of induction, and the number of other objects increases following the application of each constructor. We cannot take the number of points or lines as such a measure, because the expression that is obtained as a result of adding a single point or a single line to a PLCA expression may not be a PLCA expression.

An alternative method of generating a new area is to add a path to the outer part of the *outermost*. That is, we take two points on the current *outermost* and combine these with a path in the exterior region of *outermost*. In this case, *outermost* changes during each step where a constructor is applied. Because the construction of a new *outermost* is the base case in an inductive definition, we cannot succeed in a proof if we change the definition of *outermost* during each step. Therefore, we do not adopt this method.

We now describe the construction. The idea of construction is based on drawing a figure. Although we demonstrate the construction process on a figure to provide an intuitive discussion, the construction itself is performed symbolically.

A constructor *single_loop* is for a base case, and corresponds to the simplest target figure with one area. There are only two circuits: the outermost circuit and the inner side thereof. Consider an arbitrary path *path*, such that $start(path) = x$, $end(path) = y$, and $inner\_lines(path) = [l_0^+, \ldots, l_n^+]$. Then we create new circuits *outermost* such that $outermost.lines = [l^+, l_0^+, \ldots, l_n^+]$ and c such that $c.lines = [l_n^-, \ldots, l_0^-, l^-]$, where $l.points = [y, x]$. We also create a new area a such that $a.circuit = \{c\}$ (Fig. 7).

Formally, *single_loop* is defined as follows:

$$path = \langle x, y, ip, [l_0^+, \ldots, l_n^+] \rangle \land x \neq y \land n \geq 1$$
$$\rightarrow \quad e = \langle P, L, C, A, o \rangle$$

where

$$P = inner\_points(path),$$
$$L = inner\_lines(path) \cup \{l\},$$
$$C = \{c, outermost\},$$
$$A = \{a\},$$
$$o = outermost,$$
$$l.points = [y, x],$$
$$outermost.lines = [l^+, l_0^+, \ldots, l_n^+]$$
$$c.lines = [l_n^-, \ldots, l_0^-, l^-],$$
$$a.circuit = \{c\}.$$

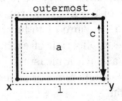

Fig. 7. The constructor *single_loop*.

Next, we define *add_loop*. Consider an arbitrary area a (Fig. 8(a)). Take an arbitrary path *path*, such that $start(path) = x$, $end(path) = y$ and *inner_lines* $(path) = [l_0^+, \ldots, l_n^+]$. Make a line l such that $l.points = [y, x]$ (Fig. 8(b)). Then make new circuits c_1 and c_2 such that $c_1.lines = [l^+, l_0^+, \ldots, l_n^+]$, and $c_2.lines = [l_n^-, \ldots, l_0^-, l^-]$. Add c_1 to $a_1.circuits$ and c_2 to $a_2.circuits$ (Fig. 8(c)). As a result, a is divided into two areas, a_1 and a_2 (the hatched part). The points and lines contained in *path* are added accordingly. If a contains more than one circuit, all of them remain in a_1, and a_2 contains none.

Formally, *add_loop* is defined as follows:

$$e = \langle P, L, C, A, o \rangle \land$$
$$path = \langle x, y, ip, [l_0^+, \ldots, l_n^+] \rangle \land x \neq y \land n \geq 1 \land a \in A \land \forall p(p \in ip \rightarrow p \notin P)$$
$$\rightarrow \quad e' = \langle P', L', C', A', o' \rangle$$

where

$$P' = P \cup inner\_points(path),$$
$$L' = L \cup inner\_lines(path) \cup \{l\},$$
$$C' = C \cup \{c_1, c_2\},$$
$$A' = A \setminus a \cup \{a_1, a_2\},$$
$$o' = o,$$
$$l.points = [y, x]$$
$$c_1.lines = [l^+, l_0^+, \ldots, l_n^+],$$
$$c_2.lines = [l_n^-, \ldots, l_0^-, l^-],$$
$$a_1.circuit = a.circuits \cup \{c_1\},$$
$$a_2.circuit = \{c_2\}.$$

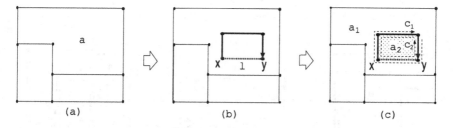

Fig. 8. The constructor *add_loop*.

Next, we define *add_path*. Consider a circuit c such that $c \in a.circuits$, and two points y, z on c. Here y and z may be identical. Because a circuit-segment is a path, consider a circuit-segment $cs \sqsubseteq c$ such that $start(cs) = y$, $end(cs) = z$. Then c is divided into two circuit-segments: cs and cs'. Let $c.lines = [ll_0^+ \ldots, ll_m^+]$, $cs = [ll_0^+ \ldots, ll_k^+]$ $(0 \leq k \leq m)$ and $cs' = [ll_{k+1}^+ \ldots, ll_m^+]$ (Fig. 9(a)). Take an arbitrary path *path*, such that $start(path) = s$, $end(path) = e$ and $inner\_lines(path) = [l_0^+, \ldots, l_n^+]$. Make lines l_s and l_e such that $l_s.points = [s, y]$ and $l_e.points = [z, e]$, respectively (Fig. 9(b)). Then make new circuits c_1 and c_2 such that $c_1.lines = [l_s^-, l_0^+, \ldots, l_n^+, l_e, ll_{k+1}^+ \ldots, ll_m^+]$ and $c_2.lines = [l_e^+, l_n^-, \ldots, l_0^-, l_s^+, ll_0^+ \ldots, ll_k^+]$. Add c_1 to $a_1.circuits$ and add c_2 to $a_2.circuits$ (Fig. 8(c)). As a result, a is divided into two areas, a_1 and a_2 (the hatched part), c is eliminated, and two new circuits are created. The points and lines contained in *path* are added and the objects are changed. If a contains circuits other than c, all of them remain in a_1, and a_2 contains none.

Formally, *add_path* is defined as follows:

$$e = \langle P, L, C, A, o \rangle \wedge$$
$$path = \langle s, e, ip, [l_0^+, \ldots, l_n^+] \rangle \wedge s \neq e \wedge n \geq 0 \wedge a \in A \wedge \forall p(p \in ip \rightarrow p \notin P) \wedge$$
$$c \in a.circuits \wedge c.lines = [ll_0^+ \ldots, ll_m^+]$$
$$\rightarrow \quad e' = \langle P', L', C', A', o' \rangle$$

where

$$P' = P \cup inner\_points(path),$$
$$L' = L \cup inner\_lines(path) \cup \{l_s, l_e\},$$
$$C' = C \setminus c \cup \{c_1, c_2\},$$
$$A' = A \setminus a \cup \{a_1, a_2\},$$
$$o' = o,$$
$$l_s.points = [s, y],$$
$$l_e.points = [z, e],$$
$$c_1.lines = [l_s^-, l_0^+, \ldots, l_n^+, l_e^-, ll_{k+1}^+ \ldots, ll_m^+],$$
$$c_2.lines = [l_e^+, l_n^-, \ldots, l_0^-, l_s^+, ll_0^+ \ldots, ll_k^+],$$
$$a_1.circuit = a.circuits \cup \{c_1\},$$
$$a_2.circuit = \{c_2\}.$$

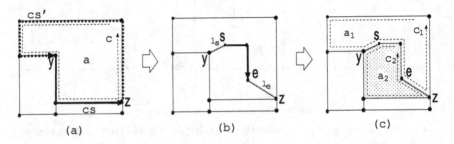

Fig. 9. The constructor *add_path*.

Note that *add_loop* is applied to a specific area, whereas *add_path* is applied to a specific circuit and two points on it.

Definition 10 (IPLCA). *PLCA expressions constructed by the above three constructors are said to be* Inductive PLCA (IPLCA).

4 Proof of Formalization

Here we prove that IPLCA coincides with planar PLCA.

4.1 Proof of Planarity

We first prove that IPLCA is planar. From Theorem 2, we prove the following theorem.

Theorem 3. *If e is an IPLCA expression, e is (i) consistent, (ii) PLCA-connected, and (iii) PLCA-Euler.*

We implement IPLCA and prove these three properties using the proof assistant Coq [2]. Coq is based on typed logic adopted for higher-order functions. The data types and functions are defined in recursive form, and the proof proceeds by connecting suitable tactics. The definition of IPLCA and the proof of Theorem 3 required approximately 5500 lines of code in total. As for consistency, we combine several conditions in a single formula and verify them simultaneously. As for PLCA-connectivity, the proof is somewhat involved, and we prove it by decomposing it into several sub-lemmas. As for PLCA-Euler, the proof is straightforward, since we only need to convert the numbers that appear in the formula. The advantage of using Coq is to certify the correctness of the formalization. We do not show the detail of the proof here, since it is out of the focus of this paper. The entire code is shown in [12].

4.2   Proof of Realizability

We prove that a planar PLCA is IPLCA. This means that any target figure can be drawn by applying the constructors of IPLCA in a suitable order. For example, consider Fig. 10. If we apply *add_loop* first, we cannot successively apply constructors, because any intermediate figure is not the target figure (Fig. 10(a)). However, if we apply *add_path* first, we can successively add areas by applying *add_path* again (Fig. 10(b)). In proving mechanically, we search all the possible cases and show an instance in each case.

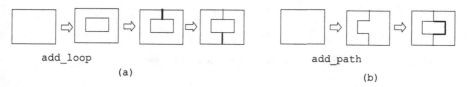

add_loop

(a)

add_path

(b)

Fig. 10. Constructing figures (a) by first applying *add_loop*, and (b) by first applying *add_path*.

Theorem 4. *A planar PLCA is IPLCA.*

Proof. We prove the theorem using induction on the number of areas of a given planar PLCA.

(Base case) The number of areas is 1.
     This is clearly a base case of IPLCA, and is constructed by applying *single_loop*.

(Induction step) The number of areas is $n + 1$.
     The principle of our proof via induction is as follows. For a planar PLCA e, of which the number of areas is $n+1$, we remove a suitable area a such that we can form a planar PLCA e', of which the number of areas is n. Because e' is IPLCA from the induction hypothesis, we can apply *add_loop* or *add_path* to obtain e. We proceed the proof based on this principle. The point of the proof is that we

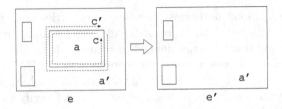

Fig. 11. Removing an area with case 1.

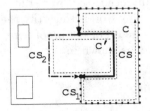

Fig. 12. Circuit-segments in case 2. Circuit c is divided into cs and cs_1, and circuit c' is divided into $inv(cs)$ and cs_2.

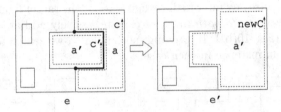

Fig. 13. Removing an area with case 2.

can find a suitable area. We can take an area a with a single circuit c from e by Lemma 1. There exists c' such that $|S_{MSCS}(c, c')| = 1$, from Lemma 2. Assume that $c' = outermost$. Since the number of areas of e is more than one, a contains more than one circuit, which is a contradiction. Therefore, $c' \neq outermost$.

Case 1. $S_{MSCS}(c, c') = \{c.lines\}$.

In this case, we remove a, c, c', and all objects on c and c' to obtain a planar PLCA e' such that $|e'.areas| = n$. Let a' be an area such that $c' \in a'.circuits$ holds. Note that since $c' \neq outermost$, e' has an $outermost$. Here e' is IPLCA from the induction hypothesis. Then we can construct e by applying the constructor add_loop on a' (Fig. 11).

Case 2. $S_{MSCS}(c, c') \neq \{c.lines\}$.

Let $S_{MSCS}(c, c') = \{cs\}$. In this case, c is divided into two circuit-segments cs and cs_1, and c' is divided into two circuit-segments $inv(cs)$ and cs_2 (Fig. 12). We remove a, c, c', and all objects on c and c', and add a circuit $newC$ by appending cs_1 and cs_2. We obtain a planar PLCA expression e' such that $|e'.areas| = n$. e'

is IPLCA from the induction hypothesis. Then we can construct e by applying the constructor add_path on $newC$, $start(cs_1)$ and $end(cs_1)$ (Fig. 13).

5 Related Work

There exist several symbolic expressions other than qualitative spatial representations for a figure on a two-dimensional plane, including computational geometry [1] and graph theory [13]. Different from qualitative spatial representations, the main objective of computational geometry is to analyze the complexity of algorithms for problems expressed in terms of geometry and to develop efficient ones, rather than to recognize or to analyze the characteristics of a figure. Graph theory can be used to provide symbolic expressions of spatial data. The topological structure of spatial data can be represented as a graph by treating spatial objects, such as points and lines, as nodes and the relationships between them as edges. There exists a condition to determine the planarity of a given graph; however, in general, a graph does not contain any information on an area, and therefore we only know that we can embed a graph by locating areas properly. In contrast, a PLCA expression places constraints on the locations of areas. In this respect, a PLCA expression is more specific than a graph.

One of the challenges for symbolic expressions of a figure on a two-dimensional plane is the concept of a *hypermap*. A hypermap is an algebraic structure that represents objects and relationships between them, and can be used to distinguish the topological and geometric aspects. There are several works that use a hypermap and give a formalization and a proof of the properties of these aspects using proof assistants. Gonthier et al. formalized and proved the four-color theorem and showed a proof [11]. In this work, planar subdivisions are described by a hypermap. Dufourd applied a hypermap to formalize and to prove a Jordan curve theorem [6]. He also showed a treatment of surface subdivision and planarity based on a hypermap [7]. Brun et al. showed a derivation of a program to compute a convex-hull for a given set of points from their specification using a hypermap [4]. They specified the algorithm and proved its correctness using a structural induction. Hypermap is a strong method for providing a mechanical proof of the topological or geometric properties in a symbolic form; however, the representation is too complicated to understand intuitively.

6 Conclusion

We have described a method of constructing a PLCA expression inductively, and have proved that the defined class coincides with that of planar PCLA. Formalization and part of the proof was implemented using the proof assistant Coq. Our main contribution is giving a computational model to a qualitative spatial representation, which is the first attempt in the research field on qualitative spatial reasoning.

Here, we discuss the realizability of a PLCA expression on a two-dimensional plane. We are considering its realizability on surfaces such as a sphere or a torus as well.

Mechanical proof using a proof assistant provides a rigorous proof of correctness of the formalization. In future, we will complete the mechanical proof of the part currently done manually.

Acknowledgements. This work is supported by JSPS KAKENHI Grant Number 25330274.

References

1. de Berg, M., van Kreveld, M., Overmars, M., Schwarzkopf, O.: Computational Geometry. Springer, Heidelberg (1997)
2. Bertot, Y., Castéran, P.: Interactive Theorem Proving and Program Development - Coq'Art: The Calculus of Inductive Constructions. Springer, Heidelberg (1998)
3. Borgo, S.: RCC and the theory of simple regions in $\mathbb{R}^2$. In: Tenbrink, T., Stell, J., Galton, A., Wood, Z. (eds.) COSIT 2013. LNCS, vol. 8116, pp. 457–474. Springer, Heidelberg (2013)
4. Brun, C., Dufourd, J.-F., Magaud, N.: Designing and proving correct a convex hull algorithm with hypermaps in coq. Comput. Geom.: Theory Appl. **45**(8), 436–457 (2012)
5. Cohn, A.G., Renz, J.: Qualitative spatial reasoning. In: Harmelen, F., Lifschitz, V., Porter, B. (eds.) Handbook of Knowledge Representation. Chap. 13, pp. 551–596. Elsevier, Amsterdam (2007)
6. Dufourd, J.-F.: An intuitionistic proof of a discrete form of the jordan curve theorem formalized in coq with combinatorial hypermaps. J. Autom. Reason. **43**(1), 19–51 (2009)
7. Dufourd, J.-F., Bertot, Y.: Formal study of plane delaunay triangulation. In: Kaufmann, M., Paulson, L.C. (eds.) ITP 2010. LNCS, vol. 6172, pp. 211–226. Springer, Heidelberg (2010)
8. Egenhofer, M., Herring, J.: Categorizing binary topological relations between regions, lines, and points in geographic databases. Department of Surveying Engineering, University of Maine (1995)
9. Forbus, K.D.: Qualitative process theory. Artif. Intell. **24**(1–3), 85–168 (1984)
10. Freksa, C.: Conceptual neighborhood and its role in temporal and spatial reasoning. In: Proceedings of the IMACS Workshop on Decision Support Systems and Qualitative Reasoning, pp. 181–187 (1991)
11. Gonthier, G.: Formal proof - the four color theorem. Not. AMS **55**(11), 1382–1393 (2008)
12. Goto, M., Moriguchi, S., Takahashi, K.: Formalization of IPLCA. http://ist.ksc.kwansei.ac.jp/~ktaka/IPLCA2015Mar
13. Harary, F.: Graph Theory. Addison-Wesley, Reading (1969)
14. Hazarika, S.: Qualitative Spatio-Temporal Representation and Reasoning: Trends and Future Directions. IGI Publishers, USA (2012)
15. Kosniowski, C.: A First Course in Algebraic Topology. Cambridge University Press, Cambridge (1980)
16. Ligozat, G.: Qualitative Spatial and Temporal Reasoning. Wiley, London (2011)

17. Randell, D.A., Cui, Z., Cohn, A.G.: A spatial logic based on regions and connection. In: Proceedings of the Third International Conference on Principles of Knowledge Representation and Reasoning (KR92), pp. 165–176 (1992)
18. Renz, J.: Qualitative Spatial Reasoning with Topological Information. LNAI, vol. 2293. Springer, Heidelberg (2002)
19. Stock, O. (ed.): Spatial and Temporal Reasoning. Kluwer Academic Publishers, Dordrecht (1997)
20. Takahashi, K.: PLCA: a framework for qualitative spatial reasoning based on connection patterns of regions. In: [14], Chap. 2, pp. 63–96 (2012)
21. Takahashi, K., Sumitomo, T.: The qualitative treatment of spatial data. Int. J. Artif. Intell. Tools **16**(4), 661–682 (2007)
22. Takahashi, K., Sumitomo, T., Takeuti, I.: On embedding a qualitative representation in a two-dimensional plane. Spat. Cogn. Comput. **8**(1–2), 4–26 (2008)

Offline Norm Evolution

Magnus Hjelmblom[1,2](✉)

[1] Faculty of Engineering and Sustainable Development,
University of Gävle, Gävle, Sweden
mbm@hig.se
[2] Department of Computer and Systems Sciences, Stockholm University,
Stockholm, Sweden

Abstract. An approach to the pre-runtime design of normative systems for a class of problem-solving norm-regulated multi-agent systems is suggested. The basic idea is to employ evolutionary mechanisms to evolve efficient normative systems for so-called norm-regulated DALMASes, as part of the design process. The DALMAS architecture uses an algebraic approach to normative systems, in which normative consequences are based on an extended set of one-agent types of normative positions, which is given a semantics in terms of prohibition of certain types of state transitions. To illustrate the approach, a genetic algorithm is used to evolve norms for an example system. Furthermore, some approaches to reducing the algorithm's search space, including to employ a notion of 'operational equivalence' of norms, are discussed. It is demonstrated that an evolutionary algorithm may be a useful tool when designing norms for problem-solving multi-agent systems.

Keywords: Norm-regulated multi-agent system · Normative MAS · DALMAS · Norm evolution · Evolutionary algorithm

1 Introduction

Agent-based modelling and simulation is an active field of study which, for example, may offer methods for solving complex optimization problems. In this setting, agents are required to cooperate to solve the problem at hand. In complex systems with adjustable agent autonomy, sophisticated planning can often be replaced by norms; see for example [21]. The study of norm-regulated multi-agent systems, often referred to as normative MAS, has also attracted a lot of attention. The NorMAS roadmap [3] is a comprehensive introduction to and overview of the field. The combination of agent-based modelling and simulation and normative MAS is a promising field of study [4].

It is often desirable to replace planning (and replanning), since it may be a complex and time-consuming task, especially in collaborative environments. On the other hand, designing good normative systems is also a challenge. The approach suggested here, whose basic ideas were outlined in [20, pp. 164f], is to use evolutionary mechanisms, employed in a genetic algorithm, to aid the 'off-line'

© Springer International Publishing Switzerland 2015
B. Duval et al. (Eds.): ICAART 2015, LNAI 9494, pp. 316–333, 2015.
DOI: 10.1007/978-3-319-27947-3_17

Table 1. One-agent types of normative positions.

$\mathbf{T}_1(x, F)$: May Do(x, F) & May$[\neg$Do(x, F) & $\neg$Do$(x, \neg F)]$ & May Do$(x, \neg F)$

$\mathbf{T}_2(x, F)$: May Do(x, F) & May$[\neg$Do(x, F) & $\neg$Do$(x, \neg F)]$ & $\neg$May Do$(x, \neg F)$

$\mathbf{T}_3(x, F)$: May Do(x, F) & $\neg$May$[\neg$Do(x, F) & $\neg$Do$(x, \neg F)]$ & May Do$(x, \neg F)$

$\mathbf{T}_4(x, F)$: $\neg$May Do(x, F) & May$[\neg$Do(x, F) & $\neg$Do$(x, \neg F)]$ & May Do$(x, \neg F)$

$\mathbf{T}_5(x, F)$: May Do(x, F) & $\neg$May$[\neg$Do(x, F) & $\neg$Do$(x, \neg F)]$ & $\neg$May Do$(x, \neg F)$

$\mathbf{T}_6(x, F)$: $\neg$May Do(x, F) & May$[\neg$Do(x, F) & $\neg$Do$(x, \neg F)]$ & $\neg$May Do$(x, \neg F)$

$\mathbf{T}_7(x, F)$: $\neg$May Do(x, F) & $\neg$May$[\neg$Do(x, F) & $\neg$Do$(x, \neg F)]$ & May Do$(x, \neg F)$

(i.e., pre-runtime) design of normative systems for problem-solving multi-agent systems based on the DALMAS architecture for norm-regulated MAS. The normative framework of a DALMAS is based on an algebraic version of the Kanger-Lindahl theory of normative positions, which is well suited as the logical foundation for normative systems in a MAS context, since the types of normative positions are mutually exclusive and jointly exhaustive in the logical sense.

The paper is structured as follows. Section 1.2 briefly introduces the algebraic version of the theory of normative positions, and in Sect. 1.3, previous work on the DALMAS architecture is presented. Section 2 introduces an example DALMAS which will be used in Sect. 3 to demonstrate how to employ evolutionary mechanisms in the process of designing norms, by applying an evolutionary algorithm to this example. Section 4 concludes and suggests some lines of future work.

1.1 Related Work

The runtime emergence of norms within artificial social systems has attracted the attention of many researchers; see, e.g., [2]. However, evolving normative systems as part of the process of designing norm-regulated MAS is not as well studied, although evolutionary approaches for learning behaviour patterns or strategies for coordination have been successfully used in, e.g., the RoboCup[1] domain; see for example [6,17,18] . In fact, the simple decision policies evolved by Di Pietro et al. for the RoboCup *Keepaway* game can be regarded as simple normative systems consisting of production rules which prescribe certain behaviours in certain situations.

1.2 One-Agent Types of Normative Positions

The Kanger-Lindahl theory of normative positions is based on Kanger's 'deontic action-logic'; see for example [14]. The theory, further developed by Lindahl [15], contains three systems of types of normative positions, based on the logic of the action operator Do and the deontic operator Shall. The simplest of these systems is a system of seven 'one-agent types' of normative positions.

---

[1] http://www.robocup.org.

Do(x, F) is commonly read as 'x sees to it that F' or 'x brings it about that F', where F is a proposition regarding some state of affairs. The logical properties assumed for Do is that it is the smallest system containing propositional logic, closed under logical equivalence and containing the axiom schema Do(x, F) → F, which tries to capture the notion of *successful* action; if x 'sees to it' or 'brings about' that F, then F is indeed the case.

Each of the three statements

(i) Do(x, F),
(ii) Do($x, \neg F$), and
(iii) $\neg$Do(x, F) & $\neg$Do($x, \neg F$),

implies the negation of each of the others, and the disjunction of all three is a tautology. Each of (i) – (iii) can be prefixed with either May or $\neg$May, where May F is defined as $\neg$Shall$\neg F$, and basic conjunctions containing one statement from each such pair can be formed. By iterated construction of basic conjunctions, a set of eight conjunctions (of which one is self-contradictory) is obtained. The consistent 'maxi-conjunctions' are listed in Table 1.

In a series of papers, comprehensively summarized in [16], Lindahl and Odelstad have combined the theory of normative positions with an algebraic approach to normative systems. Their idea is to use the one-agent types of normative positions as operators on descriptive *conditions* to get deontic conditions. A ν-ary condition d can be true or false of ν agents $x_1, ..., x_\nu$. Thus, $d(x_1, ..., x_\nu)$ is a state of affairs which may be true or false. (To facilitate the presentation, X_ν will often be used as an abbreviation for the argument sequence $x_1, ..., x_\nu$.) In the special case when the sequence of agents is empty, i.e. $\nu = 0$, d represents a proposition which may be true or false. Note that negations d', conjunctions $(c \wedge d)$, and disjunctions $(c \vee d)$ can be formed in the following way:

$$d'(X_\nu) \text{ iff } \neg d(X_\nu),$$
$$(c \wedge d)(X_\nu) \text{ iff } [c(X_p) \text{ and } d(X_q)], \text{ and}$$
$$(c \vee d)(X_\nu) \text{ iff } [c(X_p) \text{ or } d(X_q)],$$

where $\nu = \max(p, q)$.[2] Therefore, it is possible to construct Boolean algebras of conditions. A Boolean algebra together with an implicative relation R fulfilling certain conditions, forms a so-called *Boolean quasiordering* (*Bqo*). As an application of their Theory of Joining-Systems (TJS), Lindahl and Odelstad define the notion of a *normative position condition-implication structure*, abbreviated *np-cis*, which is based on *Bqo*'s on descriptive and deontic conditions, so-called *cis-Bqo*'s. For details on Boolean quasiorderings, condition implication structures and *np-cis*'es, see for example [16] or [20].

---

[2] The free variables in $c(x_1, ..., x_p)$ must be the same, and in the same order, as the free variables in $d(x_1, ..., x_q)$, but it is not necessary that c and d have the same arity. Cf. [20, p.146].

Table 2. 'Reduced extended' types of one-agent normative positions.

$\mathbf{P}_1(x, F)$: $\mathrm{MayDo}(x, F)$ & $\mathrm{May}\Lambda(x, F)$ & $\mathrm{May}\Omega(x, F)$ & $\mathrm{MayDo}(x, \neg F)$

$\mathbf{P}_{2\Lambda}(x, F)$: $\mathrm{MayDo}(x, F)$ & $\mathrm{May}\Lambda(x, F)$ & $\neg\mathrm{May}\Omega(x, F)$ & $\neg\mathrm{MayDo}(x, \neg F)$

$\mathbf{P}_{2\Omega}(x, F)$: $\mathrm{MayDo}(x, F)$ & $\neg\mathrm{May}\Lambda(x, F)$ & $\mathrm{May}\Omega(x, F)$ & $\neg\mathrm{MayDo}(x, \neg F)$

$\mathbf{P}_{4\Lambda}(x, F)$: $\neg\mathrm{MayDo}(x, F)$ & $\mathrm{May}\Lambda(x, F)$ & $\neg\mathrm{May}\Omega(x, F)$ & $\mathrm{MayDo}(x, \neg F)$

$\mathbf{P}_{4\Omega}(x, F)$: $\neg\mathrm{MayDo}(x, F)$ & $\neg\mathrm{May}\Lambda(x, F)$ & $\mathrm{May}\Omega(x, F)$ & $\mathrm{MayDo}(x, \neg F)$

$\mathbf{P}_5(x, F)$: $\mathrm{Shall\ Do}(x, F)$

$\mathbf{P}_{6\Lambda}(x, F)$: $\mathrm{Shall\ }\Lambda(x, F)$

$\mathbf{P}_{6\Omega}(x, F)$: $\mathrm{Shall\ }\Omega(x, F)$

$\mathbf{P}_7(x, F)$: $\mathrm{Shall\ Do}(x, \neg F)$

1.3   Previous Work

DALMAS [20] is an abstract architecture for a class of norm-regulated multi-agent systems. A deterministic DALMAS is a simple multi-agent system in which the actions of an agent are connected to transitions between system states. In a deterministic DALMAS the agents take turns to act; only one agent at a time may perform an action. By allowing 'do nothing' actions and accelerating the turn-taking, systems with close to asynchronous behaviour can be obtained. A special kind of DALMAS is the *norm-regulated simple deterministic* DALMAS, which employs what is often referred to as 'negative permission', by letting its *deontic structure* (i.e., the set of permissible acts) consist of all acts that are not explicitly prohibited by a normative system $\mathcal{N}$. The DALMAS's *preference structure* consists of the most preferable (according to the agent's utility function) of the acts in the deontic structure. In short, a DALMAS agent's behaviour is regulated by the combination of a normative system and a utility function; this 'agent oeconomicus norma'[3] chooses the most desirable act, according to the utility function, within the 'room for manouver' determined by the norms. The DALMAS's normative framework is based on an algebraic version of the Kanger-Lindahl theory of normative positions, in which normative consequences are formulated by applying normative operators to descriptive conditions. (See Sect. 1.2.) From these general normative conditions follow normative sentences regarding specific states of affairs, which in turn result in permission or prohibition of individual actions in specific situations. (See for example [19, 20] for an introduction.) Hence, the norms in the DALMAS architecture play a different role, and is represented in a fundamentally different way, than, e.g., the decision rules in the *RoboCup* setting (see Sect. 1.1).

Since the agents in a deterministic DALMAS take turns to act, each individual step in a run of a DALMAS may be characterized by an ordered 5-tuple $S = \langle x, s, A, \Omega, S \rangle$ whose components are a set of states S, a state s, an agent-set $\Omega = \{x_1, ..., x_n\}$, the acting ('moving') agent x, and an action-set $A = \{a_1, ..., a_m\}$.[4]

---

[3] Cf. [19, Sect. 1.8.3].

[4] In [9], such a tuple is called a *transition system situation*.

Table 3. Basic transition types.

I. $d(X_\nu; s) \,\&\, d(X_\nu; s^+)$

II. $\neg d(X_\nu; s) \,\&\, d(X_\nu; s^+)$

III. $d(X_\nu; s) \,\&\, \neg d(X_\nu; s^+)$

IV. $\neg d(X_\nu; s) \,\&\, \neg d(X_\nu; s^+)$

In this setting, a may be regarded as a function such that $a(x, s) = s^+$ means that s^+ is the resulting state when x performs act a in state s. In the following, the abbreviation s^+ will be used for $a(x, s)$ when there is no need for an explicit reference to the action a and the acting agent x. As already mentioned, there is no simultaneous action by other agents (including the 'environment', which may be regarded as a special kind of agent). Furthermore, we assume that a ν-ary condition d is true or false on ν agents $x_1, ..., x_\nu \in \Omega$ in s; with the abbreviation X_ν for the agent sequence, this will be written $d(X_\nu; s)$.

Let the situation $\langle x, s \rangle$ be characterized by the moving agent x and the state s in a norm-regulated simple deterministic DALMAS . It is possible in the DALMAS architecture to distinguish between the moving agent and the agent to which normative condition applies[5], but to facilitate the presentation it is assumed in the sequel that norms always apply to the moving agent x in a situation $\langle x, s \rangle$. A norm in $\mathcal{N}$ is represented by an ordered pair $\langle c, Nd \rangle$, where the (descriptive) condition c on a situation $\langle x, s \rangle$ is the *ground* of the norm and the (normative) condition Nd on $\langle x, s \rangle$ is its *consequence*; see, e.g., [20]. Nd is formed by applying a 'norm-creating' operator N to the descriptive condition d.

In the following, the normative framework of the DALMASes employed is based on the notion of an *np9-cis* [12, Sect. 2.2.1], a structure similar to the *np-cis* defined by Lindahl and Odelstad, but based on the 'reduced extended' set of types of normative positions shown in Table 2. It is argued in [12] that a semantics for the normative framework of a DALMAS can be formed by defining a set of 'transition type operators' C_k^a, $k \in \{1, 2\Lambda, 2\Omega, 4\Lambda, 4\Omega, 5, 6\Lambda, 6\Omega, 7\}$, based on Table 4, and a set of corresponding 'transition type prohibition operators' P_k, such that $P_k d(X_\nu; x, s)$ is intended to mean that if $C_k^a d(X_\nu; x, s)$ holds, then a is prohibited for x in $\langle x, s \rangle$. In effect, $P_k d(X_\nu; x, s)$ implies a prohibition of zero, one or two of the four 'basic transition types' (see Table 3, where s^+ refers to the resulting state when the acting agent performs its act) with regard to the state of affairs $d(X_\nu)$. For example, $\langle c, P_k d \rangle$, where c and d can have different arity, represents the sentence

$$\forall x_1, x_2, ..., x_\nu \in \Omega : c(x_1, x_2, ..., x_p; x, s) \to P_k d(x_1, x_2, ..., x_q; x, s)$$

where Ω is the set of agents, x is the acting agent (to which the norm applies) in the situation $\langle x, s \rangle$, and $\nu = \max(p, q)$. If the condition specified by the ground of a norm for some agents in some situation, then the (normative) consequence

---

[5] Cf. the remark in [10, p. 84].

Table 4. Transition type prohibition operators and transition type conditions.

Operators		$Prohibited_a(x, s)$ if
P_1	-	-
$P_{2\Lambda}$	$C_{2\Lambda}^a$	$d(X_\nu; s) \& \neg d(X_\nu; a(x, s))$
$P_{2\Omega}$	$C_{2\Omega}^a$	$\neg d(X_\nu; s) \& \neg d(X_\nu; a(x, s))$
$P_{4\Lambda}$	$C_{4\Lambda}^a$	$\neg d(X_\nu; s) \& d(X_\nu; a(x, s))$
$P_{4\Omega}$	$C_{4\Omega}^a$	$d(X_\nu; s) \& d(X_\nu; a(x, s))$
P_5	C_5^a	$\neg d(X_\nu; a(x, s))$
$P_{6\Lambda}$	$C_{6\Lambda}^a$	$\neg(d(X_\nu; s) \leftrightarrow d(X_\nu; a(x, s)))$
$P_{6\Omega}$	$C_{6\Omega}^a$	$d(X_\nu; s) \leftrightarrow d(X_\nu; a(x, s))$
P_7	C_7^a	$d(X_\nu; a(x, s))$

Table 5. Possible changes of Lap_n.

State of affairs	Possible state of affairs in next state
$Lap_0(x_1, x_2)$	$Lap_0(x_1, x_2), Lap_1(x_1, x_2), Lap_2(x_1, x_2), Lap_3(x_1, x_2)$
$Lap_1(x_1, x_2)$	$Lap_0(x_1, x_2), Lap_1(x_1, x_2), Lap_2(x_1, x_2)$
$Lap_2(x_1, x_2)$	$Lap_0(x_1, x_2), Lap_1(x_1, x_2), Lap_2(x_1, x_2), Lap_3(x_1, x_2), Lap_4(x_1, x_2)$
$Lap_3(x_1, x_2)$	$Lap_0(x_1, x_2), Lap_2(x_1, x_2), Lap_3(x_1, x_2), Lap_4(x_1, x_2), Lap_6(x_1, x_2)$
$Lap_4(x_1, x_2)$	$Lap_2(x_1, x_2), Lap_4(x_1, x_2), Lap_6(x_1, x_2)$
$Lap_6(x_1, x_2)$	$Lap_3(x_1, x_2), Lap_4(x_1, x_2), Lap_6(x_1, x_2), Lap_9(x_1, x_2)$
$x_1 =' x_2 \& Lap_9(x_1, x_2)$	$Lap_6(x_1, x_2), Lap_9(x_1, x_2)$

of the norm is in effect in that situation. If the normative system $\mathcal{N}$ contains a norm whose ground holds in the situation $\langle x, s \rangle$ and whose consequence prohibits the type of transition represented by x performing action a, then a is prohibited for x in $\langle x, s \rangle$:

$$Prohibited_{x,s}(a) \text{ according to } \mathcal{N}$$
if there is a p-ary condition c
and a q-ary condition d
and a $k \in \{1, 2\Lambda, 2\Omega, 4\Lambda, 4\Omega, 5, 6\Lambda, 6\Omega, 7\}$,
such that $\langle c, P_k d \rangle$ is a norm in $\mathcal{N}$,
and there are $x_1, ..., x_\nu$ such that
$$c(x_1, ..., x_p; x, s) \& C_k^a d(x_1, ..., x_q; x, s),$$
where $\nu = \max(p, q)$.

Hence, if $c(x_1, ..., x_p; x, s)$ for some sequence of agents $x_1, ..., x_\nu$, then the normative condition $P_k d(x_1, ..., x_q; x, s)$ is 'in effect'. Thus, if $C_k^a d(x_1, ..., x_q; x, s)$ holds, then a is prohibited for x in s. (Cf. the examples in Sect. 3.1.) Table 4 contains the nine norm-building operators P_k, together with the corresponding C_k^a operators and the result of applying them to $d(x_1, ..., x_q; s)$; cf. Table VI in [11].

A general-level Java/Prolog implementation of the DALMAS architecture has been developed, to facilitate the implementation of specific systems. The Colour & Form system, the Waste-collector system and the Forest Cleaner system are three specific systems that have been implemented using this framework. The reader is referred to [7,8,13,20] for a description of these systems and their instrumentalizations.

The approach to normative systems employed in this framework is ideally suited for evolution of normative systems, since the nine 'reduced extended' types of normative positions are mutually exclusive and jointly exhaustive in the logical sense. Therefore each conceivable normative system, consisting of conditional norms based on descriptive conditions selected from a set of potential grounds and normative conditions selected from a set of potential consequences, could become a candidate for evaluation in the execution of an evolutionary algorithm. This idea will be further explored in the following sections.

2   Example: Explorer DALMAS

Let us consider a class of systems of agents operating in an environment consisting of a grid of squares ordered in rows and columns, in which each square is assigned a pair of integer coordinates. Let us assume that the joint goal of the agents is to explore as much as possible of the grid using a fixed number of moves. An agent can *stay* in the current square, i.e., do nothing, or *move* one square in one of four directions (east, north, west, south) as long as it stays within the boundaries of the grid. In other words, in a given situation, an action is feasible if and only if it does not move the agent off limits. It should of course be noted that these simple systems (in the following referred to as Explorer DALMASes) in themselves are of limited interest, but the idea here is to illustrate how evolutionary mechanisms could be used in the process of designing normative systems for problem-solving MAS.

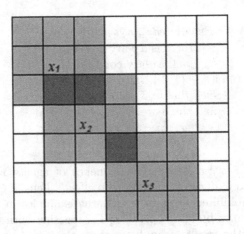

Fig. 1. Overlap of the protected spheres for three agents.

To simulate a situation with limited possibilites for communication between agents and only local knowledge of the environment, we further assume that an agent only knows the status (visited or unvisited) of the immediately surrounding squares, and the location of other agents within two squares. An agent's preference is represented by a very simple utility function such that moving to an unvisited square is preferred over moving to a visited square, and stay is the least preferred action. In the case of a tie between equally preferred actions, one of them is randomly selected. This means that all agents have the same utility function.

To make the situation more concrete, let us assume that the size of the grid is $c \times r$ squares and place three agents at square $(1, 1)$, the leftmost lowest square. Note that this system can be considered as an instance of the Waste-collector system [13, 20], in which visited (resp., unvisited) squares are represented by 0 (resp., 1) units of 'waste'. The higher number of 'waste' carried by an agent, the higher number of unvisited squares have been entered by that agent. It would not be a very difficult task to design a plan where the agents take turns to act in such a way that all remaining $cr - 1$ squares are visited in $cr - 1$ moves. But if the environment gets changed, e.g., is resized or reshaped, the plan must be recalculated. What if we let norms replace plans in this class of environments? Let us investigate the interplay between the agents' utility functions, representing their 'desires', and a normative system which determines their 'room for manouvre'. One idea is to base norms on the spatial relationship between the agents, potentially restricting how the agents may move in the proximity of other agents. We define the condition Lap_n, $n \in \{0, 1, 2, 3, 4, 6, 9\}$, with the intended meaning that $Lap_n(x_i, x_j; s)$ holds if and only if the *protected spheres* of agents x_i and x_j overlap with n squares in a state s. The protected sphere consists of the agent's square plus the eight surrounding squares; see Fig. 1, which illustrates a state in which $Lap_2(x_1, x_2)$, $Lap_1(x_2, x_3)$, and $Lap_0(x_1, x_3)$ holds. Table 5 shows how the overlap can change from one state to another, given the five available actions. Note that $Lap_n(x_i, x_j)$ implies $x_i =' x_j$ for $n < 9$, and $x_i = x_j$ implies $Lap_9(x_i, x_j)$. Furthermore, $Lap_n(x_i, x_j)$ implies $\neg Lap_m(x_i, x_j)$ for $n \neq m$. In other words, $Lap_n R ='$ for $n < 9$, $= R Lap_9$, and $Lap_n R Lap'_m$ for $n \neq m$, where d' is the negation of the condition d and R is the implicative relation on conditions which defines the *cis-Bqo*'s of grounds and consequences of the normative system.

Now let the 'elementary' conditions Lap_0, Lap_1, Lap_2, Lap_3, Lap_4, Lap_6, together with the 'non-elementary' condition $(=' \wedge Lap_9)$, form a set of potential descriptive grounds for conditional norms. The set of potential normative consequences corresponding to each ground is constructed by applying the norm-building operators P_1, $P_{2\Lambda}$, ..., P_7 (see Sect. 1.3) to the conditions listed in the corresponding rows in Table 5. Thus, the potential consequences for, e.g., Lap_1 are $P_1 Lap_0$,..., $P_7 Lap_0$, $P_1 Lap_1$,..., $P_7 Lap_1$, and $P_1 Lap_2$,..., $P_7 Lap_2$. Note that it would be meaningless to, e.g., let $P_i Lap_4$ be a potential consequence for Lap_0, since none of the available acts can change the state of the system in such a way that $Lap_0(x_i, x_j)$ holds in one state and $Lap_4(x_i, x_j)$ holds in the next state.

With these building blocks available, normative systems for Explorer DALMASes can be constructed. Let us employ the following scheme: For each condition c in the leftmost column of Table 5, one norm $\langle M_1 c, P_i d \rangle$ is added to the normative system for each condition d in the rightmost column.[6] E.g., for Lap_0 we add four norms: $\langle M_1 Lap_0, P_{k_0} Lap_0 \rangle$, $\langle M_1 Lap_0, P_{k_1} Lap_1 \rangle$, $\langle M_1 Lap_0, P_{k_2} Lap_2 \rangle$, and $\langle M_1 Lap_0, P_{k_3} Lap_3 \rangle$. Note that, as regards the ground $(=' \wedge Lap_9)$, one of $\langle M_1 (=' \wedge Lap_9), P_{k_0} Lap_9 \rangle$ and $\langle M_1 (=' \wedge Lap_9), P_{k_1} Lap_6 \rangle$ is redundant, and can therefore be removed.[7] This gives a total of 24 norms. Note, however, that not all normative systems formed in this way are *coherent*. To begin with, some sets of rules may be contradictory, according to the intended meaning of the P_i operators, but the problem of coherence (sometimes referred to as 'absence of conflicts') cannot simply be reduced to logical consistency; see for example [1]. We will return to this issue in Sect. 3.1.

We would now like to find the best normative system, i.e., the normative system that, together with the simple utility function described earlier, on average makes the Explorer system most efficient. The following measure of efficiency will be employed: the normative system is applied to three different Explorer DALMASes, operating on grids of (almost) equal sizes but different shapes: 6×8 squares, 7×7 squares, and 10×5 squares, respectively. On each grid, three agents are initially placed on square $(1, 1)$. A k-event run of each of these three systems will be performed, where k is the number of unvisited squares from the beginning, i.e., $k = cr - 1$. For each run, the ratio between the total number of visited squares and the total number of unvisited squares in the beginning is calculated. If the normative system is not coherent, in the sense that, at some point during the run, all actions (including stay) become prohibited for the acting agent, then the evaluation score is set to 0. The score of the normative system under evaluation is then the average of the three ratios obtained. We have now obtained an optimization problem which may be solved with the help of an evolutionary algorithm.

3   Evolution of Explorer Norms

Evolutionary algorithms (EA), being a subfield of evolutionary computation, use the principles of biological evolution (such as reproduction, mutation, recombination, and selection) to solve problems on computers. For a comprehensive introduction to this field the reader is referred to, e.g., [22]. In the Explorer

---

[6] The 'move operator' M_κ, where κ is less than or equal to the arity of the condition to which it is applied, identifies the agent to which the normative condition applies with the moving agent x in the situation $\langle x, s \rangle$, as well as with the κth agent in the argument sequence X_ν. For example, $M_1 Lap_0(x_1, x_2, x_3; x, s)$ holds if and only if $Lap_0(x_1, x_2; s)$ holds, and $x_1 = x_3$, and $x_3 = x$. See, e.g., [9] for an explanation.

[7] This is due to the fact that $Lap_6 R Lap_9'$ and $Lap_9 R Lap_6'$. Thus, if a certain type of normative position holds regarding Lap_9, then this completely determines the type of normative position regarding Lap_6, or vice versa. For example, when Lap_9 holds, if $P_7 Lap_6$, then it must follow that $P_5 Lap_9$.

DALMAS setting, there is some randomness in the agents' choices of actions, and in such 'noisy' domains, evolutionary algorithms are known to work well [5]. We thus implement a basic genetic algorithm (one of the most common forms of EAs) for Explorer DALMAS norms:

1. **Genesis.** Create an initial population of n candidate normative systems, half of which are entirely randomly generated and half of which consist of P_1-consequences (the most permissive consequences) only. Each candidate is represented by a character string consisting of 24 characters, one for each norm, from $\{'1', ..., '9'\}$, where '1' represents P_1, '2' represents P_{2A}, '3' represents $P_{2\Omega}$, '4' represents P_{4A}, etc.

2. **Evaluation.** Evaluate each member of the population, by translating the character string to a normative system according to the scheme presented in Sect. 2, running three different systems regulated by this normative system and using as fitness function the average of the evaluation scores of the three runs. For example, a 'chromosome' starting with "371529..." is translated to the following normative system:
$\{\langle M_1(='\wedge Lap_9), P_{2\Omega}Lap_9\rangle, \quad \langle M_1Lap_6, P_{6A}Lap_9\rangle, \quad \langle M_1Lap_6, P_1Lap_6\rangle, \langle M_1Lap_6, P_{4\Omega}Lap_4\rangle, \langle M_1Lap_6, P_{2A}Lap_3\rangle, \langle M_1Lap_4, P_7Lap_6\rangle, ...\}$

3. **Survival of the Fittest.** Select a number of members of the evaluated population, favouring those with higher fitness scores, to be the parents of the next generation.

4. **Evolution.** Generate a new population of offspring by randomly altering and combining elements of the parent candidates. The evolution is performed by the two basic evolutionary operators *cross-over* and *mutation*.

5. **Iteration.** Repeat steps 2–4 until the termination condition (see Table 6) is met.

The evolutionary algorithm was implemented using the Java-based Watchmaker framework for evolutionary computation[8] together with a slightly adapted Java/Prolog implementation of the Waste-collector system [7,13].[9] The latter was used in step 2 to perform the k-event runs of Explorer systems to be evaluated.

3.1   Result

The algorithm was run with the parameter values shown in Table 6; the execution time on an ordinary laptop was 5–6 h. The graph in Fig. 2 shows the fitness values (evaluation scores) of the best normative system, as well as the average fitness values, in each generation. We can see that, initially, the best fitness (which is obtained by a normative system with P_1-consequences only, i.e., a normative system which allows everything) is around 0.78. Up to around generation 25, we can see a slow but quite steady improvement in the best fitness values, although

---

[8] http://watchmaker.uncommons.org/.

[9] The source code is available for download via http://drpa.se/norms/nrtssit, together with a log of a run of the algorithm.

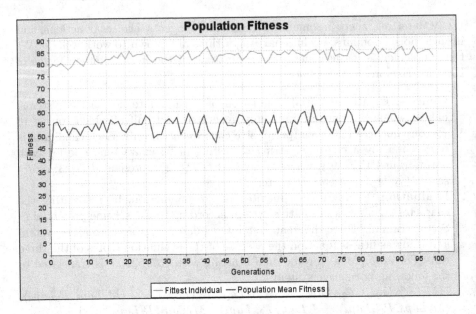

Fig. 2. Evolution progress. Upper curve shows fitness of best individual, lower curve shows mean fitness. Algorithm parameter values are shown in Table 6. A log of the run is available for download via http://drpa.se/norms/nrtssit/.

the impact of the slight randomness in the agents' choices of actions is clear. The highest scores, just above 0.86, which roughly corresponds to three more visited squares per run, are obtained in generations 41 and 78. After 25 generations there seems to be no significant improvement.

According to the log, the best normative system in generation 41 (with P_1-norms omitted for brevity) is translated to

$$\langle M_1(='\ \wedge Lap_9), P_{2\Omega} Lap_9 \rangle, \langle M_1 Lap_6, P_{6\Lambda} Lap_9 \rangle, \langle M_1 Lap_4, P_{6\Omega} Lap_4 \rangle,$$
$$\langle M_1 Lap_3, P_{2\Lambda} Lap_6 \rangle, \langle M_1 Lap_2, P_{6\Lambda} Lap_4 \rangle, \langle M_1 Lap_2, P_{4\Omega} Lap_3 \rangle,$$
$$\langle M_1 Lap_1, P_{4\Omega} Lap_2 \rangle, \langle M_1 Lap_0, P_{4\Lambda} Lap_1 \rangle.$$

A closer look at the log reveals that, of the best candidates with a fitness over 0.85,

(1) all but one (13 out of 14) contain either $\langle M_1 Lap_6, P_{6\Lambda} Lap_9 \rangle$ or $\langle M_1 Lap_6, P_{4\Lambda} Lap_9 \rangle$, and

(2) all but three contain $\langle M_1 Lap_2, P_{6\Lambda} Lap_4 \rangle$ or $\langle M_1 Lap_2, P_{4\Lambda} Lap_4 \rangle$.

Let us first consider (1). The intended meaning of $\langle M_1 Lap_6, P_{6\Lambda} Lap_9 \rangle$ is that if $Lap_6(x_1, x_2; s)$ for some agents x_1, x_2, and x_3 such that $x_1 = x_3$ and x_1 is the moving agent x, then the normative condition $P_{6\Lambda} Lap_9(x_1, x_2, x_3; x, s)$ holds, and thus, according to the definition of $C_{6\Lambda}^a$ (see row 7 in Table 4) action a is prohibited for x if

Table 6. Choice of parameter values.

Parameter	Value
Population size	100 individuals
Termination condition	100 generations evolved
Level of elitism	25 %
Crossover probability	0.7
Crossover points	6
Mutation probability	0.05
Selection strategy	Roulette wheel selection

$$\neg Lap_9(x, x_2; s) \,\&\, Lap_9(x, x_2; a(x, s))$$

or

$$Lap_9(x, x_2; s) \,\&\, \neg Lap_9(x, x_2; a(x, s)).$$

Now, when $Lap_6(x, x_2; s)$, the second disjunct never becomes true, since $Lap_6 \, R \, Lap_9'$ (i.e., Lap_6 implies Lap_9'); hence a is prohibited for x if

$$\neg Lap_9(x, x_2; s) \,\&\, Lap_9(x, x_2; a(x, s)).$$

Since $\neg Lap_9(x, x_2; s)$ follows from $Lap_6(x, x_2; s)$, a is prohibited for x if $Lap_9(x, x_2; a(x, s))$. Similarly, the meaning of $\langle M_1 Lap_6, P_{4\Lambda} Lap_9 \rangle$ is that if Lap_6 $(x_1, x_2; s)$ for some agents x_1, x_2, and x_3, such that $x_1 = x_3$ and $x_3 = x$, then $P_{4\Lambda} Lap_9(x_1, x_2, x_3; x, s)$ holds, and thus (see Table 4, row 4) a is prohibited for x if

$$\neg Lap_9(x, x_2; s) \,\&\, Lap_9(x, x_2; a(x, s));$$

i.e., when $Lap_6(x, x_2; s)$, it follows that $\neg Lap_9(x, x_2; s)$, and thus a is prohibited for x if $Lap_9(x, x_2; a(x, s))$. Hence, $\langle M_1 Lap_6, P_{6\Lambda} Lap_9 \rangle$ and $\langle M_1 Lap_6, P_{4\Lambda} Lap_9 \rangle$ are 'operationally equivalent' in the Explorer DALMAS setting, in the sense that they prohibit the same actions in the same situation. Furthermore, both are operationally equivalent to $\langle M_1 Lap_6, P_7 Lap_9 \rangle$ with the intended interpretation that if Lap_6 then the moving agent shall see to it that not Lap_9. A similar case can be made for (2); $\langle M_1 Lap_2, P_{6\Lambda} Lap_4 \rangle$, $\langle M_1 Lap_2, P_{4\Lambda} Lap_4 \rangle$ and $\langle M_1 Lap_2, P_7 Lap_4 \rangle$ are operationally equivalent and thus interchangeable in this setting. The notion of operational equivalence of norms is further discussed in Sect. 3.2.

It is showed by (1) and (2) that, in some settings, the set of consequences may contain redundancy. This is an effect of the fact that, in this particular setting, the set of grounds and the set of consequences are constructed from the same set of conditions. Whether this is a problem or not is probably dependent on the particular setting. We may also note that, for example, the meaning of $\langle M_1 Lap_0, P_{4\Omega} Lap_2 \rangle$ would be that if $Lap_0(x_1, x_2; s)$ for some agents x_1, x_2, and x_3, such that $x_1 = x_3$ and $x_3 = x$, then $P_{4\Omega} Lap_2(x_1, x_2, x_3; x, s)$ holds, and thus (see Table 2, row 5) a is prohibited for x if

$$Lap_2(x, x_2; s) \,\&\, Lap_2(x, x_2; a(x, s)).$$

Now, $Lap_2(x_1, x_2; s)$ & $Lap_2(x_1, x_2; a(x, s))$ can never become true when Lap_0 $(x_1, x_2; s)$, since $Lap_0 \, R \, Lap'_2$. Hence, $\langle M_1 Lap_0, P_{4\Omega} Lap_2 \rangle$ will never prohibit any actions, and is thus operationally equivalent to, $\langle M_1 Lap_0, P_1 Lap_2 \rangle$ in this setting. This illustrates another kind of redundancy. Another consequence of employing negative permission is that normative systems may evolve which are incoherent (see Sect. 1.3) according to the underlying logic of the P_k operators, but still meaningful in an 'operational' sense. A discussion of these matters is beyond the scope of this paper, but a more precise representation of genes and a more careful design of the genetic operators could avoid or at least reduce logical incoherence and redundancy in the setting at hand. This could, potentially, significantly reduce the search space for the evolutionary algorithm. For this purpose, the mechanisms for norm addition and subtraction described in [16, Sect. 4.3] might be very useful, as well as a more thorough analysis of the relationships between potential grounds and consequences, in order to exploit the possibility of operational equivalence of norms (Sect. 3.2).

Based on the above analysis, the following set of Explorer norms (again, P_1-norms are omitted) is suggested: $\{\langle M_1 Lap_6, P_7 Lap_9 \rangle, \langle M_1 Lap_2, P_7 Lap_4 \rangle\}$. The intended interpretation is

(1) $\forall x, y : Lap_6(x, y; s) \rightarrow P_7 Lap_9(x, y, x; x, s))$; and
(2) $\forall x, y : Lap_2(x, y; s) \rightarrow P_7 Lap_4(x, y, x; x, s))$.

Using the deontic operator Shall and the action operator Do, these norms are expressed as follows: (1) For all x, y: if $Lap_6(x, y)$, and x is the moving agent, then $\text{Shall Do}(x, \neg Lap_9(x, y))$; and (2) For all x, y: if $Lap_2(x, y)$, and x is the moving agent, then $\text{Shall Do}(x, \neg Lap_4(x, y))$; cf. [11,20]. This represents the following simple set of 'rules of thumb': (1) If you stand in the square next to another agent's square, you shall act so that you do not end up in the same location as the other agent, and (2) if your protected sphere overlaps another agent's protected sphere with two squares, you shall act so that the overlap does not increase to four.

Test runs indicate that the average improvement with this very simple normative system compared with a system with no restrictions is two to three additional squares visited. As the Explorer DALMAS example was chosen primarily for demonstration purposes, we shall be content with the simple analysis performed here. In more complex scenarios, other more powerful (e.g., statistical) methods could be useful.

3.2   Discussion

Validation of the suggested approach to the design of normative systems for problem-solving MAS is, of course, a non-trivial problem. One aspect of this problem is the difficulty of applying this approach, but most important is probably to focus on the quality of the results it produces, i.e., to validate the systems obtained by applying the approach. The performance of norm-regulated MAS designed in this way could, for example, be compared with the performance of systems (norm-regulated systems as well as, e.g., planning systems) designed by hand. Such comparisons require domain-specific performance measures, which makes a general-level (i.e., domain independent) validation very difficult, if not impossible. Even within a specific domain, validation is non-trivial and sensitivity analyses are required. A good starting-point is to consider every tool in the evolutionary toolbox, together with a thorough analysis of the domain at hand, to increase the chance of evolving the optimal normative system. First, the parameters controlling the evolutionary algorithm may be varied: the population size, the number of evolved generations, the level of elitism (i.e., the portion of the best candidates which are allowed to survive into the next generation), the probability of crossover, the number of crossover points, and the selection strategy (e.g., tournament selection instead of roulette wheel). Other ideas include using other representations of chromosomes, such as tree-based representations to allow for normative systems with a variable number of norms, or (as has already been mentioned) more carefully designed evolutionary operators that exclude redundant and/or incoherent candidates from evaluation. More advanced schemes, such as island evolution (where several populations are evolved in parallel, with a small probability of 'migration' between such 'islands') or cooling (where the crossover and mutation probabilities gradually decrease), could also be tried. One example of a more careful design of an evolutionary operator is to restrict the mutation operator by the notion of 'deontic paths' [15, pp. 110ff] between types of normative positions. In short, the deontic path follows the edges in the Hasse diagram of the relation 'less free than' on types of normative positions; cf. [15, p. 105] and [12, Fig. 1]. The restriction could be that a gene which represents a type operator P_i applied to a descriptive condition d, may only be changed by mutation to represent a new operator P_j in such a way that P_j lies immediately above or below P_i on the deontic path between them. This could bring more stability into the evolution process, since the effects of mutations would be less dramatic.

Furthermore, the parameters for the particular setting may also be varied. For example, one might want to consider grounds and consequences based on other conditions. In the Explorer DALMAS domain one could try, e.g., Lap_n conditions based on larger protected spheres (since it seems reasonable to expect that a normative system based on small protected spheres will be most 'effective' when the agents are relatively close to each other), or generalized versions of Lap_n conditions involving three or more agents. Other ideas are to allow individual utility functions for each agent, or evolving the utility function and the normative system in parallel. In general, special treatment is required for domains such as the Explorer DALMAS where the fitness evaluations are 'noisy', i.e., subject to some degree of randomness. To deal with noisy fitness evaluations, a number of techniques are available, for example increasing the population size, and resampling and averaging the fitness. [6, Sect. 3.3] As described in Sect. 2, a variant of the latter technique is used in the Explorer DALMAS fitness evaluations. Another option regarding the evaluation function is to allow more or less variation regarding, e.g., grid sizes or shapes, number of agents, number of events per run and number of runs per normative system. However, large populations, in combination with expensive fitness calculations in each generation, are computationally challenging. The *moving average* approach by Di Pietro et al. can be used to reduce the number of samples needed per generation, and thus allow for running more generations in a given run-time. When a candidate is generated for the first time, its 'fitness array' is initialized with n fitness evaluations. For each new generation, the evaluation score is calculated only once, and the oldest score in the fitness array is replaced with the new score. A candidate's fitness is then the average of the evaluation scores in the fitness array.

Operational Equivalence of Norms. It was observed in Sect. 3.1 that norms where grounds and consequences are based on the same set of descriptive conditions can become equivalent in the sense that they have exactly the same effect in the same situations. Let us investigate this further. First, recall the definitions of the C_i^a operators in Table 4, and note the following:

$$C_5^a c(X_\nu, x_{\nu+1}; x, s) \text{ iff } [c(X_\nu; s) \ \& \ \neg c(X_\nu; a(x, s))] \text{ or } [\neg c(X_\nu; s) \ \& \ \neg c(X_\nu; a(x, s))]$$
$$C_{6\Lambda}^a c(X_\nu, x_{\nu+1}; x, s) \text{ iff } [c(X_\nu; s) \ \& \ \neg c(X_\nu; a(x, s))] \text{ or } [\neg c(X_\nu; s) \ \& \ c(X_\nu; a(x, s))]$$
$$C_{6\Omega}^a c(X_\nu, x_{\nu+1}; x, s) \text{ iff } [c(X_\nu; s) \ \& \ c(X_\nu; a(x, s))] \text{ or } [\neg c(X_\nu; s) \ \& \ \neg c(X_\nu; a(x, s))]$$
$$C_7^a c(X_\nu, x_{\nu+1}; x, s) \text{ iff } [c(X_\nu; s) \ \& \ c(X_\nu; a(x, s))] \text{ or } [\neg c(X_\nu; s) \ \& \ c(X_\nu; a(x, s))]$$

Now suppose for example that $c \in C$, the set of potential grounds, but also $c \in D$, the set of descriptive conditions underlying the set of potential normative consequences. Let M_κ be a 'move operator', for example M_1, such that $\kappa \leq \nu$, and suppose that c is true of some agents $x_1, ..., x_\nu$ in a state s. We may then note the following:

(1) $C_{2\Omega}^a c(X_\nu, x_{\nu+1}; x, s)$, and $C_{4\Lambda}^a c(X_\nu, x_{\nu+1}; x, s)$ are false whenever $c(X_\nu; s)$. Hence, the set of actions a that would be prohibited by $\langle M_\kappa c, P_{2\Omega} c \rangle$, resp. $\langle M_\kappa c, P_{4\Lambda} c \rangle$, is exactly the same as the set of actions that would be prohibited by $\langle M_\kappa c, P_1 c \rangle$, *viz.* the empty set.

(2) The second disjunct of $C_{6\Lambda}^a c(X_\nu, x_{\nu+1}; x, s)$ and the second disjunct of $C_5^a c$ $(X_\nu, x_{\nu+1}; x, s)$ must be false. Hence, if $c(X_\nu; s)$, then $C_{6\Lambda}^a c(X_\nu, x_{\nu+1}; x, s)$ iff $C_{2\Lambda}^a c(X_\nu, x_{\nu+1}; x, s)$ iff $C_5^a c(X_\nu, x_{\nu+1}; x, s)$, which means that the actions that would be prohibited by $\langle M_\kappa c, P_{2\Lambda} c \rangle$, $\langle M_\kappa c, P_5 c \rangle$, and $\langle M_\kappa c, P_{6\Lambda} c \rangle$, are exactly the same.

(3) The second disjunct of $C_{6\Omega}^a c(X_\nu, x_{\nu+1}; x, s)$ and the second disjunct of $C_7^a c$ $(X_\nu, x_{\nu+1}; x, s)$ must be false. Hence, if $c(X_\nu; s)$, then $C_{6\Omega}^a c(X_\nu, x_{\nu+1}; x, s)$ iff $C_{4\Omega}^a c(X_\nu, x_{\nu+1}; x, s)$ iff $C_7^a c(X_\nu, x_{\nu+1}; x, s)$; so the actions that would be prohibited by $\langle M_\kappa c, P_{4\Omega} c \rangle$, $\langle M_\kappa c, P_{6\Omega} c \rangle$, and $\langle M_\kappa c, P_7 c \rangle$, are exactly the same. In other words, given that $c(X_\nu)$ holds, $P_{2\Omega}$, $P_{4\Lambda}$, and P_1 are 'equally prohibitive', and the same holds for $P_{2\Lambda}$, $P_{4\Omega}$, and P_5, resp. $P_{2\Lambda}$, $P_{6\Omega}$, and P_7. Now suppose that $\neg c(X_\nu)$ holds for some agents $x_1, ..., x_\nu$ and some act a in s:

(4) Since $C_{2\Lambda}^a c(X_\nu, x_{\nu+1}; x, s)$ and $C_{4\Omega}^a c(X_\nu, x_{\nu+1}; x, s)$ are false whenever $\neg c$ $(X_\nu; s)$, the set of actions that would be prohibited by $\langle M_\kappa c', P_{2\Lambda} c \rangle$, resp.

$\langle Mc', P_{4\Omega}c\rangle$, is exactly the same as the set of actions that would be prohibited by $\langle M_\kappa c', P_1 c\rangle$, *viz.* the empty set.

(5) The second disjunct of $C^a_{6\Lambda}c(X_\nu, x_{\nu+1}; x, s)$ and the first disjunct of $C^a_7 c(X_\nu, x_{\nu+1}; x, s)$ must be false. Hence, if $\neg c(X_\nu; s)$, then $C^a_{6\Lambda}c(X_\nu, x_{\nu+1}; x, s)$ iff $C^a_{4\Lambda}c(X_\nu, x_{\nu+1}; x, s)$ iff $C^a_7 c(X_\nu, x_{\nu+1}; x, s)$, which means that the actions that would be prohibited by $\langle M_\kappa c', P_{4\Lambda}c\rangle$, and $\langle M_\kappa c', P_{6\Lambda}c\rangle$, and $\langle M_\kappa c', P_7 c\rangle$, are exactly the same.

(6) The first disjunct of $C^a_{6\Omega}c(X_\nu, x_{\nu+1}; x, s)$ and the first disjunct of $C^a_5 c(X_\nu, x_{\nu+1}; x, s)$ must be false. Hence, if $\neg c(X_\nu; s)$, then $C^a_{6\Omega}c(X_\nu, x_{\nu+1}; x, s)$ iff $C^a_{2\Omega}c(X_\nu, x_{\nu+1}; x, s)$ iff $C^a_5 c(X_\nu, x_{\nu+1}; x, s)$; therefore, the actions that would be prohibited by $\langle M_\kappa c', P_{2\Omega}c\rangle$, $\langle M_\kappa c', P_{6\Omega}c\rangle$, and $\langle M_\kappa c', P_5 c\rangle$ are exactly the same.

Thus, if $\neg c(X_\nu)$ holds, then $P_{2\Lambda}$, $P_{4\Omega}$, and P_1 are equally prohibitive, and the same holds for $P_{4\Lambda}$, $P_{6\Lambda}$, and P_7, resp. $P_{2\Lambda}$, P_5, and $P_{6\Omega}$. It seems plausible that 'equally prohibitive' could be a suitable foundation for a notion of operational equivalence of norms. It is straightforward to generalize the above arguments to cases where $c \, R \, d$ or $c \, R \, d'$, i.e., where c implies d, resp., c implies d'.

4 Conclusion and Future Work

Concrete advice on how to use evolutionary mechanisms as part of the pre-runtime design of normative systems for problem-solving MAS were presented. The idea behind the methodology sketched here is to use a top-down approach of selecting (a subset of) the most 'efficient' norms from an evolved normative system, rather than a bottom-up approach of designing a normative system entirely from scratch. To illustrate the idea, a simple system, based on the DALMAS architecture for norm-regulated MAS was employed as part of the evaluation step of an evolutionary algorithm. The results show that an evolutionary algorithm has the potential of being a useful tool when designing normative systems for problem-solving MAS.

Ideas for future work include trying to formalize and further investigate the notion of operational equivalence of norms, which was introduced in Sect. 3.2. Also left for future work is further validation of the suggested methodology, for example by applying the methodology in other domains in which the grounds of the norms and the consequences are based on different sets of descriptive conditions, or by further validating the evolved normative system for the Explorer DALMAS. One could experiment with different domain-specific parameters as well as evolutionary algorithm parameters, as suggested in Sect. 3.2, to see if better solutions can be found and thus gain more support for the ideas suggested here. It could be interesting to, e.g., explore normative systems of variable size and evaluation functions which impose a penalty for large normative systems, since in many cases it could be desirable to rely on a small number of 'rules of thumb' and avoid overly complex normative systems which may become expensive in terms of calculations. Investigating the possibility to design more accurate evolutionary operators, for example by exploiting the fact that certain norms are operationally equivalent in the Explorer DALMAS setting, also seems like a promising idea.

Acknowledgements. The author is very grateful to Jan Odelstad and Magnus Boman for valuable ideas and suggestions, to participants of ICAART 2015 for discussions in relation to this paper, and to the organizers of the conference for the opportunity to expand the conference paper.

References

1. Alechina, N., Bassiliades, N., Dastani, M., Vos, M.D., Logan, B., Mera, S., Morris-Martin, A., Schapachnik, F.: Computational models for normative multi-agent systems. In: Andrighetto, G., Governatori, G., Noriega, P., van der Torre, L.W.N. (eds.) Normative Multi-Agent Systems, Dagstuhl Follow-Ups, vol. 4, pp. 71–92. Schloss Dagstuhl-Leibniz-Zentrum fuer Informatik, Dagstuhl, Germany (2013). http://drops.dagstuhl.de/opus/volltexte/2013/4000
2. Andrighetto, G., Castelfranchi, C., Mayor, E., McBreen, J., Lopez-Sanchez, M., Parsons, S.: (Social) Norm dynamics. In: Andrighetto, G., Governatori, G., Noriega, P., van der Torre, L.W.N. (eds.) Normative Multi-Agent Systems, Dagstuhl Follow-Ups, vol. 4, pp. 135–170. Schloss Dagstuhl-Leibniz-Zentrum fuer Informatik, Dagstuhl, Germany (2013). http://drops.dagstuhl.de/opus/volltexte/2013/4002
3. Andrighetto, G., Governatori, G., Noriega, P., van der Torre, L.W.: Normative multi-agent systems. Dagstuhl Follow-Ups. vol. 4. Schloss Dagstuhl-Leibniz-Zentrum fuer Informatik (2013). http://www.dagstuhl.de/dagpub/978-3-939897-51-4
4. Balke, T., Cranefield, S., Tosto, G.D., Mahmoud, S., Paolucci, M., Savarimuthu, B.T.R., Verhagen, H.: Simulation and NorMAS. In: Andrighetto, G., Governatori, G., Noriega, P., van der Torre, L.W.N. (eds.) Normative Multi-Agent Systems, Dagstuhl Follow-Ups, vol. 4, pp. 171–189. Schloss Dagstuhl-Leibniz-Zentrum fuer Informatik, Dagstuhl, Germany (2013). http://drops.dagstuhl.de/opus/volltexte/2013/4003
5. Darwen, P.: Computationally intensive and noisy tasks: co-evolutionary learning and temporal difference learning on backgammon. In: Proceedings of the 2000 Congress on Evolutionary Computation, vol. 2, pp. 872–879 (2000)
6. Di Pietro, A., While, R.L., Barone, L.: Learning in robocup keepaway using evolutionary algorithms. GECCO **2**, 1065–1072 (2002)
7. Hjelmblom, M.: Deontic action-logic multi-agent systems in Prolog. Technical report 30, University of Gävle, Division of Computer Science (2008). http://urn.kb.se/resolve?urn=urn:nbn:se:hig:diva-1475
8. Hjelmblom, M.: State transitions and normative positions within normative systems. Technical report 37, University of Gävle, Department of Industrial Development, IT and Land Management (2011). http://urn.kb.se/resolve?urn=urn:nbn:se:hig:diva-10595
9. Hjelmblom, M.: Norm-regulated transition system situations. In: Filipe, J., Fred, A. (eds.) Proceedings of the 5th International Conference on Agents and Artificial Intelligence, ICAART 2013, pp. 109–117. SciTePress, Portugal (2013). http://urn.kb.se/resolve?urn=urn:nbn:se:hig:diva-13987

10. Hjelmblom, M.: Instrumentalization of norm-regulated transition system situations. In: Filipe, J., Fred, A. (eds.) ICAART 2013. CCIS, vol. 449, pp. 80–94. Springer, Heidelberg (2014). http://dx.doi.org/10.1007/978-3-662-44440-5_5
11. Hjelmblom, M.: Normative positions within norm-regulated transition system situations. In: 2014 IEEE/WIC/ACM International Joint Conferences on Web Intelligence (WI) and Intelligent Agent Technologies (IAT), vol. 3, pp. 238–245, August 2014
12. Hjelmblom, M.: Normative positions in multi-agent systems (2015). Submitted to Web Intelligence and Agent Systems: An International Journal (WIAS)
13. Hjelmblom, M., Odelstad, J.: jDALMAS: A java/prolog framework for deontic action-logic multi-agent systems. In: Håkansson, A., Nguyen, N.T., Hartung, R.L., Howlett, R.J., Jain, L.C. (eds.) KES-AMSTA 2009. LNCS, vol. 5559, pp. 110–119. Springer, Heidelberg (2009)
14. Kanger, S.: Law and logic. Theoria 38(3), 105–132 (1972). http://dx.doi.org/10.1111/j.1755-2567.1972.tb00928.x
15. Lindahl, L.: Position and change: a study in law and logic. Synthese library, D. Reidel Pub. Co. (1977). http://www.google.com/books?id=_QwWhOK8aY0C
16. Lindahl, L., Odelstad, J.: The theory of joining-systems. In: Gabbay, D., Horthy, J., Parent, X., van der Meyden, R., van der Torre, L. (eds.) Handbook of Deontic Logic, Chap. 9, vol. 1, pp. 545–634. College Publications, London (2013)
17. Luke, S., Hohn, C., Farris, J., Jackson, G., Hendler, J.: Co-evolving soccer softbot team coordination with genetic programming. In: Kitano, H. (ed.) RoboCup 1997. LNCS, vol. 1395, pp. 398–411. Springer, Heidelberg (1998). http://dx.doi.org/10.1007/3-540-64473-3_76
18. Nakashima, T., Takatani, M., Udo, M., Ishibuchi, H.: An evolutionary approach for strategy learning in robocup soccer. In: 2004 IEEE International Conference on Systems, Man and Cybernetics, vol. 2, pp. 2023–2028. IEEE (2004)
19. Odelstad, J.: Many-Sorted Implicative Conceptual Systems. Ph.D. thesis, Royal Institute of Technology, Sweden (2008). qC 20100901
20. Odelstad, J., Boman, M.: Algebras for agent norm-regulation. Ann. Math. Artif. Intell. 42, 141–166 (2004). doi:10.1023/B:AMAI.0000034525.49481.4a
21. Verhagen, H., Boman, M.: Norms can replace plans. In: IJCAI 1999 Workshop on Adjustable, Autonomous Systems (1999)
22. Whitley, D.: An overview of evolutionary algorithms: practical issues and common pitfalls. Inf. Softw. Technol. 43(14), 817–831 (2001). http://www.sciencedirect.com/science/article/pii/S0950584901001884

Parsing with Partially Known Grammar

Ife Adebara[1], Veronica Dahl[1,3](✉), and Sergio Tessaris[2]

[1] Department of Computer Science, Simon Fraser University,
University Drive, Burnaby 8888, Canada
iadebara@sfu.ca, veronica@cs.sfu.ca
[2] Faculty of Computer Science, Free University of Bozen-Bolzano,
Piazza Domenicani 3, 39100 Bolzano, Italy
tessaris@inf.unibz.it
[3] Institute of Software Engineering and Compiler Construction,
University of Ulm, Ulm, Germany

Abstract. We address the problem of making syntactic sense of text for which the grammar has only partial information. Our proposed methodology is to adapt a recent formalism, Womb Grammars, into parsing creative text that departs from the grammar at hand, or which cannot rely on a complete grammar being available. We argue that unspecified information can be detected with appropriate ontologies together with our adaptation of a recently introduced constraint-based methodology for acquiring linguistic information on a given language from that of another. Our implementation tool is CHRG (Constraint Handling Rule Grammars). We examine as well possible extensions to multilingual text parsing. Our proposed methodology exploits the descriptive power of constraints both for defining sentence acceptability and for inferring lexical knowledge from a word's sentential context, even when foreign.

Keywords: Partial grammars · Womb grammars · Ontologies · Imperfect querying · Mixed language text · Constraint acquisition · Universal grammar · Parsing · CHRG (Constraint Handling Rule Grammars) · Constraint based grammars · Property grammars

1 Introduction

Social media promotes communication across countries, multiplying the opportunities for users to spontaneously mix syntax, lexicons and jargons. Also, there are domains where syntactic arrangements different from the standard arrangement are acceptable. These factors, together with the increasing infiltration of English words and specific group jargons into technical and even every day communications in many other languages, results in the need for ever more flexible parsers if we are to succeed in extracting information from text in timely fashion. Yet we are quite far from being able to address the challenges inherent in

This research was supported by NSERC Discovery grant 31611024 and was started during a visit by Veronica Dahl and Sergio Tessaris to Universidade Nova de Lisboa.

multilingual and creative text. In fact, one of the worst nightmares for linguistics is that of trying to parse textual sources that do not respect the grammar.

Traditional parsers focus on constructing syntactic trees for complete and correct sentences in a given language. More flexible parsing models can be arrived at in economic fashion by giving up syntactic trees as a focus and focusing instead on *grammar constraints*, also called *properties*. For instance, if we were to work with tree-oriented rules such as:

```
np --> det, adj, n.
```

their adaptation into a language where nouns must precede adjectives would require changing every rule where these two constituents are involved. In contrast, by expressing the same rule in terms of separate constraints, we only need to change the precedence constraint into saying that adjectives must precede nouns, and the modification carries over to the entire grammar without further ado.

In this paper we propose to combine Womb Grammar parsing—a property-based methodology for multilingual parsing developed by Dahl and Miralles [10]-with ontologies, in view of further specifying partial information which can be lexical or structural, in an automatic manner.

The remainder of this paper is organized as follows: Sect. 2 discusses our motivation; Sect. 3 overviews the relevant background; Sect. 4 presents our methodology; and Sect. 5 present our concluding remarks.

2   Motivation

Taking into account the way humans speak and the way we interact via social media, it is very important to propose parsing techniques that are able to parse non-canonical input. Among the potential benefits are the consequent improvement of information retrieval tools, and the possibility of treating hybrid, cross-cultural jargons, which are becoming ubiquitous with the proliferation of texting and of social media communications.

Program transformation is one of the research areas that has received fair attention in the past few years in CHR literature. It has been successfully used in particular for simplifying program development (e.g. [19] studies how to transform transaction-augmented CHR programs into CHR ones); for program optimization; and for mechanizing the generation of programs with certain desired features. Grammar transformation on the other hand is just as promising at least all of these subfields, but has been fairly neglected so far.

The encouraging results in using grammar transformation to induce a target language's grammar from that of a known grammar plus appropriate corpuses [10] have motivated us to adapt this same methodology of grammar transformation to the needs of partially known grammar parsing.

3 Background

3.1 Womb Grammars

Womb Grammars [10] were designed for inducing a target language's syntax from the known syntax of a source language plus a representative corpus of correct sentences in the target language. As such they can be considered a kind of self-modifying grammar, whose approach is quite different from that of predecessors (e.g. [15] resorts heavily to push-down automata; [7], while being more declarative, are an extension of attribute grammars.) Womb grammars, in contrast, are constraint-based: they derive a target language's syntax by observing the list of violated properties that are output when correct sentences in the target language are fed to the source grammar, and correcting that grammar so that these properties are no longer violated. WGs have been useful in various applications such as second language tutoring [2], language acquisition [12] and bio-inspired computation [1].

Using linguistic information from one language for the task of describing another language has historically yielded good results, albeit for specific tasks–such as disambiguating the other language [5], or fixing morphological or syntactic differences by modifying tree-based rules [16]–rather than for syntax induction.

This usually requires parallel corpora, an interesting exception being [9], where information from the models of two languages is shared to train parsers for two languages at a time, jointly. This is accomplished by tying grammar weights in the two hidden grammars, and is useful for learning dependency structure in an unsupervised empirical Bayesian framework.

Most of these approaches have in common the target of inferring *syntactic trees*. As exemplified above and discussed for instance in [4], constraint-based formalisms that make it possible to evaluate each constraint separately are advantageous in comparison with classical, tree-based derivation methods. For instance the Property Grammar framework [3] defines phrase acceptability in terms of the properties or constraints that must be satisfied by groups of categories. For instance, English noun phrases can be described through a few constraints such as precedence (a determiner must precede a noun, an adjective must precede a noun), uniqueness (there must be at most one determiner), exclusion (an adjective phrase must not coexist with a superlative), obligation (a noun phrase must contain the head noun), and so on. Rather than resulting in either a parse tree or failure, such frameworks characterize a sentence through the list of the constraints a phrase satisfies and the list of constraints it violates, so that even incorrect or incomplete phrases will be parsed.

For partially known grammars, this flexibility comes in very handy, but must be complemented, as we shall argue, with ontological information. Ontologies are nowadays part of the essential tools for natural language processing. It is well understood that semantic models can be exploited in order to improve and share lexical resources [14]. The ability of representing and maintaing the relations between words and semantic concepts is crucial for charting and using models of language. In our work we build upon the advances in this research area in order to use ontological knowledge-sharing to fill the gaps in our target lexicon.

In the original Womb Grammar formalism, we had two languages: the source language, of which both the syntax and the lexicon were known, and the target language, of which only the lexicon and a correct input corpus were known. Here we still assume a main language such as English, but it might be creatively cross fertilized with multilingual contributions, both in structure and lexicon, from other languages.

Since Womb Grammars are implemented in CHRG, we now briefly summarize the subset of CHRG relevant to understanding the code.

3.2   CHRG

CHRGs, or Constraint handling Rule Grammars [6], are a grammatical interface to CHR, providing it what DCGs provide to Prolog—namely, they invisibly handle input and output strings for the user. In addition, they include constructs to access those strings dynamically, and the possibility of reasoning in non-classical ways, with abduction or with resource-based assumptions.

For the purposes of this paper, we only use two types of CHRG rules, which parallel the CHR rules of propagation and simplification, and are respectively defined as follows:

A propagation rule is of the form

$$\alpha \ -\backslash \ \beta \ /- \ \gamma \ :: > \ G \ | \ \delta.$$

The part of the rule preceding the arrow $:: >$ is called the head, G the guard, and δ the body; $\alpha, \beta, \gamma, \delta$ are sequences of grammar symbols and constraints so that β contains at least one grammar symbol, and δ contains exactly one grammar symbol which is a nonterminal (and perhaps constraints); α (γ) is called *left (right) context* and β the *core* of the head; G is a conjunction of built-in constraints as in CHR and no variable in G can occur in δ. If left or right context is empty, the corresponding marker is left out and if G is empty (interpreted as **true**), the vertical bar is left out. The convention from DCG is adopted that constraints (i.e., non-grammatical stuff) in head and body of a rule are enclosed by curly brackets. Gaps and parallel match are not allowed in rule bodies. A gap in the rule head is noted "...". Gaps are used to establish references between two long distant elements.

A *simplification (grammar) rule* is similar to a propagation rule except that the arrow is replaced by $< : >$.

4   Our Proposed Methodology

The main difficulty in adapting our methodology is that the target language's input can no longer be considered correct. We shall first consider lexical and structural intrusions separately, and then discuss how to deal with them jointly.

4.1 Failure-Driven Parsing

Notation. As said, our implementation of Womb Grammars [10] is done in terms of CHRG. During our explanation below we show some actual code for completeness, but our description should be intuitively clear that the main ideas can be followed independently from the code.

Parsing Strategy. Each word is stored in a CHRG symbol word/3, along with its category and traits (i.e. word(n, [sing,masc], livre)).

Grammar constraints are entered in terms of a CHRG constraint g/1, whose argument stores each possible grammar property. For instance, an English noun phrase parser would include the constraints:

```
g(obligatority(n)), g(constituency(det)),
g(precedence(det,adj)), g(unicity(det)),
g(requirement(n,det)), g(dependence(det,n))
```

Our proposal adopts the Direct PG parsing strategy introduced in [11], in which constraints are tested only for failure. In contrast, all previous methods exhaustively test each constraint for all constituents that can participate in it.

Concretely, a notion not unlike obligation can be used to identify new phrases, and those phrases can be tentatively expanded from nearby constituents.

For each tentatively expanded phrase, all other constraints are tested for *failure* only. The phrase is allowed to expand only if either no constraint fails, or all constraints that fail have been declared as relaxable. Exhaustive satisfaction check is thus replaced by a smart guided search for a falsifying assignment. This is appropriate provided that the set of satisfied constraints is the exact complement of the set of failed constraints - an assumption that seems reasonable, and that we make.

Should we need to explicitly output those constraints that hold, they can be inferred from the list of constraints that must be satisfied plus those output as unsatisfied, at less computational cost than the usual practice of evaluating all constraints between every pair of constituents, or of adding heuristics to reduce the search space.

This is significant because deep parsing with Property Grammars is theoretically exponential in the number of categories of the grammar and the size of the sentence to parse [18]. Since all previous approaches to PG parsing (except for Womb Parsing) have to calculate all constraints between every pair of constituents, and since the number of failed constraints will in general be much smaller than the number of satisfied constraints, any parsing methodology that manages to mostly check the failed ones will have a substantial efficiency advantage.

Violation Detection. Properties are weeded out upon detection of a violation by CHRG rules that look for them, e.g. an input noun phrase where an adjective precedes a noun will provoke deletion of the constraint g(precedence(n,adj)) plus perhaps (if the rest of the input corpus warrants it) inclusion of the converse constraint: g(precedence(adj,n)). The following CHRG rule accomplishes that:

```
!word(C2,_,_),  ...  , !word(C1,_,_),
{g(precedence(C1,C2))} <:>
{update(precedence(C1,C2))}.
```

Note that the rule works bottom-up, and that the three dots are a facility of CHRG which allows us to skip over an unspecified substring of words. The curly brackets indicate a call to a procedure (as opposed to a grammar symbol).

The CHRG parse predicate stores and abstracts the position of each word in the sentence. In plain English, the above rule states that if a word of category C2 precedes a word of category C1, and there is a precedence rule stipulating that words of category C1 must precede words of category C2, the precedence-updating rule needs to be invoked (in CHRG syntax the symbols prefixed with exclamation points are kept, while the ones without are replaced by the body of the rule, in this case an update constraint that invokes some housekeeping procedures).

Each of the properties dealt with has similar rules associated with it.

4.2   Inferring Lexical Knowledge from Sentential Context

Let us first consider the problem of making sense of extraneous words. We assume in a first stage that we have only one language with known syntax and lexicon, and an input corpus which is correct save for the occasional intrusion of neologisms or words belonging to another language or jargon. We can adapt our Womb Grammar methodology to this situation, by running the input corpus as is and observing the list of violated properties that will be output.

Since we know everything to be correct except that some lexical items do not "belong", we know that the violated properties stem from those lexical items that failed to parse. By examining the violated properties, we can draw useful inferences about the lexical items in question.

For instance, if the head noun appears as an unknown word, among the violated properties we will read that the obligatory character of a noun phrase's noun has been violated, which can lead us to postulate that the word in question is a noun. A violated exigency property would likewise suggest that the unrecognized word has the category that is required and has not been found.

But do we Really Need Womb Grammars? It is clear that with sufficient programming effort, any computational linguistic methodology can be adapted to guess lexical categories of extraneous words from context. However in most of them, this would require a major modification of the parser. Take for instance DCGs (Definite Clause Grammars, [17]), where lexical rules would appear as exemplified by:

```
noun --> [borogove].
```

If the lexicon does not explicitly include the word "borogrove" among the nouns, the parser would simply fail when encountering it. One could admit unknown nouns through the following rule:

```
noun --> [_].
```

But since this rule would indiscriminately accept any word as a noun (and similar rules would have to be included in order to treat possible extraneous words in any other category), this approach would mislead the parser into trying countless paths that are doomed to fail, and might even generate wrong results.

In contrast, we can parse extraneous words through Womb Grammar by anonymizing the category and its features rather than the word itself, e.g. word(Category,[Number, Gender],borogrove)), which more accurately represents what we know and what we don't. The category and features will become efficiently instantiated through constraint satisfaction, taking into account all the properties that must be satisfied by this word in interaction with its context.

Of course, what would be most interesting would be to derive the meaning of the word that "does not belong". While Womb Grammars do not yet have a complete way of treating semantics, the clues they can provide regarding syntactic category can serve to guide a subsequent semantic analysis, or to bypass the need for a complete semantic analysis by the concomitant use of ontologies relevant to domain-specific uses of our parser. In general, we are not necessarily interested in capturing the exact meaning of each unrecognized word; but rather to infer its relation with known words. The problem can be casted into the (automatic) extraction of a portion of the hypernym relation involving the extraneous word using the actual document or additional sources as corpora (see [8]).

Some Examples. In the poem "Jabberwocky", by Lewis Carroll,[1] nonsense words are interspersed within English text with correct syntax. Our target lexicon, which we might call Wonderland Lexicon or WL, can be to some extent reconstructed from the surrounding English words and structure by modularly applying the constraints for English. Thus, "borogoves" must be labelled as a noun in order not to violate a noun phrase's exigency for a head noun.

In other noun phrases, the extraneous words can be recognized only as adjectives. This is the case for "the manxome foe" and "his vorpal sword", once the following constraints are applied: adjectives must precede nouns, a noun phrase can have only one head noun, determiners are also unique within a noun phrase.

In the case of "the slithy toves", where there are two WL words, the constraint that the head noun is obligatory implies that one of these two words is a noun, and the noun must be "toves" rather than "slithy" (which is identified as an adjective as in the two previous examples) in order not to violate the precedence constraint between nouns and adjectives.

In other cases we may not be able to unambiguously determine the category, for instance the WL word "frabjous" preceding the English word "day" may

---

[1] See http://www.poetryfoundation.org/poem/171647.

remain ambiguous no matter how we parse it, if it satisfies all the constraints either as a determiner or as an adjective.[2]

Two of the poem's noun phrases ("the Jubjub bird" and "the Tumtum tree") provide ontological as well as lexical information (under the reasonable assumption that capitalised words must be proper nouns, coupled with the fact that as proper nouns, these words do not violate any constraints). Our adaptation of Womb Grammars includes a starting-point, domain dependent ontology (which could, of course, initially be empty), which can be augmented with such ontological information as the facts that Tumtums are trees and Jubjubs are birds. Similarly, input such as "Vrilligs are vampires" would result in additions to the ontology besides in lexical recognition.

It could be that some input allows us even to equate some extraneous words with their English equivalents. For instance, if instead of having in the same poem the noun phrases "his vorpal sword" and "the vorpal blade", we'd encountered "his vorpal sword" and "the cutting blade", we could bet on approximate synonymy between "vorpal" and "cutting", on the basis of our English ontology having established semantic similarity between "sword" and "blade".

Similarly, extraneous words that repeat might allow a domain-dependent ontology to help determine their meaning. Taking once more the example of "his vorpal sword" and "the vorpal blade", by consulting the ontology besides the constraints, we can not only determine that "vorpal" is an adjective, but also that it probably refers to some quality of cutting objects. It would be most interesting to carefully study under which conditions such ontological inferences would be warranted.

4.3 Inferring Extraneous Structures

We have said that Womb Grammars figure out the syntax of a target language from that of a source language by "correcting" the latter's syntax to include properties that were violated by the input corpus. Another variant of Womb Grammars, which we call Universal Womb Grammars, does not rely on a specific source language, but uses instead the set of all properties that are possible between any two constituents – a kind of universal syntax. This universal grammar contains contradictory properties, for instance it will state both that a constituent A must precede another constituent B, and that B must precede A. One or both of these properties will be weeded out by processing the input corpus, which is assumed to be correct and representative.

When dealing only with lexical intrusions, our solution discussed in the previous section does not affect the assumption, made by Womb Grammars, that the input corpus is correct: we merely postulate an anonymous category and features, and let constraint solving automatically find out from context which are the "correct" ones (correct in the sense of our multilingual or neologism-creating environment) to associate to an extraneous word.

---

[2] Which precise constraints are defined for a given language subset is left to the grammar designer; those in this paper are meant to exemplify more than to prescribe.

Extraneous structures, particularly if coexisting with extraneous lexicon, might be more difficult to deal with, because we rely upon the structural constraints being correct in order to infer an unknown category (e.g. the constraint that adjectives must precede nouns helps to determine that the word "vorpal" functions as an adjective in Lewis Carrol's poem). Therefore, in this section we assume there are no extraneous words and we only deal with extraneous structures. We shall then try to combine both approaches.

We assume, with no loss of generality, that the main language is English and that it is being infiltrated with structures of other languages—the same considerations apply if the main language is another one.

One possibility is to use the Hybrid Womb Grammar approach with the user's mother tongue as target language and English as the source language, thus obtaining a parser for the mixed language, through training a hybrid Womb Grammar with a user-produced representative corpus of sentences. We can then run an input corpus that is representative of the user's talk (e.g. Spanglish) and this will result in a Spanglish grammar adapted to the user in question. Thereafter, this user will be able to create all the neologisms he wants, given that the structures used, although they may be incorrect for either Spanish or English, will be adequately represented in the Spanglish grammar obtained, which is tailored to this user.

Mixed Language Text Parsing

The Training Phase. Before being able to parse a user's mixed use of two languages, we propose to obtain a parser for the mixed language, through training a hybrid Womb Grammar with a user-produced representative corpus of sentences. Let L^S (the source language) be the main language used in the text we want to parse, e.g. English. Its syntactic component will be noted L^S_{syntax}, and its lexical component, L^S_{lex}.

Let L^T be the user's mother tongue. We want to obtain the syntax for the user's blending of L^S and L^T. Let us call this mixed language L^M.

Since we have made the assumption that during this training phase we have no extraneous words (that is, no words that do not appear in the lexicon), we have two options: we can either require that the user do not include them in the training phase, so that the target lexicon will be that of English ($L^M_{lex}=L^S_{lex}$) or we can simply extend the target lexicon to include both the source language's and that of the user's mother tongue ($L^M_{lex} = L^S_{lex} \cup L^T_{lex}$). Whichever of these two options we take, let us call the mixed language's lexicon (L^M_{lex}). We can feed a sufficiently representative corpus L^M_{corpus} of sentences in L^M that the user has produced, to a hybrid parser consisting of L^S_{syntax} and L^M_{lex}. This will result in some of the sentences being marked as incorrect by the parser. An analysis of the constraints these "incorrect" sentences violate can subsequently reveal how to transform L^S_{syntax} so it accepts as correct the sentences in the corpus of L_M—i.e., how to transform it into L^M_{syntax}. Figures 1 and 2 respectively show our problem and our proposed solution through Hybrid Parsing in schematic form.

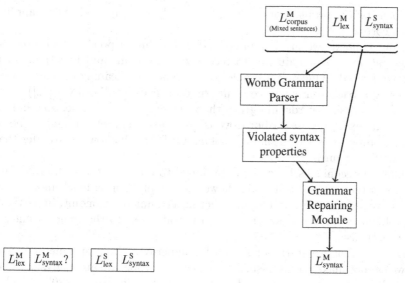

Fig. 1. The problem   Fig. 2. The solution.

For example, let $L^S = English$ and $L^T = French$, and let us assume that English adjectives always precede the noun they modify, while in French they always post-cede it (an oversimplification, just for illustration purposes). Thus "the blue book" is correct English, whereas in French we would more readily say "le livre bleu".

If we plug the French lexicon and the English syntax constraints into our Womb Grammar parser, and run a representative corpus of (correct) French noun phrases by the resulting hybrid parser, the said precedence property will be declared unsatisfied when hitting phrases such as "le livre bleu". The grammar repairing module can then look at the entire list of unsatisfied constraints, and produce the missing syntactic component of L^T's parser by modifying the constraints in L^S_{syntax} so that none are violated by the corpus sentences.

Some of the necessary modifications are easy to identify and to perform, e.g. for accepting "le livre bleu" we only need to delete the (English) precedence requirement of adjective over noun (noted $adj < n$). However, subtler modifications may be in order, perhaps requiring some statistical analysis in a second round of parsing: if in our L^M corpus, which we have assumed representative, *all* adjectives appear after the noun they modify, French is sure to include the reverse precedence property as in English: $n < adj$. So in this case, not only do we need to delete $adj < n$, but we also need to add $n < adj$.

4.4   Extracting Domain Knowledge from Text Corpora

Extracting domain knowledge from text corpora is an active research area which involves several communities (see e.g. [8] for an overview). For our purposes we'll focus on the problem of building a (partial) hypernym relation graph from textual corpora.

In our context, we are not interested in building a precise structured conceptualization of a domain but to recognize hypernyms and hyponyms of the extraneous words. Once we are able to recognise the meaning of related words (e.g. using a background source of information like EuroWordNet [22]) we can classify the missing words and grasp their meaning. For example, searching the web for the exact phrase "a borogove is" returns a snippet containing the sentence "a borogove is a thin shabby-looking bird" which allows us to infer that a "borogove" is a bird.

Different techniques have been developed to optimize the task of acquiring semantic structuring of a domain; however, our problem is much more limited because we are not interested in constructing a complete taxonomy. In particular, the problems of precision and recall will not affect us to the same extent as in the general case.

The fact that we start our search for hypernyms from specific *seed* words and we cannot make strong assumptions on the corpora we are analysing, makes approaches based on hyponym patterns a natural choice (see [13,20]). The basic idea is to search the corpora for specific textual patterns which explicitly identify a hyponym relation between terms (e.g., "such authors as $\langle X \rangle$"). Hyponym patterns can be pre-defined or extracted from corpora using known taxonomies (e.g., [20]). For our purposes we can reuse known patterns and apply them to the text source being parsed or external sources like Wikipedia or a web search engine [21].

5   Conclusion

We have shown how to use the combined power of Womb grammars plus ontologies in order to make syntactic sense of text for which the grammar we dispose of has only partial information. As well, we have delineated how we could extend these abilities into semantics.

While in this paper we have focused on a specific language's grammar, it might be useful to be able to consult in a second stage the relevant fragment (e.g. that of noun phrases if the extraneous word belongs to one) of a universal grammar. This will be the case for instance if the word that seems not to belong in the text exhibits some property that does not exist in the text's main language. When this is the case, there will be no way to assign for some word a category that is in line with the surrounding ones and results in no more properties being violated.

Our work may have interesting connections with Chomskys innate theory of language, which states that all children share the same internal constraints which characterize narrowly the grammar they are going to construct, and exposure to a specific language determines their specialization into the specific rules for that language.

These internal constraints, if the theory is correct, characterize what may be seen as a latent universal language. Womb grammars may help to uncover its constraints phrase by phrase, perhaps relative to families of language, or help shed light upon specific problems, such as phylogenetic classification.

References

1. Becerra-Bonache, L., Dahl, V., Jiménez-López, M.D.: Womb grammars as a bio-inspired model for grammar induction. In: Bajo Perez, J., Corchado Rodríguez, J.M., Mathieu, P., Campbell, A., Ortega, A., Adam, E., Navarro, E.M., Arndt, S., Moreno, M.N., Soto, S.V., Julián, V. (eds.) Trends in Practical Applications of Heterogeneous Multi-agent Systems. The PAAMS Collection. AISC, vol. 293, pp. 79–86. Springer International Publishing, Heidelberg (2014)
2. Becerra Bonache, L., Dahl, V., Miralles, J.E.: On second language tutoring through womb grammars. In: Rojas, I., Joya, G., Gabestany, J. (eds.) IWANN 2013, Part I. LNCS, vol. 7902, pp. 189–197. Springer, Heidelberg (2013). http://dx.doi.org/10.1007/978-3-642-38679-4_18
3. Blache, P.: Property grammars: a fully constraint-based theory. In: Christiansen, H., Skadhauge, P.R., Villadsen, J. (eds.) CSLP 2005. LNCS (LNAI), vol. 3438, pp. 1–16. Springer, Heidelberg (2005)
4. Blache, P., Guénot, M.L., Vanrullen, T.: A corpus-based technique for grammar development. In: ICCL, pp. 123–131 (2003). https://halv3-preprod.archives-ouvertes.fr/hal-00135437
5. Burkett, D., Klein, D.: Two languages are better than one (for syntactic parsing). In: Proceedings of the Conference on Empirical Methods in Natural Language Processing, pp. 877–886. Association for Computational Linguistics (2008)
6. Christiansen, H.: CHR grammars. TPLP 5(4–5), 467–501 (2005)
7. Christiansen, H.: Adaptable grammars for non-context-free languages. In: Bio-Inspired Models for Natural and Formal Languages, pp. 33–51. Cambridge Scholars Publishing (2011)
8. Clark, M., Kim, Y., Kruschwitz, U., Song, D., Albakour, D., Dignum, S., Beresi, U.C., Fasli, M., De Roeck, A.: Automatically structuring domain knowledge from text: an overview of current research. Inf. Process. Manag. 48(3), 552–568 (2012)
9. Cohen, S.B., Smith, N.A.: Covariance in unsupervised learning of probabilistic grammars. J. Mach. Learn. Res. 11, 3017–3051 (2010)
10. Dahl, V., Miralles, J.: Womb grammars: constraint solving for grammar induction. In: Sneyers, J., Frühwirth, T. (eds.) Proceedings of the 9th Workshop on Constraint Handling Rules. vol. Technical report CW 624, Department of Computer Science, K.U. Leuven, pp. 32–40 (2012)
11. Dahl, V., Blache, P.: Directly executable constraint based grammars. In: Proceedings of the Journees Francophones de Programmation en Logique avec Contraintes, JFPLC 2004 (2004)
12. Dahl, V., Miralles, E., Becerra, L.: On language acquisition through womb grammars. In: 7th International Workshop on Constraint Solving and Language Processing, pp. 99–105 (2012)
13. Hovy, E., Kozareva, Z., Riloff, E.: Toward completeness in concept extraction and classification. In: Proceedings of the 2009 Conference on Empirical Methods in Natural Language Processing, vol. 2, pp. 948–957. Association for Computational Linguistics (2009)
14. Huang, C., Calzolari, N., Gangemi, A.: Ontology and the Lexicon: A Natural Language Processing Perspective. Studies in Natural Language Processing. Cambridge University Press, Cambridge (2010)

15. Jackson, Q.T.: Adapting to Babel: Adaptivity and Context-Sensitivity in Parsing. Verlag: Ibis Publishing, Plymouth (2006)
16. Nicolas, L., Molinero, M.A., Sagot, B., Sánchez Trigo, E., De La Clergerie, É., Alonso Pardo, M., Farré, J., Miquel-Vergès, J.: Towards efficient production of linguistic resources: the Victoria Project. In: Proceedings of the International Conference RANLP-2009, pp. 318–323. Association for Computational Linguistics, Borovets (2009). https://hal.inria.fr/inria-00553259
17. Pereira, F.C., Warren, D.H.: Definite clause grammars for language analysis—a survey of the formalism and a comparison with augmented transition networks. Artif. Intell. **13**(3), 231–278 (1980)
18. van Rullen, T.: Vers une analyse syntaxique a granularite variable. Ph.D. thesis, Université de Provence (2005) (2005)
19. Schrijvers, T., Sulzmann, M.: Transactions in constraint handling rules. In: Garcia de la Banda, M., Pontelli, E. (eds.) ICLP 2008. LNCS, vol. 5366, pp. 516–530. Springer, Heidelberg (2008)
20. Snow, R., Jurafsky, D., Ng, A.Y.: Learning syntactic patterns for automatic hypernym discovery. In: Advances in Neural Information Processing Systems, vol. 17 (2004)
21. Snow, R., Jurafsky, D., Ng, A.Y.: Semantic taxonomy induction from heterogenous evidence. In: Proceedings of the 21st International Conference on Computational Linguistics and the 44th Annual Meeting of the Association for Computational Linguistics, pp. 801–808. ACL-44, Association for Computational Linguistics, Stroudsburg (2006). http://dx.doi.org/10.3115/1220175.1220276
22. Vossen, P.: EuroWordNet: a multilingual database of autonomous and language-specific wordnets connected via an inter-lingualindex. Int. J. Lexicography **17**(2), 161–173 (2004). http://dx.doi.org/10.1093/ijl/17.2.161

Author Index

Adebara, Ife 334
Adoe, Fadel 262
Aehnelt, Mario 207
Aggoune-Mtalaa, Wassila 145
Anders, Gerrit 223
Ang, E. Mei 100

Bader, Sebastian 207
Barták, Roman 185
Benelallam, Imade 20
Bouyakhf, El Houssine 20

Cabri, Giacomo 58
Capodieci, Nicola 58
Chen, Yingke 262

da Silva, Flavio S. Correa 284
Dahl, Veronica 334
Doshi, Prashant 262
Dranidis, Dimitris 37
Drugan, Madalina M. 128

EL Khattabi, Ghizlane 20
Erraji, Zakarya 20

Goto, Mizuki 298

Habbas, Zineb 145
Hjelmblom, Magnus 316

Iida, Hiroyuki 100
Ishitobi, Taichi 100

Jakubův, Jan 245

Kefalas, Petros 37
Khalid, Mohd Nor Akmal 100

Kiyohara, Tatsuya 163
Komenda, Antonín 245

Lakemeyer, Gerhard 79
Leonardi, Letizia 58

Meyer, Thomas 3, 79
Miwa, Hiroyoshi 298

Ntika, Marina 37

Ohsuga, Akihiko 163
Orihara, Ryohei 163

Puviani, Mariachiara 58

Reif, Wolfgang 223
Rens, Gavin 3, 79
Robertson, David S. 284

Sadeg, Lamia 145
Sakellariou, Ilias 37
Sei, Yuichi 163
Siefert, Florian 223

Tahara, Yasuyuki 163
Takahashi, Kazuko 298
Tessaris, Sergio 334
Tožička, Jan 245

Vasconcelos, Wamberto W. 284
Vlk, Marek 185

Yusof, Umi Kalsom 100

Printed in the United States
By Bookmasters

Printed in the United States
By Bookmasters